CONSCIOUSNESS AND MIND

D1615381

CONSCIOUSNESS AND MIND

DAVID M. ROSENTHAL

CLARENDON PRESS • OXFORD

OXFORD

UNIVERSITY PRESS

Great Clarendon Street, Oxford OX2 6DP

Oxford University Press is a department of the University of Oxford.
It furthers the University's objective of excellence in research, scholarship,
and education by publishing worldwide in

Oxford New York

Auckland Cape Town Dar es Salaam Hong Kong Karachi
Kuala Lumpur Madrid Melbourne Mexico City Nairobi
New Delhi Shanghai Taipei Toronto

With offices in

Argentina Austria Brazil Chile Czech Republic France Greece
Guatemala Hungary Italy Japan Poland Portugal Singapore
South Korea Switzerland Thailand Turkey Ukraine Vietnam

Oxford is a registered trademark of Oxford University Press
in the UK and in certain other countries

Published in the United States
by Oxford University Press Inc., New York

© David M. Rosenthal, 2005

The moral rights of the author have been asserted
Database right Oxford University Press (maker)

First published 2005

All rights reserved. No part of this publication may be reproduced,
stored in a retrieval system, or transmitted, in any form or by any means,
without the prior permission in writing of Oxford University Press,
or as expressly permitted by law, or under terms agreed with the appropriate
reprographics rights organizations. Enquiries concerning reproduction
outside the scope of the above should be sent to the Rights Department,
Oxford University Press, at the address above

You must not circulate this book in any other binding or cover
and you must impose this same condition on any acquirer

British Library Cataloguing in Publication Data

Data available

Library of Congress Cataloging in Publication Data
Rosenthal, David M.
Consciousness and mind / David M. Rosenthal.
p. cm.
Includes bibliographical references and index.
1. Consciousness. 2. Thought and thinking. I. Title.
B808.9.R675 2006 126–dc22 2005020562

Typeset by Laserwords Private Limited, Chennai, India
Printed in Great Britain
on acid-free paper by
Biddles Ltd, King's Lynn, Norfolk

ISBN 0-19-823697-2 978-0-19-823697-9
ISBN 0-19-823696-4 (Pbk.) 978-0-19-823696-2 (Pbk.)

To the memory of my father
and to my son, Joshua,
who in different ways
inspired and enriched
this work

Preface

I first sketched the higher-order-thought theory of consciousness toward the end of an article about mind-body materialism, to help defuse the challenge consciousness seems to pose for materialism. That brief discussion left many questions unaddressed, and I set out to develop the theory in "Two Concepts of Consciousness," reprinted here as chapter 1. My main goal there was to show how the theory can handle our pretheoretic intuitions, sometimes by predicting those intuitions and in other cases by showing why intuitions that seem compelling are nonetheless erroneous.

I also came to see how the theory facilitates the fruitful investigation of the many connections consciousness has with other mental phenomena. One group of connections has to do with mental qualities. Discussions of consciousness often take off from unquestioned assumptions about the nature of mental qualities, assumptions that constrain subsequent theory and so make a mystery of consciousness. The appeal to higher-order thoughts suggests ways to work in the opposite direction, using the theory to point toward an account of mental qualities that conforms to both commonsense ideas and scientific findings about qualitative consciousness. In doing this, the theory helps undermine the assumptions about mental qualities that cause difficulty. These matters are the focus of chapters 5, 6, and 7.

A second group of issues has to do with the ways consciousness interacts with thought, speech, and the self-interpretation that thoughts about ourselves sometimes involve. The appeal to higher-order thoughts makes possible informative explanations of things that it's unlikely any other theory can handle, such as why a state's being conscious coincides with its being reportable, why thoughts are always conscious when they're expressed verbally, and why our conscious mental lives appear unified. Such topics dominate a number of the remaining chapters.

I am grateful to many friends, colleagues, and students for fruitful conversations about the issues discussed here, and especially to Ned Block, Austen Clark, Martin Davies, Dan Dennett, Zoltán Dienes, Jerry Fodor, Pierre Jacob, Tony Marcel, Douglas Meehan, Sidney Morgenbesser, Adam Morton, Josef Perner, Georges Rey, Edmund Rolls, Peter Ross, Eckart Scheerer, Robert Schwartz, Sydney Shoemaker, Josh Weisberg, and Larry Weiskrantz. And I am grateful to David Pereplyotchik for preparing the index and for very many helpful comments.

All but two of these essays have appeared in print before, though several of those appear here in revised or expanded form. I am grateful to the editors and publishers who kindly granted permission to reprint previously published material.

Details of original publication follow.

1. "Two Concepts of Consciousness," *Philosophical Studies*, 49, 3 (May 1986): 329–359 (here with minor revisions).

Contents

Introduction

I. THE EXPLANATORY DIVISION OF LABOR

Despite dramatic recent advances in studying the mind, there is still strikingly little consensus about the nature of consciousness. Doubtless this is in part because theorists often use the term 'conscious' for different phenomena, and don't always clarify which they are talking about. And even when they do, they often fail to characterize the relevant phenomena in terms that are neutral as regards competing theories, and subsequent theorizing inherits the bias of those characterizations. These problems in picking out and describing the phenomena hinder efforts to reach agreement about consciousness.

But there is another, more substantive matter that also contributes to that lack of consensus. Theoretical explanation often benefits from an explanatory division of labor in which we focus on some aspects of a phenomenon while temporarily putting others aside. This strategy has been no less fruitful in the study of mind than it has in other areas. Thus some mental phenomena, such as perceiving, exhibit both intentional and qualitative mental properties, but it has proved highly useful to investigate each type of property independently of the other.

There is some reluctance, however, to apply this strategy of divide and conquer in the case of consciousness. Whereas we typically study intentionality and qualitative character independently of one another, theorists often resist considering consciousness apart from other features of mental functioning.

One sign of this resistance is the widespread use of the phrase 'what it's like' as a test for whether one is talking about consciousness at all, since that all but ubiquitous rubric in effect yokes consciousness to mental qualities. There is something it's like for one to be in a mental state only if that state not only is conscious, but also exhibits some qualitative character. And at least on many construals, the related notion of phenomenal consciousness also applies to both consciousness and mental quality as though they are indissolubly tied together.

The popularity of the phrases 'what it's like' and 'phenomenal consciousness' reflects a tendency to see consciousness and qualitative character as inseparable. Whether they actually are is a matter of controversy, which cannot be settled by stipulation or the use of seductive phrases. But, even if the two properties did always occur together, it might nonetheless be theoretically fruitful to treat them independently, and we shouldn't set things up in a way that rules out doing so. Intentionality and qualitative character occur inseparably in perceiving, but it's useful even there to consider each property on its own. Why, then, is there such resistance to such an approach in the study of consciousness?

The answer very likely has to do with a persistent tendency to think about consciousness as a matter of the mind's being transparent to itself, and so as giving us infallible and exhaustive knowledge about our own mental functioning. This epistemological conception encourages thinking about consciousness in terms of the mental properties it provides access to, rather than as itself an independent mental property. The idea that such access is transparent, moreover, makes it tempting to think that there's nothing useful or informative to say about the nature of that access. The epistemological conception of consciousness shifts attention onto the mental properties we're conscious of, and away from consciousness itself as a subject of independent study.

The idea that we have transparent access to our own mental functioning has for some time now been regarded with well-deserved skepticism. It's widely acknowledged that we are sometimes wrong about what mental states we are in, and that others occasionally know what states we are in well enough to correct our errors. First-person access to one's own mind is of course different in kind from the access we have to the minds of others, and it's usually fairly accurate; but it is neither infallible nor incorrigible.

Nonetheless, thinking about consciousness often proceeds as though we do have absolute epistemic privilege about our own mental states. Thus theoretical discussions often appeal to phenomenological appearances as though they are by themselves sufficient to settle questions about consciousness. But, if consciousness isn't always accurate about the states we're conscious of, there's even less reason to think that it's always right about itself. The way our mental lives appear to consciousness is an important datum that any theoretical account must do justice to, but it's not decisive about the nature either of mental functioning or of consciousness.

Even if consciousness were inseparable from the mental properties it gives us access to, it might be useful, as already noted, to study consciousness independently of those properties. But the states to which consciousness gives us access do in any case sometimes occur separately from consciousness, since those states sometimes occur without being conscious. So consciousness must be something over and above the mental properties and states that we're conscious of. This casts further doubt on the idea that such access is either infallible or exhaustive.

It's generally agreed that thoughts, doubts, wonderings, and other intentional states sometimes occur without being conscious. But there is ample reason to hold that the same is true of qualitative states as well. I'll say a bit more about this below; for now it's enough to note just that subliminal perceiving and peripheral vision, which aren't conscious, plainly involve mental qualities. Not only do we describe them in qualitative terms; we do so because they typically carry the kind of information that's distinctive of conscious qualitative states. Qualitative mental states do sometimes occur without being conscious.

Consciousness tells us only about states that are conscious. But intentional and qualitative states sometimes occur without being conscious. So there must be third-person considerations that show that these states occur when they aren't conscious.

Those considerations will overrule consciousness when it comes to the occurrence of states that aren't conscious, since according to consciousness the only mental states we are in are conscious states. Consciousness is not decisive even about the occurrence of mental states.

We know about intentional and qualitative states that aren't conscious from various third-person considerations. Indeed, third-person considerations tell us things that we couldn't learn from consciousness, such as what distinctive causal connections mental states have with nonmental events. Such third-person considerations will apply to states that are conscious no less than to states that aren't. And, even though the third-person information we have about what conscious states we are in typically agrees with consciousness, the two do occasionally conflict. So we can expect that third-person information will sometimes overrule consciousness even about conscious states, as it does in connection with mental states that aren't conscious.

Because mental states sometimes occur without being conscious, we must treat consciousness as an independent phenomenon, independent, that is, of the mental properties and states to which it affords access. And, since mental states occur both consciously and not, we must explain what the difference between these two ways of occurring consists in. Indeed, explaining that difference will be a central goal of any theory of consciousness, which will guide the way the theory handles other questions as well.

One major aim of chapter 1 is to show that conceiving of consciousness as independent of the intentional and qualitative properties of conscious states is a crucial first step in explaining consciousness. But it's sometimes urged that a state's being conscious is necessary for it to be a mental state in the first place, and that only consciousness allows us to distinguish genuinely mental states from mere subpersonal or information-processing surrogates. So chapter 1 also argues that we get a more satisfactory mark of the mental by appealing to intentional and qualitative properties themselves, independently of consciousness. Chapter 3 takes up the question of how the intentionality of mental states differs from the intentionality of things that aren't strictly speaking mental at all, such as speech acts, paintings, and tone poems. And chapters 5, 6, and 7, develop an account of mental qualities that's independent of whether the states that have such qualities are conscious.

II. THE TRANSITIVITY PRINCIPLE AND HIGHER-ORDER THOUGHTS

Explaining what it is in virtue of which conscious states differ from mental states that aren't conscious is the principal goal of a theory of consciousness. And it's fairly straightforward to get a start on that question. When a mental state is conscious, the individual that's in that state is conscious of it; when a mental state fails to be conscious, that individual is in no way whatever conscious of that state.

That this is so is evident from cases in which an individual is in some mental state, but not in any way conscious of being in it. It sometimes happens that one sincerely denies being in some mental state, even though one acts in a way that makes it plain that one is in that state. One's behavior may clearly show that one thinks or desires something or that one feels happy or sad, despite one's sincere, consistent denials. The natural conclusion is that one is in that state but the state isn't conscious.

A mental state fails to be conscious if one is in no way conscious of it. So a state is conscious only if one is in some way conscious of that state. A mental state's being conscious consists, at least in part, in one's being conscious of it.

The term 'conscious' appears here both in describing the phenomenon being explained and in the explanation itself. Still, the explanation is not circular. An individual's being conscious *of* something is different from a *mental state's being conscious*. One is conscious of something when one is in a mental state that pertains to that thing in a suitable way, and it's by no means obvious that a state must itself be conscious to make one conscious of something. To keep straight about these two uses of 'conscious', I'll refer to a mental state's being conscious as *state consciousness*, and to an individual's being conscious *of* something as *transitive consciousness*.[1] And I'll call the observation that mental states are conscious only if one is in some way conscious of them the *transitivity principle*.

By specifying how conscious states differ from mental states that aren't conscious, the transitivity principle provides the beginning of an explanation of state consciousness. But it does more than that. Mental states are conscious in different ways; what it's like for one to have a conscious sensation of red, for example, differs from what it's like for one to have a conscious sensation of green. Since a state's being conscious consists of one's being in some way conscious of it, we can explain differences in how various states are conscious by appeal to differences in the way we are conscious of those states. There being something it's like for one to have a sensation of red, for example, will consist in one's being conscious of that sensation *as* a sensation of red; similarly for other kinds of case.

We are conscious of things when we are in mental states that represent those things in some suitable way. We might be conscious of something by seeing it or sensing it in some other way, or by having an appropriate thought about it. The transitivity principle doesn't itself tell us in which of these ways we are conscious of mental states when those states are conscious.

Still, any theory that respects the transitivity principle will hold that a state's being conscious consists in one's being in some kind of higher-order mental state that represents that state. The prevalence of various forms of higher-order theory reflects a widespread if sometimes tacit recognition that the transitivity principle does define what it is for a state to be conscious. The different types of higher-order theory can be seen as differing mainly about how best to implement the transitivity principle, that is, about how it is that we are conscious of a mental state when that state is conscious.[2]

[1] Cf. Wittgenstein's related use of 'transitive' in *The Blue and Brown Books*, Oxford: Basil Blackwell, 1958, 2nd edn. 1969, 22.
[2] See my "Varieties of Higher-Order Theory," in Rocco J. Gennaro, ed., *Higher-Order Theories of Consciousness*, Amsterdam and Philadelphia: John Benjamins Publishers, 2004, pp. 17–44, and other contributions to that collection.

The term 'conscious' was not generally applied to mental states until the late nineteenth century, when it became widely recognized that mental states sometimes occur without one's being conscious of them. But the idea underlying the transitivity principle has a long history. Descartes and Locke routinely speak of our being conscious of all our mental states, and Aristotle insisted that thinking always involves thinking that one thinks and perceiving involves perceiving that one perceives.[3] These claims plainly imply what we would put by saying that all mental states are conscious states.

Indeed, denying the transitivity principle would mean having to come up with an alternative account of how conscious states differ from mental states that aren't conscious, and it's unclear that there is any acceptable alternative. One might urge that a state's being conscious is not a matter of one's being conscious of that state, but rather of the state's making one transitively conscious of something. But perceiving isn't always conscious, even though it always makes one conscious of things. The transitivity principle is very likely the only credible way to explain how conscious states differ from mental states that aren't conscious.

Perceiving and sensing things is one way of being conscious of them, and it's generally the first way that comes to mind. Perhaps because of that, traditional discussions have implemented the transitivity principle by appeal to that way of being conscious of things. On the so-called inner-sense theory, we are conscious of our conscious mental states by sensing or perceiving them. Chapters 4 and 7 argue that the inner-sense model cannot be sustained;[4] sensing and perceiving involve mental qualities, but no higher-order mental qualities figure in the way we are conscious of our conscious states.

But sensing and perceiving are not the only ways of being conscious of things. We are also conscious of something when we have a thought about it. It may be that not every thought results in one's being conscious of the thing it is about; perhaps when a thought represents something as being distant in space or time, having that thought doesn't result in one's being conscious of that thing. But when a thought represents something as being present, having that thought does make one conscious of that thing. We know of no third way of being conscious of things. Since we don't sense or perceive our conscious states, it must be that we are conscious of those states by having thoughts about them. And, because these thoughts are about other mental states, we can call them *higher-order thoughts* (HOTs).

When a state is conscious, we have a compelling subjective sense that we are directly conscious of that state, that nothing mediates between the state and our consciousness of it. Traditional discussions have usually taken this subjective sense at face

[3] e.g. Aristotle, *de Anima*, Γ2, 425*b*12–20; *Nicomachean Ethics*, IX, 9, 1170a29–a34; *The Philosophical Writings of Descartes*, tr. John Cottingham, Robert Stoothoff, and Dugald Murdoch, vol. II, Cambridge: Cambridge University Press, 1984–91, 113 and 171–2; and John Locke, *Essay Concerning Human Understanding*, ed. from the 4th (1700) edn. by Peter H. Nidditch, Oxford: Oxford University Press, 1975, II, i, 19, II, i, 10–12, and IV, vii, 4.
[4] In §II of each of those chapters; see also "Varieties of Higher-Order Theory," §§II–IV.

value, but there is no basis for doing so. We also have a compelling sense that we perceive things directly, though we know that there is much that mediates between the things we perceive and our perceiving of them.

In the case of perceiving, our sense of immediacy stems from our seldom being conscious of any mediating factors. The same is doubtless true for mental states' being conscious; we aren't conscious of anything as mediating between mental states and our consciousness of them, and that results in a subjective sense that such consciousness is direct. All we need to explain is that subjective immediacy of consciousness, not any alleged underlying immediacy. And we can explain that subjective immediacy by noting that, when a state is conscious, we're never conscious of an accompanying HOT as relying on some inferential process.

Because having a HOT that one is in some state is a way of being conscious of oneself as being in that state, HOTs implement the transitivity principle. Mere dispositions to have such HOTs, by contrast, would not do so. Being disposed to have a thought about something results not in one's being conscious of that thing, but only in one's being disposed to be.

HOTs require relatively minimal conceptual resources. So nonlinguistic beings, including human infants, might well have HOTs, and thereby be in mental states that are conscious. The HOTs of such beings would not result in their being conscious of their mental states in the rich way in which we're typically conscious of ours, but there is no reason to think that they ever are conscious of their mental states in that rich way. Moreover, the HOTs of creatures without language might never make them conscious of their mental states in respect of the intentional content of those states. But, again, we have no reason to think they ever are conscious of their mental states in respect of their intentional content. Indeed, the considerations that have led some to contend that nonlinguistic beings don't have thoughts at all typically at best support only doubts about whether they have any conscious thoughts.

The HOT hypothesis is arguably the only acceptable way to implement the transitivity principle. But even apart from such argument by elimination, there are also compelling positive reasons to adopt the hypothesis. One family of reasons has to do with linguistic behavior. For creatures who, like ourselves, have the ability to say what mental states they are in, a reliable mark of a state's being conscious is that one can report being in that state. We routinely rely on this reportability criterion both in everyday life and in experimental work in psychology.

Whenever we say anything, our speech acts express corresponding intentional states that we are in, and reports of mental states are no exception. So, saying "I am in such-and-such a mental state" expresses one's thought that one is in that state, and that thought is itself a HOT. Since statements that one is in some mental state are typically spontaneous, moreover, we typically aren't conscious of any mediating inference that leads to our thinking that we're in that state. So the reportability of conscious states actually helps sustain the HOT hypothesis about what such consciousness consists in. Conscious states are noninferentially reportable because such reports express the HOTs in virtue of which we're conscious of those states. Chapter 2 develops this argument in detail, and chapter 3 explores the connection between intentional states and speech acts on which the argument relies.

Several subsequent chapters say more about the connection between consciousness and speech. Whenever we say anything, the intentional state we thereby express is conscious. Chapter 10 shows how the HOT hypothesis can explain both that regularity and also certain systematic exceptions to it, and chapter 11 considers how that regularity applies to the special case of the emotions. Chapter 9 explores the relationship between consciousness and speech in connection with Moore's paradox, which involves the impossibility of saying things of the form 'It's raining but I don't think it is'. The HOT theory handles all these phenomena in a natural, informative way, and it's unlikely that any other theory of consciousness can explain them at all.

Because the HOT theory appeals to higher-order intentional states, it's natural to expect that the theory will be in its element in explaining the connection between consciousness and speech. But the theory has a number of advantages in explaining qualitative consciousness as well.

Often when we perceive things, we're conscious of our perceptual experience in a less detailed or fine-grained way than we might be. When we see something red, our perceptual state registers the particular shade of red of the thing we see. But our experience is often conscious not in respect of that specific shade, but in respect only of some generic, all-purpose red. We're conscious of our experience of the specific shade *as* a generic experience of red. The way we're conscious of our perceptions is often far less fine-grained than the actual character of those perceptions.

That a perception actually has more specific qualitative character than one is conscious of it as having may become evident from focusing attentively on a visual perception, and thereby coming to be conscious of it in respect of the more specific shade. But, even if we remain conscious of the experience in the more generic way, we sometimes later recognize a specific shade as the very one that we had seen earlier. So the earlier experience must itself have had the more fine-grained perceptual character, even though we weren't at the time conscious of it in that way. Moreover, when two sensations differ in shade only slightly, we're often conscious of the shades as different only when they occur together. Still, the sensations presumably have the same mental properties even when they occur separately and we aren't conscious of them as different.

Such disparities between our perceptions and the way we're conscious of them aren't limited to shades of color. When walking through the woods, one's visual states must represent fallen branches and other obstacles in fair amount of detail if one is to avoid tripping over them. But what it's like for one seldom reflects much, if any, of that visual detail. Here again the qualitative character of our perceptions exhibits more detail than we are conscious of them as having.

The same kind of thing happens also with thoughts and other intentional states. Sometimes when we consciously think something, we recall having had that thought at some earlier time, but having not then been clear about just what the thought was. We had the thought consciously, but without being conscious in a clear way of its intentional content. It may also sometimes happen that the content of the earlier thought was itself unclear or confused. But sometimes it seems that we were simply confused about what content the thought actually had. We feel we recognize that the later thought is the very thought we had earlier, despite our having not then been conscious of its content in a clear way. And the earlier thought may indeed have inter-acted with others in ways that would only have been possible for a thought with that specific content.

In all these cases, the ways we're conscious of our thoughts and experiences diverge from the mental nature of the states themselves; we are conscious of those states in ways that don't fully or accurately reflect their mental properties. Such disparities plainly point to the transitivity principle. We can best explain why we're not always conscious of mental states in ways that fully reflect their mental nature by construing the way a state is conscious in terms of the way one is conscious of the state. And this calls for some sort of higher-order theory.

But not every theory that conforms to the transitivity principle is equally well-suited to deal with these disparities. Some theories construe the higher-order content as an aspect of the first-order state itself. But in that case it's not obvious why that higher-order content would vary, sometimes representing the first-order mental prop-erties fully and accurately, and at other times less so.

Higher-order sensing and perceiving fail for other reasons. But distinct HOTs are well-suited to explain the disparity between the way states are conscious and their actual mental properties. The way a state is conscious—in the qualitative case, what it's like for one to be in that state—is a matter of the way one's HOT describes the state. It's a matter of what state one is conscious of oneself as being in. Chapters 4, 6, 7, and 8 show how the HOT theory handles divergence between qualitative states and the way we're conscious of them, and chapters 4 and 12 discuss such disparities in both qualitative and intentional cases.

Our sensations and perceptions are caused by the things we sense and perceive. So we can think of sensing and perceiving as monitoring those perceptible objects and properties. And, since it's natural to think about being conscious of things in terms of perceiving and sensing them, higher-order theories are often seen as involving some kind of monitoring, in which the first-order states cause the higher-order states that monitor them.

But this monitoring picture is gratuitous. The principal advantage of higher-order theories is that they implement the transitivity principle; they capture the truism that a state's being conscious is a matter of one's being conscious of oneself as being in that state. And one can be conscious of oneself as being in a state even when that state doesn't cause one's consciousness of it.

First-order states are doubtless often implicated in causing higher-order states. But other factors, such as confabulation and self-deception, may independently figure in the causing of such higher-order states; so higher-order states may sometimes rep-resent us as being in states that we aren't actually in. This further conflicts with the monitoring picture, on which the monitored states determine the content of the higher-order states that do the monitoring, and so determine how those higher-order states represent our stream of consciousness.

The monitoring picture would, if true, explain how higher-order states arise, and why they usually are accurate. But we have no independent reason to think that such a monitoring mechanism actually exists. And the HOT hypothesis suggests in any case a more informative explanation of why higher-order states are so often accurate. I'll return to this question in section IV.

It is sometimes urged that a HOT can make a first-order state conscious only if the HOT is itself conscious, and that would lead to vicious regress. This misconstrues the situation. Conscious states don't inherit their consciousness from higher-order states; rather, a state's being conscious consists simply in one's being conscious of oneself as being in that state, and that happens by having a HOT that one is in that state. Nor must a HOT itself be conscious to make us conscious of its target. We're conscious of things even when we see them subliminally, though we're not in such cases aware that we're conscious of those things. Similarly with HOTs and their mental targets.

We're seldom aware of having HOTs, which is what we should expect. Not all thoughts are conscious, and we're aware only of those which are. And a HOT would be conscious only when one has a third-order thought about it, and we can assume that such third-order thoughts are rare. Our being unaware of most of our HOTs, moreover, doesn't deprive the theory of support, since the theory doesn't rely mainly on introspective input. Rather, HOTs are theoretical posits. We are occasionally conscious of them, but we establish their occurrence in general by appeal to the explanatory strength of the theory that posits them.

Since the theory relies for support on its explanatory advantages, it doesn't appeal to, nor is it intended to reflect, any conceptual or metaphysically necessary truths. The claim that conscious states are states we're conscious of ourselves as being in by having HOTs about them is a theoretical claim justified by its explanatory power, not a metaphysical truth or a result of conceptual analysis. The theory does if correct reflect the nature of things, but only in the way that theoretical claims generally do.

Theoretical explanations must take into account the pretheoretic, commonsense intuitions we have about things and try to accommodate them wherever possible. But we must take care that the intuitions we seek to accommodate are not simply disguised theoretical claims. It's arguable that that is so, for example, with the idea that we can conceive of an inversion of mental qualities that's undetectable by others, or of beings physically indistinguishable from us that nonetheless lack conscious mental qualities. These alleged intuitions arguably reflect controversial theoretical views. I'll return to quality inversion in the next section.

Taking account of intuitions that are genuinely pretheoretic, moreover, doesn't always mean taking those intuitions to be accurate. Intuitions are strongly held pretheoretic beliefs; it's important to explain why we have those beliefs, but the best way to do that often does not rely on their being true. The intuition that consciousness is an intrinsic property of mental states, for example, doubtless results simply from our seldom being conscious of the distinct higher-order states in virtue of which our mental states are conscious. Genuinely pretheoretic intuitions are data, not self-evident truths.

III. QUALITATIVE CONSCIOUSNESS
AND HOMOMORPHISM THEORY

Some who accept that the HOT hypothesis explains the consciousness of intentional states nonetheless insist that the hypothesis fails for qualitative states. Indeed, some go further and reject altogether the transitivity principle for qualitative states. An intentional state's being conscious, they concede, consists in one's being conscious of it. And, since qualitative character doesn't figure in the way we're conscious of intentional states, we may well be conscious of them by way of HOTs.

But conscious qualitative states, they argue, are different. There is something that it's like for one to be in conscious qualitative states, and nothing it's like for one to be in a qualitative state that isn't conscious, assuming that such a thing is even possible. And, since HOTs, like thoughts in general, have no qualitative character themselves, how could having a HOT about a qualitative state result in there being something it's like for one to be in that state?

Another consideration seems to point to the same conclusion. HOTs differ solely in respect of conceptual content. But there seem to be more differences in conscious qualitative character than it's possible to capture by way of concepts. And if that's so, HOTs can't be responsible for all the fine-grained differences that occur in conscious mental qualities. Indeed, if we can't capture conscious mental qualities conceptually, perhaps qualitative character is ineffable, and so not susceptible to any informative explanation whatever.

The apparent ineffability of mental qualities suggests, moreover, that qualitative character may, after all, be inseparable from consciousness. If we can't uniquely capture mental qualities by our concepts, the only way we could refer to those qualities at all would be in terms of the conscious qualitative states we're in on particular occasions. And if we can't even talk about qualitative character apart from consciousness, perhaps the two are after all inseparable. Indeed, the claim that qualitative character is ineffable is very likely in this way the main source of the idea that qualitative character is inseparable from consciousness. So those who see the two as inseparable seldom even try to give an informative characterization of either.

If mental qualities were inseparable from consciousness, consciousness would be an aspect of the very nature of every qualitative state. So this inseparability thesis might make it tempting to see qualitative states as in some way conscious independently of any mental access we have to them. But mental qualities seem inseparable from consciousness only insofar as it seems that we can talk about those qualities only by talking about our conscious qualitative states.

If qualitative character is indeed ineffable, the HOT hypothesis must be wrong. HOTs differ only in respect of conceptual content. So, if HOTs are responsible for there being something it's like for one to be in qualitative states of various sorts, it must be possible to capture in conceptual terms all the differences among mental qualities of which we're conscious. And it's also likely that we can dispel the sense many theorists have that consciousness is inseparable from qualitative character only if we can show that qualitative character is not ineffable. So to sustain the HOT hypothesis, we need an account of mental qualities on which we can capture them and the differences among them in conceptual terms.

It's not hard to see the general form that such an account must take. Suppose you consciously see several red objects of slightly different shades, and so have conscious visual sensations of those shades. And suppose I ask you to characterize what it's like for you to have each of these conscious experiences. Even though you will seldom have single words for each shade, you still can answer that question informatively. Your answer will typically invoke various comparisons; you'll say, for example, that the one on the left is a bit lighter than the top one, and that the one on the right has a bit more yellow in it than the others.

Such comparisons plainly trade on qualitative differences that we can capture conceptually. The comparative concepts that figure in such descriptions, moreover, can be used to refine the distinctions we draw to the limits of what we can consciously distinguish. There is no reason to doubt that sufficiently rich comparisons can in every case uniquely individuate the mental qualities in question. Though we seldom have distinct concepts corresponding to each variation in mental qualities, we still can capture conceptually all the differences that occur among our conscious qualitative states.

We can supplement these comparisons, moreover, by referring to mental qualities that are distinctive of perceiving particular types of object. Thus we might refer to one mental quality of yellow as that which occurs when we see lemons, and another in terms of the color of bananas. And we often combine both devices, describing conscious qualitative properties both comparatively and by reference to the characteristic perceptible properties of familiar objects.

These two devices point towards a general theory of qualitative character that enables us to capture mental qualities in conceptual terms. On that theory, we fix the family of mental qualities characteristic of each sensory modality by reference to the family of perceptible properties to which the modality in question enables us to have perceptual access. And we fix the mental qualities within each family by way of the similarities and differences among the relevant perceptible properties.

Consider visual qualities. Vision enables us to perceive various physical colors. These physical colors are reflectance properties, but we can also describe them in terms of the ways they resemble and differ from one another in respect of our ability to discriminate among them. Given human discriminative abilities, for example, physical red is closer to physical orange than either of those is to physical green. And there are myriad other such comparative generalizations. The similarities and differences among these visible properties in respect of our ability to discriminate among them determine a quality space of physical colors.

For an organism to discriminate physical colors, it must be in perceptual states that reflect the structure of that quality space. So those states must themselves resemble and differ from one another in ways that are homomorphic to the similarities and differences among the physical colors that the organism can discriminate. These perceptual states make visual discrimination possible by resembling and differing from one another in ways that reflect the discriminable similarities and differences among the physical colors. Since the organism has perceptual access to the physical colors by way of those states, they are the visual qualitative states for that organism. And the properties in respect of which those states resemble and differ among themselves are the mental qualities for that organism that pertain to vision.

We can fix each mental color quality, then, by reference to its position in a quality space whose constituent properties exhibit similarities and differences homomorphic to the similarities and differences that define the quality space of perceptible physical colors. Physical red is determined by the characteristic ways it resembles and differs from other discriminable properties in the quality space of perceptible colors. So mental red is that mental quality whose similarities and differences from other properties in the quality space of mental colors are homomorphic to the similarities and differences that define physical red. Similarly for the mental qualities of the other sensory modalities, and indeed for the mental qualities of bodily sensations as well.

This *homomorphism theory* of mental qualities allows us to individuate conceptually the mental qualities that figure both in perceptual discrimination and in conscious qualitative experience. The theory relies on describing mental qualities comparatively and also by reference to perceptible properties, fixing each mental quality partly by reference to the relevant family of perceptible properties and in comparative terms within those families. Chapters 5, 6, and 7 develop this account of mental qualities.

Because it enables us to individuate mental qualities conceptually, homomorphism theory refutes the contention that qualitative character is ineffable. It also shows how HOTs could make one conscious of states in respect of their particular mental qualities. A HOT will describe a sensation of red, for example, as resembling and differing from others in its family in ways that parallel the similarities and differences that perceptible red has to other perceptible colors. And in general, HOTs will describe each mental quality in terms of its location in a space of mental qualities defined by relations of similarity and difference that are homomorphic to those of the perceptible properties which those mental qualities enable one to perceive.

This account fits well with the way we actually describe what it's like for us to see red. We describe what it's like for us to see red in terms of the ways in which that conscious experience resembles and differs from other color experiences. Having a HOT that one is in a state that resembles and differs from others in those characteristic ways makes one conscious of oneself as having a conscious experience of red.

Post-Galilean physics demands that all physical properties be described in mathematical terms. But our commonsense conception of the perceptible properties of physical objects represents many of them as qualitative in a way that seems to resist such mathematical description. One traditional response has been to urge that those perceptible physical qualities which seem to resist mathematical description are actually just mental qualities of our sensations. This strategy of reconstruing problematic physical properties as mental is a major source of the sense that there is a prima facie conflict between something's being mental and its being physical.

Unseen physical colors and other commonsense perceptible properties of which we're not conscious don't require any such reconstrual, since perceptible properties of which we aren't conscious don't seem intuitively to resist mathematical description. Reconstruing commonsense qualities seems called for only for those qualities of which we are conscious. So the mental qualities that such reconstrual would result in would have consciousness already built into them. Chapter 6 examines this view of mental qualities as relocated perceptible properties, and shows that both that view and the surprising consequence about consciousness are avoidable.

Both homomorphism theory and the traditional relocation story characterize mental qualities by reference to commonsense perceptible properties. But, unlike the relocation story, homomorphism theory doesn't require qualitative states to be conscious. A state's having qualitative character, on that account, is solely a matter of the role that state plays in perceiving, and perceiving need not be conscious. So homomorphism theory sustains the idea that qualitative character can occur without being conscious.

The theory also helps make sense of cases in which the way one is conscious of a qualitative state isn't fully accurate, or even accurate at all. A state's qualitative character consists in the properties that figure in that state's perceptual role. How one is conscious of such a state is an independent matter, which is arguably due to the HOT one has about it. Because mental qualities aren't ineffable, there's no reason to assimilate qualitative character to the way we're conscious of it, and hence no reason to think that disparities between qualities and the way we're conscious of them cannot occur.

The way one is conscious of a qualitative state is distinct from and independent of the qualitative properties of that state. Still, when qualitative states are conscious, the states we are conscious of ourselves as being in are just those which figure in perceiving. The combination of homomorphism theory with the HOT hypothesis reflects this connection between perceptual role and subjective consciousness. Our HOTs make us conscious of ourselves as being in qualitative states in respect of mental qualities that play particular roles in perceiving, that is, in respect of the similarities and differences that determine those perceptual roles. So the combined theory avoids the distortions of theories that rely solely on the way we're conscious of mental qualities or solely on perceptual role.

Theories on which we fix mental qualities solely by way of consciousness wrongly suggest that qualitative states cannot occur without being conscious. They also make it seem that we can conceive of conscious mental qualities' being inverted in a way undetectable by others, since third-person considerations are irrelevant on such theories to the individuation of such qualities. Indeed, because such inversion is by hypothesis undetectable by way of any third-person considerations, all available third-person evidence would tell against such inversion. So the claim that inversion is nonetheless conceivable reflects a tacit assumption that first-person access to qualitative states overrules the totality of third-person evidence.

The combination of the HOT hypothesis and homomorphism theory precludes such inversion. If what it's like for me to have sensations of red and green were inverted relative to what it's like for you, our HOTs would be inverted in that way. But those HOTs describe the qualitative states they are about in terms of their perceptual roles, and perceptual roles cannot invert, since any shift in them would be detectable by others. So an inversion of HOTs would itself result in a detectable mismatch of those HOTs with the perceptual thoughts we have about the corresponding physical colors.

To somebody convinced that such inversion is at least conceivable, this will tell decisively against the present theory. But such inversion would be undetectable by third-person means. So the only reason one could have to think that such inversion is even conceivable would be the idea that what quality a state has is solely a matter of how one is conscious of it, independent of its perceptual role. And, without independent support, that stipulation begs the question against the present theory. Chapters 6 and 7 take up issues about inverted and absent qualities. And chapter 7 also briefly considers what light homomorphism theory sheds on the question of what one would learn on first consciously seeing a particular color.

The way qualitative states are conscious is a matter of how one's HOTs about those states characterize them. But that doesn't require HOTs themselves to have qualitative character. Qualitative states are conscious because one is conscious of oneself as being in states with various mental qualities. And being conscious of oneself as being in a state with qualitative character doesn't mean that one's consciousness of oneself as being in that state itself has qualitative character. We are conscious of ourselves as being in qualitative states simply by having HOTs that represent us as being in such states.

Intentional states are responsible for there being something it's like for one to be in qualitative states, and for differences in what it's like for one to be in states of various sorts. But the HOT hypothesis is not a representationalist view, on which the only way we're ever aware of qualities is by having thoughts about perceptible physical properties. For one thing, we are also aware of such perceptible properties by having sensations that exhibit the corresponding mental qualities. Moreover, there are qualitative properties we are aware of other than the commonsense perceptible properties of physical objects; HOTs make us aware of ourselves as being in states with mental qualities, which are distinct from perceptible physical properties. Chapters 4 (§V) and 7 (§IV) elaborate on the difference between the HOT hypothesis and representationalism.

IV. CONSCIOUSNESS, SELF-INTERPRETATION, AND UNITY

The appearances of consciousness reflect the contents of our HOTs; what it's like for one be in a particular mental state is a matter of how one's HOT represents that state. And the way we are conscious of ourselves as being in various mental states is not always accurate, nor does it reveal everything about one's current state of mind. The appearances of consciousness give us a particular picture of that state of mind; we are conscious of ourselves *as* being in various mental states. So the HOTs in virtue of which one is thus conscious of oneself constitute a kind of self-interpretation; they are an interpretation of one's current state of mind.

Reluctance to see consciousness as a matter of self-interpretation doubtless stems in large measure from the traditional picture of consciousness as infallible and exhaustive. Consciousness on that view isn't merely interpretive; it doesn't simply give us a particular take on our current state of mind, but the real goods. Since such epistemic privilege does not actually obtain, however, there is little reason to reject an interpretive picture.

If consciousness were authoritative about what mental states we are in, an interpretive picture of consciousness would imply that it's also a matter of interpretation what mental states we actually are in. But there is a prima facie conflict between thinking that consciousness is interpretive and the view that it's authoritative. It's natural to think of consciousness as interpretive in part because consciousness isn't always accurate, and hence not authoritative. Consciousness is self-interpretation in respect of what mental states we are in, but whether the states themselves actually occur is independent of such self-interpretation.

We have reason to regard consciousness as interpretive even apart from the inaccuracies and incompleteness of consciousness. The higher-order states in virtue of which we are conscious of ourselves as being in various mental states are distinct from those first-order targets, and they describe those targets. So those higher-order states inevitably constitute a construal of what first-order states one is in. Conscious states are the states one is conscious of oneself as being in; we interpret our own mental states no less than we interpret those of others.[5] Chapters 4, 8, and 12 develop this connection between consciousness and self-interpretation.

Consciousness is not always accurate. Still, the way we are conscious of ourselves as being in various mental states typically is reasonably accurate, judged by the independent standards available to us. Why should that be so? If HOTs are self-interpretations about what mental states we are in, why should such self-interpretations generally be accurate? What explains the frequent match between the mental states we are in and the HOTs in virtue of which we're conscious of them?

Explaining the relative accuracy of the way we are conscious of the mental states we are in is an important challenge for any higher-order theory. If the relevant higher-order states are distinct from their targets, those targets will doubtless often figure in causing the higher-order states; but why do those causal connections result in accurate higher-order states? As noted earlier, some higher-order theorists seek to meet this challenge by appeal to a monitoring mechanism, perhaps of some quasi-perceptual sort. But without independent reason to think that some such dedicated mechanism exists, simply positing an accurate monitoring mechanism amounts to no more than stipulating a solution to the problem. Others have urged that consciousness is accurate because the higher-order content is not distinct from their first-order targets, but internal to those states. But there is again no independent warrant for this move, which in any case makes it mysterious that consciousness varies in how accurate it is.

The HOT hypothesis suggests a more satisfactory explanation of why we're so often conscious of our mental states, and why so often in a relatively accurate way. Consider an individual that has concepts for intentional states and applies those concepts fluently, but always on the basis of third-person considerations. This individual routinely and habitually relies solely on observed behavior and stimuli to

---

[5] Recall W. V. Quine's related insistence that "radical translation begins at home" ("Ontological Relativity," in *Ontological Relativity and Other Essays*, New York and London: Columbia University Press, 1969, 46; cf. *Word and Object*, Cambridge, Massachusetts: MIT Press, 1960, 78).

determine not only what intentional states others are in, but also what states it itself is in.

When this individual has the thought that it's raining, the way it behaves and its knowledge of the ambient situation tend to lead to its also having the thought, "I have the thought that it's raining." The fluent, habitual application to itself, on a third-person basis, of concepts for intentional states facilitates HOTs about its intentional states, HOTs that are reasonably accurate. And we can hypothesize that we came to be able fluently to apply concepts for intentional states to ourselves on the basis of an earlier ability to apply such concepts to both others and ourselves by consciously inferring from observable behavior and stimuli.

Similar factors facilitate HOTs about qualitative states. It's likely that we initially came to think of ourselves as being in qualitative states by noting occasional errors about the things we take to be in our immediate environment. Such errors could be due only to our having been in states that misrepresent environmental objects, states with the systematic similarities and differences characteristic of qualitative states. Taking note of perceptual errors leads to our thinking of ourselves as being in qualitative states.

Consider, then, an individual that has come to ascribe qualitative states both to itself and to others. When that individual is in a state with the mental quality red, it typically also has a perceptual thought that there is something red in front of it. So thinking that there is something red in front of it is by itself reasonably good evidence for that individual that it is in a state with the corresponding mental quality.

Such an individual will come to ascribe qualitative states to itself in an increasingly habitual way, simply on the basis of its having corresponding perceptual thoughts. As that happens, the individual's having those perceptual thoughts will by itself come to dispose the individual to have HOTs that it's in the relevant qualitative states. Simply having the perceptual thought that something in front of it is red comes to facilitate its having a HOT that it is in a state with the mental quality red.

As a result, the qualitative states of such an individual will often be conscious, and often in relatively accurate ways. First-order mental states play a causal role in such facilitation of HOTs not by way of some dedicated monitoring mechanism, but because of habitual connections that HOTs come to have with other intentional states. State consciousness is self-interpretation, but there are substantial psychological pressures toward accurate self-interpretation. Chapters 7 and 10 briefly discuss this facilitation of accurate HOTs.

Other psychological factors sometimes result in our self-interpretations' being erroneous in respect of what mental states we are in. So consciousness is not always accurate. Chapters 4, 7, and 8 discuss such confabulatory self-interpretation. But the pressures toward accuracy generally keep things from getting out of hand without any need to posit a dedicated monitoring mechanism or some special epistemic properties of consciousness.

Self-interpretation occurs not only in connection with what states we are conscious of ourselves as being in, but also in the way we are conscious of ourselves. There is the uninteresting unity that the mental states of each individual have, which consists simply in their all being states of a single biological organism. But conscious states seem also to exhibit a more challenging kind of unity that is specifically relevant to consciousness; they seem all to be states of a single conscious self.

Hume notoriously cast doubt on any such idea of a self. Because we never perceive a self, Hume urged that what we call the self is "nothing but a bundle or collection of different perceptions."[6] But this difficulty about the self results simply from Hume's conceiving of consciousness, and hence self-consciousness, in perceptual terms. The HOT hypothesis explains awareness of the self not perceptually, but by appeal to our having thoughts about the self. The content of each HOT is that one is, oneself, in a particular state; so one is conscious of one's mental states by having thoughts about oneself as being in those states. HOTs are seldom conscious, but when they are we have a reflective, introspective awareness of the self. HOTs make us conscious not only of our mental states, but also of the self that is in those states.

The subjective unity of consciousness results from the way these HOTs operate. Each HOT ascribes the state it is about to a particular self, and absent any counter-vailing reason, we take the self to which each HOT ascribes a state to be the same from one HOT to the next. So we are conscious of the self to which each HOT ascribes its target state as being the same as the self to which other HOTs ascribe their targets. Because we interpret the self as being the same from one HOT to another, we are conscious of all our conscious states as belonging to the same self. The apparent unity of consciousness is a matter of our interpreting all our conscious states as states of a single self. Chapter 13 develops and defends this account of conscious unity.

Our consciousness of ourselves as acting freely is also a matter of such self-interpretation. Because we're seldom conscious of the mental antecedents of our conscious intentions and desires, we're rarely conscious of those intentions and desires as being caused. So they appear to us as uncaused, and in that way free. This idea of freedom seems compelling to us because of the way we're conscious of our intentions and desires. Chapter 13 also develops this explanation.

It's natural to assume that the causal role of intentional states is a function of just their content and mental attitude, independent of whether those states are conscious. Still, there is a temptation to think that consciousness has a function, so that the consciousness of our beliefs and desires makes a difference to our reasoning and planning. But it's likely that what makes such a difference is only the content of these states, and not their being conscious. Indeed, there is convincing evidence that we become conscious of our decisions only after those decisions have been formed. Very likely it seems that our consciousness of our beliefs and desires makes a difference in our behavior because the only states we're conscious of as playing roles in reasoning and planning are conscious states. So we conclude that such consciousness makes a difference to the role those states play in behavior.

State consciousness is a matter of the way we are conscious of ourselves as being in various mental states. When the state we are conscious of ourselves as being in

---

[6] David Hume, *A Treatise of Human Nature* [1739], ed. L. A. Selby-Bigge, Oxford: Clarendon Press, 1888, I, IV, vi, 252.

is qualitative, what it's like for us is determined by the way we are conscious of the state. Similarly, the appearance of unity of consciousness, freedom of the will, and a function for consciousness all result from the way we are conscious of our mental states. We are conscious of those states as belonging to a single conscious self, as being uncaused, and as playing various roles in reasoning. The best explanation of all these things is that we are conscious of our mental states by having HOTs that describe the states in those ways.

PART I

EXPLAINING CONSCIOUSNESS

1

Two Concepts of Consciousness

No mental phenomenon is more central than consciousness to an adequate understanding of the mind. Nor does any mental phenomenon seem more stubbornly to resist theoretical treatment.

Consciousness is so basic to the way we think about the mind that it can be tempting to suppose that no mental states exist that are not conscious states. Indeed, it may even seem mysterious what sort of thing a mental state might be if it is not a conscious state. On this way of looking at things, if any mental states do lack consciousness, they are exceptional cases that call for special explanation or qualification. Perhaps dispositional or cognitive states exist that are not conscious, but nonetheless count as mental states. But if so, such states would be derivatively mental, owing their mental status solely to their connection with conscious states. And perhaps it makes sense to postulate nonconscious versions of ordinary mental states, as some psychological theories do. But if consciousness is central to mentality in the way this picture insists, any such states are at best degenerate examples of mentality, and thus peripheral to our concept of mind.

This picture is both inviting and familiar. But there are other features of the way we normally think about mind which result in a rather different conception of the relation between consciousness and mentality. We often know, without being told, what another person is thinking or feeling. And we sometimes know this even when that person actually is not aware, at least at first, of having those feelings or thoughts. There is nothing anomalous or puzzling about such cases. Even if it is only seldom that we know the mental states of others better than they do, when we do, the mental states in question are not degenerate or derivative examples of mentality. Moreover, conscious states are simply mental states we are conscious of being in. So when we are aware that somebody thinks or feels something that that person is initially unaware of thinking or feeling, those thoughts and feelings are at first mental states that are not also conscious states. These considerations suggest a way of looking at things on which we have no more reason to identify being a mental state with being a conscious state than we have to identify physical objects with physical objects that somebody sees. Consciousness is a feature of many mental states but, on this picture, it is not necessary or even central to a state's being a mental state. Consciousness seems central to mentality only because it is so basic to how we know our own mental states. But how we know about things is often an unreliable guide to their nature.

These two alternative pictures of the connection between consciousness and mentality have different implications about what sort of explanation is possible of what it is for a mental state to be a conscious state. If we take the view that consciousness is not a necessary feature of mental states, then we cannot define mental states as conscious states. Accordingly, we must seek some other account of what makes a state a mental state. But once we have an account of mentality that does not appeal to consciousness, we can then try to explain what conscious states are by building upon that very account of mentality. In particular, it then makes sense to try to formulate nontrivial necessary and sufficient conditions for a mental state to be a conscious state. On this conception of mentality and consciousness, it is open for us to proceed sequentially in this way, first defining mentality and then consciousness.

No such procedure, however, is possible if instead we adopt the view that being a mental state is at bottom the same as being a conscious state. For we cannot then explain what makes conscious states conscious by appeal to a prior account of mentality, since on that view mentality presupposes consciousness itself. Any attempt to explain consciousness by formulating necessary and sufficient conditions for a mental state to be conscious will thus automatically fail. If consciousness is already built into mentality, any such explanation will be uninformative. If not, then, on the present view, the conception of mind on which our explanation of consciousness is based will unavoidably be radically defective. It is plain that there is no third way; nothing that is not mental can help to explain consciousness. So, if consciousness is essential to mentality, no informative, nontrivial explanation of consciousness is possible at all. Moreover, since we cannot then proceed sequentially, explaining mentality first and then consciousness, the gulf that seems to separate mind and consciousness from the rest of reality will appear impossible to bridge. Thomas Nagel succinctly expresses this view when he writes that "[c]onsciousness is what makes the mind–body problem really intractable."[1]

Although it seems effectively to preclude our giving any informative explanation of consciousness, the view that consciousness is essential to all mental states does have apparent advantages. For one thing, that view, which has strong affinities with the Cartesian view of mind, fits well with many of our commonsense intuitions about the mental. And perhaps that view even does greater justice to those intuitions than a view of the mind on which not all mental states are conscious. These two competing pictures of mind and consciousness seem to present us, therefore, with a difficult choice. We can opt to save our presystematic intuitions at the cost of being unable to explain consciousness. Or we can hold open the possibility of giving a satisfactory explanation, but risk being less faithful to our commonsense intuitions about what mental states are.

One reaction to this quandary is simply to accept the more Cartesian of the two pictures, and accept that an illuminating explanation of consciousness will simply prove impossible. This traditional response is now hard to credit. Mind and consciousness are continuous with other natural phenomena of which we can give impressively powerful explanations. And it is difficult to believe that a singularity in

---

[1] "What Is It Like to Be a Bat?", *The Philosophical Review*, LXXXIII, 4 (October 1974): 435–450; reprinted in Nagel's *Mortal Questions*, Cambridge and New York: Cambridge University Press, 1979, pp. 165–180, at p. 165. Page references to Nagel will be to *Mortal Questions* and, unless otherwise indicated, to that article.

nature could exist that would utterly and permanently resist all attempts to explain it. For these reasons, some more recent writers have chosen, instead, simply to abandon commonsense intuitions about mind when they conflict with our explanatory goals. Physics does not aspire to reconstruct all our presystematic intuitions about the things around us. Why, proponents of this eliminativist approach ask, should the science of mind proceed differently?[2]

But we should, wherever possible, seek to explain our commonsense intuitions rather than just explain them away. And we should hesitate to jettison our presystematic conceptions of things, whether mental or physical, unless efforts to do justice to them have decisively failed. Indeed, even physical theories must square as much as possible with our commonsense picture of physical reality. In what follows, I argue that we need embrace neither the Cartesian nor the eliminativist stance toward the consciousness of mental states. Instead, we can both be faithful to our presystematic intuitions about consciousness and mind and, at the same time, construct useful, informative explanations of those phenomena. In section I, I develop the two pictures sketched above. In particular, I articulate the two different definitions of mentality itself that comprise the core of those two pictures. I then use the non-Cartesian concept of mind and consciousness to construct a systematic and theoretically satisfying explanation of what it is for a mental state to be conscious—an explanation, that is, of what it is that distinguishes conscious from nonconscious mental states. I show further how the definition of mentality central to each of the two pictures determines a distinct conception of consciousness, and how the Cartesian concept of consciousness makes any informative explanation of consciousness impossible. In sections II and III, then, I go on to argue that the non-Cartesian explanation can save the phenomenological appearances and explain the data of consciousness as well as the more familiar Cartesian picture. And I argue there that the standard considerations that favor the Cartesian view are baseless. In section IV I conclude with some observations about consciousness and our knowledge of the mental, and about the actual significance of the insights that underlie the Cartesian picture.

I.

All mental states, of whatever sort, exhibit properties of one of two types: intentional properties and phenomenal, or sensory, properties. Something has an intentional property if it has propositional content, or if it is about something. Sensory properties, by contrast, are less homogeneous. Examples are the redness of a visual sensation and the sharp painful quality of certain bodily sensations. Some mental states may have both intentional and phenomenal properties. But whatever else is true of mental states, it is plain that we would not count a state as a mental state at all unless it had some intentional property or some phenomenal property.

[2] Richard Rorty and Paul M. Churchland, among others, have championed this view; see Rorty's *Philosophy and the Mirror of Nature*, Princeton: Princeton University Press, 1979, Part I, and Churchland's *Scientific Realism and the Plasticity of Mind*, Cambridge: Cambridge University Press, 1979.

Something close to the converse holds as well. For one thing, only mental states can have phenomenal properties. Although we use words such as 'red' and 'round' to refer to properties of physical objects as well as to properties of mental states, we refer to different properties in the two cases. The introspectible redness of a visual sensation is not the same property as the perceptible redness of a tomato, for example, since each can occur in the absence of the other. Moreover, mental states are not objects at all, and therefore cannot have the same properties of shape and color that physical objects have. Indeed, we do not even use quality words the same way when we talk about mental states and about physical objects. We speak interchangeably about red sensations and sensations of red, but it makes no nonmetaphorical sense to talk about tomatoes of red. Similar considerations apply to properties that are special to bodily sensations. Knives and aches may both be dull, but the dullness of a knife, unlike that of an ache, has to do with the shape of its edge. Phenomenal properties, properly so called, are unique to mental states.[3]

Things are slightly less straightforward with intentional properties, since items other than mental states can exhibit intentionality. Speech acts and works of art, for example, can be about things and can have propositional content. But except for mental states themselves, nothing has intentional properties other than those modes and products of behavior which express intentional mental states. So it is reasonable to hold that these modes and products of behavior derive their intentionality from the mental states they express. As Roderick M. Chisholm puts it, "thoughts are a 'source of intentionality'—i.e., nothing would be intentional were it not for the fact that thoughts are intentional."[4] So, even though intentional properties belong to things other than mental states, they do so only derivatively. Accordingly, all mental states have intentional or sensory properties, and sensory properties belong only to mental states and intentional properties nonderivatively to mental states alone. We thus have a compelling basis for defining mental states as just those states which have either intentionality or phenomenal quality.

There are, however, objections to this way of delineating the distinctively mental which seem to favor a mark of the mental based on consciousness instead. For one thing, a mark of the mental that relies solely on intentional and phenomenal properties may seem to underplay the special access we have to our own mental states. Even if all mental states do exhibit intentional or sensory features, one might urge that the more revealing mark of the mental would somehow appeal, instead, to that special access. On such a mark, what is essential to mental states would not be intentional

---

[3] In a review of Frank Jackson's *Perception* (*The Journal of Philosophy*, LXXXII, 1 [January 1985]: 28–41), I argue in detail that words for such qualities have this double use. On this point see also G. E. Moore, "A Reply to My Critics," in *The Philosophy of G. E. Moore*, ed. Paul Arthur Schilpp, La Salle, Illinois: Open Court, 1942, pp. 535–677, pp. 655–658; and Thomas Reid, *Essays on the Intellectual Powers of Man*, ed. Baruch A. Brody, Cambridge, Massachusetts: MIT Press, 1969, II, xvi, 244.

[4] "Chisholm-Sellars Correspondence on Intentionality," in *Minnesota Studies in the Philosophy of Science*, II, ed. Herbert Feigl, Michael Scriven, and Grover Maxwell, Minneapolis: University of Minnesota Press, 1958, pp. 521–539, at p. 533. In "Intentionality," ch. 3 in this volume, I argue that this claim is defensible if it is construed in strictly causal terms.

or sensory character, but consciousness itself. Moreover, if we take the possession of either sensory or intentional properties to be definitive of the mental, we must then explain why we regard this disjunctive mark as determining the mental. Why do we construe as a single category the class of states that have one or the other of these two kinds of properties? It does not help to note that some mental states, for example, perceptual states, have both sorts of characteristic. Despite the existence of such mongrel cases, it seems unlikely that pure phenomenal states, such as pains, have anything interesting in common with pure intentional states, such as beliefs. And we can avoid this difficulty if, instead, we take consciousness to be what makes a state a mental state. Finally, the characteristically mental differences among kinds of mental states are all differences in what intentional or sensory properties those states have. So those properties may seem to figure more naturally in an account of how we distinguish among types of mental state than in an account of how mental states differ from everything else. These various considerations all suggest that an account of mind in terms of consciousness may be preferable to an account that appeals to intentionality and phenomenal character.

Moreover, defining mentality in terms of consciousness need not involve any circularity. We can say what it is to be a conscious state in a way that does not explicitly mention being mental. A state is conscious if whoever is in it is to some degree aware of being in it in a way that does not rely on inference, as that is ordinarily conceived, or on some sort of sensory input. Conscious states are simply those states to which we have noninferential and nonsensory access.†

People do, of course, have many more beliefs and preferences, at any given time, than occur in their stream of consciousness. And the nonconscious beliefs and preferences must always have intentional properties. But this need not be decisive against taking consciousness as our mark of the mental. For we can construe beliefs and preferences as actual mental states only when they are conscious. On other occasions we could regard them to be merely dispositions for actual mental states to occur; in those cases, we can say, one is simply disposed to have occurrent thoughts and desires.

Consciousness is intuitively far more crucial for sensory states than for intentional states. This disparity is something we must explain if we take consciousness as the mark of all mental states. Construing nonconscious beliefs and preferences not as actual mental states but as mere dispositions to be in such states helps us give a suitable explanation. Sensory states normally result from short-term stimulations; so we have little reason to talk about our being disposed to be in particular types of sensory state.

---

† The qualification about inference "as ordinarily conceived" was intended to restrict attention to inference of which we are conscious; see, e.g., n. 27 in "Thinking that One Thinks," ch. 2 in this volume.

Sensory access must not be restricted to the five exteroceptive senses, as Jerome A. Shaffer suggests, in "defining 'mental events' as those which can be justifiably reported without appeal to observation via the five senses" ("Persons and Their Bodies," *The Philosophical Review*, LXXV, 1 [January 1966]: 59–77, p. 61). We are aware of the ordinary movements of our limbs or the perturbations of our viscera independently of exteroceptive sensing, and we don't want those bodily events caught in the net of conscious states. But proprioceptive and enteroceptive sensing does figure in our being aware of those bodily conditions. [Daggered notes added in 2005.]

By contrast, we are often disposed to be in intentional states of various kinds. Since we are typically not conscious of being thus disposed, the tie between consciousness and mentality may at first sight seem less strong with intentional than with sensory states. But that tie may apply equally to both sorts of state if we count only nondispositional states as mental states, properly speaking. For when we focus on short-term, episodic intentional states, the commonsense intuition that mental states must be conscious is no less compelling than it is in the case of phenomenal states.

The two marks of the mental just sketched are independent of each other, and both lay claim to long and well-established histories. Thus writers with Cartesian leanings have generally favored some mark based on consciousness, while those in a more naturalist, Aristotelian tradition have tended to rely instead on some such mark as intentionality or sensory character. For it is a roughly Aristotelian idea that the mental is somehow dependent on highly organized forms of life, in something like the way in which life itself emerges in highly organized forms of material existence. And this idea suggests that one should try to delimit the mental in terms of the various distinctively mental kinds of functioning and, thus, by reference to the intentional and phenomenal characteristics of mental states. To the Aristotelian, such a mark has the advantage of inviting one to conceive of the mental as continuous with other natural phenomena. Thus Aristotle's own account of psychological phenomena gives great prominence to sense perception, thereby stressing the continuity between the mental and the biological.

The Cartesian tradition, by contrast, conceives of the mental as one of the two jointly exhaustive categories of existence, standing in stark opposition to everything physical. And on this view it is tempting to select some single essential feature, such as consciousness, to be the mark of the mental. For this kind of mark will stress the sharp contrast between mental and physical, and play down the differences among types of mental state compared to how different all mental states are from everything else. In this spirit, Descartes takes nonperceptual, propositional states to be the paradigm of the mental and, notoriously, has great difficulty in explaining how perception can involve both mental and bodily states.

Although both marks of the mental have enjoyed widespread acceptance, it is crucial which mark we adopt if our goal is to give an explanation of consciousness. Conscious states are simply mental states we are conscious of being in. And, in general, our being conscious of something is just a matter of our having a thought of some sort about it.[†] Accordingly, it is natural to identify a mental state's being conscious with one's having a roughly contemporaneous thought that one is in that mental state. When a mental state is conscious, one's awareness of it is, intuitively,

---

[†] Elsewhere I consider and argue against the possibility that we are conscious of our conscious mental states by perceiving or sensing them. See, e.g., "Introspection and Self-Interpretation," ch. 4 in this volume, § II; "The Independence of Consciousness and Sensory Quality," ch. 5 in this volume, § IV; "Sensory Quality and the Relocation Story," ch. 6 in this volume, § III; "Varieties of Higher-Order Theory," in *Higher-Order Theories of Consciousness*, ed. Rocco J. Gennaro, Amsterdam and Philadelphia: John Benjamins Publishers, 2004, pp. 17–44, §§ II–IV; and "Perceptual and Cognitive Models of Consciousness," *Journal of the American Psychoanalytic Association*, 45, 3 (Summer 1997): 740–746.

immediate in some way. So we can stipulate that the contemporaneous thought one has is not mediated by any inference or perceptual input.[†] We are then in a position to advance a useful, informative explanation of what makes conscious states conscious. Since a mental state is conscious if it is accompanied by a suitable higher-order thought, we can explain a mental state's being conscious by hypothesizing that the mental state itself causes that higher-order thought to occur.[‡]

At first sight it may seem that counterexamples to this explanation are rife. Although we are usually, when awake, in some conscious mental state or other, we rarely notice having any higher-order thoughts of the sort this explanation postulates. Typically, mental states occur in our stream of consciousness without our also having any evident thought that we are in those states. But such cases are not counterexamples unless we presuppose, contrary to the present explanation, that all mental states are conscious states. For otherwise, there will be no reason to assume that the higher-order thoughts that our explanation posits would, in general, be conscious thoughts. On this explanation, a mental state is conscious if one has a suitable second-order thought. So that second-order thought would itself be a conscious thought only if one also had a third-order thought that one had the second-order thought. And it begs the question against that account to assume that these higher-order thoughts are usually, or even often, conscious thoughts. If a mental state's being conscious does consist in one's having a suitable higher-order thought, there is no reason to expect that this thought would ordinarily be a conscious thought. Indeed, we would expect, instead, that the third-order thoughts that confer consciousness on such second-order thoughts would be relatively rare; it is hard to hold in mind a thought about a thought that is in turn about a thought. So the present account correctly predicts that we would seldom be aware of our second-order thoughts, and this actually helps confirm the account.

It is important to distinguish a mental state's being conscious from our being introspectively aware of that state. Higher-order thoughts are sometimes invoked to explain introspection, which is a special case of consciousness.[5] But

---

[†] As above, independence from inference should be understood as independence from inference of which one is conscious.

It is arguable that we need not exclude perceptual input, since whenever perception figures in our being aware of a mental state, inference will as well, and in subsequent discussions I frame this condition without mention of observation. We are sometimes aware without conscious inference of the throbbing of our veins and positions and movements of our limbs. And even when we are, these bodily conditions don't count as conscious states. But that is because those conditions aren't mental states in the first place. Because those conditions exhibit neither intentional nor qualitative properties, they don't make us conscious *of* anything; only mental states make us conscious *of* things. So, even when we are spontaneously and noninferentially conscious of being in nonmental states, we do not count them as conscious states.

[‡] By the time this paper first appeared, I had come to reject the idea that a state's being conscious requires some causal connection between that state and the accompanying higher-order thought. See, e.g., note 25 in "Thinking that One Thinks," ch. 2 in this volume, and "Higher-Order Thoughts and the Appendage Theory of Consciousness," *Philosophical Psychology*, VI, 2 (1993): 155–167, pp. 161–163.

[5] See, e.g., David M. Armstrong, *A Materialist Theory of the Mind*, New York: Humanities Press, 1968, 92–115 and 323–327, and "What Is Consciousness?", in Armstrong's *The Nature of Mind*

introspection is a more complex phenomenon than the ordinary consciousness of mental states. Intuitively, a mental state's being conscious means just that it occurs in our stream of consciousness. Introspection, by contrast, involves consciously and deliberately paying attention to our contemporaneous mental states. As Ryle remarks, "introspection is an attentive operation and one which is only occasionally performed, whereas consciousness is supposed to be a constant element of all mental processes."[6] Normally when mental states occur in one's stream of consciousness, one is unaware of having any higher-order thoughts about them. But when we are reflectively or introspectively aware of a mental state, we are aware not only of being in that mental state; we are also aware that we are aware of being in it. The Cartesian picture of mind and consciousness thus tacitly conflates a mental state's being conscious with our being introspectively aware of it. For on that picture the consciousness of a mental state is inseparable from that mental state. So reflective awareness, which is being aware both of a mental state and of one's awareness of that state, will be inseparable from awareness of the state which is not thus reflective. Here our commonsense intuitions diverge from the Cartesian view that consciousness is essential to mental states, since the two kinds of awareness plainly do differ.

Introspection is consciously and deliberately paying attention to mental states that are in our stream of consciousness. So, whatever else one holds about consciousness, it is natural to explain introspection as one's having a conscious higher-order thought that one is in the mental state that one is introspectively aware of. So, if these higher-order thoughts all had to be conscious, we could invoke them only to explain introspective consciousness. For only when we are introspectively aware of a mental state are we also aware of our higher-order thoughts. But higher-order thoughts are not automatically conscious, any more than other mental states are. They are conscious only when we have a yet higher-order thought that we have such a thought. So there is no difficulty about using higher-order thoughts to explain not only reflective or introspective awareness, but also what it is for a mental state just to be in our stream of consciousness without our also consciously focusing on it. Introspective awareness of a particular mental state is having a thought that one is in that mental state, and also a thought that one has that thought. Having a conscious mental state without introspectively focusing on it is having the second-order thought without the third-order thought. It may seem slightly odd that each of these hierarchies of conscious mental states has a nonconscious thought at its top. But whatever air of paradox there seems to be here is dispelled by the commonsense truism that we cannot be conscious of everything at once.

One might urge against the present account that higher-order thoughts are unnecessary to explain the consciousness of mental states. Intuitively, a mental

and Other Essays, Ithaca, New York: Cornell University Press, 1980, pp. 55–67, at pp. 59–61; David Lewis, "An Argument for the Identity Theory," *The Journal of Philosophy*, LXIII, 1 (January 6, 1969): 17–25, p. 21, and "Psychophysical and Theoretical Identifications," *Australasian Journal of Philosophy*, 50, 3 (December 1972): 249–258, p. 258; and Wilfrid Sellars, "Empiricism and the Philosophy of Mind," in Sellars' *Science, Perception and Reality*, London: Routledge & Kegan Paul and New York: Humanities Press, 1963, pp. 127–196, at pp. 188–189 and 194–195.

[6] Gilbert Ryle, *The Concept of Mind*, London: Hutchinson & Co., 1949, 164.

state is conscious if it is introspectible. And one might conclude from this that, to explain such consciousness, we need not posit actual higher-order thoughts, but only dispositions to have such thoughts. A mental state is conscious, on this suggestion, if one is disposed to think that one is in that state.[7] But there are several difficulties with such a dispositional account. For one thing, the consciousness of mental states is phenomenologically occurrent. Since consciousness does not appear to be dispositional, it is ad hoc simply to posit a disposition that comes and goes as needed. We cannot, of course, save all the phenomenological appearances, but we should prefer to do so when we can. Moreover, it is unclear what explanatory work a disposition to have a higher-order thought would do, except when one actually had that thought, and the disposition would then be superfluous.

In any case, the present account readily enables us to explain the intuition that a state's being conscious means that it is introspectible. To introspect a mental state is to have a conscious thought about that state. So introspection is having a thought about some mental state one is in and, also, a yet higher-order thought that makes the first thought conscious. It is a feature of our experience that, when a mental state is conscious, we can readily come to have a conscious thought about that mental state. On the present account, we do not come to have a new thought about that mental state; we simply come to be conscious of a thought we already had, albeit nonconsciously. Higher-order thoughts are mental states we can become aware of more or less at will. A state's being conscious therefore amounts to its being introspectible. Only if being unaware of a higher-order thought meant that one simply did not have that thought would we have reason to try to make do with dispositions, rather than the actual thoughts themselves.

On the present account, conscious mental states are mental states that [are accompanied by and often]† cause the occurrence of higher-order thoughts that one is in those mental states. And, since those higher-order thoughts are distinct from the mental states that are conscious, those thoughts can presumably occur even when the mental states that the higher-order thoughts purport to be about do not exist. But such occurrences would not constitute an objection to this account. It is reasonable to suppose that such false higher-order thoughts would be both rare and pathological.‡ Nor would they be undetectable if they did occur. We can determine the presence of

---

[7] Allen Hazen has urged this line especially forcefully, in correspondence. Also, see Kant's claim that the representation 'I think' must be able to accompany all other representations (*K.d.R.V.*, B131–2; cf. B406, though Kant insists that the representation 'I think' is a nonempirical [B132] or transcendental [B401, A343] representation).

† Added in 2005.

‡ Since this paper first appeared I have come to think that such misrepresentation by higher-order thoughts of the states they are about is neither all that rare nor pathological, and that it may well be relatively routine. See, e.g., "Introspection and Self-Interpretation," § VI; "Sensory Quality and the Relocation Story," § V; "Sensory Qualities, Consciousness, and Perception," ch. 7 in this volume, §§ V and VII; and "First-Person Operationalism and Mental Taxonomy," ch. 9 in this volume, § IV.

See also my "Consciousness, Content, and Metacognitive Judgments," *Consciousness and Cognition*, 9, 2, Part 1 (June 2000), pp. 203–214, § V; "Metacognition and Higher-Order Thoughts," *Consciousness and Cognition*, 9, 2, Part 1 (June 2000), pp. 231–242, § IV;

nonconscious mental states by way of their causal connections with behavior and stimuli, and with other mental states, both conscious and not. Similarly, we can detect the absence of mental states by virtue of the causal connections they would have with such other events.

By itself, the present account of consciousness does not imply a materialist or naturalist theory of mind. Indeed, the account is compatible with even a thoroughgoing Cartesian dualism of substances. But it does square nicely with materialist views. For the account holds that what makes conscious mental states conscious is their causing higher-order thoughts that one is in those mental states. And the materialist can reasonably maintain that this causal pattern is due to suitable neural connections.

Moreover, the materialist can argue that intentional and sensory properties are themselves simply special sorts of physical properties. For one thing, arguments that these mental properties are not physical properties usually rely on the unstated and question-begging assumption that anything mental is automatically nonphysical. Independent support for this supposition is seldom attempted. Even more important, however, the characteristics that are supposed to show that intentional or sensory properties are not physical turn out, on scrutiny, to be characteristics that various indisputably physical properties also exhibit.[8] So even if no developed, satisfactory account of these properties is presently at hand, there is no reason to doubt that accurate accounts will be forthcoming that are compatible with a thoroughgoing naturalist view of mind. Together with the present explanation of the consciousness of mental states, this should make possible a reasonably comprehensive naturalist theory of mind.

It is a welcome benefit of the present account that it is hospitable to naturalist theories, but this is not its main strength. Rather, its principal advantage is just that it enables us to explain what it is for a mental state to be a conscious state. The present explanation, moreover, has precise empirical consequences that one could reasonably hope to test. For it implies not only that conscious mental states are accompanied by distinct higher-order thoughts, but also that some causal mechanism exists that connects conscious mental states to the corresponding higher-order thoughts.

Such an explanation is possible only if we adopt the non-Cartesian view that intentional and sensory character are jointly the mark of the mental. If, instead, we were to follow the Cartesian tradition in regarding consciousness itself as the key to mentality, no account of consciousness in terms of higher-order thoughts could succeed. For then one would have to deny that a mental state could occur without its being conscious. As Descartes put it, "no thought can exist in us of which we are not conscious at the very moment it exists in us."[9] But, if all mental states

---

and "Consciousness and Metacognition," in *Metarepresentation: A Multidisciplinary Perspective*, Proceedings of the Tenth Vancouver Cognitive Science Conference, ed. Daniel Sperber, New York: Oxford University Press, 2000, pp. 265–295, § V.

[8] For a detailed argument to this effect, see my "Mentality and Neutrality," *The Journal of Philosophy*, LXXIII, 13 (July 15, 1976): 386–415, § I.

[9] *Fourth Replies, Oeuvres de Descartes*, ed. Charles Adam and Paul Tannery, Paris: J. Vrin, 1964–75 [henceforth "*AT*"], VII, 246; see René Descartes, *The Philosophical Writings of Descartes*, tr. John Cottingham, Robert Stoothoff, and Dugald Murdoch (vol. III with Anthony Kenny), 3

are conscious and a higher-order thought exists for every conscious mental state, serious, insurmountable difficulties immediately ensue. For one thing, there would be denumerably many distinct higher-order thoughts corresponding to every conscious mental state. No mental state could be conscious without being accompanied by a higher-order thought. But that thought would itself have to be conscious, and so a yet higher-order thought would be necessary. This regress would never halt. It strains credulity to suppose that human beings can have infinitely many conscious thoughts at a particular time. And even if we could, it is hardly sensible to explain a mental state's being conscious by way of such an infinite series.

Even more damaging consequences follow for an account in terms of higher-order thoughts if all mental states are conscious states. As noted above, we are not normally aware of the higher-order thoughts that, on such an account, make mental states conscious. But, if all mental states were conscious, we would be aware of any higher-order thoughts that we have. So we could not explain why we typically seem not to have such thoughts by saying that they are simply not conscious thoughts. By requiring that all mental states be conscious states, the Cartesian conception of mentality rules out our explaining consciousness by reference to higher-order thoughts.

If consciousness were what makes a state a mental state, therefore, any account that represents that consciousness as being due to a connection that conscious mental states have with some other mental state would be radically misguided. For that other mental state would then itself have to be conscious, and we would have to invoke yet another mental state to explain its being conscious. A vicious regress would thus be unavoidable. So long as we hold that all mental states are conscious, we can prevent that regress only by maintaining that the consciousness of a mental state is not a relation that state bears to some other mental state, but rather an intrinsic property. Moreover, if consciousness is what makes mental states mental, it will be viciously circular to explain that consciousness in terms of a relation that conscious mental states bear to other mental states, since those other mental states would themselves then have to be conscious. It is plain that we cannot explain or analyze consciousness at all unless we can do so in terms of some sort of mental phenomenon. So, if consciousness is what makes a state a mental state, consciousness will not only be an intrinsic, nonrelational property of all mental states; it will be unanalyzable as well. It will, as Russell disparagingly put it, be "a pervading quality of psychical phenomena."[10] Indeed, if being mental means being conscious, we can invoke no mental phenomenon whatever to explain what it is for a state to be a conscious state. Since no nonmental phenomenon can help, it seems plain that, on the Cartesian concept of mentality, no informative explanation is possible of what it is for a mental state to be conscious.

---

volumes, Cambridge: Cambridge University Press, 1984–91 [henceforth "*C*"], II, 171. See also the Geometrical Exposition of the *Second Replies*: "the word 'thought' applies to all that exists in us in such a way that we are immediately conscious of it" (*AT* VII, 160; see C II, 113), and elsewhere, e.g. *First Replies*, AT VII, 107 (*C* II, 77), Letter to Mersenne, *AT* III, 273 (*C* III, 165), *Fourth Replies*, *AT* VII, 232 (*C* II, 162), and *Principles* I, ix, *AT* VIII-1, 7 (*C* I, 195).

[10] Bertrand Russell, *The Analysis of Mind*, London: George Allen & Unwin and New York: Humanities Press, 1921, p. 9.

Since consciousness is a matter of our noninferential and nonsensory knowledge of our mental states, it is tempting to describe the issue in terms of such notions as incorrigibility, infallibility, and privacy.[11] But the foregoing obstacles to explaining consciousness do not derive from any such epistemic matters. Rather, they result simply from the Cartesian idea that all mental states are conscious states.

On the Cartesian concept of mentality and consciousness, consciousness is essential to mental states. It is therefore a nonrelational property of those states that is very likely unanalyzable as well. That this conception prevents us from explaining consciousness in any useful way is the most compelling reason we can have for adopting, instead, a non-Cartesian mark of the mental. But there are other reasons as well to prefer a non-Cartesian mark. For one thing, it is impossible to conceive of a mental state, whether or not it is conscious, that lacks both intentional and sensory properties. So, even though it may not always be easy to imagine one's being in a mental state that is not conscious, intentional and sensory properties are evidently more central to our concept of a mental state than consciousness is. So, even though the characteristically mental differences among mental states are, as noted earlier, a function of their intentional and sensory properties, those properties are not only important for explaining how we distinguish among the various types of mental state. They are also necessary for explaining how mental states differ from everything nonmental.

The Cartesian might concede that we can have no notion of a mental state that has neither intentional nor phenomenal character, but go on to insist that we also can have no idea of what it would be like to be in a nonconscious mental state even if it does have intentional or sensory properties. But knowing what it would be like to be in such a state is not relevant here. Knowing what it is like to be in a state is knowing what it is like to be aware of being in that state. So, if the state in question is not a conscious mental state, there will be no such thing as what it is like to be in it, at least in the relevant sense of that idiom. This does not show, however, that intentional and phenomenal states cannot lack consciousness. Conscious states resemble and differ in respect of their intentional or phenomenal features. Accordingly, nonconscious mental states will simply be states that resemble and differ from one another in exactly these ways, but without one's being noninferentially aware of their existence and character.

Indeed, it is indisputable that inner states that resemble and differ in just these ways do occur outside our stream of consciousness. Many sorts of mental state, such as beliefs, desires, hopes, expectations, aspirations, various emotions, and arguably even some bodily feelings such as aches, often occur in us without our noticing their presence. And the only thing that makes these states the kinds of states they are is the intentional and phenomenal properties they have. So we must explain what it is for these states to be mental not by reference to consciousness, but by appeal to their

---

[11] See, e.g., Rorty's argument "that incorrigibility is the best candidate" for a satisfactory mark of the "sorts of entities [that] make up the content of the stream of consciousness" ("Incorrigibility as the Mark of the Mental," *The Journal of Philosophy*, LXVII, 12 [June 25, 1970]: 399–424, pp. 406–407; cf. also Rorty's *Philosophy and the Mirror of Nature*, e.g., pp. 88–96, and Part I, *passim*).

having phenomenal or intentional character. As noted above, we can deny that some of these mental phenomena are properly speaking mental states at all, and instead construe them as mere dispositions for mental states to occur. But states of these sorts often have a strong effect on our actual behavior, and even influence the course and content of our stream of consciousness. These mental phenomena must presumably be nondispositional states at least on those occasions when they exercise such causal influence. So the only reason to regard them as mere dispositions would be a question-begging concern to sustain the theory that all mental states are conscious states.

Perhaps the Cartesian will counter that, even if nonconscious intentional states are unproblematic, the idea that a mental state could have sensory character and yet not be conscious is simply unintelligible. For it may seem that the very idea of a nonconscious state with sensory qualities is, in effect, a contradiction in terms. What seems to make intelligible the idea of a mental state's having phenomenal qualities at all is our immediate awareness of how such states feel or what they are like for those who are in them. This issue will receive extended consideration in section III. For now, however, it is enough to note that, even if we understand what it is for a state to have sensory quality only because we are familiar with cases in which we are conscious of being in such states, it hardly follows that nonconscious sensory states cannot occur. That we understand a kind of phenomenon by way of a particular kind of case does not show that cases of other sorts are impossible.

II.

On the Cartesian view, consciousness is definitive of the mental. This concept of mentality implies that consciousness cannot be a relational characteristic of mental states, and that it may well be inexplicable as well. The difficulty in explaining consciousness on that view actually results from the Cartesian strategy for dealing with mental phenomena. The main strength of the Cartesian picture is that it closely matches our presystematic, commonsense intuitions. But it achieves this close match by building those intuitions into our very concepts of mind and consciousness. And this automatically trivializes any explanation we might then give of them. We cannot very well give non-question-begging accounts of intuitions that we incorporate definitionally into our very concepts. Explanations based on the Cartesian conceptions of mind and consciousness thus rely heavily, and ineliminably, on interdefinition of such terms as 'mind', 'consciousness', 'subjectivity', and 'self'. Such interdefinition may be useful in marking out a range of interconnected phenomena, but it cannot do much to help explain the phenomena thus delineated.

On the non-Cartesian concept, by contrast, consciousness is not essential to mental states, and thus consciousness may well be an extrinsic characteristic of whatever mental states have it. The Cartesian conception achieves its close match with common sense at the cost of ruling out any useful explanation. No such trade-off is necessary on the non-Cartesian picture. The non-Cartesian has no trouble in giving a theoretically satisfying explanation of consciousness. And it is possible to show that this account enables us to save the phenomenological appearances at least roughly as well as the Cartesian can. Moreover, objections to an account cast in terms of higher-order thoughts can be convincingly met. In this section and the next I consider some of the most pressing of these objections, and also argue that such an account does do justice to the phenomenological data. In the present section I take up various general questions about the adequacy of the non-Cartesian account; in section III I address issues that pertain specifically to sensory qualities and to subjectivity.

One especially notable feature of our presystematic view of consciousness which the Cartesian conception seems to capture perspicuously is the close connection between being in a conscious state and being conscious of oneself. An account in terms of higher-order thoughts has no trouble here. If a mental state's being conscious consists of having a higher-order thought that one is in that mental state, being in a conscious state will imply having a thought about oneself. But being conscious of oneself is simply having a thought about oneself. So being in a conscious mental state is automatically sufficient for one to be conscious of oneself.

Any reasonable account of consciousness will presumably insist on this connection. But the Cartesian can say little that is informative about why the connection should hold. An account that appeals to higher-order thoughts has no such difficulty. Moreover, there is a well-motivated reason why the higher-order thought that the non-Cartesian invokes must be a thought about oneself. To confer consciousness of a particular mental state, the higher-order thought must be about that very mental state. And the only way for a thought to be about a particular mental state is for it to be about somebody's being in that state. Otherwise, the thought would just be about that type of mental state, and not about the particular token of it. So, in the case at hand, the higher-order thought must be a thought that one is, oneself, in that mental state.[12]

Having a thought that one is, oneself, in a particular mental state does not by itself presuppose any prior conception of the self or of some sort of unity of consciousness. Rather, the present view allows us to explain these conceptions as themselves actually arising from our being in conscious mental states. For we can construe the second-order thoughts as each being a thought to the effect that whatever individual has this very thought is also in the target mental state.[†] And, if a fair number of these

---

[12] As Hector-Neri Castañeda and G. E. M. Anscombe have pointed out, believing something of oneself must involve the mental analogue of the indirect reflexive construction, represented here by 'oneself' (Castañeda: "On the Logic of Attributions of Self-Knowledge to Others," *The Journal of Philosophy*, LXV, 15 [August 8, 1968]: 439–456 and elsewhere; Anscombe: "The First Person," in *Mind and Language*, ed. Samuel Guttenplan, Oxford: Oxford University Press, 1975, pp. 45–65). Even when George believes that somebody who turns out to be George is *F* it may not be true that George believes that he, himself, is *F*. For example, George may truly believe somebody is *F* while wrongly believing that that person is not George, himself. Or he may not even believe of himself that he is George. Unlike token-reflexive constructions, these terms involve anaphora. But the clauses that contain them are grammatical transforms of sentences that do contain genuine token reflexives.

[†] I no longer accept my earlier suggestion that we can construe higher-order thoughts as having the explicit content that whatever individual has this very thought is also in the target mental state. As Thomas Natsoulas has pointed out, if all higher-order thoughts were about themselves in that way, that might make one conscious of them all, and if it did they would all be conscious. See his

thoughts are conscious thoughts, it is plausible to suppose that a sense of the unity of consciousness will, in time, emerge.

If one held the Cartesian view that all mental states are conscious, invoking higher-order thoughts would issue in the vicious regress noted in section I. So, if one is tempted by both these moves, one might try to adjust things in order to avoid that outcome. The most promising way to do so would be simply to insist that the higher-order thoughts in virtue of which we are conscious of conscious mental states are actually part of those conscious states themselves. Every conscious mental state would then be, in part, about itself, and our knowledge that we are in such states would be due to that self-reference. Metaphorically, we would then conclude that a mental state's knowing itself is, in Ryle's apt metaphors, a matter of its being "self-intimating" (158) or "self-luminous" (159).[13]

This line of reasoning is particularly inviting, since it suggests that the Cartesian can, after all, give some nontrivial explanation of the consciousness of mental states. Conscious mental states are conscious, on this account, because they are about themselves. And this self-reference is intrinsic; it does not result from some connection those states have with other mental states. But anything that would support the view that conscious mental states are conscious because they know, or are in part about, themselves would provide equally good evidence that consciousness is due to an accompanying higher-order thought. Moreover, we have no nonarbitrary way to tell when one mental state is a part of another.

There is, accordingly, no reason to uphold the idea that our awareness of conscious states is a part of those states other than a desire to sustain the Cartesian contention that all mental states are conscious states. And, if conscious states do have parts in this way, the question arises whether all the parts of such states must be conscious, or only some. If all, then the awareness of the mental state will have to be conscious. A regress would thus arise that is exactly parallel to that which arose when we construed the awareness of conscious mental states as due to a distinct higher-order thought. The only advantage of an account on which that awareness is a part of the conscious mental state is if the awareness is a nonconscious part of the conscious state. This reinforces the conclusion that there is no nonarbitrary way to distinguish this view from an account in terms of higher-order thoughts. And it undercuts the idea that the Cartesian can formulate an informative explanation of consciousness along these

"What is Wrong with the Appendage Theory of Consciousness?", *Philosophical Psychology*, VI, 2 (June 1993): 137–154, p. 23, and my reply, "Higher-Order Thoughts and the Appendage Theory of Consciousness," *Philosophical Psychology*, VI, 2 (June 1993): 155–167.

For more on this issue and on the unity of consciousness, see "Unity of Consciousness and the Self," ch. 13 in this volume. On the unity of consciousness and related phenomena, see also "Introspection and Self-Interpretation," §VII; "Being Conscious of Ourselves," *The Monist*, 87, 2 (April 2004): 159–181; and "Persons, Minds, and Consciousness," in *The Philosophy of Marjorie Grene*, ed. Randall E. Auxier and Lewis E. Hahn, La Salle, Illinois: Open Court, 2002, pp. 199–220, §§ IV–V.

[13] See Franz Brentano, *Psychology from an Empirical Standpoint*, tr. Antos C. Rancurello *et al.*, London: Routledge & Kegan Paul and New York: Humanities Press, 1973, pp. 129–30.

lines. Since the Cartesian explanation would work only if the part of each conscious
state that makes it conscious were itself conscious, the regress is unavoidable.

One reason that consciousness seems intrinsic to our sensory states is that it is difficult to isolate that consciousness as a distinct component of our mental experience.
When we try to focus on the consciousness of a particular sensory state, we typically
end up picking out only the sensory state we are conscious of, instead. As Moore usefully put it, consciousness is "transparent," or "diaphanous."[14] Since efforts to pick
out consciousness itself issue instead in the states we are conscious of, it is tempting to conclude that the consciousness is actually part of those states. But the present
account gives a better explanation of the diaphanous character of consciousness. We
normally focus on the sensory state and not on our consciousness of it only because
that consciousness consists in our having a higher-order thought, and that thought is
usually not itself a conscious thought.

There is a strong intuitive sense that the consciousness of mental states is somehow
reflexive, or self-referential. But we need not invoke the idea that conscious states are
conscious of themselves to explain this intuition. For a mental state to be conscious,
the corresponding higher-order thought must be a thought about oneself, that is, a
thought about the mental being that is in that conscious state. So, as noted above, we
can construe that thought as being, in part, about itself. For it is reasonable to regard
the content of the thought as being that whatever individual has this very thought is
also in the specified mental state. The sense that there is something reflexive about the
consciousness of mental states is thus not due to the conscious state's being directed
upon itself, as is often supposed. Rather, it is the higher-order thought that confers
such consciousness that is actually self-directed.

The foregoing objections have all challenged whether an account based on higher-
order thoughts can do justice to various ways we think about consciousness. But one
might also question whether higher-order thoughts are enough to make mental states
conscious. Here a difficulty seems to arise about mental states that are repressed. By
hypothesis such states are not conscious. But it might seem that mental states can be
repressed even if one has higher-order thoughts about them. Higher-order thoughts
could not then be what makes mental states conscious. A person who has a repressed
feeling may nonetheless take pleasure, albeit unconscious pleasure, from having that
repressed feeling. But to take pleasure in something we must presumably think that
it is so. So that person will have a higher-order thought about the repressed feeling.[15]
Moreover, it appears intuitively that the feeling cannot remain unconscious unless
the pleasure taken in it also does. And this suggests that, contrary to the present
account, a higher-order thought can confer consciousness only if that thought is itself
already conscious.

But genuine counterexamples along these lines are not all that easy to come up
with. Despite the foregoing suggestion, one can take pleasure in something without
having any actual thought about it. I cannot, of course, take pleasure in something

---

[14] G. E. Moore, "The Refutation of Idealism," in his *Philosophical Studies*, London: Routledge &
Kegan Paul, 1922, pp. 1–30, at pp. 20 and 25.
[15] I am grateful to Georges Rey and Eric Wefald for independently raising this point.

I disbelieve or doubt,[16] but that does not imply the actual occurrence of a thought that it is so. Indeed, we frequently form no actual thought about the things in which we take pleasure. Sometimes, by 'thought', we mean only to speak of propositional contents, as when I talk about some thought you put forth. Taking pleasure is a propositional mental state; so taking pleasure in something does involve a thought about it, in the sense of a proposition. But it hardly follows that one also has a thought in the sense of a particular kind of mental state. Having a thought in that sense is the holding of an assertive mental attitude, which need not occur when one takes pleasure in something. So, in the foregoing example, we have no reason to suppose that the person would actually have any higher-order thought about the repressed feeling.

The difference between taking pleasure in a mental state and having an actual thought about it is crucial for the present account of consciousness. It is natural to hold that being aware of something means having a thought about it, not taking pleasure in it. And one can take pleasure in something without knowing what it is that gives one pleasure. One may have no idea why one feels good, or be mistaken about why. One may even be unaware of feeling good at all if one is sufficiently distracted or other factors interfere. So taking pleasure in something is compatible with being unaware of that thing. Such considerations also apply to putative counterexamples based on other sorts of higher-order mental states. For example, repressed feelings are, presumably, always accompanied by higher-order desires not to be in them. But desires that something not be so do not, in general, imply any awareness that it is.

Conceiving of nonconscious mental states on the model of the repressed cases is doubly misleading. For one thing, it ignores factors that in such cases presumably block consciousness. Moreover, it also conceals a tacit Cartesian premise. For it suggests that consciousness is the norm: Unless exceptional pressures intervene, a mental state will automatically be conscious. Consciousness is to be assumed unless some external factor prevents it. Thus, on this model, we can explain the forces that interfere with consciousness, but consciousness itself may very likely be inexplicable.[17]

---

[16] On this point, see Robert M. Gordon's illuminating "Emotions and Knowledge," *The Journal of Philosophy*, LXVI, 13 (July 3, 1969): 408–413, and "The Aboutness of Emotions," *American Philosophical Quarterly*, 11, 1 (January 1974): 27–36.

[17] It is noteworthy that this very attitude appears even in Freud's own writings. Freud does, indeed, "energetically den[y] the equation between what is psychical and what is conscious" ("Some Elementary Lessons in Psycho-Analysis," in *The Complete Psychological Works of Sigmund Freud*, tr. and ed. James Strachey, London: The Hogarth Press, 1966–74 [henceforth "*Works*"], XXIII, pp. 279–286, at p. 283. And he understood that to do so one must define the mental in terms of phenomenal and intentional character; thus he insisted that "all the categories which we employ to describe conscious mental acts ... can be applied" equally well to unconscious mental states ("The Unconscious," *Works*, XIV, pp. 166–215, at p. 168). Moreover, he maintained that "[t]he psychical, whatever its nature may be, is itself unconscious" ("Some Elementary Lessons," p. 283), and so, "[l]ike the physical, the psychical is not necessarily in reality what it appears to us to be" ("The Unconscious," p. 171; cf. "Some Elementary Lessons," p. 282, and *The Interpretation of Dreams*, *Works*, V, p. 613). But despite all this, Freud operated with a surprisingly Cartesian concept of consciousness. Consciousness, he wrote, is a "unique, indescribable" quality of mental states ("Some Elementary Lessons," p. 282), and "the fact of consciousness" "defies all explanation

III.

Whatever one holds about intentional states, it may seem altogether unacceptable to try to explain the consciousness of sensory states by way of higher-order thoughts. Consciousness seems virtually inseparable from sensory qualities, in a way that does not seem so for intentional properties. Indeed, as noted at the end of section I, it may seem almost contradictory to speak of sensory states' lacking consciousness. This intimate tie between sensory quality and consciousness seems to hold for all sensory states, but appears strongest with somatic sensations, such as pain. Saul A. Kripke succinctly captures this intuition when he insists that "[f]or a sensation to be *felt* as pain is for it to *be* pain"[18] and, conversely, that "for [something] to exist without being *felt as pain* is for it to exist without there *being any* pain."[19] And, more generally, Kripke seems to insist that for something to be a sensation of any sort it must be felt in a particular way (*NN* p. 146).

Since consciousness seems more closely tied to sensations than to intentional states, it is tempting to consider a restricted form of the Cartesian view, on which all sensations are conscious but not all intentional states are.[20] This restricted thesis would still allow one to explain consciousness in terms of higher-order thoughts; no regress would arise, because then those thoughts could themselves be nonconscious. But the Cartesian view holds not only that all mental states are conscious, but also that consciousness is an intrinsic property of mental states. And if it is, an explanation in terms of higher-order thoughts is impossible, and all the problems about giving an informative explanation of consciousness will arise. So even if not all mental states are conscious, it is important to see whether consciousness is intrinsic to those which are.

We can, however, explain our tendency to associate consciousness and sensory qualities without having to suppose that consciousness is intrinsic to sensory states, or even that all sensory states are conscious. We are chiefly concerned to know what bodily sensations we and others have because they are highly useful indicators of bodily and general well being. People cannot tell us about their nonconscious sensations, and bodily sensations usually have negligible effect on behavior unless they

---

or description" (*An Outline of Psycho-Analysis, Works*, XXIII, pp. 141–208, at p. 157). In thus regarding consciousness as unanalyzable, Freud seems to have uncritically accepted the core of the Cartesian doctrine he strove to discredit. (To dissociate the present account from Freud's views I eschew here the colloquial 'unconscious mental state' in favor of the somewhat awkward term 'nonconscious'.)

[18] "Identity and Necessity," in *Identity and Individuation*, ed. Milton K. Munitz, New York: New York University Press, 1971, pp. 135–64 [henceforth "IN"], at p. 163, n. 18; emphasis original here and elsewhere.

[19] *Naming and Necessity*, Cambridge, Massachusetts: Harvard University Press, 1980 [henceforth "*NN*"], p. 151. Compare Reid, *Essays*, II, xvi, p. 243: "When [a sensation] is not felt, it is not. There is no difference between a sensation and the feeling of it; they are one and the same thing."

[20] Even Freud does not hold that feelings can strictly speaking be unconscious, though he sees no difficulty about unconscious intentional states (*The Ego and the Id, Works*, XIX, pp. 3–68, at pp. 22–23; cf. *An Outline*, p. 197).

are conscious. So nonconscious sensations are not much use as cues to such well-being, and we thus have little, if any, interest in pains or other somatic sensations, except when they are conscious.

Things are different with other sorts of mental states, even perceptual sensations. It is often useful to know somebody's thoughts, emotions, and perceptual sensations, even when that person is unaware of them. Moreover, when mental states are not conscious, our interest in knowing about them is greatest with propositional states, less with emotions, less still with perceptual sensations, and far the least with somatic sensations. Strikingly, our sense that consciousness is intrinsic to mental states increases accordingly. The less useful it is to know about a particular kind of mental state even when the person is unaware of it, the more compelling is our intuition that that kind of mental state must be conscious. This correlation is telling evidence that, even in the case of pains and other somatic sensations, the idea that being mental entails being conscious is just a reflection of our usual interests, and not a matter of the meanings of our words or of the nature of the mental itself.

Some of our idiomatic ways of describing somatic sensations do entail consciousness. Something's hurting, for example, implies awareness of the hurt. And perhaps one cannot correctly say that somebody is in pain unless that person knows it. Phrases such as 'what a sensation is like' and 'how a sensation feels' reinforce this impression, since they refer both to a sensory quality and to our awareness of it, and seem thus to yoke the two together. But when one is in pain or when something hurts, we not only are in a sensory state, but are also aware that we are. And our idiomatic descriptions of these situations have no bearing on whether that very kind of sensory state may sometimes occur without one's being aware of it. Perhaps we would then withhold from such states the epithet 'pain'. But those states would still resemble and differ from other nonconscious states in just those ways in which conscious pains resemble and differ from other conscious sensory states. And that is what it is for a state to have sensory qualities. The intuitive simplicity of those qualities might tempt one to hold that consciousness also is simple and, hence, an intrinsic characteristic of sensory states. But it is question begging to suppose that the apparent simplicity of sensory qualities tells us anything about the nature of our consciousness of them.

Examples of sensory states that sometimes occur without consciousness are not hard to come by. When a headache lasts several hours, one is seldom aware of it for that entire time. Distractions occur, and one pays attention to other things, or just forgets for a bit. But we do not conclude that each headache literally ceases to exist when it temporarily stops being part of our stream of consciousness, and that such a person has only a sequence of discontinuous, brief headaches. Rather, when that happens, our headache is for a time literally a nonconscious ache.[21] The same holds even more vividly for mild pains and minor bodily discomforts. So, to insist that nonconscious states are just not mental states, or that they cannot have sensory qualities, is not, as Kripke seems to urge (e.g., *NN* 152–3), the elucidation of decisive

---

[21] Thus it is a parody for Wittgenstein to suppose that all we could mean by an unconscious toothache, e.g., is "a certain state of decay in a tooth, not accompanied by what we commonly call toothache" (*The Blue and Brown Books*, Oxford: Basil Blackwell, 1958, p. 22).

and defensible presystematic intuitions, but only the tacit expression of the Cartesian definition of mind.

Indeed, an account in terms of higher-order thoughts actually helps explain the phenomenological appearances. If a sensory state's being conscious is its being accompanied by a suitable higher-order thought, that thought will be about the very quality we are conscious of. It will be a thought that one is in a state that has that quality. So it will indeed be impossible to describe that consciousness without mentioning the quality. An account in terms of higher-order thoughts actually helps explain why the qualities of our conscious experiences seem inseparable from our consciousness of them.

Moreover, we typically come to make more fine-grained discriminations as we master more subtle concepts pertaining to various distinct sensory qualities. Experiences from wine tasting to hearing music illustrate this process vividly. An account in terms of higher-order thoughts explains the bearing these concepts have on our very awareness of sensory differences. If consciousness is intrinsic to sensory states, the relevance of concepts remains mysterious. The Cartesian might just deny that sensory differences exist when we are unaware of them. But it will be even more difficult to explain how learning new concepts can actually cause sensory qualities to arise that previously did not exist.

Perhaps the strongest objection to an account in terms of higher-order thoughts is that there are creatures with conscious sensations whose ability to have any thoughts at all may be in doubt. Infants and most nonhuman animals presumably have a relatively rudimentary ability to think, but plainly do have conscious sensations. But one need not have much ability to think to be able to have a thought that one has a particular sensation. Infants and nonhuman animals can discriminate among external objects, and master regularities pertaining to them. So most of these beings can presumably form thoughts about such objects, albeit primitive thoughts that are very likely not conscious. No more is needed to have thoughts about one's more salient sensory experiences. Infants and nonhuman animals doubtless lack the concepts required for drawing many distinctions among their sensory states. But, as just noted, one can be aware of sensory states and yet unaware of many of the sensory qualities in virtue of which those states differ.

The common tendency to link the ability to think with the ability to express thoughts in speech may account for the doubts we can fall into about whether infants and nonhuman animals can think at all. But the capacity for speech is hardly necessary for thinking. It is often reasonable to interpret nonlinguistic behavior, of other people and of non-language-using creatures alike, in terms of the propositional content and mental attitude we take it to express. Such behavior is convincing evidence of the occurrence of intentional states.

Forming higher-order thoughts about one's own propositional mental states takes a lot more than having such thoughts about one's sensations. For one thing, the concept of a mental state with propositional content is more complex than the concept of a sensory experience. And picking out particular intentional states demands an elaborate system of concepts, whereas referring to salient sensory experiences does not. An account in terms of higher-order thoughts fits well with these points. Infants and most nonhuman species lack the ability to have the more complex higher-order thoughts needed to make intentional states conscious, though they presumably can form higher-order thoughts about their sensory states. And, though these beings seem plainly to have conscious sensations, we have little reason to suppose that their intentional states are also conscious.[†] Indeed, these considerations help explain why we associate consciousness so much more strongly with sensory than with intentional states. Conscious sensory states arise far more readily, since higher-order thoughts about them are far easier to have.

Some animal species, however, lack the ability to think at all. And this may seem to support Nagel's contention that conscious "experience is present in animals lacking language and thought" (167, n. 3). But being a conscious creature does not entail being in conscious mental states. For an organism to be conscious means only that it is awake and mentally responsive to sensory stimuli (cf. Ryle *The Concept of Mind*, 156–7). To be mentally responsive does require that one be in mental states. And to be mentally responsive to sensory stimuli may even mean that one is in some way conscious of the objects or events that are providing such stimulation. But a creature can be in mental states without being in conscious mental states, and can be conscious of external or bodily events without also being aware of its own mental states.

Conscious experiences, as Nagel has stressed, manifest a certain subjectivity. We each experience our sensory states in a way nobody else does and from a point of view nobody else shares. It is notoriously difficult to articulate these differences. But we understand their occurrence reasonably well, and it is far from clear that such subjectivity causes any problem for the present account.

One way differences arise in sensory experiences is from variations in sense organs or other aspects of physical makeup. Experiences also vary from individual to individual because of such factors as background and previous experience. When these factors diverge markedly, aspects of our sensory experiences may as well. When the individuals belong to distinct species, this effect may be quite dramatic. But hard as it is to pin down precisely what these differences amount to, they do not bear specifically on the consciousness of the experiences in question. Rather, the variations are due to differences in the mental context in which the experiences occur, or, when biological endowment is at issue, they are actual differences in the sensory qualities of those experiences. Nagel holds that "the subjective character of experience" is a matter of what "it is like to *be* a particular organism — [what] it is like *for* that organism" (166). But the present account can accommodate this idea. What it is like to be a particular conscious individual is a matter of the sensory qualities of that individual's conscious experiences and the mental context in which those experiences occur. The consciousness of those experiences, by contrast, is simply that individual's being aware of having the experiences.[22]

[†] I.e., we have little reason to think that, if infants are in intentional states that lack qualitative character, those states are conscious.

[22] On difficulties in Nagel's discussion and, especially, his notion of a point of view, see my "Reductionism and Knowledge," in *How Many Questions?: Essays in Honor of Sidney Morgenbesser*,

According to Nagel, "[a]ny reductionist program has to be based on an analysis of what is to be reduced. If the analysis leaves something out, the problem will be falsely posed" (167). Indeed, no account that is even "logically compatible with" the absence of consciousness could, Nagel contends, be correct (166; "Panpsychism," 189). And the present account is reductionist, since it seeks to explain conscious mental states ultimately in terms of mental states that are not conscious. But that account aims only at explaining consciousness, and not also at conceptual analysis. And satisfactory explanations do not, *pace* Nagel, require full analyses of the relevant concepts. Explanation, in science and everyday contexts alike, must generally proceed without benefit of complete conceptual analyses.

Nagel's language is strongly evocative of that sense we have of ourselves which can make it appear difficult to see how, as conscious selves, we could find ourselves located among the physical furniture of the universe. When we focus on ourselves in this way, there seems to be nothing more basic to our nature than consciousness itself. If nothing were more basic to us than consciousness, there would be nothing more basic in terms of which we could explain consciousness. All we could then do would be to try to make consciousness more comprehensible by eliciting a sense of the phenomenon in a variety of different ways. Analyzing concepts would be central to any such project, and Nagel's demand for conceptual analysis would then make sense. But consciousness could be essential to our nature only if all mental states are conscious states. If a fair number of our mental states are not conscious, we cannot define our mental natures in terms of consciousness, and there will be nonconscious mental phenomena in terms of which we can explain consciousness itself.

The puzzled cognitive disorientation that can result from reflecting on the gulf that seems to separate physical reality from consciousness makes any noncircular explanation of consciousness seem inadequate. How could any explanation of consciousness in terms of nonconscious phenomena help us to understand how consciousness can exist in the physical universe, or how physical beings like ourselves can have conscious states? But no other explanation can do better with these quandaries so long as an unbridgeable gulf seems to divide the conscious from the merely physical. To understand how consciousness can occur in physical things, we must dissolve the intuitive force of that gulf. And we can do so only by explaining the consciousness of mental states in terms of mental states that are not conscious. For the stark discontinuity between conscious mental states and physical reality does not also arise when we consider only nonconscious mental states. And once we have explained consciousness by reference to nonconscious mental states, we may well be able also to explain nonconscious mental states in terms of phenomena that are not mental at all.

IV.

The central place consciousness has in our conception of the mental is doubtless due in large measure to the way we know about mind in general, and in particular about

ed. Leigh S. Cauman, Isaac Levi, Charles Parsons, and Robert Schwartz, Indianapolis: Hackett Publishing Co., 1983, pp. 276–300.

our own mental states. We get most of that knowledge, directly or indirectly, from introspection.[†] And we have introspective access to mental states only when they are conscious. Since our chief source of knowledge about the mind tells us only about conscious mental states, it is natural to infer that consciousness is an important feature of mental phenomena.

But stronger claims are sometimes made about the epistemic status of introspection. Introspection may seem particularly well adapted to its subject matter, since most of our knowledge of mind derives from introspection and all introspective knowledge is about mind. This close fit may tempt some to hold that introspection is a privileged source of knowledge that is somehow immune from error. If so, perhaps introspection reveals the essential nature of mental states. And, since introspection tells us only about conscious mental states, perhaps consciousness is itself a part of that essential nature. But inviting as these Cartesian conclusions may be, they are without foundation. Introspection is simply the having of conscious thoughts that one is in particular mental states. Those thoughts can by themselves no more reveal the essences of those states than having a conscious perceptual thought that a table is in front of one can reveal the essence of the table. Nor can we infer anything from the close fit between introspection and its subject matter. Sight is equally well adapted to knowing about colored physical objects. But there are other ways to know about those objects. And even though sight informs us only about illuminated objects, we can hardly conclude that only illuminated objects are colored.

Introspective apprehension seems, however, to differ from perceptual knowledge in a way that undermines this analogy. Perception is never entirely direct. Some causal process always mediates, even in ostensibly direct perception, between our perceptual experience and what we perceive. Introspection, by contrast, may seem wholly unmediated. And if it is, there would be no way for error or distortion to enter the introspective process. There would thus be no difference between how our mental states appear to us and how they really are. Mental states would have no nonintrospectible nature, and introspection would be an infallible and exhaustive source of knowledge about the mind. Nagel evidently endorses this view when he claims that "[t]he idea of moving from appearance to reality seems to make no sense" in the case of conscious experiences (174). Kripke too seems to hold that introspection is different from perception in this way. Thus he writes:

although we can say that we pick out [physical] heat contingently by the contingent property that it affects us in such and such a way, we cannot similarly say that we pick out pain contingently by the fact that it affects us in such and such a way ("IN" 161; cf. *NN* 150–2).

[†] I would now put this more cautiously. Plainly we learn much of what we know about mental functioning from introspective consciousness, but much that we know is a matter of the many complex connections mental states have with one another and with behavior and stimuli. And we need not in any case rely on introspective consciousness. See, e.g., "Sensory Qualities, Consciousness, and Perception," § IV.

We could not, Kripke contends, have been aware of our pains in a way different from the way we actually are.[†]

Introspection is the reflective awareness of our mental states. So, the only way introspective apprehension of those states might be entirely unmediated would be for consciousness to be a part, or at least an intrinsic property, of such states. For nothing could then come between a mental state and our being conscious of it, nor between our being thus conscious and our also having reflective consciousness. But as noted in section II, that view is indefensible. Accordingly, consciousness must be a relational property, for example, the property of being accompanied by higher-order thoughts. And some causal process must therefore mediate between mental states and our awareness of them—in Kripke's example, between a pain and "the fact that it affects us in such and such a way." And, since mental states might have been connected causally to different higher-order thoughts, we might have been aware of mental states differently from the way we are. The appearance of mental states will not, therefore, automatically coincide with their reality. Indeed, since the way mental states appear is a matter of our introspective awareness of them, their appearance and reality could be the same only if our consciousness of mental states were a part or an intrinsic property of those states.

These considerations notwithstanding, we do rely heavily on introspection in picking out and describing mental states. And introspection tells us about nothing except conscious mental states. So even though consciousness is not what distinguishes mental states from everything else, it is reasonable to hold that it is by reference to a range of conscious states that we fix the extension of the term 'mental'. Similarly, even though the various kinds of mental state can all occur nonconsciously, it is also reasonable to suppose that we fix the extensions of our terms for the different kinds of mental state by way of the conscious cases. As Kripke and Hilary Putnam have stressed, what fixes the extension of a general term can turn out to be distinct from what is essential to the items in that extension.[23] And, just as the way we know about things is not, in general, a reliable guide to their nature, so the way we pick out things is not, either. So, even if we fix the extensions of terms for mental states by way of the conscious instances, we could still discover that the states so determined are not all conscious and that what is actually essential to all such states is just their sensory or intentional properties.

The idea that we fix mental extensions by way of the conscious cases plainly supports the non-Cartesian picture. But it also helps explain why consciousness seems so crucial to our mental concepts. And it even enables us to explain why we group sensory and intentional states together as mental states, despite its seeming that they have little intrinsic in common. We do so because in both cases we fix extensions by way of states to which we have noninferential and nonobservational access.

[†] Cp. also Descartes's insistence that our awareness of our own mental states is always immediate (*Second Replies, AT* VII 160 [*C* II 113]).

[23] *NN* 54–9, "IN" 156–161, and Putnam, "The Meaning of 'Meaning'," in Putnam's *Philosophical Papers*, vol. 2, Cambridge: Cambridge University Press, 1975, pp. 215–271, pp. 223–235.

Kripke contends that what fixes the reference of terms for sensory states cannot diverge from what is essential to those states (*NN* 149–54; "IN" 157–61). Thus, he insists, "[i]f any phenomenon is picked out in exactly the same way that we pick out pain, then that phenomenon *is* pain." [24] But what fixes the extension of 'pain' must coincide with what is essential to pains only if it is necessary that pains affect us in the way they do. And this would be necessary only if consciousness were intrinsic to them. It therefore begs the question to base the Cartesian picture on an insistence that what fixes the extensions of mental terms cannot diverge from the essences of mental states. Kripke offers no independent support for that insistence.

Relative to what we now know about other natural phenomena, we still have strikingly scant understanding of the nature of the mental. So introspection looms large as a source of information, just as sense perception was a more central source of knowledge about physical reality before the flourishing of the relevant systematic sciences. But, since not all knowledge about mind is derived from introspection, we have no more reason to suppose that mental states have no nonintrospectible nature than that the nature of physical objects is wholly perceptible. Nor, therefore, have we any reason to hold that the essences of mental states must be what fixes the extensions of mental terms. It is reasonable to conclude that whatever temptation we have to accord absolute epistemic authority to introspection derives solely from our relative ignorance about the mind. Only because we now know so little about mental processes does it make sense to suppose that, in the case of mental states, appearance and reality coincide. Accordingly, we have no reason to continue to favor that picture, or to reject an explanation of consciousness based on higher-order thoughts. [25]

---

[24] *NN* 153; cf. "IN" 162–3. Again, cf. Reid, *Essays*, II, xvi, p. 243: A "sensation can be nothing else than it is felt to be. Its very essence consists in being felt." Cf. also J. J. C. Smart: "[t]o say that a process is an ache is simply to classify it with other processes that are felt to be similar" ("Materialism," *The Journal of Philosophy*, LX, 22 [October 24, 1963]: 651–662, p. 655). It is striking that this Cartesian claim about our mental concepts should be shared by theorists who, in other respects, diverge as sharply and as thoroughly as do Smart and Kripke. That it is so shared suggests that this claim may underlie much of what is, in different ways, unintuitive about each of those theories.

[25] I am greatly indebted to many friends and colleagues for comments on earlier versions of this paper, most especially to Margaret Atherton, Adam Morton, and Robert Schwartz.

2

Thinking that One Thinks

I. INTRODUCTORY

There are two distinct kinds of things we describe as being conscious or not conscious, and when we describe the two kinds of thing as being conscious we attribute two distinct properties. The term 'conscious' thus conceals a certain ambiguity.

In one use, we speak of mental states as being conscious or not conscious. Mental states, such as thoughts, desires, emotions, and sensations, are conscious if we are aware of them in some intuitively immediate way. But we also apply the term 'conscious' to the creatures that are in those mental states. A creature's being conscious consists, roughly, of its being awake and being mentally responsive. Plainly, this property of being conscious is distinct from the property a mental state may have.

It is the notion of a mental state's being conscious that occasions such difficulty in understanding what consciousness amounts to. It is the consciousness of mental states, as Thomas Nagel points out, that makes understanding the nature of those states seem difficult, or even impossible.[1] If we bracket or ignore the consciousness of mental states, the problem of how to explain their nature will no longer seem intractable. Our explanation will then proceed simply in terms of the intentional or sensory content mental states have, without reference to their being conscious. Because the notion of consciousness that applies to mental states is the more difficult of the two to explain, it is that notion which I shall be concerned with in what follows.

By contrast, no special problems impede our understanding what it is for a creature to be a conscious creature. A creature's being conscious means that it is awake and mentally responsive. Being awake is presumably an unproblematic biological notion. And being mentally responsive amounts simply to being in some mental state or other. That will occasion no special difficulty unless those states are themselves conscious states, and if they are we can trace the difficulty to the notion of a mental state's being conscious, rather than a creature's being conscious.

It is possible, however, to dispel our sense that special difficulties face any explanation of what it is for mental states to be conscious. The sense that such consciousness is somehow intractable derives at bottom from the tacit, and unnecessary, assumption that all mental states are conscious states. If being a conscious state did coincide with being a mental state, we would then be unable to rely on any prior account of mentality in trying to explain what it is for mental states to be conscious. For if the concept of mind we started from had consciousness already built in, the resulting

---

[1] "What Is It Like to Be a Bat?", *The Philosophical Review*, LXXXIII, 4 (October 1974): 435–450.

explanation would be circular, and if it did not, our explanation would rest upon a conception of mentality that, by hypothesis, is defective. There is no third way; we plainly can explain consciousness only in terms of what is mental. So if mental states are all conscious, no informative, nontrivial explanation of such consciousness is possible.

This result perfectly suits Cartesian theorists. If we can give no informative explanation of consciousness, the gulf that intuitively separates mind and consciousness from the rest of reality will seem impossible to bridge. Our explanations will thus be limited to tracing the conceptual connections holding among such terms as 'mind', 'consciousness', 'subjectivity', and 'self'. Cartesians such as Nagel and Colin McGinn[2] encourage us to embrace this limitation by evoking that sense we have of ourselves on which consciousness is the most central feature of our existence. If consciousness were the most basic aspect of our nature, why should we expect to be able to explain it in terms of anything more basic?

The sense that consciousness is thus basic is closely tied to the idea that mental states are all conscious states. And if mental states are not all conscious, the foregoing difficulty dissolves. We can then seek first to explain the nature of those mental states which are not conscious, and build on that understanding of nonconscious mental states to arrive at an informative account of what it is for a mental state to be conscious. In particular, if consciousness is not essential to a state's being a mental state, we can reasonably identify a state's being mental with its having either intentional or sensory character. And this account does not presuppose that such states are conscious. A mental state's being conscious, moreover, is our being aware of that state in a suitably immediate way. So we can then go on to argue that a mental state's being conscious is its being accompanied by a roughly simultaneous higher-order thought about that very mental state. On this account, not all mental states are conscious, and we can explain how the conscious ones differ from those which are not. It is this hypothesis which I shall defend here.

On this account, we explain the property of a mental state's being conscious in terms of our being conscious of that state. In general, being conscious of something means having a thought about it or a sensation of it. One may be conscious of a chair, for example, by thinking something about the chair or by having some sensation of it. Sensations will not help with the present concern. Although discussions of consciousness often make metaphorical appeal to so-called inner sense, no such sense actually exists. We may conclude that mental states are conscious by virtue of our having suitable thoughts about them.

It might be supposed that higher-order thoughts can help explain introspective or reflective consciousness, but not the so-called simple consciousness our mental states have in virtually every moment of our waking lives. Indeed, the connection between higher-order thoughts and introspection has sometimes been drawn. Writers such as D. M. Armstrong, Daniel C. Dennett, David Lewis, and Wilfrid Sellars[3] have urged

---

[2] *The Problem of Consciousness*, Oxford: Basil Blackwell, 1991.

[3] D. M. Armstrong, *A Materialist Theory of the Mind*, New York: Humanities Press, 1968; second revised edition, London: Routledge & Kegan Paul, 1993, pp. 94–107 and 323–338, and "What

that being introspectively aware of a mental state means having a roughly simultaneous thought about that state. And Dennett,[4] in a probing discussion of higher-order
thoughts, uses that notion to explicate the concept of a person.[5]

If higher-order thoughts could explain only introspective consciousness, that
would not do much to dispel the apparent difficulties in the notion of what it is
for a mental state to be conscious. Introspective consciousness occurs when we pay
deliberate, reflective attention to some mental state. That is relatively rare, and is a lot
more elaborate than the nonreflective, phenomenologically immediate awareness we
have of mental states in everyday life.

I have argued elsewhere,[6] however, that we can in fact explain the ordinary, nonintrospective consciousness of mental states in terms of higher-order thoughts.[7] On my
account, a mental state is conscious—nonintrospectively conscious—just in case one
has a roughly contemporaneous thought to the effect that one is in that very mental
state. Since not all mental states are conscious, it is open for not all of those higher-
order thoughts to be conscious thoughts, though having such a thought will always
mean that the lower-order thought it is about is conscious.

An account of introspective consciousness follows naturally. Introspection is the
attentive, deliberately focused consciousness of one's mental states. So introspecting
a mental state is not just being aware of it, but being actually conscious that one
is thus aware. Since a state's being conscious is its being accompanied by a suitable
higher-order thought, introspective consciousness occurs when a mental state is
accompanied both by such a second-order thought, and also by a yet higher-order
thought that one has that second-order thought. A mental state is conscious, but
not introspectively conscious, when the higher-order thought it is accompanied by
is itself not conscious. Introspective consciousness is the special case in which that

---

is Consciousness?", in *The Nature of Mind*, Ithaca, New York: Cornell University Press, 1980, pp.
55–67, esp. pp. 59–63; Daniel C. Dennett, "Toward a Cognitive Theory of Consciousness," in
Minnesota Studies in the Philosophy of Science, IX, ed. C. Wade Savage, Minneapolis: University
of Minnesota Press, 1978, pp. 201–228, esp. pp. 216–222; David Lewis, "An Argument for the
Identity Theory," in *Philosophical Papers*, I, New York: Oxford University Press, 1983, pp. 99–107,
at p. 21, and "Psychophysical and Theoretical Identifications," *Australasian Journal of Philosophy*,
50, 3 (December 1972): 249–258, p. 258; and Wilfrid Sellars, "Empiricism and the Philosophy of
Mind," in *Science, Perception and Reality*, London: Routledge & Kegan Paul, 1963, pp. 127–196,
at pp. 188–189 and 194–195.

[4] Daniel C. Dennett, "Conditions of Personhood," in *The Identities of Persons*, ed. Amélie
Oksenberg Rorty, Berkeley: University of California Press, 1976, pp. 175–196, esp. pp. 181–186.

[5] D. H. Mellor appeals to higher-order believing to explain not merely our introspective
consciousness of beliefs, but the ordinary, nonintrospective consciousness beliefs often have
("Conscious Belief," *Proceedings of the Aristotelian Society*, New Series, LXXVIII [1977–8]: 87–101;
and "Consciousness and Degrees of Belief," *Prospects for Pragmatism*, ed. D. H. Mellor, Cambridge:
Cambridge University Press, 1980, pp. 139–173). But he holds that this view, for which he argues
forcefully, applies only to the case of conscious believing, and not to other mental states as well.

[6] "Two Concepts of Consciousness," ch. 1 in this volume, and "A Theory of Consciousness,"
in *The Nature of Consciousness: Philosophical Debates* ed. Ned Block, Owen Flanagan, and Güven
Güzeldere, Cambridge, Massachusetts: MIT Press, 1997, pp. 729–753.

[7] In "Toward a Cognitive Theory of Consciousness," Dennett develops a related strategy for
avoiding the difficulty about consciousness being an intrinsic feature of mental representations.

second-order thought is also conscious. It is only if we assume that higher-order thoughts themselves must all be conscious that higher-order thoughts will seem useful in explaining introspective consciousness, but not ordinary nonintrospective consciousness.

In previous work[8] I have mainly argued that an account of consciousness in terms of higher-order thoughts can save the phenomenological appearances and explain the data of introspection even more successfully than the traditional Cartesian view. Here I develop a wholly different kind of argument—one that more directly and decisively supports an account in terms of higher-order thoughts. The next section sets out the background and premises of this argument, and section III puts forth the actual argument. The last three sections, then, defend the argument against various objections.

II. EXPRESSING AND REPORTING

Saying something and thinking it are intimately connected.[9] If one says something meaningfully and sincerely, one thereby expresses some thought that one has, and the thought and speech act will have the same propositional content.[†] The speech act and thought will also in cases of sincere speech have the same force; both, that is, will be a matter of affirming, suspecting, wondering, denying, doubting, and the like. We usually speak of people expressing their thoughts; by an innocent metonymy, it is natural to talk also of a person's speech act as itself expressing, or giving expression to, the person's thought.[10]

But it is also possible to communicate what we think in another way, by saying something that does not literally express the thought we have. Instead of expressing our thoughts, we can describe them. If I think that the door is open, for example, I can convey this thought to you simply by saying 'The door is open'; that speech act will express my thought. But I could equally well convey the very same thought by saying, instead, 'I think the door is open'. Similarly, I can communicate my suspicion that the door is open either by expressing my suspicion or by explicitly telling you about it. I express the suspicion simply by saying, for example, that the door may well be open, whereas I would be explicitly telling you that I have that suspicion if I said that I suspect that it is open.

---

[8] "Two Concepts of Consciousness" and "A Theory of Consciousness."

[9] See my "Intentionality," ch. 3 in this volume; John R. Searle, *Intentionality: An Essay in the Philosophy of Mind*, Cambridge: Cambridge University Press, 1983, ch. 1; Wilfrid Sellars, "Notes on Intentionality," *The Journal of Philosophy*, LXI, 21 (November 12, 1964): 655–665; and Zeno Vendler, *Res Cogitans*, Ithaca, New York: Cornell University Press, 1972.

[†] Or roughly the same; see "Content, Interpretation, and Consciousness," ch. 12 in this volume, §§II–III. [Added in 2005.]

[10] There are differences. If the expressing is deliberate, it may be more natural to say that the person expresses the mental state; otherwise one may say instead that the person's behavior expresses that state. On these two ways of speaking, see William Alston, "Expressing," in *Philosophy in America* ed. Max Black, Ithaca, New York: Cornell University Press, 1965, pp. 15–34, esp. pp. 17–18, 23–26.

I use 'thought' throughout as a generic term covering all types of propositional mental states, and 'say' as a generic verb to cover all kinds of speech act, whatever the illocutionary force.

In every case, the speech act that expresses my thought has the same force and the same propositional content as the thought itself. But, if I say that I think the door is open, the propositional content of my speech act is not that the door is open; it is that I think it is open. And if I say I suspect the door is open, my speech act tells of a suspicion. But my speech act then has the force, not of a suspicion, but of an assertion. In saying I suspect something, I report, rather than express, my suspicion.

In general terms, then, I can convey my thought that *p* either just by saying that *p*, or by saying that I think that *p*.[11] These two ways of conveying our thoughts to others are plainly distinct; still, it is easy to conflate them. This is because the conditions in which I could assert that *p* are the same as the conditions in which I could tell you that I think that *p*. Any conditions that warranted my saying that *p* would equally warrant my saying that I think that *p*, and conversely. Things are the same for other speech acts, and the mental states they express, even when their force is not that of asserting something. The conditions for appropriately expressing doubt, suspicion, or wonder are the same as those for explicitly reporting that one is in those mental states, at least when such social considerations as tact and discretion are not at issue.[12]

But the truth conditions for saying that *p* and saying that one thinks that *p* are, of course, dramatically different. That these truth conditions differ, even though the corresponding performance conditions are the same, is vividly captured by G. E. Moore's observation that the sentence ⌜*p*, but I don't think that *p*⌝, though not literally a contradiction, is still plainly absurd.[13] Such a sentence cannot have coherent conditions of assertibility, since the thought I seem to express by saying that *p* is precisely the thought I deny I have by going on to say that I don't think that *p*. Parallel remarks hold for speech acts other than assertions; I cannot, for example, coherently say 'Thank you, but I am not grateful'.[14] And, though I can perhaps

---

[11] Cf. Dennett's related distinction between reporting and expressing in *Content and Consciousness*, New York: Humanities Press, 1969, esp. §13, though Dennett's concern there is with introspective, rather than simple, consciousness.

[12] Strictly speaking, it may be that the performance conditions for saying that one thinks that *p* are not identical with, but rather include, the performance conditions for saying that *p*. This refinement is irrelevant in what follows.

[13] G. E. Moore, "A Reply to My Critics," in *The Philosophy of G. E. Moore*, ed. Paul Arthur Schilpp, New York: Tudor, 1942 (2nd edn. 1952), pp. 533–677, at p. 543, and "Russell's 'Theory of Descriptions'," in *The Philosophy of Bertrand Russell*, ed. Paul Arthur Schilpp, New York: Tudor, 1944, pp. 175–226, at p. 204. Moore uses believing, rather than thinking, as his example, but the point is the same. On Moore's paradox (so called by Ludwig Wittgenstein, *Philosophical Investigations*, tr. G. E. M. Anscombe, New York: Macmillan, 1953, Part II, §x), see Max Black, "Saying and Disbelieving," in *Philosophy and Analysis*, ed. Margaret MacDonald, Oxford: Basil Blackwell, 1954, pp. 109–119; M. F. Burnyeat, "Belief in Speech," *Proceedings of the Aristotelian Society*, New Series, LXVIII (1967–8): 227–248; and Wittgenstein, part II, §x. (For more on Moore's paradox, see "Moore's Paradox and Consciousness," ch. 9 in this volume.)

[14] *Pace* Mellor, who claims that Moore's paradox "has no analogue for the other attitudes" (D. H. Mellor, "What Is Computational Psychology?", *Proceedings of the Aristotelian Society*, Supplementary Volume LVIII (1984): 37–53, p. 38). Mellor also restricts his account of consciousness to the case of believing (see n. 5 above). As will emerge in §III, the generalization of Moore's paradox shows that this restriction is unwarranted.

actually have both thoughts simultaneously, I could not coherently convey both at once. Nor could I think them in, so to speak, the same mental breath. If the truth conditions for reporting thoughts and expressing them were not distinct, Moore's example would be not merely absurd, but an actual contradiction. We can infer to the distinction between expressing and reporting propositional states as the best explanation of why Moore's paradox is not an actual contradiction.[15]

Moore's paradox also helps with an earlier point, that all sincere speech acts express mental states with the same force and propositional content. If reporting and expressing were the same, Moore's paradox would be contradictory. If, on the other hand, I could say that *p* without thereby expressing the thought I have that *p*, Moore's paradox would even not be problematic, in whatever way. There would be no difficulty about saying that *p* and going on to deny that I have any such thought. We can thus infer to the claim that sincere speech acts express corresponding thoughts as the best explanation of Moore's-paradox sentences' being in some way absurd.

In ordinary conversation, however, we typically focus more on conditions of assertibility and other conditions for correct performance than on truth conditions. And as just noted, this may lead us to elide the difference between expressing our mental states and reporting them. This point will be crucial to dealing with certain objections in sections V, VI, and VI. For now, an example will do. People untrained in logic generally regard literal contradictions as meaningless. It is wrong, however, to suppose, as many do, that this betrays some confusion of meaning with truth. It is simply that, until we are taught otherwise, we tend to rely on conditions of assertibility, rather than conditions of truth. Since a contradictory sentence lacks coherent conditions of assertibility, we can perform no meaningful speech act with it. The

---

[15] It may seem possible to explain this absurdity without appeal to any such distinction. On a Gricean view, my sincerely saying something involves my intending that my hearer believe that I believe what I say. Such a view thus implies that I cannot at once sincerely say that *p* and say that I do not believe it. (See Mellor, "Conscious Belief," pp. 96–97; cf. "Consciousness and Degrees of Belief," p. 148.) But Moore's paradox strikes us as absurd independent of any context of communication; it is absurd because it lacks coherent conditions of assertibility.

  Insincere speech on the Gricean picture involves my intending you to believe that I believe something that in fact I do not (see Mellor, "Consciousness and Degrees of Belief," p. 148). But it is more reasonable to regard insincere speech acts as in fact a degenerate kind of speech, similar to reciting lines in a play. Like play acting, insincere speech is a kind of pretense; in both cases, one in effect pretends to perform normal speech acts. Thus J. L. Austin ("Other Minds," in *Philosophical Papers*, third edition, Oxford: Oxford University Press, 1979 [second edition. 1970; first edition. 1961], pp. 70–116, at pp. 101–103 [pp. 69–71 in first edition]) describes a sense of 'promise' and related words in which if I speak insincerely I do not promise. (Cf. Austin's *How to Do Things with Words*, second edition, Cambridge, Massachusetts: Harvard University Press, 1975 [first edition, 1962], pp. 48–50 and 136–137 [pp. 135–136 in the first edition], in which he urges that an insincere speech act, though it succeeds, is defective (*How to Do Things with Words*, pp. 15–16 and Lecture IV, esp. pp. 39–45).) Also see my "Intentionality," esp. §§II, III, and V, and Postscript.

  There is also nothing automatically problematic about one's speaking insincerely in ways that betray that insincerity. So one cannot express the absurdity, as Moore once proposed ("A Reply to My Critics," pp. 542–543), as due to one's betraying one's insincerity if one says something with the form of Moore's paradox.

sentence itself is false, and so must have semantic meaning. But nobody could mean anything by asserting it.

The distinction between expressing and reporting is pivotal to the argument I want to advance for the theory that a mental state's being conscious consists in its being accompanied by a suitable higher-order thought. So it is important to see whether that distinction applies not only to our thoughts, doubts, suspicions, and the like, but to all our conscious mental states.

It turns out that it does. One way to convey one's desires and emotions is to express them.[16] One does this both by the things one says and by one's facial expressions, gestures, choice of words, and tones of voice. But one can also communicate these states by explicitly reporting that one is in the state in question. In the case of one's thoughts, the thought and its expression are about the same things, and the two have the same propositional content and the same truth conditions—they are true under the same circumstances. This holds also for emotions and desires; to the extent to which one's desire for food or fear of a tiger are about the food and the tiger, one's expressions of these states will be as well.[17] The same goes for whatever propositional content these states may have. But one's report of being in such a mental state is never about the very thing that the mental state itself is about. Rather, any such report must be about the mental state, and its propositional content is that one is now, oneself, in that very mental state.[18]

Sensations are a special case. Sensations have no propositional content, and are therefore not about things. Still, there is one kind of sensation that we plainly express nonverbally, namely, our bodily sensations such as pain. And these sensations may even be expressible in speech. We use various interjections, for example, to express pains, and perhaps this counts as speech. If so, such an expression of a bodily sensation would not diverge from the sensation expressed in respect of propositional content, since neither the sensation nor its expression has any propositional content. And reports of bodily sensations, such as 'It hurts', are about those sensations, and have propositional content in a way exactly parallel to reports of other mental states. So it is

[16] Stuart Hampshire, "Feeling and Expression," in *Freedom of Mind*, Princeton: Princeton University Press, 1971, pp. 143–159.

[17] This is plainly true of verbal expressions, and it is plausible for nonverbal expressions as well.

[18] It is not sufficient that the report be about somebody who happens to be oneself. Rather, the report must be about oneself, as such; that is, it must be a report that the being that is in the mental state is oneself. For discussions of the special sort of reference involved, see G. E. M. Anscombe, "The First Person," in *Mind and Language*, ed. Samuel Guttenplan, Oxford: Oxford University Press, 1975, pp. 45–65; Steven E. Boër and William G. Lycan, "Who, Me?", *The Philosophical Review*, LXXXIX, 3 (July 1980): 427–466; Hector-Neri Castañeda, "On the Logic of Attributions of Self-Knowledge to Others," *The Journal of Philosophy*, LXV, 15 (August 8, 1968): 439–456; Roderick M. Chisholm, *The First Person*, Minneapolis: University of Minnesota Press, 1981; David Lewis, "Attitudes *De Dicto* and *De Se*," *The Philosophical Review*, LXXXVIII, 4 (October 1979): 513–543; and John Perry, "The Problem of the Essential Indexical," *Noûs*, XIII, 1 (March 1979): 3–21.

not surprising that the sentence 'Ouch, but nothing hurts' is like a standard Moore's-paradox sentence in being absurd, but not contradictory.[19]

Whereas bodily sensations are plainly expressible nonverbally and possibly verbally as well, neither sort of expressing is possible in the case of perceptual sensations. No speech act or other form of behavior can express, for example, a sense impression of red. At best, a sense impression may occasion the comment that some observable object is red or, more rarely, that one has a red afterimage or hallucination. But such remarks at best report red objects or red sense impressions; they will not express any sensation at all, but rather a thought about a red object or red sense impression. Perhaps it seems that one expresses a perceptual sensation when a startled cry is provoked by one's sensing a sharp or rapidly moving object. But this is hardly a clear case of one's expressing a perceptual sensation, as opposed to expressing, for example, one's feeling of fear. Or it may seem that saying 'Ah' as one savors a wine or settles into one's bath should count as a verbal expression of the relevant perceptual sensations.[20] But it is perhaps more reasonable to regard such borderline cases as expressing a bodily sensation of pleasure that accompanies the perceptual sensations in question.

The problem is that perceptual sensations seldom have any effect on our behavior except when they are part of our perceiving something. But when one perceives something, one's behavior, both verbal and nonverbal, expresses the propositional content of the perception, and not its sensory quality. One can always isolate the sensory content for special attention. But even then, what one says and does will express one's thought about the sensory quality, and not the quality itself.

Sense impressions enter our mental lives, therefore, in a kind of truncated way, compared with other sorts of mental states. We express every other kind of mental state in fairly standard ways, sometimes even when we are not conscious of that state. Perhaps it is this odd feature of perceptual sensations that has made some follow Descartes in doubting whether sensations are mental states at all.

But our concern is with the distinction between reporting and expressing. In particular, we want to know whether expressions of mental states invariably have the same content as the states themselves, whereas reports of mental states always diverge in content from the states they are about. And the foregoing considerations show that sense impressions are not counterexamples to this generalization. Even though we speak of perceptual sensations as being "of" various sorts of perceptible objects,[21] such sensations are not actually about anything. And reports of sense impressions are, again, about those impressions, and their propositional content conforms to the pattern described earlier.

---

[19] Care is necessary here. Sentences such as 'It hurts' may at first glance seem to express pains, rather than report them. But since 'Ouch' expresses one's pain rather than reporting it, it is reasonable to explain why 'Ouch, but nothing hurts' is not contradictory by taking 'It hurts' to report one's pain, and not express it.

[20] This was suggested by Daniel Dennett.

[21] See Wilfrid Sellars, "Empiricism and the Philosophy of Mind," in *Science, Perception and Reality*, London: Routledge & Kegan Paul, 1963, pp. 127–196, at pp. 154–155.

There is a view often associated with Wittgenstein that might be thought to cast doubt on the distinction between expressing and reporting one's mental states. In *Philosophical Investigations* Wittgenstein seems to have held, roughly, that although one can report that some other person is, for example, in pain, in one's own case one can only express the pain, and not report it as well.[22] If so, sentences like 'I am in pain', which ostensibly report bodily sensations, actually just express them.

But however suggestive this idea may be, it is plainly possible to report explicitly that we are in such states. And it is indisputable that others sometimes assert of us that we are, or are not, in particular mental states, and we sometimes explicitly contradict what they say. It is not just that we undermine what they say, as I might by saying 'Ouch' when you say I am not in pain. Rather, we literally deny what others say about us. If we were unable to report on our own states of mind, but could only express them, this direct denial of the ascriptions others make about us would be impossible. If you deny that I am in pain and I simply say 'Ouch', we have not thus far contradicted each other.[23]

---

[22] Part I, §§244, 256, 310, 377; cf. Norman Malcolm, "Knowledge of Other Minds," in *Knowledge and Certainty*, Englewood Cliffs: Prentice-Hall, 1963, 130–140, pp. 138–140; and Norman Malcolm, "Wittgenstein's *Philosophical Investigations*," in *Knowledge and Certainty*, Englewood Cliffs: Prentice-Hall, 1963, pp. 96–129, at pp. 105–117.

In an illuminating discussion, Jay F. Rosenberg ("Speaking Lions," *Canadian Journal of Philosophy*, VII, 1 [March 1977]: 155–160) argues that it is characteristic of speech acts such as 'I am in pain' that we have no criteria for their being true independent of our criteria for their being performed truthfully, i.e., sincerely. He concludes that such avowals are "report[s] judged as . . . expression[s]" (p. 159). This suggestion goes far in capturing Wittgenstein's idea, while still recognizing the reporting status of the relevant speech acts.

Intuitively, it seems out of place to evaluate expressions of feelings with respect to their cognitive credentials and success, as one might evaluate reports. Accordingly, Wittgenstein's view seems to capture whatever sense we have that speech acts such as 'I am in pain' have some special epistemic privilege.

Wittgenstein actually seems to extend the expressive theory beyond the case of sensations. See Part II, §x, p. 190: "[T]he statement 'I believe it's going to rain' has a meaning like, that is to say a use like, 'It's going to rain'." Sentences that ostensibly report one's own beliefs, like those which ostensibly report one's own sensations, would then really just express those beliefs and sensations.

[23] Parallel remarks hold for Wittgenstein's claim about 'I believe it's going to rain'. See also §VI, p. 69.

It may seem that the expressive theory works better with 'I am in pain' and its kindred than with 'I am not in pain'. Perhaps one can contradict such negative remarks, but not the affirmative counterparts. Moreover, 'I am not in pain' must express my thought that I am not in pain, since if I am not in pain, there is nothing else for it to express. But in both cases, whatever inappropriateness exists in my contesting your word about your own mental states disappears if we imagine that I speak first. There is nothing intuitively amiss if I say you are not in pain and you insist you are, or I say you are and you deny that. Moreover, you would then be contradicting what you would say if, instead, you agreed with me that you are not in pain. Even if the expressive theory applies only to affirmative sentences, it cannot accommodate these facts.

Although 'I am in pain' and ⌐I think that *p*⌐ express thoughts about my pain and about my thought that *p*, they may have the same conditions of use as saying 'Ouch' and saying that *p*, respectively. My saying that I am in pain or that I think that *p* will then be appropriate when, and only when, I am in pain or think that *p*. These considerations would explain our sense that these speech acts are somehow privileged, and even capture the kernel of truth in Wittgenstein's stronger claim that we never report, but only express, our bodily sensations.

We may thus conclude that, for creatures with the requisite linguistic capability, reporting mental states is possible, and that such a report differs in content from a verbal expression of that state. Not all types of mental state can be verbally expressed; perceptual sensations, for example, cannot be, and it is not clear what to say about bodily sensations. But creatures with the requisite linguistic ability can verbally express all other types of mental state, and in every case the verbal expression has the same propositional content as the state being expressed, and an illocutionary force corresponding to the state's mental attitude.

III. THE ARGUMENT

Distinguishing clearly between expressing one's mental states and reporting them has important consequences about consciousness. Whenever one says something meaningfully and sincerely, one's speech act expresses some thought that one has. Speech acts that do not express one's thoughts either are parrotingly produced, as in something recited by rote, or else are cases of intent to deceive or dissimulate. So, whenever one meaningfully and sincerely reports being in some mental state, one's very report invariably expresses some thought that one has.

Moreover, speech acts that are meaningful and sincere express thoughts that have the same propositional content as the speech acts. So whenever one meaningfully and sincerely reports being in some particular mental state, one thereby expresses one's thought that one is, oneself, in that mental state. Unless one's words expressed that higher-order thought, the ostensible report would fail to be an actual speech act, rather than a piece of parroting behavior. The ability to report being in particular mental states requires the ability to express higher-order thoughts that one is in those states. Clarity about the distinction between expressing and reporting points toward those very higher-order thoughts needed for the theory of consciousness I am defending.

There is an even more intimate tie, however, between the question of what it is for a mental state to be conscious and the distinction between expressing and reporting mental states. The ability to report being in a mental state of course presupposes moderately sophisticated capacities to communicate. But, given that a creature has suitable communicative ability, it will be able to report being in a particular mental state just in case that state is, intuitively, a conscious mental state. If the state is not a conscious state, it will be unavailable to one as the topic of a sincere report about the current contents of one's mind. And if the mental state is conscious, one will be aware of it and hence able to report that one is in it. The ability to report being in a particular mental state therefore corresponds to what we intuitively think of as that state's being in our stream of consciousness.[24]

---

[24] Cf. Dennett, *Content and Consciousness*, New York: Humanities Press, 1969, ch. vi, and "Toward a Cognitive Theory of Consciousness," esp. §§III–IV.

Robert Van Gulick has urged that we detach self-consciousness from the ability to report ("A Functionalist Plea for Self-Consciousness," *The Philosophical Review*, XCVII, 2 [April 1988]:

But the ability to report being in a particular mental state is the same as the ability to express one's thought that one is in that mental state. So a mental state's being conscious will be the same as one's having the ability to express one's higher-order thought that one is in that mental state. It is unclear how one could have the ability to express some particular thought without actually having that thought. The best explanation of our ability to express the higher-order thought in question is plainly that one actually has that thought.

The converse holds as well. When a mental state is not conscious, we cannot report on it, and thus we cannot express higher-order thoughts about it. The best explanation of our inability to express higher-order thoughts about nonconscious mental states is that when the states are not conscious no such higher-order thought exists. And, if conscious mental states are invariably accompanied by suitable higher-order thoughts, but nonconscious mental states never are, we have every reason to conclude that a mental state's being conscious consists simply in its being accompanied by such a higher-order thought.[25]

If a mental state is conscious, one can both express that state and report that one is in it. But when a mental state is not in one's stream of consciousness, even though one cannot then report being in that state, one can often still express it, at least non-verbally. One's nonverbal behavior often betrays nonconscious mental states, by giving unwitting expression to them. A person may sometimes even explicitly deny being in a particular mental state whose presence is made overwhelmingly obvious by some nonverbal expression of it; we have all had occasion to remark, with the Queen in *Hamlet*, that somebody "doth protest too much" (III, ii, 240).[26] This kind of

---

149–181, p. 160). But Van Gulick identifies self-consciousness in terms of the subpersonal possession of "reflexive meta-psychological information" (pp. 160 ff.); self-consciousness occurs whenever a mental state has informational content that involves some other mental state. This notion covers far more than the intuitive notion of a conscious mental state, which is under present consideration. So even if Van Gulick's defined notion is independent of any abilities to report, nothing follows about our intuitive notion of a conscious state.

[25] In "Two Concepts of Consciousness," toward the end of §I, I assumed that a mental state's being conscious required not only that it be accompanied by such a higher-order thought, but also that it cause that higher-order thought. This causal requirement may seem natural enough; after all, what else would cause that higher-order thought? But the requirement is unmotivated. Being in a conscious state requires only that one be conscious of being in that state; the causal antecedents of being thus conscious do not matter to whether the state one is conscious of being in is, intuitively, a conscious state.

The causal requirement may seem tempting as a simulation of the essential connection Cartesians see between mental states and their being conscious. But this weaker connection is still problematic. If mental states cause accompanying higher-order thoughts, why do many mental states occur without them? We might posit causal factors that block the causal connection, but that wrongly makes being conscious the normal condition for mental states. It is more natural to suppose that higher-order thoughts are caused by a coincidence of mental factors, many of which are causally independent of the state in question. [See, however, "Why Are Verbally Expressed Thoughts Conscious?", ch. 10 in this volume, §V, on why the targets higher-order thoughts are about often are among the causes of those higher-order thoughts. —Added in 2005.]

[26] Sometimes even one's speech acts will give unwitting expression to mental states one is not conscious of; Freudian slips are the obvious example. But here things are more complicated. When

occurrence shows that the abilities to express and report one's mental states need not coincide, any more than the mere ability to express a mental state nonverbally implies that that state is conscious.

The kind of consciousness we are focusing on is that special awareness we all have of our own mental states which is intuitively immediate, and seems to require no particular act of attention. Common sense puts few constraints on what positive account we should give of this intuitive immediacy. But part of our sense of immediacy plainly results from the awareness's being independent of both inference and observation, at least as these are ordinarily conceived.[27] And we must exclude both proprioceptive and visceral observation, as well as observation by way of the five exteroceptive senses.

Because our behavior can express mental states we are unaware of being in, others can learn about such states by observation and inference. So occasionally others can point out to us that we are in some mental state we had not previously noticed—say, that we are irritated or pleased. But the feeling of pleasure or irritation is not a conscious mental state if one's awareness of it relies solely on ordinary observation and inference, as the other person's knowledge does. The feeling would become conscious only if we also came to know, nonobservationally and noninferentially, that the other person's comment is correct. For my mental state to be conscious, my higher-order thought about it must not be based on inference, at least not on any inference of which I am aware.[28]

Typically one's higher-order thoughts are not themselves conscious thoughts. Indeed, our feeling that the consciousness of mental states is somehow immediate is most vivid in just those cases in which the higher-order thought is not conscious. This is because conscious higher-order thoughts normally distract us from the mental states they are about,[29] so that those states no longer occupy center stage in our stream of consciousness. But when we are unaware of having any higher-order thought, we

a speech act unwittingly expresses a nonconscious mental state, one is aware of the content of one's speech act. So the content of the speech act is distinct from the content of the nonconscious state it betrays. Indeed, it is probable that, with systematic exceptions, whenever one expresses a thought verbally, that thought will be conscious. (On the explanation of this generalization, and on why it does not threaten the argument of this section, see "Why Are Verbally Expressed Thoughts Conscious?" and my "Consciousness and Speech," MS.) It is therefore natural to understand these cases on the model of nonverbal expressing. One's speech act reveals one's nonconscious state not by functioning linguistically, but by being a piece of nonverbal behavior that gives nonverbal expression to that state.

[27] Perhaps, as Gilbert Harman (*Thought*, Princeton: Princeton University Press, 1973) convincingly urges, much of our knowledge derives from nonconscious inference. If so, such nonconscious inference may well underlie the presence of the higher-order thoughts that make mental states conscious. Such nonconscious inferences are not precluded here, since they would not interfere with the intuitive immediacy of such consciousness.

[28] Dennett has remarked (personal communication) that there will be penumbral cases in which one simply cannot tell whether or not one's higher-order thought is based on inference, so understood. This is no problem; in such cases one will plausibly also be unsure whether or not to count one's mental state as a conscious state.

[29] As Gilbert Ryle (*The Concept of Mind*, London: Hutchinson & Co., 1949, p. 165; cf. p. 197) in effect observed, though he talks simply of higher-order mental activities, and omits the qualification that they be conscious. It is important for a theory of consciousness in terms of higher-order

lack any sense of how we came to know about the conscious mental state. It is this very feeling of mystery about how we come to be aware of conscious mental states which encourages us to regard such consciousness as phenomenologically immediate.[30]

Is it necessary for a creature to have something as elaborate as human linguistic ability to be able to report its mental states? It is sometimes urged that we would not regard a creature's signals as making assertions unless those signals were embedded in something like human language. If so, nonhuman terrestrial animals would be unable to report their mental states.

But the ability to make assertions may well not require such elaborate resources. In particular, the syntactic complexity and semantic compositionality that permit the prodigious expressive powers characteristic of human language may not be necessary to performing simpler speech acts. It is far from obvious that a creature must be able to express the seemingly unlimited range of things that humans can to be capable of performing any speech acts at all. One factor that is more important is whether the creature can differentially express distinct mental attitudes. This ability seems more important to the core idea of what is involved in performing a speech act than the range and complexity of thoughts a creature can express. Another factor is whether there is some measure of conventionality about what various signals convey and a suitable degree of deliberate, voluntary choice about when the signal is used.[31]

It will take more, however, to report one's mental states than to be able to perform other sorts of speech acts. Unless a creature's signals exhibited a fairly sophisticated compositional structure, perhaps nothing would justify us in concluding that it was reporting its mental states, rather than just expressing them. Norman Malcolm's well-known distinction between thinking and having thoughts seems to capture the distinction. Malcolm contends that nonlinguistic animals can think, but cannot have

---

thoughts that nonconscious higher-order thoughts do not distract one from the mental states they are about.

[30] There is another way in which the consciousness of conscious mental states seems intuitively immediate. In the case of nonconscious mental states, it is arguable that their belonging to a particular subject is no more problematic than the bond between physical objects and their properties. But when a mental state is conscious, it is tempting to insist that there is more to say about how it belongs to a particular subject.

The present theory explains what is phenomenologically special about the way in which conscious mental states belong to their subjects. Propositional states, both conscious and nonconscious, intuitively seem bound to their subjects by their mental attitudes; the attitude is a kind of relation joining a thinking subject to its thoughts. And sensory mental states, whether conscious or not, seem similarly tied to their subjects by occurring within a field of experience, which connects these mental states to others of the same and different sensory modalities. But conscious states seem tied to their subjects in some way above and beyond the bond they have in common with nonconscious states. We can explain this additional tie that such consciousness seems to add as due to the content of the accompanying higher-order thought. That higher-order thought is a thought to the effect that one is, oneself, in the mental state in question. Because such higher-order thoughts are both about oneself and the mental state one is in, they carry with them the sense that the tie between one's mental state and oneself is stronger when the state is conscious than when it is not.

[31] When the means of expressing thoughts is not all that systematic, as with all the nonhuman terrestrial animals we know about, we will want to see more conventionality and deliberateness to be convinced that speech acts are occurring.

thoughts. As he describes the difference, thinking seems to correspond to intentional states one can express but not report, whereas having thoughts corresponds to those one can report as well.[32] So what Malcolm calls thinking will be nonconscious thinking, and the having of thoughts will be conscious thinking.[33]

In any case, even if reporting one's mental states did require a communicative system with the full resources of human language, that would not show that creatures that cannot report their mental states have no conscious mental states. Being able to report a mental state means being able to express a higher-order thought about that state. Most creatures presumably have far more thoughts than they can express; the inability to express a thought hardly means that no such thought occurs. So if a creature were unable to express any of its higher-order thoughts, that would not imply that it had none.

The ability to report mental states is important here only because we understand what it is for a mental state to be conscious by appeal to creatures who can say what mental states they are in. We fix the extensions of terms for the various types of mental state by way of the conscious cases. We understand what it is for a mental state to be of this type or that by reference to conscious examples of that type of mental state, both our own and those of others. But we often fix the extensions of terms by way of a range of phenomena narrower than those to which the terms apply. So using the conscious cases to fix the extensions of our terms for mental states does not show that all such states are conscious.

Similarly, we fix the reference of the term 'conscious' itself, as it applies to mental states, by the special case of creatures like ourselves that can report being in such states. But this does not show that creatures that cannot make such reports cannot be in conscious mental states. The connection between a state's being conscious and our being able to report that state reflects the fact that conscious states are accompanied by thoughts about those states and we can express those thoughts. In the human case, we may describe the ability to have higher-order thoughts in terms of the language system having access to certain mental states.[34] But what matters to a state's being conscious is the higher-order thought, not the resulting ability to report.[35]

---

[32] "Thoughtless Brutes," in *Thought and Knowledge*, Ithaca: Cornell University Press, 1977, pp. 40–57, §II. Malcolm would not put it this way, since his inclination there towards an expressive theory of first-person ascriptions of mental states leads him, in effect, to assimilate reporting and expressing. And this, together with a view of expressive ability modeled on human language, lead him in turn to a rather restrictive view of the mentality of nonhuman animals (§III).

[33] As noted above (n. 17), verbally expressed thoughts are typically conscious. But when a creature lacks the ability to report its mental states, verbally expressing them may well imply nothing about whether the state expressed is conscious. This point is exploited in "Why Are Verbally Expressed Thoughts Conscious?".

[34] See, e.g., Dennett, "Toward a Cognitive Theory of Consciousness," §§III–IV.

[35] Indeed, Dennett in "Toward a Cognitive Theory of Consciousness" (e.g., p. 217) also puts his point in terms of the having of thoughts—what he calls "thinkings."

These considerations show that, *pace* Van Gulick (p. 162), the fact that many mental states of nonlinguistic creatures are conscious provides no reason to deny the connection between a state's being conscious and the ability for creatures with suitable linguistic endowment to report on that state.

IV. A DISPOSITIONAL ALTERNATIVE

On the foregoing argument, conscious mental states are those mental states we are able to report, and any such report must express a higher-order thought about the conscious state in question. It may seem, however, that these considerations do not support the conclusion that higher-order thoughts actually accompany all conscious states. Rather, they may support only the weaker conclusion that a higher-order thought must be able to accompany every conscious state. If so, the foregoing argument would show, instead, that a mental state's being conscious consists only in a disposition to have such a higher-order thought, and not in its actual occurrence.

This conclusion seems to receive support from an independent line of argument. Conscious mental states are mental states we can readily introspect, pretty much at will. So it is reasonable to think of a mental state's being conscious as a matter of our being able to become introspectively aware of it; conscious states are normally[36] introspectible states. Moreover, it is natural to think of being introspectible as a dispositional property. So it may seem but a short step to the conclusion that a mental state's being conscious is, itself, a dispositional property: a disposition to have higher-order thoughts about one's mental states. Similarly, conscious states are those we can report, and it is natural also to think of being reportable as a dispositional property.[37]

These considerations recall Kant's well-known claim that the representation 'I think' must be able to accompany all other representations.[38] Kant insists that the representation 'I think' be a nonempirical (B132) or transcendental representation (B401, A343); the possibility of its accompanying all other representations is a condition for those representations all being mine, united in one center of consciousness (B132–5, esp. B134; on mental states' belonging to a subject, see n. 30 above). But this qualification is irrelevant for present purposes, since the reflexive representation Kant has in mind is presumably like other, more mundane thoughts in that a sincere, meaningful speech act could express it.

Kant does not say in so many words that a representation's being conscious is due to its being able to be accompanied by the representation 'I think'. But there is reason to think he holds this. The representation 'I think' must accompany all other representations because we could not otherwise explain what it is for my representations to be mine. And he seems to hold that a mental state's being mine coincides with its being conscious.[39]

Kant's dictum therefore suggests an account of a mental state's being conscious in terms of higher-order thoughts. But Kant does not say that the representation 'I

---

[36] I.e., normally for creatures like us that have the capacity for being introspectively conscious of their mental states.

[37] I am especially indebted to Daniel Dennett for pressing on me the virtues of some form of a dispositional view, and also for many other helpful reactions to drafts of this paper.

[38] Immanuel Kant, *Critique of Pure Reason*, second edition, tr. and ed. Paul Guyer and Allen W. Wood, Cambridge: Cambridge University Press, 1998, B131–138; cf. B157–159, A122–3, B406.

[39] Kant explicitly allows that I need not be conscious of my representations as being mine (B132). So, if its being mine is its being nonintrospectively conscious, my being aware of it as mine would be my introspecting it.

think' actually accompanies all other representations, but only that it must be able to do so. His view is therefore a version of the dispositional account just sketched: A mental state's being conscious is not its being actually accompanied by a suitable higher-order thought, but its being able to be thus accompanied.

This dispositional view, however, does not readily square with our intuitive idea of what it is for a mental state to be conscious. A mental state's being conscious is our being conscious of being in that state in a suitably immediate way. And being conscious of things generally is occurrent, not dispositional. On the present theory, we are conscious of being in mental states when they are conscious states because we have higher-order thoughts about those states. Merely being disposed to have such thoughts would not make us conscious of the states in question; we must have actual, occurrent higher-order thoughts. Having a disposition to have a thought about a chair could not make one conscious of the chair; how could having a disposition to have a higher-order thought about a mental state make one conscious of that state? This conclusion accords well with our commonsense intuitions, on which, whatever being conscious may amount to, it seems to be a clear case of a nondispositional, occurrent property of mental states.

Moreover, the fact that conscious states are all introspectible and reportable does not show that a state's being conscious is solely a dispositional matter. Being conscious can perfectly well be a nondispositional, occurrent property of mental states and yet involve dispositions. One and the same property can often be described in both dispositional and occurrent terms. Something's being red plainly involves various dispositions, such as causing bulls to charge. And perhaps something's being flammable or soluble consists in something's having a certain physical makeup, though we pick out those properties by way of a disposition to burn or dissolve. Similarly, a mental state's being conscious is an occurrent property, even though it involves such dispositions as being introspectible and reportable.[40]

Positing occurrent higher-order thoughts as accompanying all conscious states also readily explains why those states are introspectible and reportable. It is my ability to express my thoughts verbally that enables me to report on the mental states my higher-order thoughts are about. And it is because my higher-order thoughts can become conscious that I can come to introspect the mental states those thoughts are about. This second point will figure below toward the end of this section.

On the present theory, a mental state's being conscious is a relational property—the property of being accompanied by a higher-order thought. This accords poorly with common sense, which seems to represent being conscious as

---

[40] There are additional sources of confusion. Something can plausibly be dispositional from the point of view of common sense and occurrent from the point of view of a scientific treatment, or conversely. Similarly, something can count as an occurrent property from the vantage point of science and common sense but figure dispositionally within a functional or computational description, or again conversely. Moreover, it is sometimes difficult to draw any useful distinction between short-term dispositions and occurrent properties. In claiming that a mental state's being conscious is its being actually accompanied by a suitable higher-order thought, the present theory is operating with our ordinary folk-psychological categories and concepts. Still, such higher-order thoughts might correspond to something dispositional when we move to scientific theory.

nonrelational. Why should it matter, then, that common sense represents a mental state's being conscious as occurrent, and not dispositional?

Commonsense considerations are hardly decisive, and may well be overruled by theory. But we should try to do some sort of justice to those intuitions. There are different ways to do this. The present theory preserves the intuition that consciousness is occurrent. And, though it does not preserve the idea that consciousness is nonrelational, the theory does explain why that idea is so appealing. Consciousness seems to be nonrelational because we are generally unaware of the higher-order thought that makes a mental state conscious, and thus unaware of the relation by virtue of which that consciousness is conferred.

An apparent advantage of the dispositional view stems from the difficulty in accepting the existence of so many higher-order thoughts. At most waking moments we are in a multitude of conscious states; it seems extravagant to posit a distinct higher-order thought for each of those conscious states. When a mental state is conscious, we plainly have the ability to think about it, but it seems equally plain that we do not actually think about all our conscious states. A dispositional account circumvents this difficulty by requiring only that we be disposed to have a higher-order thought about each conscious state, and not that we actually have all those thoughts.

But this line of reasoning rests on a mistake. Thinking about something is not just having a train of thoughts about it, but having a conscious train of thoughts about it. We seldom think, in that way, about any of our conscious states. But the higher-order thoughts the theory posits are typically not conscious thoughts. The intuitive difficulty about how many higher-order thoughts we could have arises only on the assumption that those thoughts must be conscious; higher-order thoughts of which we are unaware will pose no problem. The worry about positing too many higher-order thoughts comes from thinking that these thoughts would fill up our conscious capacity, and then some; we would have no room in consciousness for anything else. But this is a real worry only on the assumption that all thoughts are automatically conscious thoughts.[41]

A mental state's being conscious consists in one's being conscious of being in that state. Being conscious of being in a mental-state type will not do; I must be conscious of being in the relevant token of that type. A dispositional account faces a difficulty here, since it is far from clear how a disposition to have a higher-order thought can refer to one mental-state token rather than another. Perhaps a dispositional account will require not that the disposition refers to a mental-state token, but that it is a disposition to have a higher-order thought that refers to it.[42]

---

[41] One might hold that the distinction between occurrent thoughts and dispositions to have them coincides with the distinction between conscious and nonconscious thoughts. If so, occurrent thoughts could never be nonconscious. The only way, then, to put the present theory would be in terms of dispositions to have higher-order thoughts, since these thoughts are typically nonconscious. (I am grateful to Ernest Sosa for pressing this point.) But it is not easy to see how one might independently substantiate this Cartesian denial of nonconscious occurrent mental states.

[42] I am grateful to Martin Davies for this point.

Still, if such a disposition is responsible for a mental state's being conscious, the disposition must somehow connect with the right mental state, and it is unclear how that can take place.

This problem becomes especially intractable in the case of sensations. No higher-order thoughts could capture all the subtle variations of sensory quality we consciously experience. So higher-order thoughts must refer to sensory states demonstratively,[†] perhaps as occupying this or that position in the relevant sensory field. It is especially unclear how mere dispositions to have higher-order thoughts could accomplish this.

A headache or other bodily sensation may last an entire day, even though one is only intermittently conscious of it. The point is not merely that one introspects or pays attention to headaches only intermittently; a day-long headache is unlikely to be constantly in one's stream of consciousness in any way at all. And, in general, sensory states need not be conscious states. The distinctive sensory qualities of such states are simply those properties in virtue of which we distinguish among sensations as having distinct sensory content. There is no reason to hold that these differences can obtain only when the sensation is conscious. The distinctive sensory properties of nonconscious sensations resemble and differ in just the ways that those of conscious sensations resemble and differ, differing only in that the one group is conscious, whereas the other is not.[43]

Explaining the intermittent consciousness of such a headache is easy if we appeal to occurrent higher-order thoughts; occurrent thoughts come and go. So one and the same mental state, such as a headache, could persist, sometimes accompanied by a higher-order thought, sometimes not. Mental states would accordingly enter and leave our stream of consciousness. Dispositions seem less well-suited to this task. Because they are more long lasting, dispositions seem intuitively less likely to come and go with the desired frequency, as occurrent higher-order thoughts might.

The argument of section III also tells against a dispositional account. A mental state's being conscious is manifested by reports that one is in that state, and to be

---

[†] I would now reject this appeal to demonstrative reference, and appeal instead to the theory of mental qualities developed in Part II, which provides a way for higher-order thoughts to refer to the qualities they are about. See esp. "Sensory Qualities, Consciousness, and Perception," §V. [Added in 2005.]

[43] For more on sensory quality see "Two Concepts of Consciousness," §III; "A Theory of Consciousness," §II; and my "The Colors and Shapes of Visual Experiences," in *Consciousness and Intentionality: Models and Modalities of Attribution*, ed. Denis Fisette, Dordrecht: Kluwer Academic Publishers, 1999, pp. 95–118.

Norton Nelkin, if I understand him, holds that sensory states, though they can occur nonconsciously, always have what he calls phenomenologicality, and thus are invariably felt ("Unconscious Sensations," *Philosophical Psychology*, II, 2 [1989]: 129–141, p. 139). It is unclear in what sense nonconscious states might be felt. Apart from these issues, Nelkin presents a view very similar to that defended here, though he advances different arguments for it. [See also Norton Nelkin, *Consciousness and the Origins of Thought*, Cambridge: Cambridge University Press, 1996, and my discussion of Nelkin's views in "Apperception, Sensation, and Dissociability," *Mind and Language*, 12, 2 (June 1997): 206–222. —Added in 2005.]

meaningful these reports must express corresponding thoughts about those mental states. And speech acts plainly do not express mere dispositions to have thoughts.[44]

Conscious states can normally be introspected. And one might argue that even though this does not imply a dispositional account, a dispositional account is necessary to explain why it is so. But that is a mistake. A state is introspectible if it can become an object of introspection. And introspecting a state consists in being aware of that state, and also being conscious that one is thus aware. So introspecting is having a conscious thought about a mental state. On the present theory, a state's being conscious is its being accompanied by a suitable higher-order thought. Those higher-order thoughts are typically not conscious; but once one has such a higher-order thought, it can itself become conscious. And its being conscious results in the mental state it is about being introspectively conscious. Conscious states are introspectible because higher-order thoughts can themselves become conscious thoughts.

If all mental states were conscious states, however, this explanation would be unavailable. There would then be no difference between having a conscious thought about one's mental state and having a thought about it, *tout court*. So one could not explain why a state's being conscious coincides with its being introspectible by saying that the accompanying higher-order thought is not conscious but can become so. Moreover, introspecting would simply be having such a thought, and a mental state would be introspectible just in case one were disposed to have such a thought about it. A state's being nonintrospectively conscious could not then consist in having a higher-order thought, on pain of collapsing the distinction between being introspectively and nonintrospectively conscious. We would thus have to say that a state's being nonintrospectively conscious consists in one's being disposed to have such a thought.

The idea that a state's being a conscious state consists in a disposition to have a suitable higher-order thought does not explicitly presuppose that mental states are always conscious. But the foregoing considerations suggest that this Cartesian picture may underlie much of the appeal a dispositional theory has. Only if we tacitly assume all mental states are conscious will the dispositional account be needed to explain why conscious states are introspectible. But the assumption that all mental states are conscious is plainly question begging in the context of evaluating the present theory.[45]

---

[44] The argument that speech acts express corresponding thoughts relied on Moore's paradox; 'It's raining but I don't think so' lacks coherent performance conditions because one cannot meaningfully say it's raining and not think it is. So one could argue that meaningful speech acts must express dispositions to have the relevant thought, since 'It's raining but I'm not disposed to think so' also lacks coherent performance conditions. But this shows at best that meaningful speech acts express both corresponding thoughts and dispositions to have such thoughts, since whenever the dispositional version of Moore's paradox works, the nondispositional version will as well.

Indeed, the dispositional version works presumably only because the corresponding nondispositional version does. Since 'I'm not disposed to think so' is stronger than 'I don't think so', if 'It's raining but I don't think so' is problematic, 'It's raining but I'm not disposed to think so' must be as well. So the reason meaningful speech acts are accompanied by dispositions to have higher-order thoughts is that they are accompanied by the actual thoughts themselves.

[45] Introspecting a mental state means having a conscious higher-order thought, and nonconscious mental states are presumably unaccompanied by higher-order thoughts, whether conscious or not.

V. ARE HIGHER-ORDER THOUGHTS POSSIBLE?

The objection just considered sought to show that conscious mental states need not be accompanied by occurrent higher-order thoughts. But there are other considerations that seem actually to cast doubt on whether such higher-order thoughts are possible at all. When a conscious mental state is a thought, the mental analogue of performance conditions will be the same for that thought as for the higher-order thought about it. No circumstances exist in which I can appropriately think that *p*, but not appropriately think that I think that *p*. Perhaps, moreover, the right way to individuate mental states is by reference to these mental analogues of performance conditions. If so, the ostensibly higher-order thought would be indistinguishable from the thought it purports to be about; the conditions for having a thought about a thought would be the same as those for just having that thought. The very idea of distinct higher-order thoughts about other thoughts would accordingly be incoherent.

Brentano (1973, p. 127) actually advances just such an argument, applying it even to the case of perceiving.[46] Thus he maintains that my hearing a sound and my thought that I hear it are one and the same mental act. And he goes on to insist that the very content of that perception must be contained in the content of any higher-order thought about it, thus reasoning from performance conditions to mental content. Accordingly, he concludes, every mental state is, in part, about itself; in his words, all mental acts "apprehend [themselves, albeit] indirectly" (128). Every mental state, in addition to having its standard nature, will also function as a higher-order thought about itself.

This idea is not uncommon. Locke seems to express it when he writes that "thinking consists in being conscious that one thinks."[47] Some such idea seems also to underlie Descartes's and Hobbes's insistence that it is absurd to suppose that one

---

Moreover, a state's being nonintrospectively conscious involves less than its being introspectively conscious, but more than its not being conscious at all. So it may seem that only a disposition to have a higher-order thought could fit in between a conscious higher-order thought and its absence. But the Cartesian assumption that all mental states are conscious again figures in this reasoning. Such a disposition is the natural intermediate between a conscious higher-order thought and none at all only if we tacitly rule out the possibility of a higher-order thought that is not conscious.

[46] Franz Brentano, *Psychology from an Empirical Standpoint*, tr. Antos C. Rancurello, D. B. Terrell, and Linda L. McAlister, London: Routledge & Kegan Paul, 1973.

As Brentano puts it, we must choose whether to individuate propositional mental states (presentations) in terms of their (propositional) object or the mental act of the presentation.

Brentano credits Aristotle with the idea. Aristotle's actual argument (Aristotle, *de Anima*, with translation, introduction, and notes by R. D. Hicks, Cambridge: Cambridge University Press, 1907, III, 2, 425b 13–14), which Brentano adapts, is that if the sense by which we see that we see is not sight, then the sense of sight and the other sense would both have color as their proper object, and distinct senses cannot share the same proper object.

[47] John Locke, *An Essay Concerning Human Understanding*, by John Locke, edited from the fourth edition by Peter H. Nidditch, Oxford: Oxford University Press, 1975, II, i, 19. Cf. I, ii, 5; II, i, 10–12; II, x, 2; and IV, vii, 4. On Locke's reflexive model of consciousness see also II, xx, 1 and II, xxvii, 9.

thought could ever be about another.[48] If higher-order thoughts must be a part or aspect of the mental states they are about, an account of consciousness in terms of distinct higher-order thoughts will be unintelligible.[49]

It is useful to see Brentano's argument as the mental analogue of Wittgenstein's idea in *Philosophical Investigations* that meaning is use.[50] Understanding how sentences are correctly used is knowing their performance conditions. So focusing on use will suggest typing speech acts by reference to performance conditions, rather than by such semantic features as truth conditions or propositional content. This fits well with Wittgenstein's suggestion, noted at the end of section II, that one cannot report, but can only express one's own pains and other bodily sensations. 'I am in pain' is indistinguishable from 'Ouch' in respect of performance conditions; so if one focuses solely on performance conditions, it is natural to type the two together.

This has consequences for how we think about consciousness. 'It hurts' and 'I am in pain' plainly have propositional content; they are about one's pain, and thus express one's thought that one is in pain, that is, they express one's awareness of being in pain. And saying 'Ouch' plainly expresses one's pain. So if 'I am in pain' were on a par with 'Ouch', it too would express one's pain, as well as expressing one's awareness of being in pain. Accordingly, sentences such as 'I am in pain' and 'It hurts' intuitively seem to yoke together the pain and one's awareness of it, suggesting that the two actually cannot occur separately.[51]

---

[48] For both, see *Third Replies*, René Descartes, *Oeuvres*, ed. Charles Adam and Paul Tannery, 11 volumes, Paris: J. Vrin, 1964–76, VII, 175; and *The Philosophical Writings of Descartes*, tr. John Cottingham, Robert Stoothoff, and Dugald Murdoch (and Anthony Kenny in vol. III), 3 volumes, Cambridge: Cambridge University Press, 1984–91, II, 124; though see also *Seventh Replies*, *Oeuvres*, VII, 559 (*Philosophical Writings*, II, 382).

[49] This conclusion echoes a certain interpretation of the thesis that knowing implies knowing one knows. On that interpretation, there is nothing to such second-order knowing above and beyond first-order knowing itself. Here, too, stressing performance conditions over propositional content seems to be at issue: The force of saying or thinking that I know is equivalent to that of saying or thinking that I know that I know, even if their propositional contents differ. Historically, however, this view has generally encouraged claims about the transparency of mind to itself, rather than *vice versa*. And if knowing can be tacit, the idea that knowing implies knowing one knows is independent of such claims of transparency.

[50] Applied, however, to sentence-sized, rather than word-sized, mental units: "The meaning of a word is its use in the language" (Part I, §43). See also n. 22. Wittgenstein's denial that there is anything to meaning above and beyond use amounts, in effect, to denying that anything other than performance conditions figures in these issues. In that respect, Brentano's argument is less clean, since he allows an independent role for propositional content. Just as Moore's paradox helps show that reporting and expressing are distinct (see p. 51), so it helps show that content is distinct from force, or performance conditions. It seems impossible to explain the difference between 'It's raining but I don't believe it' and 'It's raining and it's not raining' without invoking some distinction between force and content.

Rosenberg's idea that our criteria for the truth of avowals are the same as our criteria for the truthfulness of their performance (n. 22) also involves a move from semantics to performance conditions.

[51] Another consequence of the Wittgensteinian focus on performance conditions, and the consequent idea that ostensible reports actually express one's sensations has to do with J. J. C. Smart's

But there is more to a mental state than the mental analogue of its performance conditions. When we individuate mental states, we must also take into account their truth conditions, if any, and their propositional content. Two states are the same only if their semantic properties and performance conditions are the same. Brentano's argument hinges on the idea that it is sufficient for two states to be the same that they have the same mental analogue of performance conditions. That argument cannot therefore be sustained, and there is thus no incoherence in the idea of higher-order thoughts distinct from the thoughts they are about. Indeed, mental attitude is by itself sufficient to undermine Brentano's argument. Suppose the higher-order thought is about a suspicion or doubt; that state will perforce have a mental attitude distinct from any higher-order thought, since higher-order thoughts will invariably have the mental attitude corresponding to an assertion.

There is in any case a somewhat idle air to Brentano's claim that higher-order thoughts are part of the mental states they refer to. How could we ever show, in a non-question-begging way, that a higher-order thought is part of the mental state it is about, rather than that the two are just distinct, concurrent states? It would be more tempting to hold this if all mental states were conscious. If we trace a state's being conscious to the presence of a higher-order thought and every mental state is conscious, there will be a higher-order thought for every mental state. Since no mental state would then occur without its higher-order thought, it might seem inviting to hold that higher-order thought to be part of the state itself. But, if higher-order thoughts are distinct mental states, we can explain why we are generally unaware of them only by saying that such thoughts are usually not conscious thoughts. And this explanation would be unavailable if all mental states were conscious. It begs the question against the present theory to suppose all mental states are conscious, and in any case we have excellent reason to hold that mental states exist that are not conscious states.

There is an even more dramatic way to see how the view suggested by Brentano and Locke goes wrong. If every mental state is conscious and every conscious mental state is, in part, about itself, every mental state without exception will, in part, be about itself. Those who endorse this reflexive model of consciousness presumably find this consequence acceptable. But there is a further implication that has generally

---

well-known topic-neutral translations of sentences that refer to sensations. According to Smart, the statement 'I have a yellowish-orange afterimage' is roughly equivalent to 'Something is going on in me like what goes on in me when I am visually stimulated by an orange' ("Sensations and Brain Processes," in *The Philosophy of Mind*, ed. V. C. Chappell, Englewood Cliffs: Prentice-Hall, 1962, pp. 160–172, at p. 167). Smart's critics have rightly stressed that these sentences differ in truth conditions, but perhaps they are, after all, equivalent in respect of performance conditions.

Smart sometimes describes the relevant sentences as reports (p. 168; cf. pp. 170–171), but he also concedes finding congenial the " 'expressive' account of sensation statements" often attributed to Wittgenstein (p. 162; see the next paragraph in the text). Seeing these statements as expressions rather than reports of perceptual sensations may explain Smart's persistence in casting his topic-neutral accounts in the first-person singular, a feature of Smart's treatment that other advocates of the topic-neutral approach have not followed, and that critics have not noted. Still, since statements such as 'I have a yellowish-orange afterimage' report, rather than express our sensations, this reconstruction cannot justify Smart's topic-neutral program.

not been noted. To say anything meaningfully and sincerely, one's speech act must express some thought that has the same force and the same propositional content. So, if every mental state is, in part, about itself, it will be impossible to say anything at all that is not, in part, literally about one's own mental states.

Locke actually seems to endorse something like this when he claims that the primary use of words is to refer to the ideas in one's mind.[52] Indeed, in advancing this view, Locke seems deliberately to assimilate expressing one's ideas to reporting them. As he puts it, "the *Words* [a person] speak[s] (with any meaning) . . . *stand for the* Ideas *he has*, and which he would express by them."[53] Words, on this account, are about the very ideas they express.

This assimilation of reporting and expressing recalls Locke's reflexive model of consciousness, though his doctrine about words and ideas derives not from that model but from his views about meaning. Locke's semantic theory thus fits well with his views about consciousness. Because words apply primarily to the speaker's ideas, all speech acts will be about the speaker's mental states. It is interesting to note in this connection that J. R. Ross has argued, on grammatical grounds, that the deep structure of every declarative sentence is dominated by the pronoun 'I' plus some verb of linguistic performance,[54] as though every such sentence implicitly reported its own illocutionary force and meaning.

But just because particular grammatical or semantic theories fit neatly with the reflexive model of consciousness does not mean that those theories provide any support for that model. The conclusion that the reflexive picture of consciousness forces on us is truly extravagant: Every speech act, to be meaningful and sincere, must literally refer to one of the speaker's own mental states. It is hard to see how any grammatical or semantic theory could render this claim acceptable.

VI. IS REPORTING DISTINCT FROM EXPRESSING?

Stressing performance conditions over propositional content raises doubts about whether a higher-order thought can really be distinct from the thought it is about. But there is another source for such doubts. We sometimes use verbs of mental attitude in ways that may appear to undercut the sharp distinction between expressing and reporting, on which the argument of section III relied. And if reporting and expressing a mental state are the same, a speech act such as saying 'I think it's raining' will indifferently express both the ostensible higher-order thought that I think it's raining and the thought that it's raining. Those thoughts will then arguably be the same, since an unambiguous speech act presumably expresses a single thought.

[52] I owe this observation to Margaret Atherton. See Locke, III, ii, 2–3; words all 'apply to' (III, ii, 2), 'are signs of', 'signify', only one's own ideas. Note, however, that Locke's claim is that terms refer to the ideas they express, and is not directly about complete sentences.

[53] III, ii, 3. "Nor can any one apply them . . . immediately to any thing else, but the *Ideas*, that he himself hath" (III, ii, 2).

[54] John Robert Ross, "On Declarative Sentences," in *Readings in English Transformational Grammar*, ed. Roderick A. Jacobs and Peter S. Rosenbaum, Waltham, Massachusetts: Ginn & Co., 1970, pp. 222–272.

The problem is this. I can express my doubt about something by saying, for example, that it may not be so. But, even when I say 'I doubt it' or, more explicitly, ⌜I doubt that *p*⌝, it seems natural to take me to be expressing my doubt, and not just reporting what mental state I am in. Similarly, if I say that I suppose or choose something, or sympathize with somebody, it is natural again to see this as actually expressing my supposition, choice, or sympathy, and not just telling you about the contents of my mind. A parody will illustrate the point especially vividly. If you ask me whether it is raining and I say 'I think so', it would be bizarre to take me to be talking about my mental state, rather than the weather. (See n. 22.)

This challenge is important. Higher-order thoughts entered our account of consciousness because conscious mental states are those we can report noninferentially. And those putative reports will not be actual speech acts unless they express thoughts about the conscious mental states in question. But if such ostensibly higher-order remarks are not really second-order reports about our mental states at all, but only express those states, those remarks will not express any higher-order thoughts.

This conclusion would thus vindicate the Cartesian claim that consciousness is intrinsic to mental states. The second-order character of such remarks would be a surface illusion, and would not imply the existence of any distinct second-order thoughts. More important, these ostensibly second-order remarks would presumably also report the very mental states they express. The speech act 'I doubt it' would both express and report one's doubt, so that the doubt itself would have both the content of the doubt and the content that one had that doubt. Every conscious mental state would be, in part, about itself; consciousness would be a reflexive feature of mental states, in Ryle's apt words, a matter of their being "self-intimating" or "self-luminous" (159). We would then have no choice but to swallow the strikingly unintuitive consequence noted earlier about sincere speech acts' invariably referring to the speaker's own mental states.

It is worth noting that not all ostensible reports follow the pattern illustrated above. If I say that I gather, deduce, covet, or recognize something, it is not all that tempting to hold that I thereby express, rather than report, my mental state. And if I say that I expect, want, understand, or suspect something, it is plain that I am then explicitly talking about my mental states, and not merely, as we say, "speaking my mind"—not just expressing those states.

But even in cases such as saying that I think, doubt, suppose, or choose something, the tendency to take my remarks to express, rather than report, my mental states misleads. As already noted (pp. 51 and 67), that temptation stems from focusing on the performance conditions of such sentences at the expense of their distinctively semantic characteristics—their truth conditions and propositional content. The sentences 'I doubt it' and 'I think so' may superficially seem to express one's doubts and thoughts, and to be about whatever those doubts and thoughts are about. But this is because the circumstances in which one can appropriately say that something

[55] Cf., e.g., Alston, "Expressing," esp. p. 16.

may not be so are the same as those for saying that one doubts it; similarly for saying that something is so and saying that one thinks it is.[56]

Once again, meanings and truth conditions tell a different story. If I am asked whether it is raining and I say I think so, my remark is not semantically equivalent to saying 'Yes, it's raining'.[57] The sentence 'It's raining but I don't think so' is absurd, but not contradictory; the sentence 'I think it's raining but I don't think so', by contrast, is an actual contradiction.[58] Moreover, if you say that I believe, doubt, suppose or choose something, I can deny what you say, and in so doing I would contradict what I would have said if instead I agreed with you. And agreeing with you would naturally take the form of saying that I believe, doubt, suppose, or choose that thing.

The distinction between reporting and verbally expressing one's mental states is crucial to the argument of section III. Given the failure of the most plausible attempts to undermine that distinction, we may conclude that the argument successfully supports a theory of consciousness in terms of higher-order thoughts.[59]

---

[56] Cf. Vendler's argument: "the utterance *I say that I order you to go home* (if it is acceptable at all) amounts to the same speech-act as the utterance *I order you to go home*. Similarly, to think that *p* and to think that one thinks that *p* (if we can speak of such a thing) are the same thought" (*Res Cogitans*, pp. 193–4; see also pp. 50–51). Vendler is plainly relying here on performance conditions and their mental analogues.

The same holds for a related matter. If one held that ⌜I think that *p*⌝ expresses, rather than reports my thought that *p*, one might urge that ⌜I don't think that *p*⌝ expresses my thought that it's not the case that *p*. Perhaps this would explain why we use 'I don't think ...' and its kindred not to deny we think that *p*, but to say we think *p* isn't so. But again, performance conditions explain this more successfully: It is normally appropriate to deny we think that *p* only when we think it isn't so.

[57] As Austin points out, 'I think he did it' can be a statement about myself, in contrast to 'I state he did it', which cannot (*How to Do Things with Words*, second edition, p. 134; p. 135 in the first edition).

[58] Similarly, as noted above (pp. 52–53), 'Ouch, but I'm not in pain', unlike 'I'm in pain, but I'm not in pain', is like a standard Moore's-paradox sentence: absurd but not contradictory. See n. 19 and pp. 54 and 66.

[59] Much of the work on this paper, resulting in the penultimate draft, was done while I was a fellow at the Center for Interdisciplinary Research (ZiF), University of Bielefeld, Germany, in 1989–90. I am indebted to the Center for generous support and exceptionally congenial and stimulating surroundings.

Previous drafts were read at Tufts, Columbia, The University of Wisconsin at Milwaukee, and the August 1989 Joint Conference of the Sociedad Filosófica Ibero-Americana and the Sociedad Argentina de Análisis Filosófico, in Buenos Aires. I am grateful to friends and colleagues in those audiences for helpful reactions, and to Martin Davies for useful comments on a penultimate draft. Special thanks to Daniel Dennett.

3

Intentionality

I. INTRODUCTION

Thought and speech are intimately connected, in ways that make the study of each shed light on the other. But the nature of that connection, and of the illumination it casts, are vexed issues that are the subject of considerable controversy.

At the level of our platitudinous background knowledge about these things, speech is the expression of thought. And understanding what such expressing involves is central to understanding the relation between thinking and speaking. Part of what it is for a speech act to express a mental state is that the speech act accurately captures the mental state and can convey to others what mental state it is. And for this to occur, the speech act at least must have propositional content that somehow reflects that of the mental state, and perhaps must have other such properties as well.

Speech acts must not only resemble the thoughts they express; they must also differ in important ways. Speech plainly cannot occur without thought, but thought unexpressed in speech can and often does occur. A satisfactory account of the relation between speech and thinking must, accordingly, do justice both to the resemblance between speech and thought and to this difference between them.

This asymmetry between thinking and speech may appear to imply that the study of speech must be based on the study of thought. Thus, one might argue, if thought can occur without speech but not conversely, thought must somehow be more basic than speech. Moreover, if speech is at bottom the expression of thought, perhaps we cannot understand the nature of speech without knowing what it is for something to express thought. And we cannot understand that unless we know what thought is. On this view, thought is prior to speech, and the primacy of thought implies that to understand speech we must first understand the nature of thinking.

But, if the asymmetry of the expressing relation suggests that we cannot understand speech without understanding thought, the way speech acts must correspond to the thoughts they express suggests that we can proceed in either direction. Since speech and thinking share their most important properties, we should be able to learn equally about each by studying the other. If so, we need not follow the Cartesian suggestion that the study of thought must precede the study of speech.

In what follows, I defend an account of the relation between speech and thought according to which the priority that thinking does have implies nothing about how we must study them. We need not understand speech only by appeal to the nature of thought. I begin by discussing, in section II, how speech acts must resemble, in crucial respects, the mental states they express. In section III, then, I advance a strictly causal explanation of what it is for a speech act to express a thought. On this suggestion, a speech act expresses a thought just in case the thought causes the speech act, and the two have the same or corresponding intentional properties, in the manner sketched in section II. If this causal account proves to be defensible, we will have no reason to suppose we must study thinking before we can understand speech. Thought is only causally prior to speech, and causal priorities do not, by themselves, dictate how we should study things.

To sustain this conclusion, I take up, in section IV, claims by various authors that thought is prior to speech in a way that we cannot explain in causal terms. On these claims, the basis for this priority is that the intentionality of thought is intrinsic, whereas the intentionality of speech is not. I argue that these claims about intrinsic intentionality, and the noncausal primacy of thinking, are both unfounded. Section V examines insincere speech, which is a useful test case for a theory of the relation between speech and thought. For, if we hold that insincere speech acts express thoughts the speaker does not have, it is difficult to see how such expressing can be a causal matter. Section VI, then, considers the question of whether a causal account suffices to give a satisfactory explanation of intentionality, or whether we need, in addition, some thesis about intrinsic intentionality and the noncausal primacy of thought. In section VII, finally, I urge that we can best understand the force of the idea that thought is noncausally prior to speech if we appeal to the way we are automatically aware of our own thoughts and speech acts. And I conclude by arguing that this suggestion is compatible with an account of such primacy cast in strictly causal terms.

II. THE CORRESPONDENCE OF THOUGHT AND SPEECH

One way that thinking and speech resemble each other pertains to their propositional content. Whenever I think something, I can express what I think by saying it. My speech act then has the very same content as my mental state.[1] And whenever I perform a speech act, what I say expresses something that I am thinking, at least if I speak sincerely. To sincerely say it's raining, I must also think it is; and again my speech act expresses my thought. For a speech act to express a mental state, the two must have the same propositional content.

But the expression of thought by speech goes beyond just expressing content. To see this, it is important to distinguish two ways we put words to our mental states, and convey those thoughts to others. For example, I can express my belief that it's raining by asserting that it's raining. But if, instead, I only expect it to rain, I can express my expectation as well, by saying it will probably rain. And, in general, I can

---

[1] In what follows I use 'mental state' to refer only to intentional mental states, thereby excluding nonintentional mental states such as bodily sensations. I also frequently use 'thought' not to refer just to beliefs and similar mental states, but as a generic term for intentional mental states of any sort, regardless of the kind of propositional attitude they exemplify.

express in words the whole range of propositional attitudes that I can hold. If I say something you did was nice, I express my gratitude. If I say that something is nice, I express my admiration or pleasure; if I say it would be nice to have, I express my desire. In each such case, my speech act not only conveys the content of my mental state; it also captures my mental attitude.

When I convey the content and mental attitude of my thoughts in the ways just illustrated, I do not explicitly mention those thoughts. Sometimes, my speech act simply has the same content, and has an illocutionary force parallel to my mental attitude. Other times, I may modify the content of my speech act so as to capture my mental attitude, as when I say that something would be nice to have, rather than that it just is nice. I can also, however, put words to my mental states by explicitly describing them. I can convey my expectation of rain by making a prediction that expresses my expectation; I can say, for example, that rain is likely. But another way to convey that expectation is just to say, straight-out, that I expect rain. These two kinds of speech act are not equivalent. The truth conditions of 'Rain is likely' differ from those of 'I expect it to rain', and either can be true without the other's also being true. But the two speech acts both convey the same mental state. Consequently, the conditions in which one can correctly perform the two speech acts are the same. Similar remarks hold of other kinds of mental state. I can convey my gratitude either by saying 'Thank you' or by telling you that I am grateful. I can express admiration of something either by saying that it is nice or by saying that I admire it. The conditions under which we can appropriately perform such pairs of speech acts will always be the same.

This divergence of truth conditions from performance conditions emerges particularly vividly in connection with what Wittgenstein called Moore's paradox.[2] As Moore noted, even though the sentence 'It's raining but I don't believe it is' is not an actual contradiction, we cannot use it to make a coherent assertion. There are circumstances in which the sentence would be true, but none in which anybody could use it to say so. Its truth conditions thus differ from its conditions for coherent assertibility. Such sentences resemble 'I do not exist', which I cannot assert even though it can be, and indeed has been, true.[3] Parallel considerations affect other

---

[2] Ludwig Wittgenstein, *Philosophical Investigations*, New York: Macmillan, 1953, II, 190. See G. E. Moore, "Russell's 'Theory of Descriptions'," in *The Philosophy of Bertrand Russell*, ed. Paul Arthur Schilpp, New York: Tudor, 1944, pp. 177–225, at p. 204.

[3] Since the problem about such sentences is assertibility and assertion is an expression of thought, these considerations suggest an inviting way to explain Descartes's insistence that "this statement, 'I am, I exist', is necessarily true every time it is produced by me, or mentally conceived" (René Descartes, *The Philosophical Writings of Descartes*, tr. John Cottingham, Robert Stoothoff, and Dugald Murdoch (vol. III with Anthony Kenny), 3 volumes, Cambridge: Cambridge University Press, 1984–91, II, 17; see René Descartes, *Oeuvres de Descartes*, ed. Charles Adam and Paul Tannery, Paris: J. Vrin, 1964–75, VII, 25). I argue for such an account of the *cogito* at the end of "Will and the Theory of Judgment," in *Essays on Descartes' Meditations*, ed. Amélie O. Rorty, Berkeley: University of California Press, 1986, pp. 405–434, § IV, and, more extensively, in "Judgment, Mind, and Will in Descartes," Report No. 29/1990, Center for Interdisciplinary Research (ZiF), University of Bielefeld, § VII.

mental attitudes and the illocutionary acts that express them. I cannot coherently say 'Thank you but I feel no gratitude', or 'Rain is likely, but I don't expect it'. If someone were to produce such forms of words, we would automatically try to interpret those words nonliterally, or as having been used ironically or with some other oblique force. Only thus can we regard the speaker as having performed any speech act at all.

It is important to stress that there are grammatical forms of words that one can utter and yet perform no speech act. Otherwise, we could not explain what goes wrong with sentences such as 'It's raining but I don't believe it' and 'I do not exist' by saying that the literal meanings of these sentences prevent us from using them to say anything. But indisputable examples of this phenomenon are easy to come by. If somebody assertively utters a blatant contradiction, such as 'It's raining and it isn't raining', that utterance does not, on its face, constitute the comprehensible asserting of anything. If such a case actually occurred, we might try to take the person to be saying something that goes beyond those words, for example, that it is raining in one place but not another. But if the speaker insisted that we take those words literally and rejected any helping reconstrual, we would be unable to understand what illocutionary act was being performed.

Things are different, of course, with a covert contradiction. People can, and do, say contradictory things without explicitly realizing that that is what they are doing. But if a contradiction is so blatant that its falsehood cannot be missed, we cannot use it, at least not in any literal way, to make an assertion. The impossibility of using a blatant contradiction to say anything explains the commonsense reaction people typically have to such cases. People do not normally say that contradictory assertions are false, or even necessarily false; they say, instead, that they are meaningless. This is not the crude error it is often supposed to be, but only the result of focusing on speech acts rather than on sentence types. Contradictory sentence types are plainly false, but the speech acts that result when one tries to assert them literally are meaningless. There is no way to understand the speech act, and thus no meaning we can give it. These considerations are, in effect, a commonsense counterpart of W. V. Quine's observation that no translation can be acceptable if it results in our rendering as elementary contradictions sentences that people actually assert.[4] The point is unexceptionable once we note that translations must, in part, tell us how to construe people's speech acts. Since there is no way to regard the assertion of a blatant contradiction as a coherent speech act, any translation that leads us to construe utterances this way must be in error.

Manifest contradictions are not the only cases of meaningful, grammatical sentences whose literal meaning blocks the performance of any coherent speech act. Any time we cannot construe the content of a person's speech act as a literal match of the sentence in question, the conditions for the coherent performance of a speech act cannot be met. Part of what distinguishes such cases is that hearers automatically try to reconstrue the speech act as having some content or illocutionary force different from those which the grammatical and lexical properties of the sentence indicate.

---

[4] *Word and Object*, Cambridge, Massachusetts: MIT Press, 1960, pp. 58–59.

This desire to reconstrue, however, occurs in other kinds of cases as well. But when the sentence is perfectly grammatical, and there is nothing about the context of its being uttered that explains the hearers' tendency to reconstrue, then no speech act is possible that has the literal content and force of the sentence in question. The sentences that exemplify Moore's paradox are prime examples of this phenomenon. If somebody actually uttered 'It's raining, but I don't believe it', we would very likely try to reconstrue the speech act. Perhaps, for example, the speaker wants to say only how very surprising it is. Perhaps somebody who utters 'Thank you but I feel no gratitude' means not to thank anybody, but only to produce, albeit grudgingly, the proper formula. Unless we reconstrue these examples in some such way, one cannot understand the person as performing any speech act whatever.

To explain the divergence manifest in Moore's paradox between truth conditions and conditions for the coherent performance of speech acts, we must distinguish expressing mental states from reporting that one is in them. 'It's raining' expresses, but does not report, one's belief that it's raining. By contrast, 'I believe it's raining' reports that belief, but does not express it. One cannot therefore assert 'It's raining but I don't believe it is', since the second conjunct denies that I have the very belief that the first conjunct purports to express. If expressing were not distinct from reporting, the first conjunct would both express and report one's belief, whereas the second conjunct would still deny that any such belief exists. So on this construal the sentence would be contradictory, which it plainly is not. Accordingly, a correct explanation of Moore's paradox is impossible unless we recognize that reporting a mental state is distinct from expressing it.

We tend to use verbs of illocutionary act in a way that may blur the difference between expressing and reporting one's mental states. Rather than say that rain is likely or that something you did was good, I can make my illocutionary force explicit by saying 'I predict rain' or 'I commend what you did', perhaps with the formulaic 'hereby' inserted where appropriate. But 'I predict rain' and 'Rain is likely' not only make the same prediction; they also express the same mental state, namely, my expectation of rain. Similarly, saying that something is good and that I commend it both express the same mental state, namely, my approval.

These considerations may tempt one to hold that the phrase 'I predict' is something like an optional variant of 'is likely', and 'I commend' a variant of 'is good'. One might then go on to infer that 'I expect' and 'I approve' are just other such variants, and that when predictive illocutionary force is already present, both 'I expect' and 'I predict', like 'I commend' and 'I approve', are merely ornamental pleonasms. It would follow that 'I expect rain' does not report my expectation, but rather expresses it, by making a prediction. Similarly, we would conclude that 'I approve of this' expresses, rather than reports, my approval.

Some such reasoning appears to have influenced Wittgenstein's assessment of such cases. According to Wittgenstein, "the statement 'I believe it's going to rain' has a meaning like, that is to say a use like, 'It's going to rain'." He concludes: " 'I say', ... in 'I say it will rain today', ... simply comes to the same thing as the assertion 'It will ...' " (II, pp. 190, 192). If we take the use of linguistic expressions as central to their semantic character, it will be difficult not to assimilate reporting mental states to expressing them.[5]

But the considerations raised earlier are still decisive. Whatever we may think about meaning and use, the use of a sentence is plainly distinct from its truth conditions. The sentences 'I hereby predict rain', 'Rain is likely', and 'I expect rain' are all three alike with respect to conditions of appropriate use. But their truth conditions indisputably diverge. Indeed, we can construct Moore's paradox using any pair from among this triad of sentences. We can assert neither 'I hereby predict rain but rain isn't likely' nor 'I expect rain but I predict it won't rain', though neither sentence is contradictory.

The identity of conditions of correct use despite divergence of truth conditions not only shows that expressing mental states differs from reporting them. It also confirms that for a speech act to express a mental state the speech act must, in addition to sharing its propositional content with the mental state, have an illocutionary force that reflects the attitude of that mental state. For the paradox will arise using any mental attitude together with the corresponding illocutionary force. Only if expressing a mental state implies that the illocutionary force of the speech act reflects the attitude of the mental state is it open to us to explain Moore's paradox as due to the denial in one conjunct of a mental state that the other conjunct purports to express. No alternative explanation is available that is equally compelling.

That illocutionary force expresses mental attitude is also shown by impressive parallels that hold between verbs of illocutionary act and those of propositional attitude, and the grammatical complements that various verbs of each kind require. These syntactic and semantic parallels, and their importance, have recently been articulated in elegant and illuminating detail by Zeno Vendler and John R. Searle.[6]

The parallelism between mental attitude and illocutionary force strongly supports the view that satisfactory accounts of speech acts and mental states must proceed hand in hand. We can learn about either by appeal to the other. Traditional arguments for the interdependence of such accounts have generally stressed the impossibility of explaining what it is for either mental states or speech acts to have propositional content without presupposing a notion of propositional content common to both. The difficulty resembles that which Quine finds in breaking out of the family of terms that

---

[5] This view suggests a way to help clarify Wittgenstein's well-known but puzzling suggestion that we construe such sentences as 'I am in pain' not as straightforward assertions that one is in pain but as expressions of that pain, on a continuum with such natural expressions as crying (Part I, 244). Whatever reasons we have to hold that 'I believe it's raining' expresses my belief rather than reporting it should equally help to show that 'I am in pain' expresses, rather than reports, my pain. But see Wittgenstein's distrust of this analogy at Part I, 317.

[6] Zeno Vendler, *Res Cogitans*, Ithaca, New York: Cornell University Press, 1972, chs. 2 and 3; John R. Searle, *Intentionality: An Essay in the Philosophy of Mind*, Cambridge: Cambridge University Press, 1983, 166 and 175, and "A Taxonomy of Illocutionary Acts," in *Minnesota Studies in the Philosophy of Science*, VII, ed. Keith Gunderson, Minneapolis: University of Minnesota Press, 1975, pp. 344–369, *passim*. Unless otherwise indicated, references to Searle are to *Intentionality*; all references to Vendler are to *Res Cogitans*.

ascribe synonymy and analyticity.[7] The parallelism of mental attitude and illocutionary force complements traditional appeals to propositional content in supporting the claim that speech acts and mental states together form a family whose members cannot be explained except by appeal to other members of that family.

Indeed, parallels of illocutionary force and mental attitude tell us more about thought and speech, and the way they are connected, than can parallels that involve propositional content. For one thing, the way we classify mental states is a function of differences in mental attitudes, and we also classify speech acts into kinds on the basis of differences in illocutionary force. Propositional content tells us relatively little about how the various sorts of mental state and speech act differ from one another. More important, as Moore's paradox shows, a match between illocutionary force and mental attitude is necessary for a speech act to express a mental state. That match is central to the tie between thought and speech.

III. THE PRIMACY OF THOUGHT

The claim that thought and speech are interdependent is unexceptionable. And, since speech acts have properties that correspond to those of the mental states they express, knowing about either will help us understand the other. But a compelling intuition exists that, whatever parallels there are between the properties of speech and thought, the nature of speech is dependent on thought, but not conversely. When a speech act expresses a mental state, the two do indeed have corresponding properties. But the speech act, on this intuition, somehow owes its properties to the mental state. We can understand speech only as the expression of thought. So we can explain speech by reference to thought, but we cannot explain thinking by appeal to speech.

The idea that thinking is, in some such way, more basic than speech has been formulated with particular force and clarity by Roderick M. Chisholm. According to Chisholm, "nothing would be intentional were it not for the fact that thoughts are intentional," although "[t]houghts would be intentional even if there were no linguistic entities." So "[t]houghts are a 'source of intentionality'," whereas speech acts are not.[8] Accordingly, we cannot "explicate the intentional character of believing and other psychological attitudes by reference to certain features of language." Rather, we must "explicate the intentional characteristics of language by reference to believing and to other psychological attitudes" (521).

---

[7] On analyticity and synonymy, see "Two Dogmas of Empiricism," reprinted as ch. 2 of *From a Logical Point of View*, Cambridge, Massachusetts: Harvard University Press, 1980. Quine formulates the analogous difficulty about intentional mental states in *Word and Object*, p. 221.

In "Talking about Thinking," *Philosophical Studies*, 24, 5 (September 1973): 283–313, I argue that the difficulty about intentional mental states is insuperable. On the interdependence between speech and thinking, see also Donald Davidson, "Thought and Talk," in *Mind and Language*, ed. Samuel Guttenplan, Oxford: Oxford University Press, 1975, pp. 7–23.

[8] Roderick M. Chisholm, "Intentionality and the Mental," in *Minnesota Studies in the Philosophy of Science*, II, ed. Herbert Feigl, Michael Scriven, and Grover Maxwell, Minneapolis: University of Minnesota Press, 1958, pp. 507–539 [in part, correspondence with Wilfrid Sellars], p. 533. All references to Chisholm are to this work.

The view that thought has primacy over speech is not new. It is of course present in Descartes, and can be found in Aristotle.[9] And more recently, such primacy has been championed by Vendler and by Searle. Both Vendler and Searle concede that, because speech has a physical realization that is readily observable, speech is intersubjectively more accessible than thought (Vendler, 3; Searle, 5). But greater epistemic accessibility does not always indicate a more fundamental nature. And Searle and Vendler both insist, with Chisholm, that thinking is more basic than speech in some way that reflects the nature of both processes.

That thinking is in some way prior to speech seems plain, and it is natural to try to explain this priority by appeal to the asymmetry of the expressing relation. Speech expresses thoughts, but thoughts do not express speech. Indeed, nothing whatever expresses speech, and thinking itself does not express anything, at least not in the way in which speech expresses mental states. Thoughts can therefore exist unaccompanied by any other sorts of intentional items, whereas speech is parasitic on thinking. In this spirit, Searle maintains that the intentionality of thinking is intrinsic, as opposed to the derived intentionality of speech. For a person's meaning something cannot "stand on its own in the way that [a person's] believing" something, for example, can (29).

By itself, however, this appeal to expressing raises more questions than it resolves. We cannot explain the primacy of thought over speech simply by saying that speech acts express thoughts unless we know what such expressing consists in, and why it exhibits the asymmetry it does. Parallels between verbs of propositional attitude and illocutionary act help little here. Without some actual account of what the relation of expressing involves, 'expressing' is hardly more than a label for whatever it is that explains and underlies that parallelism.

Moreover, a satisfactory explanation of expressing, for these purposes, must show how the expression of mental states by speech results in the primacy of thought. Not every asymmetric relation implies that one of the relata is somehow more fundamental than the other. And the primacy that such expressing implies must square both with the interdependence of thought and talk, and with the greater intersubjective accessibility of speech. An account of expressing which met these conditions would be able to explain satisfactorily the kind of primacy thought has, and why it has it.

The account that immediately suggests itself relies on causal connections. On this proposal, a speech act expresses a mental state just if, in addition to having the right propositional content and illocutionary force, the mental state is causally necessary for the speech act to occur. If thought does cause speech, speech cannot occur without thought. So thought is causally prior to speech. This suggestion fits nicely with our having better intersubjective access to speech. Effects are often more readily observable than their causes, and we often learn much about the nature of causes by studying effects. The direction of epistemic primacy is often opposite to that of causation.

    [9] Descartes, *Discourse*, V *Philosophical Writings*, I, 140–1; *Oeuvres*, VI, 56–59; and in letters to the Marquess of Newcastle and to More (*Philosophical Writings*, III, 302–304 and 365–366, respectively). Aristotle: *de Interpretatione*, 16a3–8 (*Aristotle's Categories and* De Interpretatione, tr. J. L. Ackrill, Oxford: Clarendon Press, 1963, p. 43).

A causal account of expressing also squares well with the interdependence of thought and speech. For one thing, we not only learn about causes from examining their effects, but also about effects from looking at their causes. More important, however, that interdependence is due chiefly to the impossibility of breaking out of the family of illocutionary acts and propositional attitudes when we explain any of its members. The explanations that tie us to that family, however, are not causal, but conceptual explanations. They are explanations of what it is to be this sort of illocutionary act or that kind of propositional attitude. The situation is similar with many natural processes and properties—for example, with colors. We cannot explain what it is, phenomenally, to be some particular color except by reference to other colors. But this is a limitation on what we can explain conceptually, not causally. Causal explanations of color are of course possible that do not themselves refer to color. Similarly, the conceptual interdependence of thought and speech has no bearing on what causal links may connect them.

But an even stronger case can be made for a causal account of expressing. There are features of our commonsense views about the relation between thinking and speech that it is hard to see how to explain except by reference to the idea that speech acts causally depend on the mental states they express. Mental states often go unexpressed, and utterances occur that express no mental state, for example, when they consist in words that someone merely recites without thought. And a person may think two distinct things, each expressible by the same words, and yet use those words to express only one of the two mental states. So mere accompaniment of a thought by a corresponding speech act does not suffice for the speech act to express that very thought. Expressing is not like resembling. A speech act does not express a mental state just by having the right properties. There must also be some specific tie between the two.

Moreover, we must explain a person's performance of a speech act by appeal, in part, to that person's being in that particular mental state. Indeed, genuine speech acts, as opposed to mindlessly recited utterances, presumably cannot even occur in the absence of mental states that have the same content and a corresponding mental attitude. If mental states do not cause the speech acts that express them, these features of the relation between thought and speech must remain puzzling.

Sometimes we speak of a speech act's expressing a belief without meaning to talk about any particular mental state that the speech act expresses. Instead, we may mean only that the speech act has the propositional content that such a belief would have. To describe a statement as expressing the belief that it's raining may be just a way of describing it in terms of its propositional content, and not by reference to some particular state of believing. In such cases, we do not speak of any particular state of believing. Rather, we mention a type of mental state, some token of which the speech act presumably expresses.[10]

---

[10] On this distinction, see Wilfrid Sellars, "Notes on Intentionality," *The Journal of Philosophy*, LXI, 21 (November 12, 1964): 655–665 (reprinted with minor changes in Wilfrid Sellars, *Philosophical Perspectives*, Springfield, Illinois: Charles Thomas, 1967, 308–320; and *Science and Metaphysics*, London: Routledge & Kegan Paul, 1968, ch. III). See also Wilfrid Sellars, *Science, Perception and Reality*, London: Routledge & Kegan Paul, 1963, esp. chs. 2, 5, and 11.

Similar remarks hold for other kinds of illocutionary force. We can describe a speech act as expressing the expectation that it will rain, for example, without meaning to describe it in terms of any relation it bears to a specific mental state. We may, instead, only mean to specify the content and force of the speech act. That is, we may mean to say no more than that it is the kind of speech act that expresses mental states that are, in turn, instances of expecting it to rain. We can, in general, say that a speech act expresses something in order to describe its relation to a mental state, or just simply to say what kind of speech act it is. .

An example of the second way of speaking occurs when we say that a speech act expresses a proposition. Here it is plain that we mean only to be talking about the speech act and its content, and not also about any mental state. Typically when we mean to be specifying the character of the speech act, we say what kind of force it has as well, as when we say the speech act expresses the belief that it's raining or the expectation that it will. But it will be convenient, and help us avoid ambiguity, to speak of expressing a proposition when what we mean is not to speak of a particular mental state that the speech act expresses, but to say what its force and content are.

The distinction between expressing mental states and expressing propositions will assume special importance in subsequent sections. For now it is enough to note that the distinction can help dispel whatever doubts we may have about whether speech acts are caused by the mental states they express. These doubts stem from the correct observation that we can describe a speech act as expressing beliefs, expectations, and the like without implying anything about a causal tie with some particular mental state. But to so describe a speech act is to do no more than specify, somewhat obliquely, its propositional content and illocutionary force. By contrast, when we actually do say that a speech act expresses some particular mental state, we cannot explain the tie to an individual mental state unless we presuppose a causal connection.

An illustration of how this distinction can help us understand the relation between speech and thought arises in connection with the point, just noted, that mere accompaniment is not enough for a speech act to express a mental state. Suppose I speak the words 'It's raining' and, at the same time, have the thought that it's raining. It may seem impossible not to conclude that my words express my thought. In ordinary cases, of course, my words do just that. But this is not always the case. All that we can be certain of, in the case under consideration, is that my words have the same propositional content as my mental state, that is, that my words express the proposition that my thought expresses. We cannot conclude that my words also express that very act of thinking. It is possible to use 'thought' in such cases to refer either to the act of thinking or to its propositional content, and confusion can result.

Once again, Moore's paradox helps out. In section II, we used Moore's paradox to show that expressing a mental state is distinct from reporting that one is in it. Only if the two kinds of speech act are distinct can we avoid construing sentences like 'It's raining but I don't believe it is' as contradictions. But, if speech acts could occur in

It will be evident throughout that the present discussion has been strongly influenced by Sellars' important and penetrating work on these topics.

the absence of corresponding mental states, the opposite difficulty would arise in trying to explain Moore's paradox. For then not only would Moore's-paradox sentences not be contradictory; we would be unable to construe them even as being in any way problematic. If speech acts need not be accompanied by corresponding mental states, there would be no difficulty about one's simply asserting that it's raining, but that one has no corresponding belief.

Accordingly, to explain Moore's paradox we must suppose that speech acts cannot occur in the absence of corresponding mental states. And, as noted above, the best explanation of this regularity is that speech acts are causally dependent on such mental states. So the best explanation of Moore's paradox will imply a causal connection between speech acts and the mental states they express. This should not be surprising. If the connection between the two conjuncts of Moore's paradox were conceptual or analytic, we would once again have difficulty in explaining why such sentences are not contradictions. Indeed, we would have difficulty even in explaining why parallel problems do not affect sentences like 'George says that it's raining, but he doesn't believe it is'. Such sentences are slightly odd, but we can explain such oddity as due not to any analytic connection between speech and thinking, but to our background knowledge that speech always does express mental states. Our background knowledge about speech and thought is so well-entrenched as to be taken for granted. And any sentence that offends against such a well-entrenched piece of background knowledge will strike us as somewhat odd.[11]

One might insist, however, that Moore's paradox, and the regularity that speech acts cannot occur without corresponding mental states, both reflect the very way we think about mental states and speech acts. And if so, one might object, causal connections could not underlie or help explain either the paradox or that regularity. Causal connections are empirical, and so could have gone unknown by us. Thus they cannot, on this objection, underlie our conceptions about things.

But it is hard to imagine that the causal ties that bind speech to thought could escape our notice. And causal connections often do influence the ways we conceive of things. Indeed, if there were any area in which causal ties would be likely to shape our conceptions, it would presumably have to do with our conceptions about the mental. For our introspective awareness of our own mental states very likely detects, or at least is somehow responsive to, such causal ties. And our introspective sense that such causal ties obtain will doubtless affect how we think about speech and thought.

Accordingly, it is arguable that a causal account of the expression of thought by speech does all one could ask to explain the primacy of thought. In particular, it seems to do justice to Chisholm's point that, although thinking would be intentional without speech, speech without thought would not be. It is natural to take subjunctive and counterfactual conditionals to express causal connections. So we can understand

---

[11] Searle also appeals to Moore's paradox to show that all speech acts must express mental states. He writes: "[I]t is logically odd, though not self-contradictory, to perform the speech act and deny the presence of the corresponding Intentional state" (9). But he leaves unexplained what this oddity consists in and, if it is logical, how it differs from analyticity. In any case, since Searle takes the oddity to be logical and not a feature of the relation between thinking and speech, it is unclear why, on his account, there is no difficulty with third-person counterparts.

Chisholm to be claiming that, whereas speech is causally dependent on thought, no opposite dependence obtains. Similarly, we can offer a causal construal of Searle's observation that "I couldn't make a statement without expressing a belief or a promise without expressing an intention" (28), and Vendler's insistence that speech involves "putting thought into words" (44).

But one can concede that thought causes speech without also accepting that this causal tie is all there is to the primacy of thought. And all three authors insist that thought is primary in a way that is not at all causal. Thus Chisholm maintains that the meaning of linguistic items "is to be analyzed in terms of" the content of thoughts, and not conversely (524; cf. 529, 523). Vendler echoes this claim when he writes that "the full analysis of the [notion] of saying something . . . inevitably involves a concept which . . . essentially corresponds to the Cartesian idea of thought" (4). Searle too endorses this asymmetry with respect to analyzability: "the direction of logical analysis is to explain language in terms of [the] Intentionality [of the mental]." We can, Searle concedes, use language heuristically to explain the intentionality of mental states, but "the relation of logical dependence is precisely the reverse" (5). Thus "speakers' meaning should be entirely definable in terms of . . . forms of Intentionality that are not intrinsically linguistic" (160). These claims suggest that, though thought and speech may belong to the same conceptual family, within that family thought has pride of place. If so, the primacy of thought will not be solely causal, but conceptual as well. And if thinking is conceptually prior to speech, perhaps we can understand the nature of speech only by reference to thought.

An initial response to these claims would be that what looks like conceptual priority is actually just a causal connection that is so much a part of our lives that we tend to take it for granted. Truths so ordinary as to be axiomatic often seem conceptual. Such conflation of causal with conceptual matters occurs in more mundane areas. It may seem to be a conceptual truth that the sky is blue simply because its terrestrial color figures so centrally in our everyday picture of how things are. Similarly, we so take it for granted that thought causally underlies speech that this primacy can seem conceptual. Any causal connection that we take to be partially constitutive of our picture of reality will seem to us, as Hume observed, to be grounded in our concepts.

IV. INTRINSIC INTENTIONALITY

We may fairly regard the foregoing considerations as placing upon advocates of conceptual primacy the burden of showing that the priority they champion is actually conceptual, and not due simply to causal connections. But it is arguably precipitous to convict the advocates of conceptual primacy of conflating platitudinous truths with conceptual connections. Even if such confusion does underlie claims of conceptual priority, we must address directly the reasons these authors have given for such primacy. To sustain a claim of conceptual primacy one must show that there is some feature of thought or speech we cannot explain or do justice to if the priority of thought is only causal. So we must see whether any such feature exists. The insistence on conceptual priority seems to be based largely on the idea that the intentionality of thinking, unlike that of speech, is in some way intrinsic. If thinking is intrinsically intentional and speech is not, then perhaps some conceptual connection exists between thinking and intentionality that does not hold between intentionality and speech.

The idea that thoughts, unlike speech acts, are intrinsically intentional has considerable intuitive appeal. But, to evaluate the force of that intuition, we must first specify what it means for intentionality to be intrinsic. One way to articulate the idea of intrinsic intentionality is by appeal to an apparent disparity between speech and thought with respect to physical realization. Speech acts cannot occur except by virtue of the production of specific sentences, which have determinate phonetic features. And sentences can occur parrotingly, as when one mouths words without meaning anything by them. So words with determinate phonetic features can occur without exhibiting any intentionality, whereas the opposite is impossible. Words cannot manifest intentionality without having phonetic properties, or other equivalent observable properties.

By contrast, there may seem to be no properties that thinking must manifest in order to be intentional. Indeed, introspection suggests that, aside from causal or temporal properties, thoughts have no properties whatever except for their mental attitudes and propositional contents. As Vendler puts it, there is no "mental 'medium'" (44), in the way words are the medium of speech. So it may be tempting to conclude that thought, unlike speech, is intrinsically intentional.

Perhaps Vendler is right that thinking involves nothing we would call a "mental 'medium'." But the intentional character of thoughts no more exhausts their nature than the intentionality of speech acts exhausts theirs. Thoughts have a multitude of causal ties, some to mental events and others to nonmental, physical events. The best explanation of these causal connections is that thoughts themselves have certain nonmental, physical properties. For even if one regarded the intentionality of thoughts as some sort of nonphysical property, it would be mysterious how thoughts could be connected causally with physical states and events unless thoughts also have physical properties that enable these connections to hold. There is presumably nothing about the intentional properties themselves that explains these causal connections. So thoughts must have some nonintentional properties that make the connections possible. And, if thoughts must have nonintentional properties, physical properties that pertain to the central nervous system are easily the most likely candidates. Indeed, it is reasonable to insist, with Searle,[12] that the mental as we know it has a biological basis. And we can most readily explain how biological processes could issue in thinking if we suppose that thoughts themselves have suitable physical characteristics.

Like Donald Davidson's well-known argument for anomalous monism, the foregoing argument infers to what we must assume if we are to explain causal interactions between mental and bodily events.[13] But the present argument circumvents Davidson's difficult thesis about the impossibility of psychophysical laws. It may seem

---

[12] P. 160, and ch. 10; see also John R. Searle, "Mind, Brains, and Programs," *The Behavioral and Brain Sciences*, 3, 3 (September 1980): 417–57 (with commentaries and response).

[13] Donald Davidson, "Mental Events," in *Experience and Theory*, ed. Lawrence Foster and J. W. Swanson, Amherst: The University of Massachusetts Press, 1970, pp. 79–101.

that the use of this thesis as a premise enables Davidson to establish a conclusion stronger than the foregoing argument can reach. Anomalous monism is the claim that intentional mental events are actually physical events, whereas the conclusion reached here, that intentional mental states have physical properties, may seem to be weaker. But the difference is illusory. The bodily events that Davidson holds are identical with mental events are physical only because they have physical properties that enable them to have causal ties with various physical events that are not also mental events. And that is exactly the conclusion reached here about mental states that interact causally with nonmental, bodily events. No reductive materialist thesis is at issue here, any more than in Davidson's argument. And, in the absence of independent argument to the contrary, there is no reason why events cannot be both mental and physical.[14]

Thoughts need not, of course, have the same physical character or embodiment in order to have the same content and mental attitude, any more than speech acts must use the same words to mean the same things. In both cases, physical properties determine intentional character only in the context of a larger systematic structure. Patterns of sounds are speech acts only relative to a language. Similarly, it is reasonable to expect that individual neural events have specific intentional properties only relative to the overall operation of the central nervous system. So, even if it is wrong to regard the physical characteristics of thinking as a "mental 'medium'," there is no significant disanalogy on this score between thought and speech. Both have nonintentional, physical characteristics. We must therefore look elsewhere for justification of the idea that the intentionality of thought, unlike that of speech, is in some way intrinsic.

Searle explicitly notes that thinking resembles speech in having physical "forms of realization." He also points out that no one-to-one correspondence exists between those forms of realization and the intentional character of particular speech acts (15). Nonetheless, he holds that the intentionality of thought is *"intrinsic,"* as opposed to the *"derived"* intentionality of speech acts (27). And, since he speaks of thought as being prior to speech in respect of logical dependence and definability, we must see whether his distinction between being intrinsic and derived supports a view that thought has a kind of primacy that goes beyond mere causal priority.

The intentionality of mental states is intrinsic, according to Searle, because "[t]o characterize them as [mental states] is already to ascribe Intentionality to them." By contrast,

speech acts have a physical level of realization, *qua* speech acts, that is not intrinsically intentional. There is nothing intrinsically Intentional about the products of the utterance act, that is, the noises that come out of my mouth or the marks I make on paper.

---

[14] Davidson's denial of the possibility of psychophysical laws does, however, allow him to claim a priori status for his conclusion about mental events. On there being no difficulty about events' being both mental and physical, see my "Mentality and Neutrality," *The Journal of Philosophy*, LXXIII, 13 (July 15, 1976): 386–415.

It may be worth noting that, since the present argument makes no appeal to laws or regularities under which causally connected events must fall, it does not conflict with Searle's contention that when causal connections involve intentional states, they can obtain in the absence of a corresponding universal regularity (135; see 117 and ch. 4, *passim*).

Speech acts, on Searle's view, are "entities such as marks and sounds that are, construed in one way, just physical phenomena . . . like any other" (27). The intentionality of mental states is intrinsic because to describe them as mental states is to describe them as intentional. The intentionality of speech acts is derived because a description in terms of their physical realization implies nothing about intentionality.

But, as Searle concedes, intentional mental states, no less than speech acts, have some physical realization or other. So we could use that physical realization to refer to those states if only we knew enough neurology. And, even knowing no neurology, we can describe mental states in terms that imply nothing about intentionality. We can, for example, describe them as states that cause particular pieces of behavior. Searle is right that we seldom talk about our thoughts except in terms of their intentional character, whereas we do have occasion to describe illocutionary acts in nonintentional terms. But to sustain his distinction between intrinsic and derived intentionality, it is not enough that physical realization should sometimes figure in characterizations of speech, but seldom if ever in descriptions of thinking. Searle must present some way in which physical realization matters to the very nature of speech, but not to that of thought.

We can, of course, describe speech acts in terms of their intentional character, rather than their physical realization. Indeed, that is our standard practice. To specify a speech act in *oratio obliqua* is to characterize it solely by reference to its illocutionary force and propositional content. Moreover, direct discourse describes speech acts not just in terms of their physical realization, but by way of intentional character as well. A direct quotation tells us not only the exact words, but the content and illocutionary force as well.

So to evoke his intuition about the derived intentionality of speech, Searle must get us to abstract from the intentionality of speech, and focus only on its physical realization. Accordingly, he puts his point in terms of "the products of the utterance act[s]" (27), rather than in terms of illocutionary acts. The marks and sounds we produce when we use language can also occur in the absence of any intentional speech act. And, even when we produce marks and sounds by way of performing such speech acts, it is implausible to regard the marks and sounds on their own as bearers of intentionality. But the actual speech acts, by contrast, are intentional. For speech acts all have propositional content and illocutionary force. Indeed, no nonintentional utterance would count as an illocutionary act. The disparity Searle sees between the intentionality of thought and that of speech is illusory.

If we focus on speech acts simply as marks and sounds, we need to explain how those physical phenomena could have intentional character. Since marks and sounds are not always intentional, those which are must somehow derive their intentionality. The "problem of meaning," Searle suggests, is the question of how they do so. But Searle also holds that no parallel problem obtains for thinking (27; cf. 167 ff. and Chisholm, 524). This is puzzling, since, as Searle concedes, thinking also has physical realization. So the question will also arise about how neural states of the relevant kind can have intentional character. The explanation of how speech acts derive intentionality from mental states cannot help support the idea that the intentionality of thought is different in status from that of speech.

It is important here to distinguish two problems. Some marks and sounds are intentional and others are not. So the question arises of what it is about those marks and sounds which are intentional in virtue of which they differ from those which are not. But there is a second, distinct question about how it is possible for such things as marks and sounds to have intentional character at all.

The two questions are sometimes run together, perhaps in part because it is tempting to try to answer both by appeal to intrinsic intentionality or the primacy of thought. But the two questions are plainly distinct. One cannot even pose the question about what it is that makes intentional marks and sounds intentional unless one brackets the other question, about how it is that sounds and marks can have intentional character in the first place.

Even if one believed that we can satisfactorily resolve the question of how sounds and marks can be intentional by appeal to some connection that those marks and sounds have with mental states, a parallel problem automatically arises all over again with the mental states themselves. If marks and sounds can be intentional because of their causal tie with mental states, what is it that can explain how neural events themselves can be intentional? Unless there is some way to block this question, the appeal to mental states only postpones the problem; it does not resolve it.

Moreover, the question about how marks and sounds can be intentional is not the only problem about speech acts that has a parallel for mental states. Once we see that a question arises about how neural events can be intentional, the question will also arise of what makes intentional neural events intentional. The two parallel problems that apply to mental states are arguably more pressing, since there is no move we can make, analogous to the move from speech to thinking, that can help out here. The existence of these problems may make it tempting to postulate that the intentionality of mental states is, after all, intrinsic. If we can see no place that such intentionality could come from, must we not conclude that it is intrinsic, rather than derived? But without some independent reason to hold that the intentionality of mental states really is intrinsic, and an explanation of what being intrinsic amounts to here, such a claim is merely the label for the problem, and cannot provide a solution.

This line of reasoning does illustrate, however, how we may be misled by not taking account of the difference between expressing mental states and expressing propositions. Suppose we set out to explain how marks and sounds can be intentional by appeal to their expressing mental states. We may then seek to make an analogous move for the case of mental states themselves, and propose to explain how neural events can be intentional on the basis of their expressing propositions. But the analogy here is unfounded. To say that some event, whether neural or linguistic, expresses a proposition is just to say that it has propositional content. To explain how neural events can be intentional by reference to their expressing of propositions is viciously circular.

Again, if we focus on speech acts simply as marks and sounds, one might claim that sentences are relevantly unlike thoughts. For we can individuate sentences without reference to intentionality, but we cannot do so with thoughts. When we do individuate a sentence independently of its intentional character, however, we leave open what speech act the sentence realizes, just as we presumably would have to be noncommittal about what mental properties a mental state has if we were to specify the state in solely neural or causal terms. No disanalogy occurs here that can sustain Searle's claims about intrinsic and derived intentionality. And, in the absence of some other way to substantiate such claims, we cannot use them to support the thesis that thought is conceptually prior to speech, and not just prior causally.

One can occasionally get the impression from what Searle writes that he believes the derived intentionality of speech acts not to be genuine intentionality at all. And, if one focuses on mere sounds and marks, rather than on actual speech acts, it is understandable that one might reach that conclusion. But genuine speech, as Searle himself explicitly insists (e.g., 169), is more than simply sounds. Speech is the producing of sounds, in those cases, in which the very acts of producing have propositional content and illocutionary force.

Similarly, by saying that the intentionality is intrinsic, Searle may mean only to say that its intentionality is not a relational property. Thinking is intrinsically intentional because, on this construal, its having some propositional content and mental attitude does not consist in its bearing some relation to something else. Speech would thus have derived intentionality, presumably because, on Searle's account, its having any sort of intentional character consists in its bearing a certain relation to the thoughts it expresses. On this suggestion, derived intentionality is relational, or extrinsic, intentionality.

But there is a difference between what it is for something to have a particular characteristic and what causes it to have that characteristic. Mental states cause speech acts to be intentional; without those causes, speech acts would not be intentional at all. But it does not follow that the intentionality that speech acts do have consists in a relation they bear to those causes, any more than the movement of a billiard ball consists of a relation that billiard ball bears to the cause of that motion. Indeed, many thoughts are caused, either by other thoughts or by nonmental, bodily states such as perceptual stimulations. But we do not conclude that the intentionality of these mental states consists in their bearing some relation to their causes.

As noted in section III, Searle holds that a person's meaning something cannot "stand on its own in the way that [a person's] believing" something can (28). For "John couldn't mean that *p* unless he was saying or doing something *by way of which* he meant that *p*, whereas John can simply believe that *p* without doing anything.... In order to mean that *p*, there must be some overt action" (29). But these considerations do not help show that thinking exhibits a kind of intentionality different either in kind or in status from the intentionality of illocutionary acts. To explain these observations, all we need is the causal tie between speech and thought. Meaning something cannot "stand on its own" because meaningful performances depend causally on the mental states those performances express.

V. INSINCERE SPEECH

Insincere speech provides a pivotal test case for any account of the relation between speech and thought. When we speak insincerely, the connection between what we say and what we think is not the same as it is when our speech acts are sincere. So to give an account of the intentional character of insincere speech requires that we examine our commonsense, presystematic intuitions about the connection between thought and speech, and the justification we have for holding them.

According to Searle, "a lie or other insincere speech act consists in performing a speech act, and thereby expressing an Intentional state, where one does not have the Intentional state that one expresses" (10). Vendler makes a similar claim. Insincere speech, he holds, expresses thoughts that the speaker does not have (37).

These remarks, if correct, cast doubt on our being able to give a causal explanation of what it is for a speech act to express a mental state. If speech acts express mental states even when we speak insincerely, no causal relation can, in general, connect speech acts with the mental states they express. Speaking insincerely is just saying something we do not think. So when we speak insincerely, there is no corresponding mental state to cause our speech. Moreover, if we cannot construe expressing causally, we must find some other way to explain what it is for speech to express thought. And the most inviting alternative may very likely seem to be an explanation that postulates some conceptual relation that ties speech acts to the mental states they express. Having to appeal to this sort of conceptual tie would, in turn, lend support to the idea that thought is conceptually prior to speech, rather than causally prior. So how we account for insincere speech has an important bearing on whether a causal explanation of expressing can succeed. We must therefore examine Searle's and Vendler's claims about insincere speech acts in some detail.

At first sight, the view that insincere speech expresses thoughts that the speaker does not have may seem intuitively compelling. Some such view is roughly what most people would say, if asked to explain insincerity. But on closer scrutiny it is unclear that we can make clear sense of that idea. For one thing, if a person who lies lacks the mental state that the lie is supposed to express, how can the lie express it? One person's lie cannot express another's mental state. So it is no help that somebody else may have the relevant thought. The claim that insincere speech acts express mental states that the speaker is not in implies that such speech acts express mental states that do not even exist. How this can happen is a mystery. And it is a mystery whatever one's view may be about what it is for speech to express thinking. 'Expresses', in 'This speech act expresses that mental state', does not generate a referentially opaque context.

This puzzle becomes particularly acute if one holds, with Chisholm, Vendler, and Searle, that speech acts derive their intentionality from the mental states they express. If no such mental state exists, an insincere speech act will, in Chisholm's phrase, have no source of intentionality. The speech act will therefore end up having no intentional character. Searle and Vendler both explicitly reject this conclusion. As Searle puts it, an "insincere speech act . . . express[es] an Intentional state" (10). But it is hard to see how, on their view, one can avoid it. Nor, it will emerge, should we want to.

Searle notes that "it is possible to perform a statement while lying." To think otherwise is simply to "confuse the intention to make a statement with the intention to make a true statement" (168). For to make a statement, Searle tells us, is to represent things in a certain way. And one can readily choose to represent things as being different from the way one takes them to be. These sensible observations seem to capture accurately the way we ordinarily talk about stating, asserting, and the like. But Searle also holds that one cannot "make a statement without expressing a belief" (28). And this claim lands us back with the problem about how speech acts can express nonexistent mental states.

A satisfactory account of intentionality must somehow resolve these opposing pressures. It must explain our inclination to regard insincere speech as having intentional character, and thereby explain Searle's observation that, at least in casual usage, we speak of the telling of lies as cases of making statements. But it must also recognize the oddness of insisting that insincere speech acts derive their intentionality by expressing mental states that do not exist.

As noted earlier, we sometimes use such terms as 'thought' and 'belief' not to speak of mental states, but to describe the propositional content of a mental state, at least as long as the mental attitude or illocutionary force is appropriate. This ambiguity will help explain the force of the intuition that lies express beliefs that the speaker does not have, while enabling us to avoid puzzles about nonexistent mental states. For we need not interpret that intuition to mean anything about the expressing of mental states by insincere speech acts. Rather, the intuition may amount just to the idea that even insincere speech acts have propositional content. There is no problem about attributing to an insincere speech act propositional content that is shared by none of the speaker's mental states. To say such a speech act has propositional content is simply to talk about the semantic character of the sentence in question. Propositional content in such cases results not from any connection the speech act has with any mental state, but from the way people typically use the relevant form of words in the language in question. In the case of insincere speech, one's speech act does, indeed, express a belief, but only in the sense of expressing a proposition. It does not express a mental state. So the intuition that even lies express beliefs tells us nothing about the relation of thinking to speech.

Insincere speech is intentional, therefore, only in an attenuated way, by virtue of the role other tokens of the relevant sentence types play in the language. Indeed, although sincere speech is intentional in just the way mental states are, insincere speech exemplifies something we can reasonably think of as derived, as opposed to intrinsic, intentionality. Insincere speech acts count as intentional only because they are token of a type of utterance, other tokens of which are intentional directly.

When somebody lies, we tend to describe that person as stating something, albeit insincerely. And, as argued in section II, all speech acts express mental states. These natural observations seem to imply, once again, that insincere speech expresses nonexistent mental states. But when one tells a lie, one states something only in the somewhat attenuated sense that the sentence that one utters is a token of a type we ordinarily use to make statements. The sentence token itself is not used, in such a case, with the illocutionary force of a statement. Only thus can we avoid the conclusion that we always believe the content of our lies. Parallel remarks hold for insincere speech acts that seem to exhibit other types of illocutionary force.

The foregoing considerations suggest that a promising account of insincere speech would model it not on the making of statements at all, but on the rehearsed speech of actors. Actors are not typically in the mental states of their characters, and so the utterances of actors do not normally express those mental states. Rather, actors in effect pretend to perform illocutionary acts of stating, requesting, commanding, and the like, in accordance with the demands of their parts. Actors may even pretend to think the thoughts of their characters. But pretending to think something is not the same as actually thinking it, any more than pretending to say something is the same as actually saying it. If an actor does happen to think something that corresponds to the lines of a character, it is incidental to the actor's uttering those lines. When an actor playing Macbeth utters 'I have done the deed', he does not believe he has killed Duncan. Nor does the actor, himself, actually say he has. If an actor did not merely pretend to say and think the things the character is supposed to think and say, but actually said and thought those things, we would very likely question the actor's sanity.

Similarly, when we speak insincerely, we simulate illocutionary acts. Pretense in this case is not the real thing. When one lies, one intends to deceive. Moreover, we intend our lies to deceive not just about whether our utterances are true, but also about what we actually believe. We try to get our audience to accept that we believe our utterances are true, when we really believe they are not. Thus we hope to deceive our audience into thinking that we are trying to tell them something, and to keep from them that we are, instead, trying to deceive them. It is at best a misleading ellipsis to say in such a situation that the speaker has made a statement. To insincerely make a statement is to pretend to make a statement.

It is convenient to use the words for ordinary illocutionary acts to describe what happens when we speak insincerely. For, except in special cases such as lying, there is simply no term for the insincere counterpart of an illocutionary act. So, when context makes it clear what we are saying, it is an innocuous shorthand to speak of an insincere simulation of a prediction or question, for example, as a prediction or question, without qualification. But it hardly follows that insincere speech consists of the actual performance of illocutionary acts. We also use such language to describe the speech of actors, without meaning thereby to elide the difference, in that case, between pretense and the real thing. Indeed, we even speak as though the fictional character an actor plays were a real person. Similarly, we describe, by an equally innocuous courtesy, both insincere utterances and lines recited in playacting as though they were genuine illocutionary acts.

One reason why insincere speech acts may seem more like actual illocutionary acts than like the speech of actors is that an actor's goal is just the simulation itself. When we speak insincerely, our goal is not primarily to simulate, but to deceive. And it may seem natural to describe speech as simulated only when the speaker's goal is simply to simulate. But this difference in how we ordinarily describe things is not telling. Even if the aim of insincere speech is primarily to deceive, simulation is a means to that end. We simulate ordinary illocutionary acts, hoping, in part, to get our audience to think that we have performed the real thing.

Sometimes insincere speech acts have much the same effects as their sincere counterparts. As J. L. Austin observed, we tend to count an insincere promise as a case of promising, though we also regard it as infelicitous.[15] But we do not count such cases as promising because the sincere and insincere cases are the same kinds of speech act. Partly we do so because, as just noted, we have no special word for insincere promises. But we also do so because we hold people responsible the same way, whether they speak sincerely or not. If I try to deceive you in thinking that I am sincerely promising something, I am responsible for my speech act just as though I had been sincere. The same holds for lying. You will hold me responsible for my lie just as if it had been a sincere statement. But responsibility is not a reliable guide to how we classify things, and lies and insincere promises are not genuine statements and promises.

We can reinforce this conclusion by turning again to the comparison between insincere speech and the rehearsed speech of actors. Though we hold each other responsible for our insincere speech acts, nobody would think of holding actors responsible for the illocutionary acts of their characters. We cannot explain this difference as due to the simulated nature of actors' speech, since we do hold people responsible for simulations. The difference here is rather that actors have no intention to deceive, and context makes it unlikely that their utterances would fool anybody. We peg responsibility to considerations of intention and probable outcome, not to types of speech act.

It might appear that insincere speech acts are genuine speech acts because the insincerity, properly understood, attaches not to the speech act but to the speaker. If I insincerely tell you something, the insincerity is a matter of my state of mind in speaking to you. My act of telling you something is perfectly genuine, one might urge. In telling you what I believe is false, however, I myself am not being genuine. But this objection trades on a false dichotomy about how adverbs operate. If I do something carelessly or willfully or generously, both my action and I are careless or willful or generous. Similarly with my saying something insincerely. Nor, of course, can we infer from my saying something insincerely that I say it, *tout court*. Adverbs do not, in general, detach.

One might maintain, however, that whatever the case about insincere speech, genuine speech acts can occur unaccompanied by corresponding mental states. And if this is so, the causal account of expressing will not do justice even to sincere speech acts. Thus one might urge that, in general, we can choose to say whatever we please, regardless of what our mental states may be. One can, for example, say "The moon is made of green cheese," or even "2 + 2 = 5," if one so chooses. And plainly there is no question of one's believing these things. But saying such things would not be genuine speech acts. Rather, if one uttered such things, they would simply be cases, once more, of simulated assertion. If somebody were to produce these words, we would automatically assume either that the person somehow misspoke, or that no real illocutionary act was in question. We would either try to construe the utterance nonliterally or ironically, so as to allow us to attribute to the speaker some genuine speech act, or we would simply dismiss the person's words as not worth taking seriously. As Vendler

---

[15] *How To Do Things with Words*, Cambridge, Massachusetts: Harvard University Press, 1962, p. 16.

stresses, saying something, in such cases, is the saying of words and sentences, and "none of these 'sayings' will carry an illocutionary force" (25; cf. 93).

When one speaks sincerely, what one says corresponds to some mental state that one is in. Indeed, this is what it is for a speech act to be sincere. We can only understand a speech act to be sincere if we suppose that the speaker is in a corresponding mental state. But in section II we argued that all speech acts express corresponding mental states. Moreover, the argument there did not hinge on whether or not the speech act is sincere. It was simply that if speech acts did not invariably express corresponding mental states, we could not explain why we cannot coherently assert, for example, 'It's raining but I don't believe it is'. Thus, suppose that not all speech acts do express corresponding mental states. Then there should be no difficulty about my saying that it's raining, albeit perhaps insincerely, and immediately going on to say that I don't believe it. But I cannot do so. Accordingly, the conditions for a speech act's being sincere coincide, in this respect, with the conditions for something to be a genuine speech act at all. In both cases, one's speech must express a corresponding mental state. As Vendler and Searle both note, for something to be a genuine speech act, "one must mean what one says" (Vendler, 26; see Searle, 69).

If I say that it's raining and go on to say also that I don't believe it, I simply betray my insincerity. That, one might object, is all that goes wrong in Moore's paradox. Indeed, Moore himself seems, at one point, to offer such a diagnosis.[16] But this suggestion cannot be correct. There is nothing problematic about one's speaking insincerely in ways that betray one's insincerity. The difficulty with Moore's paradox is not just that one avows one's own insincerity. If I say it's raining and go on to say I don't believe it, I tell you that I did not mean what I said, that is, that I did not actually perform the illocutionary act that I purported to. Only if sincerity is presupposed in the performing of genuine illocutionary acts can we explain why this is so.

These considerations may seem to provide the basis, after all, for insisting on a conceptual connection between thinking and speaking. It is part of our conception of genuine speech acts that they express actual mental states that the speaker is in. We do not count any utterance that does not do this as an actual speech act. But how we conceive of things and how we classify them often does not reflect any analytic connections among our concepts, but only well-entrenched background knowledge about those things. We do not count as water anything that is not H_2O, nor anything as gold whose atomic number is not 79, though no analytic or conceptual truths underlie our refusal to do so. And, as noted in section III, there are strong theoretical reasons to conclude that no conceptual or analytic truth explains the connection between thought and speech, either. If it did, we could not explain why 'George says it's raining but does not believe it is' is not a contradiction.

Once again, focusing on speech as simply marks and sounds misleads. If speech acts were merely utterance acts, the kind of simulation that occurs both when actors recite lines and when we speak insincerely would not make the resulting utterance a case of simulated speech. Whatever simulation there is in such cases, genuine uttering does

[16] G. E. Moore, "A Reply to My Critics," in *The Philosophy of G. E. Moore*, ed. Paul Arthur Schilpp, La Salle, Illinois: Open Court, 1942, pp. 533–677, at pp. 542–543.

occur. But mere uttering does not suffice for the performance of an illocutionary act. Uttering can and indisputably does occur unaccompanied by any illocutionary force.

VI. EXPLAINING INTENTIONALITY

The foregoing discussion of insincere speech not only helps sustain a causal account of expressing and of the primacy of thinking over speech. It also has a useful implication about the status of the distinction between expressing mental states and expressing propositions. Unless we invoke that distinction, we cannot explain our common-sense, presystematic intuition that insincere speech expresses thoughts we do not have. The distinction between expressing mental states and expressing propositions is therefore not the product of abstruse considerations of limited application. Rather, our double use of words for mental states, to refer to mental states or to their propositional content, emerges in the course of the very attempt to understand the ways we ordinarily describe thinking and speaking.

We may expect, therefore, that the distinction between expressing mental states and expressing propositions will be central to any satisfactory explanation of the relation between thinking and talking. This turns out to be so. In particular, once we see that thoughts, beliefs, and the like may be either mental states or propositions, we are in a position to explain the powerful temptation we have to subscribe to claims about the intrinsic intentionality of thinking, and the noncausal priority of thought over speech.

Propositional content is simply intentional content. Such content cannot, presumably, occur on its own, since it is only a characteristic of concrete mental states or speech acts. We conceive of such content by abstracting from particular mental states or speech acts that have that content. Since we conceive of propositional content in abstraction from particular mental states and speech acts, it is independent of any other aspect of speech or thinking. So a thought, in the sense of a propositional content, is no more than some intentional property or other. Thoughts, understood as propositional contents, are therefore as intrinsically intentional as anything could be.

Conflating thoughts in the sense of mental states with thoughts in the sense of propositions can therefore lead us, albeit tacitly, from the unexceptionable but unexciting claim that propositions are intrinsically intentional to the interesting but indefensible claim that mental states are. We saw in section V that the only way to explain Searle's and Vendler's views about insincere speech is to appeal to such a conflation. It is therefore a natural speculation that this conflation also underlies their insistence on the intrinsic intentionality of mental states.

The same ambiguity also helps explain the pull of the idea that thought is prior to speech in some noncausal way. Thoughts in the sense of propositional contents are, indeed, conceptually prior to speech. We cannot understand what it is for something to be a genuine speech act unless we understand what it is to have propositional content. But mental states are, in this respect, no different from speech. We can understand what it is for something to be an intentional mental state only if we grasp what it is to have propositional content. If one fails to notice that 'thought', 'belief', and the like can refer either to mental states or to propositional contents, one might conclude, wrongly, that thoughts in the sense of intentional mental states are also conceptually prior to speech acts.

One might question, however, whether a causal account of expressing, and of the primacy of thought, enables us to deal satisfactorily with all the questions we have about the relation of speech to thinking. In particular, a causal account might seem not to do justice to our sense that we must in some way make reference to thinking in order to explain the intentionality of speech. And if it does not, perhaps we must appeal to some sort of noncausal primacy of thought or to intrinsic intentionality.

In section IV we distinguished two questions about intentionality. One was the problem of how such things as marks and sounds can have intentional character at all. A parallel problem arises, as we saw, for mental states if those states have physical characteristics. But we can bracket that concern and ask the more limited question of how those sounds and marks which are intentional differ from those which are not. What is it that accounts for the intentionality of those speech events that do have intentional character? Again, we can pose a parallel problem about thoughts, if thoughts have physical realization. What is it in virtue of which those neural events which are intentional differ from those which are not?

These various questions are not entirely independent. How we answer each will influence, to some extent, the way we can answer the others. But it is tempting to try to answer the question of how intentional marks and sounds differ from those which are not intentional in strictly causal terms. The intentional cases are caused by mental states that have the same content and a corresponding mental attitude, whereas the nonintentional cases are not. Indeed, not only do mental states cause corresponding speech acts; they presumably also cause those speech acts to have whatever properties they have that enable them to be intentional. So mental states actually cause those performances to be intentional. Mental states are thus a causal source of intentionality.

Mental states not only cause speech acts and other behavior. They also cause other mental states. Indeed, we can introspectively discern that this is so. We are often aware that thinking one thing causes us to think another. And, introspection aside, it would be strange if mental states had such a multitude of causal connections with various bodily events but not with one another. Suppose, then, that the mental states that cause speech acts also cause them to have the intentional character they have. There is no reason to think that the way mental states cause speech acts differs from the way they cause other mental states. So it will be equally natural to suppose that when one mental state causes another it also causes that other mental state to have the particular intentional character it has.

These considerations have consequences about intrinsic and derived intentionality. We cannot reasonably hold that the intentionality of thoughts is intrinsic if those thoughts are causes of other thoughts, but derived if they are effects. For one thing, many mental states are both causes and effects of other mental states. Moreover, the distinction between intrinsic and derived intentionality does not, intuitively, fit with any difference we know to hold between those mental states which cause other mental states and those which are caused. But mental states are sources of intentionality for speech acts in just the way they are sources of intentionality for other mental states. In each case, they confer intentionality by causing the speech act or other mental state to have whatever properties it has in virtue of which it has its intentional character. So we cannot sustain a distinction between intrinsic and derived intentionality by appeal to the idea that thinking is the source of the intentionality of speech.

The causes of speech acts are not themselves speech acts. And this may seem to provide a disanalogy between thought and speech that would allow us to characterize as intrinsic even the intentionality of those thoughts which are caused by other thoughts. Thus we might urge that something has derived intentionality only when it is different in kind from the source of its intentionality. Speech acts have derived intentionality, on this suggestion, but those mental states whose intentionality is caused by other mental states would nonetheless have intentionality that is intrinsic. But there is no reason to think that whether something differs in kind from the source of its intentionality matters to whether the intentionality of that thing is intrinsic or derived. Indeed, to determine whether it does matter, we would need some independent grasp of the distinction between intrinsic and derived, which we lack.

In any case, there are other reasons to reject the idea that something is intrinsically intentional if it causes something different in kind to be intentional. Some mental states are caused by other mental states. But some are caused by nonmental, bodily events, such as perceptual stimulations of various kinds. We cannot conclude that such causes of mental states have intrinsic intentionality, since these causes are not even intentional. The distinction between intrinsic and derived intentionality cannot, therefore, enable us to explain anything about the intentionality of speech that we cannot explain by the causal theory of expressing.

Even if we can give a satisfactory causal explanation of how those sounds and marks which are intentional differ from those which are not, there is also the problem about how such things can have intentional properties at all. As already noted, this problem arises equally for thoughts. Since we can, in principle, describe mental states in neurological terms, we must explain how such things as neural events can be intentional.

If mental states had no nonintentional, physical features, no such problem would arise for them. There would be nothing to being a mental state other than being intentional. To ask how it is possible for mental states to be intentional would then be just to ask how intentional states can be intentional. We can sensibly formulate the problem of how mental states can be intentional only if we can describe such states in nonintentional terms.

Accordingly, if mental states had no nonintentional, physical features, the status of the intentionality of thought would differ from that of the intentionality of speech. For speech acts plainly do have nonintentional, physical features. So the question about how such things can be intentional would still arise for speech, though not for thought. This disparity would justify our thinking of the intentionality of thought as intrinsic. We could maintain that something is intrinsically intentional just if the question about how it can be intentional does not arise. Intentionality is intrinsic, on this suggestion, when it is pure—unaccompanied and undiluted by nonintentional properties other than causal connections and spatiotemporal location.

But, if mental states with no nonintentional features did exist, we would need to explain how such states are possible. And we would have the additional burden of explaining how such states can interact with nonintentional bodily states. So, even though no question would arise about how mental states can be intentional, we would have to explain at least as much if the intentionality of mental states were pure, in the foregoing sense, as we would if mental states have properties other than their intentionality. The idea that we need not explain something's being a certain way if its being that way is all there is to it is an unfortunate legacy of Aristotle's unmoved mover, adapted with disastrous results in Descartes's postulation of a substance whose sole nature is thinking. And the idea of thoughts that have no characteristics other than their intentionality is no more than a further adaptation from substances to states.

Indeed, the difficulties we encountered above in discussing the question of how speech acts come to be intentional suggests that there may well be something misconceived about that question. There is no difficulty about how speech acts get to be intentional if that question is simply the question of how speech acts come to exist. But if, instead, it is the question of how intentionality can come to belong to states or events that also have physical properties, the situation is less clear. But the correct answer here must, in any case, depend on what it is for something, whether speech act or mental state, to be intentional.

Insofar as we want to explain how such things as speech acts and mental states can be intentional at all, and what it is for them to be so, we should expect that whatever understanding we gain about the intentionality of one will help us explain the intentionality of the other. We can come to understand why intentional performances occur at all, and why particular ones do, by appeal to the mental states that cause them. But there is no reason to expect more help from mental states than from speech acts about what it is for something to be intentional, or how it is possible for particular kinds of states and events to be so. A satisfactory explanation of intentionality must accordingly stress the interdependence of thinking and speech, rather than rely on the causal asymmetry between them.

Indeed, it is arguable that speech acts inherit their intentionality from mental states by being part of an overall causal network that involves those mental states. If so, mental states would be responsible for the intentionality of speech acts in a way that goes beyond merely causing their occurrence. But even this line of argument cannot help establish any priority of thought over speech. Whatever considerations might go to show that the intentionality of speech acts derives from their having suitable causal connections with other intentional states and events would also apply to the mental states themselves. Moreover, it is arguable that what makes something a mental state is its causal connections with other mental states and with behavior and sensory stimulation.[17] If so, then not only is the intentionality of speech acts due to their causal

[17] For an especially effective defense of this view, see David Lewis, "An Argument for the Identity Theory," *The Journal of Philosophy*, LXIII, 1 (January 6, 1966): 17–25, and "Psychophysical and Theoretical Identifications," *The Australasian Journal of Philosophy*, L, 3 (December 1972): 249–258.

connections with thoughts; the intentionality of mental states themselves consists, in part, in the causal relations those states bear to speech acts. Accordingly, the causal network containing both mental states and speech acts will yield no priority for either thought or speech beyond the circumstance that mental states cause speech acts.

VII. INTENTIONALITY AND SELF-AWARENESS

If the preceding argument is correct, we have no reason to suppose that our ability to explain intentionality will be impaired if we forgo claims about intrinsic intentionality and the noncausal primacy of thinking. There is, however, a difference between speech and thought which does support a kind of primacy for thinking, and which also helps explain the force of the intuition that thoughts are intrinsically intentional. We are ordinarily aware, without having to infer or observe anything, of what we say and of much of what we think. This awareness, moreover, is not couched in terms of the physical features of either our mental states or our speech acts. We are, of course, ignorant of the physical realizations of our thoughts. And our automatic awareness of what we say typically involves no conscious attention to the words we use. We are often fully aware of what we have said, but either cannot recall our actual words or must concentrate to do so. And, even when we do know what words we spoke, we rarely determine what we have said on the basis of our knowing those words.

Now insincere speech aside, whenever we say anything we are in a mental state with the same propositional content and some corresponding mental attitude. Since we do not normally determine what we say by inferring it from our words, the best explanation of our effortless awareness of what we say is that we are aware of what we think, and aware that we gave expression to that mental state in speech. Accordingly, our automatic awareness of what we say is less direct, by two steps, than our awareness of what we think.

A number of factors nicely corroborate this account. Notoriously, we have comparative difficulty remembering the content of our lies. We more often make mistakes about our lies than we do about our sincere statements, and they sometimes slip our mind altogether. Our account predicts this. When we lie, we get no help from any automatic awareness of the mental state our speech expresses, as we do with sincere speech acts. For no such mental state exists. Accordingly, our awareness of our lies is more studied than our awareness of sincere speech, and we would therefore expect, correctly, that we would have a harder time accurately recalling them.

Moreover, although others must sometimes tell us how to take their words, we need never do this for ourselves. We know automatically what construction to place on our own words. The best explanation of this knowledge is, again, that we come to be aware of what we say by being aware of what mental state our words express. We may, of course, occasionally have to do something like figure out what our own words amount to. If my thought is confused, I may have to sort out what, as we might put it, I really meant by my words. But even then I do not so much figure out what it was I said as figure out what I should have said. And, if I am inarticulate, or misspeak, then my words may be confused even though the thought itself is not. Indeed, I can presumably distinguish cases in which my thought is confused from those in which only my words are precisely because my awareness of my mental state makes me aware of how to take my words.

Cases of misspeaking and confusion aside, the match between thinking and speech typically seems flawless.[†] Our words make clear the content of our thoughts, and illocutionary verbs indicate our mental attitudes. Nonverbal behavior, by contrast, seems unable to keep up with the detailed and subtle accuracy with which speech conveys thought.[18] We tend even to attribute to our thoughts the syntactic structure of the speech acts that express them, though it is plain on reflection that we have no reason to suppose that thoughts have much of the complex compositional structure that sentences exhibit.

The best explanation of this sense of seamless match between thought and speech is, once again, that we know what we say because we know in the first instance what we think, and know also that our speech expresses those thoughts. The situation is analogous with nonverbal behavior. We are also automatically aware of our nonverbal actions; we do not have to watch ourselves, or infer from anything, to know what actions we perform (see Searle, 88–9). This awareness results from our knowing what we intend, and knowing that our actions have given expression to those intentions.

If our awareness of what we say derives in this way from our awareness of what we think, we can understand why thought should seem to be prior to speech in a way that goes beyond the fact that mental states cause speech acts. This additional primacy of thought is due to our deriving our awareness of what we say from our awareness of what we think. Such primacy is basically an epistemic matter. But it also has to do with the nature of thinking itself. Our automatic awareness of our own mental states is presumably possible, in part, because of the nature of mental states themselves. And our ability to rely on that awareness to know our own speech acts doubtless tells us something, in addition, about the connection between thinking and speech.

These considerations can also help explain the appeal of the idea that the intentionality of thought is intrinsic. There are two ways we learn about what we say: by our awareness of the thought expressed, and by our words. But, without neurological knowledge far beyond anything we now have, we can have no such double access to our own thoughts. So, for practical purposes, we can regard the intentionality of mental states as if it were intrinsic. For, given our current knowledge, our thoughts have no nontrivial properties other than those we apprehend introspectively.

Since our automatic awareness of what we say relies on our automatic awareness of what we think, but not conversely, we can sustain an epistemic version of the primacy of thought, and a pragmatic version of something resembling the intrinsic intentionality of thought. But things would be different if intentional mental states were necessarily conscious, as some have urged. On the present suggestion, the primacy of thought and the intrinsic character of its intentionality stem from the

---

[†] I would now qualify this claim of a flawless match; see "Content, Interpretation, and Consciousness," ch. 12 in this volume, § III. [Added in 2005.]

[18] Compare Wittgenstein's observation: "Suppose we think while we talk or write—I mean, as we normally do—we shall not in general say that we think quicker than we talk, but the thought seems *not to be separate* from the expression" (I, 318; emphasis in original).

way we are conscious of our own intentional states. So, if that consciousness is a necessary feature of our intentional states, then the primacy of thought and the intrinsic character of its intentionality would arguably be necessary as well. Indeed, if intentional states are necessarily conscious, it is reasonable to suppose that such consciousness would be a necessary consequence of the intentionality of such states. Such intentionality would then itself arguably be a necessary feature of the states that have it.

These considerations provide one more way to explain the appeal that such primacy, and intrinsic intentionality, have for us. One who holds with Descartes that thinking is necessarily conscious[19] will very likely also insist on the primacy of thought, and the intrinsic intentionality, which seem both to follow from such necessary consciousness. Indeed, the idea that intentional states are invariably conscious plays a pivotal role in Vendler's discussion (50, 155, 161, and 191–193), though Searle equally explicitly disavows that idea (2).

Searle's disavowal is undoubtedly correct. Many, indeed probably most, of our intentional mental states occur outside our stream of consciousness. Nor is there any reason to suppose that any necessary connection does hold between a mental state's being intentional and its being conscious. It is arguable, instead, that a mental state's being a conscious state is just a matter of its causing a roughly contemporaneous second-order thought to the effect that one is in that very mental state.[20] Indeed, this account of what it is for a mental state to be a conscious state is intuitively most compelling in the case of intentional mental states. On this view, the consciousness of intentional states is indeed the result of intentionality. But although such consciousness is a result of intentionality, it is not a result of the intentionality of the states that are conscious. Rather such consciousness is due to the intentionality of the second-order thoughts about such cases. Moreover, although neither thought nor speech is conceptually prior to the other, on this view, those thoughts which are conscious do have a primacy that is doubly causal. For that primacy consists in those thoughts' causing both the speech acts that express them and the higher-order thoughts that make them conscious.

---

[19] For example: "it is not possible for there to be in us any thought of which, at the moment it is in us, we are not conscious" (*Fourth Replies: Philosophical Writings* II, 171; *Oeuvres*, VII, 246).
[20] I defend this view in detail in "Two Concepts of Consciousness," ch. 1 in this volume, and "Thinking that One Thinks," ch. 2 in this volume.

Postscript to "Intentionality" (1989)

My general aim in "Intentionality" is to defend a causal theory of expressing—that is, a causal theory of what it is for a speech act to express a propositional mental state. On this theory, every genuine speech act expresses some mental state. Two conditions must be satisfied for a speech act to express a mental state. The propositional content and mental attitude of that mental state must correspond to the speech act's meaning and illocutionary force; and the mental state must cause the speech act in some suitable way.

When one speaks insincerely, one doesn't believe what one says. No corresponding mental state exists, and so none causes the speech performance. The causal theory therefore implies that insincere vocal performances do not qualify as genuine speech acts. I argue in section V of "Intentionality" that, despite initial appearances, this conclusion is actually correct. Insincere speech performances are degenerate speech acts, and so are not counterexamples to the claim that genuine speech acts occur only in the presence of corresponding mental states.

As noted in section V, ordinary usage seems not to sanction this conclusion. We generally do not describe insincere speech as defective. But this is hardly decisive. It may well be convenient to talk as though insincere speech were on a par with sincere speech acts, but doing so elides a crucial distinction.

On the argument of section V, we must understand insincere speech on the model of play acting. If I play Hamlet and speak some lines, nobody would contend that I really say or think those things. Nor does any other real person. But we do regard the character I am playing as both saying and thinking these things. These fictional thoughts and speech acts occur in my fictional character's mind and mouth, though not in my own. A fictional character's saying and thinking things is, of course, a pretense; we pretend that Hamlet says and thinks the relevant things.

Much the same thing happens when I speak insincerely. There, too, I play a role. But now things are more complicated, since this time my character is a fictional version of myself. We regard my fictional self as actually saying and thinking the things I insincerely pretend to say and think, even though my real self does neither. Because the character I play is now a sincere but fictional version of myself, it is easy to disregard the distinction between my real and fictional selves. This encourages us to describe insincere speech performances as though they were genuine speech acts, rather than pretense. But assimilating insincere speech to the sincere case is no more than a convenience; saying something insincerely is merely pretending to say it.

This account of insincere speech allows us to explain the expressing of thoughts by speech acts in causal terms. Still, one might object that if it were possible to explain the connection between speech and thought without having to accord second-class status to insincere speech, we should prefer such an explanation. And it may seem that just such an explanation is possible if we adopt a roughly Gricean theory of utterance meaning.[1] This postscript argues that a challenge along these lines cannot succeed.

On a Gricean theory, an utterance's meaning something is a matter of a speaker's having certain intentions. I mean something by my utterance if I intend my audience to respond in a certain way because it recognizes that I so intend. The various conditions that Grice and others have introduced to disarm counterexamples do not affect the present argument. What is crucial is that a Gricean account of utterance meaning treats sincere and insincere utterances uniformly. Whether I speak sincerely or insincerely, I intend you to take me to have a particular intention, and therefore to respond in a certain way. Insincere utterances will thus have meaning in just the way that sincere utterances do.

Not only does a Gricean theory give a uniform treatment of sincere and insincere speech; it also seems to be no less successful than my causal theory in dealing with Moore's paradox. I had invoked Moore's paradox in section V to defend the claim that genuine speech cannot occur in the absence of corresponding thoughts. I argued there that this claim provided the best explanation of why Moore's-paradox sentences have no coherent conditions of assertibility. To have assertibility conditions, 'It's raining but I don't believe it' must have truth conditions, and for the whole sentence to be true the second conjunct must be. But if the second conjunct were true, there would be no thought corresponding to the first conjunct. On the causal theory, the sentence would therefore make no assertion. The best explanation of why Moore's paradox could not have coherent assertibility conditions is that it couldn't be true and also successfully assert anything.

But a Gricean theory can also deal effectively with Moore's paradox. On a Gricean theory, one cannot say insincerely what cannot be said sincerely. That is because when I speak insincerely, I intend you to take my speech act to be sincere. If it is impossible for tokens of a particular sentence type to be used to perform a sincere illocutionary act, I cannot hope to use such a token to produce in you the right response. Accordingly, I cannot intend to do so. So I cannot use it even to say something insincerely.

A Gricean theory can therefore explain what's wrong with Moore's paradox. It is plainly impossible to say anything sincerely by uttering a sentence like 'It's raining but I don't believe it'. Since Moore's-paradox sentences cannot be used to perform sincere speech acts, those sentences lack coherent conditions of assertibility. This Gricean explanation of Moore's paradox does represent insincere speech as parasitic on sincere speech acts, since a sentence type can be used insincerely only if it can be used to speak sincerely, but the converse does not hold. Nonetheless, the explanation does not imply that insincere speech performances are defective as speech acts. The causal theory's explanation of Moore's paradox may accordingly be no better than that which comes out of a Gricean theory.

---

[1] Paul Grice, "Meaning," *The Philosophical Review*, LXVI, 3 (July 1957): 377–388; "Utterer's Meaning and Intentions," *The Philosophical Review*, LXXVIII, 2 (April 1969): 147–177; and "Utterer's Meaning, Sentence-Meaning, and Word-Meaning," *Foundations of Language*, IV (1968): 225–242; and Stephen R. Schiffer, *Meaning*, Oxford: Clarendon Press, 1972. See also Schiffer's *Remnants of Meaning*, Cambridge, Massachusetts: MIT/Bradford Books, 1987.

I am grateful to Schiffer for putting this objection especially forcefully.

A Gricean theory can do all this because it explains what utterances mean not in terms of the propositional mental states those utterances express, but by appeal to one's intending that one's audience take one to be in such propositional states. A uniform treatment of sincere and insincere speech is therefore possible.

Moreover, a Gricean theory may seem to be in direct competition with the causal theory defended in "Intentionality." Both theories posit a connection between every genuine speech act and a propositional mental state in virtue of which the speech act has meaning. On a Gricean theory, when one asserts that it's raining, the mental state that confers meaning on one's speech act is an intention that one's audience take one to believe that it's raining. On my theory, one's sincere assertions that it's raining have meaning because they are caused by one's believing that it's raining. The basic difference between the two theories seems to be the way they treat insincere speech.

But the primary goal in "Intentionality" is to explain what it is for a speech act to express a thought. It is reasonable to expect such a theory also to tell us what it is for a speech act to mean what it does. But the converse need not hold. A theory of utterance meaning may fail to tell us what it is for a speech act to express a thought. A Gricean theory seems to do just that.

On a Gricean theory, the mental state that is responsible for an utterance's having meaning cannot, in general, be the mental state that the utterance expresses. Assertions, for example, express beliefs, not intentions. And, more generally, the mental state a speech act expresses has the same propositional content as the speech act and a mental attitude corresponding to the speech act's illocutionary force. So, even if we accepted that a Gricean theory correctly explains what it is for an utterance to mean something, that explanation would not help us understand what it is for a speech act to express a mental state.

This conclusion may seem too quick. After all, if I intend my audience to respond to my utterance that it's raining by taking me to believe that it's raining, doesn't the thought that it's raining play a role in my intention? In one sense, yes. The proposition that it's raining does figure in that intention. And we often use 'thought' to refer to propositions, and describe sentences as expressing thoughts in the sense of expressing propositions. But what is at issue here is not how speech acts express propositions, but how they express propositional mental states. And if we restrict 'thought' so that it applies only to propositional mental states, one's Gricean intention may well fail to be accompanied by any thought that it's raining. Indeed, that is just what happens when we speak insincerely. On a Gricean theory, insincere utterances are accompanied by Gricean intentions, but not by corresponding beliefs.

A speech act expresses a proposition just in case that proposition is the semantic meaning of the sentence type used to perform the speech act. So a speech act will express a proposition if the relevant sentence type has some semantic meaning; the speaker need be in no mental state that corresponds to the speech act. But sincerity is just a matter of whether or not such a corresponding mental state occurs. And speech acts cannot express mental states the speaker is not in. So it is precisely because a Gricean theory treats sincere and insincere speech uniformly that it cannot explain what it is for a speech act to express a propositional mental state. Such a theory cannot, therefore, help circumvent the conclusion that insincere utterances are defective cases of speech.

4

Introspection and Self-Interpretation

I. INTRODUCTION

Introspection is a process by which people have focused access to their own mental states. We have access, of course, to all our conscious states, since a mental state's being conscious in the first place means in part that one is conscious of that state. That we are conscious of all our conscious states is evident from the fact that, if one is altogether unaware of a state, that state does not count as a conscious state. But our introspective access to a mental state is something more than that state's simply being conscious. Access to a state is distinctively introspective only when it is deliberate, attentive, and reflective.

It is sometimes held that all mental states are introspectible, that is, subject to introspective access. But there are two distinct ways to understand this claim, which are not always distinguished. When we introspect a state, we attend to it in respect of its mental properties, its intentional content and mental attitude in the case of intentional states and its sensory modality and qualitative properties in the case of sensory states. So mental states are the right kind of states to be subjects of introspective awareness, and we can readily imagine introspecting any state that has these mental properties.

But a state's being introspectible can also mean that one is actually able to introspect the state. And it may well be that individual mental states occur that we cannot, for whatever reason, access introspectively. Many mental states occur without being conscious at all, and perhaps there are mechanisms or other factors that actually prevent some of these states from becoming conscious. And, if a state cannot come to be conscious at all, it cannot become introspectively conscious. It might even be that in some cases states that are conscious but not introspectively so cannot, because of some mechanism or other factor, come to be introspectively conscious. Mental states are all the right kinds of things to be subjects of introspective consciousness, but it may be that specific factors prevent some of them from ever becoming introspectively conscious.

Introspective access to our mental states is subjectively unmediated, in that nothing seems, from a subjective point of view, to mediate between one's state and one's introspective consciousness of it. Such access also seems, subjectively, to be within our control, in that nothing more is needed for one to become introspectively aware of a state than for one to decide to be.

The introspective access one has to one's own mental states seems to afford the only access anybody has to what mental states one is in other than inferences from one's behavior. Such inferences are, of course, notoriously fallible. So it is tempting to conclude that introspection provides an epistemically privileged way to determine what mental states a person is in. Nothing, it may seem, could overrule a person's introspective pronouncements. Indeed, an even stronger conclusion seems to some to be warranted. It is arguable that we need some independent way to tell whether inferences from behavior to mental states are correct. So, since introspection is evidently the only alternative way we have to tell what mental states a person is in, it may seem inviting to conclude that introspection is not only privileged, but decisive.

But this traditional line of argument is unconvincing. We rely both on introspective access and behavioral inference to determine what mental states a person is in, but neither route to this information need be infallible. It could well be instead that we simply establish what mental state somebody is in by taking into account all available information, both introspective and inferential. That would not guarantee a decisive conclusion about what mental state the person is in, but that is the way generally with empirical information. Introspection is no less fallible and subject to correction than are third-person considerations. Just as there is no way to determine the existence and behavior of subatomic particles independent of balancing observation and theoretical inference, so we cannot determine what mental states a person is in independently of balancing introspection with third-person evidence.

For these and other reasons, I will not discuss the alleged special epistemic status that some theorists have held introspective access has, nor the distinctive methodological role introspection is sometimes held to play. Instead, I shall focus on trying to characterize the nature of introspection and, in particular, its relation to other mental phenomena. I begin in section II by urging that the widespread theoretical model of introspection on which it is a kind of inner perceiving fails, and that introspecting must therefore be a kind of conscious, attentive thinking about our own mental states. In section III I turn to the contrast mentioned at the outset between introspective consciousness of our conscious states and our ordinary, unreflective access to those states. Section IV, then, discusses whether we ever are, properly speaking, conscious in a first-person way of our own mental states, and section V takes up a challenge about what the content of such introspective consciousness of our mental states could be. In section VI, I discuss confabulatory introspective reports and the interpretive character of introspection. I conclude in section VII with some brief remarks about introspection in connection with personhood and the unity of consciousness.

II. THE PERCEPTUAL MODEL

Introspection gives us conscious access to our mental states. But what sort of process or mechanism is responsible for that conscious access? There is a popular idea that introspection is a kind of "inner sense"[1] or inner perception of our mental states. This perceptual model, which reflects the very etymology of 'introspect' (from the

---

[1] In Kant's useful phrase: *Critique of Pure Reason*, tr. and ed. Paul Guyer and Allen W. Wood, Cambridge: Cambridge University Press, 1998, p. 174, A22/B37.

Latin *spicere* [look] and *intra* [within]), derives considerable plausibility from the idea that introspecting is a kind of internal monitoring of one's mental states. Just as exteroceptive perception monitors the external environment and proprioception monitors the positions and movements of our limbs, so introspection performs a parallel monitoring function for the contents of our minds.

We know of no organ that subserves introspection in the way the eyes subserve the transduction of visual information and the ears auditory information. But this is hardly decisive. For one thing, there might well be some relatively modular portion of the brain that subserves introspective monitoring by being sensitive to the occurrence of conscious mental states. But even if that is not the case, not all perceiving proceeds by way of such organs; proprioception, for example, relies on no dedicated organ.

Indeed, exteroceptive, proprioceptive, and enteroceptive perception seem intuitively to have so little in common that one might well wonder what it is in virtue of which we count all of them as kinds of perceiving. Two things seem necessary. One is that all three involve the monitoring of some process or condition. The other is that they all seem to proceed by way of some kind of qualitative property that reflects the state or condition being monitored. There is in each case a distinctive state whose very qualitative character serves to carry the relevant information.

One thing that encourages a perceptual model of introspection is the temptation to regard introspecting as a clear case of monitoring. I shall argue in section VI that thinking of introspection as a kind of monitoring misleads us in serious ways about the nature of introspection. But independent of that question, it is plain that introspecting does not involve any distinctive feel or other qualitative property. This is especially obvious when we introspect intentional states, such as thoughts and desires. Such purely intentional states have no qualitative aspect, and nothing qualitative occurs when we are introspectively conscious of them. When we introspect qualitative states, we are aware of those states in respect of the qualities they seem to exhibit. Still, the only qualities that figure in our introspecting such states are those of the states themselves; there are no additional qualities by means of which introspection represents the qualities of the states it makes us aware of. Introspecting adds no additional sensory qualities of its own.

Sensory quality is not an incidental aspect of perceiving. Perceiving represents bodily or environmental states of affairs, but one need not represent these states of affairs by perceiving them. One can instead represent the state of affairs by thought, by simply thinking that it obtains. Perceiving a red object or one's arm's being extended differs from simply thinking that a red object is in front of one or that one's arm is extended because in perceiving we represent those states of affairs in part by the qualitative character of the perception. Thinking, by contrast, involves no such qualitative aspect. If we could subtract from perceiving its qualitative properties, we would be left just with our thinking about the state of affairs in question.

William Lycan has argued that the lack of qualitative properties is not decisive here, and that the monitoring function of introspection by itself suffices for introspection to count as a kind of perceiving, or at least as relevantly like perception.[2] And he urges that, just as perceiving monitors the environment, so introspecting monitors one's mental states. But being a kind of monitoring does not establish any useful resemblance to perception. Bodily processes often track states of affairs, by occurring whenever the state of affairs obtains and not otherwise, and indeed by occurring with an intensity that reflects that of the condition being monitored; states of the liver, for example, track blood glucose levels. Any bodily state that carries the requisite information monitors the condition in question, but few such states do so by perceiving that condition; states of the liver do not perceive glucose levels, except metaphorically. More than monitoring is necessary for a state to count as perceiving.

An advocate of the perceptual model might urge that, even if not all monitoring is perceiving, perhaps all mental monitoring is. But even when monitoring does take place by way of mental processes, the states that carry the relevant information could be thoughts, rather than perceptions. Suppose we were so constituted that our thoughts about whether a particular state of affairs obtains tracked that very state of affairs; our thoughts about whether the state of affairs obtains would be reliable indicators of whether it does. Those thoughts, then, would monitor that state of affairs. There would be no temptation to regard the mental states in virtue of which this monitoring takes place as perceptions. We have an independent mark of whether a mental state is a thought or a perception; perceptions, unlike thoughts, involve sensory qualities. Standard cases of mental monitoring are typically perceptual, but that does not mean that all mental monitoring is.

Lycan recognizes that introspection involves no qualitative properties, but denies that this speaks against a perceptual model since, on his view, qualitative properties are not necessary to perceiving. Lycan's view here relies on his view about what the qualitative properties of perceiving consist in. "[S]ensory properties presented in first-order states are," he maintains, "the represented features of physical objects; e.g., the color presented in a (first-order) visual perception is [just] the represented color of the physical object."[3] But if introspection monitors anything, it monitors mental states, not physical objects. So, if Lycan is right that first-order perceptual states have no qualitative properties, but only represent those of perceived objects, there is no reason to expect the perceiving of first-order mental states to have qualitative properties either. That introspecting involves no qualitative character of its own does not, he concludes, undermine the perceptual model of introspecting.

I discuss such representationalist views of mental qualities in section V. But whatever the merits of representationalism about mental qualities, anybody who adopts that view must still draw the ordinary distinctions between, for example, a visual perception of a red object and a nonperceptual thought that there is a red object in front of one. Both mental states represent the color of the object, and both

---

[2] William G. Lycan, *Consciousness and Experience*, Cambridge, Massachusetts: MIT Press/Bradford Books, 1996, p. 28. Lycan relies only on exteroceptive perception in developing his perceptual model of introspection.

[3] *Consciousness and Experience*, pp. 28–9. Lycan refers here to his extended discussion of this view in *Consciousness*, Cambridge, Massachusetts: MIT Press/Bradford Books, 1987, ch. 8.

represent the object as being in front of one. We cannot distinguish the two by saying that perceiving a red object, unlike merely thinking that such an object is in front of one, represents one as responding visually to the object.[4] Seeing represents only the object's visible properties, not also the modality of one's access to it. However one draws the distinction between perceiving something and thinking of it as present, it seems clear that introspecting will fall not on the side of perceiving, but of thinking about something as present.

Introspection occurs when we focus our attention on some particular mental occurrence. The attended mental occurrence is already conscious; introspection does not transform a state that was not conscious at all into one we introspect. Introspecting a state is, rather, our focusing on that state from among the range of those which are already within our stream of consciousness. This suggests one more reason why many theorists see introspection in perceptual terms; the most convenient model for attentively focusing on something is selective attention in vision, hearing, and the other perceptual modalities.

But directing one's attention to something need not be a matter of perceiving at all. Even if I am looking straight at something, I may not be attending to it; I attend to it by consciously thinking about it in a concentrated, detailed way. Attention is often a matter of where one's conscious thoughts are focused. And this is likely the case when we introspect. When we introspect a state, we typically become conscious of it in respect of its detailed mental properties; we mentally describe it in terms of those salient distinguishing characteristics. And mentally describing something is a matter of having thoughts about it. One introspects being in a mental state by having conscious thoughts to the effect that one is in a state with the relevant mental properties.

In any case, the absence of introspective qualities is by itself enough to show that introspection is not a kind of perceptual monitoring. Still, introspection does give us access to our mental states by making us conscious of those states. The only way it could do this other than by responding perceptually to the states is by way of thoughts to the effect that we are in those states. Introspection is not the perceiving of our mental states, but the having of thoughts about them.

III. INTROSPECTIVE AND NONINTROSPECTIVE CONSCIOUSNESS

A mental state's being introspectively conscious differs from the way in which mental states ordinarily are conscious in everyday life. A state is introspectively conscious only when one is conscious of it in an attentive, deliberate, focused way, whereas states are nonintrospectively conscious when our awareness of them is relatively casual, fleeting, diffuse, and inattentive.

---

[4] As John R. Searle in effect suggests in *Intentionality: An Essay in the Philosophy of Mind*, Cambridge: Cambridge University Press, 1983, ch. 2. Searle does not endorse representationalism about mental qualities.

Consider, for example, the conscious states that make up one's visual field at any particular moment. Though all conscious, none of these states is typically subject to the focused, deliberate attention characteristic of introspection. This is true even for states that occur in the center of our visual field, where we have foveal vision; these states have far more fine-grained detail and greater resolution than others, but still typically occur without benefit of introspective scrutiny. Similarly for our sensory input from the other sensory modalities, both exteroceptive and bodily.

Conscious intentional states are also seldom introspected. One might, for example, be considering what to do on a particular occasion, and thus having a series of thoughts and desires, many of them conscious, but it is rare in so doing that one will pause to introspect any of these conscious thoughts or desires. Introspecting is not just being conscious of a mental state; it is being conscious of it in a deliberate, focused, reflective way.

The distinction between conscious states we introspect and those we do not is often overlooked, doubtless in part because in both kinds of case we are conscious of the states in question. Indeed, the term 'introspection' is sometimes applied to both kinds of case.[5] But, however the term is used, there is plainly a distinction we must mark between the conscious states we introspect and those we do not,[6] between the states we are attentively and deliberately conscious of and those we are conscious of in only a casual and inattentive way.

Introspecting a state is not perceptual. So it must instead involve one's having a thought to the effect that one is in that state. How, then, does introspective consciousness differ from ordinary, nonintrospective consciousness? A simple, straightforward answer would be possible if part of what it is for a state to be a mental state at all were that the state be conscious. We could then say that nonintrospective consciousness is just what happens when that state occurs, without anything else, and introspection is what happens when, in addition to the state, one has an accompanying thought that one is in that state.

This simple picture may seem inviting. When we introspect, we are conscious of consciously attending to the introspected state in respect of certain mental properties, and hence conscious of having a thought about that state. When a state is nonintrospectively conscious, by contrast, we are never conscious of any such accompanying thought. And, if being a mental state is, in part, being conscious, our not being conscious of a thought is enough to show that no such thought occurs.

But this picture cannot be sustained. Mental states plainly do occur that are not in any way conscious. This is widely recognized for intentional states, such as beliefs, desires, expectations, and the like. But there is also compelling evidence that perceptual sensations also occur without being conscious. Masked priming experiments provide situations in which detailed qualitative information occurs of which subjects

[5] D. M. Armstrong, *A Materialist Theory of the Mind*, New York: Humanities Press, 1968; revised edition, London: Routledge & Kegan Paul, 1993, p. 95, and "What is Consciousness?", *Proceedings of the Russellian Society*, 3 (1978): 65–76; reprinted in expanded form in Armstrong, *The Nature of Mind*, St Lucia, Queensland: University of Queensland Press, 1980, pp. 55–67.
[6] As Armstrong himself notes; "What is Consciousness?", pp. 62–63.

are wholly unconscious, results that fit with everyday cases of peripheral vision and subliminal perceiving. And striking work with blindsight patients suggests the same conclusion.[7] Even bodily sensations, such as pains and aches, arguably occur without being conscious; if one is concentrating on something, one may be wholly unaware of a pain evident to others by one's behavior.

So, we need to explain not only how introspectively conscious mental states differ from those which are nonintrospectively conscious, but also how both of those differ from states that are not conscious at all. In addition, since not all thoughts are conscious, one's not being conscious of any thought about a mental state cannot show that no such thought occurs; at most it can show that, if any such thought does occur, it is not a conscious thought. A more complicated picture is needed to explain this threefold distinction between states that are introspectively conscious, those which are nonintrospectively conscious, and those which are not conscious at all.

When a state is conscious, whether introspectively or not, we are conscious of that state. As noted at the outset, no state of which one was in no way at all conscious would count as being conscious, introspectively, nonintrospectively, or in any other way. So we have a way to approach our threefold distinction. When a state is not conscious, we are not conscious of it at all. And a state's being nonintrospectively conscious must differ from our introspecting a state in virtue of the different ways we are conscious of those states.

It is sometimes held that explaining a state's being conscious, in whatever way, in terms of one's being conscious of it is unavoidably circular, since that is simply explaining consciousness by appeal to consciousness.[8] But there are two distinct notions of consciousness that figure in this explanation. We are conscious *of* many things other than mental states; whenever we perceive something or think about it as present, we are conscious *of* that thing. Moreover, we understand what it is to have thoughts about things and to perceive them independently of understanding what it is for mental states to be conscious. So we understand what it is to be conscious *of* a state independently of a state's being a conscious state. There is no circularity in the explanation.

A state will be introspectively or nonintrospectively conscious depending on how one is conscious of that state. What difference in how we are conscious of our mental states is relevant here? Introspecting a state involves one's having a thought about that state as having certain mental properties. Since the thought is about the state as one's own current state, it is about that state as present. This explains how it is that introspecting a state makes one conscious of it.

---

[7] For early work on masked priming, see Anthony J. Marcel, "Conscious and Unconscious Perception: Experiments on Visual Masking and Word Recognition," *Cognitive Psychology*, 15 (1983): 197–237, and "Conscious and Unconscious Perception: An Approach to the Relations between Phenomenal Experience and Perceptual Processes," *Cognitive Psychology*, 15 (1983): 238–300.

For work on the phenomenon of blindsight, see Lawrence Weiskrantz, *Blindsight: A Case Study and Implications*, Oxford: Oxford University Press, 1986, and *Consciousness Lost and Found: A Neuropsychological Exploration*, Oxford: Oxford University Press, 1997.

[8] See, e.g., Alvin I. Goldman, "Consciousness, Folk Psychology, and Cognitive Science," *Consciousness and Cognition*, 2, 4 (December 1993): 364–382, p. 366.

When we introspect a state, we are conscious of it in a way that seems attentive, focused, deliberate, and reflective. When a state is conscious but not introspectively conscious, by contrast, we are conscious of it in a way that is relatively fleeting, diffuse, casual, and inattentive. Introspective and nonintrospective consciousness do not seem to differ in any other ways. There is no other phenomenological or subjective difference, and no theoretical reason to posit any additional difference.

The natural conclusion is that both nonintrospective and introspective consciousness involve an accompanying thought about the target state, but that the cases differ because of differences in the accompanying thought. When we introspect a state, the accompanying thought is attentive, conscious, and deliberate, whereas the accompanying thought when a state is nonintrospectively conscious is fleeting, casual, and inattentive. In addition, since we are unaware of any accompanying thoughts when our mental states are only nonintrospectively conscious, the accompanying thought in that case is not a conscious thought.

This account of nonintrospective consciousness is just the higher-order-thought (HOT) hypothesis about such consciousness that I have developed elsewhere.[9] But it is worth stressing that the present argument does not rely on that hypothesis to explain introspective awareness. Rather, the argument here goes in the opposite direction. An independent account of introspective awareness, together with the need to explain the difference between introspective and nonintrospective consciousness, by themselves led us to the HOT hypothesis.

Indeed, the HOT hypothesis about nonintrospective consciousness is very likely the only credible way to explain how a state's being nonintrospectively conscious is weaker than introspection but stronger than a state's not being conscious at all. On that hypothesis, a state is nonintrospectively conscious just in case it is accompanied by a HOT that is not itself conscious. By contrast, a state is introspectively conscious if it is accompanied by a HOT that is conscious. And it fails to be conscious at all if no HOT, conscious or not, accompanies it.

It might be thought that there is another way to explain how ordinary, nonintrospective consciousness falls in between introspection and a state's not being conscious at all. Perhaps a state is nonintrospectively conscious not if it is actually accompanied by a HOT, but rather if there is a disposition for such a HOT to occur. A state would be introspectively conscious, then, if accompanied by an occurrent HOT. This view about nonintrospective consciousness has been advanced by Peter Carruthers, who argues that only dispositions for actual HOTs to occur are necessary for mental states to be conscious, not the actual HOTs themselves.[10]

---

[9] "Two Concepts of Consciousness," ch. 1 in this volume; "The Independence of Consciousness and Sensory Quality," ch. 5 in this volume; "Thinking that One Thinks," ch. 2 in this volume; "A Theory of Consciousness," in *The Nature of Consciousness: Philosophical Debates*, ed. Ned Block, Owen Flanagan, and Güven Güzeldere, Cambridge, Massachusetts: MIT Press, 1997, pp. 729–753; and "Consciousness and Its Expression," ch. 11 in this volume.

[10] E.g., in Peter Carruthers, *Language, Thought, and Consciousness: An Essay in Philosophical Psychology*, Cambridge: Cambridge University Press, 1996, and *Phenomenal Consciousness: A Naturalistic Theory*, Cambridge: Cambridge University Press, 2000. Carruthers's actual formulation

This dispositional version of the HOT model may seem inviting. When a mental state is conscious, it seems phenomenologically that there is no HOT present but that one could readily occur. But that phenomenological appearance is irrelevant. HOTs are posited as the best explanation of what it is for a mental state to be a conscious state, not because we find them in our stream of consciousness. Indeed, since the HOTs posited to explain nonintrospective consciousness are themselves not conscious thoughts, we would expect to be phenomenologically unaware of them. And, in any case, a dispositional variant of the HOT hypothesis cannot work. Since a disposition to have a thought about something cannot make one conscious of that thing, dispositions to have HOTs cannot explain how we come to be conscious of our conscious mental states.[11]

I mentioned at the outset that introspection makes us aware of our mental states in a way that seems, from a first-person point of view, to be unmediated. We can readily explain this subjective sense that introspection is direct and unmediated by stipulating that the conscious HOTs in virtue of which we introspect mental states do not rely on any inference of which we are aware. Similarly, as I have argued elsewhere, for the nonconscious HOTs that explain nonintrospective awareness. We need not suppose

appeals to dispositional HOTs, but it is unclear what a dispositional thought could be other than a disposition for an episodic thought to occur.

Carruthers also argues that appeal to dispositions would allay a concern that there is insufficient computational capacity to accommodate HOTs for all our conscious states. But it is unclear why dispositions to have HOTs would take up less cortical space than the HOTs themselves. It is also unclear why, with our huge cortical resources, there is reason for such concern. But if there is, it may well be that many HOTs operate wholesale on bunches of conscious states. This is phenomenologically plausible, since our conscious states seem to be conscious in clusters, and focusing on a small area seems to withdraw consciousness from previously conscious peripheral states. I return to this possibility in §VII, in connection with the apparent unity of consciousness.

[11] It is likely that such appeal to dispositions is, at bottom, a way to avoid confronting the popular intuition that thoughts are invariably conscious. Theorists tempted by the idea that mental states are all conscious sometimes appeal to dispositions to try to disarm arguments that nonconscious mental states actually occur. Dispositions to be in occurrent mental states play much the same causal roles as those played by the occurrent mental states themselves. So such theorists, while holding onto the claim that all occurrent mental states are conscious, allow for nonconscious dispositional states corresponding to the ordinary conscious versions. It is tempting to see Carruthers's explanation of conscious states by way of dispositions to have HOTs as a way to avoid positing occurrent, but nonconscious, HOTs.

A well-known example of appeal to dispositions in place of nonconscious mental states can be found in Searle's connection principle, on which all intentional states are potentially conscious. On that principle, nonconscious states can have only an ersatz intentionality derived from their connection with intentional states that are conscious. A state is never intentional without being conscious, according to Searle, since not being conscious would deprive it of its subjectivity. See John R. Searle, "Consciousness, Explanatory Inversion, and Cognitive Science," *The Behavioral and Brain Sciences*, 13, 4 (December 1990): 585–696. Searle's argument for the connection principle relies on his claim that only conscious states can differ in the way they represent the same thing. But how a state represents something will have effects on behavior and other mental states whether or not the state in question is conscious.

For another example of holding that a mental phenomenon can fail to be conscious only if it is dispositional, see Norman Malcolm, "Thoughtless Brutes," *Proceedings and Addresses of The American Philosophical Association*, 1972–3, XLVI (November 1973): 5–20, esp. §ii.

in either case that nothing actually does mediate between the HOT and its target, only that nothing seems subjectively to mediate.

The same holds for our subjective sense that our introspective awareness of mental states is attentive, focused, and deliberate. It seems to us when we introspect a state that we are conscious of the state in a distinctively attentive way and that this is the result of a deliberate decision to focus on the state in question. We are conscious of ourselves *as* deliberately attending to our mental states. But being conscious of one-self *as* deliberately attending to something does not establish that one actually is.[12] It is an independent question whether the way one is conscious of an introspected state engages any mechanisms of attention. Indeed, the argument of section VI raises a doubt about whether introspective consciousness is, properly speaking, attentive.

There is even a question about how reliable our subjective sense is that introspecting is deliberate. In the case of overt actions, being deliberate is a matter of the action's resulting from a process of deliberation, at least part of which is normally conscious. Such conscious deliberation seldom if ever precedes our introspectively focusing on a mental state. Perhaps being deliberate amounts to something else in this case, but it is not clear just what that might be.

Sometimes attention is drawn to a mental occurrence by some external stimulus; a bright flash of light may, for example, cause one to focus on the almost painful brightness of the resulting visual sensation. By contrast, no external event seems to figure in our focusing on a mental state when we introspect. This suggests that our subjective sense that introspective focusing is deliberate may be due just to its resulting from wholly inner factors, factors of which we typically remain unaware.[13]

What is clear, however, is that when we introspect a state, we are not only conscious of the state, but also conscious that we are thus conscious. We are aware, when we introspect, that we are focusing on the state in question. In ordinary, nonintrospective consciousness, by contrast, we are conscious of the conscious state, since otherwise it would not be a conscious state at all, but we are not also aware of being so conscious. Our being conscious of our mental states passes, in these cases, without any apparent notice.

Ned Block has sometimes characterized the HOT hypothesis as suited to explain a special type of consciousness, which he calls monitoring consciousness.[14] This

---

[12] It is natural to construe the phrases 'conscious of' and 'conscious that' as factive, so that one is not conscious of something unless that thing exists, and not conscious that something is the case unless it is. But even if being conscious of something is factive in that way, being conscious of something *as* having a particular property does not imply that it has that property.

In any case, many verbs that are usually used factively also get used nonfactively; we speak of seeing pink elephants, as well as things about whose existence we are noncommittal. It is likely that, whatever the ordinary usage of 'conscious of' and 'conscious that', we must treat these phrases as being nonfactive in developing a satisfactory account of what it is for a mental state to be conscious.

[13] More precisely, though we may sometimes speculate about what led to our introspecting a state, we are never introspectively aware of the process leading to our introspective awareness.

It might seem more accurate to describe introspective focusing as voluntary, rather than deliberate. But this characterization is misleading, since introspective focusing is not properly an action at all.

[14] E.g., "On a Confusion about a Function of Consciousness," *The Behavioral and Brain Sciences*, 18, 2 (June 1995): 227–247, with Author's Response, "How Many Concepts of Consciousness?", 272–287, p. 235.

characterization may be due in part to Lycan's and Armstrong's appeal to higher-order perceiving to explaining what they see as the monitoring aspect of introspective consciousness. Block characterizes such monitoring consciousness as metacognitive, and at one point identifies it with attention (279). These remarks strongly suggest that Block's notion of monitoring consciousness is just introspective, as against ordinary, nonintrospective consciousness.[15]

But the notion of consciousness that the HOT hypothesis seeks to explain is in the first instance not that of introspective consciousness, but that of ordinary, inattentive, fleeting, nonintrospective consciousness. Nor does the HOT hypothesis offer any explanation whatever about attention. A mental state is nonintrospectively conscious, on that hypothesis, if it is accompanied by a HOT that is not, itself, a conscious thought. Introspection is the special case in which that HOT is conscious, which happens when a yet higher-order thought occurs—a third-order thought about the second-order thought. One would see the HOT hypothesis as a dedicated explanation of introspective consciousness only if one tacitly assumed that any HOTs one has would have to be conscious thoughts.

IV. ARE WE CONSCIOUS OF OUR MENTAL STATES?

When a state is conscious, whether introspectively or not, one is conscious of being in that state. Such states differ from those which are not conscious, since in those cases one is not conscious of the state, at least not in the seemingly immediate way characteristic of conscious states. The difference between introspective and nonintrospective consciousness, then, is due to a difference in how we are conscious of states in the two kinds of case.

It is sometimes argued, however, that a mental state's being conscious does not consist in our being conscious of that state and, indeed, that conscious states actually exist of which we are not conscious. An ingenious argument for this conclusion has been put forth by Fred Dretske. Adapting his case in inessential ways, consider two scenes, one consisting of ten trees and another just like it but with one tree missing. Suppose that you consciously see first one scene and then the other, and that in each case you consciously see all the trees. But suppose that, despite all this, you notice no difference between the two scenes. This kind of thing happens all the time; we often consciously see everything in a scene and then everything in a slightly later version of that scene, altered in some small, unnoticed way.

Dretske assumes that, since you consciously see all the trees in each scene, you have conscious experiences not only of both scenes but of all the trees in each. Still, there is some part of the conscious experience of ten trees that is not part of the conscious experience of nine trees, and that part is, itself, a conscious experience: a conscious experience of a tree. Since you notice no difference between the scenes, you are not

---

[15] Block's apparent identification of monitoring with attentive introspection would also explain his claim that monitoring consciousness is somewhat intellectualized (234), as well as his denial that monitoring consciousness figures either in phenomenal or access consciousness (279, 280).

conscious of the difference between them. But the conscious experience of the extra tree is the only difference between the two overall conscious experiences. Accordingly, Dretske concludes, you are not conscious of that experience of the extra tree. And, because the experience of the extra tree is a conscious experience, there is a conscious experience of which you are not conscious.[16]

But this conclusion is unwarranted. It is notorious that one can be conscious of something in one respect but not in another. And this happens when we are conscious of our mental states just as with anything else. One might, for example, be conscious of a particular visual experience as an experience of a blurry patch, but not as an experience of a particular kind of object, say, a table. Yet it might be that that very experience, though not conscious *as* an experience of a table, is nonetheless an experience of a table. It might leave memory traces of a table, detectable by its priming effects. Similarly, one might be conscious of the experience of the extra tree *as* an experience of a tree, or even just *as* part of one's overall experience, but not conscious of it *as* the thing that makes the difference between the experiences of the two scenes.[17] Indeed, this is very likely the best explanation of what happens in the case Dretske constructs.[18]

Since Dretske holds that a mental state's being conscious does not consist in one's being conscious of that state, he must have some other account of what it is for a state to be conscious. He suggests that a state's being conscious consists, instead, in its being a state in virtue of which one is conscious of something or conscious that something is the case ("Conscious Experience," 280). This proposal has the disadvantage that no mental state could then fail to be conscious, since every mental state is such that being in it makes one either conscious of something or conscious that something is the case.

---

[16] Fred Dretske, "Conscious Experience," *Mind*, 102, 406 (April 1993): 263–283, pp. 272–275; reprinted in Dretske, *Perception, Knowledge, and Belief*, Cambridge: Cambridge University Press, 2000, pp. 113–137. Cf. Fred Dretske, *Naturalizing the Mind*, Cambridge, Massachusetts: MIT Press/Bradford Books, 1995, pp. 112–113.

[17] Dretske in effect concedes that this can happen, since he holds that being conscious of a difference always amounts to being conscious "that such a difference exists" ("Conscious Experience," p. 275; cf. 266–7). And, as he notes, being aware of the thing in virtue of which the experiences differ does not mean being aware that they differ in that way (275).

[18] Striking experimental work on so-called change blindness shows that subjects can consciously and attentively see two scenes that differ in some respect, often highly salient, without being at all conscious of the respect in which they differ. For a sample of this literature, see John Grimes, "On the Failure to Detect Changes in Scenes across Saccades," *Perception*, ed. Kathleen Akins, New York: Oxford University Press, 1996, pp. 89–110; Ronald A. Rensink, J. Kevin O'Regan, and James J. Clark, "To See or Not To See: The Need for Attention to Perceive Changes in Scenes," *Psychological Science*, 8, 5 (September 1997): 368–373; Daniël J. Simons, "Current Approaches to Change Blindness," *Visual Cognition*, 7 (2000): 1–16; *Change Blindness and Visual Memory: A Special Issue of the Journal Visual Cognition* (book version of the journal issue), Philadelphia: Psychology Press, 2000; Ronald A. Rensink, J. Kevin O'Regan, and James J. Clark, "On the Failure to Detect Changes in Scenes Across Brief Interruptions," *Visual Cognition*, 7 (2000): 127–145; and Daniel T. Levin, Nausheen Momen, Sarah B. Drivdahl, and Daniel J. Simons, "Change Blindness Blindness: The Metacognitive Error of Overestimating Change-Detection Ability," *Visual Cognition*, 7, Special Issue on Change Blindness and Visual Memory (2000): 397–412.

More pressing for present purposes, if a state's being conscious is not a matter of one's being conscious of it, Dretske must also offer an account of introspection which does not imply that we are conscious of the states we introspect. On Dretske's proposal, introspection resembles what he calls displaced perception. Just as we come to know how full a car's gas tank is by looking at the gauge, so one comes to know what visual experience one has by noticing what physical object one is seeing. One comes thereby to be conscious *that* one is in a particular mental state, but not conscious *of* that state.[19]

Coming to be conscious that one is in a particular state presumably means having a thought to that effect; so on Dretske's account introspecting a mental state means having a thought that one is that state. In introspecting a visual state, for example, one extrapolates from the physical object one sees to a thought that one has the resulting visual experience. Still, when one introspects, the inference by which this extrapolation takes places is presumably never a conscious inference; it is never an inference of which one is conscious. Moreover, one's thought that one has the visual experience will, on Dretske's view, be a conscious thought, since he holds that any state in virtue of which one is conscious that something is the case is a conscious state.

So, on Dretske's view, introspecting a state consists in having a conscious, noninferential thought to the effect that one is in that state. That conscious HOT is inferred from some thought about the thing that the introspected experience is about; one infers from a thought about the object one sees to a thought that one sees that object. Perhaps that is often the origin of the thoughts by means of which we introspect our conscious states, though I will argue in section VI that our introspective awareness often arises in other ways. That question aside, Dretske's view differs from that defended above only in its commitment to the idea that mental states are all conscious, which cannot be sustained.

According to Dretske, when one introspects a state one is not conscious *of* that state, but conscious only *that* one is in that state. But it is tempting to think that whenever one is conscious *that* a state of affairs obtains, one is thereby conscious of whatever things are involved in its obtaining. Dretske's denial that we are conscious of the states we introspect is accordingly very likely due to his desire to reject a perceptual model of what happens when we introspect our mental states. Displaced perception is not perception, properly speaking, but something we infer from a perception.

Like Dretske, Searle also holds that we are never conscious of our mental states, again in large measure because he adopts a perceptual model of what it is to be conscious of something. Being conscious of something, he assumes, is a matter of observing it. But "where conscious subjectivity is concerned," he argues, "there is no distinction between the observation and the thing observed, between the perception and the object perceived." He concludes that no distinction is tenable between the

[19] Fred Dretske, "Introspection," *Proceedings of the Aristotelian Society*, CXV (1994/5): 263–278, and *Naturalizing the Mind*, ch. 2. See also "The Mind's Awareness of Itself," *Philosophical Studies*, 95, 1–2 (August 1999): 103–124; reprinted in Dretske, *Perception, Knowledge, and Belief*, Cambridge: Cambridge University Press, 2000, pp. 158–177.

introspecting of a state and the state introspected; any "introspection I have of my own conscious state is itself that conscious state."[20]

Searle argues that the distinction between introspecting and the introspected state collapses because we can describe consciousness only in terms of what it is consciousness of (96). This has a certain plausibility. Since consciousness is a matter of the way things appear to us, we must describe it in terms of those things. We describe consciousness in terms of its content.

But we cannot describe consciousness by only describing the things that appear to us; we must also describe the way they appear to us and, indeed, the fact that they do appear to us. We must also say how we are conscious of the things we are conscious of. Suppose that I consciously see a red object; I may describe my consciousness simply as being of a red object. But there are different ways one can be visually conscious of red objects. My being conscious of it might be focused and careful or casual and offhand; I might be conscious of it in respect of its specific hue, brightness, and environmental contrasts, but my consciousness might not register those features. There are differences in the ways we are conscious of things that do not reduce to the contents of our consciousness. And we are not only conscious of things in these various ways, but also conscious that we are conscious of things in one way rather than in another. There is more to say about our being conscious of things than just what things we are conscious of.

On Searle's construal of being conscious of things as a matter of observing them, it is plausible that we are never conscious of our conscious states, since we never observe those states, properly speaking. But this undermines only the perceptual model of introspective and nonintrospective consciousness, which, however inviting metaphorically, we have already seen to be indefensible.

Indeed, Searle concedes as much. "[I]f by 'introspection' we mean simply thinking about our own mental states, then there is no objection to introspection. It happens all the time, and is crucial for any form of self-knowledge." Searle would very likely also concede that our thoughts about our own mental states can sometimes be subjectively unmediated. His complaint is with the perceptual model of introspection and with the idea that it has some special epistemic standing, with introspection construed as "a special capacity, just like vision only less colorful" (144). Like Dretske, Searle adopts a view on introspection that differs from that put forth above only in denying that mental states ever occur without being conscious.

Dretske and Searle both construe being conscious of things on a perceptual model, in effect denying that having thoughts about our mental states constitutes a way of being conscious of those states. But having a thought about something does, under the right circumstances, make one conscious of that thing. Perhaps having a thought about Julius Caesar does not make one conscious of him, properly speaking. But that is because Caesar is not present and we do not think of him as being present. Similarly,

---

[20] John R. Searle, *The Rediscovery of the Mind*, Cambridge, Massachusetts: MIT Press, 1992, p. 97. Cf. p. 144: "In the case of vision, we have a clear distinction between the object seen and the visual experience.... But we can't make that distinction for the act of introspection of one's own conscious mental states." Cf. also p. 96.

we do not describe ourselves as conscious of the abstract objects we think about. But when we think about something as being present, we are thereby conscious of it. Suppose that you and I are in the same room, but you neither see me nor hear me or sense me in any other way. Still, if you realize I am there and have a thought about my being there, you are thereby conscious of me. And HOTs represent their targets concretely and as present, since they represent one as currently being in particular token mental states.

V. THE CONTENT OF INTROSPECTION

When a mental state is conscious, whether introspectively or not, one is conscious of being in that state. But we are never conscious of our conscious states perceptually. Dretske and Searle recognize that, but, since they conceive of being conscious of things perceptually, they deny that we are ever conscious of our conscious states.

That denial leads Searle to insist that any "introspection I have of my own conscious state is itself that conscious state"; if being conscious of something is perceiving it, the only things we are conscious of are the things we perceive by way of our conscious perceptual states. Introspective awareness of conscious states is still possible, according to Searle and Dretske, if it is not construed perceptually but in terms of having thoughts about our conscious states.

But a more thoroughgoing challenge is available to the idea that introspection makes us conscious of our mental states, a challenge about what it is we are conscious of when we seem to introspect. That question arises especially vividly in connection with perceptual experiences. As G. E. Moore noted, consciousness seems to be "transparent" or "diaphanous,"[21] in that when we try to focus on our conscious perceptual states, it may seem that we simply look through those states to the things we perceive in virtue of those states. As Searle notes, it seems that we can describe our perceptions only in terms of what they are perceptions of. When we try to focus on the visual sensation we have in seeing a red tomato, it may seem that we end up focusing only on the tomato itself and its redness.

These considerations lead Searle to conclude that there is no distinction between introspecting a state and the state introspected. But one could cast one's conclusion in slightly different terms. Instead of maintaining that introspecting is nothing over and above the introspected state, one could simply insist that, when we do seem to introspect an experience, the only properties we are aware of are the properties of the things that experience represents. As Gilbert Harman puts it, when you have a conscious experience of seeing a red tomato, "[y]ou have no conscious access to the qualities of your experience by which it represents the redness of the tomato. You are aware [only] of the redness of the tomato."[22]

---

[21] G. E. Moore, "The Refutation of Idealism," in Moore, *Philosophical Studies*, London: Routledge & Kegan Paul, 1922, pp. 1–30, at pp. 20 and 25.

[22] Gilbert Harman, "Explaining Objective Color in Terms of Subjective Reactions," *Philosophical Issues: Perception*, 7 (1996): 1–17, p. 8; reprinted in Alex Byrne and David Hilbert, eds., *Readings*

Perhaps Harman's remark pertains only to perceptual awareness; the only property one sees or perceives when one has a conscious visual experience of a red tomato is the redness of the tomato. But there are other ways to be aware of properties when they are instantiated, and when we conceive of awareness more broadly, the redness of the tomato is not the only property one can be aware of. One may also sometimes be aware of properties of the visual experience itself.

If one has an experience of a red tomato, for example, one could come to be aware that one has that experience. And then one will be aware of the property the experience has of representing the redness of the tomato. And, if it is a visual experience of a red tomato, the experience will represent that redness in a way unlike the way a nonperceptual thought might represent that redness. Nonperceptual thoughts represent redness simply by being about that color, whereas visual experiences represent it in a distinctively qualitative way. So, when one is aware of having an experience of a red tomato, one is aware of the experience's representing the redness in that distinctively qualitative way.

As Harman notes, a visual experience of the redness of a tomato is not red in the way the tomato is. But that does not preclude its having some mental quality, distinct from the red of the tomato but characteristic of the visual sensations we have when we see red objects in standard conditions of illumination. Mental qualities are unlike the perceptible qualities of physical objects in several ways. For one thing, they are properties of states, rather than objects. Equally important, they are not perceptible; we do not come to be aware of them by perceiving them. The question of whether we might be perceptually aware of our perceptual experiences and their qualitative properties seems, indeed, to arise only because of this misconception about mental qualitative properties. Only if mental qualities resembled the perceptible properties of physical objects in being literally perceptible could one suppose that we might be perceptually aware of them.

Although mental qualities are distinct types of property from the perceptible properties of physical objects, we fix the reference to mental qualities by appeal to their perceptible physical counterparts. The distinguishing mental quality of red sensations, for example, resembles and differs from other mental color properties in ways that parallel the ways in which the perceptible red of physical objects resembles and differs from other physical color properties. Thus the mental quality of red

on Color, volume 1: The Philosophy of Color, Cambridge, Massachusetts: MIT/Bradford, 1997, pp. 247–261. Cf. the similar representationalist views put forth by Lycan, *Consciousness and Experience*, ch. 4. (see §II, above), and Armstrong, *The Nature of Mind*, ch. 9.

Sydney Shoemaker has developed a somewhat qualified representationalism in "Introspection and Phenomenal Character," *Philosophical Topics*, 29, 2 (Winter 2001): 247–273. Earlier versions of that view occur in Shoemaker, "Introspection and 'Inner Sense'," *Philosophy and Phenomenological Research*, LIV (1994): 249–314, reprinted in Shoemaker, *The First-Person Perspective and Other Essays*, Cambridge: Cambridge University Press, 1996, pp. 201–268; "Phenomenal Character," *Noûs*, 28 (1994): 21–38; and "Phenomenal Character Revisited," *Philosophy and Phenomenological Research*, LX, 2 (2000): 465–468.

I am grateful to Shoemaker, personal communication, for pressing various issues about representationalism.

resembles mental orange more than mental green just as physical red is closer to physical orange than to physical green; similarly with the qualitative properties of other perceptual modalities. The similarities and differences that matter here are those which figure in our commonsense taxonomies, not the similarities and differences that hold among reflectance properties or wavelengths of visible light, described in terms of physical theory.[23]

It is these mental qualities by which perceptual experiences, unlike nonperceptual thoughts, represent things in a distinctively qualitative way. Harman insists, however, we "have no conscious access to the qualities of your experience by which it represents the redness of the tomato." He concludes that we have no idea whether experiences represent things by means of such mental qualities, since we are never aware of any.

But, if we do not model these qualities on the perceptible properties of physical objects, thereby restricting ourselves to perceptual awareness, there is no reason to expect we would never be aware of these qualities. We sometimes have thoughts about our experiences, thoughts that sometimes characterize the experiences as the sort that visually represent red physical objects. And to have a thought about an experience as visually representing a red object is to have a thought about the experience as representing that object qualitatively, that is, by way of its having some mental quality.

When one has a thought that one's own experience visually represents a red physical object, that thought need not be in any way consciously inferential or based on theory; it might well be independent of any inference of which one is conscious. From a first-person point of view, any such thought would seem unmediated and spontaneous. And it is the having of just such thoughts that makes one introspectively conscious of one's experiences. Such a thought, moreover, by representing the experience as itself visually representing a red physical object, makes one conscious of the experience *as* being of the type that qualitatively represents red objects. And being an experience of that type simply is having the relevant mental quality. So, being conscious of oneself as having a sensation of that type is automatically being conscious of oneself as having a sensation with the quality of mental red, and thus of the mental quality itself. One can be noninferentially, and therefore directly, conscious of the qualitative character of experiences themselves.

Introspection is the awareness of one's own mental states in a way that is deliberate, attentive, and reflective. When one consciously sees a red tomato, one is conscious of the tomato. And, since the experience involved in perceiving the tomato is a conscious experience, one is conscious also of that experience, though in a casual, fleeting, and inattentive way that normally escapes one's notice. It is ordinarily the tomato, not the experience, that could come to attract one's attention.

But one's attention can shift away from the tomato and onto the experience itself. Suppose, for whatever reason, that one concentrates not on the tomato but on one's

---

[23] I have developed this account of the qualitative properties of sensations in "The Independence of Consciousness and Sensory Quality," ch. 5 in this volume; "The Colors and Shapes of Visual Experiences," in *Consciousness and Intentionality: Models and Modalities of Attribution*, ed. Denis Fisette, Dordrecht: Kluwer Academic Publishers, 1999, pp. 95–118; and "Sensory Quality and the Relocation Story," ch. 6 in this volume. See also Wilfrid Sellars, *Science, Perception and Reality*, London: Routledge & Kegan Paul, 1963, chs. 2, 3, and 5.

experiencing of it and, in particular, on the sensory aspect of one's experiencing. Then one will be attentively, deliberately, and reflectively conscious of the qualitative character of one's experience in virtue of which one is experiencing the tomato. One thereby introspects one's experience of a tomato.

Shifts of attention are often a matter of what one looks at. That model of attention might suggest that, if one shifts one's attention from the tomato to introspecting one's experience of it, that shift must be a matter of casting one's gaze inside, as though looking at the sensation rather than the tomato. But shifts of attention are not always strictly perceptual; they are often due to higher cortical processes, including shifts of what one's thoughts concentrate on, rather than what one perceptually focuses on. This is what happens when one shifts one's attention from the tomato to introspecting one's experience of it. One comes to introspect the experience by having a thought about it that occupies center stage in one's attention. One comes to be conscious of oneself as consciously focusing one's attention on the experience itself, and not the tomato.

This focusing on a mental state in virtue of which one perceives something, as against the thing one perceives, is the relatively unusual occurrence Husserl described as the bracketing of conscious states from the objects they represent.[24] Such bracketing of the mental state from what it represents consists simply in one's focusing on it as such, thereby diverting attention from the object represented. One is still conscious in introspecting of both the mental state and the represented object, just as one is conscious of both when one consciously sees a tomato in the ordinary, unreflective way. Consciously seeing means having a conscious experience, and that means being conscious of the experience. But in ordinary, unreflective cases the experience one is conscious of attracts no attention, and one does not notice at all that one is conscious of it.

The difference between one's consciously seeing a tomato in that ordinary, unreflective way and one's introspecting one's sensation of the tomato is a matter of what one concentrates one's attention on. And that, in turn, is a matter of what thoughts dominate one's attention. No introspection occurs if one's dominant conscious thoughts are about the tomato. But if, instead, they are about one's having a particular type of visual experience, one is introspectively conscious of that experience.

When one shifts one's attention from the tomato to one's visual experience of it, it does not seem, subjectively, that some new quality arises in one's stream of consciousness. This may well seem to underwrite Harman's insistence that the only quality one is aware of in either case is that of the tomato. But that is too quick. As noted earlier, we can be conscious of a particular thing in various ways. When one sees a red tomato consciously but unreflectively, one conceptualizes the quality one is aware of as a property of the tomato. So that is how one is conscious of that quality. One thinks of the quality differently when one's attention has shifted from the tomato to one's

[24] Edmund Husserl, *Ideas Pertaining to a Pure Phenomenology and to a Phenomenological Philosophy*, I, tr. Ted E. Klein and William E. Pohl, The Hague and Boston: Martinus Nijhoff, 1980 (original published in 1913), book I, §2.

experience of it. One then reconceptualizes the quality one is aware of as a property of the experience; one then becomes conscious of that quality as the qualitative aspect of an experience, in virtue of which that experience represents a red tomato. Whether one is conscious of the quality one is aware of as a physical property or as a mental property of an experience depends on how one's dominant conscious thoughts represent that quality.

When we consciously but nonintrospectively see a tomato, we conceptualize the quality we are aware of as a property of the tomato itself. Does that mean that we project onto the tomato a property of the qualitative state, a property which the tomato does not actually have? The projectivist view about color, recently defended by Paul A. Boghossian and J. David Velleman, among others, claims exactly that. According to them, "the intentional content of visual experience represents external objects as possessing colour qualities that belong, in fact, only to regions of the visual field." Such projectivism holds that the content of our visual experiences is systematically in error with respect to the properties it attributes to perceived physical objects.[25]

But conceptualizing the qualities we are aware of in visual experience as belonging to perceived objects involves no such projection. Nor is there any systematic error in thinking of those qualities as properties of perceived objects, though there is, as already noted, a systematic ambiguity we must watch for in the way we use color words. We use our color vocabulary to attribute physical properties to the objects we perceive, properties which those objects have in themselves independently of whether anybody perceives them. But we also use those very same color words to describe the visual experiences we have of those objects. Since color words ascribe two distinct types of property, one to perceived objects and the other to our visual experiences of them, there is no occasion to project the mental properties of visual experiences onto perceived physical objects.

We attribute the qualities we are aware of in nonintrospectively conscious experience to the physical objects we experience. So whether we project mental qualities onto physical objects will depend on just what qualities we are aware of when we see something consciously, but without introspecting the experience. It may be tempting to hold that the qualities we are aware of in such cases are the properties of the experiences themselves, since the qualities, as we experience them, occur only in perceiving. Indeed, we are perceptually aware of the independently occurring color properties of perceived objects only by way of the mental qualities of our experiences, in virtue of which the colors of perceived objects appear to us. The properties we perceive physical

[25] Paul A. Boghossian and J. David Velleman, "Colour as a Secondary Quality," *Mind*, XCVIII, 389 (January 1989): 81–103, p. 95; reprinted in Alex Byrne and David Hilbert, eds., *Readings on Color, volume 1: The Philosophy of Color*, Cambridge, Massachusetts: MIT/Bradford, 1997, pp. 81–103. They continue: "The most plausible hypothesis about what somebody means when he calls something red, in an everyday context, is that he is reporting what his eyes tell him. And according to our account, what his eyes tell him is that the thing has a particular visual quality, a quality that does not actually inhere in external objects but is a quality of his visual field" (100). Boghossian and Velleman claim Galileo, Locke, Newton, and Hume as early exponents of such projectivism about color (pp. 96–97, and esp. nn. 15 and 16).

I am grateful to Christopher S. Hill for raising the issue about projectivism.

objects to have present themselves to experience by way of the mental qualities of those experiences.

But in nonintrospectively conscious experience, our conscious thoughts are not about those mental qualities, but about the properties we take the perceived objects to have, independently of whether anybody experiences those properties and, if so, in what way. And our conscious thoughts are about those independently occurring physical properties not *as* they appear to us, but *as* they occur independently of any perceptual process. So the properties we consciously attribute to perceived objects in these cases are not the mental appearances of physical properties, but the physical properties themselves, as they occur independently of being perceived.

Only when we introspect our experiences do we have conscious thoughts about the mental qualities that are the appearances of the independently occurring physical properties. But in those cases we attribute the mental qualities we have conscious thoughts about to our qualitative experiences, not to the objects we perceive. The idea that we project mental qualities onto perceived physical objects derives from conflating introspectively conscious experience, in which we attribute mental qualities, with nonintrospectively conscious cases, which are about perceived physical objects.

So, when we consciously but nonintrospectively see a red tomato and conceptualize the red quality we are aware of as a property of the tomato, we attribute to the tomato the quality *as it is independent of perception, not as we experience it*. Even if we are unclear about just what redness consists in independent of its being perceived, our visual experience attributes to the tomato only the independently occurring property, not the property as it appears in experience. There is no projection onto the tomato of the way that property appears to us. And, since we attribute to those objects only the properties themselves, not the face they present to perceptual experience, there is no systematic error in our interpreting the qualities we are aware of in experience as belonging to the objects we perceive.[26]

When an experience is introspectively conscious, we have conscious thoughts about the experience itself. So we then conceptualize the quality we are aware of as a property of the experience itself. Even so, we still describe that quality in terms of what the experience represents. When we describe an experience as being red, we are describing it as being an experience of the sort that represents red physical objects. But as noted earlier, experiences represent things in virtue of the mental qualities they have;

---

[26] Pre-Galilean common sense acknowledges the distinction between perceptible properties as they are in themselves and as they appear to us. Thus, Aristotle distinguishes the potentiality of physical colors and other so-called proper sensibles, which is independent of their being perceived, from the way those perceptible properties are actualized in perception (e.g., *De Anima*, III, 2, 425b26–426a1). So the post-Galilean temptation to deny color to physical objects does not result from any prior failure to countenance that difference. Rather, that temptation is due to another, independent Aristotelian claim, that the color properties actualized in physical objects are the very same properties as color qualities actualized in the soul (ibid.). And the post-Galilean insistence that physical reality is mathematically describable precludes those properties being the same. But the need to deny color properties to physical objects is removed once we recognize that the perceptible colors of physical objects are distinct kinds of property from the mental colors of visual experiences.

For more on these issues, see "Sensory Quality and the Relocation Story."

only thus could they represent things in the distinctively qualitative way that differs from just having a nonperceptual thought. So being aware of an experience as being the type that represents red objects is being aware of it as having the relevant mental quality. So, even when we are aware of these properties in representational terms, we are aware of them as mental qualities.

One might suppose that the property we are directly aware of is the red of the physical object, whereas we are only indirectly aware of the corresponding mental quality, since we conceive of that mental quality by reference to the perceptible physical property. Every mental quality is of a particular mental type in virtue of its resembling and differing from other qualities of that sensory modality in ways that parallel the ways the corresponding perceptible property resembles and differs from others in its perceptible family. So being aware of a mental quality as being of some particular qualitative type is being aware of it in respect of those similarities and differences. But the directness that matters for being introspectively aware of mental states and their properties is subjective; it is just that nothing consciously mediates between our awareness and the quality we are aware of. And one need not be aware of any particular instance of a perceptible physical property to be aware of a mental quality in respect of such similarities and differences.

Whether one simply sees a tomato consciously or introspects one's experience of the tomato is a function of how one's dominant conscious thoughts represent the situation. Similar remarks apply to the introspecting of our intentional states. Suppose I am consciously thinking about a particular situation or a decision I made or the solution to a problem. If my conscious thoughts are just about the situation, decision, or solution, no introspecting occurs. I take no conscious note of the thoughts I have, only what those thoughts are about.

But if, for whatever reason, I shift my attention and come consciously to think about the thoughts I have about the situation, decision, or solution, I become introspectively aware of those thoughts. I may think about those thoughts for any number of reasons, perhaps because something about the thoughts surprises me, because they seem unclear, or because I come to wonder why I have those particular thoughts. I do not stop having the thoughts about the situation, decision, or solution; it is just that those thoughts no longer dominate my conscious thinking, but have become the subject matter of my dominant conscious thoughts. By consciously and deliberately focusing on those thoughts, rather than on what they are about, I come to be introspectively conscious of them. Introspection is not a special faculty, whose access to our mental states resembles our perceptual access to the objects around us. Rather, it is our thinking about our own mental states in a reflective, deliberate, and attentive manner.

VI. INTROSPECTION AS SELF-INTERPRETATION

Whenever one is conscious of something, one is conscious of that thing in some respect. This is so whether one is conscious of something perceptually or by having a thought about it as being present. One never perceives or thinks about anything in respect of every aspect of the thing.

This applies to being introspectively conscious of one's mental states. A mental state's being conscious, whether introspectively or not, consists in one's being conscious of that state. So the respects in which one is conscious of it will determine how the state presents itself to consciousness. The state will be conscious in these respects and not in others.

Suppose I consciously see a red physical object. I may be conscious of the exact shade of red. But I may instead be conscious of the object simply as being of some indiscriminate shade of red. The object itself has, of course, some exact shade of red, but the way I am conscious of the object may or may not reflect that exact shade. I may be conscious of the object *as* having that exact shade or *just as* an object with some indiscriminate shade of red.

Similarly with the way we are conscious of our conscious states. I may be conscious of an experience of red in respect of its exact shade, but I may be conscious of it only as being of some indiscriminate shade. Whichever way I am conscious of the experience, that is what it's like for me to have that experience. How I am conscious of a sensory experience determines what it's like for me to be in it. And, even when I am conscious of the experience only as being of some indiscriminate shade, the experience itself, moreover, independently of my being conscious of it, has a mental quality with some exact shade. In most cases and perhaps in all, my attentively focusing on the experience would suffice to make me conscious of that exact shade, just as with the colors of physical objects.[27]

The way we are conscious of mental states and their properties in respect of different properties figured in the argument of section V. When one consciously sees a red tomato, one's experience has a red qualitative aspect. But how one is conscious of that qualitative aspect depends on whether one is introspectively conscious of the experience. In the ordinary, unreflective case, one is aware of the experience only *as* representing the tomato; one's dominant conscious thoughts represent the quality *as* a property of the tomato. But when, instead, one is introspectively conscious of the experience, one is conscious of the situation in respect of the properties of that experience. So one's dominant conscious thoughts represent the very same qualitative aspect *as* a property of the experience itself.

All this accords with the HOT model of both introspective and nonintrospective consciousness. The difference between consciously seeing a red tomato in the ordinary, unreflective way and being introspectively aware of the experience is a matter of what HOTs occur in the two cases. When one consciously but unreflectively sees the tomato, one has a HOT about one's experience, but that HOT is not attentive or deliberate. Indeed, that HOT is not even conscious; one's having it wholly escapes one's notice, making one's awareness of the experience inattentive, casual, and fleeting. When one introspects the experience, on the other hand, the HOT one has about that experience is both conscious and attentive. HOTs allow a straightforward and economical explanation of the difference between the two situations.

---

[27] This is not just a matter of focusing attentively on the exact shade of a physical object's color; focusing attentively on hallucinatory sensory experiences is also enough to reveal the exact shade of the mental quality.

I argued in section II that even if we construe introspection as a kind of monitoring of our conscious states, we need not adopt a perceptual model of how such monitoring occurs. It might instead be that introspection is the having of conscious HOTs. If these conscious HOTs were caused by target states by way of some suitable mental mechanism, they would be reliable indicators of the presence of those states. The resulting introspective awareness would be a kind of monitoring of those targets.

Some reliable causal mechanism is required for introspective awareness to constitute a kind of monitoring, whether that awareness is a matter of some process that resembles perceiving or a matter of having HOTs. It could be, as Lycan urges, that the "awareness is a product of attention mechanisms,"[28] though the mechanisms could also be of some other sort. But whatever the case about that, introspective awareness is a kind of monitoring only if some mechanism normally leads from introspected states to introspective awareness.

Doubtless introspected states are sometimes causally implicated in our introspective awareness of them. But it is likely that introspective awareness sometimes arises uncaused by any target state and, more important, that no causal mechanism normally plays a role in leading from target state to one's introspective awareness of it. This is best seen by noting a way in which introspective awareness is often in error. In well-known work on confabulatory introspective awareness, subjects report being in intentional states that there is convincing evidence do not even occur. Typically they report beliefs and desires that would make *ex post facto* sense of their behavior, often in ways that enable them to appear, both to themselves and to others, in some favorable light. Subjects literally confabulate stories not only about the causes of their being in particular intentional states, but actually about what intentional states they are in.[29]

The subjects in these cases seem to invent states to be conscious of themselves as being in, states that fit with a particular picture they have either of their motivations and character or of some take on their social environment. It is not surprising that people sometimes invent stories about themselves in this way. What is striking is that subjects in these cases take themselves to be reporting on beliefs and desires to which they have direct, unmediated introspective access. The process of introspecting delivers erroneous results that conform to the way subjects want to see themselves.

It is difficult to see such confabulation as due to some failure of a monitoring mechanism. It is hard to believe that mishaps in such a mechanism lead to subjects' being introspectively aware of themselves as having just those beliefs and desires which accord with the way they wish to see themselves. Far more likely, this confabulation of wished-for beliefs and desires is on a par with ordinary cases of

[28] *Consciousness and Experience*, p. 30.
[29] The classic study is Richard E. Nisbett and Timothy DeCamp Wilson, "Telling More than We Can Know: Verbal Reports on Mental Processes," *Psychological Review*, LXXXIV, 3 (May 1977): 231–259. Many studies have followed; see, e.g., Peter A. White, "Knowing More than We Can Tell: 'Introspective Access' and Causal Report Accuracy 10 Years Later," *British Journal of Psychology*, 79, 1 (February 1988): 13–45; and Timothy D. Wilson, Sara D. Hodges, and Suzanne J. LaFleur, "Effects of Introspecting about Reasons: Inferring Attitudes from Accessible Thoughts," *Journal of Personality and Social Psychology*, 69 (1995): 16–28.

self-deception. People interpret themselves in ways that fit with how they want to see themselves and the situations they are in; they become convinced of things about themselves that we have independent reason to doubt or disbelieve.

Such confabulation differs from ordinary self-deception because it results in introspective awareness. Subjects take themselves to be focusing consciously on the contents of their mental lives, and they take these introspective efforts to result in their being conscious of the confabulated states. The HOT model again allows a reasonable and economical explanation. Ordinary self-deception consists of having thoughts that result from one's desire to see things in a certain light. Confabulatory introspective awareness is just a special case of that. It is the case in which one has conscious self-deceptive thoughts about one's own mental states, thoughts whose inferential and motivational antecedents are not themselves conscious. One consciously interprets oneself as being in particular mental states and, because one is unaware of any inference or motivation leading to that self-interpretation, one is introspectively aware of oneself as being in those states.

Erroneous introspective reports are the handle we have on what underlies such introspective awareness, since self-deceptive self-interpretation sometimes leads us to be introspectively aware of ourselves as being in mental states we are not actually in. But many largely accurate cases of introspective awareness doubtless also result from such self-interpretation. People interpret themselves in the light of their situation and past experience, and some of these self-interpretations have to do with what mental states they are in. As long as one remains unaware of whatever inference and motivation leads to these self-interpretations about one's mental states, the self-interpretations will seem, from a first-person point of view, to be spontaneous and unmediated. They will seem to arise from just asking oneself what mental states one is in, from a deliberate decision to focus on the states in question by casting one's mental eye inward. But it is likely that such introspective awareness results in substantial measure from desires to see ourselves in a certain light. Introspection is often, if not always, a process of conscious self-interpretation.

Much interpretation of ourselves occurs without being at all conscious. What is special to introspective self-interpretation is that it is conscious and it pertains to one's own conscious states. Interpreting things in a particular way, whether consciously or not, typically results in those things' seeming to one to be that way. Similarly with self-interpretation in respect of one's own mental states. If one interprets oneself as believing something or wanting a particular thing, typically that is how one seems to oneself to be. Introspective self-interpretation is the conscious case, in which one's interpretation results in one's consciously seeing oneself as being in particular conscious states.

Erroneous introspective self-interpretation occurs not only in introspecting intentional states, but qualitative states as well. Being introspectively aware of an experience of red as simply being of some indiscriminate shade is a case in point. Since there is every reason to suppose that the mental quality of the experience is of some determinate shade, our introspective awareness of the experience is in that respect erroneous. Our relative lack of attention to the state leads us to interpret ourselves as being in a state whose very nature is indeterminate.

A more dramatic case of mistaken introspective self-interpretation of qualitative states sometimes occurs in dental treatment. Patients occasionally seem, from a first-person point of view, to feel pain, although the relevant nerves are dead, missing, or anesthetized. The best explanation is that the patients are conscious of their sensations of vibration and fear *as* being sensations of pain. The apprehensive expectation of pain influences how these patients are conscious of sensations that would in ordinary circumstance be clear and unmistakable. Once this explanation is given and drilling resumes, patients are conscious of the sensations as being sensations of vibration and fear. Still, their memory of what it had been like for them to have the earlier experience remains unchanged, confirming that what it's like for one to be in a qualitative state is a function of how one's introspective self-interpretation represents the qualitative character of that state.[30]

Consider again the qualitative aspect I am conscious of when I see a red tomato. When I consciously but unreflectively see the tomato, my HOT is not conscious. So the only conscious thought I have relevant to my seeing the tomato is my thought about the tomato itself, which represents it as being red. My only relevant conscious thought interprets the quality I am conscious of as a perceptible physical property of the tomato. By contrast, when I introspect my experience of the tomato, my HOT about that experience is conscious, resulting in an additional conscious thought relevant to my experience of the tomato. And that conscious HOT construes the qualitative aspect of my stream of consciousness not as a property of the tomato, but as a mental property of my sensation. The qualitative aspect I had previously interpreted as a physical property of the tomato I now consciously reinterpret as a mental quality.

VII. PERSONHOOD AND THE UNITY OF CONSCIOUSNESS

Mental functioning is a necessary condition, but plainly not sufficient, for a creature to be a person. Many animals that fall short of being persons nonetheless function mentally, sometimes in fairly elaborate ways. Nor is being in mental states that are conscious by itself sufficient to be a person; it is likely that creatures such as higher mammals are in many conscious states without being persons. Human beings are

---

[30] There are two places at which error might enter erroneous introspective awareness. It might be that one's initial HOT is mistaken about what mental state one is in or that one's introspective third-order thought is mistaken about what state one is conscious of oneself as being in. In the second case, one would have an accurate second-order thought but an erroneous third-order thought.

Perhaps confabulatory error can enter at the higher, introspective level. But it is not easy to see a reason to think that it happens there, as opposed to at the level of ordinary, unreflective consciousness. Nor it is easy to see how that question could be decisively settled short of isolating the different thought events neuroscientifically.

Eric Schwitzgebel has argued (personal communication) that the third-order level is more likely, but his argument seems to rest on his assumption that mental states, though not automatically subjects of introspective consciousness, are invariably conscious. See also Eric Schwitzgebel and Michael S. Gordon, "How Well Do We Know Our Own Conscious Experience?: The Case of Human Echolocation," *Philosophical Topics*, 28, 2 (Fall 2000): 235–246.

the only terrestrial animals we know of that qualify as persons, but being a person is plainly not the same as being human. It is likely that creatures exist elsewhere that we would not hesitate to count as persons, and certainly such creatures could exist.

What, then, distinguishes persons from other creatures with conscious mental states? One central condition is the capacity not just to be in mental states that are conscious, but to be introspectively conscious of some of those states. Doubtless there is also an ethical dimension to our pretheoretic notion of what it is for a creature to be a person; perhaps, for example, one must be able to assume responsibility or see oneself and others in an ethical light. But whatever the case about that, part of what it is to be a person is having the kind of reflective consciousness that gives one a sense of oneself as a being with a reasonably coherent, unified mental life. Seeing one's mental life as coherent and unified is a crucial necessary condition for a creature to be a person.

A creature can have a greater or lesser capacity for introspective awareness and can vary in the degree to which that capacity results in its seeing itself as having a unified, coherent mental life. Indeed, it is unlikely that there is a single measure of coherence and unity of a mental life, so that a creature's sense of such unity and coherence might well be greater in one respect and less in another. It would be arbitrary to set any particular level or kind of introspective coherence as necessary for a creature to qualify as a person. So introspective unity and coherence, like any other mark of what it is to be a person, admits of degrees. The possibility of a creature's being a person to a greater or lesser extent conforms to our pretheoretic thinking about being a person. Though we count all human beings as persons, it is likely that distant ancestors of ours were persons to some degree, though not as fully as we are, and doubtless the same is true of other, nonterrestrial creatures as well.

Several factors result in the sense we have of our mental lives as unified. One kind of unity occurs independently of any introspective consciousness and contributes little if anything to our sense of mental unity. As already noted,[31] our HOTs operate on many of our mental states not singly, but in large bunches. A vivid example of this occurs in the cocktail-party effect, in which one becomes suddenly conscious of hearing one's name in a conversation that one had until then consciously heard only as part of a background din. One must have been hearing the articulated words of the relevant conversation, though not consciously, since one's attention was drawn to the use of one's name. Indeed, one's name's occurring in any number of other conversations would have exactly the same effect, even though one was also conscious of those conversations only as part of the background noise. So one must have been hearing articulated words in all those conversations, though not consciously. Though what it's like for one is just the hearing of a background din, one must nonconsciously be hearing very many individual words.

Once again, the HOT model offers an economical and credible explanation. One's HOTs group many auditory sensations together, making them conscious only as an unarticulated bunch. The same doubtless happens with many visual sensations that

---

[31] In connection with Carruthers's dispositional version of the HOT hypothesis, n. 10.

lie outside the area of foveation; one sees things in large bunches, though an item of special attention can visually jump out at one. Similarly as well as with the other sensory modalities. Doubtless such grouping of perceptual sensations occurs in many creatures other than humans, and occurs independently of any introspective awareness. Perhaps it contributes slightly to a creature's sense of mental unity, since it may produce the impression of being able to focus instantly anywhere in a unified field of sensory experiences. But it is unlikely that this kind of unity contributes anything to what it is for a creature to be a person, since such grouping of sensory experiences is gained at the expense of a drastic loss of conscious information.

There is another way in which we are conscious of our conscious states in bunches which does produce some sense of unity and coherence among those states. When qualitative states are conscious, we are typically conscious of those states not just individually, but in respect of their spatial relations to other states of the same sensory modality. The resulting unity of our sensory fields does not depend on introspective consciousness, nor is it special to persons; many creatures that are not persons have such unity.[32]

There is, however, yet another way in which we are conscious of our conscious states in groups, and this not only results in a distinctive sense of unity among those states, but seems also to rely on our introspective awareness of those states. When we consciously reason, we are often conscious of one intentional state as leading to another. This is not just a matter of our being conscious of the various intentional states themselves; we are, in addition, conscious that these conscious intentional states exhibit a certain connectedness in our thinking. This sense of unity and coherence in one's reasoning is part of what it is to be a person. One could imagine this sense of unity occurring without introspective awareness; perhaps one could be conscious of one's intentional states as inferentially connected simply by having a single HOT about them all. But it is overwhelmingly likely that the awareness of such connections arises often, perhaps always, as a result of our being reflectively conscious of intentional states that are already individually conscious on their own.

Another factor that induces a sense of mental unity that is relevant to being a person is even more closely tied to introspective consciousness. Every HOT represents one as being in some particular mental state, since each is a thought to the effect that one is, oneself, in that target state. So each HOT makes us conscious of its target as belonging to a self. Our HOTs do not involve any particular conception of the self to which they assign their targets. Indeed, the self that one is noninferentially conscious of mental states as belonging to is no more than a raw bearer of such states; one is not

---

[32] Note that no sense of the unity or coherence of consciousness will result simply from one's qualitative states' standing in some spatial relations to one another. Such a sense arises only if one is conscious of those states as standing in those relations. Indeed, their actually standing in such relations is not even necessary for such a sense; all that matters is that they are conscious *as* standing in those relations. See "Unity of Consciousness and the Self," ch. 13 in this volume.

For problems about the way we are conscious of qualitative states as spatially unified within sensory fields, see my "Color, Mental Location, and the Visual Field," *Consciousness and Cognition*, 9, 4 (April 2000): 85–93, §IV, and "Sensory Qualities, Consciousness, and Perception," ch. 7 in this volume, §§IV and VII.

conscious of that self in any other way. And because one is not conscious of that bearer in respect of any other properties, one has a sense that all mental states of which one is noninferentially conscious belong to the same bearer. Since there is nothing that distinguishes the bearer to which one HOT assigns its target from the bearers to which others assign theirs, the HOTs seem to assign their targets all to the same self.

As long as one's HOTs are not themselves conscious thoughts, one is not conscious of their seeming all to assign their targets to a single self. But, when one comes to be introspectively conscious of one's mental states, one thereby becomes conscious of those HOTs, and therefore conscious of those HOTs' seeming to assign their targets all to the same subject. Introspective consciousness leads to our being aware of the way our conscious states are represented as belonging to a single self.[33]

It may well be that the self we become conscious of our mental states as belonging to is merely notional; perhaps there is nothing that all one's conscious states belong to other than the entire organism. But that does not matter for present purposes. Being a person is, at least in part, a matter of being conscious of oneself *as* having a reasonably unified, coherent mental life. And introspective consciousness results in a sense of one's conscious states *as* all belonging to a single subject. Every HOT, even when not itself conscious, represents its target as belonging to a bearer indistinguishable from those to which other HOTs assign their targets. And introspective consciousness makes us aware of this feature of the way our HOTs represent their targets. HOTs in effect interpret the states they are about as all belonging to a single self whether or not any such self exists.[34]

Introspective awareness interacts with speech in a way that seems to underwrite the traditional idea of mental states as transparent to the self. Being able to express one's introspective consciousness in speech amounts to being able to report the mental states one introspects. If, for example, one is introspectively aware of thinking that p, one can say that one thinks that p.

Saying that one thinks that p is plainly not semantically the same as simply saying that p, since the two speech acts differ markedly in truth conditions. Still, the two types of speech act have roughly the same conditions of use, or performance conditions. So there is a tendency to regard the two speech acts as being in some way equivalent. This tendency has dramatic consequences.

Every speech act expresses an intentional state that has the same content and a mental attitude that corresponds to the illocutionary force of the speech act. So, if one regards saying that one thinks that p as equivalent to saying that p, one will extrapolate

---

[33] It is worth noting that Hume's famous problem about the self resulted from his tacit adoption of a specifically perceptual model of introspecting; one cannot find a self when one seeks it perceptually. See David Hume, *A Treatise of Human Nature*, ed. L. A. Selby-Bigge, Oxford: Clarendon Press, 1888, I, IV, vi, 252.

[34] I discuss these issues about personhood and the unity of consciousness at greater length in "Persons, Minds, and Consciousness," in *The Philosophy of Marjorie Grene*, in *The Library of Living Philosophers*, ed. Randall E. Auxier and Lewis E. Hahn, La Salle, Illinois: Open Court, 2002, pp. 199–220, in "Unity of Consciousness and the Self," ch. 13 in this volume, and in "Subjective Character and Reflexive Content," Book Symposium on John Perry's *Knowledge, Possibility, and Consciousness*, *Philosophy and Phenomenological Research*, 68, 1 (January 2004): 191–198.

to the corresponding thoughts; one will also regard the thought that p as equivalent to the thought that one thinks that p. But that would mean that the thought that p would not only have its ordinary content, but would also be literally about itself; the thought would thus constitute an awareness of itself. Seeing the speech acts of saying that p and saying that one thinks that p as equivalent gives rise to the traditional idea that intentional states are all transparent to the mind.

The temptation to assimilate the two types of speech act arises only when a creature has the ability to express its introspective consciousness in speech. Only then can one report one's intentional states noninferentially, and thereby treat the two speech acts as having roughly the same use. But, despite that rough performance-conditional equivalence, the two speech acts do differ semantically. The illusion of Cartesian transparency that comes with the ability to express one's introspective consciousness in speech results from failing to note that there is more to the role speech acts play than their conditions of use.[35]

---

[35] For more on the implications for consciousness of the distinction between these two types of speech act, see "Thinking that One Thinks" and "Why Are Verbally Expressed Thoughts Conscious?", chs. 2 and 10 in this volume.

PART II

QUALITATIVE CONSCIOUSNESS AND HOMOMORPHISM THEORY

5

The Independence of Consciousness and Sensory Quality

It is often held that all sensory mental states are conscious states, and that sensory quality cannot occur in states that are not conscious. Indeed, it may seem mysterious what it could be for a state to have sensory quality if that state is not a conscious state. Consciousness, on this view, is something like a mental light, without which sensory qualities simply cannot exist. When it comes to the qualities of our sensory states, to be is to be conscious, *esse* is *percipi*.

If sensory states are all conscious, it may seem likely that the property of being conscious will be intrinsic, and essential, to having sensory quality; how better to explain why sensory states are all conscious than by assuming that being conscious is intrinsic to having sensory quality? On this picture, we can understand what it is for a state to have sensory quality only if we know what it is for that state to be conscious. And, if states with sensory quality are essentially conscious states, understanding what it is for sensory states to be conscious will presumably require knowing what sensory quality is.

Seeing the properties of being conscious and having sensory quality as thus wedded makes for unnecessary mysteries. What kind of property could it be that cannot occur except consciously? And what kind of property could the property of being conscious be if it is intrinsic to sensory qualities? Indeed, it is arguable that all the traditional problems about sensory or phenomenal quality derive from the idea that being a conscious state is intrinsic to having sensory quality. What seems difficult or intractable about sensory quality is the face it presents to consciousness—what the sensation is like for somebody who has it.

I shall argue that this picture is mistaken. The properties of being conscious and having sensory quality are independent of one another, and a satisfactory account of each property requires us to investigate them separately. In section I, I argue that, since sensory states are not all conscious states, being a conscious state cannot be intrinsic to that state's having sensory quality. Section II, then, puts forth a sketch of an account of what it is for a mental state to have sensory quality, an account on which having sensory quality does not imply being conscious. Moreover, as I show in section III, this account helps explain, and thereby disarm, the intuitive force of the idea that being conscious is an intrinsic property of sensory states. In section IV I conclude by arguing for a positive account of what it is for sensory states—and, indeed, for all mental states—to be conscious. On this account, a state's being conscious is its being accompanied by a roughly simultaneous higher-order thought that one is in the target mental state. So being conscious is an extrinsic property of those mental states which are conscious. If this account is correct, and if sensory states can occur without being conscious, we can conclude that the properties of being conscious and having sensory quality are independent of one another.

I. ARE ALL SENSORY STATES CONSCIOUS?

Descartes notoriously held that "no thought can exist in us of which we are not conscious at the very moment it exists in us."[1] It is often assumed that this Cartesian doctrine reflects our commonsense concept of mind, for sensory states as well as for thoughts. That is not so; commonsense plainly does allow room for mental states that are not conscious states. We sometimes see that somebody wants something or thinks that something is so while that person is wholly unaware of that desire or thought. Similarly with emotions; we occasionally recognize that we are sad or angry only after somebody else points it out to us. It is natural to interpret subliminal perception and peripheral vision as showing that perceptual sensations can occur without our being aware of them.[2] It is arguable that even bodily sensations such as pains can at times go wholly unnoticed, and so can exist without being conscious. When one is intermittently distracted from a headache or pain, it is natural to speak of having had a single, persistent pain or ache during the entire period. It would be odd to say that one had had a sequence of brief, distinct, but qualitatively identical pains or aches. Similarly for itches and other bodily sensations.

Pragmatic factors explain much of the intuitive pull towards thinking that sensory states are always conscious states. For one thing, our concern with the mental states of others is set in a social context that largely precludes remarking on mental states of which they are unaware. So in ordinary circumstances we tend not to pay explicit attention to such states. And of course we normally disregard whatever nonconscious sensory states we ourselves may be in.

Moreover, the intuitive idea that mental states are invariably conscious is far stronger with some types of mental state than it is with others. And it turns out that the stronger this intuition is with a particular kind of mental state, the less interest we would have in nonconscious cases of that type of mental state. The idea that mental states must be conscious is strongest with bodily sensations such as pains and tickles, less compelling with perceptual sensations, presumably still less so with emotions, and very likely weakest with intentional states such as thoughts and desires. Correspondingly, we have the least interest in nonconscious bodily

---

[1] *Fourth Replies, Oeuvres de Descartes*, ed. Charles Adam and Paul Tannery, Paris: J. Vrin, 1964–75, VII, 246. Also: "the word 'thought' applies to all that exists in us in such a way that we are immediately conscious of it" (Geometrical Exposition of the *Second Replies*, VII, 160). Descartes's reference to thoughts was meant to cover all mental states, of whatever kind.

[2] We all typically screen out the sounds of conversations other than our own. But, on the so-called cocktail-party effect, if one's name is mentioned in a screened-out conversation, one's attention often shifts immediately to that conversation. It is natural to interpret this as showing that one must have had some auditory consciousness of what was being said.

sensations, whether our own or anybody else's, and far the most in nonconscious beliefs and desires, because of their role in explaining behavior. This reinforces the diagnosis that we think mental states must be conscious largely because of our lack of interest in the nonconscious cases.

Still, these considerations may not seem sufficient to disarm completely the intuition that sensory states must be conscious. This is especially so in the case of bodily sensations such as pain. For one thing, we speak roughly interchangeably of our feeling a pain or tickle or itch and of our having the relevant sensation. And when we feel a pain or tickle or itch, must not that sensation be automatically conscious?

Such terms as 'feeling' do carry this implication of consciousness; a felt pain is perforce a conscious pain. This is true as well of something's hurting, and perhaps even of one's being in pain. But none of these things are the same as one's simply having a pain, or a pain's existing. If we are intermittently unaware of a pain by being distracted from it, we feel the pain only intermittently; similarly with its hurting and our being in pain. Still, one may well speak of having had a pain that lasted throughout the day. And if the question arises in a natural way, one may even say explicitly that one was not always aware of that pain. Common sense thus undeniably countenances the existence of nonconscious pains.[3]

We cannot of course know what it is like to have a nonconscious pain or tickle or itch.[4] But that is not relevant here. The reason we cannot know what it is like to have, for example, a nonconscious pain is simply that unless the pain is conscious there is no such thing as what it is like to have it. What it is like to have a pain, in the relevant sense of that idiom, is simply what it is like to be conscious of having that pain. So our not knowing what it is like to have pains that are not conscious cannot show that all pains are.

Nonetheless, reflection on what it is like to have sensations does suggest an important source for the view that sensations are invariably conscious. When we classify sensory states and discriminate among their various tokens, we appeal to what it is like for us to be in those states. This is equally so with bodily and perceptual sensations; we rely on such things as what it is like to be in pain, and what it is like to see red or hear a trumpet. And there is no such thing as what it is like to have these sensations unless the sensation is conscious.

If we do pick out sensory states by appeal to what it is like to be in those states, how can there be sensory states for which there is no such thing as what it is like to be in them? If the properties by reference to which we taxonomize and individuate sensory states occur only when those states are conscious, how can those states ever be nonconscious?

---

[3] One could insist here that only a single, temporally discontinuous state of pain occurs, on the model of the temporally discontinuous bursts of sound as a single siren sound. (I owe this idea to Jaegwon Kim.) But all I am arguing here is that common sense be open to nonconscious pains; plainly common sense does not insist on the discontinuous-pain interpretation.

[4] See Thomas Nagel's important article, "What Is It Like to Be a Bat?", *The Philosophical Review*, LXXXIII, 4 (October 1974): 435–450. See also Nagel's "Panpsychism," in *Mortal Questions*, Cambridge: Cambridge University Press, 1979, pp. 181–195, and *The View From Nowhere*, New York: Oxford University Press, 1986, chs. 1–4.

Care is necessary here. We do classify and discriminate among sensory states by appeal to the conscious cases. But this does not show that the properties by reference to which we classify sensory states cannot occur nonconsciously. Compare the situation in perception. We pick out physical objects, and thus classify and discriminate among them, by reference to how they appear to us. And there is no such thing as how a physical object appears to us if nobody perceives it. In the case of vision, for example, there is no such thing as the visual appearance of a physical object if nobody sees that object. Nonetheless, physical objects do have enduring properties in virtue of which they look to us as they do. One can say that the contribution physical objects make to how they look to us is their having certain colors or, more precisely, their having characteristic reflectance spectra. Physical objects have these properties whether or not anybody sees them.

Parallel remarks hold for sensory states. We classify such states by reference to what it is like to be in those states. What it is like to have a certain sensation is how that sensation appears to us. So, as with physical objects, we pick out sensory states and discriminate among them on the basis of how they appear to us. And the foregoing considerations give us no reason to insist that those states which appear to us as they do cannot occur except when they are conscious states.[5] We fix the extensions of terms for physical objects by relying on appearances that may or may not reflect the actual nature of those objects. Similarly, we fix the extensions of our terms for the various kinds of sensory state by way of the conscious cases, both our own and those of others, but this in no way shows that all sensory states are conscious states.[6]

Sensory qualities, on anybody's account, are properties that distinguish sensory states, both from one another and from everything else. All and only sensory states have sensory quality, and the various types of sensory state differ in respect of their sensory qualities. So if sensory states occur that are not conscious, being conscious cannot be intrinsic to having sensory quality.

---

[5] Just as we can say of unseen objects how they would look, we can equally well say what it would be like to be in sensory states that are not currently conscious.

[6] On the notion of fixing extensions, see Saul A. Kripke, *Naming and Necessity,* Cambridge, Massachusetts: Harvard University Press, 1980, pp. 54–59; "Identity and Necessity," in *Identity and Individuation,* ed. Milton K. Munitz, New York: New York University Press, 1971, pp. 135–164, at pp. 156–161; and Hilary Putnam "The Meaning of 'Meaning'," in Putnam's *Philosophical Papers,* vol. 2, Cambridge: Cambridge University Press, 1975, pp. 215–271, at pp. 223–235. Both Kripke and Putnam maintain that, in general, what fixes the extension of a term need not coincide with what is essential or necessary to the things in that extension.

Kripke's notorious denial of this for the case of mental states ("Identity and Necessity," pp. 157–161; *Naming and Necessity,* pp. 149–154) stems from his insistence that the way pains appear to us cannot diverge from how they really are: "For a sensation to be *felt* as pain is for it to *be* pain" ("Identity and Necessity," p. 163 n. 18; emphasis original throughout) and, conversely, that "for [something] to exist without being *felt as pain* is for it to exist without there *being any* pain" (*Naming and Necessity,* p. 151). Thus "[i]f any phenomenon is picked out in exactly the same way that we pick out pain, then that phenomenon *is* pain" (ibid. p. 153). But Kripke's contentions are correct only if it is necessary that pains affect us in the way they do, i.e., only if being conscious is intrinsic to something's being a pain. Kripke gives no independent argument for these claims.

It is crucial to avoid a merely verbal issue. Some find it tempting to hold that the term 'sensory quality' can apply only to those qualities by reference to which we say what it is like to have one or another conscious sensation. If so, nonconscious states plainly cannot have sensory quality. Similarly, sensory states might be held to be definitionally conscious states.

These convictions in no way suggest, however, that nonconscious states do not exist corresponding to sensory states. Indeed, it is natural to suppose that such non-conscious states do exist, since neural detection mechanisms must subserve conscious sensation, whatever the nature of sensation may be. Moreover, for neural states to subserve sensory states, it must be possible to taxonomize these nonconscious states so that they resemble and differ from one another in ways isomorphic to the similarities and differences among conscious sensations. Call these nonconscious states s-states, and call the properties of belonging to the equivalence classes defined by this taxonomy s-properties. What reason could there be, then, other than arbitrary verbal fiat, to withhold the terms 'sensation' and 'sensory state' from these nonconscious s-states? And what nonverbal reason could there be for refusing to apply the term 'sensory quality' to nonconscious s-properties?

Common sense often sees the important properties of things as being intrinsic to them. This tendency is especially pronounced when we know little or nothing about the nature of those properties. Thus common sense finds congenial the pre-Galilean view according to which bodies move toward a natural resting place, and having a particular natural resting place is an intrinsic property of each kind of body. It is inviting to see bodies as intrinsically tending toward upwards or downwards movement.[7] Still, we get far more accurate and powerful explanations of bodily motions if we see a body's tendency to move in terms of its relations to other bodies. Similarly, it is pretheoretically appealing to see the property of being conscious as intrinsic to sensations. But as I shall argue in section IV, it is likely that we can explain what being a conscious state consists in only if we regard being conscious as a relational property.

II. WHAT IS SENSORY QUALITY?

The foregoing considerations will, however, remain inconclusive without at least the sketch of a suitable positive account of what it is for mental states to have sensory quality. It must be possible, on such an account, for mental states to have sensory qualities whether or not those states are conscious states. Sensory qualities will occur even when sensory states are not conscious. But when states with sensory qualities are conscious, there will be something it is like to be in those states, and sensory qualities will be the properties in virtue of which that is so.

The distinctive qualities by means of which we classify sensations form families of properties that pertain to color, visual shape, sound, and so forth. The members

---

[7] Similarly, Michael McCloskey has elegantly and convincingly argued that ordinary commonsense predictions about bodily motions systematically err in ways that reveal the tacit false assumption that those motions are due to an internal force imparted by the source of motion. ("Intuitive Physics," *Scientific American*, 248, 4 [April 1983]: 114–122.)

of these families resemble and differ from one another in ways that parallel the similarities and differences among the corresponding perceptible properties of physical objects. For example, the red sensory quality of visual sensations resembles the orange sensory quality of such sensations more than either resembles the sensory green or blue of such sensations. This is so whatever else is true about such sensory qualities. A host of other relations characterize both physical color properties and the corresponding mental color properties. There is no reason to think that individual color properties of visual sensations resemble intrinsically the color properties of physical objects. Rather, it is the whole family of mental color properties that corresponds, by virtue of the relations that hold among its members, to the family of physical color properties. And it is in terms of these relations of resemblance and difference within the corresponding families that we understand the nature of both mental and physical colors.

Parallel remarks apply to the spatial properties that pertain to vision. Here it is plain that the spatial properties of physical objects have nothing intrinsic in common with the corresponding properties of visual sensations. The property of being physically round, for example, does not resemble the corresponding property of visual sensations. Still, because color cannot occur without shape, visual sensations cannot have mental colors unless they have some property that counts as the mental counterpart of physical shape.[8] Just as with mental and physical color, mental roundness and triangularity resemble and differ from each other in ways homomorphic to the similarities and differences that hold between physical roundness and triangularity. Similar observations hold for other properties of shape[9] and other sensory modalities.[10]

Such parallels hold also in the case of bodily sensations. Consider pains. The distinctive qualities of being dull, stabbing, burning, or sharp resemble and differ in ways

---

[8] And, since mental shape is plainly a different sort of property from physical shape, the connection between color and shape shows that mental color is a different sort of property from physical color.

[9] These mental analogues of physical spatial properties may well enable us to assign mental location to our visual impressions, in virtue of which they unite to form a single visual field.

[10] Various historical antecedents for these observations are available. Berkeley held that at least some terms for sensible qualities fail to apply to things univocally. Thus 'plane' and 'solid' apply primarily, on his view, to the immediate objects of touch, and only derivatively to the objects of sight. Berkeley sometimes seems to claim that such terms are radically ambiguous, as when he writes that the visual and tactile objects to which we apply these terms are "of a nature intirly different." But he also insists that planes and solids are both "equally suggested by the immediate objects of sight, [and] accordingly are themselves denominated plains and solids" (*A New Theory of Vision*, §158, in *The Works of George Berkeley*, ed. A. A. Luce and T. E. Jessop, London: Thomas Nelson & Sons, 1948, vol. I).

In *Essays on the Intellectual Powers of Man* (ed. Baruch A. Brody, Cambridge, Massachusetts: MIT Press, 1969, II, xvi) Thomas Reid claims that, when I smell a rose, "the sensation I feel, and the quality in the rose which I perceive, are both called by the same name . . . so that this name has two meanings" (243). "All the names we have for smells, tastes, sounds, and for the various degrees of heat and cold, have a like ambiguity . . . They signify both a sensation, and a quality [in physical objects] perceived by means of that sensation" (244).

And in "A Reply to My Critics," G. E. Moore insists that all words for sensible qualities are "each used in two very different senses" to refer to perceptible properties of physical objects and to the qualities of sensory experiences (*The Philosophy of G. E. Moore*, ed. Paul Arthur Schilpp, La Salle, Illinois: Open Court, 1942, pp. 535–677, at p. 657; see pp. 655–658).

that reflect the similarities and differences among the corresponding physical objects and processes. Moreover, piercing and stabbing pains are both species of sharp pains, and typically result from piercing and stabbing objects or processes. Similarly, throbbing and pounding pains are species of dull pains.[11]

It is important to emphasize that the parallels to which I am drawing attention involve the perceptible properties of physical objects, as these are conceived by common sense. We must take care not to import into our commonsense notion of these physical properties aspects that have only to do with how those properties appear to us. But subject to that qualification, the present theory takes commonsense perceptible properties at face value. This is natural; the properties in terms of which we classify sensory states are themselves commonsense properties, and are part of our macroscopic way of cutting up reality.

Moreover, such reliance on commonsense properties is legitimate in the present context, since we can hope to reconstruct these commonsense properties tolerably well in terms of scientific properties and processes. Thus we can capture the commonsense colors of physical objects in terms of the spectral reflectance of those objects multiplied by the absorption spectra of the three light-sensitive elements in the daylight visual system. An object's looking green, for example, will consist in its reflecting a distribution of wavelengths that results in a specifiable ratio of activation among those three types of cones. So an object's being green would consist in its reflecting such a distribution of wavelengths under standard conditions—say, in cloudless, midday sunlight.[12] We must still adjust for variations due to individual differences and conditions of solar illumination. But such idealizations are common in the scientific reconstruction of commonsense, macroscopic categories.

Does this mean that we can simply dispense with our commonsense conception of physical color when it comes to comparing those properties with the mental properties of visual states? Those comparisons rely on similarities and differences in the two families of properties; mental color properties resemble and differ from one another in ways homomorphic to the similarities and differences among physical color properties. Some of these parallels between the two families can be expressed in terms of ratios, rather than physical color conceived in commonsense terms. For example, when a first color is intuitively closer to a second than to a third, the corresponding ratio will very likely exhibit parallel relations.

But it may well be that important relations among members of the commonsense color family cannot be captured in terms of how close one is to another. Perhaps

---

[11] For more detail on this kind of account, see my "Armstrong's Causal Theory of Mind," in *Profiles: David Armstrong*, ed. Radu J. Bogdan, Dordrecht: D. Reidel Publishing Co., 1984, pp. 79–120, §V, at pp. 100–108; my review of *Perception: A Representative Theory* by Frank Jackson, *The Journal of Philosophy*, LXXXII, 1 (January 1985): 28–41; and "The Colors and Shapes of Visual Experiences," in *Consciousness and Intentionality: Models and Modalities of Attribution*, ed. Denis Fisette, Dordrecht: Kluwer Academic Publishers, 1999, pp. 95–118, esp. §II.

[12] Because many different combinations of wavelengths can produce the same ratio, the specific reflective properties of objects that produce a particular ratio in particular conditions of illumination may vary widely. So objects that look the same in respect of color when illuminated by daytime sunlight, e.g., may well seem to differ in color in other conditions of illumination.

a scientific taxonomy of these properties will not sustain all the relevant parallels between those properties and the corresponding mental qualities. If so, we may to this extent have to retain our commonsense conception of physical color. This is not a problem, however, for the present account. We still can hope to identify each such color that we can discriminate mathematically, in terms of the relevant ratio of activation among the three cone types. So there will be a scientific reconstruction that legitimates the normal range of commonsense physical color properties.

These observations form the basis of a sketch of what it is to have sensory quality. Sensory qualities are properties of states of organisms, families of which bear certain systematic relations to families of properties of physical objects and processes to which the organism can respond. Moreover, they are properties of which we can be conscious, in the intuitively immediate way in which we are conscious of our own mental states. Nothing in this account implies that sensory qualities can occur only when the relevant sensory states are conscious states. Moreover, since consciousness does not figure in the account, being conscious is presumably not intrinsic to a state's having sensory quality.

The overall thesis I am defending is that the properties of being conscious and having sensory quality are independent of each other. That thesis is independent of the particular account of sensory qualities I have just sketched. Any account will do on which sensory qualities are whatever properties are distinctive of the various types of sensation, properties of which we can, but need not, be conscious in a suitably immediate way.

A question arises, however, about accounts that meet this condition. Can such an account do justice to the traditional notion of sensory quality, and the traditional problems attendant on that notion? Or have we simply changed the subject, by substituting a watered-down, unproblematic notion of sensory quality for the traditional concept, and thus defined the problems away?

One way to approach this question is to ask whether such an account would square with the idea that the properties under consideration are genuinely qualitative. Being qualitative is not a very clear notion, but presumably a property's being qualitative means in part that the property is essentially the way consciousness reveals it to be. In any case, there is another example of a family of properties that common sense regards as qualitative, namely, the color properties of physical objects. Here, too, being qualitative expresses the idea that the properties in question are exactly as consciousness—in this case perceptual consciousness—reveals them to be.

Many have held that, whatever the appearances, we need not attribute genuinely qualitative colors to physical objects. We can, after all, relocate the apparent qualitative character of physical color inside, in the mind: We can say that the relevant properties of physical objects are not genuinely qualitative, but that they lead to visual sensations, whose distinctive properties are.

It is often pointed out that we cannot repeat this move; there is no place to relocate the qualitative character that the distinctive properties of sensory states seem to exhibit. But that does not matter. We need not find some way to preserve the idea that color is qualitative. We are willing to deny qualitative color to physical objects because we accept that their qualitative character, however we interpret it, is merely apparent.

It is a verdict of commonsense intuition on which we should not rely. We can say the same for the commonsense intuition that the distinctive properties of sensory states are qualitative. The inability to relocate the qualitative character of the mental properties of sensory states gives us no reason to insist that those mental properties really do have qualitative character. We need not preserve the "element of truth" in erroneous commonsense intuitions when we become convinced that these intuitions reflect only how things appear, rather than how they really are.

In any case, common sense tells us little if anything about the sensory qualities of sensory states, except that they are those properties in virtue of which we distinguish among those sensations, and that we can be more or less immediately conscious of them. Our knowing about these properties in the first instance by way of the conscious cases does not show that they cannot occur nonconsciously, nor that there is anything problematic about them. Common sense does not sustain the idea that sensory quality is problematic.

Nor is there reason to hold that the similarities and differences on which that account relies cannot obtain except when the sensation in question is conscious. We can accurately and fully capture these similarities and differences on the basis of the relevant homomorphisms, independently of whether the sensory states in question are conscious. So we have no basis for denying that sensory qualities can occur nonconsciously. Nonconscious sensory states resemble and differ in just the ways that conscious sensory states do. They diverge only in that one group is conscious and the other not.

III. WHY IT SEEMS THAT SENSORY QUALITIES MUST BE CONSCIOUS

It may be difficult to dismiss the idea that sensory properties are qualitative unless we can explain the attraction that idea has for us. Being qualitative, as just noted, expresses the idea that a property is essentially the way consciousness reveals it to be. And that suggests in turn that sensory qualities are invariably conscious. Why, after all, would consciousness reveal the essence of sensory states if such states need not be conscious?

Consciousness seems to reveal the essence of sensory qualities only because it is tempting to suppose that consciousness is our only source of knowledge about the nature of those properties. Take color. It is often held that the term 'red' applies in the first instance to a mental property of visual sensations and derivatively, if at all, to a perceptible property of physical objects.[13] We understand what it is for a tomato to be red solely by way of the tomato's having causal connections with red sensory states. Since our saying a tomato is red is then only a kind of shorthand for its having a certain tie to the mental red of sensory states, we cannot learn about that mental

[13] John Locke, *Essay Concerning Human Understanding*, III, iv, 16; Roderick M. Chisholm, *Perceiving: A Philosophical Study*, Ithaca, New York: Cornell University Press, 1957, ch. 4; Frank Jackson, *Perception: A Representative Theory*, Cambridge: Cambridge University Press, 1977, esp. ch. 6.

red from its connections to anything nonmental. We can learn about mental color only by distinctively mental means. The only available mental avenue to these properties is knowing what it is like to be in the relevant sensory states, and this depends on the relevant states' being conscious. This line of reasoning suggests that consciousness alone can reveal the nature of mental qualities, so that only conscious states can have these qualities.

The sketch of an account put forth in section II undermines this picture. On that account, the sensory qualities of sensations resemble and differ from one another in ways that parallel the similarities and differences that hold among the corresponding perceptible properties of physical objects. So knowing what it is like to be in a sensory state is not the only way to understand the nature and character of sensory qualities. We can, instead, learn about them by way of their characteristic similarities and differences, which are homomorphic to those which hold among the corresponding perceptible properties of physical objects. In particular, we can in this way know such things as that mental red resembles mental orange more than either resembles mental green or blue. Similarly for qualities special to other perceptual modalities, and to bodily sensations.

The resulting understanding of mental qualities is not restricted to the relational properties of those qualities. The similarities and differences that hold among the qualities of a particular sensory modality help characterize that modality. And within each modality, the similarity and difference relations characteristic of each mental quality help fix what is distinctive of that quality. These relations thus help us grasp the nature of the various individual qualities. Knowing the relations that define the various mental color properties, for example, will help fix what it is for a sensory state to be mentally red. Although these relations cannot tell us what it is like to experience a sensory quality, they can tell us much about what it is for a state to have such qualities.[†]

IV. EXPLAINING CONSCIOUSNESS

It might be thought that, if being conscious is intrinsic to a state's having sensory quality, at least that helps us understand what it is for sensory states to be conscious.

In fact the opposite is the case. If being conscious were an intrinsic property of sensory states, it is unlikely that we could get any informative explanation of what their being conscious consists in. No useful explanation will be possible unless we can represent the property of being conscious as having some articulated structure. But it will be hard to justify the idea that being conscious is an intrinsic property of conscious states if that property does have some informative structure. Once we assign some such structure to the property of being conscious, it will be at least as plausible to regard being conscious as an extrinsic property of mental states. So the only non-question-begging reason to see consciousness as an intrinsic property of mental states

---

[†] Since this was written, I have come to see that, because we are conscious of mental qualities in respect of these relations, they do tell us what it's like for one to experience specific qualities. See ch. 7, p. 203 and § V, *passim*. [Added in 2005.]

would be that it lacks such structure, and is thus simple and unanalyzable. And something's being simple effectively precludes our explaining it by appeal to anything else; simple properties are those we take to be primitive in our hierarchies of explanation.[14]

In any case, an account is possible of what it is for a sensory state to be conscious on which being conscious and having sensory quality are independent properties. The account applies equally well to all mental states, whether intentional or sensory, but I shall concentrate here on the sensory case.

If a state is conscious, we are conscious of being in that state. The converse also holds, at least if we are conscious of being in the mental state in a suitably unmediated way. Ruling out reliance on inference and observation will capture that intuitive immediacy.[15] So it is reasonable to hold that for a mental state to be conscious is for one to be conscious in a suitably immediate way of being in that state.

There are two ways we can be conscious of things: By perceiving them and by having thoughts about them. The perceptual model of being conscious of something cannot help here. Perceiving involves characteristic sensory qualities. So on a perceptual model, a state's being conscious will involve some characteristic quality; otherwise the comparison with perception would be idle. Since sensory states need not be conscious, their sensory qualities are independent of their being conscious. So the characteristic quality that, on the perceptual model, being conscious introduces must be distinct from the sensory qualities that sensations already have. But then it is a mystery what those new qualities could be.[16]

The only alternative is that a mental state's being conscious consists in one's having a thought that one is in that very mental state, a thought based on neither observation nor inference. (Henceforth I omit this qualification.) On this theory, the relevant higher-order thought will not itself be a conscious thought unless we have a yet higher-order thought. This explains why we are generally unaware of such higher-order thoughts. It also allows a ready distinction between a mental state's being introspectively and nonintrospectively conscious. Mental states are introspectively conscious if the relevant higher-order thought is itself a conscious thought.[17]

---

[14] Franz Brentano's idea that a mental state's being conscious is due to its being in part about itself is a rare attempt to assign informative structure to being conscious, conceived of as an intrinsic property. (*Psychology from an Empirical Standpoint*, tr. Antos C. Rancurello, D. B. Terrell, and Linda L. McAlister, London: Routledge & Kegan Paul, 1973, pp. 129–30.) But he gives no reason for his insistence that this awareness of conscious mental states is intrinsic to those states; and if it is not, the resulting theory is virtually indistinguishable from that for which I argue below. Other more decisive difficulties for Brentano's view are noted in my "A Theory of Consciousness," in *The Nature of Consciousness: Philosophical Debates*, ed. Ned Block, Owen Flanagan, and Güven Güzeldere, Cambridge, Massachusetts: MIT Press, 1997, pp. 729–753, at the outset of §VII. See also "Thinking that One Thinks," ch. 2 in this volume, §V.

[15] We need not rule out inference and observation of which we are unaware. This exception is not circular, since I explain a mental state's being conscious by reference to an independent notion of being conscious of something.

[16] These concerns are reminiscent of Aristotle's question about whether or not the sense we use to see that we see is the same as the sense of sight (*de Anima*, III 2, 425b13–14).

[17] Being conscious of something may appear to be factive. Since perceiving, unlike thinking, is arguably factive, perhaps the perceptual model is, after all, superior. But if the relevant consciousness

The relevant higher-order thoughts must be assertoric, since intentional states with other mental attitudes can occur without our being conscious of anything.[18] Nor does having a disposition to have a thought normally result in one's being conscious of anything. So it is probable that only occurrent intentional states with assertoric force will do.[19]

Relatively weak conceptual resources will suffice for a higher-order thought to refer to one's own sensory states. We refer in thought to physical objects by way of their position in our visual field. It is natural to suppose that thoughts can similarly refer to sensory states by way of their position in the relevant sensory field. Something of this sort presumably explains how higher-order thoughts can be about sensory states even though conscious differentiation of sensory detail quickly outstrips our conceptual resources.

Elsewhere I have argued that a theory based on higher-order thoughts can save the phenomenological appearances at least as well as one can with the Cartesian idea that being conscious is intrinsic to mental states generally, and to sensory states in particular.[20] In closing I shall indicate two ways this is so in the case of sensory states.

Some phenomenological data pertaining to sensory states are very likely harder to explain if we assume that being conscious is intrinsic to sensory states. There are sensory states that are conscious only some of the time, largely through shifts in attention, for example, pains from which we are temporarily distracted or auditory sensations that we screen out. The idea that being conscious is intrinsic to sensory quality in effect rules out such shifts between a state's being conscious and its not being conscious, presumably requiring some reinterpretation of the data; we might say, for

---

really is factive, we can stipulate that our higher-order thoughts are as well. Moreover, there is reason to doubt that the way we actually are conscious of our conscious mental states guarantees truth; special views about privileged access notwithstanding, we can and do make mistakes about what conscious states we are in [though not on that account about what states we are conscious of ourselves as being in—added 2005].

[18] If I doubt or wonder whether some physical object is red, I am conscious of the object; similarly if I expect, hope, or desire that it is. So perhaps if one doubts or wonders whether a mental state has some particular property, or hopes, desires, or expects that it does, one will thereby be conscious of the mental state. But it is not the doubt, wonder, hope, or desire that makes us conscious of the object. If I doubt whether that object is red, or desire or suspect that it is, I must at least think assertorically that the object is there. Similarly with doubting, hoping or expecting that my mental state has some property; I must at least have the assertoric thought that I am in that state. Having these nonassertoric attitudes will not make one conscious of being in that state except by leading to one's having an affirmative thought that one is in that state.

[19] A particular property may be described in both dispositional and nondispositional terms. Relative to the categories of folk psychology, we need nondispositional states to make mental states conscious; but at a subpersonal level we might describe those states in dispositional terms. I am grateful to Daniel Dennett for arguing the virtues of a dispositional treatment, and for much useful conversation on these topics in general.

[20] "A Theory of Consciousness"; "Two Concepts of Consciousness," ch. 1 in this volume; "Thinking that One Thinks," ch. 2 in this volume; and "Why Are Verbally Expressed Thoughts Conscious?", ch. 10 in this volume.

example, that such sensations do not literally persist. But it is probable that such gerrymandering will make a satisfactory explanation harder to come by.[21]

Other data seem even less amenable to reinterpretation on which being conscious is an intrinsic property of conscious states. We are often aware of more fine-grained differences among sensory qualities when we have more fine-grained conceptual distinctions at our disposal. Vivid examples come from wine tasting and musical experience, where conceptual sophistication seems actually to generate experiences with more finely differentiated sensory qualities. The present theory predicts this. The degree to which we are conscious of differences among sensory qualities depends on how fine grained the concepts are that figure in our higher-order thoughts. The relevant sensory states may well have been conscious before one acquired the more fine-grained concepts, but conscious only in virtue of less subtle qualities. It is unlikely that we can explain these observations except by a theory that appeals to higher-order thoughts.

On the present theory, consciousness is not only not essential to mentality; it is an esoteric development of mental capacities. Still, the intuition may persist that consciousness is somehow central to the way we think about the mind. Can we do justice to that intuition, if not by saving it at least by explaining why we have it?

As noted earlier, one way that consciousness is central to our concept of mind is that we fix the extensions of our terms for mental states, and indeed of the term 'mental' itself, by way of the conscious cases of mental states. But consciousness figures in an even more important way. Though it does not demarcate the distinctively mental, it is arguable that it provides the basis for our intuitive mark of being a person. We are the only creatures we know of that we regard as persons, but we can easily imagine discovering others that we would classify with ourselves in that way. It is not, of course, that only persons have conscious mental states; many nonhuman animals presumably do, as well. There is no reason to deny to animals without language the capacity to have suitable higher-order thoughts. The relevant higher-order thoughts do not require much richness of conceptual resources or syntactic structure.[22]

---

[21] Another example relies on a surprising fact about vision. Our visual field seems replete with visual detail throughout. This is because eye movements provide foveal vision over a wide area, and we retain the visual information thus gained. Nonetheless, at any given moment we are aware of little visual detail outside the center of our visual field. It is natural to speculate that our seeming to see much of this detail may in effect be due to our confabulating detailed visual sensations. Such confabulation would be far harder to understand if being conscious were intrinsic to sensory states.

[22] Moreover, as Daniel C. Dennett has noted, the behavior of nonlinguistic animals sometimes indicates the presence of higher-order thoughts. ("Conditions of Personhood," in *The Identities of Persons*, ed. Amélie Oksenberg Rorty, Berkeley and Los Angeles: University of California Press, 1976, pp. 175–196, at pp. 183–4.) Dennett's cases involve one animal's having a thought about another animal's thought, which in turn is about some distinct thought of the first animal. Direct evidence that an animal without language has a thought about another of its own thoughts, however, may seem difficult to come by. For methodological ideas about this kind of problem, see Lawrence Weiskrantz, "Some Contributions of Neurophysiology of Vision and Memory to the Problem of Consciousness," in *Consciousness in Contemporary Science*, ed. A. J. Marcel and E. Bisiach, Oxford: Oxford University Press, 1988, pp. 183–199, at pp. 194–197.

But we have no reason to suppose that animals other than persons are aware of whatever higher-order thoughts they may have. And if none of an animal's higher-order thoughts are conscious, it will lack the particular kind of reflective consciousness that involves some measure of rational connectedness in the way it is aware of its mental states. Being a person will, on this account, be a matter of degree, but that is as it should be. Our distant ancestors doubtless had the distinctive characteristics of people to some degree, though not as fully as we do, and the same may well be true of other creatures elsewhere.[23] Though consciousness is not essential to mentality, it is very likely crucial in this way to our concept of being a person.

The foregoing considerations suggest that a theory based on higher-order thoughts will very likely be able to save the phenomenological appearances pertaining to sensory quality. Moreover, on that account, a state's being conscious is an extrinsic property of that state. Our having good reason to explain a mental state's being conscious by appeal to accompanying higher-order thoughts thus helps sustain the view that a state's being conscious and its having sensory quality are independent properties.[24]

[23] It is worth comparing the present account of being a person to that put forth by Harry G. Frankfurt ("Freedom of the Will and the Concept of a Person," *The Journal of Philosophy*, LXVIII, 1 [January 14, 1971]: 5–20). Frankfurt holds that what distinguishes persons is their ability to have higher-order desires that some particular one of their first-order desires be effective in leading to action (pp. 6–7, 11–12). He argues that forming such higher-order desires involves identifying oneself with one, rather than another, of one's first-order desires (13). Roughly, such identification is, he maintains, what is involved in the process of deciding (16), and being able to identify oneself with one's desires in this way is also what is distinctive of being a person (16). But forming decisions is not the only way one identifies oneself in mental terms. Being a person is, rather, the more general ability to be conscious of one's thoughts that one is in a particular mental state. Consciously thinking that one is in a particular mental state is consciously identifying oneself as that being which has that mental state.

[24] I am grateful, for helpful conversation about a related paper, to the participants of the August 1989 Joint Conference of the Sociedad Filosófica Ibero-Americana and the Sociedad Argentina de Análisis Filosófico, in Buenos Aires.

This paper was written while I was a fellow in 1989–90 at the Center for Interdisciplinary Research (ZiF), University of Bielefeld, Germany. I am indebted to the Center for generous support and exceptionally congenial and stimulating surroundings during that time. I am also indebted to Peter Bieri, Daniel C. Dennett, A. H. C. van der Heijden, Jaegwon Kim, Anthony J. Marcel, Jay Rosenberg, and Lawrence Weiskrantz for helpful reactions.

6

Sensory Quality and the Relocation Story

I. FUNCTIONALISM AND QUALITATIVE STATES

More than any other aspect of mental functioning, the qualitative dimension of mind has stubbornly and persistently resisted informative explanation. Not only is there little convergence about what would count as a good theoretical approach; many believe that no satisfactory theoretical treatment of sensory states and their qualitative properties is possible at all. This emerges especially vividly in connection with functionalist theories of mind. Whatever merits functionalism may have in dealing with intentionality, qualitative mental phenomena seem to many to pose insurmountable difficulties for functionalist theories.

Perhaps the most compelling of these apparent difficulties is the claim, compellingly advanced by Ned Block and Jerry A. Fodor,[1] that functionalist accounts inevitably leave open the possibilities of so-called inverted and absent qualia. On this challenge, no functionalist specification of a creature's mental life can ensure that its sensory states exhibit any particular qualitative properties as opposed to others, nor even that it has qualia at all.[2] If so, functionalism fails as an account of the qualitative dimension of mind.

In an important series of articles, Sydney Shoemaker has explored with great subtlety and in impressive depth and detail whether functionalism can meet this pair of challenges.[3] Shoemaker argues that things are not uniform; we get different results for each of the two challenges. Functionalism cannot, he concedes, preclude quality inversion, but a suitable functionalist description can ensure that the creature described does have qualia. Shoemaker concludes that, because functionalism can dispel the difficulty about absent qualia, it can account for "what it is for mental states to have qualitative character." And, although the possibility of qualia inversion remains, a functionalist account can also explain "what it is for mental states to be in greater or lesser degree similar in qualitative character" (*FPP* 121).

---

[1] "What Psychological States Are Not," *The Philosophical Review*, LXXXI, 2 (April 1972): 159–181; reprinted with revisions in Ned Block, ed., *Readings in Philosophy of Psychology*, I, Cambridge, Massachusetts: Harvard University Press, 1980, pp. 237–250. See also Ned Block, "Are Absent Qualia Impossible?", *Philosophical Review*, LXXXIX, 2 (April 1980): 257–274, and "Inverted Earth," *Philosophical Perspectives*, IV (1990): 53–79.

[2] I include as qualitative states and sensations all states with the relevant qualitative properties, whether or not they are caused distally by external objects.

[3] "Functionalism and Qualia," *Philosophical Studies*, XXVII, 5 (May 1975): 292–315, reprinted, slightly revised, in *Readings in the Philosophy of Psychology*, I, ed. Ned Block, Cambridge,

These apparent difficulties for functionalism outstrip in intuitive force any that arise in connection with intentional states. Behavior, both verbal and nonverbal, reflects and manifests our beliefs, desires, and other intentional states, enabling a functionalist account to get considerable purchase on what it is to be in one or another type of intentional state. By contrast, what qualitative states one is in and, indeed, whether one is in any at all seem, intuitively, to be entirely independent of behavior and even stimuli.

Shoemaker's treatment of the argument from absent qualia capitalizes on connections qualitative states have with intentional states, which, he argues, make possible a functionalist specification of sufficient conditions for qualitative states to occur. These arguments are, I believe, wholly convincing, though many have remained unpersuaded. More important, such arguments tend to leave wholly undiminished the intuitive force of the idea that functionalism leaves open the possibilities of absent and inverted qualia. So it is worth asking what it is that makes these apparent possibilities seem so compelling as challenges to functionalism and related theories of mind. Why, argument aside, does it seem to many so obvious that a functionalist specification cannot preclude our mental states' having gerrymandered qualitative properties and even lacking such properties altogether?

The standard answer to this question appeals to the first-person access we have to our own qualitative states. Functionalist descriptions specify sufficient conditions for being in the various types of mental state. So such descriptions trump whatever subjective, first-person impressions we have about what states we are in. A functional description could, of course, advert to whether one believes one is in a particular type of state; but it need not, and other factors will also figure in the sufficient conditions.

This does not cause difficulty for a functionalist account of belief and desire, since we are used to the idea that our first-person access to these states is not the last word, and is sometimes mistaken. But with qualitative states it is tempting to think that one's first-person access to qualitative states overrides any possible functionalist specification for the occurrence of these states. If so, no functionalist connections that qualitative states might have with stimuli, behavior, and other mental states could guarantee the occurrence of those qualitative states. If our first-person access is truly authoritative about when we are in the various types of qualitative state, functionalist

Massachusetts: Harvard University Press, 1980, pp. 251–267, and in Shoemaker, *Identity, Cause, and Mind: Philosophical Essays*, Cambridge and New York: Cambridge University Press, 1984, expanded edition, Oxford: Clarendon Press, 2003 (henceforth *ICM*), pp. 184–205; "Phenomenal Similarity," *Critica*, 7, 20 (October 1975): 3–34, reprinted in *ICM* 159–183; "Absent Qualia are Impossible—A Reply to Block," *The Philosophical Review*, 90, 4 (October 1981): 581–599, reprinted in *ICM* 309–326; "The Inverted Spectrum," *The Journal of Philosophy*, LXXIX, 7 (July 1982): 357–381, reprinted with a postscript in *ICM* 327–357; and "Intrasubjective/Intersubjective," reprinted in Shoemaker, *The First-Person Perspective and Other Essays*, Cambridge and New York: Cambridge University Press, 1996 (henceforth *FPP*), 141–154.

See also "Qualities and Qualia: What's in the Mind?", *Philosophy and Phenomenological Research*, 50, Supplement (Fall 1990): 109–131, reprinted in *FPP* 97–120; and "Qualia and Consciousness," *Mind*, 100, 4 (October 1991): 507–524, reprinted in *FPP* 121–140.

Page references are all to versions reprinted in *ICM* and *FPP*.

ties could hold among stimulations, behavior, and nonqualitative mental states without benefit of qualitative states at all. So our intuitions seem to tell us.

This intuitive difficulty for functionalism is compelling, however, only for states with respect to which our first-person access is fully authoritative. Otherwise, a functionalist account could, after all, be decisive. This has implications about the way we think about qualitative states. We have first-person access only to mental states that are conscious. And, since the intuitive difficulty for functionalism would arise only for states for which our first-person access is authoritative, no intuitive difficulty should arise for functionalism about states that are not conscious in the first place.

This seems to fit well with the intuition that qualitative states resist functionalist treatment, since qualitative states are also often held to be states that cannot occur without being conscious. I shall shortly turn to the question of whether that is so. But suppose, for the moment without argument, that qualitative states can, after all, occur without being conscious. Only the conscious cases of such states could then sustain our strong intuitive sense that no functionalist description can guarantee the occurrence of qualitative states of particular kinds, or even any qualitative states at all. Suppose, for example, that sensations of red and green can occur nonconsciously. There is no compelling intuition that a functionalist specification of such nonconscious states cannot succeed. This does not show, of course, that a functionalist description can preclude the inversion or absence of nonconscious qualitative states, only that we have no intuitively forceful reason to doubt that this is so. Our intuitions are mute about the nonconscious cases.

We sometimes talk about a qualitative state's being conscious in terms of the metaphor of a quality's being lighted up. Put in these terms, the intuition under consideration is that no functionalist description ensures that any qualities will light up, nor if any do that a functionalist description will correctly specify the right ones. But qualitative states do not light up unless they are conscious. And there is little if any intuitive underpinning for the claim that a functionalist description could not guarantee the occurrence of nonconscious states, of whatever sort. After all, it may well be that, for a nonconscious mental state, causal considerations are all that determine whether one is in the state.

It is tempting to insist that, whatever nonconscious qualitative states might be, such states are at best mere shadows of full-bodied, conscious qualitative states. If so, consideration of such nonconscious states would show nothing about the alleged possibilities of absent and inverted qualities.[4] Even if these difficulties do not arise for such ersatz qualitative states, they might for genuinely qualitative states.

We cannot, therefore, assess these objections to functionalism without determining whether qualitative states can occur without being conscious. The occurrence of nonconscious states that are genuinely qualitative diminishes the intuitive force of the idea that functionalist descriptions cannot guarantee the occurrence of qualitative

---

[4] It is likely that the terms 'quale' and 'qualia' are predominantly used in the literature as tacitly presupposing the view that qualitative states are invariably conscious. So it is perhaps more accurate in talking about nonconscious qualitative states to speak of absent and inverted qualities, rather than qualia.

character, or the right qualitative character. We have little if any intuitive grasp of when nonconscious qualitative states would or would not occur, and if functionalism secures the nonconscious cases, why not those which are conscious as well? But, if qualitative states are always conscious, any nonconscious states would be mere simulations of qualitative states, and would leave our intuitions untouched.

If qualitative states were invariably conscious, their being conscious would then presumably be internal, or intrinsic, to their having qualitative character at all; take away the property of their being conscious and you take away whatever qualities they have. But this is not the only model of what it is for qualitative states to be conscious, and it may well not be the right model. It may instead be that a qualitative state's being conscious is a property distinct from and independent of its qualitative character. Conscious qualitative states have two mental properties; they have qualitative properties and, in addition, they have the property of their being conscious. A state could lack the second property, that of being conscious, without lacking qualitative character.

Unless there is some special tie between the property of a state's being conscious and its qualitative character, moreover, our first-person access to what states we are in presumably cannot be authoritative about that qualitative character. So there could be no intuitive basis for trusting our subjective impressions about what qualitative states we are in over the dictates of a well-confirmed functionalist description. And again, the objections from absent and inverted qualities will lose their intuitive power.

Showing that a qualitative state's being conscious is independent of that state's qualitative properties would not suffice to defend functionalism against those objections. But I am less concerned here to assess these objections than to isolate the source of their compelling intuitive character. Why do the intuitions about absent and inverted qualia seem so compelling, even dispositive? Why do those intuitions appear to remain untouched by arguments of Shoemaker and others? Because the answer seems to hinge on our first-person authority about qualitative states, we must determine whether such states can occur without being conscious. Section II addresses that question.

II. MUST QUALITATIVE STATES BE CONSCIOUS?

Qualitative states differ, of course, from intentional states in virtue of their distinctive mental properties. But they differ also in our intuitions about what it is for such states to be conscious. Whereas few would deny the occurrence of nonconscious intentional states, such a denial is common in the case of qualitative states.

One reason for this different attitude about states' being conscious has to do with the interests we have in ascribing the two kinds of states to ourselves and to others, even when those states are not conscious states. Plainly it is often useful to ascribe intentional states, such as beliefs, desires, fears, hopes, expectations, and the like, even when those states are not conscious, since such ascriptions figure in explanations of behavior. Similarly for ascribing emotions, such as joy, fear, or anger, which also exhibit intentional content. By contrast, there may seem to be relatively little reason to ascribe qualitative states that are not conscious, whether to oneself or others. It may seem as though nonconscious perceptual and bodily sensations seldom if ever explain behavior we cannot readily explain in other terms, as least where folk-psychological explanation is concerned.

Beliefs, desires, emotions, and other intentional states figure so centrally in explaining behavior even when they are not conscious that the contrast with qualitative states encourages the conclusion that folk-psychological explanations never appeal to nonconscious versions of these types of state. But the difference is one of degree, not kind. Even apart from clinical and experimental situations, we often have compelling explanatory reason to invoke nonconscious qualitative states.

Aches or pains often last for considerable periods without, however, being strong enough to intrude into consciousness for the entire time they last. It is natural to describe this by saying that the pain or ache is sometimes conscious and sometimes not. One could simply insist that the bodily sensation stops existing whenever we cease to be aware of it. But without some independent reason for thinking that this is what happens, such an insistence begs the question at hand. Nor is it easy to see what an independent reason for that claim could consist in.

Subliminal perception and peripheral vision are also examples of nonconscious qualitative states. In driving my car I may rapidly adjust to avoid a looming truck, which I may be wholly unaware of seeing. I must, however, have seen it nonconsciously, since my adjustment is often quite finely calibrated to just where the truck is. Similarly, one sometimes turns one's head to focus on somebody whose presence in one's field of vision had made it impossible to see the person consciously.[5] In such cases one must first see nonconsciously that the person was known to one, since otherwise one would not turn, and also where that person was, since one typically turns to foveate on just the right place.

Such commonsense examples are hardly decisive. Just as one can insist that pains cease when we are for a while not conscious of them, so one could maintain here that no distinctively mental state is involved. We can try to explain peripheral vision and subliminal perception by appeal not to nonconscious qualitative states but to bodily stimulations instead. But there is no reason to do so except to uphold the view that qualitative states never occur without being conscious, and once again that begs the question at hand.[6]

An objector might insist that we have no idea what kinds of states nonconscious qualitative states could be. We understand qualitative states, it might be held, only in terms of what it's like to be in those states. And if a qualitative state failed to be

---

[5] I refer to the area within which one can see distal stimuli as the field of view, in contrast with the visual field, which is one's array of visual sensations. See Austen Clark's closely related distinctions in "Three Varieties of Visual Field," *Philosophical Psychology*, 9, 4 (December 1996): 477–495 and *A Theory of Sentience*, Oxford: Clarendon Press, 2000, ch. 3, §2.

[6] Explaining these occurrences by physiological processes cannot, moreover, establish by itself that no qualitative state occurs. We would need in addition to show that those physiological processes are not themselves qualitative states. We cannot assume without argument that qualitative states cannot be physiological or the processes invoked are of the wrong kind to be qualitative states.

conscious, there would be nothing at all that it's like to be in it. So the explanatory appeal to alleged nonconscious qualitative states is empty.

But this objection is not correct. When our qualitative states are conscious and there is something it's like to be in them, we have access to specific properties of those states. We tell in that way the difference, for example, between visual sensations of red and green, and locate them within a space of mental color properties. In so doing, we appeal to our sense that the property of mental red that characterizes some visual sensations is, for example, more similar than mental green is to both mental purple and mental orange, and to many other things of that sort.

Taxonomizing visual sensations this way appeals to the way we are conscious of these sensations. But that is no reason to conclude that visual sensations cannot have these very same qualitative properties even without being conscious. We classify sensations in terms of similarities and differences among their qualitative properties. Our setting up a taxonomy by appeal to the cases we are conscious of cannot show that consciousness and sensory quality have any intimate tie. We invariably rely on the cases we are aware of when we classify and describe things.[7]

It is often assumed that pretheoretic intuition shows that qualitative states cannot occur without being conscious. But intuition cannot help here at all. Intuitions about mental functioning are a function of what we are aware of. If qualitative states do occur without being conscious, we will remain unaware of them, at least in any way that is relevant to our pretheoretic intuitions. Intuition would therefore be blind to any nonconscious qualitative states that may occur. Introspection is similarly irrelevant here, since we have introspective access only to those mental states which are conscious. Introspection would never reveal nonconscious qualitative states, whether or not such states actually occur.

Everyday examples of the sort described above help establish the existence of nonconscious qualitative states. But there is a more indirect, theoretical consideration

---

[7] We typically use the same words for color and other qualities to characterize qualitative mental states and to characterize physical objects and processes. But it is important to note that these two uses ascribe distinct properties. We use 'red', 'green', 'round', and 'square' for both visual sensations and the physical objects and processes that typically cause them, just as we use 'sharp' and 'dull' for both pains and the objects that typically cause those pains. It is indisputable that sensations cannot have the same properties of being round and square as physical objects. And, since the shape properties of visual sensations, e.g., are simply boundaries of color properties, the colors of visual sensations also cannot be the same properties as those of physical objects. For more on this, see my "The Colors and Shapes of Visual Experiences," in *Consciousness and Intentionality: Models and Modalities of Attribution*, ed. Denis Fisette, Dordrecht: Kluwer Academic Publishers, 1998, pp. 137–169, and "The Independence of Consciousness and Sensory Quality," ch. 5 in this volume, esp. §III.

Shoemaker claims that "we apply color predicates to physical objects and never to sensations, ideas, experiences, etc." ("Qualities and Qualia: What's in the Mind?," p. 98). But this seems not to be so. We seldom talk about our visual sensations at all, as against the things we see. But we do occasionally describe visual sensations as red or green, especially though not exclusively in cases of illusion or hallucination. Perhaps Shoemaker has in mind that we apply color terms to visual sensations in only an extended sense, and that may well be so. It may be, i.e., that the primary application of color terms is to physical objects and processes, and they apply in an extended way to those sensations which are typically caused by the relevant objects and processes.

that helps, as well. Suppose I am in pain and that pain is conscious, but I am not aware of whether the pain is throbbing or dull or sharp. I am aware of the pain, but not aware of it *as* throbbing or dull or sharp. Because the pain is conscious, there is something it's like to be in it; so there is no question about whether a qualitative state exists. Suppose, now, there is some physiological reason to think that the pain is throbbing, as opposed to dull or sharp. So what it's like to be in this pain actually leaves out one of its qualitative properties: that of being a throbbing pain. Similar things happen all the time with our perceptual sensations; I may have a red sensation without being conscious of my sensation as being of any particular shade of red, even though we have ample indirect reason to hold that the sensation does have some particular shade.[8]

There is no question here about whether the state under consideration is truly qualitative. Nonetheless, we fail to be in any way whatever conscious of some of the qualitative properties we have reason to suppose the state exhibits. So mental qualities can occur nonconsciously, that is, without our being at all conscious of them. And if qualitative states can occur without one's being conscious of all their mental qualities, what reason can there be to deny that such states can occur without our being conscious of any of those qualities?

We can conclude that the property of a qualitative state's being conscious is distinct from and independent of that state's qualitative properties. This has implications about what account we can give of the consciousness of qualitative states. To see this, consider a view recently advanced by Fred Dretske, on which a state's being conscious is a matter of its being a state in virtue of which one is *conscious of* something or other or *conscious that* something is the case.[9] But qualitative states enable us to be conscious of things at least in part because of the particular qualitative properties those states have. When I see a red object in front of me, I am conscious of that object in part because of the qualitative properties of my sensory state. So, if what it meant for that state to be a conscious state were simply that it makes me conscious of the object, the property of that state's being conscious would not, after all, be independent of its qualitative properties.

Dretske maintains that a state's being conscious consists in its making us conscious of something or conscious that something is the case in part because he believes that the alternative is unacceptable. The only reasonable alternative, he correctly sees, is that a mental state's being conscious consists instead in one's being conscious of that state in some suitable way. And he regards that as indefensible, since he believes he has examples of states we are in no way conscious of but which nonetheless are indisputably conscious. But there are difficulties with Dretske's examples. Although we are

---

[8] Note that the qualitative property at issue is the shade of red that characterizes the visual sensation, not the sensed physical object (see n. 7). It is, once again, question begging to deny the force of indirect reasons for holding that a pain is throbbing even though one is not conscious of it as throbbing, or that a visual sensation is of some shade even though one is not conscious of it as having that particular shade.

[9] "Conscious Experience," *Mind*, 102, 406 (April 1993): 263–283, pp. 280–1, and *Naturalizing the Mind*, Cambridge, Massachusetts: MIT Press/Bradford Books, 1995, pp. 100–1 and ch. 4, *passim*.

not conscious of the states he describes in the particular way he specifies, it does not follow that we are not conscious of those states in any relevant way. And it is arguable that we are.

In the kind of case Dretske has in mind, we have conscious visual experiences of two scenes that differ in some single way, but without our noticing consciously that they differ at all. Since we fail to notice that two scenes differ, we cannot notice the difference between our conscious visual experiences of them. We can assume that every experience has parts, and we can regard each part as itself a conscious experience; the aspect of the experiences of the two scenes is just such a part. Dretske concludes that, since we do not consciously notice the difference between the two experiences, we are not conscious of that aspect of the experiences that makes the difference between them. That part of the experiences is a conscious experience of which we are not conscious. But this is too fast. We might be conscious of the parts of the experiences that make the difference between them without thereby being conscious of those aspects *as the aspects that make that difference.* Dretske's argument is a non sequitur.[10]

There is, in any case, reason to reject the idea that a state is conscious if, in virtue of one's being in that state, one is conscious of something or conscious that something is the case. All our thoughts and sensations satisfy this condition; we are conscious of whatever our thoughts are about, and also conscious of everything that we sense. So it follows from Dretske's account that every mental state is conscious; this is widely recognized as implausible for intentional states, and we have seen that it is arguably incorrect for qualitative states as well.

The alternative, as Dretske recognizes, is that a mental state's being conscious consists in one's being conscious of it in some suitable way. Indeed, we never count a mental state conscious if we are in no way conscious of it; being conscious of a mental state is a necessary condition for it to be a conscious state. Such an account, moreover, very likely provides the only way to explain how the property of a state's being conscious can be distinct from and independent of whatever intentional and qualitative properties the state may have.

There are, of course, different ways one can be conscious of mental states. So a principal task of a theory of consciousness is to specify exactly how one must be conscious of a mental state for that state to be conscious. Elsewhere I have argued that, when a mental state is conscious, we are conscious of it by having a suitably noninferential thought about that state, what I have called a *higher-order thought.*[11] We can for now bracket the question of the specific way we are conscious of our conscious

[10] See Dretske, "Conscious Experience," pp. 272–275; cf. *Naturalizing the Mind,* Cambridge: Massachusetts: MIT Press/Bradford Books, 1995, pp. 112–13. I discuss the difficulties with Dretske's argument in detail in "Consciousness and Metacognition," in *Metarepresentation: Proceedings of the Tenth Vancouver Cognitive Science Conference,* ed. Daniel Sperber, New York: Oxford University Press, 2000, pp. 265–295, §III; "Introspection and Self-Interpretation," ch. 4 in this volume; and "Explaining Consciousness," in *Philosophy of Mind: Classical and Contemporary Readings,* ed. David J. Chalmers, New York: Oxford University Press, 2002, pp. 406–421, §I.

[11] "Two Concepts of Consciousness," ch. 1 in this volume; "Thinking that One Thinks," ch. 2 in this volume; "State Consciousness and Transitive Consciousness," *Consciousness and Cognition,* 2, 4 (December 1993): 355–363; "A Theory of Consciousness," in *The Nature of Consciousness:*

sensations, though that issue will turn out to be relevant toward the end of section IV. For present purposes all that matters is that, whatever a qualitative state's being conscious consists in, that property is independent of the state's qualitative properties.

Ned Block has argued for a position that may seem to split the difference between these two views of what it is for a mental state to be conscious. According to Block, there are two distinct things we mean in calling a mental state conscious. We call a state conscious when its content is "poised to be used as a premise in reasoning, ... [and] for [the] *rational* control of action and ... speech."[12] This property Block calls *access consciousness*. But we also call a state conscious when there is something it's like for one to be in that state; Block calls this second property *phenomenal consciousness*. And he maintains that these two properties are, conceptually at least, independent. Moreover, all qualitative states, according to Block, are phenomenally conscious, though some fail to be access conscious.

There are questions that could be raised about whether Block's distinction between access and phenomenal consciousness works in the way he suggests. It is arguable, for example, that the two notions are not independent, even conceptually, and that the two notions are best understood as referring not to two ways mental states can be conscious, but to two kinds of mental states, which are conscious in exactly the same way.[13]

But these questions aside, Block's distinction causes no difficulty for the present argument. The intuitions that absent and inverted qualia are possible derive their force from the idea that our first-person access to qualitative properties is authoritative. But we have first-person access to a state only when, in Block's terminology, that state is access conscious. Moreover, Block agrees with the foregoing argument that states can have qualitative properties even when those states are not access conscious; those are the states Block describes as phenomenally but not access conscious. Because we have no first-person access to these qualitative states—that is, no conscious access,

---

Philosophical Debates, Ned Block, Owen Flanagan, and Güven Güzeldere, Cambridge, Massachusetts: MIT Press, 1997, pp. 729–753; "Consciousness and Metacognition," in *Metarepresentation: Proceedings of the Tenth Vancouver Cognitive Science Conference*, ed. Daniel Sperber, New York: Oxford University Press, 2000, pp. 265–295; "Why Are Verbally Expressed Thoughts Conscious?", ch. 10 in this volume; and "Consciousness and its Expression," ch. 11 in this volume.

[12] "On a Confusion about a Function of Consciousness," *The Behavioral and Brain Sciences*, 18, 2 (June 1995): 227–247, p. 231; emphasis Block's. See also Block, "How Many Concepts of Consciousness?", Author's Response, ibid., 18, 2 (June 1995): 272–287; "Biology versus Computation in the Study of Consciousness" (Author's Response to Continuing Commentary), *The Behavioral and Brain Sciences*, 20, 1 (March 1997): 159–166; "How to Find the Neural Correlate of Consciousness," in *Current Issues in Philosophy of Mind*, Royal Institute of Philosophy Supplement 43, ed. Anthony O'Hear, Cambridge: Cambridge University Press, 1998, pp. 23–34; review of Dennett's *Consciousness Explained, The Journal of Philosophy*, 90, 4 (April 1993): 181–193, p. 184; "Begging the Question against Phenomenal Consciousness," *The Behavioral and Brain Sciences*, 15, 2 (June 1992): 205–6; and "Consciousness and Accessibility," *The Behavioral and Brain Sciences*, 13, 4 (December 1990): 596–8.

[13] See my "Phenomenal Consciousness and What It's Like," *The Behavioral and Brain Sciences*, 20, 1 (March 1997), pp. 64–5, and "The Kinds of Consciousness," MS, delivered at the University of Oxford Autumn School in Cognitive Neuroscience, October 1998.

intuitions about absent and inverted qualities get no purchase with them. Still, those nonconscious states have the same qualitative properties as the conscious cases. And if intuitions about absent and inverted qualities lack force with those states, they will lack force with the conscious cases as well.[14]

III. CONSCIOUS QUALITIES AND THE RELOCATION STORY

Let us take stock of the argument so far. Intuitions about absent and inverted qualia form the basis of a challenge to functionalism and related views. These intuitions derive their force from our first-person access to qualitative states. But qualitative states sometimes occur without being conscious, and there is no intuitive reason to think that functionalism leaves open the possibility of inverted or absent qualities for states that are not conscious. And, if quality inversion or absence are not intuitive worries for the nonconscious cases, why should they be for cases that are conscious?

It is worth stressing that the present concern is not about whether absent or inverted qualities are real possibilities, or if so whether functionalism can preclude them. It is simply to find out the source of the stubborn intuitive insistence that absence or inversion of qualities are possible, and not ruled out by functionalism. On the foregoing argument, that intuitive insistence is largely or entirely the result of our sense that our first-person access to the conscious cases is authoritative. This intuitive idea leaves the nonconscious cases untouched.

One could, of course, argue that the apparent possibility of absent or inverted qualities in the conscious cases should carry over to states that are not conscious. But the intuitions do not directly apply to those cases. And it is equally open to argue instead in the reverse direction. Since no intuitive case can be made that these possibilities obtain in the nonconscious cases, why take seriously the intuitions that they obtain when the states are conscious?

The force of our intuition that absent or inverted qualities are possibilities that functionalism leaves open hinges on the idea that our first-person access to qualitative

---

[14] This conclusion rests on Block's contention that we may fail to be access conscious of qualitative states. Things get more complicated, however, when we focus closely on just what phenomenal consciousness consists in. A state is phenomenally conscious if there is something it's like for one to be in that state.

But there are two ways we might understand this well-used rubric. It might mean simply that the state has qualitative properties, in which case things are exactly as described in the text. But it might instead mean having some mental access to those qualities, since the qualities in question will lack any subjective aspect unless we have such access. With no such subjective aspect, there is arguably nothing it's like to be in such a state. Phenomenal consciousness thus construed would therefore fail to correspond to anything we intuitively count as consciousness.

On this reading, moreover, phenomenal consciousness literally entails access consciousness; the two properties would no longer be conceptually independent. Still, the argument in the text would remain unaffected, since Block agrees that qualitative properties occur in the absence of access consciousness. And however we understand phenomenal consciousness, access consciousness is what matters to the force of our intuitions about inverted and absent qualia.

states is dispositive. And that rests on the idea that such states are invariably conscious. But, insofar as we are concerned with the force of intuitions, this seems only to push the difficulty one step back. Whatever the arguments of the previous section, there is a strong intuitive appeal to the claim that qualitative states are invariably conscious. Whatever the case for intentional states, many will doubtless continue to insist sensory states simply cannot occur without being conscious. What would it be, they will ask, for a state to have sensory qualities if that state is not conscious? What could such qualities be in the absence of consciousness?

Argument often leaves intuition untouched. I have urged that Shoemaker's arguments leave unaffected intuitions about absent and inverted qualia. Similarly, arguments that qualitative states occur nonconsciously may, by themselves, have little effect on contrary intuitions. Often intuitions are undercut only when we understand their source, and see that that source gives us no reason to hold the beliefs that strike us with such intuitive force.

Intuitions about absent and inverted qualities rely on another intuitive idea, that qualitative states are always conscious. So we cannot uncover the source of the intuition about absent and inverted qualities without explaining the intuitive conviction that qualitative states always occur consciously. We must try to explain why this underlying intuition is so resilient in the face of argument. What assumptions underlie the way we think about the qualitative states which make it so difficult to conceive of those qualities occurring nonconsciously?

However unyielding our intuitions on that score, it is worth noting that it would be somewhat surprising if sensory qualities were always conscious. Sensory qualities are the distinguishing properties of qualitative states, the properties in virtue of which we sort those states into types. And the properties of things standardly occur even when nobody is conscious of them. What sort of property could it be that cannot occur unless somebody is conscious of it? It cannot help to say that they are mental properties, since mental properties sometimes occur without our being in any way conscious of the instantiating states.

When we think about things in ordinary, commonsense terms, we take it for granted that physical objects have color properties such as red and green. And we assume that these color properties are physical properties of some sort. These mundane assumptions notoriously conflict with our scientific picture of physical reality. Since Galileo, that picture has been dominated by the idea of mathematically formulable laws. The properties of physical objects and processes must all be able to figure in laws that can be formulated in mathematical terms; in Galileo's vivid metaphor, the book of nature is "written in the language of mathematics."[15] The color properties of physical objects, however, seem to be irreducibly qualitative in a way that defies description in mathematical terms.[16]

---

[15] Galileo Galilei, *The Assayer*, in *Discoveries and Opinions of Galileo*, tr. Stillman Drake, Garden City, New York: Anchor Books, 1957, p. 238.

[16] There are different things mathematical description might amount to here. Galilean considerations led Descartes to insist that physical reality can be described only in geometrical terms, though of course most theorists adopt a far more relaxed constraint. Moreover, it is immediately obvious

It is often concluded that physical objects do not literally have the properties of being red and green or, if they do have such properties, they are not as common sense conceives of them. But if physical objects do not have the color properties they appear to have, how can we explain those appearances? One standard answer is that the qualitative properties physical objects seem to have belong not to those objects, but rather to sensory mental states. Physical objects appear to have qualitative properties because, when we consciously perceive those objects, those very qualitative properties do characterize the sensory states that figure in our conscious perceptual experiences. Common sense attributes qualitative properties to physical objects, properties that resist scientific treatment. We solve that problem by recasting those qualitative properties as properties of sensory states. We relocate the problematic properties from physical reality to the mind.

But that is not the end of the difficulties. Although this maneuver may succeed in banishing qualitative properties from the realm of physical objects and processes, the relocated mental properties cause problems for theories of mind. It is sometimes held that these difficulties are unavoidable. Relegating qualitative properties to the mind was meant to avoid conflict with the dictates of mathematical physics. But how can that succeed unless the relocated mental properties are nonphysical? If the relocated mental properties are physical properties of some special sort, the conflict with the Galilean paradigm will persist; we would simply have exchanged one difficulty for another. It does not help that mental qualities are qualities of states, rather than objects; if qualitative properties resist mathematical description, they will do so whatever they are properties of. And, as is often noted, there is no place to relocate these properties once they are recast as mental properties.

I shall call this account the relocation story.[17] It is familiar and standard, as is the dualist picture that underlies it. But dualism aside, the story turns out to have important implications about consciousness that seem surprisingly to have gone unnoticed, implications that emerge once we focus on exactly what it is about qualitative properties that appears to resist mathematical treatment.

On our commonsense conception, physical objects have their color properties independently of whether anybody sees the objects. But the qualitative aspect of these properties that seems to resist mathematical formulation emerges only when the colors are consciously seen. It is only the red and green of physical objects *as these are consciously perceived* that we seem to have to relocate as mental properties.[18] What intuitively resists description in mathematical terms is the qualitative aspect of physical color properties *as we are conscious of it*. When these properties are

---

which notions of mathematical description produce difficulties for qualitative properties. We need not settle these questions here, however, since the present concern is simply that the compelling intuitive sense that qualitative properties cannot be caught in whatever mathematical net is required. (I am grateful to Sidney Morgenbesser for pressing this issue.)

[17] Shoemaker's term is "displacement maneuver" ("Qualities and Qualia: What's in the Mind?", p. 99).

[18] Thus Shoemaker remarks: "colors, tastes, etc., *as we experience them*, exist only in the mind" ("Qualities and Qualia: What's in the Mind?", p. 98; emphasis Shoemaker's).

not consciously perceived, there is nothing about them that resists mathematical description. We have no intuitive sense that something is lost if we describe the color properties objects have independently of being seen in terms of surface reflectance properties and the like.

So the apparent need to relocate physical color properties arises only insofar as we consciously perceive those properties. And this affects in important ways our conception of the mental products of this relocation. On this account, we conceive of the qualitative color properties of visual sensations as relocated versions of commonsense physical colors. But we conceive of them not simply as relocated versions of physical colors, but relocated versions of physical colors *as we are conscious of them*. Seeing the mental properties of qualitative states means conceiving them on the model of the relocated physical qualities. The properties undergoing relocation, moreover, are not physical qualities *tout court*, but physical qualities *as we are conscious of them*. So the product of such relocation will be mental qualities *as we are conscious of them*. Having modeled these mental qualities on physical qualities *insofar as we are conscious of them*, consciousness will be built into the relocated mental qualities themselves.

I argued in section II that the property some qualitative states have of being conscious is independent from whatever qualitative properties those states may have. Qualitative properties are simply the distinguishing properties of qualitative states, the properties in virtue of which we classify them into mental kinds. In the conscious cases these properties allow us to discriminate states of these various kinds on the basis of our first-person access to those states. Even when they are not conscious, however, the states differ in these characteristic mental ways. But then we have no first-person access to their nature or existence. We can classify nonconscious qualitative states in respect of the same qualitative properties we use in taxonomizing conscious qualitative states, though in these cases we must pick the states out by way of theoretical or other third-person means.

The qualitative properties of these states will not, however, be independent of the states' being conscious if we conceive of qualitative properties as relocated versions of physical qualities *as they are consciously perceived*. If we model mental qualities on physical qualities insofar as we are conscious of them, we end up conceiving of those mental qualities as being intrinsically conscious.

This relocation story about the nature of mental qualities has other consequences about consciousness, as well. I argued in section II that a mental state's being conscious consists in one's being conscious of that state in some suitable way. There are, broadly speaking, two ways we are conscious of things: by perceiving them and by having thoughts about them. And there are, correspondingly, two competing theories about how we are conscious of our conscious states. On one theory, we are conscious of those states by some kind of "inner sense";[19] on the other, we have higher-order thoughts about those states.

I have argued elsewhere that inner-sense theories, which posit some kind of higher-order sensing of our conscious states, face insurmountable difficulties. Briefly, sensing

[19] For contemporary versions see D. M. Armstrong, *A Materialist Theory of the Mind*, New York: Humanities Press, 1968, second revised edition, London: Routledge & Kegan Paul, 1993; and

something requires being in a state with qualitative properties characteristic of some sensory modality. But there is no qualitative aspect characteristic of the way we are conscious of our conscious states. This is obvious when the states we are conscious of are intentional states. But it is true when we are conscious of our conscious qualitative states. Qualities do figure in our being conscious of those states. But the qualities that occur vary with the kind of state we are conscious of; there is no characteristic range of qualities corresponding to our being conscious of those states. The qualities that occur belong to the state we are conscious of rather than to the higher-order state in virtue of which we are conscious of it.[20]

Despite these considerations, the inner-sense model is the dominant account of how we are conscious of our conscious states, both traditionally and in current thinking. The relocation story helps explain why. Mental qualities, on that story, are relocated versions of certain physical properties insofar as we consciously perceive those properties. Because we are conscious of the physical properties by sensing them, it is natural to suppose that we are conscious also of the mental results of this relocation by some sort of inner sensing. Conceiving of mental qualities as products of this relocation, we think of them not only as properties we are automatically conscious of, but as properties we are *perceptually* conscious of. Adopting the relocation story leads to thinking not just that qualitative states are all conscious, but that we are conscious of them by way of inner sense.

The effect the relocation story has on how we think about the mental qualities of visual sensations plainly applies equally to the qualitative properties of auditory, gustatory, and olfactory sensations. That story represents the mental properties of all these types of sensation as relocated versions of problematic physical qualities, qualities that appear problematic only insofar as we are perceptually conscious of them. Modeling the relocated properties on physical properties *as we are conscious of them* leads to our conceiving of the mental properties of sound, taste, and smell as all necessarily conscious.

But what about the qualitative properties of bodily sensations, such as pains, aches, tickles, and itches? These qualities, it may seem, lend themselves less well to the foregoing analysis. Indeed, it may not be obvious how the relocation story applies at all

---

William G. Lycan, *Consciousness and Experience*, Cambridge, Massachusetts: MIT Press/Bradford Books, 1996. Ancestors of the view include John Locke, *Essay Concerning Human Understanding*, edited from the fourth (1700) edition by Peter H. Nidditch, Oxford: Oxford University Press, 1975, and, arguably, Immanuel Kant, *Kritik der reinen Vernunft*, ed. Raymund Schmidt, Hamburg: Felix Meiner, 1990.

[20] See "A Theory of Consciousness," pp. 739–40; "Explaining Consciousness", §II; "State Consciousness and Transitive Consciousness," pp. 360–1; and "Perceptual and Cognitive Models of Consciousness," *Journal of the American Psychoanalytic Association*, 45, 3 (Summer 1997): 740–746.

The higher-order state in virtue of which we are conscious of our conscious states is typically not, itself, a conscious state. So an inner-sense advocate might urge that higher-order qualities occur of which we are unaware. But when we introspect, we are conscious not only of the state we introspect, but of the higher-order state in virtue of which we are conscious of that target state. And we remain unaware of any higher-order qualities even when we are introspectively conscious of our qualitative states.

to the qualitative properties of pains; what relevant physical properties might we relocate as pains or other bodily sensations? This is not a small matter. Bodily sensations are prime material for the intuition that sensory qualities are invariably conscious. If the relocation story does not apply to these cases, that story cannot explain why the intuition is so unyielding.[21]

But the relocation model does apply to bodily sensations. Just as perceptual sensations make us aware of various physical objects and processes, so pains and other bodily sensations make us aware of certain conditions of our own bodies. In standard cases of feeling pain, we are aware of a bodily condition located where the pain seems phenomenologically to be located. It is, we say, the foot that hurts when we have the relevant pain. And in standard cases we describe that bodily condition using qualitative words, such as painful, burning, stabbing, and so forth. Descartes's famous Sixth Meditation appeal to phantom pains reminds us that pains are purely mental states. But we need not, on that account, detach them from the bodily conditions they reveal in standard, nonhallucinatory cases.

But if it is the foot that hurts, how do we describe that hurting in a way consonant with the constraints of mathematical physics? The relocation story has an answer. On that account, the bodily conditions our bodily sensations make us aware of have no qualitative properties at all. The foot itself does not hurt, nor are any bodily conditions properly described as painful, burning, or itchy; bodily conditions are exhaustively described mathematically. We must, on this account, recast the qualities commonsense ascribes to these bodily conditions as purely mental qualities.

But the qualities of bodily states that resist mathematical description do so only insofar as we are conscious of them. Whatever the condition of one's foot when it hurts, nothing resists mathematical formulation insofar as one remains unaware of that condition of the foot. Since we model the mental qualities of pains on bodily qualities *insofar as we are conscious of those qualities*, we will again conceive of the relocated mental qualities as necessarily conscious. With bodily sensations no less than with perceptual sensations, the relocation story explains why the intuition that sensory qualities are invariably conscious is so stubbornly recalcitrant to argument.

IV. AN ALTERNATIVE ACCOUNT OF MENTAL QUALITIES

It is of course mandatory that we reconcile somehow our commonsense conceptions of colors, painfulness, and other such qualities with our best scientific picture of physical reality. The relocation story is a familiar and widely accepted way to try to do this.[22] More important, this need to reconcile science with common sense will plainly outweigh any arguments of the sort advanced earlier in support of the occurrence of nonconscious qualitative states. Once we have settled on the best way to achieve this reconciliation, we must swallow its implications, and those implications will trump

---

[21] I am grateful to Jennifer Church for pointing out shortcomings in an earlier account of how the relocation story applies to bodily sensations.

[22] Shoemaker aptly characterizes it as "one of the clichés of the history of philosophy" ("Qualities and Qualia: What's in the Mind?", p. 98).

whatever considerations could show that qualitative states occur without being conscious. So if the relocation story is the only way or the best way to reconcile science with common sense, arguments that qualitative states are not all conscious will have little force. We will conclude that consciousness is built into sensory qualities after all.

But despite its widespread acceptance, the relocation story is not the only way to square Galilean science with common sense, nor the best way. Physical objects have various color properties. But we need not conceive of these properties, even in commonsense terms, as actually being the way they appear to us when we are conscious of them. Rather, we can regard them simply as being whatever properties physical objects have that enable us to see those objects. When we consciously see a physical object, the properties in virtue of which we discriminate that object seem to have a qualitative aspect. But that may be due not to the nature of the object's properties, but only to the nature of our conscious perceptions. We consciously respond to physical color properties qualitatively, but the physical properties themselves need not, on that account, have any intrinsic qualitative aspect.[23]

This way of thinking of physical colors and other ostensibly qualitative physical properties avoids some of the theoretical preconceptions that figure in the relocation story. And it accords more successfully with common sense, since it recognizes that the properties of physical objects are the same whether we perceive them or not. The relocation story, by contrast, in effect splits physical color properties into relocated mental qualities that reflect the qualitative aspect of physical color as we are conscious of it and an unproblematic remainder that lends itself to scientific treatment. This divided account distorts both the physical color properties and the mental color qualities modeled on them; similarly for other qualities.

I shall refer to this alternative account as *the neutral account*. On it, the colors of physical objects are whatever properties enable us to see those objects, whether consciously or not. When we fail to see these properties or we see them nonconsciously, there is nothing about the objects that in any way seems to resist mathematical description. Physical objects have the very same properties, whether we consciously see the objects or not. Since nothing about their properties resists mathematical treatment when we do not consciously see the objects, nothing resists such treatment when we do.

Pressure to relocate physical properties exists only if we tie the very nature of physical colors to the special circumstance of our consciously perceiving them. Once we recognize that the relevant physical properties are the same whether or not they are consciously perceived, no motive remains to relocate them as mental properties. And then there is temptation to model the qualitative properties of sensory states on physical properties as consciously perceived, and hence no temptation to think of mental qualities as themselves invariably conscious. The distinguishing properties of qualitative states and the perceptible properties of physical objects are both independent of our being conscious of them.

---

[23] Physical colors might simply be various light-reflecting and -emitting properties, though any such identification is independent of the present argument.

Similar considerations apply to pains and other bodily sensations. The properties of bodily conditions that pains make us aware of are whatever properties enable us to be aware in a first-person way of the relevant bodily conditions and to discriminate among types of these conditions.[24] These properties resist mathematical description only insofar as we model them on conscious cases. Once again, recognizing that the same properties occur whether or not we are conscious of them dispels the need to relocate the properties we are conscious of. And if we do not conceive of the mental qualities of pains as relocated versions of properties of bodily conditions insofar as we are conscious of those properties, there is no temptation to hold that those mental qualities cannot occur unless we are conscious of them.

The neutral account squares with our commonsense intuitions about the perceptible properties of physical objects. But does it do justice to our commonsense convictions about the qualitative properties of sensory states? The color properties of physical objects are whatever properties of those objects enable us to see those objects, whether consciously or not. How, then, should we describe the corresponding mental qualities of visual sensations?

A parallel account applies. The color properties of physical objects are whatever properties enable us to see those objects. Similarly, the mental qualities of visual sensations are whatever properties the sensations have which enable us to discriminate visually among physical objects in respect of their colors. These mental properties enable to us to make such discriminations both consciously and not; the qualitative properties of our visual sensations that figure in consciously seeing red or green objects are also responsible for our seeing those physical properties nonconsciously.

When visual sensations are conscious, however, their qualitative properties play a second role, beyond that of enabling us to discriminate among differently colored physical objects. When our sensations are conscious, we discriminate among them introspectively and sort them into types, and we do this in terms of their qualitative properties. The qualitative properties of sensory states enable us not only to discriminate among physical objects perceptually, but also to discriminate among our qualitative states themselves when they are conscious. This parallels the role played by the perceptible properties of physical objects, which enable us to discriminate perceptually among those objects.

Not all sensations are conscious, and the neutral account allows for that. Its neutrality consists in assigning the same properties to objects whether or not we are conscious of them, and the same mental qualities to sensations whether or not those states are conscious. Similar considerations hold once again for pains and other bodily sensations. Pains have the same distinguishing qualitative properties whether the pains are conscious or not, but when they are conscious we can distinguish among them by reference to those qualitative properties.

---

[24] This recalls D. M. Armstrong's useful idea that we conceive of bodily sensations on the model of our perceptual sensations; see *Bodily Sensations*, London: Routledge & Kegan Paul, 1962. (Independently, Armstrong also held there that both sorts of sensation are invariably conscious, but he has since repudiated that view.)

Physical colors are whatever properties enable us to discriminate visually among physical objects. But that does not mean that we never misperceive physical objects in respect of those colors. The same holds for the mental qualities of visual sensations. Though these qualities enable us to discriminate among different types of sensation when those sensations are conscious, such discrimination need not always be accurate.

A mental state's being conscious is an extrinsic property of that state, consisting in our being conscious of that state in some suitable way. So the possibility is open that the way we are conscious of our conscious states sometimes misrepresents them. This is no mere theoretical possibility; there is compelling reason to think that it sometimes actually happens. We are sometimes conscious in an inaccurate way of the qualitative properties of our visual sensations, and the same happens with bodily sensations. When it does happen, we are conscious of our sensations as though they have qualitative properties that they do not in fact have. The qualitative properties we are conscious of the sensations as having are not the actual properties of the sensations. Still, the qualitative properties of sensations are the kinds of properties in terms of which we discriminate from a first-person point of view among the various types of sensation. And again the same is true of pains and other bodily sensations. We will examine these possibilities more closely in section V.

When we describe a physical object as red, we say something different about that object from what we say about a visual sensation when we characterize it as red; similarly, when we describe a condition of the foot and a bodily sensation as both painful.[25] It is natural to think that when we describe a visual sensation as red, we use the word 'red' in an extended sense, derived from the case in which we characterize red physical objects.

This suggests that the relocation story may, after all, have merit. How better to explain this double use of words for the perceptible properties of physical objects and for the introspectible properties of our sensations than by the relocation story itself? If the mental red of visual sensations is the product of relocating the red of physical objects, we would expect 'red' as applied to sensations to be derived from 'red' as applied to physical objects. But the neutral account explains this double use just as easily. Since the mental red of visual sensations is whatever property of those sensations enables us to discriminate red physical objects, we would again expect the word for the mental property to be derived from the word for physical red.

The neutral account does greater justice to our commonsense intuitions than the relocation story because it holds that the color properties of physical objects are the same whether or not we perceive them. But the neutral account has another advantage as well. The relocation story, by taking physical color properties to be the way our visual consciousness represents them, in effect endorses a certain theory about the nature of these properties. It represents their reality in terms of their appearance. The neutral account, by contrast, embodies no particular theory about the color properties of physical objects, construing them simply as whatever properties of those objects

---

[25] See n. 7.

play a certain role. By eschewing special commitments about the nature of those properties, the neutral account coincides more closely to pretheoretic common sense.

V. CONSCIOUSNESS AND IDENTIFYING SENSORY QUALITIES

The relocation story distorts the perceptible properties of physical objects by conceiving of them as they appear to conscious perception, rather than as independent properties of those objects. And it distorts the mental qualities modeled on those physical properties as well, by representing them as necessarily conscious. Properties are necessarily conscious if it is in their nature that we are invariably conscious of them. It is a strikingly odd view that there should be any properties whatever that satisfy that condition. Why should being conscious of a property be necessary for that property even to exist? The relocation story explains why mental properties seem to have consciousness built in.

But the relocation story is itself gratuitous. When mathematical physics was young and its implications new, it doubtless seemed sensible to be eliminativist about those physical properties which seemed to resist mathematical description. The relocation story is just such an eliminativist view. But the temptation to be eliminativist derives from a distorted view about those relocated physical properties, on which their very nature reflects the way they appear to us.[26] And the relocation induces further distortions in the nature of the resulting mental qualities.

Rather than eliminate such commonsense physical properties, however, we can instead simply drop the distorted view about their nature. They are responsible for the appearances caused in us, though their nature need not, on that account, reflect those very appearances. So construing the perceptible properties of physical objects squares both with common sense and with the constraints of mathematical physics. We retain the properties, dispensing only with an outmoded theory about them. Here as elsewhere, the eliminativist strategy is avoidable.[27]

Our ability to discriminate visually among physical objects allows us, on the neutral account, to identify both physical and mental color properties. They are whatever properties of physical objects and visual sensations, respectively, make it possible for us to perform such discriminations. And, when our visual sensations are conscious,

---

[26] The traditional, Aristotelian conception prevalent when Galileo wrote held that unseen physical color properties exist only potentially, and are actualized only when we are perceptually conscious of them. Holding that light is the action color has on a transparent medium when we see, Aristotle writes, "in a manner light, too, converts colors which are potential into actual colors" (*de Anima*, III 5, 430a16–17; tr. R. D. Hicks, Cambridge: Cambridge University Press, 1907). Cf. II 7, 419a9–11.

[27] On the optional character of eliminativist solutions to the mind–body problem, see my "Keeping Matter in Mind," *Midwest Studies in Philosophy*, V (1980), pp. 295–322, and "The Identity Theory," in *A Companion to the Philosophy of Mind*, ed. Samuel Guttenplan, Oxford: Basil Blackwell, 1994, pp. 348–355, §III. The same features of eliminativism also undermine historicism about philosophy; see my "Philosophy and its History," in *The Institution of Philosophy*, ed. Avner Cohen and Marcelo Dascal, Peru, Illinois: Open Court, 1989, pp. 141–176, §§I and II.

their mental qualities are also the properties in virtue of which we discriminate intro-spectively among the various types of visual sensation; similarly for other modalities.

The relocation story encourages the familiar idea that each mental quality resembles some corresponding physical property. Relocated versions of perceptible physical properties would surely resemble the properties on which they are modeled. But it is widely recognized that such resemblance cannot hold. For one thing, visual sensations are states, not objects. So the qualitative properties of visual sensations are properties of states of objects, rather than properties of the objects themselves. They are the wrong sort of property to resemble properties of physical objects.

Some connection plainly holds between mental qualities and the corresponding perceptible properties of physical objects. And it is tempting to think of that connec-tion as holding property by property. That makes the idea of resemblance appealing; it is difficult to see what other kind of connection might hold one by one between mental and physical properties. But the connection need not hold one by one; it can hold instead between entire families of properties. As a first pass, we can describe the family of color properties of visual sensations as resembling and differing from one another in ways homomorphic to the ways the color properties of physical objects resemble and differ from one another.[28]

One might object, however, that this modestly holistic approach cannot succeed. Human color perception is a function of the ratio of activation that occurs among the three light-sensitive elements in the daylight visual system. An object looks red, for example, if its spectral reflectance results in a suitable distribution of wavelengths under reasonably standard conditions. But, since different combinations of wavelengths can produce the same ratio, an object's looking red in standard conditions of illumination can result from widely disparate reflectance properties.[29] Each physical color property is therefore a class of physical properties whose members produce the right ratio of wavelengths, determined as a function of the human visual system rather than anything intrinsic to the physical objects themselves. But if physical colors are such gerrymandered properties, how can they resemble and differ from one another in ways homomorphic to the ways the qualitative properties of visual sensations resemble and differ?

Plainly, therefore, similarities and differences among specific reflectance properties are not homomorphic to those among the color qualities of visual sensations. But

---

[28] See "The Colors and Shapes of Visual Experiences" and "The Independence of Consciousness and Sensory Quality" for an elaboration and defense of this approach.

A view of this sort also underlies Wilfrid Sellars' rich, subtle discussions of sensory qualities. Thus, he writes: "visual impressions stand to one another in a system of ways of resembling and differing which is structurally similar to the ways in which the colors and shapes of visible objects resemble and differ" ("Empiricism and the Philosophy of Mind," in his *Science, Perception and Reality*, London: Routledge & Kegan Paul, 1963, pp. 127–196, at p. 193). See also, in *Science, Perception and Reality*, "Being and Being Known," pp. 41–59, and "Phenomenalism," pp. 60–105, esp. 91–95, and *Foundations for a Metaphysics of Pure Process*, The Carus Lectures, *The Monist*, LXIV, 1 (January 1981): 3–90.

[29] When the conditions of illumination vary, radically different reflectance properties will produce the same ratio. So objects that look the same color in daytime sunlight, e.g., may look quite different when seen in other conditions of illumination.

suitable equivalence classes of them are. Reference to commonsense taxonomies of physical color properties is necessary to determine the right equivalence classes, but that is neither surprising nor cause for concern. Theories about macroscopic phenomena must typically appeal to commonsense classifications.[30]

An advocate of the relocation story might object that this appeal to homomorphisms presupposes the relocation model itself. We can understand why these homomorphisms would obtain if mental qualities are relocated versions of perceptible physical properties. But what else could explain such a remarkable correspondence between distinct families of properties?

Once again, however, an alternative explanation is possible. We identify the mental color qualities of visual sensations by appeal to the perceptible colors of physical objects. A visual sensation has the mental quality red, for example, if, in standard conditions of illumination, perceivers typically have sensations of that type when they see an object as red.[31] A crucial part of seeing an object as being red is that one have a perceptual thought that a red object is present to one. And having such thoughts rarely if ever occurs unless one is seeing an object as red. So visual sensations with the mental quality of red are those which typically accompany perceptual thoughts that a red object is present to one.

Particular types of sensation typically accompany perceptual thoughts that have specifiable perceptual content because they typically cause such thoughts. Which perceptual thoughts a sensation typically accompanies therefore determines how we taxonomize our perceptual sensations. For that reason, qualitative states are qualitatively similar if they typically cause perceptual thoughts that perceived objects are qualitatively similar in respect of their perceptible properties. So, as Shoemaker argues:

[W]hat makes a relationship between experiences the relationship of qualitative (phenomenological) similarity is precisely its playing a certain "functional" role in the perceptual awareness of objective similarities, namely, its tending to produce perceptual beliefs to the effect that such similarities hold ("Functionalism and Qualia," *ICM* 199–200).

We identify sensations as being qualitatively similar or different by reference to the perceptual thoughts they cause.[32]

---

[30] See "The Colors and Shapes of Visual Experiences," pp. 163–4, and "The Independence of Consciousness and Sensory Quality," pp. 24–26; also Austen Clark's useful discussion of wavelength mixture space in *Sensory Qualities*, Oxford: Clarendon Press, 1993, pp. 29–42.

[31] And if they are normal perceivers for red objects, determined by their success in visually discriminating objects as other people do.

[32] Our perceptual sensations cause perceptual thoughts that objects with particular perceptible properties are perceptually present to one whether or not the objects have those properties and, indeed, whether or not any such objects are present to one. So, as Sellars argues, the occurrence of such sensations explains the occurrence of both veridical and nonveridical perceptual thoughts.

Indeed, we conceive of perceptual sensations, according to Sellars, as states that explain the occurrence of perceptual thoughts whether or not those thoughts are veridical. So the properties in terms of which we taxonomize sensations must correspond to the various types of physical object those thoughts are about, and correspond to those objects in respect of their perceptible properties. See references in n. 28 above.

These considerations explain why the similarities and differences among mental qualities are homomorphic to those among the corresponding perceptible properties of physical objects. We classify a visual sensation as red when it is the type of sensation that normally accompanies thoughts that a red object is present to one. So our taxonomy of visual sensations reflects the way we taxonomize the color properties of physical objects. Sensations of red and green are those sorts of visual sensation which typically accompany our perceptual thoughts that a red or green object is present to one. It is in this way that the terms for physical color properties get extended to talk about and classify those visual sensations in virtue of which we see those physical colors. Our so classifying our visual sensations ensures that the similarities and differences among their mental colors of visual sensations will reflect those which hold among the perceptible colors of physical objects, as those perceptible colors are taxonomized by common sense. Similarly for other sensory modalities. We can explain these homomorphisms without appeal to the relocation story.

These homomorphisms help not only in understanding how we identify sensory qualities, but in another connection as well. The relocation story is one way in which the Galilean reconception of physical reality has encouraged an intuitively unyielding conviction that sensory qualities are invariably conscious, but it is not the only way. Commonsense explanations of learning and psychological development rely on the idea that thinking and sensing are essentially connected and, indeed, that thinking arises in some way from sensing.[33] This results in a certain tension with the demand to describe physical reality in exclusively mathematical terms. Sensations exhibit geometrical properties such as shape only in conjunction with specific content properties; visual shape is the boundary of distinct colors, and tactile shape the boundary of differences in sensed pressure or texture. So sensing resists the Galilean dissociation between mathematically describable properties and qualitative properties such as color. For thinking to capture that dissociation, therefore, intentional content must, as Descartes argued, be independent of sensory quality. Thinking must represent the mathematically describable properties of physical objects independently of the way sensing represents them.

But, if thinking is independent of sensing, sensing and its sensory qualities will seem arbitrary with respect to the cognitive functions of thought, suggesting the possibility of inverted or even absent qualities. Moreover, if sensing is unconnected to the cognitive functions of thought, it will seem that the only tie sensing has with the rest of our mental functioning would be the distinctively first-person way we are conscious of sensing. Sensing would be nothing if it is not conscious. Describing physical reality in exclusively mathematical terms leads again to the idea that sensing is necessarily conscious.

The homomorphism between the perceptible properties of physical objects and the corresponding sensory qualities of our perceptual sensations helps here, by restoring

---

[33] Perhaps by a process along the lines of Aristotle's *epagogē* (*An. Post.* II, 19, 99b35–100b5). Aristotle held that thinking is not just associated with sensory qualities, but literally involves them: "[N]oetic objects are in the sensible objects" (*de Anima*, III 8, 432a5; cf. III 7, 431a16–7, b2, I 1, 403a9–10, III 8, 432a9, 14; *de Mem.* 1, 449b31).

the connection between thinking and sensing.[34] If, for example, the mental qualities of color are homomorphic with the perceptible color properties of physical objects, those mental qualities will be related in turn to our concepts of those physical colors and, hence, our thoughts that physical objects have particular colors. So a sensation's being conscious will not be the only way it can have robust ties to the rest of our mental functioning.[35]

Frank Jackson has argued that words such as 'red' and 'round' apply to one property only, and are not equivocal as between perceptible properties of physical objects and the mental qualities of our sensations. Such a double use, he holds, would be "a linguistic accident, a fantastic fluke."[36] But the homomorphisms between corresponding families of mental and physical properties make these double uses systematic.[37] It would be a linguistic accident that 'red' refers to both a mental quality and a perceptible physical property only if the concept that figures in thoughts about red physical objects were unrelated to the sensory quality of red that figures in perceiving those objects. The idea that words such as 'red' refer only to one kind of property is of a piece with the assumption that intentional content is unconnected to sensory quality.[38]

Because the qualitative properties of sensations are homomorphic with the perceptible properties of physical objects, we can identify and taxonomize the mental qualities of qualitative states by reference to the perceptual thoughts these states typically accompany. But how does that square with the familiar idea that we identify and taxonomize qualitative states by reference to what it's like to be in them? What it's like for one to be in a qualitative state may well intuitively seem to be wholly independent of the perceptual thoughts that state typically accompanies. Indeed, if the way we are conscious of our qualitative states trumps their cognitive connections, intuitions about absent and inverted qualities result.

A slight detour will be useful here. It is sometimes held that what it's like to be in a qualitative state reveals, exhaustively and infallibly, the qualitative nature of that state. What it's like to be in a qualitative state would not, of course, reveal the state's nonqualitative properties, but it is decisive about its qualitative properties.

But as argued toward the end of the last section, consciousness need not reveal all the qualitative properties a state has, and may even get wrong those it does reveal.

---

[34] The idea of nonconceptual content provides another path for bridging that gulf; see, e.g., Christopher Peacocke, *A Study of Concepts*, Cambridge, Massachusetts: MIT Press/Bradford Books, 1992. For an earlier, different approach to this problem, see Peacocke, *Sense and Content*, Oxford: Oxford University Press, 1983.

[35] I develop this argument in "Sensation, Consciousness, and the Detachment Assumption," MS.

[36] Frank Jackson, *Perception: A Representative Theory*, Cambridge: Cambridge University Press, 1973, p. 73.

[37] See "The Colors and Shapes of Visual Experiences," §IV.

[38] Aristotle's view that perceiving consists of the organism's literally taking on the perceptible properties of the object (*de Anima*, II 5 418a4, II 11 423b31, II 12 424a18, III 2 425b23) constitutes a kind of exception, since then the object and the organism both have the same property. There would then be only one property for 'red' to refer to. And, since the sensory quality is the same property that our thoughts of red objects are about, this allows for the robust connection Aristotle recognizes between intentional content and sensory quality (see n. 33).

That consciousness fails to reveal all the qualitative properties of our qualitative states is a corollary of the occurrence of qualitative states that are not conscious at all. Qualitative states occur without being conscious, without, that is, there being anything at all it's like to be in those states. So there is no reason to suppose that, when there is something it's like to be in a qualitative state, what it's like to be in it reveals all its qualitative character.

Thus, what it's like to have a conscious pain may sometimes involve the quality of painfulness, but reveal nothing about whether that pain is throbbing, sharp, or burning. Similarly, what it's like to have a particular sensation of red may say nothing about any particular shade. In these cases, the sensation is conscious *as* a pain or a sensation of red without being conscious *as* a particular type of pain, or *as* a sensation of any particular shade of red.[39] This can shift, perhaps by attending to a sensation more or less carefully; what it's like for one to have some particular sensation can come to involve qualitative character that is more or less fine grained.

In the extreme, one can seem to be in a conscious state that does not occur at all. Dental patients occasionally report pain when physiological factors make it clear that no pain could occur. The usual explanation is that fear and the nonpainful sensation of vibration cause the patient to confabulate feeling pain. When the patient learns this explanation, what it's like for the patient no longer involves anything painful. But the patient's memory of what it was like before learning the explanation remains unchanged. Even when what it's like for one results from confabulation, it may be no less vivid and convincing than a nonconfabulatory case.

How can there be different things that it's like for one to be in one and the same qualitative state? Indeed, how can there be something it's like for one to be in a qualitative state that does not even occur? When there is something it's like for one to be in some qualitative state, consciousness represents that state in a particular way. When what it's like for one involves the quality of red but no particular shade, or painfulness but no particular kind of pain, that is how consciousness represents the state. If the way it's like for one to be in a particular state involves some qualitative property, the way one is conscious of that state represents it as having that quality. In the extreme, as in the dental case, one may be conscious of a state that does not even occur.

It is likely that an account of consciousness that appeals to *higher-order thoughts* (HOTs) provides the best explanation of this. Conscious states are states that one is conscious *of*, in some suitable way. On the HOT model, one is conscious of a conscious state by having a thought to the effect that one is in that state. This readily allows for the needed variability in the way consciousness represents one's conscious states, since thoughts can represent things in respect of a range of different properties.[40] And thoughts can, of course, represent things inaccurately, and even represent nonoccurrent things as occurring.

---

[39] Such considerations figured in the argument against Dretske in §II.

[40] One might argue that the higher-order sensing could also represent our conscious states with the required variability. But as we have seen, there are other reasons to reject that inner-sense model.

For more on the connection between HOTs and what it's like to be in qualitative states, and especially on how HOTs could be responsible for there being anything it's like for one to

Does typing qualitative states by reference to the perceptual thoughts they accompany conflict with typing those states by what it's like for us to be in them? The foregoing considerations strongly suggest not. What it's like for us to be in a specific qualitative state is determined by the way consciousness represents that state, on the HOT model, by the content of the HOT about that state. When what it's like for me is that I have a red visual sensation, my HOT represents me as having such a sensation. But how, specifically, does my HOT represent the sensation? What is that content of that HOT? The foregoing considerations suggest that my HOT represents me as being in a state of that type normally accompanied by perceptual thoughts of red physical objects. The HOT in virtue of which my sensation is conscious characterizes it in terms of typically accompanying perceptual thoughts. And that very HOT also determines what it's like for me to have the sensation. Similar considerations again apply to the other perceptual modalities and to the case of bodily sensations.

The relocation story was intended to avoid apparent conflict between the qualitative properties of physical objects and the demands of mathematical physics. Such conflict seems to emerge only when we are perceptually conscious of those physical properties. But perceiving something does not change its nature. So unperceived properties can occasion no conflict, either.

Still, the appearance of conflict is a function of the way the physical properties appear to us and that, in turn, is a matter of the character of the sensory states in virtue of which we perceive the relevant physical properties. The traditional conclusion is that the qualitative character of those states actually does conflict with the dictates of mathematical physics in just the way that the physical properties appeared to conflict. Whether or not we conceive of sensory qualities as the relocation story urges, we seem simply to have traded one difficulty in for another.

If we think of mental qualities as relocated versions of physical qualities, the story stops there; if problems persist with the mental qualities, no further relocation is possible. But if we avoid appeal to the relocation story, we avoid difficulty with mental qualities in just the way we do with physical qualities.

Physical qualities seem to resist mathematical description because of the way we are perceptually conscious of them. But the same may hold for mental qualities, as well. The way we are conscious of the qualitative properties of sensory states when those states are conscious need not reflect the character of the mental qualities. So it may well be that mental qualities appear recalcitrant to mathematical description only because of the way we are conscious of those qualities when the relevant qualitative states are conscious.

Consider the "ultimate homogeneity," in Wilfrid Sellars' useful phrase, that mental qualities appear to have, which appears to set qualitative states apart from the particulate character of ordinary physical properties.[41] But even though sensory qualities appear to us as ultimately homogeneous, they may not actually be so. They might be

be in qualitative states, see "Explaining Consciousness," esp. §§IV and V, and "The Kinds of Consciousness," §IV.

[41] Wilfrid Sellars, "Philosophy and the Scientific Image of Man," in *Frontiers of Science and Philosophy*, ed. Robert G. Colodny, Pittsburgh: University of Pittsburgh Press, 1962, pp. 35–78;

particulate, as the dependence of qualitative states on neural processes suggests, even though we are conscious of them as ultimately homogeneous. The mental properties of our sensations appear ultimately homogeneous to us simply because the way we are conscious of them smooths them out, so to speak, and elides the details of their particulate, bit-map nature.

Shoemaker has sought to contain the problem about quality inversion by appealing to the connection qualitative states have with perceptual thoughts. Because the qualitative similarities and differences that hold among our qualitative states is a function of the connection those states have with perceptual thoughts, quality inversion cannot occur without preserving these similarities and differences.

As Shoemaker notes, this does not show that no quality inversion can occur. We identify mental qualities by what it's like for us to be in states with those qualities. And we cannot preclude the possibility that what it's like for us could determine distinct sets of qualitative properties that preserve the relevant similarities and differences. But the connection HOTs have with what it's like for one to be in a qualitative state underwrites a stronger result. The HOT that determines what it's like for one to be in a particular qualitative state arguably represents that state by reference to typically accompanying perceptual thoughts. So those perceptual thoughts anchor what it's like for one to be in that state. Quality inversion could occur only if the relevant set of perceptual thoughts changed, which by hypothesis does not happen.

Adoption of the relocation story would undercut this result, since the relocation story supports the intuition that qualitative states are invariably conscious. Fortunately, the relocation story, however inviting it may once have been as an initial accommodation to Galilean science, is avoidable, and the intuitions that story encouraged are very likely not warranted.[42]

reprinted in *Science, Perception and Reality*, pp. 1–40, at p. 36; see also p. 35, and "Phenomenalism," pp. 103–105. Sellars accepts the relocation story, holding that this ultimate homogeneity derives from the way common sense conceives of the perceptible properties of physical objects.

Some such view is not uncommon; cf. Peter Carruthers's claim that "perceptual information is *analogue* (that is, 'filled in' and continuous)," as against belief-contents, which "are *digital*, or chunked" (*Language, Thought, and Consciousness: An Essay in Philosophical Psychology*, Cambridge: Cambridge University Press, 1996, p. 167).

[42] Much of this paper was written during a 1998 stay at the Center for Interdisciplinary Research (ZiF), University of Bielefeld, Germany. I am grateful to the Center for providing stimulating and congenial surroundings, and to a PSC-CUNY Research Award for supporting my stay.

7

Sensory Qualities, Consciousness, and Perception

There is a popular notion, prevalent in both scientific and commonsense contexts, that qualitative mental states always occur consciously. It's plain that many types of mental state, such as thoughts, desires, beliefs, and intentions, often occur without being conscious. But qualitative states, it often is held, never do, because being conscious is in effect essential to a state's having qualitative character at all.

What's essential to something is a function of the kind of thing it is. We count a state as being qualitative only if it has qualitative properties. But on the popular view just mentioned, a state's having qualitative properties means that there is something that it's like to be in that state—something that it's like *for the subject*. And, when a state isn't conscious, there simply is nothing it's like for one to be in that state. Even Freud, who championed the idea of unconscious mental states, drew the line at qualitative states, claiming that "the possibility of . . . unconsciousness would be completely excluded so far as emotions, feelings and affects are concerned."[1]

One of my aims in this chapter will be to undermine this conception of what qualitative states are, which I argue is not only unfounded theoretically, but unsupported by any reliable commonsense intuition. Indeed, clarity about just what properties are essential to a state's being qualitative will make it plain that a state can have those properties without being conscious. I argue these things in section I. In section II, then, I sketch the higher-order-thought model of consciousness that I've developed in earlier chapters. And I argue that, contrary to what some critics have claimed, that model does justice to qualitative consciousness and, in particular, to there being something that it's like for one to be in conscious qualitative states. In section III I argue that various claims about phenomenal consciousness and about whether we can explain mental qualities are unfounded, and so cannot undermine the higher-order-thought model as applied to qualitative states.

In section IV I go on to develop a positive account of the qualitative properties of those states which fits with and sustains the arguments of the earlier sections.

---

[1] "The Unconscious," in *The Complete Psychological Works of Sigmund Freud*, tr. and ed. James Strachey, London: The Hogarth Press, 1966–74, XIV, pp. 166–215, at p. 177. And: "It is surely of the essence of an emotion, that we should be aware of it, i.e. that it should become known to consciousness" (ibid.). Thus, according to Freud, we "speak in a condensed and not entirely correct manner, of 'unconscious feelings'" (*The Ego and the Id*, XIX, pp. 3–68, at p. 22). And we do so, he held, only because the representational character of the feelings is repressed or misrepresented ("The Unconscious," pp. 177–8).

And in section V I show how that account works in tandem with the higher-order-thought theory of consciousness. Section VI takes up the conceptualization that occurs in perceiving and the different conceptualization that occurs in higher-order thoughts about qualitative states. That section also briefly sketches how the connection between those two kinds of conceptualization actually facilitates the consciousness of qualitative states. I conclude in section VII by discussing the cross-modal calibration of mental qualities, spatial sensing, representationalism, and the alleged possibility of quality inversion.

I. CONSCIOUSNESS AND QUALITATIVE PROPERTIES

To determine whether qualitative states can occur without being conscious, it's useful to get clear at the start about just what kinds of state we classify as qualitative. And it's important to guard against begging any substantive questions. Theorists sometimes use the term 'consciousness', for example, simply to refer to qualitative mental states. But either this verbal shortcut simply embodies the view that qualitative states are always conscious or, if not, it uses the term 'consciousness' in a way that's irrelevant to the issue at hand. What we want to know is whether qualitative states can fail to be conscious in the way that thoughts and other intentional states can fail to be conscious. To avoid begging this question, we need some independent handle on the application of the term 'qualitative state'.

One way to try to get such an independent handle would be by appeal to certain traditional puzzles about qualitative mental states. It's often thought that the conscious quality you call red might be the same as that which I call green and conversely, or that creatures could be functionally identical to us but lack qualitative states altogether. And it's sometimes held that, whereas explanation in other areas gives us a rational understanding of the connections among things, there can no such rational understanding of how mental qualities could result from neural or other physical processes. The possibility of inverted and absent qualities and the so-called explanatory gap are, according to Ned Block, "*routes* to [what he calls] phenomenal consciousness";[2] they enable us, he urges, to zero in on and pick out the mental phenomenon in question.

Block recognizes that such "conundra" about qualitative states "do not constitute" phenomenal consciousness (205). But it's not obvious that they can even help in picking out the target phenomena. Many theorists deny that absent or inverted qualia are possible and that any explanatory gap affects our understanding of qualitative states; plainly those theorists don't thereby deny the existence of genuine qualitative states.

---

[2] "Begging the Question against Phenomenal Consciousness," *The Behavioral and Brain Sciences*, 15, 2 (June 1992): 205–6, p. 205; emphasis Block's. On the explanatory gap see Joseph Levine, "Materialism and Qualia: The Explanatory Gap," *Pacific Philosophical Quarterly*, LXIV, 4 (October 1983): 354–361, "On Leaving Out What It's Like," in *Consciousness: Psychological and Philosophical Essays*, ed. Martin Davies and Glyn W. Humphreys, Oxford: Basil Blackwell, 1993, pp. 121–136, and *Purple Haze: The Puzzle of Consciousness*, New York: Oxford University Press, 2001, esp. ch. 3.

What we need is a way to pick out the phenomena under consideration which is neutral with respect to different theoretical convictions, including positions one can take about an explanatory gap and whether absent or inverted qualities are possible.

Another approach to understanding what it is for a state to be qualitative would be to appeal to the function perceptual qualitative states have in transmitting to the mind perceptual information about the environment. Qualitative states are those mental states in virtue of which we respond mentally to the properties of environmental objects and processes. This is doubtless right, but we need to take care in how we understand this suggestion, since it invites a mistaken inference about consciousness. There are, in addition to qualitative states, many nonmental, purely physiological states that also figure in transmitting information about environmental objects to the mind; how are we to distinguish the qualitative mental states from those nonmental, physiological states? Here it may be tempting to appeal to consciousness, and hold that qualitative states, unlike those nonmental, purely physiological states, are essentially and invariably conscious. Indeed, arguments that qualitative states can occur without being conscious are often met by the dogged insistence that any such nonconscious states would simply not be mental, but rather mere physiological surrogates of genuine qualitative states.

It's worth pausing over another possible answer to the concern about distinguishing qualitative states from various nonmental, purely physiological concomitants. We might say that qualitative states differ from the nonmental, physiological states that figure in transmitting perceptual information to the mind simply because the qualitative states have mental qualities and the nonmental, merely physiological states don't. Again, this is right, but it only pushes the question one step back; how do we distinguish these mental qualities from the distinguishing properties of those nonmental, physiological states? This invites once more the appeal to consciousness, on which mental qualities are simply those properties which occur consciously; why, it may be asked, would we count any property as qualitative if it's not a conscious property?

I'll argue in section IV that a useful, informative account of mental qualitative properties is possible which is wholly independent of a state's being conscious. But even apart from such an account, it's plain that distinguishing qualitative properties from the properties of nonmental, physiological states does not require that such qualities are always conscious. To be qualitative, a property need not always occur consciously; it must simply be able to occur consciously. Nonmental, physiological properties, by contrast, are never conscious. Qualitative properties are potentially conscious, not invariably or essentially conscious.[3]

This preliminary characterization of qualitative mental states requires distinguishing between the properties in virtue of which we typically pick things out and the

---

[3] The psychological architecture of a particular type of organism may block states with those properties from occurring consciously. The current suggestion is independent of such considerations; some states simply aren't of such a type that could occur consciously, regardless of what psychological architecture they are embedded in. A property is qualitative if states with that property could occur consciously in an organism whose architecture allows it.

properties that are essential to the things thus picked out. Because we often pick out qualitative states introspectively, that is, by reference to the way we are conscious of them, it's natural to see them as states whose properties sometimes occur consciously. But that doesn't imply that occurring consciously is essential to the states and properties we pick out in this way. Qualitative states are distinctively mental not because they must be conscious but because they may be.[4]

Because we sometimes individuate mental states by reference to the way we're conscious of those states, it may be tempting to see it as essential to all mental states that they can occur consciously. But there is a better account of what it is for a state to be mental, which invokes consciousness in a different way. A state is mental if, in virtue of being in that state, one is conscious *of* something as being present or conscious *that* something is the case.[5] Any such state will have characteristic intentional or qualitative properties; it will be a case of perceiving or sensing something or of thinking about something as being present.

Not all states with intentional or qualitative properties are states in virtue of which one is conscious of something or conscious that something is the case. But all states in virtue of which we're conscious of things do have qualitative or intentional properties. And that suggests that we count all states with those properties as being mental, even if one isn't, simply in virtue of being in those states, conscious of anything or conscious that something is the case. A state is mental if it has intentional content and mental attitude or if it has some qualitative property. It may not always be clear whether a state has qualitative character; but we can rule out any state that doesn't exhibit characteristic interactions with many other mental states. In any case,

It's important to distinguish this observation from John R. Searle's well-known view that a state, to be genuinely intentional, must be at least potentially conscious. Searle notes that the way an intentional state represents things, say, as being water or as being H_2O, must make a difference to the subject. And he urges that only conscious states can make such a difference. So nonconscious states can count as intentional only by a kind of courtesy, in virtue of their having some possible connection with consciousness. (John R. Searle, "Consciousness, Explanatory Inversion, and Cognitive Science," *The Behavioral and Brain Sciences*, 13, 4 [December 1990]: 585–696; with open peer commentary, and Searle's reply: "Who is Computing with the Brain?", ibid., 632–642.)

On the present suggestion, by contrast, states can be qualitative and intentional fully and without qualification even if they aren't conscious, though it must be possible for any state of either type to occur consciously.

Searle is of course right that the ways intentional states represent things must make a difference to the subject. But intentional states need not be conscious to make such a difference. Nonconscious intentional states can also make a psychological difference, as a result of having ties with other intentional states and with verbal and nonverbal behavior. It might even be that nonconscious intentional states will make a difference to one's conscious states, by way of these connections with other states. See my "On Being Accessible to Consciousness," *The Behavioral and Brain Sciences*, 13, 4 (December 1990): 621–2.

[4] For more on the application to such cases of the distinction between what's essential to qualitative states and how we pick them out, see "Two Concepts of Consciousness," ch. 1 in this volume, §IV.

[5] I'll argue in §II that we know what it is to be conscious *of* something or *that* something is the case independently of knowing what it is for a mental state to be a conscious state.

the account of qualitative properties I'll develop in section IV will make clear that we needn't ever pick out or individuate qualitative mental states by reference to the way we're conscious of them.[6]

This conclusion fits with many empirical findings, as well as what's obvious from everyday life. Phenomena such as peripheral vision, subliminal perception, and blindsight all testify to the occurrence of qualitative states that aren't conscious. One could, of course, simply dig in one's heels and insist that only nonmental states occur in these cases. But this stand is highly unintuitive, since we routinely characterize all these cases in distinctively qualitative terms. We subliminally see things in respect of their color and shape, and we may subliminally recognize a voice by its pitch and timbre. It's not that we couldn't explain all this by appeal only to nonmental, physiological states. But it's plain that trying to do so would be grinding a controversial theoretical axe, not saving some pretheoretic, commonsense intuition.

II. CONSCIOUS QUALITIES AND HIGHER-ORDER THOUGHTS

Qualitative states sometimes occur without being conscious. So it's natural to conclude that the property of being conscious is not intrinsic to such states. One could insist that consciousness is an intrinsic property only of those qualitative states which are conscious, but that move would unduly complicate any account we might give, and would arguably be theoretically *ad hoc* and unmotivated.[7]

The idea that a mental state's being conscious is an extrinsic, or relational,[8] property of that state fits strikingly well with the way we actually talk about consciousness. We count a person's mental states as conscious only when that person is conscious, in some way or other, *of* those states. We never classify as conscious a state of which the subject is wholly unaware. So a necessary condition for a state to be conscious is that one is conscious of that state in some suitable way. The hard part will be to specify just what that suitable way is. But if we can do that, we'll have a condition of a state's being conscious that's not only necessary, but sufficient as well. And, whatever that suitable way of being conscious of our conscious states turns out to be, a state's being conscious will be extrinsic to that state.[9]

---

[6] So I now reject the suggestion in "Two Concepts of Consciousness," §III, that we might have to taxonomize qualitative properties by appeal to the way we're conscious of them.

[7] There is in addition striking evidence from functional brain imaging that a state's being conscious is an extrinsic property of that state. Chris D. Frith and Uta Frith report a number of studies in which asking subjects to report their mental states resulted in neural activation in medial frontal cortex. The states reported ranged from pains and tickles to emotions aroused by pictures and spontaneous thoughts, and other cortical areas subserve those states. Since reporting a mental state involves that state's being conscious, such consciousness very likely involves a cortical area distinct from that of the state itself. See "Interacting Minds—A Biological Basis," *Science*, 286, i5445 (November 26, 1999): 1692–1695, p. 1693.

[8] There will be reason to retreat on the claim that a state's being conscious is strictly speaking relational; see §V. But the required modification won't affect the point that a state's being conscious is in any case not an intrinsic property of that state.

[9] *Pace* Brentano, who builds being conscious of one's mental states into the states themselves. But this move, if it is not merely stipulative, requires some independent test of whether one's being

Amie Thomasson has argued that conscious states are not states one is conscious of, but rather states that one is in consciously.[10] But this doesn't help unless we have an independent argument that one's being in a state consciously doesn't consist simply in one's being conscious of oneself as being in that state. And somebody who urges that being in a state consciously is somehow more basic must in any case contend with the foregoing argument, on which one's not being at all conscious of a state is sufficient for that state not to be conscious. We sometimes have evidence, as with subliminal perception, that somebody is in a particular mental state even though that person firmly denies being in it. That's enough to conclude that the person isn't conscious of being in that state. And, if not being conscious of a state is sufficient for that state not to be conscious, being in some suitable way conscious of a mental state is perforce a necessary condition for that state to be conscious.

Fred Dretske has argued in a number of places that a state's being conscious is not a matter of one's being conscious of that state.[11] But maintaining that has a serious cost. Some mental states occur without being conscious; so we must account for the difference between mental states that are conscious and those which are not. And Dretske's view precludes the most natural explanation, that a state is conscious if one in conscious of it in some suitable way. Dretske has therefore urged an alternative account, on which a mental state's being conscious consists in its being a state in virtue of being in which one is conscious of something.[12] But it's arguable that this account implies that all perceiving is conscious, since perceiving something automatically makes one conscious of it.

---

conscious of a state is intrinsic to that state, and it's not obvious that any convincing test would generate the result Brentano wants.

Indeed, Brentano's own test runs afoul of insurmountable problems. According to him, mental states are individuated by reference to the mental attitude involved, such as believing, wondering, doubting, and the like; more than one mental attitude implies more than one mental state. (Franz Brentano, *Psychology from an Empirical Standpoint*, tr. Antos C. Rancurello, D. B. Terrell, and Linda L. McAlister, London: Routledge & Kegan Paul, 1973, pp. 127–8.) But it's clear that doubting or wondering about a mental state doesn't make one conscious of that state. So when the state that's conscious is itself a case of doubting or wondering, one's being conscious of that state will have to involve some distinct mental attitude, and hence will be a distinct state. Brentano's favored example is one of hearing a sound, which obscures the point about mental attitude.

For more on this, see "Thinking that One Thinks," ch. 2 in this volume, §V, and "Varieties of Higher-Order Theory," in *Higher-Order Theories of Consciousness*, ed. Rocco J. Gennaro, Amsterdam and Philadelphia: John Benjamins Publishers, 2004, pp. 17–44, §V.

[10] Amie L. Thomasson, "After Brentano: A One-Level Theory of Consciousness," *European Journal of Philosophy*, 8, 2 (August 2000): 190–209, pp. 203–4. I am grateful to Dan Zahavi for bringing this argument to my attention.

[11] E.g., "Conscious Experience," *Mind*, 102, 406 (April 1993): 263–283; reprinted in Dretske, *Perception, Knowledge, and Belief*, Cambridge: Cambridge University Press, 2000, pp. 113–137, and *Naturalizing the Mind*, MIT Press/Bradford Books, 1995, ch. 4.

I discuss Dretske's arguments in "Introspection and Self-Interpretation," ch. 4 in this volume, §IV, "Sensory Quality and the Relocation Story," ch. 6 in this volume, §II, and "Consciousness and Metacognition," in *Metarepresentation: A Multidisciplinary Perspective*, ed. Daniel Sperber, New York: Oxford University Press, 2000, pp. 265–295, §III.

[12] "Conscious Experience," pp. 280–1; *Naturalizing the Mind*, pp. 100–1. This echoes the account proposed above of a state's being mental, as against being conscious.

To meet this difficulty, Dretske has recently amplified his account of the difference between conscious perceiving and perceiving that isn't conscious, by invoking rationality. Perceiving is conscious, he suggests, if a subject can cite the fact perceived as a justifying reason for doing something. That contrasts with blindsight and subliminal perceiving, in which subjects perform above chance in response to perceptual input but cannot cite the content of the perceiving as a justifying reason for such performance. Indeed, since such subjects deny seeing anything relevant, they offer no justifying reasons for whatever remarks they make about possible stimuli, but regard those remarks simply as guesses. Dretske takes the absence of such justifying reasons to indicate perceiving that isn't conscious.[13]

But subjects' inability to give a justifying reason may not show that they have no such reason, but only that they aren't conscious of whatever justifying reason they do have. We often do things without being able to give a justifying reason, even though others may know what justifying reason is operative for us, which we would offer if only we were conscious of it. Indeed, we may ourselves come in due course to be conscious of that justifying reason. Dretske might urge that a consideration counts as a justifying reason only if one can offer it, but it counts against that claim that we often do things without being clear what our reason is for doing them. Offering something as a reason requires being conscious that one thinks that thing, and that one thinks it as a reason for doing something. And, when the consideration is some perceptual input, that requires being conscious of the perceiving. All this helps confirm that what matters to perceiving's being conscious is whether one is conscious of the perceiving.

Dretske argues that one's ability to offer a justifying reason reflects the connection conscious perceiving has with rational agency, since blindsight subjects sometimes seem unable to initiate rational action based on stimuli in their blind field.[14] But when conscious vision is wholly unavailable, stimuli present to blindsight sometimes do result in rational action.[15] Rational action can result from both conscious and nonconscious vision.

Until relatively recently people did not apply the one-place predicate, 'conscious', to mental states, but instead spoke only of being conscious *of* those states. Thus Descartes never speaks of a thought's being conscious, but only of one's being immediately or directly conscious of a thought. Applying the one-place predicate to mental states seems to have been a nineteenth-century neologism introduced to draw the distinction between mental states that we are and are not directly conscious of. A dedicated term to mark that contrast became useful only when it came to be widely recognized that we are not conscious of all our own mental states.

---

[13] "Perception without Awareness," in *Perceptual Experience*, ed. Tamar Szabo Gendler and John Hawthorne, Oxford: Oxford University Press, forthcoming, §IV.

[14] Anthony J. Marcel, e.g., cites a thirsty blindsight subject who won't reach for a glass of water located in his blind field; "Consciousness and Processing: Choosing and Testing a Null Hypothesis," *The Behavioral and Brain Sciences*, 9, 1 (March 1986): 40–1.

[15] As Nicholas Humphrey describes in the case of the rhesus monkey, Helen, whose entire primary visual cortex had been surgically ablated. Helen "could, for example, run around a room full of furniture picking up currants from the floor, and she could reach out and catch a passing fly" (*Consciousness Regained*, Oxford: Oxford University Press, 1983, p. 38; see also pp. 19–20).

There are two ways we are ordinarily conscious of things: by sensing them and by thinking about them as being present. I may, for example, be conscious of somebody by seeing that person or simply by thinking about the person as being nearby.[16] We know of no other way of being conscious of things, and it would be theoretically idle to insist that we're conscious of our conscious states in some third way without having some independent idea of what that third way consists in.

In which of the two ways we do know about, then, are we conscious of our mental states when those states are conscious? The traditional reply, both in philosophy and psychology, has been that we sense those mental states. But this "inner sense" model of consciousness, championed by writers from John Locke to David Armstrong,[17] faces serious difficulties. Sensations all belong to one or another sensory modality; but what could be the modality of those sensations in virtue of which we might sense our conscious mental states? Stipulating that there's a dedicated modality for sensing all our conscious states is no better than simply saying we're conscious of our conscious states in some way we know not what. And it's implausible that we sense our conscious states by any of the ordinary sensory modalities.[18]

Even more telling, when a sensation is conscious, the qualities that occur are those of the first-order sensation we are conscious of, not of some higher-order sensation

---

[16] Very likely we regard thoughts as making one conscious only of things they describe as being present because of an analogy with sensing. (I am grateful here to Robert Lutzker.) Sensing always represents things as being present, and sensing is arguably the more fundamental way of being conscious of things, at least in part because it's the more basic and widespread form of mental functioning.

Having a thought about Napoleon doesn't make one conscious of him unless one thinks about him as being present. Still, one might suppose that having a thought that he was emperor makes one conscious *of* his having been emperor, despite one's not thinking about that state of affairs as being present. (I am grateful to Douglas Meehan for this suggestion.) But one's being conscious of a state of affairs doesn't amount to anything over and above one's being conscious *that* the state of affairs obtains; it is not a way of being conscious *of* anything.

[17] John Locke, *An Essay Concerning Human Understanding*, edited from the fourth (1700) edition by Peter H. Nidditch, Oxford: Oxford University Press, 1975, II, I, 4, p. 105, and II, xxvii, 9, p. 335; D. M. Armstrong, "The Causal Theory of Mind" and "What is Consciousness?", in his *The Nature of Mind*, St Lucia, Queensland: University of Queensland Press, 1980, pp. 16–31 and pp. 55–67. See also William G. Lycan, *Consciousness and Experience*, Cambridge, Massachusetts: MIT Press/Bradford Books, 1996.

Locke's remark that it's "impossible for any one to perceive, without perceiving, that he does perceive" echoes Aristotle at *de Anima*, Γ2, 425b12–20, and *Nicomachean Ethics* IX, 9, 1170a29–a34. The term 'inner sense' derives from Kant, *Critique of Pure Reason*, tr. Werner S. Pluhar, Indianapolis: Hackett Publishing Co., 1996, A22/B37, p. 77.

[18] Aristotle holds that perceptible color and sound occur in the sense organs when we perceive. That suggests to him that we see our visual perceptions and hear our auditory perceptions, but in a way different from the way in which we see and hear sights and sounds (*de Anima*, Γ2, 425b12–25). The difference he has in mind between the two ways of seeing and hearing may correspond to the difference in the ways color and sound occur in perceptible objects and in sense organs, since he thinks that the properties we perceive objects to have occur in the sense organs, though without their ordinary matter. See, e.g., *de Anima*, B12, 424a17–26.

But Aristotle's view here is unconvincing. Sensing doesn't occur by way of the occurrence of color, sound, and other perceptible properties in our sense organs or any other part of our bodies.

in virtue of which we sense the first-order state.[19] But sensations always have some qualitative property or another. So the higher-order states in virtue of which we are conscious of our conscious sensations cannot themselves be sensations.[20] The only alternative is that they are thoughts. We are conscious of our conscious sensations, and of our conscious mental states generally, by having *higher-order thoughts* (HOTs) about those states.

The way we are conscious of our conscious states appears to us to be spontaneous and unmediated; hence the traditional dictum that we are directly or immediately conscious of those states. But the traditional dictum overshoots. We don't count a state as conscious if we become conscious of it by consciously observing our behavior, by applying a theory to ourselves, or by relying on somebody else's observation. That's because in each of these cases a conscious inference mediates our becoming conscious of our mental state.

We count a state as being conscious only when we are conscious of it independently of any such conscious inference—any inference, that is, of which we are conscious. One must be conscious of the state in a way that does not rely on conscious inference.[21] The traditional dictum overshoots because a state's being conscious does not

---

[19] A state's being conscious requires being conscious of that state, but not that one is also conscious of the higher-order state in virtue of which one is conscious of the first-order state. So one might urge that the only reason we don't think that any higher-order qualities occur is that we aren't conscious of those higher-order qualities or of the sensations that have them.

When we introspect a conscious state, however, we are conscious not only of the first-order state, but also of the higher-order state. We are conscious of being conscious of the first-order state. (For more on introspection, see "Introspection and Self-Interpretation," ch. 4 in this volume.) But even then we aren't conscious of any higher-order sensory qualities.

One can be conscious of things in one respect but not another. So perhaps such introspecting makes us conscious *that* we're conscious of a mental state without thereby making us also conscious of *how* we're conscious of that state. That would leave open the possibility that we are conscious of our conscious states by sensing them even though introspection does not reveal that that's how we're conscious of them, nor what qualitative properties such higher-order sensing involves. (I am grateful to Meehan for pressing this objection.)

But it's doubtful that one can be conscious of being conscious of something without being conscious of some feature or other in respect of which one is conscious of that thing. So, if one senses some object or state, being conscious of one's being conscious of it would require that one be conscious of sensing it. And one can be conscious of sensing something only if one is conscious of some qualitative property in virtue of which one senses it.

[20] Lycan concedes that those higher-order states do not involve qualitative character, but insists that they are nonetheless more like perceptions than like thoughts ("The Superiority of HOP to HOT," in *Higher-Order Theories of Consciousness*, ed. Gennaro, pp. 93–113, §§V–VI). But his specific suggestions about how the higher-order states more closely resemble perceptions are unconvincing. See my "Varieties of Higher-Order Theory," §III.

Doubtless an inner-sense theory has appeal in large measure because sensing is the more basic way in which creatures are conscious of things. It may even be by analogy with sensing that we count a thought as making us conscious of something only if that thought represents the thing as present to us, since sensing always represents what's sensed as being present. But sensing and perceiving do not, despite this more basic character, figure in the way we are conscious of our conscious states.

[21] Even if some conscious inference does occur, a state would be conscious if one is also conscious of it in some way that's independent of any conscious inference.

preclude something's mediating between the state and one's being conscious of it so long as one isn't conscious of that mediation. What's required is subjective independence of inference, not causal independence. I'll call a HOT *noninferential* when one has that HOT independent of conscious inference. So a mental state's being conscious consists in one's having a noninferential HOT about that state.

For a state to count as conscious, I must be conscious of it in a way that seems, subjectively, to be unmediated. But the state must also be a mental state; we do not count as conscious any nonmental state, even if one is conscious of it in a way that seems to one unmediated. This doesn't require that one have a concept of a property as being mental. One can be conscious of a mental property without being conscious of it *as mental,* just as one can be conscious of qualitative states without having a specific concept of such a state.

Still, why must a state be mental for it to count as a conscious state? The best explanation is that it is only in virtue of being in mental states that we are conscious of things and conscious that something is the case. We apply 'conscious' to a state only if it's the kind of state in virtue of being in which we are conscious of something or that something is so.

We are not ordinarily conscious of ourselves as having HOTs about our conscious mental states. But that's exactly what the model predicts. We would be conscious of ourselves as having such HOTs only if those thoughts were themselves conscious. But as with other mental states, HOTs are conscious only when we have yet higher-order thoughts about them, which presumably seldom happens. On the HOT hypothesis, a mental state is conscious because an accompanying HOT makes one conscious of oneself as being in that state. But that hypothesis does not rely on our being introspectively aware of those HOTs, but rather on the explanatory work that the hypothesis can do. HOTs are theoretical posits, whose existence is established by the explanatory success of the theory that posits them.

One reason some have favored a theory such as Brentano's, on which a state's being conscious is built into the state itself, is that we thereby avoid a regress in which the first-order state is conscious in virtue of a second-order state, which is in turn conscious in virtue of a third-order state, and so forth. But since the second-order thought needn't be conscious, no such regress threatens.[22]

The conscious dependence on inference that prevents a state from being conscious does not require that one be conscious of a specific inference on which the HOT relies. A state would fail to be conscious even if one simply had a conscious sense that there is some relevant inference, at least if one weren't also conscious of the state independently of that sense of there being some such inference. I'm grateful to Ned Block for this observation.

[22] One might wonder why building consciousness into the state would forestall such regress, since, if we are in turn conscious of that consciousness, some third-order consciousness would in any case be required. And, if the higher-order consciousness needn't itself be conscious, that's what cuts off the regress, whether or not the higher-order consciousness is internal to the state.

Brentano, however, urges that the awareness of the state is an awareness both of the first-order aspects of the state and of the awareness itself (p. 129); the reflexivity of the higher-order consciousness is what terminates the regress. The more telling difficulty is that internal higher-order consciousness doesn't square with individuating mental states by way of mental attitude. See n. 9.

One might object that a HOT cannot confer on its target the property of being conscious unless that HOT is itself conscious. But that idea, reminiscent of the scholastic dictum that there can be only as much reality in an effect as there is in a cause, is groundless. HOTs do not transfer the property of being conscious from themselves to their targets; indeed, they don't induce any change whatever in those targets. Rather, they make their targets conscious because a state's being conscious consists simply in one's being suitably conscious of oneself as being in that state, and having a HOT is the right way of being conscious of oneself as being in a state.

There are various refinements we can add to this HOT model of consciousness. HOTs cannot be dispositional, for example, since being disposed to have a thought about something as being present doesn't make one conscious of that thing.[23] More interesting, the mental attitude of a HOT must be assertoric; wondering and doubting about things, for example, do not by themselves make one conscious of those things. That's why unconsciously feeling guilty about wanting something would not alone result in that desire's being conscious, since feeling guilty about something does not involve an assertoric attitude. Similarly, the strikingly accurate forced-choice guessing that subjects perform in tests for blindsight and for subliminal vision in masked priming experiments also cannot make the relevant visual states conscious. Even if these guesses are occasionally about what visual state one is in, guessing about something doesn't make one conscious of it.[24]

---

[23] *Pace* Peter Carruthers, *Phenomenal Consciousness: A Naturalistic Theory*, Cambridge: Cambridge University Press, 2000. For more on the difficulties facing dispositional higher-order theories, see "Thinking that One Thinks," § IV.

Carruthers argues that occurrent HOTs would result in cognitive overload, which dispositional HOTs would avoid. But we have no reason to think that we lack cortical resources sufficient for occurrent HOTs. Nor is it at first sight obvious why dispositions, which are themselves states, would require fewer cognitive resources.

Carruthers's answer appeals to his view about intentional content, on which a state's content is in part a matter of that state's being disposed to cause other states and behavior. And he posits that first-order states are available to a mind-reading subsystem, so that given the theory of content, such availability will by itself confer higher-order content on those states. But many states occur sometimes consciously and at other times not. And, if a state's being conscious results from its being available to the mind-reading subsystem, it's unclear why that state would ever occur without being conscious, since ties to that subsystem would presumably be fairly stable. Shifts in such availability, moreover, would be at least as demanding on cognitive resources as occurrent HOTs.

Because the first-order states end up having higher-order content on Carruthers's theory, he can explain our being conscious of those first-order states. But, since the first-order states do have higher-order content, it's strictly speaking the theory of content, and not the theory of consciousness, that appeals to dispositions. In any case, it's preferable if we can have a theory of consciousness that does not rely on a controversial theory of intentional content.

For more on Carruthers's theory, see "Varieties of Higher-Order Theory," §IV.

[24] Such forced-choice guessing is ordinarily about the presence of external stimuli, not the occurrence of visual states, since these subjects routinely deny being in any relevant visual states. But a sufficiently knowledgeable and experienced subject might also sometimes guess about what visual states are occurring.

Guessing is a complicated phenomenon. Guessing often fails to make one conscious of things because of the lack of conviction. But guessing does sometimes involve some measure of conviction.

Rather than pursue such refinements further,[25] let me turn directly to the way the HOT model applies to sensations and their mental qualities. The HOT hypothesis explains how conscious states differ from those which aren't conscious; we are conscious of our conscious states by having a HOT about them, and there is no HOT to make us conscious of states that aren't conscious.

But the HOT hypothesis also explains differences in what it's like for one to be in different qualitative states. What it's like for one to be in a qualitative state is a matter of how one is conscious of that state. If I am conscious of myself as having a sensation with the mental quality red, that will be what it's like for me, and similarly for every other mental quality. And how we are conscious of our qualitative states is a matter of how our HOTs characterize those states. There being something it's like for me to be in a state with a particular mental quality is a matter of my having a HOT that characterizes a state I am in as having that mental quality.

Even when qualitative states are conscious, we are conscious of their mental qualities in more or less refined ways. When one has a sensation of red, for example, one is sometimes conscious of it in respect of a highly specific shade of red, and sometimes simply in respect of some nondescript shade; similarly for saturation and brightness.

How one is conscious of the sensation is of course partly a function of the sensation itself. The sensation might simply have more or less refined qualities due to the specific stimulus conditions, and the way one is conscious of the sensation might just follow suit. Discussions of qualitative consciousness seem to take this as the typical case, possibly because they tacitly assume that the way a qualitative state is conscious is intrinsic to the state itself.

But how we're conscious of our sensations can also vary with other factors, such as attention, interest, passing distractions, and experience at discerning various mental qualities. Even when perceptual conditions don't vary, so we can assume that the sensation and its qualities are constant, we may be conscious of those qualities in a relatively refined way or in a relatively undiscriminating way. Indeed, cases occur in

Even in these cases, however, it differs from asserting, since one will be disposed to regard one's hunch as not relying on anything firm.

An experienced, knowledgeable subject might not merely guess with conviction about occurrent mental states, but even outright affirm that they occur. Still, since such assertions would rely on the subject's conscious inference from dispositions to guess about stimuli, the resulting awareness of those states would not be subjectively unmediated, and the states would not be conscious.

For more on such guessing, see Zoltán Dienes and Josef Perner, "Assumptions of a Subjective Measure of Consciousness: Three Mappings," in *Higher-Order Theories of Consciousness*, ed. Gennaro, pp. 173–199, Zoltán Dienes, "Assumptions of Subjective Measures of Unconscious Mental States: Higher-Order Thoughts and Bias," *Journal of Consciousness Studies*, 11, 9 (September 2004): 25–45; and Marcel, "Slippage in the Unity of Consciousness," in Gregory R. Bock and Joan Marsh, eds., *Experimental and Theoretical Studies of Consciousness*, Ciba Foundation Symposium No. 174, Chichester: John Wiley & Sons, 1993, pp. 168–186.

[25] For more on the HOT model generally, see "Two Concepts of Consciousness"; "The Independence of Consciousness and Sensory Quality," ch. 5 in this volume; "Thinking that One Thinks"; "Varieties of Higher-Order Theory"; and "Explaining Consciousness," in *Philosophy of Mind: Classical and Contemporary Readings*, ed. David J. Chalmers, New York: Oxford University Press, 2002, pp. 406–421.

which increased attention to one's sensation seems by itself dramatically to enhance the way one is conscious of the qualities of the sensation.

The HOT model readily explains such variation in the way we are conscious of our qualitative states. When I have a HOT about such a state, that HOT represents me as being in a certain type of state. My HOT may simply be to the effect that I have a red sensation, but it may instead be that I have a bright, saturated, claret red sensation. How I represent to myself the sensation I have determines what it's like for me to have it. Differences in my HOTs result in differences in what it's like for me to have my qualitative states.

The HOT model not only allows us to explain such variation in how we're conscious of our conscious sensations; there are some cases that it's unlikely any other model could handle. It sometimes happens that learning new words for the qualities of our sensations actually affects how we are conscious of those sensations. Consider learning to taste wines. Being told words for gustatory qualities sometimes actually leads to one's coming to be aware of those qualities; one comes to be aware of such gustatory qualities as sharp, tannin, or robust by having verbal pegs on which to hang those conscious experiences.

The same happens with other sensory modalities as well. One may not be conscious of any differences between the auditory sensations that result from hearing oboes and clarinets until one learns words for the different qualities. Learning those terms will then sometimes lead to one's being conscious of the sensory qualities as being of distinct types.

Perhaps repeated experience is also sometimes responsible for our sensations coming to seem to have more refined qualities. But other times learning new words for mental qualities seems by itself to bring out those conscious qualities. It's highly implausible that learning the new words actually generates the new qualities and we're then automatically conscious of them. What mechanism might explain such generation of new qualities?[26] Far more likely is that our having new ways to describe our mental qualities results in our being conscious in new ways of qualities that were already there.[27] But the words we use simply reflect the thoughts we have, in this case thoughts about our mental qualities. So the qualities in respect of which our qualitative states in these cases are just the qualities our thoughts represent those states

---

[26] Repeated exposure to stimuli of a particular type sometimes results in so-called perceptual learning, in which we do come to have a correspondingly new type of mental quality. But that mechanism is unlikely to be operative here. For one thing, the effect of learning the new words is typically quite dramatic and occurs immediately after learning the new word. And in any case the learning of new words plays no role in perceptual learning.

[27] Which process is operative is in any case subject to empirical test, since nonconscious qualitative states often have priming effects that can reveal their occurrence. So such effects might show whether the relevant mental qualities had occurred prior to the learning of the new words and the qualities' becoming conscious.

On priming, see, e.g., Marcel, "Conscious and Unconscious Perception: An Approach to the Relations between Phenomenal Experience and Perceptual Processes," *Cognitive Psychology* 15 (1983): 238–300, and "Conscious and Unconscious Perception: Experiments on Visual Masking and Word Recognition," *Cognitive Psychology*, 15 (1983): 197–237.

as having. A qualitative state's being conscious *as* having one quality or another is a matter of one's having a HOT about the state *as having that quality.*[28]

The woodwind and wine cases are unusual, and so may seem not to reflect what normally happens when we come to be conscious of mental qualities and the differences among them. But these cases are special only in that we seldom learn to discriminate sensory qualities late enough in life for us to notice how the process works. We come to be conscious of most qualitative differences long before we have any overt vocabulary in which to express our thoughts about the relevant qualities. But absence of verbal expression does not mean that there are no thoughts about those qualitative states. And, since we know of no other mechanism by which we might become conscious of differences among qualitative properties, it's likely that things always happen in roughly the way they do in the wine and woodwind cases.

Being conscious of fine-grained differences among mental qualities by way of HOTs requires having the conceptual resources needed to capture those qualitative differences. But one might question whether we have such fine-grained conceptual resources. Plainly we don't have individual words for all the slight variations in qualitative variation we can consciously discern. Since mastery of words is the usual mark of having concepts, the lack of such words suggests a lack of the corresponding concepts.

We plainly don't have single words or concepts for all the mental colors or other qualities we can discriminate, whether presented one by one or simultaneously. But it hardly follows that we lack the conceptual resources to differentiate between any two qualities that we can consciously distinguish. Though we have a relatively small stock of noncomparative concepts for mental qualities, by supplementing those noncomparative concepts with comparative concepts, we have ample resources to distinguish conceptually any qualities we can consciously discern. Thus two discriminable shades of red may differ because one is slightly darker, slightly bluer or more yellow, slightly brighter, or slightly more like the color of some particular type of object. We have a huge range of comparative concepts available for HOTs to use in representing distinct qualitative properties. We get additional leverage from concepts for qualities characteristic of particular types of physical object, such as the yellow of bananas as against the yellow of lemons. But the most fine-grained discriminations doubtless always rely in significant measure on comparative concepts.

Our use of comparative concepts for qualities to supplement our smaller stock of noncomparative concepts also helps with another challenge. Diana Raffman has drawn attention to our ability to judge whether two simultaneously presented qualities are the same or different far more accurately than we can identify, recognize, or remember those very same qualities when they occur one by one.[29] We can often

---

[28] In the wine-tasting and musical-experience cases, people do typically focus on the character of their experiences; so the new words one learns apply to those experiences, and not the wines or physical sounds.

[29] "On the Persistence of Phenomenology," in *Conscious Experience*, ed. Thomas Metzinger, Exeter, UK: Imprint Academic, 1995, pp. 293–308, at p. 295. On color memory, see, e.g., Jules

discriminate two nearly identical shades of red seen together even if we can't tell which of the two we're seeing when each occurs by itself.

Raffman uses this phenomenon to argue against the view that subjective qualities are nothing more than mental descriptions of physical properties.[30] But it may also suggest a difficulty for the HOT hypothesis. If a state is conscious in virtue of one's having a HOT about that state, why would such HOTs make one conscious of qualitative states in respect of very fine-grained differences when those states occur together, but not when they occur separately? We can assume that HOTs typically arise in response to the qualitative states they are about; if so, why would qualitative states cause less fine-grained HOTs when the states occur one by one than when they occur together? Why would the intentional content of our HOTs differ depending on whether their target qualitative states occur singly or together?

There is no problem in recognizing, identifying, and remembering colors when they are as different as red and orange, or blue and purple; there we have individual, noncomparative concepts to rely on. A difficulty arises only when our qualitative states differ in color only slightly, and we lack any noncomparative concepts for those slight variations. In these cases, we're likely to be conscious of slight differences only when we have available for comparison two or more simultaneous qualities. We are conscious of variations for which we have noncomparative concepts whether the qualities occur together or on their own. But, when qualitative differences are so slight that we capture them only using comparative concepts as well, then we are conscious of those slight differences only when the qualities occur together. This strongly suggests that what matters to the way we're conscious of these qualities is the kind of concept we have available to individuate the qualities.

Even when seeing two very similar colors together results in two plainly different conscious color experiences, moreover, it may well be that seeing each separately would result in color experiences that are subjectively indistinguishable. This is just what the HOT hypothesis predicts. When we see the two together, our conscious experiences of them differ because of the comparative concepts that figure in our HOTs. When we see the very same colors separately, there is seldom any way to apply the relevant comparative concepts; so the resulting conscious experiences are subjectively the same. This again is a striking confirmation of the HOT hypothesis.

The difference between cases in which we have noncomparative concepts to characterize mental qualities and cases in which we must in addition rely on comparative concepts actually reflects a difference in the way we experience things phenomenologically. When we are aware of the differences between two very close qualities for which we have no single words, it seems subjectively as though we are aware of the difference only comparatively; when noncomparative concepts will do, it doesn't seem that way.

Davidoff, *Cognition through Color*, Cambridge, Massachusetts: MIT Press/Bradford Books, 1991, pp. 108–9, and references given there.

[30] This echoes a representationalist account, on which the only mental properties we are introspectively aware of are intentional properties. For more on representationalism, see §VII.

III. PHENOMENALITY AND THE EXPLANATORY GAP

In a number of influential articles, Block has argued that qualitative states are conscious in a way that's wholly independent of any awareness we have of those states, and indeed independent of any mental access we might have to them. He calls this special kind of consciousness *phenomenal consciousness*[31] or, more recently, *phenomenality*,[32] and he distinguishes it from two other kinds of consciousness, which he calls *access* and *monitoring* consciousness. A state's being access conscious consists in its content's being "poised to be used as a premise in reasoning, . . . [and] for [the] *rational* control of action and . . . speech."[33] And a state exhibits monitoring consciousness "just in case it is the object of another of the subject's states, for example one has a thought to the effect that one has that experience" ("Paradox and Cross Purposes," p. 205).

It is unclear, however, that Block's notion of access consciousness actually picks out any phenomenon that we intuitively regard as a kind of consciousness. Though our classifying a state as conscious does often go hand in hand with its having content that's poised to influence speech, action, and reasoning, the two properties often don't go together. Many states that we would in no intuitive way count as conscious nonetheless have content that's poised for use in reasoning and the rational control of action and speech. Mental states need not be conscious in order to have a significant, active influence on our reasoning, action, and speech. A state's being conscious, in whatever way, is one thing and its role in mental processing another.

Since what Block calls access consciousness is itself independent of any intuitive notion of consciousness, we can expect that it will occur, as Block maintains, independently of phenomenality. But there are also complications about phenomenality and what Block calls monitoring consciousness. A state exhibits monitoring consciousness if it's the object of another of the subject's states. So, if phenomenality does occur independently of monitoring consciousness, it occurs independently of any HOTs. And if phenomenality is indeed a kind of consciousness, then qualitative states exhibit that kind of consciousness even when unaccompanied by HOTs.

Block's notion of monitoring consciousness, however, conceals a crucial ambiguity. Block intends that concept to apply only to cases in which it's intuitively obvious that one mental state is the object of another. And that restricts consideration to cases in which the higher-order state is itself conscious; it's not monitoring consciousness if

---

[31] "On a Confusion about a Function of Consciousness," *The Behavioral and Brain Sciences*, 18, 2 (June 1995): 227–247; review of Daniel C. Dennett, *Consciousness Explained*, *The Journal of Philosophy*, XC, 4 (April 1993): 181–193, p. 184; "Begging the Question against Phenomenal Consciousness"; and "Consciousness and Accessibility," *The Behavioral and Brain Sciences*, XIII, 4 (December 1990): 596–598.

[32] "Paradox and Cross Purposes in Recent Work on Consciousness," *Cognition*, 79, 1–2 (April 2001): 197–219, p. 202.

[33] "On a Confusion about a Function of Consciousness," p. 231, emphasis Block's.

one is in no way at all aware of the higher-order state. So Block's claim that phenom-enality occurs without monitoring consciousness means only that it occurs without conscious monitoring.

But this in no way conflicts with the HOT model. HOTs are seldom conscious, nor need they be conscious for one to be conscious of their target states, and hence for those targets to be conscious states.[34] So the occurrence of phenomenality without conscious monitoring doesn't tell against the HOT hypothesis. The hypothesis would face difficulty only if conscious qualitative states occurred independently even of higher-order states that were not conscious. But there is no reason to think that this ever occurs. Indeed, we could have no intuitive, commonsense reason to think that it ever does occur. Since we are unaware of any monitoring that isn't conscious, there could be no subjective difference between a case in which nonconscious monitoring occurs and a case in which it doesn't, no difference, that is, from the point of view of consciousness itself.

There can be no subjective reason to think that phenomenality occurs without nonconscious monitoring states. But Block urges that theoretical considerations show that phenomenality does occur in the absence of higher-order monitoring, whether conscious or not. In the condition known as visual extinction, subjects presented with identical objects on both sides of their field of vision report seeing only one, though there is compelling evidence that subjects are also perceptually responsive to the stim-ulus they report not seeing.[35] Block takes this to be a case of phenomenality without monitoring; subjects "have phenomenal experience . . . without knowing it" ("Para-dox and Cross Purposes," p. 203).

But this interpretation is at odds with Block's official definition of phenomenality as there being something "it is like to have an experience" (202). What it's like to have an experience is, in the relevant sense, what it's like *for one* to have that experience. And if one isn't in any way aware of an experience, there simply isn't anything it's like for one to have it.[36] Since subjects aren't in any way aware of the relevant experiences

---

[34] We are often conscious of things without being conscious of the states in virtue of which we are conscious of those things. If I respond to something that I see only subliminally, I am conscious of that thing, though not, as we might say, consciously aware of it. Indeed, I would presumably have been unable to respond to it at all if I was in no way conscious of it.

[35] E.g., the object not consciously seen nonetheless primes for consciously seeing other stimuli.

[36] Replying elsewhere to this point, Block has argued that the relevant way in which there's something it's like to have a conscious experience does not involve there being anything it's like *for the subject*. The additional phrase, he insists, implies having access to oneself, which is unnecessary for phenomenality ("Biology versus Computation in the Study of Consciousness," *The Behavioral and Brain Sciences*, 20, 1 [March 1997]: 159–166, p. 162).

But there being something it's like *for one* does not imply explicit conscious access to oneself. And some access to oneself, albeit perhaps only nonconscious, must occur if there being something it's like is to be distinctively subjective. The way in which there is something it's like to have an experience will involve subjectivity only if there is more to it than, e.g., what it's like for something to be a table. We can capture the difference, as Thomas Nagel has noted, only if the subjective case involves there being something that it's like *for one*. See his "What Is It Like to Be a Bat?", *The Philosophical Review*, LXXXIII, 4 (October 1974): 435–450; reprinted in Nagel, *Mortal Questions*, Cambridge: Cambridge University Press, 1979, pp. 165–180, at p. 166.

in visual extinction, there is nothing it's like for them to have those experiences, and hence no phenomenality, at least on the best understanding of Block's notion. There are nonconscious states with qualitative properties, but there is nothing it's like for one to have those qualitative properties if one is in no way whatever aware of them.[37]

There is an important ambiguity in Block's notion of phenomenality. There is what we can call the *thick* phenomenality that occurs when there is something it's like for one to have an experience. But there is also the *thin* phenomenality that occurs when one is wholly unaware of an experience. Such thin phenomenality consists in mental qualities of which we aren't in any way conscious.

It's reasonable to speculate that Block's insistence that phenomenality occurs without monitoring or access consciousness rests on conflating those two things. Because thick phenomenality involves there being something it's like for one to have an experience, it cannot occur without one's being in some suitable way conscious of the state. And that requires one to be in some higher-order state in virtue of which one is conscious of the state that exhibits thick phenomenality. The thin phenomenality that occurs, for example, in visual extinction does occur independently of one's having any relevant mental access to it. And, since it involves only mental qualities of which one is unaware, there is nothing it's like for one to have them. All this fits comfortably with the HOT hypothesis.

Because one is in no way conscious of the thin phenomenality that occurs in visual extinction, it is not intuitively a kind of consciousness at all. Thick phenomenality does involve qualitative states' being conscious. But, even so, it is best not seen as a distinct kind of consciousness, but simply as a special case of the way mental states are conscious in general. It is the case in which the state that's conscious is qualitative, as against those in which the conscious state is intentional and nonqualitative. There is only one way mental states are conscious, though the states that are conscious fall into the two broad categories of the qualitative and the intentional.[38]

---

[37] These considerations aside, higher-order conceptual states may well figure in any explanation of visual extinction. Extinction typically occurs only when subjects are presented with two objects of the same type, even when the two have different colors or shapes. See Robert Rafal and Lynn Robertson, "The Neurology of Visual Neglect," *The Cognitive Neurosciences*, ed. Michael S. Gazzaniga *et al.*, Cambridge, Massachusetts: MIT Press, 1995, pp. 625–648, at pp. 625–6. So, for a sensation to be extinguished, the subject must conceptualize the thing sensed as being of the same type as the thing sensed by another of the subject's current sensations. And that conceptualization must play a role in the extinction of one sensation, since the two objects must be conceptualized as being of the same type for extinction to occur. So the conceptualization of the objects sensed as being of the same type may well affect the way we conceptualize the two states, themselves. Some higher-order conceptualization may well in some way figure in visual extinction.

[38] The theoretical intuition that what it is for a state to be conscious is different for intentional and qualitative states may be due to the different kinds of process that give rise to HOTs for states of the two sorts. I discuss the process that facilitates HOTs about qualitative states in §VI, below, and the somewhat different process that facilitates HOTs about intentional states in "Why Are Verbally Expressed Thoughts Conscious?", ch. 10 in this volume, §5.

I discuss Block's views at greater length in "How Many Kinds of Consciousness," *Consciousness and Cognition*, 11, 4 (December 2002): 653–665, and in "The Kinds of Consciousness", MS, delivered at the University of Oxford Autumn School in Cognitive Neuroscience, October 1998.

Block's concerns about phenomenality do not undermine the HOT model. Still, it is sometimes said on different grounds that, however well the HOT model may deal with the consciousness of thoughts and desires, it cannot capture what it is for qualitative states to be conscious. As Block stresses, there is always something it's like for one to be in a conscious qualitative state; by contrast, there is nothing it's like for one to be in a qualitative state that isn't conscious. The two kinds of case differ, on the HOT hypothesis, because HOTs accompany qualitative states only when they're conscious. But how, it may be asked, could simply having a thought make the difference between there being something it's like for one to be in a particular qualitative state and there not being anything it's like for one? How could the occurrence of a merely intentional state result in there being something it's like for one to be in a qualitative state?

We've already seen that having thoughts about one's qualitative states affects the way those states appear to consciousness. Learning new words for qualities could make a difference to how we're conscious of our qualitative states only if thoughts that these words could figure in the expression of can make such a difference. What a qualitative state is like for one is a matter of how one is conscious of it, and hence of how one represents that state to oneself. And that's a matter, in turn, of how the HOT one has about the state characterizes it. One's HOT about a qualitative state determines what it's like for one to be in that state—what it's like qualitatively.

My HOT determines whether what it's like for me is, say, having a conscious experience of magenta or a conscious experience of some nondescript red. And, since the HOT one has can make that difference, whether or not one has any relevant HOT at all can make the difference between there being something it's like for one to be in a particular state and there being nothing whatever that it's like for one. HOTs need not have qualitative character for the qualitative states they are about to be conscious states; they need simply represent those states as having qualitative character. It's in virtue of HOTs that we are conscious of ourselves as being in states with qualitative character.

Block rejects the idea that qualitative consciousness is a matter of one's being conscious of a qualitative state. We're conscious of many things noninferentially and nonobservationally even though those things don't come to exhibit qualitative consciousness. He writes: "[E]ven if I were to come to know about states of my liver noninferentially and nonobservationally (as some people know what time it is), that wouldn't make those states P[henomenally]-conscious."[39]

But, as already noted, one's coming to be conscious of a state noninferentially results in its being conscious only if the state is mental to begin with, and liver states aren't mental. Only if a state is mental will coming to be conscious of it noninferentially result in its having conscious qualitative character. Some liver states do resemble mental states in tracking and carrying information; some liver states, for example, track information about blood-glucose levels. But to be mental, a state must be either an intentional or a qualitative state. Liver states plainly don't qualify as intentional

---

[39] "How Many Concepts of Consciousness?" [Author's Response to Open Peer Commentary on "On a Confusion about a Function of Consciousness"], *The Behavioral and Brain Sciences*, 18, 2 (June 1995): 272–287, p. 280.

states; even if one held that they have something like intentional content, they lack mental attitude, which intentional states all have. And we have good reason not to count liver states as qualitative states, since they don't interact in any relevant ways with states and processes we independently know to be mental, such as perceptions, perceptual thoughts, and desires.

We can imagine things' being different, so that some liver states did interact with desires or perceptions. And perhaps those liver states would in that case be mental. Being noninferentially conscious of them would then result in there being something it's like for us to be in those states, as happens with the enteroceptive states that detect conditions of our viscera. Being noninferentially conscious of those states would result in qualitative consciousness.

Block would contest this, since he holds that coming to know noninferentially about states of one's mind doesn't result in there being something it's like for one to be in those states. But that's just what's at issue. And we cannot settle the question by appeal to introspectively based intuition. Introspection cannot reveal which mental, but nonconscious, conditions are sufficient for qualitative consciousness. For that we need an independently warranted theory. And, as we've seen, there is reason independent of this question to think that HOTs do make a difference to what it's like for one to be in qualitative states. And, since HOTs make a difference to what it's like for one to be in a qualitative state, they can even make the difference between there being something it's like for one and there being nothing it's like for one.

It's sometimes held that the HOT model portrays consciousness as being verbal and intellectual in a way that misrepresents our everyday stream of consciousness. Conscious thoughts do have a verbal air to them; we are typically conscious of thoughts in verbal terms, specifically, in terms of speech acts that would express them.[40] But thoughts that aren't conscious cannot result in any sense of anything verbal or intellectual. And HOTs are seldom conscious, especially those which occur in connection with our ordinary stream of consciousness.

Still, a sense may persist that the HOT model can't do justice to what it's like for one to be in conscious states with qualitative properties. One might seek to explain that persistent sense by appeal to the idea that the model doesn't reveal any rational connection between a qualitative state's being accompanied by a HOT and there being something it's like for one to be in that state. And one might urge that such a rational connection is needed if a qualitative state's being accompanied by a HOT is to explain what's involved in there being something it's like for one to be in that state. This objection is in the spirit of Joseph Levine's claim that there is an explanatory gap that precludes any intelligible explanation of conscious qualitative states in terms of anything physical (see n. 2, above). It also animates David Chalmers's claim that we cannot reductively explain qualitative consciousness.[41]

---

[40] See "Why Are Verbally Expressed Thoughts Conscious?", §5, and "Content, Interpretation, and Consciousness," ch. 12 in this volume, §3.

[41] David J. Chalmers, *The Conscious Mind: In Search of a Fundamental Theory*, New York: Oxford University Press, 1996.

But the objection relies on untenable demands. Connections among things seem intelligible to us only against the backdrop of a theory, whether a scientific or folk theory, which locates those connections in a larger explanatory framework. In advance of any such theory, the connections one type of thing has with another will inevitably seem arbitrary and unintelligible; connections come to seem intelligible only when theorizing forges a structure that embraces them and makes them predictable.[42] On the HOT hypothesis, a mental state's being conscious consists in one's being conscious of oneself as being in that state by having a HOT to the effect that one is in it. If that hypothesis is correct, it provides an intelligible connection between HOTs and there being something it's like for one to be in a qualitative state. Since we cannot judge whether an intelligible connection obtains independently of judging the success of some relevant theory, we cannot undermine the theory by insisting that no connection obtains independent of such a theory.

Levine urges that the situation with conscious qualitative states differs in an important way from other cases of explanation, such as that which results from establishing that water is identical with H_2O. In the water case, he insists, "once all the relevant information is supplied, any request for explanation of the identit[y] is quite unintelligible." But when we identify a type of qualitative state with some type of neural state, he maintains, "it still seems quite intelligible to wonder how it could be true, or what explains it, even after the relevant physical and functional facts are filled in" (*Purple Haze*, pp. 81–2).

But it isn't simply such facts that make the identity of water with H_2O seem intelligible, but a larger theory in which the relevant identity is embedded. If we had a successful theory that embraced both qualitative and neural states, identities between the two types of state would seem intelligible as well. The apparent disanalogy Levine notes is due only to there currently being no such widely accepted theory for qualitative and neural states. The HOT hypothesis, moreover, helps show what such a theory will look like, by describing in mental terms the higher-order states necessary for qualitative consciousness, states we can hope someday to identify in neural terms as well.

The sense that such intelligibility will not be forthcoming very likely stems in significant measure from a prior theoretical conviction that qualitative mental properties aren't the sort of properties that will ever yield to an informative account. And, if no informative account of qualitative properties is possible, no theory can forge comprehensible structures and connections that involve those qualities. If we can't say anything informative about qualitative properties, how can the connections they have with other things be rationally intelligible?

---

[42] See my "Reductionism and Knowledge," in *How Many Questions?: Essays in Honor of Sidney Morgenbesser*, ed. Leigh S. Cauman, Isaac Levi, Charles Parsons, and Robert Schwartz, Indianapolis: Hackett Publishing Co., 1983, pp. 276–300.

Even when the connections within a theory are intelligible and rational, we would still need bridge laws that connect the items the theory posits, in this case HOTs, to the items the theory is meant to explain, in this case conscious qualitative states. And those bridge laws will themselves come to seem rational and intelligible only once the success of the theory makes the explanations it provides seem obvious and familiar.

Indeed, those who advocate an explanatory gap for mental qualities seldom say anything informative about the nature of those qualitative mental properties. And that lends some support to the diagnosis of pessimism about finding intelligible connections as stemming from a conviction that no informative account of mental qualities is possible.

But not giving an informative account of what qualitative properties are is not a serious option. When theorists make claims about qualitative states and their distinguishing qualitative properties, we need to know what they're talking about if we're to be able to understand and evaluate their claims. We cannot acquiesce in the unhelpful thought that we all know the qualitative when we see it. That would amount to picking the phenomenon out in purely ostensive terms, which leaves too much open for us to tell whether we can explain the phenomenon in a way that makes it intelligible. And as we've seen, it begs important theoretical questions simply to say that qualitative properties are those which involve the traditional conundra. Indeed, absent some independent account of what qualitative properties are, we cannot even determine whether those conundra, the explanatory gap included, obtain at all. So I turn now to the task of giving an informative account of qualitative mental properties.

IV. MENTAL QUALITIES AND PERCEPTIBLE PROPERTIES

I've argued that a qualitative state's being conscious consists in one's being conscious of oneself as being in a state with the relevant qualitative properties. So we cannot appeal to such consciousness to explain what qualitative properties are, but must instead give an account of those properties that proceeds independently of whether the states that have such properties are conscious.

As we saw in section I, it overshoots to claim that qualitative states, unlike nonmental, physiological states, are invariably conscious. Rather, qualitative states are states that can occur consciously, whereas their nonmental, physiological counterparts cannot.

Sensations of red typically result from certain characteristic stimulus conditions, roughly, from visual stimulation in good illumination by red objects. Similarly for other perceptual and bodily sensations. The traditional view, articulated by Aristotle, is that the mental qualities of perceptual sensations are literally identical with the commonsense perceptible properties of physical objects.[43] But the property of being red that physical objects have is plainly not the same as the property of being red that visual sensations exhibit.[44] For one thing, sensations aren't objects at all; they

---

[43] "[S]ensing receives sensible forms without their matter" (*de Anima*, B12, 424a18–19).

[44] See my "The Colors and Shapes of Visual Experiences," in *Consciousness and Intentionality: Models and Modalities of Attribution*, ed. Denis Fisette, Dordrecht: Kluwer Academic Publishers, 1999, pp. 95–118.

The insistence that mental qualities are distinct from the commonsense perceptible properties of physical objects is by no means new. See, e.g., George Berkeley, *A New Theory of Vision*, in *The Works of George Berkeley*, ed. A. A. Luce and T. E. Jessop, London: Thomas Nelson & Sons, 1948, I, §158; Thomas Reid, *Essays on the Intellectual Powers of Man*, ed. Baruch A. Brody, Cambridge,

are states of sentient creatures, and hence states of objects. So the redness of a sensation, unlike that of a physical object, is a property not of an object, but of a state of an object.

Although the redness of perceptual sensations isn't the same property as the redness of visible objects, an echo of that Aristotelian doctrine sometimes persists in the claim that there is only one property properly called redness. Physics requires that every property of physical objects is mathematically describable, and the commonsense qualitative character of physical redness seems to resist any such mathematical description. This has led many to urge that physical objects aren't literally colored at all; colors and other qualitative properties, on this view, are actually mental qualities, not properties of physical objects. We accommodate the strictures of a mathematical physics by relocating the commonsense perceptible qualities of physical objects to the mental realm. This view echoes the Aristotelian claim in its denial that there are two distinct types of qualitative property, mental qualities and commonsense perceptible properties.

I've argued elsewhere[45] that this relocation picture distorts our understanding of mental qualities, in part because it implies that sensations are intrinsically conscious. Whatever pressure exists to relocate commonsense physical qualities applies only insofar as those properties resist mathematical description, and they resist mathematical description only when we're conscious of them. Since we need to relocate commonsense physical properties only insofar as we're conscious of them, we end up conceiving of the relocated mental versions as properties of which we are invariably conscious.

But the relocation picture and its attendant distortions is not the only way we can accommodate the demands of a mathematical physics. We can instead identify perceptible physical qualities with appropriate mathematically describable properties. Commonsense physical red, for example, will be a particular reflectance property of physical objects or, more precisely, the set of reflectance properties that yield the right ratio of stimulation for the three light-sensitive elements of the daylight visual system.[46] We cannot specify the relevant sets except by reference to the discriminative abilities characteristic of the human visual system. But that presents no problem. Commonsense physical colors are those very sets of reflectance properties, however we come to pick them out and, indeed, whether or not anybody ever does pick them out. They are objective properties that physical objects have independently of ever being perceived.

What, then, are the properties, such as redness and greenness, which characterize our visual sensations? It won't work to try to understand those mental qualities as in

---

Massachusetts: MIT Press, 1969, II, xvi, p. 244; and G. E. Moore, "A Reply to My Critics," in *The Philosophy of G. E. Moore*, ed. Paul Arthur Schilpp, La Salle, Illinois: Open Court, 1942, 535–677, at pp. 655–658.

[45] "Sensory Quality and the Relocation Story."

[46] Still more precisely, we can identify each particular commonsense color property of a physical object with the spectral reflectance of that object multiplied by the absorption spectra of the three types of cone.

some way corresponding individually to commonsense physical red and green, much less to the reflectance properties with which we identify those commonsense physical colors. The individual qualitative properties of perceptual sensations do not resemble or in any other way match their individual physical counterparts.

But there is an important correspondence at the level of families of properties. The mental qualities of red and green that visual sensations exhibit belong to a family of properties whose similarities and differences correspond to the similarities and differences that hold among the commonsense color properties of physical objects. Just as commonsense physical red, for example, is closer to orange than to blue, so the mental quality of red is closer to the mental quality of orange than it is to the mental quality of blue. Similarly for all mental qualities of color.[47]

The same holds for sensations of other modalities. In each case, the ways the various mental qualities resemble and differ from one another are homomorphic to the ways the corresponding perceptible properties of physical objects and events resemble and differ. A sensation of the sound of a trumpet, for example, resembles a sensation of the sound of a woodwind more than it does a sensation of the sound of a violin.

This homomorphism account holds even for the various types of bodily sensation. The similarities and differences that characterize perceptual sensations for each modality are homomorphic to the similarities and differences that are discriminable among the perceptible properties accessible by way of that modality. Similarly, we describe bodily sensations in terms that are borrowed from the stimuli that characteristically occasion those sensations, and do so in a way that preserves discriminable similarities and differences. The pains we call sharp and dull, for example, typically result from sharp and dull objects, just as burning or stinging pains typically result from objects that burn or sting, and tickling sensations from ticklish stimuli. And sharp pains resemble stinging pains more than dull pains and resemble dull pains more than tickles.

Such homomorphisms enable us to extrapolate even from the geometrical properties of physical objects to the mental qualities that figure in spatial sensing and perceiving. We see colors as spatially bounded by various visible sizes and shapes. So the visual sensations in virtue of which we see physical colors as thus bounded must not

---

[47] See "The Independence of Consciousness and Sensory Quality," and "Sensory Quality and the Relocation Story," chs. 5 and 6 in this volume, "The Colors and Shapes of Visual Experiences," "Explaining Consciousness," in *Philosophy of Mind: Classical and Contemporary Readings*, ed. David J. Chalmers, New York: Oxford University Press, 2002, pp. 406–421, §§III–V, and "Subjective Character and Reflexive Content," *Philosophy and Phenomenological Research*, 68, 1 (January 2004): 191–198.

Cf. Wilfrid Sellars' view that "visual impressions stand to one another in a system of ways of resembling and differing which is structurally similar to the ways in which the colours and shapes of visible objects resemble and differ" ("Empiricism and the Philosophy of Mind," in his *Science, Perception and Reality* (*SPR*), London: Routledge & Kegan Paul, 1963, pp. 127–196, at p. 193). See also Sellars' "Being and Being Known," *SPR* 41–59, "Phenomenalism," *SPR* 60–105, esp. 91–95, and "Foundations for a Metaphysics of Pure Process," *The Monist*, LXIV, 1 (January 1981): 3–90. Cf. also Christopher Peacocke's discussion of what he calls sensational properties in "Colour Concepts and Colour Experiences," *Synthèse*, LVIII, 3 (March 1984): 365–381, and *Sense and Content*, Oxford: Oxford University Press, 1983.

only have mental qualities of color, but must also have associated mental qualities of size and shape. These spatial aspects of visual states cannot be spatial properties of the sort that physical objects exhibit, since the spatial properties of visual states constitute mental boundaries of mental color qualities, not boundaries of physical objects. And to do so, those spatial properties must themselves be mental qualities of size and shape.[48]

Similarly for other modalities. Spatial mental qualities of shape and size are determined in each modality by the mental boundaries among the content qualities characteristic of that modality, color for vision, pressure and resistance for touch, and so forth. And, because the content qualities that determine mental sizes and shapes differ from one modality to another, we cannot assume that those spatial mental qualities are themselves the same properties across modalities; indeed, it would be surprising if they were. The similarities and differences among spatial mental qualities are in every modality homomorphic to those which hold among the physical properties of size and shape. But homomorphism allows for distinct sets of mental qualities to correspond to those physical sizes and shapes. And, because these spatial mental qualities are presumably distinct properties from one modality to another, the perceiving of physical objects requires that these spatial qualities be calibrated across modalities. I'll return to this cross-modal calibration in section VII.

In addition to sensing things as having size and shape, we sense things as having spatial location. But the mental qualities that pertain to spatial location behave differently in an interesting respect from other mental qualities. One can at any moment have many visual sensations that exhibit a particular type of mental color, mental size, or mental shape. But, as Austen Clark has noted, if there are mental qualities that pertain to visual location, they would each be instantiated only once, since each type of location quality would pertain to a unique position in the visual field.[49] So, unlike mental qualities of color, size, and shape, there can at any given moment be only one mental location quality of any particular type.

According to Clark, mental qualities must be able to be multiply instantiated in the way mental color qualities are. So he concludes that there are no mental qualities of location that figure in the spatial aspect of sensing.[50] But mental qualities need not be multiply instantiable in that way. Just as the mental color qualities determine visual mental qualities of size and shape, so the arrangements of those mental colors also determine various mental spatial relations; each mental color patch is above or

---

[48] Because the spatial mental qualities determine boundaries of the mental colors of qualitative states, the retinotopic adjacency relations of neural activation in primary visual cortex (V1) cannot themselves constitute those spatial mental qualities.

[49] *A Theory of Sentience*, Oxford: Oxford University Press, 2000, pp. 56–57. See also his "Feature-Placing and Proto-Objects" and "Sensing, Objects, and Awareness: Reply to Commentators," *Philosophical Psychology*, 17, 4 (December 2004): 443–469 and 553–579, in a useful issue devoted to *A Theory of Sentience*.

[50] For that reason he also rejects the notion of a visual field, construed as an array of visual mental qualities; see *A Theory of Sentience*, chs. 2 and 3, *passim*, "Feature-Placing and Proto-Objects," §II, and Clark's "Three Varieties of Visual Field," *Philosophical Psychology*, 9, 4 (December 1996): 477–495.

below and to the left or right of various others. And those mental spatial relations in turn determine the unique mental location quality that pertains to each color patch. Similarly for the other modalities.[51]

Though no mental location quality is multiply instantiated, the mental spatial relations of left, right, above, and below that determine those mental locations are multiply instantiated. And those mental relations together define a mental qualitative field for each modality. As with other mental qualities, mental spatial relations and mental locations resemble and differ from one another in ways homomorphic to the similarities and differences that hold among the perceptible spatial relations and locations of physical objects. So the mental qualities of location and the mental spatial relations that determine them are all anchored in the spatial properties of perceptible objects and properties. But as in other cases, the anchoring does not occur quality by quality, but by way of the entire family of relevant qualities. The result is a uniform treatment of spatial and content mental qualities in terms of such homomorphisms.

Visual access to shape and access to color are in part subserved by distinct cortical areas that specialize in processing the two types of information. As is well known, this fits with Anne Treisman's important finding that illusory conjunctions of color and shape sometimes occur, in which subjects see visual shapes with the colors switched. This all points to the operation early in visual processing of some mechanism that combines color and visual shape, and sometimes does so inaccurately.[52] So there is a binding problem about how the visual system produces sensations with particular mental colors and shapes.

Clark urges that such binding of mental colors with mental shapes cannot rely on mental qualities of location, since that would in turn require the binding of both mental qualities of color and shape to those of location.[53] But the relevant binding does not rely on any additional mental qualities, but rather results from subpersonal visual mechanisms that subserve the production of sensations with mental colors and shapes at particular mental locations. So the need for such binding very likely imposes no constraints on an acceptable account of those mental qualities.

Indeed, the very appeal to homomorphisms itself suggests that mental color qualities never occur without some mental shape, nor visual qualities of shape without some mental color. Mental colors resemble and differ in ways homomorphic to the similarities and differences among perceptible physical colors. And, because perceptible color patches invariably occur with some perceptible shape, those shapes are among

---

[51] In vision, though not in all modalities, the edges of the qualitative field, defined by the absence of any further mental content qualities, also figure in determining mental location.

[52] Treisman, "Features and Objects in Visual Processing," *Scientific American*, 255, 5 (November 1986): 114–125; "Features and Objects: The Fourteenth Bartlett Memorial Lecture," *Quarterly Journal of Experimental Psychology*, 40A, 2 (May 1988): 201–237; "Consciousness and Perceptual Binding," in *The Unity of Consciousness: Binding, Integration, and Dissociation*, Axel Cleeremans, ed., Oxford: Clarendon Press, pp. 95–113; and Anne Treisman and Stephen Gormican, "Feature Analysis in Early Vision: Evidence from Search Asymmetries," *Psychological Review*, 95, 1 (January 1988): 15–48.

Cf. Clark, *A Theory of Sentience*, pp. 46 and 65.

[53] *A Theory of Sentience*, pp. 62–63.

the ways perceptible color patches resemble and differ. So mental color qualities will invariably resemble and differ in corresponding ways, resulting in mental qualities of shape.[54] Similar considerations apply to mental qualities of location. These considerations help explain why, illusory conjunctions notwithstanding, visual sensations never seem to occur with mental color but no mental shape, or conversely.

This *homomorphism theory* of mental qualities does not rely on the taxonomy of perceptible properties that physics imposes on those properties.[55] The similarity metric of physics typically does not define similarities and differences among perceptible properties that correspond to the similarities and differences characteristic of an organism's mental qualities. Nor can we count in general on neural excitations' being arranged in ways that match in any relevant way the similarities and differences that define a space of mental qualities.

What's needed, rather, is a similarity metric that reflects how readily the organism discriminates the properties, which properties the organism can't differentiate, and how many qualitative differences are discernible between any two properties. These things define for each modality a quality space, which varies from one species to the next and, in slight ways that don't matter, from one individual to another.[56] What matters is not the taxonomy of physics, but the taxonomy that reflects the organism's

---

[54] For a similar argument, see Sellars, "The Adverbial Theory of the Objects of Sensation," *Metaphilosophy*, VI, 2 (April 1975): 144–160, §II.

For more on these issues, see my "Color, Mental Location, and the Visual Field," *Consciousness and Cognition*, 9, 4 (April 2001): 85–93, replying to Peter W. Ross, "The Location Problem for Color Subjectivism," *Consciousness and Cognition*, IX (2001): 42–58, who defends a view similar to Clark's.

And for more on the spatial qualities that figure in perceiving, see Douglas B. Meehan, "The Qualitative Character of Spatial Perception," Ph.D. Dissertation, CUNY Graduate Center, in preparation.

[55] For theorists who deny that physical objects can exhibit commonsense color and sound, there will be no alternative to the similarity metric that physics provides for perceptible properties. But as already noted, we can identify such commonsense perceptible properties with properties acceptable to physics and still taxonomize those properties along commonsense lines.

For reasons to reject the claim that color and sound as common sense conceives of them cannot be properties of physical objects, see "Sensory Quality and the Relocation Story."

[56] Even for mental qualities that pertain to size, shape, and spatial arrangement, the operative similarities and differences of physical space are those which the organism can discriminate by way of the sensory modality in question. They are not abstract geometrical similarities and differences. For an illuminating discussion of the difference, see Robert Schwartz, *Vision: Variations on Some Berkeleian Themes*, Oxford: Blackwell, 1994, esp. chs. 1 and 2.

On the notions of two qualities' matching or being just noticeably different, see Nelson Goodman, *The Structure of Appearance*, Cambridge, Massachusetts: Harvard University Press, 1951, pp. 222–226 and 256–258 (2nd edn., Indianapolis: Bobbs-Merrill, 1966, pp. 273–277, 311–313; 3rd edn., Dordrecht-Holland: D. Reidel Publishing Co., 1977, pp. 197–200, 226–7). Goodman convincingly argues that we must take the notion of matching as more basic. On the notion of a creature's quality space see W. V. Quine, "Natural Kinds," in his *Ontological Relativity and Other Essays*, New York and London: Columbia University Press, 1969, pp. 114–138, at pp. 123–128.

The construction of any quality space involves some choice about how to order the constituent qualities, and different methods of ordering may result in different or even incommensurable quality spaces. See, e.g., Jan J. Koenderink and Andrea J. van Doorn, "Perspectives on Colour Space," in

ability to discern similarities and differences among the properties it can perceive. In the human case, the quality space that results from our ability to discriminate perceptible properties leads to a taxonomy of mental qualities that conforms to the commonsense classifications of human folk psychology.[57]

Mental qualities are properties of states in virtue of which an organism responds to a range of perceptible properties. The individual mental qualities of each modality are defined by their positions in a quality space that's homomorphic to the quality space of the perceptible properties accessible to that modality. So, when a qualitative state is conscious, we're conscious of the qualities that distinguish that state in a way that reflects those similarities and differences. Each HOT will thus describe its target qualitative state in terms of the position that state occupies in the relevant quality space, that is, by reference to the ways in which that state resembles and differs from others in its family of qualities.

The quality spaces operative here are determined solely by the organism's discriminative abilities. But the states in virtue of which humans and other organisms discriminate perceptible properties need not be conscious states. So this dependence on discriminative abilities in no way implies that the relevant qualitative states are conscious. Qualitative states must be conscious for us to discriminate introspectively among their mental qualities. But just as physical objects have the perceptible properties whether or not any creature perceives them, so the defining similarities and differences among mental qualities hold independently of one's being conscious of those qualities.

We do sometimes appeal to conscious cases when we describe these relations of similarity and difference. But those relations are at bottom a function of an organism's discriminative powers in perceiving things, and do not depend on the deliverances of introspection. Rather, we are conscious of qualitative states in terms of the relations of similarity and difference that figure in perceiving, and introspection, which is simply a reflective way of being conscious of mental states, follows suit. HOTs describe qualitative states in terms of those similarities and differences; introspection is simply the special case in which those HOTs are conscious, so that we are conscious of their targets in a way that's attentive and deliberate.[58]

Colour Perception: Mind and the Physical World, ed. Rainer Mausfeld and Dieter Heyer, Oxford: Clarendon Press, 2003, pp. 1–56; Rainer Mausfeld, "'Colour' as Part of the Format of Different Perceptual Primitives: The Dual Coding of Colour," in Mausfeld and Heyer, pp. 381–434; and R. Duncan Luce, Donald Hoffman, Michael D'Zmura, Geoffrey Iverson, and A. Kimball Romney, eds., *Geometric Representations of Perceptual Phenomena: Papers in Honor of Tarow Indow on His 70th Birthday*, Mahwah, New Jersey: Lawrence Erlbaum Associates, 1995.

[57] So the similarities and differences among both mental qualities and the perceptible properties of physical objects will all figure in the commonsense psychological platitudes David Lewis invokes in the functionalist account he develops of mental states. See his "An Argument for the Identity Thesis," *The Journal of Philosophy*, LXIII, 1 (January 6, 1966): 17–25, "Psychophysical and Theoretical Identifications," *Australasian Journal of Philosophy*, L, 3 (December 1972): 249–258, and "Reduction of Mind," in *A Companion to the Philosophy of Mind*, ed. Samuel Guttenplan, Oxford: Basil Blackwell, 1994, pp. 412–431, reprinted in his *Papers in Metaphysics and Epistemology*, Cambridge: Cambridge University Press, 1999, pp. 291–324.

[58] See "Introspection and Self-Interpretation."

Mental qualities are properties of states that figure in the perceptual functioning of a particular sensory modality, and whose similarities and differences are homomorphic to those which hold among the properties perceptible by that modality. That gives us a way, independent of qualitative states' ever being conscious, to distinguish those states from the nonmental, physiological states that figure in transmitting perceptual information to the mind. It also allows us to distinguish among the various qualitative properties in a way that's altogether independent of consciousness. So there is no mystery about how a state can exhibit mental qualities even when it isn't conscious.

Nor is there any mystery about there being something that it's like for one to be in states with those qualities when those states are conscious. There is something it's like for one to be in a qualitative state when one is conscious of oneself as being in that state. And that's just a matter of one's having a HOT that represents one as being in a state with the relevant qualitative properties, understood in terms of their positions in the relevant quality space.

It's sometimes said that an account of qualitative consciousness should explain why each conscious qualitative state has the qualitative character it does. The present view suggests an explanation. Each mental quality is fixed by its position in a space of properties that's characteristic of the sensory modality in question. And being conscious of oneself as being in a state with that mental quality fixes the conscious qualitative character of a conscious state with that quality. Each conscious qualitative state has the conscious qualitative character it does because one is conscious of that state as occupying a position in a mental quality space homomorphic to that of a particular property in the corresponding space of perceptible properties.

Mental red is that property in the quality space of mental colors which occupies the position in that space homomorphic to the position that perceptible red occupies in the quality space of physical colors. Since the mental colors figure only in visual perception, they do not in any relevant way resemble or differ from the mental qualities of any other sensory modality.

Many of our conscious perceptual experiences, however, involve more than one sensory modality. If I consciously see and hear a car moving, the experience of the car that I am conscious of involves both visual and auditory mental qualities. This is a further strike against the inner-sense theory considered earlier of how it is that we are conscious of our conscious experiences. Since mental qualities are all specific to a single modality, higher-order sensing couldn't capture the cross-modal character that many of our perceptions exhibit. HOTs, by contrast, can readily operate across modalities. Since thoughts can have any content whatever, HOTs can make us conscious of perceptions in respect of all the mental qualities of a perception, whatever their modality. I'll say more about such cross-modal perceiving in section VII.

V. HOMOMORPHISM THEORY AND HIGHER-ORDER THOUGHTS

The appeal to homomorphisms provides just what's needed for HOTs to characterize qualitative states. The mental qualities specific to each modality are properties fixed by relations of similarity and difference that are homomorphic to those which hold among the relevant perceptible properties. Once a creature has in place a family of concepts for the properties perceptible by some modality, it can extrapolate to new concepts that apply to the states in virtue of which it perceives those properties.

Such extrapolation occurs by forming a new family of concepts for properties of states by virtue of which the creature has access to a particular range of perceptible properties. The properties the new concepts determine resemble and differ in ways homomorphic to the ways the relevant perceptible properties do. Those new concepts can then figure in HOTs in virtue of which the creature comes to be conscious of itself as being in states with the mental qualities in question. The families of concepts HOTs use to represent the mental qualities of each modality are adaptations of families of concepts that apply to the properties perceptible by that modality.

For convenience, I'll use the terms 'red', 'green', and so on to refer only to the colors of physical objects, referring to the corresponding mental qualities of visual sensations as *red**, *green**, and so forth. A mental quality counts as red* if it resembles and differs from other color* properties in ways that parallel the similarities and differences that commonsense physical red bears to other physical color properties. When a sensation is conscious *as* a red* sensation, the HOT in virtue of which one is conscious of the sensation in that way describes it in those terms. The HOT describes that target sensation as having a quality whose position in the quality space of colors* is homomorphic to the position of commonsense physical red in the quality space of physical colors.

The similarities and differences that fix each family of qualitative properties reflect the similarities and differences characteristic of the corresponding perceptible properties. Still, it may often be that an organism is not aware of differences among its mental qualities in a way that's as fine grained as the discriminations it makes among the corresponding perceptible properties. The qualitative states an organism is conscious of may not reflect all the slight differences that can figure in its perceptual functioning.

This fits with the observation in section II about wine tasting, that we can come to be conscious of our mental qualities in increasingly fine-grained ways. When that happens, the way we're conscious of our mental qualities comes to approximate more closely the similarities and differences that we can perceptually discriminate, independently of consciousness. Qualitative consciousness reflects the defining similarities and differences among the qualitative states that figure in perceiving; it does not determine those similarities and differences.

As also noted in section II, we can often consciously discern slight differences among qualities presented together, even though we wouldn't be conscious of those differences if the qualities occurred separately. The natural explanation is that we're conscious of these slight qualitative differences only comparatively; we're conscious of one mental color, for example, as being lighter or more saturated or having a bit more of some particular hue than another. And, when qualities occur together, we have a basis for such comparisons that's absent when they occur on their own.

This explanation lends support to the idea that the HOTs in virtue of which we're conscious of mental qualities are cast in terms of the very similarities and differences that according to homomorphism theory define those qualities. On homomorphism theory, the concepts in respect of which we're conscious of mental qualities are all at bottom comparative. Concepts for specific colors, such as red and green, in effect involve a quick way of referring to an especially salient region in the relevant quality space. Thus, when we're conscious of a visual state as being generically red* and not as having any more specific shade*, we're conscious of that state as belonging to a particular region of the mental quality space, but not conscious of its having any more specific location. Similarly for concepts of salient qualities in other modalities.

The HOTs in virtue of which each qualitative state is conscious characterizes that state in terms of various ways it resembles and differs from other qualitative states in its family. But it may seem that introspective consciousness conflicts with this idea. When we focus introspectively on the way we are conscious of our qualitative states, it's inviting to think that we are conscious of each state not comparatively, but only in respect of its individual mental qualities.[59]

When we introspect, we typically focus on a particular qualitative state to the exclusion of others that may at that time be in our stream of consciousness. And that may engender a sense that we are conscious of the target state solely in noncomparative terms. But our not comparing a state to other concurrent states doesn't show that we are not conscious of its mental qualities in comparative terms. We are conscious of qualitative states comparatively not because we always compare them to other concurrent qualities, but because we are conscious of them in terms of their relative locations in a relevant quality space. And we can be conscious of those relative locations in more or less fine-grained ways.

There are situations that make it obvious that this is so. One sometimes shifts introspectively between two visual qualities of very similar shades of red* so as to capture for oneself the slight difference between them. One doesn't fix the way one is conscious of each independently of how one is conscious of the other and then compare the two. Rather, it is in consciously comparing them that one captures for oneself the way one is conscious of each. Our conscious comparisons of concurrent mental qualities enhance the specificity of the way we are conscious of each.

Homomorphism theory suggests an explanation for the perceptual adaptation that occurs, for example, shortly after putting on sunglasses. Our color* sensations seem different to us just after putting sunglasses on, but we soon come to be conscious of those color* qualities in what seems to be a largely normal way. The initial difference is easy to understand. We are conscious of color* qualities in respect of the similarities and differences among them, and the color* sensations we have on first putting on sunglasses differ strikingly from those we previously had.

But that difference soon stops playing any role in how we're conscious of our visual sensations, and we come to be conscious of them only in respect of current similarities and differences, rather than in comparison with the sensations we had earlier. Since the new similarities and differences largely parallel those which ordinarily hold, we come to be conscious of the colors of things as resembling and differing in roughly

---

[59] I am grateful to David Pereplyotchik for pressing this concern.

the way they ordinarily do. So we come to see things as having their ordinary colors, and to be conscious of ourselves as having the color* sensations we would expect to have in those circumstances. Something similar doubtless happens with goggles that distort the shapes of things. As one adapts to the initial disparities between visual and tactile input, one recalibrates the shapes* of one's visual sensations by adjusting the similarities and differences that define those visual shapes*.[60]

What properties can figure in a qualitative states' being conscious? Can HOTs describe sensations not only in terms of properties that are intuitively qualitative, but other properties as well? Could a HOT, for example, describe a gustatory sensation of wine not just as tannin* or robust*, but as Merlot*, or even Merlot-1991*?[61] There is no reason why not. When HOTs describe mental qualities, they can borrow concepts for any perceptible properties we can discern and locate within some suitable quality space. Indeed, as noted earlier, we're sometimes conscious of mental qualities in terms of characteristic kinds of objects, for example, banana yellow* as against lemon yellow*. Our concepts for mental qualities trade on adapting for use in HOTs any structures of similarity and difference relations that hold among families of perceptible properties.

Since HOTs must be noninferential, the concepts they use must apply in an intuitively unmediated way. And, since concepts for mental qualities derive from concepts for perceptible properties, one must be able to apply those concepts as well in a way that's relatively fluent and automatic. The HOTs of somebody inexperienced with wine won't be able to describe gustatory states as tannin* or robust*, to say nothing of Merlot-1991*. But when one does readily discriminate perceptible similarities and differences, concepts cast in terms of parallel similarities and differences will readily pick out corresponding mental qualities, and so can figure in HOTs.

Still, it's unlikely that individual mental qualities correspond to all the things we can perceptually discriminate in a fluent way. It's unlikely, for example, that there are individual mental qualities for individual faces or for the Chrysler Building. Mental qualities resemble and differ from one another in ways parallel to the similarities and differences among the properties perceptible by that modality. But there is no family of perceptible properties the similarities and differences among which enable us to discriminate faces or buildings. Rather, the relevant visual appearances are complex constructions from many basic colors, shapes, sizes, and spatial arrangements. The distinctive unitary feel that attaches to what it's like for one to see a familiar face or building results not from the occurrence of some individual mental quality, but from

---

[60] This type of adjustment may also help explain the spatial adaptation that occurs with inverting goggles or prisms, though these cases are somewhat more complex, especially because they involve not merely cross-modal calibration, but also alterations in sensorimotor control. For a striking study of some of the complexities, see T. A. Martin, J. G. Keating, H. P. Goodkin, A. J. Bastian, and W. T. Thach, "Throwing while Looking through Prisms," *Brain*, 119 (1996): 1183–1198. I am grateful to James Bopp for calling this work to my attention. For perceptual adaptation in general see Irvin Rock, *The Nature of Perceptual Adaptation*, New York: Basic Books, 1966.

[61] I am grateful to Schwartz for pressing this concern, in "Senses and Sensation," at the 21st Annual Meeting of the Cognitive Science Society, Vancouver, August 20, 1999.

processing well downstream from whatever qualities figure in seeing and discerning those things.

Homomorphism theory provides informative descriptions of mental qualities that dispel the air of mystery that seems to surround those qualities, by helping us understand both the nature of those properties and how it is that we're conscious of them. Some theorists have recently sought to explain the way we're conscious of mental qualities by appeal to a kind of concept that's special to the way we recognize things. We sometimes recognize something even though we can't say what type of thing it is; so perhaps that's also the way we're conscious of mental qualities. Perhaps we are conscious of mental qualities by applying purely recognitional concepts to those qualities.

If we are conscious of mental qualities by way of some such purely recognitional concepts, those concepts would apply mental qualities demonstratively, solely in virtue of a quality's being of a type that one recognizes. And it's sometimes urged that the absence of any further conceptual content explains the intuitive sense we have that such qualities are somehow indescribable, while avoiding the conclusion that they are on that account mysterious. Such purely recognitional concepts might even, therefore, provide content to the higher-order states in virtue of which we are conscious of mental qualities.[62]

There is reason, however, to doubt that concepts are ever purely recognitional in this way. Even when we recognize something without knowing what type of thing it is, we always can say something about it.[63] And homomorphism theory in any case provides a more satisfactory explanation of the apparent difficulty in describing mental qualities. Mental qualities seem indescribable only because our concepts for them are at bottom comparative. But the comparative character of those concepts doesn't prevent them from figuring informatively in the way we are conscious of our mental qualities. Our comparative concepts for mental qualities reflect the comparisons we make among corresponding perceptible properties, which are in turn anchored by the properties we know objects of various sorts to have. The resulting comparative concepts for mental qualities can accordingly provide content to the HOTs in virtue of which we're conscious of our qualitative states.

Homomorphism theory determines the mental qualities that occur in each modality. Can such an approach also fix conceptual content? Arguably not.

---

[62] For examples of higher-order theories that invoke purely recognitional concepts, see Lycan, "The Superiority of HOP to HOT," p. 109, and Peter Carruthers, "HOP over FOR, HOT Theory," also in Gennaro, pp. 115–135, §III.

On purely recognitional concepts, see Brian Loar, "Phenomenal States," in Ned Block, Owen Flanagan, and Güven Güzeldere, eds., *The Nature of Consciousness: Philosophical Debates*, Cambridge, Massachusetts: MIT Press/Bradford Books, 1997, pp. 597–616.

[63] See "Varieties of Higher-Order Theory," §§III and IV.

Because 'recognize' is factive, recognizing is always accurate. So it may be that the appeal of purely recognitional concepts in this context is due in part to the continuing influence of the traditional claim that the mind is transparent to consciousness.

See also Jerry Fodor, "There Are No Recognitional Concepts—Not Even RED" and "There Are No Recognitional Concepts—Not Even RED, Part 2: The Plot Thickens," in Fodor, *In Critical Condition: Polemical Essays on Cognitive Science and the Philosophy of Mind*, Cambridge, Massachusetts: MIT Press/Bradford Books, 1998, pp. 35–47, 49–62.

Homomorphism theory fixes qualities by reference to families of similarities and differences among properties perceptible by particular modalities. But there are no such families to use in fixing intentional content. Homomorphisms cannot operate on the totality of everything one can form a concept of, since there are no well-defined similarities and differences that hold among all such things.[64]

Dogs bear no suitable relations of similarity and difference to everything else we can form a concept of; so we can't appeal to such relations to fix the concept of a dog. But maybe we can appeal instead to the ways dogs resemble and differ from things within some suitable family of things, such as mammals or animals. If so, common-sense taxonomic schemes might enable homomorphism theory to apply to conceptual content after all. Perhaps such taxomonies can provide families of similarities and differences among the things for which we have concepts, thereby fixing the concepts in corresponding families by reference to parallel similarities and differences.[65] But even if some commonsense concepts do fit into such taxonomic schemes, many concepts do not. Concepts often apply to things whose natures fall into no such well-defined families. And the commonsense concepts that do typically fit into alternative taxo-nomic schemes, and so would deliver conflicting sets of similarities and differences. Homomorphism theory cannot handle conceptual content.[66]

Qualitative states figure in perceiving things. This is so not only for ordinary per-ceptual sensations, but also for bodily sensations, in virtue of which we have percep-tual access to various discriminable bodily conditions. By reflecting the properties we perceive physical objects to have, qualitative states represent those perceived objects and properties.

But because the factors that fix qualitative properties don't determine intentional content, mental qualities don't represent things in the way intentional states do. For one thing, the representational character of mental qualities is not sentential, as intentional content is. So, the representational character that mental qualities have, according to homomorphism theory, does not sustain a representationalist theory, on which the mental character of qualitative properties is intentional.

---

[64] On some versions of meaning holism, each intentional content is a function of the implication relations that content bears to every other content. This provides a way of locating all contents within a kind of total conceptual space. But, even if one saw that space as reflecting relations of similarity and difference among its constituent contents, those relations would not be homomorphic to similarities and differences among the corresponding objects or states of affairs. Meaning holism cannot sustain the application of homomorphism theory to conceptual content.

[65] Aristotle saw thinking as continuous in nature with sensing (e.g., *de Anima*, III 4 and 8, esp. 429b13; *Posterior Analytics*, II 19, 100a3–b5). So such an appeal to traditional Aristotelian taxonomies to enable homomorphism theory to fix concepts might be especially congenial from an Aristotelian perspective, since it invites a uniform account of intentional content and qualitative properties.

[66] C. R. Gallistel has urged that we can fix intentional content by appeal to isomorphisms between the subjective probabilities of holding various intentional contents and the statistical probabilities of the corresponding states of affairs (*The Organization of Learning*, Cambridge, Massachusetts: MIT Press/Bradford Books, 1990). Whatever the merits of that proposal, those isomorphisms are not a matter of similarities and differences among contents or the corresponding states of affairs.

Each mental quality is fixed, according to homomorphism theory, by its perceptual role, rather than by the way we're conscious of it. What it's like for one to be in a state that has that mental quality, by contrast, is fixed by how one is conscious of the quality, and so by the way one's HOTs represent it.

If one conflates mental qualities with what it's like for one to be in states that have those qualities, one will insist that the very nature of qualitative properties is simply a matter of the way we're conscious of them. And that may encourage the idea that these mental properties could vary independently of perceptual role. Distinct qualitative properties might then play the same perceptual role in different individuals, or even in one individual at two different times. Indeed, perceptual functioning might then seem to be possible in the absence of mental qualities altogether. Seeing the nature of qualitative properties as depending in that way on consciousness leaves open the possibility of so-called inverted or absent qualia.

Homomorphism theory invites a different conclusion. On that view, the similarities and differences among mental qualities are homomorphic to the similarities and differences among the properties perceptible by a particular modality. So the nature of those qualities is a matter of perceptual role, independent of whether they are conscious. Homomorphism theory, moreover, constrains how different one individual's qualitative properties can be from those of another, and whether mental qualities could be absent altogether, at least without a discernible change in perceptual functioning. And these constraints will be enough to preclude absent or inverted qualia. I return to the issue about inverted qualia in section VII.

Because HOTs are distinct from the target states they make us conscious of, it's possible for HOTs to misrepresent those states. And that does sometimes happen. Such confabulatory awareness of our own intentional states plainly occurs; we can be conscious of ourselves as believing and desiring things that we don't believe or desire, as some cases of wishful thinking and self-deception make evident.[67]

But such confabulation also sometimes occurs with the qualitative states we are conscious of ourselves as being in. As we saw from the wine and woodwind cases, HOTs determine what it's like for one to be in various conscious qualitative states. So erroneous HOTs will in this case result in there being something it's like for one to be in a state that one is not actually in.

Dental patients, for example, sometimes seem to feel pain even when the relevant nerves are absent or anesthetized. The standard explanation of these cases of so-called dental fear is that the patient has fear and a sensation of vibration, but is conscious of those states as pain. Patients are conscious of themselves as being in pain, though the states that occasion their being thus conscious of themselves are actually fear and a sensation of vibration.

Once patients are told of this hypothesis and drilling resumes, they consciously experience vibration and fear. Still, the memory of the previous experience remains

---

[67] On confabulatory awareness of intentional states, see Richard E. Nisbett and Timothy DeCamp Wilson, "Telling More than We Can Know: Verbal Reports on Mental Processes," *Psychological Review*, 84, 3 (May 1977): 231–259, and Peter A. White, "Knowing More than We Can Tell: 'Introspective Access' and Causal Report Accuracy 10 Years Later," *British Journal of Psychology*, 79, 1 (February 1988): 13–45.

unaltered, underscoring that what it's like for one is a function of how one represents the state to oneself. Since the patient was conscious of the prior sensation as pain, that remains what that sensation was like for the patient.[68]

Change blindness is another dramatic case in which the qualitative state one is in diverges from the state one is conscious of oneself as being in. When John Grimes presented subjects with visual stimuli that changed in striking, salient ways during saccades, for example, a picture of a parrot that changed back and forth between brilliant red and green, the subjects frequently failed to notice these changes.[69] It's natural to assume that visual states correspond to current stimuli, so that one is in a red* state when the parrot in front of one is red and a green* state when it's green; priming studies independently support that assumption (see n. 27, above). So, when Grimes's subjects fail to notice a change, what it's like for them diverges sharply from the visual state they're in; they're conscious of themselves as being in green* states when they're in red* states, and conversely. What it's like for one diverges in these cases from the qualitative state one is actually in.

Dretske has argued that, since the changes in these cases occur during saccades and so are in effect concealed from subjects, subjects are not actually blind to those changes, but only to differences that result from the changes.[70] But there is an important way in which subjects plainly are blind to the changes themselves. As Dretske acknowledges, what subjects see in these cases corresponds to the actual stimulus; subjects see red when the parrot is red and green when it's green. But in these cases there is often no change in what it's like for the subjects even when there's a change in the color seen. That is unusual; typically what it's like for one reflects changes in what one sees. So Grimes's subjects are often in this way blind to these changes in color. Dretske might urge that what it's like for one to be in a state cannot diverge from the state itself, since as noted in section II he rejects the idea that a state's being conscious is a matter of one's being conscious of that state. But such divergence does occur in this kind of case, and with it a kind of blindness to change.

---

[68] According to Hume, states of memory and imagination are qualitative, though they have far less force and vivacity than those which occur in perceiving (David Hume, *A Treatise on Human Nature*, ed. L. A. Selby-Bigge, Oxford: Clarendon Press, 1888, pp. 8–9). But it's open to question whether most states of memory and imagination are actually qualitative at all. The HOT model allows us to capture Hume's intuition while acknowledging that question. It might be that states of memory and imagination have no qualitative properties, but our HOTs represent them as resembling perceptual states, i.e., as having pale versions of the mental qualities characteristic of actual perceiving.

[69] "On the Failure to Detect Changes in Scenes across Saccades," *Perception*, ed. Kathleen Akins, New York: Oxford University Press, 1996, pp. 89–110; for the parrot, see p. 102.

For more on change blindness and change detection, see Daniel J. Simons, "Current Approaches to Change Blindness," *Visual Cognition*, 7 (2000): 1–16; Ronald A. Rensink, "Change Detection," *Annual Review of Psychology*, 53, 1 (2002): 245–277; Daniel J. Simons and Ronald A. Rensink, "Change Blindness: Past, Present, and Future," *Trends in Cognitive Sciences*, 9, 1 (January 2005): 16–20; Daniel J. Simons, Christopher F. Chabris, and Tatiana Schnur, "Evidence for Preserved Representations in Change Blindness," *Consciousness and Cognition*, 11 (2002): 78–97; and Brian J. Scholl, Daniel J. Simons, and Daniel T. Levin, " 'Change Blindness' Blindness: An Implicit Measure of a Metacognitive Error," in *Thinking and Seeing: Visual Metacognition in Adults and Children*, ed. Daniel T. Levin, Cambridge, Massachusetts: MIT Press/Bradford Books, 2004, pp. 145–164.

[70] "Change Blindness," *Philosophical Studies*, 120, 1–3 (July–September 2004): 1–18, e.g., p. 3.

HOTs, like intentional states generally, can describe what they are about inaccurately, and they may even be about something that does not exist at all. So a question arises about what state, in the dental case, the patient's HOT is actually about. When one has a HOT that one is in pain but there isn't actually any pain, is one's HOT about the fear and sensation of vibration that do occur? Or is it simply about a notional pain, a pain that doesn't exist?

HOTs are the way we're conscious of ourselves as being in mental states. Being conscious of something by having a thought about it as present does not require any causal connection between the thought and the thing one is thereby conscious of. So we have no reason to suppose that any such a causal tie always holds between HOTs and their targets. Doubtless these targets often do figure among the causal antecedents of HOTs, but that needn't be the case.

So, even though causal ties may sometimes help determine what a HOT is actually about, we can't count on being able to appeal to that. But in most cases it won't matter what we say about this question. What matters in cases like that of dental fear is that a HOT represents one as being in pain even though one isn't. It makes no difference, subjectively or theoretically, whether we construe the HOT as being about actual sensations of vibration and fear or about a nonexistent pain.

Since there can be something it's like for one to be in a state with particular mental qualities even if no such state occurs, a mental state's being conscious is not strictly speaking a relational property of that state. A state's being conscious consists in its being a state one is conscious of oneself as being in. Still, it's convenient to speak loosely of the property of a state's being conscious as relational so as to stress that it is in any case not an intrinsic property of mental states.[71]

The content of HOTs need not, and often won't, describe the qualitative character of their target qualitative states in a complete and exhaustive way. Rather, HOTs, like all thinking and describing, play a partially interpretive role. In representing us to ourselves as being in states of various sorts, HOTs are in effect interpretations of ourselves as being in those states.

This is most obvious when there is some disparity between the states we are in and the way we are conscious of those states. The way we are conscious of being in such states is due to the way our HOTs interpret our current state of mind. But even when a HOT is accurate, it's still in part interpretive. HOTs never describe their targets in respect of all their mental properties, and they are selective not only in which properties of our conscious states they represent, but also in which states they represent at all. Ordinary consciousness seldom seems to involve any interpretive activity, but that's arguably because the HOTs that figure in such interpreting are seldom conscious, much less deliberate.[72]

---

[71] For more on this issue, see my "Metacognition and Higher-Order Thoughts," *Consciousness and Cognition*, 9, 2, Part 1 (June 2000): 231–242, § IV.

[72] On the interpretive aspect of consciousness, see "Introspection and Self-Interpretation," §VI, "Content, Interpretation, and Consciousness," and my "Consciousness, Interpretation, and Higher-Order Thought," in Patrizia Giampieri-Deutsch, ed., *Psychoanalysis as an Empirical, Interdisciplinary Science: Collected Papers on Contemporary Psychoanalytic Research*, Vienna: Verlag der österreichischen

In cases such as dental fear, consciousness literally misrepresents one type of qualitative state as another. But it seems intuitively as though there must be limits to how inaccurately we can be conscious of our qualitative states. Could a HOT represent a pain as a sensation of blue or an auditory sensation as an olfactory sensation? And if so, would that really result in what it's like for one being as though one had a sensation of blue or an olfactory sensation?

One reason to think that the states we're conscious of ourselves as being in cannot diverge too greatly from the states we are actually in is the causal role the states we are in play in our mental lives generally. Pains, for example, interact causally with other mental states whether or not we're conscious of them; for example, they distract us and cause us to desire that they stop. And it's reasonable to suppose that the HOTs in virtue of which we are conscious of ourselves as being in pain may also to some extent interact in characteristic ways with other mental states.

So, if the states we're actually in diverge too much from the states our HOTs make us conscious of ourselves as being in, the higher- and first-order states might interact in different and even conflicting ways with the rest of our mental lives. And the psychological tension this conflict would induce would very likely exert in turn some corrective influence on our HOTs, thereby limiting the degree to which those HOTs can misrepresent our first-order states. There are also more specific psychological pressures that typically constrain the HOTs we have, which I'll discuss toward the end of section VI.

Still, none of these considerations would preclude the possibility of one's occasionally being conscious of a pain as a sensation of blue. For one thing, normal constraints can go awry, so that a HOT might misrepresent a pain as a sensation of blue without any tension of the sort just sketched. Perhaps, indeed, some such thing happens in some kinds of synesthesia. A stimulus appropriate to one modality might result in conscious qualitative states that belong to two distinct modalities without actually causing both types of qualitative state. Rather, the stimulus might cause a single type of qualitative state that for whatever reason results in turn in a HOT that one has both sensations.[73]

But, even if consciousness can significantly misrepresent our qualitative states, it's natural that it should seem to us as though that cannot happen. The way our HOTs represent our qualitative states determines what it's like for us to be in those states. Suppose, then, that a HOT misrepresents a pain as a sensation of blue. And suppose

Akademie der Wissenschaften (Austrian Academy of Sciences Press), 2005, pp. 119–142, §IV.

[73] I am grateful to Schwartz for this suggestion. This idea is consonant with Simon Baron-Cohen's Neonatal Synesthesia hypothesis, on which infants until about 4 months of age "experience sensory input in an undifferentiated way" in respect to sensory modalities (Simon Baron-Cohen, "Is There a Normal Phase of Synaesthesia in Development?", *Psyche*, 2, 27 [June 1996]: http://psyche.cs.monash.edu.au/v2/psyche-2-27-baron_cohen.html).

The suggestion may conflict, however, with Richard E. Cytowic's claim that synesthesia does not result from some higher cortical function (*Synesthesia: A Union of the Senses*, New York: Springer Verlag, 1989). For more on synesthesia, see Simon Baron-Cohen and John E. Harrison, eds., *Synaesthesia: Classic and Contemporary Readings*, Oxford: Blackwell, 1996.

that no discernible mental tensions resulted from that misrepresentation. We would experience this subjectively not as a case of misrepresentation, but as an anomalous sensation, a sensation of blue inexplicably occurring in response to a normally painful stimulus. Consciousness has the last word on what it's like for one to be in the mental states one is in; indeed, it trivially has the last word, since what it's like for one to be in a qualitative state simply is how one is conscious of that state. So it never seems to us as though consciousness misrepresents those mental appearances. But having the last word on what it's like for one to be in a state does not mean having the last word on what state one is actually in. And consciousness is not authoritative about that.

One's seeing red involves one's being in a red* state. And there being something it's like for one to see red is being conscious of oneself as seeing red, and hence conscious of oneself as being in a red* state. A state's being red*, moreover, is a matter of how that state resembles and differs from other color* sensations. So being conscious of oneself as seeing red is being conscious of oneself as being in a state that resembles and differs from other states in those ways. And, since those similarities and differences reflect the way physical red resembles and differs from other perceptible colors, what it's like for one to see red depends in turn on the way one is conscious of the position physical red occupies in the space of physical colors.

So differences in the quality space of the physical colors one perceives will result in corresponding differences in the quality space of the mental color* qualities one is conscious of. What it's like for one to see red depends on the position one is conscious of physical red as having in the quality space of perceptible colors. So differences in what perceptible colors occur in that quality space will result in differences in what it's like for one to see red stimuli.

This has important consequences. Suppose that a person's visual sensations all occur in shades of black* and white*, and then that person for the first time sees something red.[74] Plainly the quality space within which that person would locate the new sensation would be strikingly different from the quality space within which normally sighted people would locate that sensation. So that person would not be conscious of the new sensation in anything like the way in which people ordinarily are. Whatever it would be like for that person to have that new sensation, there is no reason to think that it would be all that similar to what it's like for us to see red. Nor would it even be all that similar to what it would be like for one to see red for the first time if the rest of one's color quality space were otherwise like our own.

---

[74] As with Frank Jackson's well-known Mary, in "What Mary Didn't Know," *The Journal of Philosophy*, LXXXIII, 5 (May 1986): 291–295. See also his "Epiphenomenal Qualia," *Philosophical Quarterly*, XXXII, 127 (April 1982): 127–136.

Jackson has now rejected the antimaterialist conclusions of those articles. See "Postscript" to "What Mary Didn't Know," in *Contemporary Materialism: A Reader*, ed. Paul K. Moser and J. D. Trout, Routledge, 1995, 184–189; "Postscript on Qualia," in his *Mind, Method, and Conditionals: Selected Essays*, London and New York: Routledge, 1998, pp. 76–79; "Mind and Illusion," in *Minds and Persons*, ed. Anthony O'Hear, Royal Institute of Philosophy Supplement, 53, Cambridge: Cambridge University Press, 2003, pp. 251–71, and in Peter Ludlow, Yujin Nagasawa and Daniel Stoljar, eds., *There's Something about Mary: Consciousness and Frank Jackson's Knowledge Argument*, Cambridge, Massachusetts: MIT Press/Bradford Books, 2004, pp. 421–442; and "The Knowledge

Doubtless what it would be like for one to see red would be something strikingly new if one has previously seen only shades of black and white. But it's not at all obvious apart from that how we might understand what that would be like in terms of our own conscious color experiences. Still, we can describe what it's like to see red, whether for us or for somebody who previously has seen only in black and white. What it's like for one in both cases is a matter of the location the target sensation has within the quality space of one's conscious visual sensations. So one can have strictly descriptive knowledge of what it's like for an individual to see red independently of ever consciously seeing red, though such knowledge is relative to that individual's quality space of colors.

There is a natural temptation to think that one's first conscious perception of something red, having previously seen only black and white, would be much the same as what it's like for anybody else to see something red. After all, what it's like for one to see something is a matter of how one is conscious of the relevant visual state. But what's relevant to what it's like for one is how one is conscious of the state comparatively, as resembling and differing from other visual states. So differences in the comparison space will affect the way one is conscious of the target state. Only if what it's like for one to be in a qualitative state were a matter of how one is conscious of the relevant quality on its own would the first conscious perception of something red be like our own.[75]

VI. QUALITIES AND CONCEPTUALIZATION

I've spoken so far about qualitative states in a relatively generic way, without distinguishing among the various types of mental state that exhibit qualitative character, from sensations to perceptions and many or all emotions and other affective states. The mental qualities that occur in connection with affective states are beyond the scope of this discussion.[76] But it will be important to be clear about the difference between sensations and full-fledged perceptions.

Sensations are qualitative states that occur relatively early in the stream of mental processing that leads to full-fledged perceptions. But position in the processing stream is not enough to capture the difference between the two types of state. Not all states that occur later in that processing stream than sensations are perceptions; nor is it obvious that all states occurring earlier than perceptions are sensations.

The difference consists rather in the mental properties that states of those two kinds exhibit. Sensations and perceptions both have mental qualities, but perceptions, unlike sensations, also exhibit intentional content. Perceptions are qualitative states

---

Argument, Diaphanousness, and Representationalism," in *Phenomenal Concepts and Phenomenal Knowledge: New Essays on Consciousness and Physicalism*, ed. Torin Alter and Sven Walter, New York: Oxford University Press, forthcoming.

[75] I elaborate on this argument in "What Mary Wouldn't Learn," MS.

[76] For a discussion of affective states in connection with consciousness see "Consciousness and its Expression," ch. 11 in this volume.

with conceptual content, specifically content that conceptualizes whatever it is that the state's qualitative character enables one to sense.

There are two ways such conceptualized qualitative states might occur. It might be that each perception consists of two states, one a sensation that exhibits some qualitative character and the other a conceptual state that provides the relevant intentional content. But it might also be that each perception is a unitary state that exhibits both qualitative and intentional properties. Each model has its advantages and shortcomings. If each perception consists of two states, one qualitative and the other intentional, we face the difficult challenge of explaining how the two go together; the unitary model avoids that problem. But on the unitary model, we must explain how states with qualitative character come to have intentional content as well. I won't try to settle here which is the more satisfactory model, but will instead describe perceiving neutrally, as in some way involving both qualitative character and conceptual content that conceptualizes the thing being sensed.

Homomorphism theory helps distinguish qualitative states from the nonmental, purely physiological states that occur in the processing stream that transmits perceptual information to the mind. Qualitative states have mental qualities, which for each modality exhibit similarities and differences homomorphic to those which hold among the properties perceptible by that modality. But, as noted in section I, qualitative states also have characteristic interactions with other mental states. Thus, in organisms with suitable mental endowments, some purely qualitative states lead to full-fledged perceptions, whose intentional content conceptualizes whatever is sensed. Perhaps qualitative states occur in some organisms that lack the capacity for intentionality. But for a state to be qualitative, it must be that type of state which could lead to or figure in perceiving in an organism that does represent things by way of intentional content.

Perceiving adds intentional content to qualitative character. If I sense a rabbit visually, I may only have a visual sensation with certain distinctive mental qualities of color* and shape*. If I visually perceive a rabbit, I am in state with those qualitative properties, but I also conceptualize the thing I sense in some way, say, as a rabbit.

On the HOT hypothesis, a sensation's being conscious consists in its being accompanied by a HOT to the effect that one has that sensation. So a sensation's being conscious involves intentional content in addition to the qualitative character of the sensation. Perceiving also adds intentional content to a sensation, but the intentional content that perceiving adds is different from that which a HOT would contribute. Visually perceiving a rabbit involves the intentional content that a certain thing is, say, a rabbit; the intentional content of a HOT in virtue of which a sensation of a rabbit is conscious is about that sensation itself, not about the rabbit.

Though the intentional content that figures in perceiving differs from that in virtue of which a qualitative state is conscious, there is an important connection between the two. If I visually perceive something red, I conceptualize as red something that's represented by a red* qualitative state I am in. If, in addition, that perception is conscious, I also have a HOT to the effect that I'm in a state with a red* mental quality. Where my HOT characterizes its target state as being red*, the intentional content of the perception characterizes as red the thing that perception is about. HOTs characterize perceptions in terms of mental qualities that correspond to the relevant perceptible property of the object perceived.

The conceptualization that occurs in perceiving sometimes actually affects the way we are conscious of the qualitative character of our perceptions, by influencing the intentional content of our HOTs. Consider the phenomenon of color constancy. We often see a wall as having a uniform color even though close attention to select portions makes it clear that there are readily perceptible variations in sensed color from one place to another, due to shadows and irregularities of paint. These variations in sensed color seldom interfere with our perceptual judgment that the wall has a uniform color, since that judgment is a matter of how we conceptualize the wall that we sense, rather than solely a matter of the sensing itself.

This perceptual judgment about the uniform color of the wall, however, seems actually to influence how we are conscious of the relevant color* sensations. Unless we closely scrutinize a suitable small area, we tend to be conscious of our sensations of the different areas as uniform in their mental color* quality. We are conscious of our color* sensations in a way that reflects our perceptual judgment about the wall. Indeed, we are typically conscious of mental color* qualities in ways that enhance some contrasts and minimize others, smoothing out and eliding unimportant variations in accordance with what we judge the color properties of things to be.

Such constancy effects tend, moreover, to vanish when we concentrate on the qualities of our sensations as such, rather than on the object we perceive. That reinforces the idea that these effects are due to the influence of our perceptual judgments about objects on the way we are conscious of our sensations. Similar considerations suggest that constancy effects that affect the mental size* qualities of visual sensations may also be due to the perceptual judgments we make about the actual size of the objects being sensed.[77]

It may even be that these considerations enhance the perceptual adaptation effects discussed in the previous section, on which color* sensations that initially

---

[77] In the so-called moon illusion, we consciously see the moon as significantly larger when it's close to the horizon; we are actually conscious of our sensation of the moon itself as having a larger size*. This puzzling phenomenon may also be due to the influence perceptual judgments about things have on the way we're conscious of our visual sensations. On the account proposed by Lloyd Kaufman and Irvin Rock, we nonconsciously calculate an object's size as the product of its distance and the size of the retinal image it produces, conceived of as the angle subtended on the retina. But Kaufman and Rock suggest that we also nonconsciously judge the sky itself to have a somewhat flattened shape. And that results in our nonconsciously judging an object in the sky to be farther away from us when that object is nearer the horizon.

The moon subtends a constant visual angle on the retina. So, because we take things in the sky to be more distant when they're near the horizon, we judge that the size of the moon is greater when it's near the horizon. The size* quality of our visual sensation itself is presumably a direct function of the retinal angle subtended. But, since we are conscious of that size* quality as being larger when the moon is near the horizon, the inference about the size of the moon itself evidently influences the way our HOT represents the size* of the sensation. See Kaufman and Rock, "The Moon Illusion," *Scientific American*, 207, 1 (July 1962): 120–131. I am grateful to Schwartz for calling this to my attention. See also his useful discussion of size perception in *Vision: Variations on Some Berkeleian Themes*, ch. 2.

seem different after putting on sunglasses soon come to seem largely normal. Our judgments about the actual colors of things may influence the way we're conscious of the color* qualities of our sensations, once the difference in those color* qualities with and without sunglasses is no longer salient.

Somebody who holds that mental qualities are essentially conscious might hold that the current view, which distinguishes qualitative states from what it's like for one to be in those states, makes no room for genuine qualitative character. It may seem to such a person that the states I call qualitative are simply pale surrogates of genuine qualitative states, on a par with the subpersonal, nonmental states that code for various perceptible properties.

But the line between the mental and the subpersonal does not conform to that between states that are conscious and those which are not. Mental states and their distinguishing mental properties are those states and properties which conform to the commonsense taxonomy of folk psychology. By that test, the states that figure in perceiving are mental even when the perceiving isn't conscious; so states can be genuinely qualitative without being conscious. And the states determined by the similarities and differences of homomorphism theory also conform to that standard folk-psychological taxonomy, and so are genuinely qualitative.

Qualitative character is a feature of the first-order states that play a role in perception. What it's like for one to be in a state with that qualitative character, by contrast, is a matter of having a HOT distinct from the qualitative state itself. But, according to Levine, cases in which the higher-order state misrepresents its first-order target show us "what's wrong with the [higher-order] strategy of dividing consciousness, or subjectivity, from qualitative character." When such higher-order misrepresentation occurs, he urges, what it's like for one will conform either to the actual quality of the first-order state or to the quality the HOT misrepresents the first-order state as having. And each of these moves, he believes, "collapses qualitative character and subjectivity back together again."[78]

What it's like for one to be in a qualitative state is a matter of how one is conscious of oneself as being in that state. So what it's like for one will follow the way one's HOT represents one's state, even when that HOT misrepresents the state one is actually in. Levine takes this to mean that "the first-order state plays no genuine role in determining the qualitative character of the experience" (108). And he concludes that qualitative character is, on this view, solely a matter of the HOT, so that qualitative character and consciousness coincide.

But this conclusion trades on a tendentious understanding of qualitative character. Qualitative character is not invariably conscious; so it's distinct from what it's like for one to be in a qualitative state. And, because qualitative character and what it's like for one are distinct, they may diverge, as in dental fear and other cases considered in section V. So the first-order state does indeed determine qualitative character, though not what it's like for one to be in a state with that qualitative character. Qualitative

---

[78] *Purple Haze*, p. 108. As Levine notes, Karen Neander argues to much the same effect in "The Division of Phenomenal Labor: A Problem for Representational Theories of Consciousness," *Philosophical Perspectives*, 12 (Language, Mind, Ontology), 1998, 411–434, esp. p. 420.

character itself is determined by a state's perceptual role, which can be determined independently of there being anything it's like for one, for example, by priming results. What it's like for one to be in a state with qualitative character, by contrast, is an independent matter of how one is conscious of that state.

Levine's objection about distinguishing qualitative character from what it's like for one does, however, point to what may seem to some to be a significant shortcoming of the HOT model. If qualitative character can occur without there being anything it's like for one to be the relevant state, why is it that there is so often something that it's like for one to be in such states? And, if what it's like for one is distinct from qualitative character, why is the way we are conscious of our qualitative states so often accurate? If perceiving can occur without being conscious, why does it ever occur consciously? What could explain our having HOTs in the first place? And, if qualitative character is distinct from the HOTs in virtue of which we're conscious of it, why do those HOTs so often accurately reflect the actual mental qualities of our qualitative states? Unless we can answer these questions, the HOT hypothesis will rightly seem implausible.

Being in a red* state is being in a state in virtue of which one visually senses or perceives red objects, a state, that is, that resembles and differs from others in its mental family in the way red objects resemble and differ from objects of other colors. So all it takes to note that one is in a red* state is to note that one is in a state that's distinctive in that way of red objects' being in front of one. And it's sufficient to have the concept of a red* state that one have a concept of that distinctive state.

When one sees something red, there's ordinarily no reason to take note of one's being in any sort of state at all; one's relevant thoughts all have to do with the red object. But occasional errors about whether something is red will call attention to the difference between an object's being red and one's being in the state distinctive of there being a red object in front of one. And that will lead to one's having a concept of a red* state, the distinctive kind of state, that is, in virtue of which one senses red things. So the concepts that figure in HOTs about qualitative states are relatively easy to come by, given sufficient concern with objects of the relevant sort.

Perceiving involves both intentional content and qualitative character. When one perceives something red, one is in a red* state and also in a state with the intentional content, roughly, that there is something red in front of one. Suppose, then, that one not only has concepts for the mental qualities of color*, but also has a fluent, automatic command in applying those concepts. Typically when one has a perceptual thought that there is something red in front of one, one is in a red* state.[79] Indeed, one's very concept of a red* state presumably stems from having learned that it sometimes seems that something in front of one is red even though it isn't.

So given fluent command in applying the concept of a red* state, this connection between perceptual thoughts and red* states will dispose one to think that one is in such a state whenever one has a perceptual thought that there is something red in front of one. The perceptual thoughts that occur in connection with perceiving

---

[79] Not always, since perceptual thoughts sometimes adjust for nonstandard lighting and the like.

something red will actually facilitate the occurrence of HOTs that one is in a red*
state. The connection between concepts for perceptible properties and concepts for
mental qualities, together with a fluent, automatic command over those concepts,
explains both why HOTs about qualitative states so often arise and why they are so
often accurate.

Perceptual thoughts about red objects facilitate HOTs that one is in a red* qualitative state. Why, then, don't nonperceptual thoughts about red objects facilitate HOTs
that one is in such a state? Nonperceptual thoughts about red objects don't routinely
occur in connection with red* sensations. In addition, they typically differ in content from the perceptual thoughts that figure in seeing red objects. Such perceptual
thoughts have the content, roughly, that something red is in front of one; so it's natural to expect that they would facilitate a thought about a concurrent red* state. The
content of nonperceptual thoughts about red objects is, by contrast, seldom if ever
that something red is present; so such thoughts are unlikely to facilitate a HOT about
a current red* state.

As noted in section IV, though some subpersonal mechanism figures early in visual
processing to combine information about color and shape, there is reason to doubt
that colors* ever occur without visual spatial* qualities, or conversely. But, even if
early visual states do occur that have color* but no shape* or shape* but no color*,
those states are never conscious, or in any case never conscious as such. We're never
conscious of ourselves as being in visual states that exhibit color* without shape* or
shape* but no color*.

If such early visual states do occur, moreover, the facilitation story would help
explain why such states are never conscious as having color* without shape* or
conversely. Since we never perceive anything as having color without shape or shape
without color, we never have perceptual thoughts about things as having one type of
perceptible property but not the other. So the HOTs about visual qualitative states
that those perceptual thoughts facilitate would not represent those states as having
color* without shape* or shape* without color*.[80]

VII. CROSS-MODAL CALIBRATION, REPRESENTATIONALISM, AND INVERSION

Sensing occurs by way of various distinct modalities, each of which operates in connection with a dedicated sense organ. Perceiving, by contrast, often involves more
than one sensory modality. Sometimes we perceive objects by way of only one modality; some distant objects, for example, we perceive only by sight and others only
by sound. But we perceive the properties of many things by means of more than one
sensory modality, and we expect that we could in principle do so with all local objects.

---

[80] I expand on the connection between perceptual intentional content and HOTs in "The
Facilitation of Conscious States," forthcoming. On the facilitation of HOTs about intentional states,
which operates somewhat differently, see "Why Are Verbally Expressed Thoughts Conscious?", ch.
10 in this volume, §V.

We expect this in large measure because we conceptualize the things we perceive as objects and events that are accessible to more than one modality. Even when I perceive a rabbit solely by vision, I conceptualize the thing I see as something I could also sense by other modalities.

Cross-modal perceiving requires being able to coordinate inputs from distinct senses with one another, so that they all have to do with a single object. There is no sense that bridges the various modalities, common to them all; so the cross-modal character of perceiving must come from the way we conceptualize what we perceive. If I see an automobile and also hear it and touch it, I must conceptualize the various perceptible properties I sense as all belonging to one and the same object. Even when I simply see a rabbit but conceptualize what I see as something I could also hear and touch, I rely on my ability to conceptualize perceptible properties from distinct modalities as all belonging to a single object.

Such calibration of sensory inputs from distinct modalities doubtless relies heavily on what we learn early in life about the ways perceptible properties occur together, which sights go with which sounds, and the like. But the mental qualities of size*, shape*, and location* distinctive of each modality doubtless also play a crucial role in such coordination of qualities from distinct modalities.

I argued briefly in section IV that these spatial* qualities are distinct properties for each distinct modality, since they're in each case determined by the boundaries and arrangements among mental qualities specific to each modality. Visual sensations involve mental qualities of color* whose boundaries determine mental qualities of shape* and size* and whose arrangement in the visual field determine the mental quality of relative location*. Similarly, tactile sensations involve mental qualities of resistance* and texture*, whose boundaries and arrangements also determine mental qualities of shape*, size*, and relative location*.[81]

There is, however, a temptation to suppose that spatial* mental qualities are the same from one modality to another. After all, the sensed perceptible properties are in each case the same; we sense the very same properties of physical shape, size, and location by the senses of vision, hearing, and touch. In this respect, the sensing of spatial perceptible properties differs in a striking way from the sensing of color and of sound, since only one modality has access to each of those properties. And, since the spatial properties we sense are the same from one modality to another, perhaps the spatial* mental qualities that figure in such sensing are also the same across modalities.

Even homomorphism theory might seem to suggest this conclusion. For the case of spatial sensing, the perceptible properties sensed are the same across modalities. And mental qualities are properties that resemble and differ in ways homomorphic to the similarities and differences among the relevant perceptible properties. So perhaps the mental qualities that figure in sensing physical size, shape, and location are themselves the same for all the modalities.

---

[81] Cf. Berkeley's argument that the spatial* qualities of each modality are tied to the other mental qualities that are specific to that modality (*A Treatise Concerning the Principles of Human Knowledge*, I, 10, in *Works*, II, p. 45, and *Three Dialogues between Hylas and Philonous*, *Works*, II, p. 194).

But neither consideration is compelling. It doesn't matter that the perceptible properties sensed by distinct modalities are in this case the same, since distinct mental qualities might well be homomorphic to a single set of perceptible properties. There is no reason why distinct families of mental qualities cannot access the very same set of perceptible properties. Indeed, one would expect that this might well happen when the mental qualities belong to distinct modalities. The traditional Aristotelian doctrine that the properties of sensations are literally the same as those of the objects sensed would preclude this possibility. On that view, the state in virtue of which one senses some perceptible property must itself actually exhibit that very property. And that traditional view continues to exert some influence, however tacit, on our thinking. But that doctrine is without foundation.

On homomorphism theory, mental qualities play a role in sensing by way of a particular modality because they occupy positions in a quality space that's homomorphic to the quality space of the properties that modality senses. Such homomorphisms cannot determine that spatial* mental qualities are the same across modalities. And the requirement that mental qualities play a role in sensing by a particular modality points toward the opposite conclusion. Mental qualities will play a role specific to a modality only if they operate in connection with the other mental qualities specific to that modality. So the spatial* qualities of vision will operate in connection with color* qualities, those of touch in connection with qualities of resistance* and texture*, and so forth. Each modality will operate by way of a distinct set of spatial* mental qualities.

Because spatial* qualities are distinct from one modality to the next, cross-modal perceiving requires calibrating of the spatial* qualities of one modality with those of others. Is such cross-modal calibration learned? Or is it instead simply part of our innate mental endowment? The issue is essentially that posed by William Molyneux to Locke,[82] about whether somebody born blind but with tactile experience of cubes and spheres would be able, on subsequently gaining sight, to distinguish those shapes visually. Andrew Meltzoff has argued that experimental findings show that very young infants perform cross-modal calibrations of spatial information independent of any prior experience, though it's arguable that there are serious problems with those results.[83]

---

[82] Locke reports Molyneux's query in *An Essay Concerning Human Understanding*, II, ix, 8, pp. 145–6.

[83] Andrew N. Meltzoff, "Molyneux's Babies: Cross-Modal Perception, Imitation and the Mind of the Preverbal Infant," in Naomi Eilan, Rosaleen McCarthy, and Bill Brewer, eds., *Spatial Representation: Problems in Philosophy and Psychology*, Oxford: Blackwell Publishers, 1993, pp. 219–235.

Meltzoff tested one-month-old infants on two types of pacifiers, both spherical in shape but one with eight or so small protuberances. He dismisses the possibility that infants might by that age have learned to associate such tactile differences with corresponding visual differences (223). But the small protuberances have roughly the shape of tiny nipples, with which one-month-olds will have had extensive, salient experience, both visual and tactile. So we can hardly rule out the possibility that their ability to coordinate visual with tactile input in this case was learned.

Meltzoff also documents the ability of infants only 32 hours old and inexperienced with mirrors to imitate facial expressions. And he argues that this ability reveals the "capacity [of these infants]

It's in any case clear that coordination of spatial* qualities across modalities relies to some extent on experience, since inverting goggles and prisms that distort visually sensed location require the recalibration of locations sensed by sight and touch (see n. 60 above). This need to recalibrate mainly affects sensed location. But the sensing of locations, like that of size and shape, invariably relies on the sensing of differences in color, pressure, texture, or other perceptible properties special to some particular modality. Indeed, as argued in section IV, since the boundaries between mental qualities that determine mental shape* and size* also determine mental location*, whatever holds of one of these types of spatial* mental qualities will hold of the others.

As noted in section V, though qualitative states represent corresponding perceptible properties, representing by way of homomorphisms operates differently from representing by way of intentional content. So homomorphism theory doesn't sustain a representationalist view on which qualitative character is at bottom a matter of intentional content.[84]

There is another version of representationalism, however, according to which, in Sydney Shoemaker's words, "the only features of sensory states of which we are introspectively aware are intentional or representational ones."[85] Similarly, Gilbert Harman urges that, when you have an experience of seeing a red tomato, "[y]ou have no conscious access to the qualities of your experience by which it represents the redness of the tomato. You are aware [only] of the redness of the tomato."[86]

to register equivalences between the body transformations they see and the body transformations they only feel themselves make" (222). But that ability to imitate is so prodigious that it may not involve sensations of facial movements at all. Visual input in these cases may be hardwired to motor output in a way that simply bypasses such sensations, just as dedicated facial expressions of specific emotions and contagious yawning are hardwired, and don't operate by way of mediating sensations of facial movements.

One dedicated subpersonal mechanism of the sort that might subserve such imitating involves the visuomotor, or "mirror," neurons, whose firing in humans and other primates figures both in perceiving and in executing imitative behavior. See Giacomo Rizzolatti, Luciano Fadiga, Vittorio Gallese, and Leonardo Fogassi, "Premotor Cortex and the Recognition of Motor Actions," *Cognitive Brain Research*, 3, 2 (March 1996): 131–141; Vittorio Gallese, Luciano Fadiga, Leonardo Fogassi, and Giacomo Rizzolatti, "Action Recognition in the Premotor Cortex," *Brain*, 119, 2 (April 1996): 593–609; and Giacomo Rizzolatti and Laila Craighero, "The Mirror Neuron System," *Annual Review of Neuroscience*, 27 (2004): 169–192.

[84] For representationalist theories, see, e.g., Armstrong, *The Nature of Mind*, ch. 9, and Lycan, *Consciousness and Experience*, ch. 4.

[85] "Introspection and 'Inner Sense'," *Philosophy and Phenomenological Research*, LIV, 2 (June 1994): 249–314; reprinted in Shoemaker, *The First-Person Perspective and Other Essays*, Cambridge: Cambridge University Press, 1996, pp. 201–268, at p. 218. See also p. 257, and his "Phenomenal Character," *Noûs*, 28 (1994): 21–38, "Phenomenal Character Revisited," *Philosophy and Phenomenological Research*, LX, 2 (2000): 465–468, and "Introspection and Phenomenal Character," *Philosophical Topics*, 28, 2 (Fall 2000): 247–273.

I am grateful to Shoemaker, personal communication, for stressing how my view could be seen as resembling representationalism.

[86] Gilbert H. Harman, "Explaining Objective Color in terms of Subjective Reactions," *Philosophical Issues: Perception*, 7 (1996): 1–17, p. 8 (reprinted in Alex Byrne and David Hilbert, eds., *Readings on Color, volume 1: The Philosophy of Color*, Cambridge, Massachusetts: MIT Press/Bradford Books, 1997, pp. 247–261). See also "The Intrinsic Quality of Experience," *Philosophical Perspectives*,

But the current view is not representationalist on that version either. On Shoemaker's version of representationalism, the properties of qualitative states that we introspect are intentional, but that's not the case on the present account. We introspect qualitative properties as well. And, contrary to Harman's representationalist claim, we are conscious not only of the redness of the tomato, but of the mental qualities of our experience of the tomato. The higher-order states in virtue of which we are aware of such qualitative states are themselves intentional states; they are HOTs. But that doesn't sustain the representationalism put forth by Shoemaker or Harman.

Harman insists that the qualities we are aware of are never mental qualities, but only the perceptible properties of physical objects; we "are aware [only] of the redness of the tomato." When one consciously sees a red tomato, one is aware of the redness of the tomato. And there is some plausibility to Harman's claim that there is no other quality of which one is conscious. Even when one focuses introspectively on the redness, one isn't aware of any shift from one quality to another, from the redness of the tomato to the red* of the sensation. So why think that one is ever aware of a red* mental quality, as against the perceptible red of physical objects?

We are perceptually aware of the red color of the tomato. And it's plain that we aren't perceptually aware of the mental red* of any sensation. But the idea that we're only aware of perceptible red, and never of mental qualities, trades on the tacit assumption that awareness is always perceptual awareness. We perceive the redness of the tomato, but no corresponding mental quality.

But perceiving a quality is not the only way we can be conscious of it. When I consciously see a red tomato, I perceive its redness. But, since my seeing is conscious, I am also conscious of myself as seeing the red tomato. That involves my having a thought about myself as seeing the tomato. I have a thought about myself as being in a state that involves a particular form of qualitative perceiving, and hence as being in a state with mental qualitative character.

When one shifts from consciously seeing the tomato to introspecting that experience, one's attention shifts from the quality of the tomato to the quality of the state one is in. One doesn't come thereby to be perceptually conscious of a distinct quality. But, by having a conscious thought about oneself as being in a particular kind of state, one does shift attention to the quality of the conscious experience. And, since having a thought about something as being present also makes one conscious of that thing, having a thought about oneself as being in a state with a red* mental quality makes one conscious of a red* mental quality.[87]

I argued in section V that homomorphism theory, by fixing mental qualities by appeal to perceptual role rather than how we're conscious of them, undermines the idea that such qualities could vary while perceptual role remains constant. But homomorphism theory tells against the possibility of such variation in a more specific way.

---

4 (1990): 31–52; and "Qualia and Color Concepts," *Philosophical Issues: Perception*, 7 (1996): 75–79.

[87] For more on introspection and representationalism, see "Introspection and Self-Interpretation," §V.

Homomorphism theory fixes mental qualities by way of the characteristic similarities and differences each quality has to others in its family. If an inversion of mental qualities altered the distinctive pattern of similarities and differences, the new pattern would no longer be homomorphic to the similarities and differences of the relevant perceptible properties. That would alter perceptual functioning, and the inversion would then be detectable from a third-person point of view, contrary to the hypothesis that such inversion not be so detectable.

Is any inversion of mental qualities possible that preserves relations of similarity and difference? Arguably not. Such an inversion would have to be around an axis with respect to which the relevant quality space is symmetric; otherwise it would alter the relations of similarity and difference. And, if the space of mental qualities is symmetric in that way, the corresponding space of perceptible properties must be as well.

But, if the space of perceptible properties were symmetric around some axis in respect of these similarities and differences, properties on each side of that axis would be indistinguishable in respect of similarities and differences from properties on the other. So, for each perceptible property on one side of the axis, there would be some property on the other side with exactly the same relations of similarity and difference. Since we discriminate among perceptible properties in respect of their distinctive relations of similarity and difference, we would be unable to distinguish or in any way to react differently to the two members of these pairs. It would be as though one side of the axis were redundant for perceptual functioning, since the two sides would play indistinguishable perceptual roles. Any inversion around such an axis would be vacuous in respect of perceptual functioning. [88]

Undetectable inversion of mental qualities would have to take place around an axis of symmetry in respect of similarities and differences. But no such symmetry can exist in the space of mental qualities without also existing in the space of perceptible properties, and that symmetry would mean that the qualities on the two sides of the axis would be indistinguishable. So undetectable inversion of mental qualities cannot occur. But what it's like for one to be in a state with a particular mental quality is distinct from simply being in that state. What, then, about the inversion of what it's like for one to be in states with those mental qualities? Can such inversion occur undetectably?

The same conclusion holds. HOTs represent the mental qualities of our qualitative states in respect of the same patterns of similarities and differences that fix those mental qualities. So, if inversion that preserves those patterns is impossible among the qualities themselves, it will no more possible in the way HOTs represent them. If such inversion were possible, the qualities on one side of the relevant axis would be indistinguishable, from the point of view of consciousness, from the qualities on the other side. The HOT hypothesis, taken together with homomorphism theory, precludes inversion of conscious qualities undetectable from a third-person point of view.

---

[88] Some time after writing this, I came upon an argument to much the same effect in David R. Hilbert and Mark Eli Kalderon, "Color and the Inverted Spectrum," in Steven Davis, ed., *Color Perception: Philosophical, Psychological, Artistic and Computational Perspectives*, New York: Oxford University Press, 2000, pp. 187–214, §6.2.

The mental qualities that figure in achromatic perception might seem intuitively to be symmetrical, since the quality space of achromatic qualities may itself seem to be one-dimensional. But there are important asymmetries that block inversion of even the achromatic shades. For one thing, shades such as luminous gray suggest that the achromatic quality space is two-dimensional. And there are asymmetries even in the one-dimensional scale of relative luminosity. Thus the perceived gray scale in human achromatic perception is anchored only by the lightest shade, not the darkest. And the perception of black requires the presence of a contrast shade, whereas we can perceive a white ganzfeld.[89]

Shoemaker has urged that, though asymmetries in the human color quality space do preclude inversion of color qualities in humans, creatures are conceivable in which such inversion occurs.[90] But if a quality space were symmetrical in a way that allowed inversion of mental qualities, the invertible qualities would play indistinguishable roles in perceptual functioning, which would collapse perceptual distinctions. And, because qualitative states are conscious in respect of their perceptual roles, the invertible qualities would then be indistinguishable from a first-person point of view. Undetectable quality inversion is not conceivable.[91]

---

[89] On the dimensionality of the achromatic quality space, see, e.g., Rainer Mausfeld, "Color Perception: From Grassmann Codes to a Dual Code for Object and Illumination Colours," in Werner G. K. Backhaus, Reinhold Kliegl, and John S. Werner, eds., *Color Vision: Perspectives from Different Disciplines*, Berlin and New York: Walter de Gruyter, 1998, p. 223. On anchoring, see Alan L. Gilchrist, Christos Kossyfidis, Frederick Bonato, Tiziano Agostini, Joseph Cataliotti, Xiaojun Li, Branka Spehar, Vidal Annan, and Elias Economou, "An Anchoring Theory of Lightness Perception," *Psychological Review*, 106, 4 (October 1999): 795–834. On the impossibility of a black ganzfeld, see C. L. Hardin, *Color for Philosophers: Unweaving the Rainbow*, Indianapolis: Hackett Publishing Co., 1988, expanded edn., 1993, pp. 22–24. I am grateful to Josh Weisberg for pressing this issue, and to Austen Clark, Rainer Mausfeld, and Robert Schwartz for pointing me toward these findings.

[90] See "The Inverted Spectrum," *The Journal of Philosophy*, LXXIX, 7 (July 1982): 357–381; reprinted in his *Identity, Cause, and Mind: Philosophical Essays*, Cambridge: Cambridge University Press, 1984, 2nd edn., Oxford: Clarendon Press, 2003, pp. 327–357, at p. 336, and "Intrasubjective/Intersubjective," in his *The First-Person Perspective and Other Essays*, Cambridge and New York: Cambridge University Press, 1996, pp. 141–154, at p. 150.

Shoemaker also holds that, though we can determine similarity and identity of qualities within an individual by appeal to the perceptual beliefs and related behavior that qualitative states tend to cause, that won't determine which mental quality a state has. But he thinks that qualities will be the same across individuals if their functionally determined quality spaces are the same and the qualities are realized by the same physical states. ("The Inverted Spectrum," §§V and VI, and postscript.) But, if behaviorally undetectable inversion were conceivable, as Shoemaker insists, then relations of similarity and difference wouldn't after all be sufficient to fix mental qualities. And then it's unclear why specific neural states would realize specific qualities, as against qualities that simply satisfy the relevant relations of similarity and difference.

[91] Stephen Palmer has argued that, despite isomorphism of the color qualities of visual sensations across subjects, some quality inversion is possible. (S. E. Palmer, "Color, Consciousness, and the Isomorphism Constraint," *The Behavioral and Brain Sciences*, 22, 6 [December 1999]: 923–943.) According to Palmer, those mental color qualities are isomorphic across subjects because they are isomorphic to qualities in a psychophysically defined color space. These considerations lead him to adopt an "isomorphism constraint" (933), that mental qualities of qualitative states are the same

Some theorists will see this result as telling against the combination of homomorphism theory and the HOT hypothesis; if combining those theories precludes quality inversion, so much the worse for the combined theories. But the idea that such inversion is possible has no basis either in untutored, pretheoretic intuition or in empirical findings. Indeed, since the inversion must be undetectable by third-person means, how could pretheoretic intuition support such a claim? And, such third-person undetectability means that there could in any case be no empirical support for the possibility of such inversion. The idea that it is possible is simply a reflection of the theoretical conviction that mental qualities are independent of perceptual role.[92]

Theories of qualitative consciousness, like other theories, must be judged by their fruits. The combination of the HOT hypothesis and homomorphism theory yields results that conform to the dictates of folk psychology and to what we know empirically about qualitative consciousness. And it does this in a way that defuses apparent mysteries and promises to make such consciousness fit comfortably within the context of the rest of what we know about mental functioning. It's likely that this combination of theories will provide a useful framework for future research.[93]

---

across subjects only to the extent that such isomorphisms hold: "Objective behavioral methods can determine the nature of experiences up to, but not beyond, the criterion of isomorphism" (934). And he holds that such isomorphism cannot fully determine those mental qualities.

But to sustain this view, Palmer needs some independent way to tell what mental quality a state has. For that he relies solely on first-person access to those qualities, viz., on how we're conscious of the qualities. But, even leaving aside the foregoing argument that first-person access will reflect perceptual role, such first-person access plainly cannot help with intersubjective comparisons.

[92] For more on quality inversion, see "Sensory Quality and the Relocation Story," ch. 6 in this volume.

[93] Substantially earlier versions were presented at the August 1991 Cognitive Science Society in Vancouver, the Philosophy, Neuroscience, and Psychology Colloquium at Washington University in St Louis in April 2000, the July 2000 Association for the Scientific Study of Consciousness in Brussels, The Hebrew University in Jerusalem and the University of Haifa in January 2001, and as the 19th annual Dean Kolitch Memorial Lecture at the CUNY Graduate Center in December 2001. I am grateful to members of all these audiences, and especially to Robert Schwartz and Sydney Shoemaker, for helpful, challenging discussion.

PART III

CONSCIOUSNESS, EXPRESSION, AND INTERPRETATION

8

First-Person Operationalism and Mental Taxonomy

I. MULTIPLE DRAFTS AND FIRST-PERSON OPERATIONALISM

Any acceptable theory of consciousness must plainly satisfy two main constraints. It must, first of all, do reasonable justice to our commonsense, folk-psychological intuitions about consciousness and mentality. Some of these intuitions will be helpful in identifying just what phenomena the theory seeks to explain. Others the theory will predict, using its explanatory machinery. Still others the theory may be neutral about, avoiding any conflict between theory and intuition. Also, a theory may jettison certain intuitions, ruling in effect that they do not reflect the nature of conscious phenomena; but the theory must then explain why those intuitions, despite being mistaken, still strike us as compelling.

A theory of consciousness must also square with what scientific research tells us about the brain and about the conscious functioning of people and other animals. The theory must, in particular, help make it intelligible how brain mechanisms operate in producing conscious experiences, and it must take account of experimental and clinical findings.

Theories often seem to do a lot better with one of these tasks than the other. Many theorists, for example, would take Thomas Nagel's account of consciousness in terms of subjective points of view as setting a standard for successfully capturing our folk-psychological intuitions.[1] And this may well lead to the kind of skepticism Nagel himself holds about whether those commonsense intuitions can be made to fit with a scientific account of these things. Similarly, whatever the merits of neurobiological explanation, such as the suggestion by Francis Crick and Christof Koch that consciousness arises from neuronal oscillations close to 40 hertz,[2] it isn't easy to see how such explanations could do justice to our folk-psychological intuitions about consciousness. Indeed some, such as Patricia Smith Churchland, have argued

---

[1] Thomas Nagel, "What Is It Like to Be a Bat?", *The Philosophical Review*, LXXXIII, 4 (October 1974): 435–450; "Panpsychism," in *Mortal Questions*, Cambridge: Cambridge University Press, 1979, pp. 181–195; and *The View From Nowhere*, New York: Oxford University Press, 1986, chs. 1–4.

[2] "Towards a Neurobiological Theory of Consciousness," *Seminars in the Neurosciences*, 2 (1990), 263–275.

that a scientific theory of consciousness will require that many of these intuitions be rejected.[3]

Against this background, the theory of consciousness developed in Daniel Dennett's impressive and important book, *Consciousness Explained*,[4] occupies a useful middle ground. One of Dennett's main concerns is to describe a model for explaining consciousness which takes account of relevant results in experimental cognitive psychology and the neurosciences. Consciousness, he argues, results from a number of interacting brain processes, which are constantly changing due to new stimuli and feedback from other brain processes. Because the interactions among the relevant processes are continually being updated, the way consciousness represents our mental lives is not fixed from moment to moment.

At any particular moment, therefore, there may be many competing interactions among the brain processes, each capable of giving rise to consciousness. And the interactions competing at any one time may represent the contents of consciousness in different ways. Which interactions lead to conscious results, moreover, may often be a matter of chance factors, factors, that is, extrinsic to the interacting processes. Some external stimulus, or "probe," may push things in one direction or another. And often there will be a succession of interactions that yield conscious results, producing successive versions—or "drafts"—of the conscious goings-on within the person.

Dennett calls this model for explaining consciousness the Multiple Drafts model (MDM). He contrasts it with what he calls the Cartesian Theater model, on which a mental state's being conscious is a matter of its being observed, somehow, in a "theater of consciousness" (144). On the MDM, consciousness is a function of processes occurring in a distributed way throughout much of the brain, whereas the Cartesian Theater model holds that states are conscious just in case they occur at a single privileged location. Dennett argues forcefully against the Cartesian Theater model, which, he plausibly maintains, tacitly underlies the explanatory strategies used by many theorists.

Dennett is concerned not merely to make intelligible how consciousness arises in the brain, but at the same time to do justice to our folk-psychological intuitions about consciousness. But he departs from many theorists in how he gets at these intuitions. People seem to have direct access to their own introspective data; so it's tempting to claim that such data are decisive about mental reality. But introspective data differ notoriously from person to person, and even for single subjects their reliability is questionable. Dennett therefore takes the principal evidence about conscious mental phenomena to be the verbal reports people make about their mental lives. These "heterophenomenological" reports (72 ff.) provide the commonsense information about our mental lives to which a theory must do justice. Because introspectible events aren't directly accessible to others, heterophenomenological reports provide a measure of objectivity that direct reliance on introspection cannot.[5]

---

[3] "Consciousness: The Transmutation of a Concept," *Pacific Philosophical Quarterly*, LXIV, 1 (January 1983): 80–95.

[4] Daniel C. Dennett, *Consciousness Explained*, Boston, Little, Brown & Co., 1991 (*CE*). Except where otherwise indicated, page references throughout are to *CE*.

[5] Reliance on such reports is of course standard in experimental cognitive psychology.

Discounting occasional insincerity, heterophenomenological reports are authoritative about how people's mental lives seem to them. Dennett emphasizes that this doesn't mean that these reports are also authoritative about the states and processes that underlie those appearances. Even the mental events to which a subject's heterophenomenological reports ostensibly refer may not always exist. We should take heterophenomenological reports to refer to actual events only if those reports are corroborated by what we know independently, say, about brain events. Dennett's methodological reliance on heterophenomenological reports is therefore neutral about whether such reports truly describe mental events that go into a subject's first-person viewpoint, or simply express beliefs about the subject's mental events, events which may be entirely notional. It's a special strength of Dennett's approach that this neutrality enables the heterophenomenological method to bridge the traditional gulf between first- and third-person accounts of mind and consciousness. We need not, accordingly, have a theory based just on first- or third-person considerations. This approach therefore allows Dennett to weave together heterophenomenological data with the findings of neuroscience and cognitive psychology in a way that does reasonable justice to both.

Heterophenomenological reports may well provide the best evidence about how people's conscious mental lives appear to them, though these reports may not always tell us about the states and processes that underlie those appearances. But Dennett goes further, and insists that, whatever the case with underlying processes, there is nothing more to people's conscious experiences than how those experiences appear. When it comes to people's conscious mental lives, there is no distinction to be drawn between the reality of conscious experiences and how those experiences appear to those who have them. Consciousness consists in things' appearing in certain ways; so appearance is all there is to the reality of consciousness. Dennett calls this view first-person operationalism (FPO). It's a form of operationalism because appearance determines reality; but it's operationalism restricted to the first-person case, that is, to "the realm of subjectivity" (132).

Dennett regards his MDM as a form of FPO (132). But it's possible to separate Dennett's denial of the distinction between the appearance and reality of conscious experience from other aspects of his model that are independent of this denial. In what follows, I'll refer to Dennett's denial of that distinction as FPO, and I'll apply the label 'MDM' more restrictively to those aspects of his model that are independent of FPO. I'll argue that, although Dennett's MDM narrowly understood in this way is as promising a model as we now have for explaining consciousness, we need not also adopt his thesis of FPO. I'll do this by defending a model of consciousness very similar to the MDM, narrowly construed, and arguing against the addition of FPO.

II. TEMPORAL ANOMALIES AND FACTS OF THE MATTER

Perhaps the most important of the empirical findings against which Dennett tests his model has to do with the remarkable temporal anomalies he describes in chapters 5 and 6 of *CE* and in his earlier article with Marcel Kinsbourne.[6] The ability to deal satisfactorily with these anomalies is one of the greatest strengths of Dennett's MDM. So in trying to assess whether FPO is a necessary aspect of Dennett's view, it's useful to begin with these curious results.

Two anomalies will suffice to give the flavor. In color phi, a subject is presented with alternating red and green flashes on the left and right, respectively, but seems to see a single spot that moves and changes color. In the so-called cutaneous rabbit, three successive bunches of physical taps are administered, at the wrist, elbow, and upper arm, but the subject feels a sequence of single taps along the arm, evenly separated by small distances. Subjects presented only with the initial red flash on the left, or only the bunched taps at the wrist, consciously sense these things in just that way. Why is it that when these initial stimuli are followed by the others, subjects do not consciously perceive the initial red flash, nor the bunched wrist taps?

Dennett believes the MDM has the answer. On that model, conscious mental states are due to the interaction of many brain processes. These interactions are of course not instantaneous, but take some time to occur. So an interaction that would ordinarily lead to some particular conscious experience can, in effect, be derailed by a suitably timed stimulus. If presented with only a red flash on the left, the subject consciously experiences it. But the subsequent stimulus of a green flash on the right interferes with the interaction that would have led to a conscious experience of a red flash, replacing it with the conscious experience of a moving spot that changes color. Similarly with the cutaneous rabbit.

Among the intervening stimuli that may alter the course of the interactions leading to a conscious experience is the eliciting of some reaction from a subject. And a small change in timing can of course be crucial. At successive moments we may well "precipitat[e] different narratives ... [different] versions of a portion of 'the stream of consciousness'" (135). Because of this, there is no privileged moment at which eliciting a report would reveal the true nature of the subject's conscious experience. Any event that serves as a probe for a subject's heterophenomenological report may affect the contemporaneous interactions leading to specific conscious results.

Even in the temporal anomalies, when an event following the initial stimulus derails things, it might still have been possible to elicit a report of the initial stimulus if we timed our probe sufficiently precisely. In color phi, the probe would presumably have to occur after the stationary red flash affected the visual cortex, but before the first green flash interrupted the normal resulting processes. Such a probe might block the processes leading to the conscious experience of a moving spot that changes color, allowing the subject to consciously experience the initial stationary flash. But if no such probe intervenes, there will be no conscious experience of the initial stimulus.

Dennett compares the situation to the revising of texts. When a text changes through successive drafts, some features typically persist through many drafts; others

---

[6] Daniel C. Dennett and Marcel Kinsbourne, "Time and the Observer: The Where and When of Consciousness in the Brain," *The Behavioral and Brain Sciences*, 15, 2 (June 1992): 183–201. See also the Open Peer Commentary, pp. 201–234, and Dennett and Kinsbourne's Author's Response, "Escape from the Cartesian Theater," pp. 234–247.

may be so transitory as to altogether escape one's notice. Similarly with consciousness. Successive interactions among brain processes lead to different ways in which consciousness represents our mental lives, that is, to different versions of contents of consciousness. It may seem that reports of our experiences must be the last word on this matter, much as publishing a text fixes what words do and don't occur in it. This idea is especially inviting if we take heterophenomenological reports to be the best evidence about people's mental lives. But even publication fixes a text only relative to a social context, and only for a while; post-publication revision can and does occur. Similarly with reports of conscious experiences. We sometimes withdraw earlier remarks about our experiences, replacing them with claims we take to be more accurate.

It seems clear that temporal anomalies such as color phi demand some explanation along these lines. The initial stimulus sets processes in motion that, if uninterrupted, give rise to an conscious sensation of a stationary red flash. But if certain stimuli follow after a suitable temporal interval, those processes are sidetracked, and lead instead to the conscious experience of a moving spot that changes color.

When color phi occurs, there is, from a first-person viewpoint, no conscious experience of a stationary red flash. Plainly this is in some way due to the subsequent stimulus. But it seems that we can imagine two distinct types of mechanism by means of which the subsequent stimulus could have that effect. Perhaps the subsequent stimulus derails the process leading to a conscious sensation of a stationary red flash, so that no such conscious sensation ever occurs. But there's another sequence of events that would make it seem from a first-person point of view that no such conscious sensation had occurred. Perhaps the initial stimulus does reach consciousness, so that a conscious sensation of the initial flash does occur. But that conscious sensation does not last long enough to have any noticeable mental effects; it commands no attention, and when it ceases any traces in memory are immediately expunged. The first mechanism, in which the stimulus is edited out before any conscious sensation occurs, Dennett calls Stalinesque; the second sequence, in which the stimulus reaches consciousness but is immediately edited out of memory, he calls Orwellian.

It's here that FPO leads to radical results. According to FPO, there is no distinction between the reality of a conscious experience and how that experience appears. The reality of conscious states consists simply in how they seem, from a first-person point of view. Accordingly, Dennett

makes 'writing it down' in memory criterial for consciousness ... There is no reality of consciousness independent of the effects of various vehicles of content on subsequent action (and hence, of course, on memory) (p. 132).

If it seems from a first-person point of view that there has been no conscious sensation of a stationary red flash, then none has occurred.

But if the reality of conscious experiences consists in how they appear from a first-person point of view, there can be no difference between Stalinesque and Orwellian mechanisms. In color phi, the second stimulus prevents the content of a stationary red flash from occurring within the subject's first-person viewpoint. That stimulus is, at some point or other, edited out. But if 'writing it down' in memory [is] criterial for consciousness," editing a stimulus out of memory will, on criterial grounds, be indistinguishable from editing it out before it reaches consciousness. There will simply be no difference between the two. Accordingly Dennett denies that there's any difference between the Stalinesque and the Orwellian models. The difference can only be verbal, a difference between two equivalent ways of describing the same thing. When no early reaction is elicited from the subject, there is simply no fact of the matter about whether the initial stimulus ever becomes conscious. So "there are no fixed facts about the stream of consciousness independent of particular probes" (138; cf. 275).

The temporal anomalies by themselves, however, do not imply these conclusions. Explaining the anomalies does not require us to deny that there's a real difference between Stalinesque and Orwellian mechanisms nor, more generally, to adopt FPO. We can do justice to the phenomena by a more modest explanation along the lines of the MDM sketched above, on which subsequent stimuli interrupt the processes normally initiated by the original stimulus. Moreover, this interruption can be Stalinesque, preventing the occurrence of any conscious sensation corresponding to the initial stimulus, or Orwellian, in which case it will cut short the conscious sensation that occurs and remove any trace of it from memory.

In the end, the two mechanisms yield the same subjective appearances. But this doesn't mean that we cannot determine which is operative, since the order of events they posit is different. Either the stimulus is edited out before a corresponding conscious experience occurs or it isn't. And on the MDM, construed narrowly without FPO, there is an objective temporal order in which the various events occur. So the MDM thus narrowly construed suggests not only that the initial stimulus is edited out, but also that there are two distinguishable ways in which that might happen, either before or after the stimulus leads to the corresponding conscious sensation.

According to FPO, however, there are no facts of the matter about consciousness beyond those which make up one's first-person, subjective point of view. If a subject cannot distinguish two situations introspectively, then with respect to consciousness there's no difference between them.

And it may seem that the constraints of FPO are not unreasonable. By hypothesis, Stalinesque and Orwellian mechanisms do not differ in their introspectible results. Moreover, which mechanism is operative makes no difference in subjects' verbal behavior, including their heterophenomenological reports. Nor can nonverbal behavior help distinguish the two. As Dennett notes, when mental representations result in nonverbal behavior, the very same behavior may occur whether the representation occurs consciously or not (124). So, for example, neither verbal nor nonverbal behavior can determine whether or not the mental representation of a stationary red flash in color phi is conscious.

It is arguable that commonsense folk psychology distinguishes conscious mental phenomena only by way of their introspectible differences, and by the verbal and nonverbal behavior they result in. But even if that is so, theories often considerably expand our ability to discriminate among phenomena that are indistinguishable independent of theory. Suppose that a particular theory about consciousness always draws the right distinctions in problematic cases about whether particular mental states are conscious or not conscious. The theory agrees, that is, with our folk-psychological convictions. We could then apply this theory to the problematic temporal anomalies to determine, regardless of how it seems to the subject, whether a particular stimulus does or does not make it to consciousness.

We can be more specific about how a theory of consciousness can help in this way. Intuitively, it's a distinguishing mark of conscious states that whenever a mental state is conscious, we are in some way conscious *of* that state.[7] To avoid confusion, I'll refer to our being conscious *of* something, whether a mental state or anything else, as *transitive consciousness*. And I'll call the property mental states have of being conscious *state consciousness*. A state's being conscious does not, of course, require that we're attentively or introspectively conscious of it. We don't introspect or pay attention to most of our conscious states. Indeed, we forget the overwhelming majority of those states moments after they occur. Still, if one is in no way transitively conscious of a particular mental state, that state is not a conscious state.[8]

Any theory of what it is for mental states to be conscious must explain in what way we are transitively conscious of our conscious states. There must be some event that constitutes one's being transitively conscious of any conscious mental state, and a theory of consciousness must tell us what event that is. Such a theory would therefore be able to tell us, when a particular temporal anomaly occurs, whether the mechanism

[7] Fred Dretske has contested this, arguing that we often are not transitively conscious of our conscious states ("Conscious Experience," *Mind*, 102, 406 [April 1993]: 263–283, esp. 272–275, and "Are Experiences Conscious?", ch. IV of *Naturalizing the Mind*, MIT Press/Bradford Books, 1995). Instead of a mental state's being conscious if one is transitively conscious of it in some suitable way, Dretske proposes that a state's being conscious is simply a matter of its being a case of transitive consciousness (280–1). But all mental states are cases of transitive consciousness. So Dretske's alternative in effect defines all mental states as conscious states, which is implausible. Dretske's argument that we aren't always transitively conscious of our conscious states also fails to take account of the fact that we can be conscious of an experience in one respect while not being conscious of it in another. See my "Explaining Consciousness," in *Philosophy of Mind: Classical and Contemporary Readings*, ed. David J. Chalmers, New York: Oxford University Press, 2002, pp. 406–421, and "Sensory Quality and the Relocation Story," ch. 6 in this volume, § II.

John R. Searle denies that it's even possible to be conscious of our conscious mental states, though his reasons are different. "[W]here conscious subjectivity is concerned, there is no distinction between the observation and the thing observed" (*The Rediscovery of the Mind*, Cambridge, Massachusetts: MIT Press, 1992, p. 97). The context makes clear that Searle is denying not just that we can observe our conscious states, but that we are transitively conscious of them at all in the way we're conscious of other things: "We cannot get at the reality of consciousness in the way that, using consciousness, we can get at the reality of other phenomena" (96–7). Searle argues for this by appeal to the idea that we can describe consciousness only in terms of what it's consciousness *of* (96). But even if that's so, it doesn't follow that there can't be states in virtue of which we're conscious *of* our conscious states.

Searle also urges that, when we mentally represent things, the things we represent must be something ontologically objective. Since conscious states, according to Searle, are ontologically subjective, we cannot mentally represent them and so cannot be transitively conscious of them (99; cf. 87–100, 137–8, and 144–5). Because it's difficult to make clear sense of Searle's distinction between the ontologically subjective and objective and, indeed, just what ontological subjectivity amounts to, it's unclear how to evaluate this argument.

[8] For more on this, see my "State Consciousness and Transitive Consciousness," *Consciousness and Cognition*, 2, 4 (December 1993), pp. 355–363.

responsible for it is Stalinesque or Orwellian, since Orwellian mechanisms involve an event of transitive consciousness that on the Stalinesque model simply doesn't occur.

In advance of a reasonably well-confirmed theory of this sort, we have of course no way of telling which model explains color phi or the other temporal anomalies. Perhaps some anomalies are Orwellian and others Stalinesque; perhaps some have both Stalinesque and Orwellian instances. Because we cannot distinguish Stalinesque from Orwellian cases by appeal to introspection, speech, and nonverbal behavior, and we now have no suitable general theory, current experimental paradigms reflect a provisional methodological acceptance of FPO. We operate as though FPO were the case. But this methodological operationalism would be unnecessarily restrictive once we had such a theory. We would then be able to frame more fine-grained experiments based on knowing which mechanism is operative in each kind of case.

On the Orwellian model, the initial stimulus in color phi reaches consciousness but leaves no further mental traces; a conscious sensation occurs but makes no mental difference to the subject. This may seem to conflict with the commonsense observation that no mental state is conscious unless one is transitively conscious of it, even if in the most casual and inattentive way. The Orwellian model claims that sensations become conscious even though it never seems to the subject as though those sensations occur. And if the sensation doesn't, from a first-person point of view, seem to occur, how can the subject be transitively conscious of it? It seems that such a sensation could be conscious in name only, that is, in some technical sense that fails to make contact with our intuitive conception of consciousness.[9]

The Orwellian model may therefore seem to be an artificial contrivance, somewhat like Descartes's unflinching insistence that "we do not have any thoughts in sleep without being conscious of them at the moment they occur; though commonly we forget them immediately."[10] Could either claim be more than a mere verbal conceit? It doesn't help here simply to note that theories often go beyond common sense. What could we mean by a mental state's being conscious if it could be conscious without one's being in any way whatever transitively conscious of it?

But the Orwellian model does not, in fact, conflict with our commonsense conceptions. Consider the fleeting auditory and visual sensations that occupy the periphery of our consciousness. These sensations are seldom if ever introspectively conscious. But they also do not occur outside our conscious field of vision. They are conscious sensations, though we take note neither of them nor of our being conscious of them. These sensations are so transitory, moreover, that we ordinarily have no memory at all of what conscious contents occupied the peripheries of our perceptual fields, even a

---

[9] Cf. Dennett, "The Message is: There is no *Medium*," *Philosophy and Phenomenological Research*, LIII, 4 (December 1993): 919–931, pp. 929–931.

[10] Letter to Arnauld, 29 July 1648, René Descartes, *The Philosophical Writings of Descartes*, John Cottingham, Robert Stoothoff, Dugald Murdoch, and Anthony Kenny, 3 volumes, tr. Cambridge: Cambridge University Press, 1991, III, 357.

Descartes's insistence that "[b]eing conscious of our thoughts at the time when we are thinking is not the same as remembering them afterwards" stands in useful opposition to Dennett's view that " 'writing it down' in memory [is] criterial for consciousness."

moment earlier. Neither the sensations nor our transitive consciousness of them typically leave any trace in memory.

This account of things accords with common sense, which countenances a wide if somewhat indeterminate area for our conscious visual field. Because we have a strong conviction about roughly how far the field extends, and that it's visual through and through,[11] we feel convinced that many sensations near the periphery of that field are conscious. That is so despite our inability to say what sensations occur near the periphery of that field.

The Orwellian model posits states with roughly this status. The model maintains that stimuli reach consciousness but remain there so briefly that, from a first-person point of view, it doesn't seem that any such conscious sensations occur. All that's necessary for this to happen is a momentary event of being transitively conscious of the sensation, albeit too briefly to register as part of the subject's first-person point of view. Presumably this happens all the time with fleeting peripheral sensations.

Because they leave no trace in memory, it can be argued that we have no reason, from a first-person point of view, to think such conscious sensations exist at all. Of course, when we shift our attention to them, we are subjectively certain that they exist; but those are the cases that do leave traces in memory. Here, again, the appeal to theory is irrelevant, since what's at issue is our commonsense, folk-psychological view of these things.

Is it possible for a state to occur consciously even though to the subject it doesn't seem to occur? There is compelling reason to think so. We're often aware of things that don't make it into our first-person point of view. We are conscious in daily life of endless details of which we don't seem to ourselves to be conscious. The same is true with mental states. Like any other mental construct, our first-person view of ourselves leaves out much detail, enabling us to concentrate on the big picture. So there's no reason to think that every mental state we're conscious of occurs as part of our subjective view of ourselves. Still, when we're conscious of states that don't figure in that first-person picture of ourselves, those states are conscious states. The denial that the reality of conscious sensations can differ from their appearance, though central to FPO, is not part of our folk-psychological picture.

III. TRANSITIVE CONSCIOUSNESS AND THE TWO MODELS

Because a theory of consciousness must explain what events occur when we are transitively conscious of our conscious states, such a theory will help distinguish Stalinesque from Orwellian mechanisms. So explaining the temporal anomalies does not require that we adopt FPO. Nor must we deny that for each occurrence of a temporal anomaly there's a fact of the matter about whether a Stalinesque or an Orwellian mechanism is operative.

---

[11] Contrast this with the situation in which one senses that another person is looking at one. Though it's plain on reflection that we get this information visually, it doesn't intuitively seem to be visual information.

Dennett draws the contrast between Stalinesque and Orwellian mechanisms in terms of the temporal order of events: Does the editing out come before the initial stimulus reaches consciousness or after? I've argued in the previous section that there's no reason to doubt that a suitable theory can answer that question. Even so, the contrast between Stalinesque and Orwellian cases turns out to be somewhat more complicated than that. In this section, I'll argue that there's a possible mechanism for the temporal anomalies that resists ready classification either as Stalinesque or as Orwellian. What's crucial is recognizing the difference between our sensations and our transitive consciousness of those sensations. Once that distinction is clearly in place, we'll see that a firm distinction between Stalinesque and Orwellian models cannot, in general, be sustained. This will, in effect, vindicate Dennett's rejection of that distinction, though not quite for the reasons he put forth.

There is compelling reason to hold that our transitive consciousness of sensations is something distinct from the sensations themselves, even when the sensations are conscious sensations. For one thing, not all sensations are conscious. In peripheral vision and subliminal perception, and in some dissociative phenomena such as blindsight,[12] sensations occur without our being in any way transitively conscious of them. The sensations that occur in these processes are not conscious.[13] It's natural to conclude that sensations are distinct from our transitive consciousness of them, which occurs only when our sensations are conscious. Considered apart from our transitive consciousness of them, the sensations by themselves are not themselves conscious states; only the two together—sensation plus one's transitive consciousness of it—constitute a conscious state.

The heterophenomenological method may make it seem as though all mental states are conscious. Whatever may be so when mental states go unreported, the states we do report are always conscious states.[14] Since heterophenomenological reports provide the best evidence about those states, it may be tempting to conclude that no mental states could fail to be conscious. No evidence other than heterophenomenological evidence is, one may think, nearly strong enough to justify the existence of mental states that aren't conscious.

But this is too quick. Although heterophenomenological reports are our best evidence about mental states, they are not our only evidence. Nor does heterophenomenological evidence always trump other considerations. For example, other evidence can override a person's heterophenomenological denials that that person is in a particular

---

[12] See, e.g., Lawrence Weiskrantz, *Blindsight*, Oxford: Oxford University Press, 1986; "Outlooks for Blindsight: Explicit Methodologies for Implicit Processes," The Ferrier Lecture, 1989, *Proceedings of the Royal Society* B 239 (1990): 247–278; "Remembering Dissociations," in *Varieties of Memory and Consciousness: Essays in Honour of Endel Tulving*, ed. Henry L. Roediger III and F. I. M. Craik, Hillsdale, New Jersey Lawrence Erlbaum Associates, 1989, pp. 101–120; and "Introduction: Dissociated Issues," in A. D. Milner and Michael D. Rugg, eds., *The Neuropsychology of Consciousness*, New York: Academic Press, 1992.

[13] For more extended argument on this, see my "The Independence of Consciousness and Sensory Quality," ch. 5 in this volume.

[14] See my "Moore's Paradox and Consciousness," ch. 9 in this volume, and "Why Are Verbally Expressed Thoughts Conscious?" ch. 10 in this volume.

mental state. The mental states thus established would not be conscious states; het-erophenomenological denials show that the person is in no way transitively conscious of those states. And, since mental states needn't be conscious, we have reason in the conscious cases to distinguish the states from our transitive consciousness of them.

There are, in addition, theoretical reasons to distinguish sensations from our trans-itive consciousness of them. We distinguish sensations by reference to their sensory content. A sensation may, for example, be a sensation of a stationary red flash, whereas another is a sensation of a moving spot that changes color. Each such sensation may be conscious or not conscious.

When a sensation of a stationary red flash is conscious, one is transitively con-scious of that sensation. But even when one is conscious of the sensation in the way required for it to be conscious, one's consciousness of the sensation can be more or less detailed, and can represent the sensation in different ways. The way one's transit-ive consciousness of the sensation represents it, moreover, determines how it appears to one from a first-person point of view; it determines, that is, what it is like to have the sensation.

Consider, for example, the game Dennett describes of "hide the thimble" (336), in which people may look straight at the thimble they're trying to find and yet fail to register it consciously. Dennett uses this phenomenon to illustrate that it is not always clear, even from a first-person point of view, whether one is conscious of some particular thing.[15] Cases of this kind plainly occur, but they seem to cause difficulties. Whatever is true about the periphery of one's visual field, the sensory states central to that field are normally conscious. So if one is looking straight at the hidden thimble, how can one fail to see it consciously? The difficulty we have in describing this kind of case from a first-person point of view seems to lend plausibility to Dennett's claim that, independent of particular probes, there isn't any fact of the matter about what conscious experiences we have.

Distinguishing our sensations from our transitive consciousness of them helps explain this kind of case. Mental states often have more detailed content than we're transitively conscious of. This is true even of the visual sensations that occur at the center of our visual field; we're seldom if ever aware of all the sensory content such sensations contain, as casual shifts of focus reveal. This should come as no surprise. In general, being transitively conscious of something doesn't mean being transitively conscious of every aspect of the thing. We would need some special reason to make an exception of mental states and count consciousness as transparently revealing every aspect of their nature.

When I look straight at the thimble, I may well be conscious of the sensations at the center of my visual field, even though I'm not conscious of seeing a thimble. How can we explain this? It's a mistake to suppose that the sensory content of these central sensations includes no representation of the thimble. It can happen that, even though one doesn't consciously see an object, one later recalls just where it was and what it looked like. This is strong evidence that the content of our earlier visual sensations

---

[15] Recall the challenge to the Orwellian model considered at the end of the previous section.

contained a representation of the object. That aspect of our sensations wasn't conscious, but the content was nonetheless there.

But if one is conscious of sensations whose content includes a representation of the thimble, why doesn't one consciously see the thimble? The only explanation is that, although one is conscious of those sensations, one is not conscious of their content as representing a thimble. One is transitively conscious of the sensations in a way that leaves out that aspect of their content.

This sort of thing happens in many other cases as well. Consider the process by which we acquire the ability to recognize different wines, or pick out the various instruments playing in an orchestra. Normally, the two kinds of sensation are conscious even before one can tell consciously the difference between them—that is, even before they're distinguishable from a first-person point of view. It's just that the two types of sensation don't yet differ consciously. How can a sensation of an oboe and another of a clarinet both be conscious without differing consciously?

Even before one acquires these discriminative abilities, one's sensory contents must reflect the qualitative differences one is trying to learn; otherwise, one could never learn those differences. So even before one can distinguish an oboe from a clarinet, one's auditory sensations of the two instruments must differ. There will be some aspect of the sensory content of the two types of sensation that differs, even though that aspect doesn't register consciously. The two kinds of sensation are typically conscious sensations before one can consciously tell the difference between them—that is, before they're distinguishable from a first-person point of view. Even before one learns to discriminate the two sensations, one is conscious of them, though not in respect of the relevant qualitative differences. Only afterwards does one become conscious of them in respect of those differences. Again, we have reason to hold that sensations can be conscious even when one isn't transitively conscious of every aspect of their content.

Since we can be transitively conscious of our conscious sensations in different ways, there are two levels at which we must distinguish content. The sensations of which we're transitively conscious have sensory content of one sort or another, depending largely on the nature of the relevant stimuli. But even holding the sensory content of a sensation constant, we must distinguish the different contents that our transitive consciousness of those sensations can have. In the situation just considered, our transitive consciousness may represent a particular auditory sensation either as an indiscriminate woodwind sensation or in a more refined way, say, as a sensation of an oboe. In these two cases, the content of our transitive consciousness of the sensation will differ accordingly, even though the sensory content of the sensation remains unchanged. Moreover, one's first-person point of view is a function of the way one is conscious of one's sensations and other mental states. So it is the content of one's transitive consciousness of the sensation that determines how things are from a first-person point of view.

These considerations suggest a mechanism for the temporal anomalies that Dennett doesn't consider. Suppose, in color phi, that the initial stationary red flash produces in the subject a sensation of that flash. The sensory content of that sensation is of a stationary red flash. But the subject need not be transitively conscious of the sensation in that way. When distinct stimuli follow rapidly one upon another, one often isn't conscious of much detail in the resulting sensations.

Suppose, now, that the subject in color phi is transitively conscious of the initial sensation only as a sensation of a flash, and not as something stationary nor even red. After the green stimulus causes a second sensation, then the subject becomes conscious of both sensations, but still not as sensations of stationary flashes. Rather, the subject becomes transitively conscious of the two sensations together, as though fused into a single sensation of a moving spot that changes color. The content of the subject's transitive consciousness of the two sensations is that there's a single moving sensation that changes color. Strictly speaking, there is no editing here, since there's no revising of the content of the sensory states nor of the content of the subject's transitive consciousness of those states. Rather, the subjective appearance results simply from the way one comes to be transitively conscious of those states.

This mechanism resists easy classification as Stalinesque or Orwellian. On the Stalinesque model, the initial stimulus of a stationary red flash never makes it to consciousness. That's what happens in this case, since the subject never becomes transitively conscious of the initial sensation by itself, nor in respect of its sensory contents of color or motion. On the Stalinesque model, editing occurs prior to consciousness. And though strictly speaking there's no editing—that is, no revising—something like editing does occur before the initial sensation makes it to consciousness. For when the subject's transitive consciousness of that initial sensation does occur, it misrepresents the sensory content of that sensation. The transitive consciousness edits the sensations in the attenuated sense that it misrepresents them.

But this mechanism counts equally well as Orwellian. The Orwellian model stipulates that the subject becomes conscious of the sensation that results from the initial stimulus before any editing occurs. That's what happens in this case; the subject begins by being conscious of the sensation as a flash, albeit one that's indeterminate with respect to color and motion. When the second stimulus is received, the subject becomes transitively conscious of both sensations in a way that more fully reflects the sensory contents of color and motion, as a sensation of a moving spot that changes color. But on the Orwellian model, editing does occur after the first stimulus reaches consciousness. And in the mechanism under consideration, there's editing of a sort after the initial consciousness of the first sensation, since the subject's transitive consciousness changes from that of a flash with no color or motion represented to that of the spot that changes color and position.

When Dennett describes the Stalinesque and Orwellian models, he sometimes seems to allow for sensory contents' being distinct from one's transitive consciousness of those contents (e.g., 124). But Dennett holds that we need not regard the sensory contents we're transitively conscious of as distinct existences. They can, instead, be merely notional objects of the relevant transitive consciousness. What matters for consciousness is how one is transitively conscious of sensory contents, not whether distinct sensory contents exist. And if it could be that no sensory contents exist distinct from our transitive consciousness of them, we must avoid the idea that our transitive consciousness of sensory content can vary independently of the sensory content itself. For this reason, the mechanism under consideration doesn't fit comfortably with Dennett's discussion.

But if, as I've argued, sensory states can occur without being conscious states, and hence independently of one's being transitively conscious of them, the third mechanism is at least a theoretical possibility. And, because that mechanism conforms to some extent to both the Stalinesque and Orwellian models, and to neither better than the other, it is arbitrary to describe this mechanism as exemplifying either model more than the other. So the third mechanism blurs the contrast between Stalinesque and Orwellian models. Even if we suppose the objective temporal order of events fixed, it's wholly arbitrary whether to regard this mechanism as Stalinesque or Orwellian. This gives us reason, albeit different from Dennett's, to reject a firm distinction between Stalinesque and Orwellian models.[16]

IV. TRANSITIVE CONSCIOUSNESS AND FIRST-PERSON OPERATIONALISM

The foregoing argument shows that there are mechanisms it is arbitrary to count as Stalinesque or Orwellian, even when the order of events is known. But the argument does not appeal to any indeterminacy about the order of events; rather, it relies solely on the different ways we may be transitively conscious of our sensations. So the argument gives us no reason to conclude that there's no fact of the matter about the temporal order of those events. And if the argument of section I is sound, we can expect suitable theoretical developments to pin down any lack of clarity about the order of events. So even though the argument undermines a firm distinction between Stalinesque and Orwellian models, it does not support FPO.

Suppose I have a sensation of red and I'm transitively conscious of that sensation. The content of the sensation determines the sensation's character, whereas my transitive consciousness of it is responsible for there being something it's like from a first-person point of view to have that sensation. The distinction between a sensation and one's being transitively conscious of that sensation warrants a distinction between how conscious sensations appear and the way they really are.

Dennett rejects this conclusion. Seeing things this way, he urges, "creates the bizarre category of the objectively subjective—the way things actually, objectively seem to you even if they don't seem to seem that way to you" (132). Indeed, the main appeal of FPO is, he urges, that it blocks that "bizarre" consequence. Conscious experiences are a matter of things' appearing in certain ways. And according to FPO, there is no more to the reality of consciousness than the appearances our experiences present from a first-person point of view.

Dennett holds, moreover, that distinguishing between the appearance of states with content and their reality is of a piece with the Cartesian Theater model. On

---

[16] It was this way of partially undermining the contrast between Stalinesque and Orwellian models that I had in mind in "Time and Consciousness" (*The Behavioral and Brain Sciences* 15, 2 [June 1992]: 220–1), though that discussion wasn't as clear as I would like.

that model, when "vehicles of content . . . 'arrive at' the theater of consciousness, . . . [they] 'become' conscious" (144). A mental state's being conscious consists in its being observed in the theater of consciousness. The Cartesian Theater model must therefore distinguish between the reality of a mental state and how it appears. Its appearance is a function of how it's observed, whereas its reality consists in its nature independently of any such observation.

Perhaps adopting the Cartesian Theater model does commit one to distinguishing between the appearance and reality of mental states; but the converse does not hold. For one thing, the Cartesian Theater essentially involves the idea that a state's being conscious is a matter of its being located at that single place in the brain. But there can be a difference between the appearance of conscious states and their reality even if no unique location in the brain is involved.

Such unique location to one side, Dennett stigmatizes the picture he rejects as involving the notion of something's seeming to seem a certain way. But whatever initial air of oddity there is to this idea, there is good reason to sustain the distinction between how things seem and how they seem to seem. The content of one's sensory states defines how things seem to one, even when the sensory states aren't conscious. Even when they aren't conscious, sensory states have various connections with other aspects of one's mental life, both conscious and not. We sometimes see things without being conscious that we do, and our seeing things in these cases often affects us mentally. For example, seeing a truck by peripheral vision may cause one to feel startled and swerve one's car, even when one is in no way transitively conscious of seeing the truck. Such things contribute to the way things seem to one, even when one is in no way transitively conscious of their seeming that way.

When one is not at all transitively conscious of being in some sensory state, however, it will not, from a first-person point of view, seem that one is in it. That's where the second level of seeming comes in. The unconscious seeing of the truck is the first level of seeming; if one saw it consciously, that would be a second level of seeming. So, when the seeing isn't conscious, it's natural to say that things seem to us a certain way, but without seeming to seem that way. Saying this is just a way of describing the distinction between how mental states really are and how those states seem, from a first-person point of view.

These considerations allow also for a distinction between the appearance and reality of mental states that are conscious. Suppose I see the truck consciously and then, reflecting on my close call, I attend to my conscious experience of seeing the truck. I am now introspectively conscious of seeing the truck; that is, I am conscious of my sensation, and conscious also that I am conscious of that sensation. This higher-order transitive consciousness defines how my conscious sensation appears to me.

Dennett might deny that this sort of thing establishes a full-fledged distinction between the appearance and reality of mental states. Rather, it shows only that the way things seem to us is sometimes conscious and sometimes not. To distinguish between the reality of mental states and their appearance, we need cases in which their appearance and reality diverge. As long as the content of my sensation determines how I am transitively conscious of it, the reality of the sensation determines its appearance. And if that always happens, it's arguably idle to distinguish two levels of seeming.

But that does not always happen. Consider again the woodwind and thimble examples. The best explanation of those cases is that the sensory content a sensation has does not fully determine how one is transitively conscious of that content. There are, for example, two ways one might be transitively conscious of one's sensation of an oboe. One might be conscious of it indiscriminately, as a sensation of some woodwind or other. Or one might be conscious of it specifically as a sensation of an oboe. The sensory content of the sensation does not fix how one is conscious of that content, and so the two can diverge. There is sometimes a difference between a sensation's sensory content and the way one is conscious of that content—between how the oboe seems and how it seems to seem.

These cases show that our transitive consciousness of a sensory content may fail to capture everything about that content. Can we also be transitively conscious of a sensory content in a way that actually misrepresents the content? Can we in effect be mistaken about what mental states we're in? The woodwind case does not clearly involve such misrepresentation. Being conscious of an oboe sensation as a sensation of an indiscriminate woodwind is not an error in that case, especially since it only happens before one has learned to discriminate the various woodwinds. Nor does outright error occur in the thimble case; rather, the way we are transitively conscious of the sensations central to our visual field simply leaves out an important detail of their content. A clear case of error would have to involve our transitive consciousness representing the sensations as having some content they don't have, and this doesn't happen in the woodwind and thimble examples.

Dennett seems tempted to adopt the traditional view that we cannot be wrong about our mental states. If we don't, he thinks, "we lose the subjective intimacy or incorrigibility that is supposedly the hallmark of consciousness" (319). Such incorrigibility seems also to be connected with Dennett's use of his heterophenomenological method. The only neutral method for studying consciousness scientifically relies on heterophenomenological reports. And if such reports were definitive about the mental data of investigation, perhaps scientific results could never show such reports to be mistaken. Perhaps, as Richard Rorty has argued, any reason for thinking that some such report is untrue would equally be a reason to think we had misconstrued the reporter's words.[17]

But adopting the heterophenomenological method does not commit us to rejecting the possibility of real error about one's mental states. We might well have sufficient success in pinning down the use of the words used generally in somebody's heterophenomenological reports that we could simply rule out certain misuses of

---

[17] According to Rorty, when there is reason to believe somebody's report of a mental state is not true, we cannot even in principle distinguish between the person's having just misused words and having actually made a factual error about what kind of state it is. ("Mind-Body Identity, Privacy, and Categories," *The Review of Metaphysics*, XIX, 1 [September 1965]: 24–54, pp. 45–6.) This recalls W. V. Quine's well-known argument that any translation of a language which represents people as asserting bald contradictions is overwhelming evidence that the translation is wrong. ("Carnap and Logical Truth," in *The Ways of Paradox and Other Essays*, revised and enlarged edn., Cambridge, Massachusetts: Harvard University Press, 1976, pp. 107–132, at p. 109.)

language. We could then conclude that particular reports were untrue because they expressed mistaken judgments.

It's natural in any case to assume that error about our mental states does occur, and indeed that it is not all that rare. The thimble and woodwind cases show that when mental states are conscious, there can be features of those states that we could be conscious of but aren't, and it's plausible that this occurs frequently. And if that happens reasonably often, why shouldn't the way we're conscious of mental states sometimes represent them as having features they do not actually have?

One might object that distinguishing the appearance of a sensation from its reality commits us to a hierarchy of such distinctions. The reality of a sensation is independent of its being conscious, whereas its appearance is due to the way we're transitively conscious of it. And we can even be transitively conscious of our being transitively conscious of the sensation, as we are when we introspect. Here we distinguish the true nature of the appearance of the sensation from how that appearance seems to us to be. But why would things stop here? If we take these first steps, won't we risk an endless hierarchy of appearance-reality distinctions?

One might raise this worry in connection with the higher-order-thought hypothesis about consciousness that I've developed elsewhere.[18] On that hypothesis, our being transitively conscious of our conscious mental states consists in our having occurrent thoughts to the effect that we are in those mental states. So a mental state is conscious just in case it is the intentional object of a roughly contemporaneous thought—what I call "a higher-order thought." This higher-order thought must, I argue, have an assertoric mental attitude, and it may not be the result of any inference of which we are transitively conscious. This last requirement, that higher-order thoughts be independent of any conscious inference, is meant to ensure that our transitive consciousness of the mental states the higher-order thoughts are about will, from a first-person point of view, seem immediate.[19]

This concern need not, of course, be tied to the higher-order-thought hypothesis, but can be raised independently of the way any particular theory accounts for our transitive consciousness of our conscious states. The only way to avoid an endless hierarchy of distinctions between appearance and reality, on this worry, is to collapse

---

[18] See, e.g., my "A Theory of Consciousness," in *The Nature of Consciousness: Philosophical Debates*, ed. Ned Block, Owen Flanagan, and Güven Güzeldere, Cambridge, Massachusetts: MIT Press, 1997, pp. 729–753; "Thinking that One Thinks," ch. 2 in this volume; and "Two Concepts of Consciousness," ch. 1 in this volume.

Dennett has informed me (personal communication) that he is not in fact concerned about an endless hierarchy, but rather about taking the first step in distinguishing the appearance from the reality of mental states. (But see *CE* 307, and esp. 314.)

[19] Dennett raises a distinct worry specifically about the higher-order-thought hypothesis. He assumes that this theory must posit not only a higher-order thought about each conscious mental state but, in addition, a distinct higher-order belief about the state (*CE* 307, 317). As Dennett notes, beliefs are dispositional states that underlie our thoughts; in effect, they are dispositions to have certain thoughts. But being disposed to have a thought about something doesn't make one conscious of that thing. So higher-order beliefs will not figure in explaining how we are transitively conscious of our conscious mental states nor, therefore, in explaining what it is for mental states to be conscious.

the initial distinction between mental states and our transitive consciousness of them.

As already noted, introspective consciousness involves two levels of being transitively conscious of our mental states. We're transitively conscious of the state, and also transitively conscious that we are transitively conscious of it. For a distinction between appearance and reality to apply at this second level, error must again be possible at that level. And indeed introspection is often unreliable. The failure of introspectionist psychology was due less to theoretical objections than to the conflicting results that continually issued from introspectionist experiments.[20] It's also plain from everyday experience that expectations and preconceptions distort our introspective awareness of our mental states, sometimes to the point of error.

Does our ability to distinguish between mental states and being transitively conscious of them at these two levels imply an endless proliferation of levels at which we might draw that distinction? In principle yes, but not in practice. We can of course conceive of higher applications. But it's pretty clear that there's no empirical warrant for drawing that distinction at higher levels, at least in the mental life of our species. After all, it is relatively seldom that being introspectively conscious of one's mental states plays any useful role; it's far less likely that an even higher level of transitive consciousness would play any role distinct from that of introspective consciousness itself. So it's natural to suppose that such higher levels seldom if ever occur.

V. FACTS OF THE MATTER AND MENTAL TAXONOMY[21]

The argument for distinguishing mental states from our transitive consciousness of them relies mainly on noting that mental states are not always conscious, and that no state of which we are not at all transitively conscious will count as a conscious state. Since mental states occur both when we're transitively conscious of them and when we aren't, events of transitive consciousness are distinct from the mental states we're transitively conscious of.

We can reinforce the idea that mental states are distinct from the events of transitive consciousness in virtue of which those states are conscious by appealing to the content of these states. Every mental state has some distinguishing content. But the content of one's being transitively conscious of a state perforce differs from the content of that state. Suppose I think it's raining; the content of that thought is simply that it's raining. If my thought is conscious, I am transitively conscious of it; so the content of that transitive consciousness will be that I have the thought that it's raining. Similarly for other cases.

It is occasionally argued that we should not individuate mental states by way of their content. After all, the thought that it's raining and the thought that I think it's raining seem to amount to much the same thing. That is because they are the same in

[20] For a detailed survey of this failure, see William Lyons, *The Disappearance of Introspection* (Cambridge, Massachusetts: MIT Press/Bradford Books, 1986), ch. 1.
[21] Much of this section and the next derives from my "Multiple Drafts and Facts of the Matter," in *Conscious Experience*, ed. Thomas Metzinger, Exeter, UK: Imprint Academic, 1995, pp. 275–290.

respect of the mental analogue of conditions of assertibility. Any conditions in which it's appropriate to have the thought that it's raining are also conditions in which it's appropriate to think that I have that thought. And if we individuate thoughts not with respect to their content but by way of the mental analogue of their conditions of assertibility, one's conscious thought that it's raining will not be distinct from one's transitive consciousness of the thought. On this picture, such transitive consciousness turns out to be internal, somehow, to the thought.[22]

Dennett, also, resists individuating mental states the way folk psychology does, by way of content, but for different reasons. Individuating mental states that way, he notes, results in our distinguishing mental states from our transitive consciousness of them, and hence in a potential hierarchy of levels of such transitive consciousness of mental states. "[W]e end up having to postulate differences that are systematically undiscoverable by any means, from the inside or the outside," distinctions that are "systematically indiscernible in nature" (319).

Dennett emphatically does not, however, propose to individuate mental states by the mental analogue of their performance conditions. Rather, he urges that

[w]e replace the division into discrete contentful *states*—beliefs, meta-beliefs, and so forth—with a *process* that serves, over time, to ensure a good fit between an entity's internal information-bearing events and the entity's capacity to express (some of) the information in those events in speech.[23]

Describing things in terms of such processes is doubtless the right way to capture what happens at a subpersonal level of analysis. The subpersonal brain events that subserve our conscious mental lives probably are not organized in any way we could predict by relying on our folk-psychological taxonomy of ordinary mental states, whether conscious or not. Still, even if that is right at the subpersonal level, it does not follow that there is no level of description at which we should taxonomize things in terms of the folk-psychological notion of mental content.

Dennett himself occasionally seems to be committed to describing things in terms of such content. He describes the Stalinesque and Orwellian models, for example, in terms of when a stimulus reaches consciousness. And the idea of a stimulus's reaching consciousness presumably means that it is the content the stimulus produces that becomes conscious. This appeal to content is hardly decisive, however, since Dennett rejects the Stalinesque and Orwellian models; so his descriptions of them may well invoke notions he also rejects.[24]

There is a somewhat stronger reason, however, to think Dennett is committed to some notion of mental content, and thus to a distinction between mental states and our transitive consciousness of them. Throughout *CE*, Dennett speaks

---

[22] See Franz Brentano, *Psychology from an Empirical Standpoint*, tr. Antos C. Rancurello, D. B. Terrell, and Linda L. McAlister, London: Routledge & Kegan Paul, 1973, p. 127, for a traditional example of this argument.

[23] *CE* 319, emphasis Dennett's. See also "The Message is: There is no *Medium*," pp. 930–1.

[24] Similarly, though Dennett notes that the editing posited by the Orwellian model allows for a certain kind of error about what mental states we're in (*CE* 318–19), his rejection of Orwellian explanation leaves it open to him to deny the possibility of such error.

of content's being present in the brain even when it isn't conscious, that is, even when we're not conscious of it. Typically he does not use our ordinary folk-psychological terminology for these purposes. Rather, he talks of such things as "events of content-fixation" (365) "information-bearing events" (459), "content-discriminations" (113), and "vehicles of content" (144). These phrases, moreover, evidently refer to the occurrence of content of which we need not be transitively conscious. The "onsets [of content-fixations in the brain] do *not* mark the onset of consciousness of their content" (113; emphasis Dennett's).

These events of content fixation must, according to Dennett, differ in various respects from mental states as conceived of by folk psychology. For one thing, "content-fixations . . . are [each] precisely locatable in both space and time" (113); by contrast, Dennett argues that we cannot locate conscious mental phenomena precisely in time. But conscious states are states conceived of in folk-psychological terms. So Dennett must hold that events of content fixation are not the sorts of event that could be conscious.

Events of content fixation are the brain events responsible for conscious mental phenomena; they are subpersonal events that subserve mental phenomena as folk psychology taxonomizes them.[25] Nonetheless, they carry content in some way or other. Can we say anything more about exactly what kind of events they are, and how they relate to mental phenomena, folk psychologically taxonomized?

Here is one hypothesis. In the early stages of visual processing, the properties of color, form, orientation, and motion are represented in the brain independently of one another.[26] There is no special problem, moreover, about precisely locating such representations, either spatially or temporally. These independent representations of color, shape, and so forth do not occur consciously. But except perhaps for pathological cases, we never are visually aware of color or motion without shape, shape or orientation without color, and so forth. There is reason to think things are similar with other sensory modalities. It is therefore inviting to suppose that Dennett's events of content fixation may be something like these early representations.

How, then, would such events of content fixation lead to consciousness? In the early stages of vision—so-called early vision—the properties of color, motion, orientation, and shape occur independently of one another. In conscious visual states,

---

[25] On Dennett's views about subpersonal and folk-psychological levels of description, see "Three Kinds of Intentional Psychology," in Dennett's *The Intentional Stance*, Cambridge, Massachusetts: MIT Press/Bradford Books, 1987, pp. 43–68.

[26] The evidence for the independent representations of these properties in early visual processing is inferential, mainly from experiments in which subjects report seeing illusory conjunctions of the colors and shapes of distinct, simultaneous stimuli. Subjects do not report seeing either shape or color independently of the other. See Anne Treisman, "Perceptual Grouping and Attention in Visual Search for Features and for Objects," *Journal of Experimental Psychology*, 8, 2 (April 1982): 194–214; "Features and Objects: The Fourteenth Bartlett Memorial Lecture," *Quarterly Journal of Experimental Psychology*, 40A, 2 (May 1988): 201–237; and Anne Treisman and Stephen Gormican, "Feature Analysis in Early Vision: Evidence from Search Asymmetries," *Psychological Review*, 95, 1 (January 1988): 15–48.

however, taxonomized folk psychologically, these properties are combined. So it is tempting to suppose that consciousness may arise somehow in the course of subsequent integrative processes that represent those properties as unified.

This picture fits well, in a number of respects, with Dennett's MDM.[27] Dennett holds that no individual states occur that literally exhibit the contents of distinct events of content fixation, such as those in early vision (257–8). Consider any group of events of content fixation that represent independent visual properties in early vision. At any one time, there may well be several processes that might integrate the members of that group. Each process would yield a kind of draft of the contents of consciousness. As with the revising of a text, the relevant integrative processes would perform an editorial or interpretive role in bringing together the fragmentary representations of properties in early vision. Those editorial processes would serve "to ensure a good fit between an entity's internal information-bearing events and the entity's capacity to express (some of) the information in those events in speech" (319).

According to Dennett, probes at different moments may "precipitat[e] different narratives. . .: [different] versions of a portion of 'the stream of consciousness'" (135). That would occur on the present model. When distinct integrative processes coexist, each may involve a disposition to produce a different narrative about one's mental life. Editorial processes that exist concurrently might even dispose one toward conflicting narratives. Only when some particular probe intervenes will one integrative process drive out the others, thereby settling, for that moment, the facts of consciousness.

Heterophenomenological reports give us our best evidence about how people's conscious mental lives appear to them. But things aren't always as they seem. So Dennett's methodological appeal to these reports is neutral about whether sincere reports truly describe the conscious events that go into a subject's first-person viewpoint or, instead, simply express the subject's beliefs about those mental events, events which may be entirely notional.

If there are any states that do conform to the descriptions that occur in these heterophenomenological reports, they are mental states, folk psychologically conceived. And it is reasonable to follow Dennett in holding that these reports refer to actual events only if such reports are independently corroborated by what we know by objective, third-person means, for example, by what we know about such things as brain events.

Dennett apparently believes that the situation is at best mixed. Brain events exist that can be reasonably regarded as bearing content, but their content will be dramatically unlike the integrated content that folk psychology ascribes to conscious states. Certainly that is so if we understand events of content fixation on the model of the independently occurring properties of early vision, and it seems equally so however we construe events of content fixation. So perhaps what exists is simply the

---

[27] Though for other reasons, partly indicated in § VII below, Dennett would not accept this picture.

precisely locatable events of content fixation—the representations of early vision and the like—and the editorial processes that integrate those early representations. There is nothing, then, corresponding to the folk psychologically taxonomized mental states to which our heterophenomenological reports refer.

On the present hypothesis, editorial processes do not integrate content by producing actual states with unified content. Rather, they integrate by referring to each of the relevant component events of content fixation. These events can be located precisely in time; and presumably the same holds of the processes that appear to integrate those disparate events.

Folk psychology assumes that conscious states, individuated by way of their unified content, can also be located precisely in time. If so, we could locate a particular state by reference to the color, shape, location, and motion it represents. But no such unified states occur, on the present model. Indeed, the distinct events of content fixation that represent color, shape, location, and motion may well occur at distinct times. And in any case, we can assume that these independent events of content fixation will all occur earlier than the editorial process that appears to unify them.[28] So there is no unique, privileged moment at which content occurs that represents all these visual properties together.

If this model is correct, our folk-psychological taxonomy of mental states is inaccurate in certain important ways. Folk psychology posits mental states that represent in a unified way the various visual properties that are represented separately in early vision. And folk psychology supposes that these states can be located relatively precisely in time. But on this hypothesis, no such states exist. Representational events occur that we can locate precisely in time, but relative to our folk-psychological taxonomy, those representations are fragmentary. There are, in addition, processes that appear from a first-person point of view to integrate those fragmentary representations. But these processes do not result in the unified states of folk psychology.

This picture is not eliminativist with respect to mental states, taxonomized folk psychologically. To be sure, no single state or process corresponds to any conscious mental state, as folk psychology describes things. But between the subpersonal events of content fixation and the processes that appear to integrate them, we can save the subjective appearances that folk psychology describes. Events of content fixation are well-defined and precisely locatable, and the subsequent editorial processes provide the apparent folk-psychological integration of representational content. These editorial processes will, as Dennett suggests, "replace the division into discrete contentful *states*" (319). It is just that no single state or process satisfies both functions at once. This integrative model does not deny that conscious mental phenomena exist. But, as with Dennett's view, the model sees as artificial the way we ordinarily carve consciousness and mind into discrete mental states.

---

[28] This is suggestive in connection with the temporal anomalies. Thus, the explanation of our seeming to see a moving spot that changes color when the red and green flashes occur suitably separated in space and time might have to do with the timing in the brain of the events of content fixation that independently represent color, motion, and location.

VI. INTEGRATIVE PROCESSES AND CONSCIOUSNESS

Events of content fixation do not occur consciously. So consciousness must result from the editorial processes that appear to integrate those events. On the integrative model under consideration, there is nothing else that could give rise to consciousness. But why should integrative processes produce consciousness? Given that events of content fixation are not conscious to begin with, why should integrating them yield conscious results?

This problem is particularly pressing, since integrative processes often fail to produce consciousness. Cognitive theories posit many processes that integrate various representational contents, but such unification typically does not result in states that are conscious. Nor is it intuitively obvious why integration should yield consciousness. Integrative processes can explain why shape and color, for example, are represented together, but not why the resulting unified representation should be conscious. By itself, integration seems unable to explain why, from a first-person viewpoint, we seem to be in conscious states with those combined properties.

A related difficulty affects Dennett's discussion. Dennett maintains that "[t]here is no reality of consciousness independent of the effects of various vehicles of content on subsequent action (and hence, of course, on memory)" (132). Perhaps it is correct that all conscious mental phenomena leave suitable traces on action, and elsewhere in our mental lives, particularly in memory. But Dennett seems to hold that leaving such traces is not just necessary for states to be conscious, but sufficient as well. Thus he writes:

Consciousness is cerebral celebrity.... Those contents are conscious that persevere, that monopolize resources long enough to achieve certain typical and "symptomatic" effects—on memory, on the control of behavior and so forth ("The Message is: There is no *Me*dium," p. 929).

The difficulty is that mental states have many effects that are independent of whether those states are conscious or not. As noted earlier, Dennett observes that the very same nonverbal behavior may be caused either by a state that's conscious or a state that is not (124). Since conscious and nonconscious mental states can have the same effects on nonverbal behavior, having such effects will not make a state conscious. Similarly, most of the mental traces left by conscious states could equally well have been left by mental states that are not conscious. In the processes posited by cognitive theories, representational states typically have very wide-ranging mental effects even when those states are wholly nonconscious. But the general point is independent of theoretical posits. We often seem to solve difficult problems without consciously thinking about them; in these cases, many nonconscious mental states must have substantial mental effects, which in turn remain nonconscious, before the solution occurs to us consciously. The same holds for the effects mental states have on memory, effects which Dennett counts as criterial for consciousness. Occasionally we recall having seen something, and may even have a visual image of it, though at the earlier time we were not in any way conscious of seeing it. In such cases, perceiving that wasn't conscious has a significant, lasting effect on memory.

So, just as the integration of fragmentary content can occur without resulting in conscious states, so can cerebral celebrity and states' leaving traces in memory. Still, the integrative model seems to have promise. Ordinary conscious states, taxonomized folk psychologically, do represent shape, color, orientation, location, and movement as unified. If no individual brain events represent those distinct properties together, consciousness and unification somehow go hand in hand. Why should this be?

On the integrative model, properties represented separately in early vision in some way come to be represented together as a result of various editorial processes. These processes need not result in unified states with the representational properties of the relevant components; rather, they may simply refer back to each of those components. Integration may be achieved by referring to all the early representations in a unified way.

If integration occurs in this second way, the connection with consciousness is clear. Conscious mental phenomena are mental phenomena of which we're transitively conscious, in a way that from a first-person point of view seems to be immediate. By referring in a unified way to the separate representations of early vision and other such events of content fixation, integrative processes not only unify those representations, but also make us transitively conscious of them. And because these processes refer to events of content fixation as suitably integrated, they make us transitively conscious of them in just that way. To integrate events of content fixation, these editorial processes must involve some unifying intentional reference to the events. And referring to something mentally is having some sort of thought about it. So, in making us transitively conscious of events of content fixation, the editorial processes in effect involve higher-order thoughts.[29]

VII. CONSCIOUSNESS AND SPEECH

Dennett rejects the a folk-psychological taxonomy of "discrete contentful states," in favor of "a *process* that serves, over time, to ensure a good fit between an entity's internal information-bearing events and the entity's capacity to express (some of) the information in those events in speech" (319; emphasis Dennett's). What sort of fit is this? Putting aside Dennett's reasons for rejecting the taxonomy of folk psychology, just what connection does obtain between speech and our "internal information-bearing events"?

On the standard picture, speech acts express intentional states, the content of which matches that of the speech acts. This has important implications when we turn to heterophenomenological reports. Since these reports are about the mental states we take ourselves to be in, they express our transitive consciousness of those mental states. So

---

[29] To the extent that the integrative model under consideration resembles Dennett's MDM, this conclusion fits with my argument elsewhere that the higher-order-thought hypothesis has all the advantages of the MDM without being committed to FPO. (See my "Multiple Drafts and Higher-Order Thoughts," *Philosophy and Phenomenological Research*, LIII, 4 [December 1993]: 911–918.)

the content of our heterophenomenological reports is the same as the content of the corresponding events of transitive consciousness.

Dennett rejects this standard picture. Speech acts, he argues, typically do not express intentional content that is already in place; rather, our choice of words often influences the content of our thoughts (247). On this Pandemonium Model of speech production, as he calls it, the content of our speech acts does not generally match that of some previously existing intentional states. Accordingly, the content of our heterophenomenological reports seldom reflects prior events of being transitively conscious of our mental states. Instead, these reports often, perhaps always, determine the content of whatever events of transitive consciousness may occur.[30]

Dennett's principal argument against the standard picture of the relation between thought and speech is that we often discover what we think only as we say it (245). But it is likely that when we discover what we think only as we say it, that is not because the thoughts do not exist until we speak, but because often our thoughts are not conscious until we express them verbally. Doubtless, the words we use do sometimes affect the content of our thoughts, perhaps often. But even when that happens, this does not show that our heterophenomenological reports do not express prior events of transitive consciousness, but only that those reports diverge to some extent in content from those prior events of transitive consciousness.

It is likely that we often assign content to our thoughts on the basis of what we say; in effect, we read back onto our thoughts the refined distinctions of content drawn so readily in speech. But whenever one speaks, there must have been some inner state—or more likely, as Dennett urges, interactions among inner states—that are responsible for one's using the words one does. And it is reasonable to identify the thoughts one's words express with whatever states or interactions among states end up producing those words. As Dennett usefully emphasizes, we often learn what thoughts we have not by introspection but by seeing what we say. But that does not mean that there is no thought, folk psychologically conceived.

Dennett urges that "the second-order state (the better-informed state) comes to be *created* by the very process of framing the report."[31] It is unlikely that this is always so. Second-order states plainly occur without being verbally expressed, even if their content is sometimes less elaborate than that of verbally expressed second-order thoughts. In any case, heterophenomenological reports do indicate the occurrence of events of transitive consciousness with the same content as the reports, whether or not those events occur prior to the reports. Since a state's being conscious implies that one is conscious of it, it must be these events of transitive consciousness which are responsible for the consciousness of the mental states they are about.

---

[30] *CE* 315. Dennett considers in this context the higher-order-thought hypothesis, on which these events of transitive consciousness are higher-order thoughts about our mental states. It is arguable that the higher-order-thought hypothesis in effect follows from what I am calling the standard picture of the connection between speech acts and intentional states. See "Thinking that One Thinks," *passim*.

[31] *CE* 315, emphasis Dennett's. Also: "The emergence of the [verbal] expression is precisely what creates or fixes the content of higher-order thought expressed" (ibid.).

On the model I have been considering, no individual states occur that literally combine such contents as shape and color; there are only nonconscious, fragmentary events of content fixation and integrative processes that refer to those events. Nonetheless, these processes, and the higher-order thoughts they involve, enable us to explain why we seem to be in mental states as folk psychology taxonomizes them. Those mental states are the intentional objects of our editorial processes, or higher-order thoughts. They are the states we represent ourselves as being in, even if it turns out that they are simply notional.

Conscious mental states do exist on this model, but they are not the kinds of states folk psychology takes them to be. They are not conscious cases of states with integrated sensible properties, but arrays of events of content fixation of which we are transitively conscious, though we represent those arrays as though they were single states.

Dennett would have limited sympathy with these conclusions. As noted earlier, his heterophenomenological method is neutral about whether the mental events referred to by subjects' reports really exist. Still, if those reports are sincere, he maintains, they are constitutive of what it's like for the subject at that time, and hence constitutive of that subject's consciousness.[32]

The Pandemonium Model of speech production seems to support this idea. What it's like for one hinges on how one is transitively conscious of one's mental life. So, if sincere heterophenomenological reports fix the content of whatever events of transitive consciousness occur, perhaps those reports are somehow constitutive of what it's like for the subject.

As already noted, consciousness occurs even in the absence of sincere heterophenomenological reports. So in these cases Dennett might urge that what is constitutive of consciousness is the disposition to report sincerely, rather than the reports themselves. But whenever we can describe things dispositionally, there is some occurrent state or property that is responsible for the relevant dispositional behavior.[33] Since the disposition here is to make a sincere heterophenomenological report, we can assume that the relevant underlying state is simply the higher-order thought that this report would express, a thought whose content is reasonably close to that of the report.

As we saw in the thimble and woodwind cases, events of being transitively conscious of our mental states can be more or less detailed. Moreover, what determines in these cases how the subject is conscious of the mental state in question is the event of transitive consciousness, not the state or states that event of transitive consciousness is about. So, even when an event of transitive consciousness is erroneous, we can assume that that event fixes what the relevant conscious state is like for the subject. If I have a sensation of an oboe but my transitive consciousness of the sensation represents

[32] I am grateful to Dennett for emphasizing this (personal communication).
[33] Compare W. V. Quine's view that dispositional descriptions can, for theoretical purposes, be replaced by descriptions that mention enduring structural traits (*Word and Object*, Cambridge, Massachusetts: MIT Press, 1960, § 46).

it as a sensation of a clarinet, it will be just as though I have a conscious sensation of a clarinet.

Suppose, now, that the sensation is absent altogether, but an event of transitive consciousness still occurs, representing me as having a sensation of a clarinet. Since that event suffices for it to seem to me that I have such a sensation when my sensation is actually of a different sort, that event should yield the same result even if I have no relevantly similar sensation at all. Even when the sensations that events of transitive consciousness are about do not exist, those events will determine what it's like for one.

This lends plausibility to Dennett's claim that a subject's sincere heterophenomenological reports are somehow constitutive of what it's like for that subject. Events of transitive consciousness fix what it is like for the subject. So it is representing oneself as being in various particular mental states that is constitutive of one's consciousness. Heterophenomenological reports do just that.

The same considerations also lend support to the integrative model. On that model, when it seems to me that I have a conscious sensation, there is no unified sensation as folk psychology conceives of these things. Rather, there are various events of content fixation, together with my being transitively conscious of those events as suitably unified. Once again, it is the event of transitive consciousness, not the states that event pertains to, that determines what it's like for me.

What consequences does all this have for FPO? Folk psychology assumes we can assign a precise temporal location to conscious states with relatively unified representational contents, for example, visual perceptions that represent color, shape, and motion together. But that presupposes that such unified states actually exist. If what exists, instead, are various events of content fixation, we can expect that in any particular case the relevant representations of shape and color will occur at slightly different moments, and that the integrating process will occur at still another moment.

What corresponds to the conscious states posited by folk psychology, then, is an array of events and processes. So it may seem that to assign any temporal location to a conscious state, folk psychologically conceived, would require an arbitrary choice among the moments at which the relevant component events and processes occur. And the present picture would vindicate FPO; there would be no fact of the matter about the temporal location of those notional folk-psychological states.

But assigning such temporal location to the conscious states of folk psychology is not, in fact, arbitrary. Each integrating process involves being transitively conscious of the relevant component events of content fixation, as a unified whole. This points toward a nonarbitrary way to locate conscious folk-psychological states in time. Since it is the event of transitive consciousness which is responsible for a state's being conscious and determines what it's like for the subject, that event is all that matters for temporal location. Events of content fixation will occur earlier than the event of transitive consciousness. But at those earlier moments there is nothing it's like for the subject, since at those times there are only the various nonconscious mental precursors of the conscious state. So the relevant events of transitive consciousness provide determinate, nonarbitrary facts about the timing of conscious states. Since the foregoing integrative model closely resembles Dennett's MDM, narrowly construed, and we have reason to reject FPO, it seems possible that we can explain consciousness by a view along the lines of the MDM, but which avoids appeal to FPO.[34]

[34] Special thanks to Dan Dennett for exceptionally useful reactions on an earlier draft.

9

Moore's Paradox and Consciousness

I. MOORE'S PARADOX AND TRANSPARENCY

As G. E. Moore famously observed, sentences such as 'It's raining but I don't think it is', though they aren't contradictory, cannot be used to make coherent assertions.[1] The trouble with such sentences is not a matter of their truth conditions; such sentences can readily be true. Indeed, it happens often enough with each of us that we think, for example, that it isn't raining even though it is. This shows that such sentences are not literally contradictory. But even though these sentences have unproblematic truth conditions, we cannot say the same about their conditions of assertibility. There are no circumstances in which one can use such sentences to perform coherent assertoric speech acts. Situations exist in which these sentences would be true, but none in which anybody could use them to say so.

This phenomenon is known, following Wittgenstein,[2] as Moore's paradox. As some authors have noted, the difficulty arises not only with assertions, but also with speech acts whose illocutionary force is not assertoric.[3] Thus I cannot coherently say 'Thank you but I feel no gratitude' or 'Rain is likely, but I don't expect it'. If

---

[1] G. E. Moore, "A Reply to My Critics," in *The Philosophy of G. E. Moore*, ed. Paul Arthur Schilpp, New York: Tudor, 1942 [2nd edn. 1952], pp. 533–677, at p. 543; "Russell's 'Theory of Descriptions'," in *The Philosophy of Bertrand Russell*, ed. Paul Arthur Schilpp, New York: Tudor, 1944, pp. 175–226, at p. 204.

[2] Ludwig Wittgenstein, *Philosophical Investigations*, tr. G. E. M. Anscombe, New York: Macmillan, 1953, II, §x; *Remarks on the Philosophy of Psychology*, vol. I, ed. G. E. M. Anscombe and G. H. von Wright, tr. G. E. M. Anscombe, Oxford: Basil Blackwell, 1980, pp. 91–2.

Rogers Albritton has urged that what Wittgenstein regarded as paradoxical was not that such sentences as 'It's raining but I don't think it is' are troubled, but that they are troubled even though counterparts not in the first-person present tense are not. ("Comments on Moore's Paradox and Self-Knowledge," *Philosophical Studies*, 77, 2–3 [March 1995]: 229–39, at p. 239. This view recalls *Remarks on the Philosophy of Psychology*, I, 490.) But even if that's so, we can understand this paradoxical contrast only if we first understand what's defective about first-person, present-tense cases, and the correct account of those might then make the contrast no longer seem paradoxical.

[3] Max Black, "Saying and Disbelieving," *Analysis*, 13, 2 (December 1952): 25–33, pp. 32–3, reprinted in *Philosophy and Analysis*, ed. Margaret MacDonald, Oxford: Basil Blackwell, 1954, pp. 109–19, at pp. 118–91; my "Intentionality," ch. 3 in this volume, §II; John R. Searle, *Intentionality: An Essay in the Philosophy of Mind*, Cambridge: Cambridge University Press, 1983, p. 9; and Sydney Shoemaker, "On Knowing One's Own Mind," *Philosophical Perspectives: Epistemology*, 2 (1988): 183–209, pp. 204–5. D. H. Mellor claims, to the contrary, that Moore's paradox "has no analogue for the other attitudes" ("What Is Computational Psychology?", *Proceedings of the Aristotelian Society*, Supplementary Volume LVIII [1984]: 37–53, p. 38).

somebody were to produce such an utterance, we would automatically try to interpret the words nonliterally, or as having been used ironically or with some other oblique force. Only by doing so could we regard the speaker as having performed any speech act at all.[4]

One reason to trace the absurdity of Moore's paradox to the impossibility of performing any coherent speech act is that the absurdity may vanish when the very words of such sentences are embedded in a larger sentence.[5] Consider, for example, the sentence, 'Suppose it's raining but I don't think it is'. If Moore's-paradox sentences were actually contradictory, they would of course remain contradictory even when embedded in such larger contexts.

It has not generally been noted that there's an important kinship between Moore's paradox and Descartes's *cogito*. The sentence 'I don't exist' has unproblematic truth conditions. Not only is it possible for the sentence to be true; it once was true for each of us. Nonetheless, the sentence has no coherent conditions of assertibility; no circumstances exist in which one could coherently perform a speech act by assertively producing that sentence. Arguably it is this which underwrites Descartes's claim in Meditation II that "the statement 'I am, I exist' is necessarily true every time it is produced by me, or mentally conceived."[6]

Because the necessary truth of 'I exist' is conditional on my thinking or saying it, the *cogito*, like Moore's paradox, is a not a function solely of the truth conditions of the sentence 'I exist'. Rather, it's a function of the performance conditions of the corresponding speech act and, possibly, the mental analogue of these performance conditions for the corresponding propositional attitudes. A useful test is to see whether a change of grammatical tense or person relieves the difficulty. Thus, there is no problem about saying 'I *didn't* exist' (or '*won't* exist'), or 'It's raining but *you* don't think it is'.[7]

---

[4] Roy A. Sorensen has argued that we can assert certain indirect versions of Moore's paradox, e.g., 'The atheism of my mother's nieceless brother's only nephew angers God', which implies 'God exists but I believe that God does not exist'. (See his *Blindspots*, Oxford: Oxford University Press, 1988, p. 28; I am grateful to Sorensen for calling this argument to my attention.) But one can assert Sorensen's sentence only if one hasn't drawn the Moore's-paradox conclusion. And then, in effect, one would fail fully to understand its content; one would only assert that a certain sentence is true, without also asserting its content.

[5] As Wittgenstein in effect noted and, more explicitly, Albritton ("Comments," p. 228).

[6] "Necessarily" because 'I don't exist' necessarily lacks conditions of assertibility. *Oeuvres de Descartes*, ed. Charles Adam and Paul Tannery, Paris: J. Vrin, 1964–75, (henceforth *AT*), VII, 25; my translations here and below. See René Descartes, *The Philosophical Writings of Descartes*, tr. John Cottingham, Robert Stoothoff, Dugald Murdoch, and Anthony Kenny, 3 volumes, Cambridge: Cambridge University Press, 1984–91, which gives the *AT* page numbers.

[7] I develop this explanation of the *cogito* briefly in "Will and the Theory of Judgment," in *Essays on Descartes' Meditations*, ed. Amélie O. Rorty, Berkeley: University of California Press, 1986, pp. 405–434, §IV (reprinted in *Descartes's Meditations*, ed. Vere Chappell, Lanham, Maryland, and Oxford: Rowman & Littlefield, 1997, and in *Essays on Early Modern Philosophers, volume I: René Descartes*, Part II, ed. Vere Chappell, Hamden, Connecticut: Garland Publishing Co., 1992, pp. 257–286); and more extensively in "Judgment, Mind, and Will in Descartes," Report No. 29/1990, Center for Interdisciplinary Research (ZiF), University of Bielefeld, §VII.

Descartes also concluded that the "I" whose existence he had established is essentially a thinking thing. In part this is because the necessary truth of 'I exist' is conditional on my thinking or saying it. But it's also because the sentence 'I am thinking' behaves like the sentence 'I exist'. Just as the sentence 'I exist' is true every time I think it or assert it, so also is the sentence 'I am thinking'. And it might even appear that this points to a certain kind of self-knowledge. I cannot, when I'm thinking, doubt that I am thinking. So it's tempting to suppose that my being engaged in thinking is by itself enough for me to know that I am. And, because this conclusion rests on just the kind of reasoning that underwrites Moore's paradox, Moore's paradox seems relevant at least to a certain sort of self-knowledge.

Moore's paradox seems also to help us with another, more vexed, aspect of Descartes's thinking. Descartes insists that one can doubt that one has hands or a body, though he concedes it would be mad to do so (*AT* VII 19). By contrast, it may well seem that, mad or not, one simply cannot doubt such things as that $2 + 3 = 5$. But even so, one might wonder whether our inability to doubt in this case is just a fact about our mental nature, and by itself tells us nothing about the numbers. And that's what underlies Descartes's demon doubt about such things as arithmetic. Such doubting consists in the idea that, though one cannot help but mentally affirm that $2 + 3 = 5$, one can consider, on the side as it were, that this mental necessity need not correspond to the arithmetic facts.

But the very attempt to engage in any such oblique doubt falls prey to Moore's paradox, since we can describe the situation that seems to underwrite that doubt only by saying 'I think that $2 + 3 = 5$, but it isn't so'.[8] Seeing this clearly and distinctly is thus enough to defeat such doubt. Descartes remarks that the *cogito* points the way to defeating demon doubt (*AT* VII 35). This is a natural thought, since Moore's paradox defeats such doubt, and the very same considerations underlie both the *cogito* and Moore's paradox.[9]

---

[8] That is, trying to engage in such oblique doubt is in effect to try to say to oneself 'I think that $2 + 3 = 5$, but it isn't so'.

Another way to see this is that trying to doubt obliquely consists in thinking 'I think that $2 + 3 = 5$, but perhaps it isn't so', which Moore also described as paradoxical.

[9] Some things one can doubt without recourse to any such oblique maneuver; there is no difficulty in directly doubting or denying, e.g., that it's raining. Doubting that $2 + 3 = 5$, by contrast, is psychologically impossible, and Moore's paradox precludes oblique doubt. Which kinds of thing would have to be doubted obliquely if at all? Presumably truths such as those of mathematics and logic. Indeed, it's tempting to identify the things we cannot doubt directly with just those things we grasp clearly and distinctly. That is the Meditation V doctrine of impelled assent, that "I am of such a nature that, whenever I perceive something exceedingly clearly and distinctly, I am unable not to believe it to be true" (*AT* VII 69). And being unable not to believe something to be true is being unable to doubt it. Moore's paradox explains why these things cannot be doubted, by precluding even oblique doubt.

The *cogito*, according to Descartes, suggests "a general rule . . . that all that I perceive exceedingly clearly and distinctly is true" (*AT* VII 34–5). Restrict attention, for the moment, to those things which we understand exceedingly clearly and distinctly, i.e., to those things we can doubt, if at all, only obliquely. And take Moore's paradox to reveal something about our mental nature. Then, what Moore's paradox tells us is that our mental nature is such that, when we cannot doubt or deny

Let's return for a moment to self-knowledge. If being engaged in thinking is enough to know that one is thinking, then to that extent at least the mind is transparent to itself. As Descartes put it, "nothing can be in our mind of which we are not at that time conscious."[10] But this thesis of transparency is untenable. Not all our thinking is, in fact, conscious thinking. This is clear in part from results in clinical and cognitive psychology, but it's also obvious from everyday, commonsense considerations. We often consciously puzzle over a problem, for example, only to have the solution occur to us later, apparently spontaneously, without the problem having in the meantime been in any way consciously before our mind. It's hard to see how this could happen unless problem-solving thinking sometimes occurs without being conscious. Such nonconscious problem solving occurs, moreover, when we're not even aware that any thinking is going on, for example, when we're asleep. Many other commonsense considerations support the same conclusion. Simply being engaged in thinking is plainly not sufficient for that thinking to be conscious.

What, then, went wrong with the reasoning that seemed to show otherwise? It's undeniable that, just as I cannot sensibly assert 'It's raining but I don't think it is', so I cannot assert that I'm not thinking, nor, perhaps, perform the mental act of thinking

something directly, we also cannot doubt or deny it obliquely by way of the hypothesis that the impossibility of doubting directly is due to our having a defective mental nature.

This line may recall the compelling interpretation of Alan Gewirth and Harry G. Frankfurt of how Meditation III meets Arnauld's challenge of circularity. On their account, the reasoning that leads to the divine guarantee is meant to show that no challenge to the reliability of reasoning could be coherent if it relied, itself, on reasoning. (See Gewirth, "The Cartesian Circle," *The Philosophical Review*, L, 4 [July 1941]: 368–395, and Frankfurt, *Dreamers, Demons, and Madmen*, Indianapolis, Bobbs-Merrill, 1970, ch. 15. It is tempting to construe O. K. Bouwsma's well-known argument that the demon hypothesis is incoherent ["Descartes' Evil Genius," *The Philosophical Review*, LVIII, 1 (January 1949): 141–151] as in effect an ordinary-language counterpart of the reasoning Gewirth and Frankfurt ascribe to Descartes.) Similarly, our mental nature is such that we cannot cast doubt on something by casting doubt on the reliability of our mental nature.

There is another way to see Moore's paradox as informing Descartes's reasoning on these matters. Understanding something "exceedingly clearly and distinctly" is tied not only to truth, but to our being unable to doubt it. That is the Meditation V doctrine of impelled assent, that "I am of such a nature that, whenever I perceive something exceedingly clearly and distinctly, I am unable not to believe it to be true" (*AT* VII 69). And our being unable not to believe something is being unable to doubt it. An inference to the best explanation arguably yields the converse; if I cannot doubt something, even in the heroic fashion of Meditation I, that can only be because I understand it with exceeding clarity and distinctness. So our mental nature is such that the inability to doubt something, however heroically we try, is a sure sign that it's true.

The considerations that underlie Moore's paradox suggest that our mental natures are reliable in this way. I cannot say 'I don't exist' for the same type of reason I cannot say 'p but I don't believe it'. And the impossibility of asserting 'I don't exist' goes with my existing whenever I try to say it. So it may be tempting to suppose that my mental nature is such, whenever I cannot doubt something for Moore's-paradox reasons, the thing I cannot doubt is true. Arguably such reasoning underlies that of the *Meditations*.

[10] *Fourth Replies, AT* VII, 232. Descartes is aware that his reasoning establishes transparency only with respect to what mental attitudes our intentional states exhibit, and not also with respect to the content of those states, and thus explicitly qualifies his claim in the quoted passage (see also *AT* VII, pp. 246–7).

that I'm not thinking. But this hardly shows that whenever I do think, I automatically think that I'm thinking. The question of whether I'm thinking may simply not come before my mind, consciously or otherwise. Indeed, though thinking does occur during sleep, we have no reason to suppose that, when it does, the question of whether one is thinking ever occurs to one as well.

That thinking can occur without one's being aware of it is evident also from consideration of nonhuman cases. It's overwhelmingly likely that some creatures that lack the concept of thinking nonetheless have the capacity to think. Such creatures would therefore be unable ever to think that they think.

Descartes and, in a somewhat similar spirit, Donald Davidson both deny that such a thing is possible. But it's hard to see any reason for that denial that doesn't beg the question. Descartes maintains that "in order to know what doubting is, and what thinking is, only doubting or thinking is needed."[11] Presumably he is relying here on the impossibility of doubting and at the same time doubting that one is doubting. But as we've just seen, one may be unable to doubt something without, thereby, actually thinking that it's so. Davidson's argument is not much better. He writes: "Someone cannot have a belief unless he understands the possibility of being mistaken, and this requires grasping the contrast between . . . true belief and false belief." This contrast, he maintains, can in turn "emerge only in the context of interpretation."[12] But even on such an interpretationist view, it's unclear that this is required. Why isn't it enough for me to have beliefs that others, who do grasp the distinction between true and false believing, interpret me in suitable ways? Only when one's beliefs are conscious would self-interpretation be needed.[13]

Humans, of course, do often engage in thinking of a kind that would be impossible without having a concept of thinking. We sometimes think about the thinking that we or others are engaged in. Indeed, I've argued elsewhere that the way we are conscious of our conscious mental states is a matter of our having higher-order thoughts about those states.[14] But often our thinking isn't in any way conscious thinking. And such consciousness apart, it's relatively seldom that we actually think about anybody's thoughts, our own or another person's.[15] So why couldn't there be creatures whose thinking is always like our nonconscious thinking, and who moreover never think about anybody's thoughts? Such creatures might well have no concept of thinking. Though their mental lives would plainly be far less rich than

---

[11] *The Search for Truth*, AT X, 524.

[12] "Thought and Talk," reprinted in Davidson's *Inquiries into Truth and Interpretation*, Oxford, Clarendon Press, 1984, pp. 155–170, at p. 170.

[13] Or when, consciousness apart, one thinks about one's beliefs.

[14] E.g., in "Thinking that One Thinks," ch. 2 in this volume, and "A Theory of Consciousness," in *The Nature of Consciousness: Philosophical Debates*, ed. Ned Block, Owen Flanagan, and Güven Güzeldere, Cambridge, Massachusetts: MIT Press, 1997, pp. 729–753.

[15] On Paul Grice's theory of meaning, on which what we say means something if I intend my audience to believe that I believe that thing, we think about our own and others' thoughts a lot more than it might at first appear. But other considerations figure here, since as I argue below (§II), the thoughts we express in speaking are virtually always conscious. See Paul Grice, "Utterer's Meaning and Intentions," *The Philosophical Review*, LXXVIII, 2 (April 1969): 147–177.

ours, if in our case the concept of thinking applies to all our thinking, whether or not we think about it, it should equally apply to the thinking that these other, more limited creatures engage in.

Sydney Shoemaker has developed a different argument for the view that we cannot, in any straightforward way, apply our concepts for human mental phenomena to nonhuman animals. His reason is that many features of human mental phenomena are central to the very concepts of those phenomena; he regards minimal rationality as a salient example. Since nonhuman animals apparently lack the relevant minimal rationality, Shoemaker concludes that applying these concepts to nonhuman animals is "problematic."[16]

But Shoemaker's view about when we can apply various mental concepts leads to untenable results. The concepts whose application to nonhuman creatures Shoemaker sees as problematic are specifically human folk-psychological concepts. So we should expect that these concepts are tailored to human mental phenomena. But the distinctive features of human mentality that these concepts embody may well show relatively little about mental phenomena generally. For one thing, there might exist creatures whose mental states exhibited important features not shared by human mental states, for example, a minimal threshold of rationality far superior to our own. Concepts for human mental phenomena should apply unproblematically to corresponding states of such superior creatures. But on Shoemaker's view, those superior beings could not even have a concept of mind, in our sense of the word.[17]

There is in any case reason to doubt Shoemaker's claim that minimal rationality is essential to human mentality. Human mental states don't always manifest the ties with other states that subserve such rationality and hence, on Shoemaker's view, self-knowledge. But our mental concepts plainly apply to all human mental states, even when those states lack the relevant ties. So we have no reason not to apply these concepts to states of creatures, even when their states never exhibit the connections that subserve minimal rationality.

Whatever we say about nonhuman creatures, not all human thinking is conscious, nor can it always readily become conscious. So it's a mistake to expect the analogue of Moore's paradox that underlies the *cogito* to help establish any thesis about transparency. All it shows is that when creatures that have the concept of thinking do actually think, they cannot sensibly deny, in speech or in thought, that they are thinking.

---

[16] "Rationality and Self-Consciousness," in *The Opened Curtain: A U.S.-Soviet Philosophy Summit*, ed. Keith Lehrer and Ernest Sosa, Boulder, Colorado: Westview Press, 1991, pp. 127–149, at p. 145; see §§IV–V.

[17] Shoemaker evidently also thinks that the only alternative to using our concepts of human folk psychology would be to use concepts of subpersonal states "describable in the terminology of neurophysiology" ("Rationality and Self-Consciousness," p. 147). But that's far from obvious. We can avoid discredited aspects of our commonsense conception of mentality without restricting ourselves to subpersonal description; we could simply strip the unwanted features away. Similarly, if human folk-psychological concepts embody parochial features special to human mentality, we may well be able to subtract them, and use the resulting concepts to talk equally well about both our mental states and those of other creatures.

It's worth taking note of another thesis about transparency that's arguably related to Moore's paradox. It's often held that knowing something is sufficient for one to know that one knows. If so, knowing is in effect transparent to itself. Consider the sentence ⌜I know that *p* but I don't know that I know it⌝. This sentence plainly isn't contradictory; compare saying ⌜I knew that *p* but I didn't know I knew it⌝, or ⌜He knew that *p* but didn't know he knew it⌝. Still, it seems clear that there cannot be coherent conditions for asserting the first-person, present-tense version.

Strictly speaking, the sentence ⌜I know that *p* but I don't know that I know it⌝ is not quite an instance of Moore's paradox.[18] It's a substitution instance of ⌜*p* but I don't know that *p*⌝. And that sentence is implied by Moore's-paradox but doesn't imply it, since if one knows that *p* one thinks that *p*, but not conversely. So Moore's paradox is stronger than sentences of the form ⌜I know that *p* but I don't know that I know it⌝. Accordingly, it doesn't follow from Moore's-paradox sentences' having no coherent assertibility conditions that sentences of the form ⌜I know that *p* but I don't know that I know it⌝ have none.[19]

Still, perhaps Moore's paradox can help us see what is troubled about such sentences. Let knowing be true, justified believing. By Moore's paradox, saying I know that *p* makes it incoherent to deny that I believe that I know it. By the same token, if I assert that I know that *p*, it's incoherent then in the same breath to deny that it's true that I know it. As for justification, if I say I know that *p*, I take my assertion to be justified; so I can't then coherently deny knowing that I know on the ground that I'm not justified in thinking I know. Similar considerations will arguably apply to other accounts of knowing. If I say I know that *p*, for example, my speech act expresses my belief that I do, and it would be incoherent to deny that that belief tracks my knowing that *p*.[20]

Other considerations, however, cast doubt on whether Moore's paradox can help in this way. I can believe something and yet not know it, and it's perfectly coherent for me to say that, that is, to say, ⌜*p*, and I believe that *p* but don't know it⌝. And

---

[18] *Pace* John Koethe, "A Note On Moore's Paradox," *Philosophical Studies*, 34, 3 (October 1978): 303–310, p. 303.

[19] Cf. ⌜*p* ∧ ¬*p*⌝, whose lack of coherent assertibility conditions plainly doesn't carry over to all the sentences it implies.

[20] On tracking, see Robert Nozick, *Philosophical Explanations*, Cambridge, Massachusetts: Harvard University Press, 1981, pp. 172–196. On knowing that one knows, see pp. 245–247.

In *Ignorance: A Case for Scepticism*, Oxford: Clarendon Press, 1975, Peter Unger argues that we should understand what's wrong with Moore's paradox by reference to its counterpart with 'knows'. Unger argues that, in saying that *p*, one represents oneself as knowing that *p* (253), and so represents oneself as at least believing that *p* (257). Thus, e.g., if I say it's raining, it's in place to ask me how I know (263).

But in saying that *p*, one doesn't actually assert that one knows; so it's unclear what Unger means by one's representing oneself as knowing. And asking how a person knows need be no more than a challenge to that person's statement. Cf. J. L. Austin's observation that "[w]hen we make an assertion . . . , there is a sense in which we imply that we are sure of it or know it . . . , though what we imply, in a similar sense and more strictly, is only that we *believe* it" ("Other Minds," in Austin, *Philosophical Papers*, 2nd and 3rd edns., Oxford: Oxford University Press, 1970 and 1979, pp. 76–116, at p. 77 [1st edn., 1961, pp. 44–84, at p. 45]).

this suggests that Moore's paradox cannot after all help to explain what's troubled about saying ⌜p but I don't know that p⌝, and the substitution instance pertaining to knowing that one knows. Another possibility might be that the difficulty is merely pragmatic. J. L. Austin urged that, in saying one knows, one gives others a kind of guarantee,[21] and one also gives a kind of guarantee in making any assertion. So in saying ⌜p but I don't know that p⌝, one first gives a guarantee that p and then withdraws it.

Whatever the explanation of why that sentence is troubled, this cousin of Moore's paradox no more warrants concluding that knowing actually implies knowing that one knows than the *cogito* entitles us to hold that all thinking is conscious. Rather, all it shows is that we cannot coherently assert that we know something and at the same time deny knowing that we know it.[22]

II. LANGUAGE AND CONSCIOUSNESS

I'll return in section IV to the question of whether Moore's paradox does help establish some form of self-knowledge about one's own mental states. But whatever the case about that, I want now to argue that Moore's paradox does point to factors that help explain a surprising phenomenon: a case in which our thinking is, almost without exception, conscious thinking.

Whenever we say anything sincerely, we express some intentional state that we're in. If I sincerely say, for example, that it's raining, I express my thought that it's raining. Similarly with other sorts of speech act and the mental attitudes that correspond to them. If I thank you, I express my gratitude; if I say it will probably rain I express my expectation that it will. And so forth. Every sincere speech act expresses an intentional state with the same content, or nearly the same, as the speech act and a mental attitude that corresponds to the speech act's illocutionary force.

Moore's paradox reflects this connection between speech acts and the intentional states they express. I cannot use the sentence 'It's raining but I don't think it is' to make a coherent assertion precisely because the assertion that the first conjunct purports to make expresses the very intentional state that the second conjunct denies I'm in. To be used in performing a genuine conjunctive speech act, the first conjunct of a Moore's-paradox sentence would have to express a corresponding thought. But the second conjunct denies that any such thought exists, thereby denying that the whole

---

[21] "Other Minds," 2nd and 3rd edns., pp. 97–103 (1st edn., pp. 65–71).

[22] Knowing can be either active or latent; active knowing is conscious, and latent knowing is, roughly, being disposed to have active knowledge. It's seldom noted that it's only when the relevant knowing is uniformly conscious is there intuitive appeal to the claim that knowing implies knowing that one knows; when knowing is latent, that intuitive appeal vanishes. This reinforces the suggestion that the reason knowing appears to imply second-order knowing is simply because one cannot coherently represent oneself as knowing while at the same time denying that one knows that one knows, since representing oneself as knowing means that if one knows at all the knowing is conscious. And a semantic connection would not be sensitive to whether the knowing is latent or active.

sentence can be used to make any coherent assertion.[23] The same holds for the sentences 'Thank you but I'm not grateful' and 'It'll probably rain but I don't expect it to'; thanking somebody expresses one's gratitude, and saying something will probably happen expresses one's expectation. Similarly for versions of Moore's paradox derived from other illocutionary forces and the mental attitudes that correspond to them.

Many of our intentional states are not in any way conscious states. But when we express our intentional states in speech, those states are always conscious, or almost always. Suppose I think it's raining. My thought may or may not be conscious. But if I verbally express that thought by asserting that it's raining, the thought is invariably conscious. Indeed, with an exception that I'll mention in closing, any intentional state that I express with a speech act will be a conscious intentional state.

Intentional states are expressed not only by speech, but also by many forms of nonverbal behavior. Taking an umbrella may express my belief that it will rain, or my desire not to get wet, or both. Facial expressions and bodily movements of various kinds may express my delight in something or my dislike of it, my fear of something or my anticipation of some future event. In all these cases the intentional state my nonverbal behavior expresses may well be conscious; but it may also fail to be. I may take the umbrella absently, "without thinking," as we might say—that is, without thinking consciously. And one's facial expressions and bodily movements often betray delight, distaste, fear, and expectations of which one is, oneself, wholly unaware.

This difference between expressing intentional states verbally and expressing them by one's nonverbal behavior is striking. When an intentional state is expressed in speech, it's always conscious, but when it's expressed nonverbally it needn't be. Doubtless this contrast helped to persuade Descartes and others that language and consciousness are both essential to mentality. It's tempting to think and talk about intentional states in terms of the speech acts that would express them, since doing so enables us to describe the content and the mental attitude of intentional states with an accuracy and precision not otherwise available.[24] And if we describe our own intentional states and those of others by reference to speech acts that would express those states, we may take the further step of thinking about all intentional states as though they were expressed in speech, and hence conscious. But as we've seen, there is ample evidence that our commonsense, folk-psychological conceptions don't require that all intentional states are conscious, and indeed ample evidence that many of them are not.

It might be argued that slips of the tongue, such as those said to occur in Freudian parapraxis, cause difficulty here. Such slips, it may seem, express thoughts of which

---

[23] So even though when one successfully says that *p* one is conscious of one's thought that *p*, the trouble with Moore's paradox does not on my view result, as Albritton suggests ("Comments," p. 237), from one's being conscious of the belief the first conjunct purports to express.

[24] Indeed, it's likely that when we describe intentional states in terms of the content and illocutionary force of speech acts that might express those states, we draw more fine-grained distinctions among those states than their nature warrants. We project distinctions among our words back onto the intentional states those words express, even though nothing about the intentional states themselves would allow us to distinguish them so finely. For more on this, see "Content, Interpretation, and Consciousness," ch. 12 in this volume.

we're not conscious. If so, the thoughts our speech acts express sometimes aren't conscious. But there would also be another problem. The latent content such slips supposedly express is typically distinct from the manifest content that matches the semantic meaning of the speech act. So the content of these speech acts would diverge from the content of the intentional states they express. Of course, the latent thought expressed by one's slip is often conscious; witness the conscious embarrassment sometimes caused by the realization of what one's slip reveals. Even so, it's arguable that the content of the speech acts involved in such slips corresponds not to the latent content, but to the manifest content.

But in fact things are more complicated. Suppose an unintended word intrudes into one's performing of a speech act, thereby revealing some nonconscious thought that one has. The occurrence of that word is best construed not as an integral part of the speech act, but in effect as a piece of nonverbal behavior. It's on a par with cases in which one's tone, or other aspects of one's utterances, unintentionally betray one's nonconscious intentional states. The way we utter things often reveals our intentional states without, thereby, expressing them verbally. The latent thought in these cases is simply a causal factor, somewhat like an external noise, which interferes with the correct expression of the conscious thought that corresponds to the speech act. So the slips that occur in parapraxis are not counterexamples to the foregoing generalizations.[25]

It's important here to distinguish between verbally expressing an intentional state and reporting that state. Although verbally expressing our intentional states and reporting them are both ways of conveying to others what intentional states we're in, there are important differences between these two ways. When I think it's raining, I verbally express my thought by saying that it's raining. My verbal expression has the same content as the intentional state it expresses and an illocutionary force that corresponds to the mental attitude of the intentional state. By contrast, I report my thought that it's raining when I explicitly say that I have that thought, for example, when I say 'I think it's raining'. So the content of my thought inevitably differs from that of a speech act that reports the thought.

The contrast between reporting and expressing one's intentional states emerges most decisively, however, with intentional states that have a nonassertoric mental attitude. If I wonder whether it'll rain, I express my state of wondering by saying 'Will it rain?'. By contrast, I report my wondering by saying 'I wonder whether it'll rain'. Here the illocutionary force of the speech act that verbally expresses my intentional state is that of a question, corresponding to the mental attitude of wondering. The illocutionary force of my report, on the other hand, is assertoric, as it is with all reports of intentional states.

Again, Moore's paradox is helpful. I cannot assertively produce the sentence 'It's raining but I don't think it is' because asserting the first conjunct would express an intentional state that the second conjunct denies I am in. Suppose, now, that there were no difference between reporting an intentional state and verbally expressing it. Then my denial that I am in the intentional state of thinking that it's raining would

---

[25] For more on parapraxis, see "Consciousness and Its Expression," ch. 11 in this volume.

be tantamount simply to expressing the thought that it's not raining. Accordingly, the Moore's-paradox sentence would be equivalent to 'It's raining and it's not raining', which is an actual contradiction. But the truth conditions of Moore's-paradox sentences specify occasions on which they are true. To avoid this result, we must distinguish reporting our intentional states from verbally expressing them.

Mark Crimmins has produced an intriguing and instructive example of an assertible sentence syntactically indistinguishable from ordinary cases of Moore's paradox. Suppose I know you, know you under one guise not to be an idiot, and also know that I know you under some other guise. I don't know what that other guise is, but I do know that I believe that the person I know under that other guise is an idiot. Addressing you as the person I know not to be an idiot, I can then sensibly assert 'I falsely believe that you're an idiot'. This is equivalent to 'You aren't an idiot but I believe you are an idiot', which is syntactically just like a case of Moore's paradox, but it isn't at all absurd.[26]

The foregoing explanation makes clear why Crimmins's case is not an example of Moore's paradox. If, in the circumstances just described, I say 'You aren't an idiot but I believe you are', the first conjunct expresses my thought that you aren't an idiot. But that thought is not relevant to the intentional state I report with the second conjunct. The intentional state a speech act expresses must be a nondispositional, occurrent state that I'm in at roughly the time of the speech act. But when I say 'You aren't an idiot but I believe you are', the belief I report that you're an idiot is only a belief I'm disposed to have under other circumstances.[27] Indeed, Crimmins's case helps underscore that the intentional state that a genuine illocutionary act expresses must be an occurrent state, and not a mere disposition to be in that state. This need to distinguish between dispositional and occurrent beliefs will be important again in section IV, in connection with the consciousness of beliefs.

Ordinary usage of verbs of propositional attitude may sometimes seem to run together reporting with the expressing of our intentional states. For example, when one says 'I choose this one' or 'I sympathize with you', it may seem that one's speech act expresses one's choice or sympathy, rather than reporting those states. This is because these mental verbs have a performative aspect. When I say 'I do' in a marriage ceremony, my speech act is my doing. Similarly, if I say 'I sympathize with you', my speech act is a case of sympathizing, and often it's my saying 'I choose this' that counts as my making my choice. Even mental verbs such as 'doubt' and 'suppose' seem to follow this pattern. In saying ⌜I doubt (or suppose) that *p*⌝, I perform a conversational act of doubting or supposing.

But these verbs not only have a performative aspect, but a truth-stating, constative aspect as well. And when we take the truth conditions of these sentences into

[26] See "I Falsely Believe that *p*," *Analysis*, 52 (July 1992): 191.
[27] One might insist that the guise under which I think you're an idiot affects the content of the belief I report, so that in this way, too, the belief I report is irrelevant to the thought I express in saying you're not an idiot. But this line of argument is controversial, since one might also urge that the use of the indexical 'you' cancels in these cases any relevance of guises to content
See my "Moore's Paradox and Crimmins's Case," *Analysis*, 62, 2 (April 2002): 167–171.

consideration, it's clear that such speech acts report the relevant attitudes. Indeed, if they didn't, Moore's paradox would otherwise be an outright contradiction. The performative aspect of such verbs no more entitles us to ignore their truth-stating aspect than their performance conditions do.

Verbally expressing an intentional state is, with a certain type of exception, a sufficient condition for that state to be conscious.[28] But distinguishing between reporting our intentional states and expressing them points toward a second connection between consciousness and speech. When a creature has the requisite concepts and linguistic ability, a mental state's being conscious is sufficient for the creature to be able to report being in that state.

This second connection between language and consciousness is to be expected. Conscious mental states satisfy two conditions: we're conscious of being in them, and the way we're conscious of them seems to us to be immediate. We needn't, of course, be conscious of our conscious states in a way that's at all attentive or focused; we're no more than peripherally conscious of the vast majority of our conscious states. But when mental states occur of which we are not in any way conscious, those states are not conscious states. And, given the requisite concepts and linguistic ability, being conscious of something is sufficient for being able to report about it.

What about the other way around? Being able to report about a mental state is not sufficient for that state to be conscious, because a state's being conscious requires not just that one is conscious of the state, but also that one is conscious of it in a way that from an intuitive point of view is immediate. Being able to report some mental state one is in solely because of behavioral evidence or solely because one takes somebody else's word for it is not sufficient for the state to be a conscious state.

This intuitive immediacy, however, does not amount to much. Our consciousness of our own mental states will be intuitively immediate if we're conscious of them in a way that doesn't rely on any inference, at least not on any inference of which we are aware.[29] So, although being able to report on a state doesn't suffice for that state to be conscious, being able to report on it noninferentially does.

III. VERBALLY EXPRESSED THOUGHTS

We are now in a position to explain why verbally expressed intentional states are invariably conscious. Moore's paradox is absurd because the speech acts of asserting that *p* and asserting that I think that *p*, though they differ in respect of truth

---

[28] See "Why Are Verbally Expressed Thoughts Conscious?", ch. 10 in this volume.

[29] There's no circularity in this last qualification, since we're explaining what it is for a state to be conscious in terms of what it is we're conscious *of*. A state is conscious just in case one is conscious of being in that state, and conscious of that in a way that's independent of any inference of which one is, in turn, conscious.

All that matters for a state to be conscious is that one be conscious of it in a way that does not rely on any conscious inference. It doesn't prevent the state from being conscious if, in addition, one is conscious of an inference that would make one conscious of the state if the subjectively unmediated awareness of it weren't operative.

conditions, have roughly the same conditions of assertibility. Any circumstances in which I could say that *p* are circumstances in which I could say I think that *p*. And with a qualification[30] that won't affect the argument here, the converse holds as well.

More important, this performance-conditional equivalence is second nature for us. We automatically take saying $\ulcorner p \urcorner$ and saying $\ulcorner$ I think that $p \urcorner$ to amount to much the same thing insofar as conditions of assertibility are concerned. Indeed, we tend to slip insensibly between saying the one and saying the other, and may even have difficulty recalling on any particular occasion which of the two forms we used. It's a matter of well-entrenched linguistic habit that the two are interchangeable in this way.[31] And it's because this performance-conditional equivalence is second nature to us that Moore's paradox is not just absurd, but intuitively jarring. We know automatically that no circumstances can exist in which somebody could sensibly say that *p* but deny thinking that *p*.

The relevant performance-conditional equivalence emerges in the absurdity of the following conversation. Suppose I ask you whether it's raining, you say 'I think so', and I remonstrate that I asked not about your intentional states but about the weather. That's a bad joke in roughly the way Moore's paradox is, though it's harder here to imagine any charitable reinterpretation that would save things. And it's jarring in just the way Moore's paradox is, because in that context we automatically regard your saying 'I think so' as performance conditionally equivalent to your saying that it's raining. Indeed, it's so automatic as to be second nature.

Suppose I think that it's raining, and I express my thought by saying 'It's raining'. Because saying 'It's raining' is performance conditionally equivalent to saying 'I think it's raining', it would have served essentially the same purpose if I'd said that I think it's raining. More important, because that equivalence is second nature for us, I might as easily have said the other; in most circumstances it's a matter of complete indifference, both to you and to me, which of the two I say.

Now put performance conditions to one side for a moment, and think instead about truth conditions. What makes the sentence 'I think it's raining' true isn't the rain, but my being in a certain intentional state. Its being true requires that I think it's raining. So if I were to say 'I think it's raining', however we may take that remark in respect of performance conditions, I am literally telling you about one of my intentional states. I am reporting a certain thought.

So, when I express my thought that it's raining by saying 'It's raining', I could equally well have reported my thought that it's raining. And because it's second nature for us that saying 'It's raining' is performance conditionally equivalent to saying 'I think it's raining', if I had said 'I think it's raining', my report would not have been based on any inference, at least not on any inference of which I was conscious.[32] So, whenever I actually say 'It's raining', I could equally well have noninferentially

---

[30] $\ulcorner$ I think that $p \urcorner$ can, of course, be used to qualify the firmness of one's conviction that *p* is the case, in ways that simply asserting that *p* doesn't.

[31] There is more, however, than mere linguistic habit; see "Why Are Verbally Expressed Thoughts Conscious?", §V.

[32] I take that qualification for granted in what follows.

reported my thought that it's raining. My thought that it's raining would accordingly be noninferentially reportable.

But as we've seen, noninferential reportability is sufficient for a state to be a conscious state. So, given that it's second nature for us that saying 'It's raining' is performance conditionally equivalent to saying 'I think it's raining', whenever I verbally express any intentional state, that state will be conscious. And, since Moore's paradox is a reflection of that performance conditional equivalence, we have used the factors that underlie Moore's paradox to explain why verbally expressed intentional states are always conscious.

Let me briefly rehearse the argument once more. I've urged that Moore's paradox is absurd because saying ⌜p⌝ is performance conditionally equivalent to saying ⌜I think that p⌝. And it's intuitively jarring because that equivalence is so automatically a part of how we use these words. Given the equivalence, whenever I say ⌜p⌝, I could equally well have said ⌜I think that p⌝. But to say ⌜I think that p⌝ is, literally, to report one's thought that p. And because it's second nature that saying ⌜p⌝ is performance conditionally equivalent to saying ⌜I think that p⌝, saying ⌜I think that p⌝ would be reporting one's thought noninferentially. Being able to report an intentional state noninferentially, however, is sufficient for that state to be conscious. So the factors operative in the absurdity of Moore's paradox also explain why all verbally expressed intentional states are conscious.

The explanation applies equally to intentional states whose mental attitude is not assertoric. If I ask, 'Is it raining?', for example, the performance-conditional equivalence that underlies Moore's paradox shows that I might equally well have said 'I wonder whether it's raining'. If I say 'Close the door', I could instead have said in so many words that I want you to close it. Whenever I verbally express these intentional states, I'm able also to report those states noninferentially; similarly for states with other mental attitudes. An intentional state's being verbally expressed is sufficient for it to be conscious.

The connection between an intentional state's being expressed and its being conscious holds only, as we've seen, when the state is expressed in speech. States expressed by nonverbal behavior often aren't conscious. It will reinforce the foregoing explanation if we can use it to show why things are different with the two kinds of expressing.

Unlike speech acts, the pieces of nonverbal behavior that express our intentional states do not have established performance conditions. Taking my umbrella may in certain circumstances be odd or irrational or inappropriate, but not because it contravenes performance conditions. Nonverbal acts have no performance conditions, in part because they have nothing that corresponds to illocutionary force, and performance conditions are relative to illocutionary force.

Taking my umbrella has no performance conditions. So even if that action nonverbally expresses, say, my desire not to get wet, the action cannot have the same performance conditions as a speech act that reports the desire I nonverbally express. Taking my umbrella will therefore not be interchangeable, as a matter of well-entrenched linguistic habit, with the making of such a report. I might well perform the action of taking the umbrella even when I could not readily report the desire that action expresses. Similarly with other cases of nonverbally expressing our intentional states. An intentional state's being nonverbally expressed is not, therefore, sufficient for that state to be conscious.

We could perhaps imagine a piece of nonverbal behavior becoming so well-entrenched in our social practices that we came to see that behavior as having performance conditions. For example, taking an umbrella might come not simply to indicate the likelihood of rain,[33] but actually to mean semantically that it's going to rain. If taking an umbrella also came somehow to have illocutionary force, that action might then be performance conditionally equivalent to reporting one's thought that it's going to rain. It's arguable that if that equivalence also became second nature, one would be unable to take an umbrella without one's thought that it's going to rain being conscious. Intuitions about this kind of case, however, are unlikely to be firm enough to test this idea, since it's so unlikely that this kind of thing would ever happen.

I've argued that Moore's paradox is absurd because every speech act is roughly equivalent, in respect of performance conditions, to a report of the intentional state that the speech act expresses. But one might wonder whether the trouble with Moore's paradox is simpler than this. Perhaps all that's wrong is that one cannot say 'It's raining but I don't think it is' without betraying one's insincerity in making the utterance. Making such an utterance would in effect then be simply self-defeating, relative to our normal purposes in asserting things. Indeed, Moore himself at one point suggests this kind of diagnosis.[34]

Many speech acts telegraph their insincerity. What is supposed to be different about Moore's paradox, on this account, is that it does so solely as a result of its semantic properties, and not, for example, because of the way it's uttered. This explanation seems to fit well with Paul Grice's idea that my meaning something involves intending that my hearer believe that I believe what I say. If Grice is right, I couldn't mean that *p* if I also said I don't believe it, and if I can't mean that *p*, I can't say it sincerely.[35]

But this won't work as a diagnosis of Moore's paradox. Suppose one utters the sentence 'It's raining' and also indicates somehow that one doesn't think it's raining. One then betrays one's insincerity in uttering 'It's raining'. But this is not the relevant situation. Moore's paradox is a matter not of saying simply 'It's raining', but of saying 'It's raining but I don't think it is'. If I say 'It's raining' and then as an aside say 'I don't believe it's raining', one of my two utterances is presumably insincere. But to understand Moore's paradox we must know what's wrong with trying to join the two within a single illocutionary act. And it cannot simply be the impossibility of sincerely asserting the conjunction, since that's also true of actual contradictions.

---

[33] As with Paul Grice's "natural" meaning; see his "Meaning," *The Philosophical Review*, LXVI, 3 (July 1957): 377–88.

[34] "A Reply to My Critics," pp. 542–43.

[35] Paul Grice, "Utterer's Meaning and Intentions." Mellor endorses this explanation; see "Conscious Belief," *Proceedings of the Aristotelian Society*, New Series, LXXXVIII (1977–8): 87–101, pp. 96–7, and "Consciousness and Degrees of Belief," in his *Matters of Metaphysics*, Cambridge: Cambridge University Press, 1991, pp. 30–60, at p. 38. See also M. F. Burnyeat, "Belief in Speech," *Proceedings of the Aristotelian Society*, New Series, LXVIII (1967–8): 227–48.

Sincerity matters in communicating. But Moore's paradox is absurd independent of any context of communication; it's absurd even in soliloquy, where betrayals of insincerity are irrelevant. One cannot say even to oneself 'It's raining but I don't think it is'.[36] We can best explain this independence from any context of communication, as well as the absurdity of trying to assert the relevant conjunction, by appeal to the performance-conditional equivalence I've been relying on.

This equivalence holds, I've urged, because of a connection between speech acts and the intentional states they express. All sincere speech acts express corresponding intentional states. We cannot coherently assert 'It's raining but I don't think it is' because what the first conjunct purports to assert expresses the intentional state that the second conjunct denies I am in.

But I've cast the regularity about speech acts' expressing intentional states solely in terms of sincere speech. So doesn't my account also rely on sincerity? It is arguable that the qualification about sincerity can be dropped. When my utterance of the sentence 'It's raining' is a lie, none of my assertoric intentional states has the content *it's raining*; there is then no actual intentional state for my words to express. Still, don't I in that kind of case *say* it's raining? Only in a qualified way. 'Say' and related verbs of illocutionary act are sometimes used in a weak sense, as roughly equivalent to 'utter'; saying in this sense involves no illocutionary act. When we recite lines in a poem or a play, for example, we seldom if ever produce them with illocutionary force, though typically we pretend to; in these cases we say things in only the weak sense. When an actor utters 'My heart is in the coffin there with Caesar', nobody would take him to be performing an actual illocutionary act, despite his pretense to do so. As Frege remarked, "stage assertion is only sham assertion."[37]

Insincere speech also operates in this way. When we speak insincerely we pretend to be in intentional states that don't exist, and thereby pretend to perform the relevant illocutionary acts. Lying and play acting differ, of course, in the motives we have for pretending; so in lying my pretense isn't candid, as it is in play acting. Moreover, in lying the character I play is a fictional version of myself, one who actually believes the things I pretend to assert. So when I speak insincerely, it's only in the reciting sense that I say anything. As Austin has noted, when I insincerely say 'I promise', strictly speaking I don't promise, but only say I do.[38]

[36] For more shortcomings of the appeal to sincerity, and of a Gricean explanation, see Jay David Atlas, "G. E. Moore's Paradox: Assertion, Self-Reference, the Gödel Sentence and the Ordinary Concept of Belief," MS, Department of Philosophy and Department of Linguistics and Cognitive Science, Pomona College, Claremont, California.

[37] Gottlob Frege, "Thoughts," in *Logical Investigations*, tr. P. T. Geach and R. H. Stoothoff, New Haven: Yale University Press, 1977, pp. 1–30, at p. 8.

[38] "Other Minds," *Philosophical Papers*, 2nd and 3rd edns., pp. 101–103 (1st edn., pp. 69–71). Similarly, Black notes that "[a] man who lies is trying to deceive his hearers by behaving like somebody who makes an honest assertion." Thus "the making of an utterance [in a certain tone of voice] in the absence of the corresponding knowledge or belief is properly treated as a violation of the language" ("Saying and Disbelieving," pp. 116–17). I argue this at length in "Intentionality," §V, and Postscript.

One might reject this account of insincere speech on the ground that it treats sincere and insincere speech differently. And we can have a uniform account of sincere and insincere speech if we adopt the Gricean view on which an utterance means something if one intends one's audience to believe that one believes that thing. But such a view has significant disadvantages. Since insincere utterances don't result from intentional states that have the same content, a uniform treatment cannot explain what it is for one's illocutionary acts to express one's thoughts.[39] So the connection speech has to the thoughts one has must, on such an account, be oblique. And the account must appeal to a context of communication, even though sincere and insincere speech acts alike can occur independently of any such context. It is better not to force sincere and insincere speech to submit to a uniform account, and to accept that genuine illocutionary acts all express corresponding intentional states.[40]

Moore's paradox is absurd because the speech act of saying $\ulcorner p \urcorner$ has the same performance conditions as the speech act of saying $\ulcorner$I think that $p\urcorner$. And that performance-conditional equivalence holds, in turn, because speech acts all express corresponding intentional states. Insincere utterances, that is, utterances that do not express corresponding intentional states, arguably do not involve genuine illocutionary acts. But even if that view about insincere speech is wrong, and we need the qualification about sincerity, the main argument is unaffected. Nor, in that case, would sincerity figure directly in explaining Moore's paradox. What performance conditions an utterance has doesn't depend on whether that utterance is sincere. And it's performance conditions that make Moore's paradox absurd.

What, then, is the status of the regularity about speech acts' expressing corresponding intentional states? It cannot be purely a conceptual matter, a matter of nothing more than the meanings of the relevant words. If it were part of the meaning of 'assert' that assertions express corresponding beliefs, Moore's paradox would not simply have problematic performance conditions, but would be an outright contradiction.[41] Nonetheless, it's somehow a part of the way we automatically think about asserting and other speech acts. The only alternative is that the connection between speech acts and corresponding intentional states is a particularly well-entrenched part of our folk-psychological conceptions.[42]

---

[39] Speech acts can express thoughts, on such an account, in the sense that they express abstract propositions; but the account cannot capture what it is for speech acts to express intentional states.

[40] See "Intentionality," Postscript.

[41] One might argue that, even if 'assert' had such a meaning, the sentence isn't an outright contradiction because it doesn't actually use the word 'assert'. Compare one's at once running and saying 'I'm not moving fast'; there's no contradiction there, even though 'run' in part means to move fast. Similarly with 'It's raining but I'm not asserting it', which purports to combine the act of asserting with the denial that I'm performing that act.

But these considerations are not decisive. If 'assert' meant in part that one thinks the relevant content, then the sentence 'I assert that it's raining but I don't think it is', which uses both 'assert' and 'think', would be a contradiction. That it's instead an instance of Moore's paradox argues against the meaning hypothesis.

[42] It's worth noting that we speak not only about speech acts' expressing intentional states, but also about their expressing abstract thoughts, i.e., propositions. And we sometimes describe both

Those who diagnose Moore's paradox as being conceptually defective sometimes urge that the only alternative to that view is an account on which Moore's paradox "merely . . . depict[s] situations which we take to be extremely unlikely."[43] But here as elsewhere, the dichotomy between the conceptual and the merely empirical misleads. Much that's intuitively impossible runs counter not to established semantic connections, but only deeply entrenched background beliefs about the way things are.

For a speech act to express an intentional state is, in part, for that state to be among the causal factors leading to the speech act. When I say that it's raining, many things causally contribute to my saying it. But if my speech act verbally expresses my thought that it's raining, my having that thought is one of the causal factors that lead to my saying it. I've argued that this connection between speech and thinking is, for us, so strongly second nature that simply saying that *p* inevitably makes it immediately obvious to one that one thinks that *p*. And the very same connection is responsible for there being no coherent performance conditions for asserting Moore's paradox.

IV. MOORE'S PARADOX AND SELF-KNOWLEDGE

It's impossible, even when speaking to oneself, to assert 'It's raining but I don't think it is'. Moreover, it may well seem that it's no less impossible to think that thing assertorically. Just as there are no coherent conditions for asserting 'It's raining but I don't think it is', so, it is plausible to insist, there is no coherent mental analogue of assertibility conditions for thinking 'It's raining but I don't think it is'.

But the tie between speech acts and the intentional states they express cannot by itself explain why it should be impossible to think Moore's paradox. That's because the tie between speech acts and intentional states cannot explain anything about the mental analogue of assertibility conditions. Nor does that tie itself have any suitable mental analogue. Because asserting expresses a corresponding belief, it's impossible to assert anything without believing it. But it's plainly possible to think something without thinking that one thinks it. Indeed, I've urged that this typically happens when our thoughts aren't conscious. So we cannot explain the impossibility of thinking Moore's paradox by appeal to the same factors that explain the impossibility of saying it.

It's sometimes held that a satisfactory account of Moore's paradox must give a uniform explanation both of why we cannot say it and why we cannot think it. This requirement would preclude explaining even the linguistic version of Moore's paradox by reference to performance conditions. Proponents of a uniform treatment typically also insist that semantic contradictoriness somehow underlies Moore's

in the same terms. Thus to say an assertion expresses a particular belief may mean either that it expresses an intentional state or that it has a certain content and an assertoric illocutionary force. Because Moore's paradox is cast in terms of the speaker's intentional states, it's only the expressing of those states that's relevant here.

[43] Jane Heal, "Moore's Paradox: A Wittgensteinian Approach," *Mind*, CIII, 409 (January 1994): 5–24, p. 6. Cf. Albritton's contrast between sentences that involve some "linguistic malpractice" and those which are just very surprising ("Comments," p. 238).

paradox. Since speech acts and intentional states share their content, a uniform explanation will very likely have to appeal to semantic factors.[44] But there seems no reason to adopt this uniformity requirement apart from an insistence on a purely semantic explanation, which in this context is question begging.[45]

It's obvious that we cannot coherently assert Moore's paradox. And I've assumed, with many others, that we also cannot think it. But perhaps that's not all that obvious. How might one try to show that we cannot think something that has the content of Moore's paradox? By trying and failing? By pretheoretic intuition about what we can think? These methods seem unlikely to help.

Our judgments about what we think typically rely on what we are disposed to say.[46] Perhaps, therefore, the judgment that we cannot think things with the content of Moore's paradox is simply a reflection of our judgment that we cannot assert Moore's paradox. And, if that's all the impossibility of thinking Moore's paradox amounts to, a uniform explanation follows automatically. But, because it results from this trivial projection of what we can say onto what we can think, that uniformity is similarly trivial and uninformative. And it can also impose no special constraints on a correct explanation of Moore's paradox.

It is plausible that there is nothing more than this to the impossibility of thinking Moore's paradox. But suppose, instead, that there is something more. How, then,

---

[44] E.g., Heal, who bases her claim that a common explanation is required on her observation that "the idea that someone realises the sentences to be true of him or herself" is just as strange as the idea of somebody's asserting such a sentence (p. 6). But this misrepresents the purely mental version of Moore's paradox; thinking that p is not the same as thinking that the sentence $\ulcorner p \urcorner$ is true of something. One can think a sentence only if one can consider asserting that sentence; one can't think the sentence $\ulcorner p$ but I don't believe it $\urcorner$ is true of oneself, precisely because one can't consider asserting it. By contrast, the mental version of Moore's paradox has to do with my thinking the content that p but I don't believe it, independently of any overt sentences. And it may be possible to do that even if it's impossible to think that the corresponding sentence is true.

It may well be, however, that the temptation to think that the trouble with Moore's paradox in thought is more than just its irrationality derives just from describing the case in this way.

Shoemaker argues that explaining what's wrong with thinking Moore's paradox would automatically explain what's wrong with saying it ("Moore's Paradox and Self-Knowledge," *Philosophical Studies*, 77, 2–3 [March 1995]: 211–228 [reprinted in Shoemaker, *The First-Person Perspective and Other Essays*, Cambridge: Cambridge University Press, 1996, pp. 74–93], §I). But this ignores the possibility, argued for here, that believing Moore's paradox is less defective than asserting it; asserting something may well require more than just believing it.

[45] Koethe advances a different requirement for uniform explanation, using it to reject an explanation of Moore's paradox similar to the one presented here (pp. 303–305). According to Koethe, a satisfactory explanation must cover cases such as $\ulcorner p$ but I don't know that $p \urcorner$. But as noted earlier, it's arguable that such a sentence is not an example of Moore's paradox at all. The sentence $\ulcorner I$ don't know that $p \urcorner$ is notoriously ambiguous, as between $\ulcorner \neg$ (I know that p) $\urcorner$ and $\ulcorner I$ know that $\neg p \urcorner$. Koethe has in mind $\ulcorner p$ but $\neg$ (I know that p) $\urcorner$, which is weaker than $\ulcorner p$ but I don't think that $p \urcorner$; it's likely that it sounds odd not because it isn't assertible, but only because the second conjunct carries the suggestion that the speaker has some doubt about the first conjunct. It's also possible that asserting $\ulcorner p$ but I don't know that $p \urcorner$ sounds odd because the speaker might mean $\ulcorner p$ but I know that $\neg p \urcorner$, which actually implies a contradiction.

[46] See "Content, Interpretation, and Consciousness."

could we explain that impossibility? It seems we would have to appeal to a certain rationality that governs much of our thinking. We can perfectly well have the thought that *p* without thinking that we have it. But it's irrational to think both that *p* and that one doesn't think that *p*. So, if the question arises about whether one thinks that *p* and one does actually think it, it would then be irrational to hold that one doesn't. So it would be irrational to have an assertoric thought that conjoined those two contents.[47] Only insofar as we are rational in this particular way is thinking Moore's paradox absurd.

Rationality does not dictate that whenever one thinks something the question will arise about whether one thinks it; much of our thinking occurs without any such reflection, and much that occurs that way is rational. And, when that question doesn't arise, it's generally possible to think that *p* without thinking that one thinks it. The first-order thought will presumably then not be conscious. But insofar as we are rational in this way, if one has some particular thought and it's possible for the question to arise as to whether one has it, it must also be possible for the relevant higher-order thought to occur. As Kant insisted, in the case of rational beings "the representation '*I think*' . . . must be capable of accompanying all other representations. . . ."[48]

Sydney Shoemaker has argued for an even stronger connection between rationality and our having thoughts about our thoughts. Adopting the functionalist view that believing and desiring are defined in terms of certain connections with actions, sensory input, and other mental states, Shoemaker argues that these connections actually constitute a certain minimal rationality. Moreover, he urges that beliefs and desires do more than simply cause the behavior with which they're rationally connected; they also "rationalize" that behavior. And to rationalize a course of action, beliefs and desires must refer to it.

But rationality applies not merely to overt actions, but also to the very mental activities of believing and desiring, themselves. Just as having certain beliefs and desires may make a certain course of action rational, so too it may be rational to adopt certain beliefs and desires given that we have certain others. But as with overt courses of action, we do not count as rational a person's adopting or changing certain beliefs or desires unless others of the person's beliefs and desires rationalize that adoption or change of beliefs and desires. And the beliefs and desires that do this rationalizing will have to refer to those which are rationally adopted. The rational fixation of beliefs and desires requires one to have higher-order beliefs about the first-order beliefs and

---

[47] When the two contents are thought separately, one's thought that *p* might not be conscious, and one might then mistakenly think that one doesn't think that *p*. But that's irrelevant, since thinking Moore's paradox requires combining the contents in one conjunctive thought.

[48] Immanuel Kant, *Critique of Pure Reason*, tr. and ed. Paul Guyer and Allen W. Wood, Cambridge: Cambridge University Press, 1998, B132.

In §I, I argued that the factors that explain Moore's paradox also underlie the *cogito*. But Descartes's demon can cause doubt by undermining rationality. So, if the impossibility of thinking Moore's paradox rests on rationality and the *cogito* relies on the same factors, then there is some question about whether the *cogito* can, after all, effectively resist the demon.

desires one rationally fixes. Accordingly, such rationality cannot occur without our being conscious of our first-order beliefs and desires.[49]

As Shoemaker notes, one could deny that rationality in the adopting of beliefs and desires is due to explicit rationalizing by higher-order beliefs and desires. Perhaps rationality here requires only that the causal relations that hold among our first-order beliefs and desires conform to rational standards.[50] It's far more plausible that beliefs and desires are states whose causal ties tend to conform to patterns we count as rational than that they are definitionally states whose rational fixation requires the causal influence of higher-order beliefs and desires. Perhaps, then, rationality doesn't require us to have higher-order beliefs.

But even if rationalization of the sort Shoemaker describes does occur, there's another difficulty with his argument. Beliefs and desires are sometimes occurrent, but often they're dispositional. In their dispositional versions, belief and desire are simply dispositions to be in the relevant occurrent intentional states. And the beliefs and desires that rationalize actions will often be dispositional in just this way. But simply being disposed to have an occurrent belief or desire about something doesn't make us conscious of that thing. So, when the higher-order thoughts and desires that rationalize our adoption of certain first-order beliefs and desires are merely dispositional, they won't make us conscious of the first-order states. So they won't make those first-order states conscious states. Moreover, there could be creatures for which that's how it always happens. In the human case, the higher-order beliefs and desires that rationalize other intentional states are often occurrent. But rationality would not be compromised if the higher-order states were always dispositional. Intentional states can be rational without being conscious; indeed a creature could exist for which all rationality among its intentional states was that way.[51]

Connections between rationality and consciousness to one side, Shoemaker has developed an ingenious and probing argument that links Moore's paradox to one's having first-person access to one's mental states.[52] He defines as self-blind a being that has our concepts of mental phenomena and can therefore ascribe to itself mental states, but which has no first-person access to its mental states. A self-blind individual could come to believe that it's in some particular mental state, but only in a characteristically third-person way. Such an individual, moreover, might be presented with highly compelling third-person evidence both that it's raining and also that it doesn't believe that it's raining. Since the self-blind creature lacks any first-person access, this

[49] "On Knowing One's Own Mind," pp. 188–191; see also "Rationality and Self-Consciousness," p. 126, and "First-Person Access," *Philosophical Perspectives: Action Theory and Philosophy of Mind*, 4 (1990): 187–142, p. 206.

[50] "On Knowing One's Own Mind," p. 193.

[51] If self-knowledge could be latent (see n. 22), then rationalizing dispositional states might yield latent self-knowledge. It's likely, however, that only active, conscious knowing can count as self-knowledge. Similarly, nothing counts as first-person access unless we're conscious of having the access.

[52] The most extensive development of this provocative argument occurs in "On Knowing One's Own Mind," esp. pp. 193–198.

third-person evidence would give it good reason to assert 'It's raining but I don't think it is'.

Shoemaker argues, however, that Moore's paradox would be absurd even for a self-blind creature, so defined. He urges that such an individual, simply by being conceptually unimpaired, would recognize the absurdity of Moore's paradox; on my account, that would mean recognizing the performance-conditional connections between saying that *p* and saying ⌜I think that *p*⌝. But then, Shoemaker urges, our ostensibly self-blind individual would be indistinguishable from somebody that does have ordinary first-person access. And if this is so, self-blindness is not a possibility, after all; any creature with our mental concepts and the ability to ascribe mental states to itself in a third-person way would be able to do so in a first-person way as well. First-person access to one's own mental states would follow from that conceptual capacity alone.[53]

For creatures relevantly like us, all verbally expressed intentional states are conscious. So any such creatures will have first-person access to all their verbally expressed intentional states. The factors that explain Moore's paradox, I've argued, also underlie this connection between verbal expression and consciousness. But very few of our intentional states are actually expressed in speech; indeed, few come close to being so expressed. Moore's paradox, moreover, arguably pertains in the first instance to whether certain speech acts can be performed. So even if a self-blind creature does have first-person access to its verbally expressed intentional states, it's unclear why merely recognizing the absurdity of Moore's paradox would extend such first-person access to intentional states that aren't expressed in speech.

Moreover, even a self-blind individual that recognized the absurdity of Moore's paradox might not be like us in the ways required for it to have first-person access even to its verbally expressed intentional states. By the definition of self-blindness, such an individual would have our mental concepts, and be able to believe of itself that it's in various mental states. And, as Shoemaker's argument makes clear, it will have the ability to express its intentional states in speech. But on the argument I put forth earlier, that's not sufficient for all the self-blind individual's verbally expressed thoughts to be conscious. It's also necessary that the performance-conditional equivalence between saying that *p* and saying ⌜I think that *p*⌝ is second nature to that individual.

This is important because, if that connection is not second nature, the access an individual has to its verbally expressed thoughts will be based on some conscious inference. And access that's thus consciously mediated would be characteristically third-person access, even if it's access to the individual's own states. It would therefore not make one's verbally expressed thoughts conscious. And since genuine self-knowledge requires conscious first-person access, it would not result in self-knowledge, either.

---

[53] This conclusion recalls a remark of Wittgenstein's, though he and Shoemaker rely on very different arguments. Wittgenstein claimed that "it is possible to think out circumstances in which ... someone [could] say 'It is raining and I don't believe it'." Such a situation, he thought, would be one in which one could say: "Judging from what I say, *this* is what I believe." But I could say this, he insisted, only if my "behaviour indicat[ed] that two people were speaking through my mouth" (*Philosophical Investigations*, II, 192). In effect, he held, one cannot be a unified individual and also be in a position to say such a thing, and thus to judge from the outside what beliefs one has.

Shoemaker often writes as though sensitivity to the absurdity of Moore's paradox would be a direct result of having unimpaired conceptual capacities.[54] If so, the relevant performance-conditional equivalences would presumably be conceptual truths; they would thus be second nature for us. I've argued against this idea. It's difficult to see how to explain Moore's paradox by appeal to the meanings of words like 'assert' and 'think' without construing it as an outright contradiction. It's more plausible, I think, to see the connection between asserting and believing as part of our folk-psychological knowledge about these things—part of a folk theory so well-entrenched as to constitute commonly shared background knowledge. The relevant conceptual competence is necessary, but not sufficient, for the performance-conditional equivalence. If this is right, our self-blind creature's access to its own mental states would be mediated by a conscious inference that relies on the relevant folk-theoretic connection.

But even if the relevant tie between thinking and asserting were an exclusively conceptual matter and not part of folk theory, our self-blind individual might still have to rely on some conscious inference for access to its own mental states. Conceptual truths function in effect as null premises in inference. So any inference that relies solely on such truths would be automatic. But the self-blind individual's inference would rely on more than the conceptual connection between speech and thinking. That inference would go from that conceptual connection plus the fact that the individual asserts that p to that individual's thinking that p. Indeed, Shoemaker sometimes seems to envisage the need for some conscious inference. "[I]t ought to possible," he writes at one point, "to get [our self-blind creature] to recognize that the assertive utterance of Moore-paradoxical sentences involves some sort of logical impropriety."[55]

Perhaps, however, the relevant inference would after a time come to be second nature, and would therefore no longer be conscious. The resulting access that the self-blind individual would have to at least those of its thoughts which are verbally expressed would then not be based on any inference of which it was aware. Such access would therefore be indistinguishable from the first-person access we have to our conscious states. But the concept of self-blindness does not ensure that the required inference would ever stop being conscious. And if it didn't, the self-blind individual would continue to be limited to having only third-person access to its mental states.

Shoemaker argues that any individual with mental concepts "will be aware of having [mental states] when it does, or at least will become aware of this under certain conditions (e.g., if it reflects on the matter)."[56] Shoemaker may be assuming here that "reflect[ing] on the matter" is enough to raise the question whether one is in a certain

---

[54] E.g., "Rationality and Self-Consciousness," p. 134.

[55] "On Knowing One's Own Mind," p. 194. Elsewhere he describes a plainly conscious inference that would take the putatively self-blind individual from believing that p to having a motive for saying, indifferently, 'p' or 'I believe that p'. Arguably, Shoemaker begs the question there, since the individual's conscious reasoning from its having the belief that p presumably presupposes that the belief is conscious.

[56] "On Knowing One's Own Mind," p. 19.

280 Consciousness, Expression, and Interpretation

mental state. And that, along with the particular kind of rationality discussed earlier in this section would be sufficient for one to be aware that one is in that state.

But reflection will not, in general, raise the question of whether one is in a particular mental state unless, independently of reflection, one already has access to the state. If one's access to the state is characteristically third-person, reflection cannot transform that into first-person access, since that would mean making one unaware of the relevant third-person considerations. And it begs the question at hand to invoke reflection if one must already have first-person access.

According to Wittgenstein, Moore's paradox is absurd because "the statement 'I believe it's going to rain' has a meaning like, that is to say a use like, 'It's going to rain'."[57] This is in effect to construe the speech act 'I believe it's going to rain' as expressing my belief that it's going to rain, rather than as reporting that belief. On this account, Moore's paradox is absurd because it is a straightforward contradiction, rather than because of anything about the conditions for using such sentences to perform successful speech acts.

This view about Moore's paradox can be seen as having consequences for self-knowledge. If I make no claim about my mental states when I say 'I believe it's raining', my remark cannot be challenged on that score. That fits with the air of incorrigibility such remarks have, even though they would then not actually express any knowledge about one's beliefs.[58]

But this view notoriously faces serious difficulties. On it, for example, I cannot literally deny another person's claim that I don't believe that it's raining.[59] Shoemaker's argument, by contrast, appeals to no such diagnosis, and he countenances both genuine self-knowledge and the semantic difference between ⌈p⌉ and ⌈I think that p⌉. Still, it's not clear exactly what the semantic difference between these two amounts to if conceptual competence alone is enough to take one automatically from one to the other.

I've argued that Moore's paradox sheds light on our first-person access by pointing to those factors which explain why all verbally expressed intentional states are conscious. But as I also mentioned, there's an exception to that regularity. Suppose I assert 'I think it's raining'. Speech acts express intentional states with the same content;[60] so here my speech act expresses my thought that I think it's raining. It expresses, that is, a higher-order thought to the effect that I have the thought that

---

[57] *Philosophical Investigations*, II, p. 190. Indeed, Wittgenstein understands Moore's paradox exclusively in terms of use: "Moore's paradox can be put like this: the expression 'I believe that this is the case' is used like the assertion 'This is the case'; and yet the *hypothesis* that I believe this is the case is not used like the hypothesis that this is the case" (p. 190). Cf. *Remarks on the Philosophy of Psychology*, I, pp. 91–96.

[58] Cf. Wittgenstein's better-known claim that saying 'I'm in pain', like crying 'Ouch', expresses rather than reports my pain (*Philosophical Investigations*, §§244, 256). And if no speech act reports our states of pain, we cannot be said to have knowledge of them (§246). Here the sense of incorrigibility is stronger, since one can deny 'It's raining', but not 'Ouch'.

[59] Or that I'm not in pain. Moreover, as noted above, collapsing the distinction between reporting and expressing leads to construing Moore's paradox as an outright contradiction.

[60] Or roughly the same; see "Content, Interpretation, and Consciousness," §§11–111.

it's raining. But that's not the thought I'm typically aware of having when I say I think it's raining. Rather, when I say I think it's raining, the thought I'm ordinarily conscious of is my first-order thought that it's raining. When I perform a speech act whose content is that I'm in some intentional state, the state that's conscious is not the state my speech act expresses, but the state it reports. It's not surprising that the thought I report is conscious, since a state's being conscious coincides with my being able to report it noninferentially, and if I so report it I plainly can. The question is why the higher-order thought that my report expresses isn't also conscious.

This is an important exception. It's doubtless this kind of case that has encouraged some to assimilate the reporting of mental states to the verbal expression of those states. As I remarked earlier, Moore's paradox helps resist that tendency; if reports and verbal expressions weren't different, Moore's paradox would be an actual contradiction, which it isn't. Still the exception demands explanation. That, however, is a task for another occasion.[61]

---

[61] I address this question in "Why Are Verbally Expressed Thoughts Conscious?"

This is an expanded version of a paper read at the American Philosophical Association, Pacific Division, Symposium on Moore's Paradox and Self-Knowledge, April 1994, in Los Angeles. The shorter version appears, slightly revised, in *Philosophical Studies* 77, 2–3 (1994 Pacific Division APA special issue) (March 1995), pp. 195–209, under the title "Self-Knowledge and Moore's Paradox," along with the contributions of the other symposiasts, Sydney Shoemaker, "Moore's Paradox and Self-Knowledge," pp. 211–228, and Rogers Albritton, "Comments on Moore's Paradox and Self-Knowledge," pp. 229–239.

[The present version is expanded, in turn, from the longer version that appeared in *Philosophical Perspectives*, 9 (1995): 313–333. Added 2005.]

10

Why Are Verbally Expressed Thoughts Conscious?

I. THE PROBLEM

Suppose I think it's going to rain, and leaving my home I take my umbrella. My act of taking my umbrella expresses my thought that it's going to rain.

One way this can all happen is that I consciously think it's going to rain and deliberately get my umbrella to take with me. But it need not happen this way. I may be late and preoccupied with what I must do that day. So I may reach for my umbrella and take it with me automatically—without thinking, as we might say. In this case I may not even be aware of my thought that it's going to rain; it may be a nonconscious thought. Nonconscious thoughts often cause appropriate actions, and when that happens the action typically expresses the thought that causes it.[1]

Now suppose again that I think it's going to rain. But this time, instead of performing some action, I simply tell you that it's going to rain. Here my thought that it's going to rain is expressed not by any action, but by my speech act. I may even tell you this in an offhand, automatic way; still, if I express my thought by performing some speech act, the thought I thereby express is always a conscious thought.[2] In this respect, verbally expressing a thought differs strikingly from expressing that thought nonverbally. However offhandedly I may tell you that it's going to rain, the thought I thereby express is always a conscious thought.

There seems, however, to be an exception to this generalization. Let's alter the case so that I tell you not that it's going to rain, but rather that I think it's going to. It is natural to take this speech act to express a certain sort of higher-order thought, a thought whose content is about another thought. Here, my speech act expresses not the thought that it will rain, but rather the thought that I think that it will rain.

---

[1] Whenever a piece of nonverbal behavior expresses a thought, it's appropriate to engage in the nonverbal behavior, given the thought and the thought's causing the behavior. But these two conditions may well not be sufficient for a piece of behavior to express a thought; perhaps not every appropriate action caused by a thought expresses that thought. It won't matter to the following argument what additional conditions might be needed for a nonverbal action to express a thought.

[2] This commonsense generalization has largely gone unnoticed; D. H. Mellor does, however, observe that this connection holds for the special case of sincere speech acts. See D. H. Mellor, "Conscious Belief," *Proceedings of the Aristotelian Society*, New Series, LXXXVIII (1977–8): 87–101, p. 96; and "Consciousness and Degrees of Belief," in Mellor, ed., *Prospects for Pragmatism: Essays in Memory of F. P. Ramsey*, Cambridge: Cambridge University Press, 1980, 139–173, p. 148.

It might of course be that my higher-order thought—my thought, that is, that I think it's going to rain—is a conscious thought. But it seems clear that in this kind of case it need not be. We often say that we think it's going to rain even when we are wholly unaware of having any such higher-order thought. Verbally expressing such higher-order thoughts seems thus to be an exception to the generalization that, whenever I express my thoughts in speech, those thoughts are conscious thoughts.

These observations apply not only to assertoric thoughts, such as the thought that it's going to rain, but to any intentional state, whatever its mental attitude. Thus the observations apply, for example, to doubting, desiring, expecting, anticipating, wondering, suspecting, and the like.

Why must verbally expressed intentional states be conscious? And why does this generalization hold for the verbal expression of intentional states, but not when those states are expressed solely by nonverbal means? Why, finally, does the generalization break down in the case of higher-order thoughts of the sort just described? It is these questions I address in this paper.

In section II, I consider a naive answer to these questions and argue that it is inadequate. I conclude that the facts just noted demand an explanation that relies essentially on the nature of consciousness and the verbal expression of thoughts. In section III, then, I advance a theory of what it is for a mental state to be a conscious state, and an argument for that theory that reveals important connections between such consciousness and verbal expression. In section IV, I show how this theory, and the argument that supports it, allow us to explain all three observations that connect the expression of thought with consciousness. I conclude in section V by placing that solution in the context of some general observations about consciousness, thought, and speech.

II. THE NAIVE ANSWER

One commonsense reaction to these observations may be that they are due simply to the way one's speech directs attention to one's own thoughts. When I say something, my very act of saying it calls attention to the fact that I think that thing. Even if my thought that it's going to rain had not been a conscious thought, my saying it's going to rain would have made it conscious by directing my attention to what it is I think. On this account, that is all there is to the connection between my saying something and the consciousness of the thought I thereby express.

This reply suggests answers to the other two questions as well. The reason my thoughts need not be conscious even when I express them nonverbally is that nonverbal behavior does not always direct my attention to the thought that lies behind the behavior. And the reason my higher-order thoughts may fail to be conscious even when I express them verbally is that my saying that I think it's going to rain normally calls attention not to my higher-order thought, but to the thought that higher-order thought is about. Typically, my saying that I think it's going to rain calls attention to my first-order thought that it's going to rain, rather than to my higher-order thought that I think it's going to rain.

This last idea suggests, moreover, that we may have falsely posed the problem about the expressing of higher-order thoughts. Saying it's going to rain normally has the same force as saying that I think it's going to, setting aside whatever slight additional hesitation the second formulation may convey. Bracketing such hesitation, which won't matter in what follows, the two assertions have what we can call the same performance conditions—the same conditions in which it would be appropriate to make the assertions. So perhaps the two remarks express the very same thought: the thought that it's going to rain. If so, then when I say 'I think it's going to rain', I do not, after all, express my thought that I think it's going to rain, but instead express only my thought that it's going to rain. There is then no problem about why I can say I think it's going to rain even when I have no relevant conscious higher-order thought.

These naive answers are inviting, and have the merit of proceeding independently of any special theories about consciousness, verbal expression, and their connection. And as a general rule, the more we can explain while remaining neutral about potentially controversial theories, the better.

Nonetheless, the naive answers will not do. After all, why does speaking call attention to the thought expressed, while nonverbally expressing the thought does not? Unless we can explain that, the naive approach does little more than postpone giving an informative solution to our problem. Indeed, in the absence of such further explanation, it may well be that we have simply redescribed in different terms the observations with which we began. After all, what is there, in the current context, to something's calling attention to a thought other than something's making that thought conscious? The naive answer might help if recasting things in terms of directing attention to the thought itself suggested a substantive explanation. But it's notorious that what is involved in shifting attention is at best no more tractable than consciousness.

As with nonverbal actions, we perform speech acts in ways that range from relatively automatically to fully deliberately, and the verbal expressing of intentional states is no exception. If one expresses an intentional state in a relatively deliberate way, that may indeed go hand in hand with one's shifting one's attention to that intentional state. But most speech acts that verbally express our intentional states are far from deliberate. Rather, they occur without any attentive focus on the thought we are expressing; ordinarily if we are concentrating on anything at all, it's the subject matter at hand, and perhaps the goal of informing, convincing, or otherwise affecting another person. So there's no reason to expect that such nondeliberate, automatic speech acts will call attention to the thoughts they express. But verbally expressed thoughts are conscious whether the verbal expressing is deliberate or instead automatic and unthinking.

An advocate of the naive answer might reply that speech acts are never as automatic as nonverbal behavior often is. We do sometimes perform nonverbal actions without being aware of doing so, but when we say something we are invariably conscious of saying that thing. So we are conscious, at least to some degree, of the thought our speech act expresses. But this again simply puts off the real explanation; why are we always conscious of our speech acts? Speech acts are, after all, kinds of actions; they are actions of asserting, asking, demanding, predicting, retracting, and the like. If we can perform nonverbal actions, such as taking umbrellas, without being conscious of doing so, why isn't that also possible for verbal actions?

These considerations suggest that no naive answer of the sort just proposed will do. We need an account that goes deeply enough into the nature of expressing to reflect the relevant difference between verbal and nonverbal expressions. And we need an account that goes far enough into the connection between expressing and consciousness to show how the difference between the two kinds of expressing bears on what we must in each case be conscious of.

The naive answer fails also to explain why the higher-order case, in which one says that one thinks that it's going to rain, rather than simply that it's going to rain, is an exception. We cannot explain why verbally expressed thoughts are conscious but not when expressed nonverbally by appeal to whether or not the expression calls attention to the thought. So we cannot then go on to invoke the more specific explanation that my thinking it's going to rain calls attention to my thought that it will rain, rather than to my higher-order thought that I think it will.

But in this case there is a related naive answer sketched earlier. Perhaps saying 'I think it's going to rain' does not, after all, express the higher-order thought that I think it's going to rain, but rather expresses only the first-order thought that it's going to rain. Can this view be sustained?

As already noted, the remarks 'It's going to rain' and 'I think it's going to rain' have the same performance conditions; any circumstances in which it would be appropriate to say one thing would also be circumstances in which it would be appropriate to say the other. But the two do not at all have the same semantic properties. They mean different things, and have distinct truth conditions.

Similar observations hold of the thought that it's going to rain and the thought that I think it is. The circumstances in which it would be appropriate to think these two thoughts are the same; in effect, the mental analogue of performance conditions for speech acts is the same for the two thoughts. But, as with the corresponding speech acts, the two thoughts have distinct truth conditions. And on any commonsense account their content is distinct.[3] Moreover, the distinct contents of this pair of thoughts presumably matches the semantic properties of the corresponding pair of speech acts. This gives us reason to insist that the remark 'I think that it's going to rain' expresses not the thought that it's going to rain, but the thought that I think it will.

---

[3] Since we are evaluating the naive response to our problem, it is theoretically uninformed folk psychology that matters here.

Brian Loar has argued that the concepts in such a first-order thought will occur in the corresponding higher-order thought, and concludes that the conceptual role of the lower-order thought is included in that of the higher-order thought ("Subjective Intentionality," *Philosophical Topics*, XV, 1 [Spring 1987]: 89–124, p. 103). But a higher-order thought will include more concepts than the first-order thought; it will, in addition to those they share, have concepts that pertain to one's having a thought. So the conceptual role of the higher-order thought will be distinct from that of the first-order thought it is about.

There is another way to reach the same result. When a speech act expresses an intentional state, not only are the contents of both the state and the speech act the same; the speech act and thought also have the same force. Both, that is, will involve suspecting, denying, wondering, affirming, doubting, and the like. Whenever a speech act expresses an intentional state, the illocutionary force of the speech act corresponds to the mental attitude of that intentional state.

When the thought in question is assertoric, considerations of force do not matter; the thought that it's going to rain and the thought that I think it is have the same force. But nonassertoric intentional states are expressed by speech acts that have the corresponding, nonassertoric illocutionary force. Suppose I doubt it's going to rain. If I then say 'I doubt it will rain', my speech act is assertoric; it asserts that I doubt that thing. My speech act must therefore express the assertoric thought that I doubt it will rain; it cannot express the nonassertoric intentional state of my doubting. So we cannot explain why verbally expressed higher-order thoughts need not be conscious by insisting that ostensibly higher-order speech acts do not actually express higher-order thoughts, but only lower-level thoughts.

Every speech act expresses an intentional state that has the same content and a mental attitude that corresponds to that speech act's illocutionary force. Indeed, it's typical to understand the content and mental attitude of intentional states by reference to the content and illocutionary force of the speech act that would best express those states. The correspondence of the content and illocutionary force of speech acts with the content and mental attitude of intentional states is built into the very way we ascribe content to intentional states.[4]

III. CONSCIOUSNESS AND HIGHER-ORDER THOUGHTS

Since the naive answer fails, we must try to find a more probing explanation of both the generalization about the consciousness and verbal expression of thoughts and the exception about higher-order thoughts. The best hope for this is an explanation that addresses what it is for a thought to be conscious. Only then can we expect to understand the connection between verbally expressing a thought and that thought's being conscious.

Conscious states are mental states we are conscious of. There are two models for what it is to be conscious of things; we are conscious of something when we sense that thing and when we think about it as being present. The sensory model creates

---

[4] For more on the way the properties of speech acts correspond to those of the intentional states they express, see "Intentionality," ch. 3 in this volume. For more on the way we interpret the mental properties of intentional states by reference to the speech acts that express them, see "Content, Interpretation, and Consciousness," ch. 12 in this volume.

Zeno Vendler has an extensive and highly illuminating treatment of the parallel between intentional states and the speech acts that express them in *Res Cogitans*, Ithaca, New York: Cornell University Press, 1972, ch. 3. The idea that we understand the intentional character of mental states in terms of the semantic character of the speech acts that would express those states is arguably the best explanation of the striking parallels that Vendler details.

unnecessary difficulties in this context; sensing always involves some mental quality, and being conscious of a mental state involves no qualities above and beyond those of the mental state we are conscious of. The only alternative is that a mental state's being conscious consists in its being accompanied by a *higher-order thought* (HOT) to the effect that one is in that very mental state. These HOTs must be assertoric, since nonassertoric intentional states do not, by themselves, make one conscious of things. And they must also be occurrent, since having a dispositional thought is being disposed to have an occurrent thought, and merely being thus disposed again doesn't make one conscious of anything.[5]

A compelling argument is available that supports this conclusion. This argument relies on independently defensible premises about what it is to express and to report a thought.[6] So the argument points the way to building a bridge between consciousness and the expressing of thoughts. I develop the argument here in three steps, each of which connects with the issues raised above about expressing one's intentional states.

Expressing One's Mind

I begin with the connection between speech acts and the intentional states they express. Sincere, meaningful speech acts invariably express intentional states. Whenever one says something sincerely and meaningfully, one is in some intentional state that has the very same content as one's speech act (or at least very similar; see chapter 12). Moreover, as noted in section II, the illocutionary force of every sincere speech act corresponds to the mental attitude of the intentional state expressed by that speech act. But it is sameness of content that matters for our purposes here.

The well-known phenomenon of Moore's paradox provides evidence for the conclusion that no sincere speech act can occur unless the speaker is in an intentional state whose content coincides with that of the speech act. As Moore noted, sentences such as 'It's raining but I don't think so', though not contradictory, are nonetheless absurd.[7] They are absurd in that no such sentence can be used to perform a coherent speech act. Such a sentence has no coherent performance conditions that would allow

---

[5] In "Two Concepts of Consciousness" (ch. 1 in this volume) I argue that this kind of account can save our folk-psychological intuitions at least as successfully as any alternative theory; in "A Theory of Consciousness" (in *The Nature of Consciousness: Philosophical Debates*, ed. Ned Block, Owen Flanagan, and Güven Güzeldere, Cambridge, Massachusetts: MIT Press/Bradford Books, 1997, pp. 729–753) and "Explaining Consciousness" (in *Philosophy of Mind: Classical and Contemporary Readings*, ed. David J. Chalmers, New York: Oxford University Press, 2002, pp. 406–421), I show that independently well-motivated constraints on a satisfactory theory require us to adopt this one. In "Varieties of Higher-Order Theory," in *Higher-Order Theories of Consciousness*, ed. Rocco J. Gennaro, Amsterdam and Philadelphia: John Benjamins Publishers, 2004, pp. 17–44, I argue that this account is superior to other higher-order theories of consciousness.

Mellor puts forth a somewhat similar account ("Conscious Belief" and "Consciousness and Degrees of Belief"), though he argues that it applies only to conscious believing, and not to mental states generally.

[6] As above, I use 'thought' generically to cover all intentional states, regardless of their mental attitude.

[7] G. E. Moore, "A Reply to My Critics," in *The Philosophy of G. E. Moore*, ed. Paul Arthur Schilpp, New York: Tudor, 1942, 2nd edn. 1952, pp. 533–677, at p. 543; and "Russell's 'Theory

for the performing of any speech act. We can best explain this lack of performance conditions on the assumption that all sincere speech acts express intentional states that have the same force and intentional content. The sentence 'It's raining but I don't think so' is absurd because the corresponding speech act would purport to express an intentional state that it's raining and also purport to deny that one is in that state.[8]

It is even arguable that, unless a speech act expresses a thought that the speaker actually has, it is a degenerate kind of speech. Insincere speech, like lines uttered in play acting, is basically performed by rote; in both kinds of case one pretends to perform normal speech acts. When I play the part of Hamlet, the lines I utter express no actual thoughts; rather, the audience and I both pretend that my lines express thoughts of my fictional character. Similarly, when I speak insincerely, I pretend that my utterances express the thoughts of the fictional person I am pretending to be—roughly, a person just like me except for believing the things I pretend to say.[9] This is why, in insincere speech and play acting alike, one needs to depend more on one's exact words to remember what one has said, since there is no thought behind

---

of Descriptions'," in *The Philosophy of Bertrand Russell*, ed. Paul Arthur Schilpp, New York: Tudor Publishing Company, 1944, pp. 175–226, at p. 204.

See also "Moore's Paradox and Consciousness," ch. 8 in this volume, my "Moore's Paradox and Crimmins's Case," *Analysis*, 62, 2 (April 2002): 167–171, and "The *Meditations* and Moore's Paradox," MS.

[8] Parallel remarks hold for speech acts that have nonassertoric illocutionary force; I cannot, e.g., coherently say 'Thank you, but I am not grateful'. (*Pace* Mellor, who claims that Moore's paradox "has no analogue for the other attitudes" [D. H. Mellor, "What Is Computational Psychology?", *Proceedings of the Aristotelian Society*, Supplementary Volume LVIII (1984): 37–53, p. 38]. It is notable that Mellor similarly restricts his account of consciousness to the case of believing; see n. 5, above.)

One might instead seek to explain the absurdity of these sentences by appeal to Gricean considerations. On a Gricean view, my sincerely saying something involves my intending that my hearer believe that I believe what I say. (See, e.g., Paul Grice, "Utterer's Meaning and Intentions," *The Philosophical Review*, LXXVIII, 2 [April 1969]: 147–177.) So I cannot at once sincerely say both that *p* and that I do not believe it. (See Mellor, "Conscious Belief," pp. 96–7; cf. "Consciousness and Degrees of Belief," p. 148.) But Moore's paradox is absurd independent of any context of communication; it is absurd because it lacks coherent conditions of assertibility. (For more on the Gricean view, see the Postscript to "Intentionality.")

If I say it's raining and go on to say I don't believe it, I betray my insincerity. One might object that this is all that goes wrong in Moore's paradox. Moore himself offered such a diagnosis at one point ("A Reply to My Critics," pp. 542–3). But that cannot be correct, since there is in general nothing problematic about one's speaking insincerely in ways that betray one's insincerity. One can even do so knowingly. This underscores the inadequacy of a Gricean explanation, since one could not on that account knowingly betray the insincerity of one's speech.

[9] Such pretend speech is, in Wilfrid Sellars' useful phrase, produced parrotingly ("Notes on Intentionality," *The Journal of Philosophy*, LXI, 21 [November 12, 1964], 655–665, p. 657).

On these issues, see "Intentionality," esp. §§II, III, V, and the Postscript.

Bruce Bridgeman has urged (personal communication) that there may be types of speech production intermediate between genuine speech acts and pretend speech, as when one reads a newspaper article aloud to somebody else. But the sense that such cases are intermediate very likely results simply from their occurring in both ways; though reading a newspaper aloud to somebody is sometimes merely parroting, it also sometimes occurs with genuine illocutionary force.

those words to rely on. But this point is unnecessary for the present argument. No more is needed here than that, when speech is sincere, it expresses intentional states whose content matches that of our speech acts.

Slips of the tongue and Freudian parapraxis may seem, however, to be exceptions to this rule. Such slips sometimes reveal thoughts markedly different from what one consciously meant to say, and perhaps when that happens the content of the spoken slip differs from that of the thought it expresses. But such slips are not counterexamples to the generalization that speech acts express thoughts with the same content. When such a slip occurs, the consciously intended content that matches the semantic meaning of the uncorrupted speech act differs from the content of the thought the slip reveals. But a remark can reveal a thought without thereby verbally expressing it, as when one's tone of voice in saying something reveals a thought distinct from, or even unconnected to, the thought that remark expresses. Slips of the tongue are like that; they reveal thoughts beyond those they express. A slip may sometimes reveal a thought the speaker consciously intended to conceal, and in some cases of that sort the remark may verbally express no intentional state at all, but be a straightforward case of insincere speech.[10]

Expressing and Reporting

The second step in the argument invokes the HOTs described earlier. Expressing is the most common and straightforward way to convey our intentional states to others. If I say 'The door is open', my speech act conveys my thought that the door is open by expressing that very state. But this is not the only way to convey my thought. I could convey it equally well by saying instead 'I think the door is open'. The same goes for intentional states with mental attitudes other than that of belief. I can, for example, communicate my suspicion that the door is open either by expressing my suspicion or by explicitly telling you about it. Saying that the door may well be open would express the suspicion, whereas saying that I suspect the door is open would explicitly report that I have that suspicion.[11]

It is easy to conflate these two distinct ways of conveying our intentional states to others. As noted in section II, the performance conditions for asserting that *p* are the same as those for telling you that I think that *p*. Bracketing whatever hesitation one form of words may sometimes suggest, any conditions in which it's appropriate to

---

[10] For more on parapraxis, see "Consciousness and Its Expression," ch. 11 in this volume, §V.

[11] On this distinction, see, e.g., Sellars, "Empiricism and the Philosophy of Mind," in his *Science, Perception and Reality*, London: Routledge & Kegan Paul, 1963, pp. 127–196, §§viii, x, and xv, and Daniel C. Dennett, *Content and Consciousness*, New York: Humanities Press, 1969, §13.

When subjects in psychological experiments are instructed to respond with particular nonverbal signals if they perceive something, it's not always obvious whether that nonverbal response constitutes a report of such perceiving or merely expresses it. Consider Anthony J. Marcel's report of hemianopic subjects who responded most sensitively to stimuli with an eye blink, less so with a button press, and least sensitively when they responded verbally ("Slippage in the Unity of Consciousness," in Gregory R. Bock and Joan Marsh, eds., *Experimental and Theoretical Studies of Consciousness*, Ciba Foundation Symposium No. 174, Chichester: John Wiley & Sons, 1993, pp. 168–186). It's tempting to explain this divergence by supposing that the eye blinks and button presses functioned as nonverbal expressions of subjects' perceptions, whereas the verbal responses were explicit reports.

say one thing would equally be conditions in which it's appropriate to say the other. Once again, the point generalizes beyond the case of assertoric intentional states. The conditions for appropriately expressing doubt, suspicion, wonder, and other mental attitudes are the same as those for explicitly reporting that one is in those intentional states.

Unreflective, colloquial usage may seem to suggest that when I say ⌜I think that *p*⌝, my speech act simply expresses my thought that *p*, and not my thought that I think that *p*. If I say 'I think it's raining', we normally take my speech act to be about the weather, not just about my mind. And if I say 'I doubt it's raining', doesn't my speech act express that doubt, rather than a HOT that I have the doubt? Similarly, it may seem that saying 'I choose this one' and 'I sympathize with you' express one's choice and sympathy, rather than merely reporting those states.

But these intuitions result from focusing solely on performance conditions, to the exclusion of the semantic properties of sentences.[12] As noted above, the speech acts one performs with the sentences 'I think that it's raining' and 'I doubt that it's raining' are performance conditionally equivalent to those one performs with the sentences 'It's raining' and 'It's probably not raining'. But these pairs plainly have distinct truth conditions, and so are semantically distinct. Similarly with the pairs 'I choose this one' and 'I'll take this one', and 'I sympathize with you' and 'That's too bad'.[13]

Once again Moore's paradox helps. Sentences such as 'It's raining but I don't think so' and 'It's surely raining but I doubt it' reveal the relevant differences in truth conditions. More generally, if the sentence ⌜*p*, but I don't think that *p*⌝ could be used to perform a coherent speech act, that speech act would first express one's thought that *p* and then immediately go on to report that one had no such thought. So, if reporting and expressing were the same, then to say ⌜*p*, but I don't think that *p*⌝ would in effect be both to report the thought and also to report its absence. Moore's paradox would then be not merely absurd, but an actual contradiction. Only if expressing thoughts is distinct from reporting them can we explain why Moore's paradox is not an actual contradiction.

Reporting and Consciousness

The distinction between expressing and reporting one's intentional states has important implications for the question of what it is for mental states to be conscious. It's generally recognized that one can report a mental state one is in just in case that state is conscious. This connection has firm grounding in pretheoretic intuition, and is used

---

[12] Beginning students often take statements such as 'It's raining and it's not raining' to be meaningless, rather than meaningful but false. This too is best understood as a result of focusing on performance conditions, rather than the semantic meaning of sentences. It's tempting to see such sentences as meaningless because uttering such sentences would lack speaker's meaning.

[13] Saying that one sympathizes, doubts, or chooses has a performative aspect; as with 'I do', said in wedding ceremony, to say 'I choose' is to choose, and similarly with these other verbs. But these remarks also all succeed in making statements: that one chooses, doubts, or sympathizes. And the truth conditions of each statement again underscores that it reports a corresponding intentional state.

in experimental work as a reliable indicator of whether a mental state is conscious.[14] If a state is not conscious, it will be unavailable to one as the topic of a sincere report about the current contents of one's mind. And if it is conscious, one will be aware of it and hence able to report on it. The ability to report a particular mental state coincides with what we intuitively think of as that state's being in our stream of consciousness.

The connection between consciousness and reportability holds for creatures with the relevant linguistic abilities, such as ourselves. But that needn't limit our application of 'conscious state'. We can use the connection with reportability to fix the extension of the term 'conscious state' by reference to our own case. But what fixes the extension of 'conscious state' need not coincide with what is essential to such states.[15] So we can then discover what is essential to conscious states, and go on to apply the term also to creatures that lack the ability to report their mental states.

It is important to stress that the relevant reporting of one's mental states is intuitively unmediated. This is crucial to ensure the intuitive immediacy of consciousness. Reports of mental states reflect our consciousness of those states only if those reports do not appear to rely on inference or observation, only, that is, only if we are not conscious of the reports as relying on inference or observation. But excluding conscious inference is enough, since conscious observational mediation itself always relies on some inference of which one is aware.

But the ability noninferentially to report a particular mental state is the same as the ability to express verbally one's noninferential thought that one is in that state. So, for creatures with the relevant linguistic ability, a state's being conscious will coincide with one's having the ability verbally to express a noninferential HOT that one is in that state. The best explanation of one's having that ability is that the HOT one is able to express occurs, even if it is unexpressed. Given that explanation, a mental state's being conscious actually implies the presence of the very noninferential HOT that the current theory posits.

When a mental state is not conscious, we cannot report being in it. But that is equivalent to our being unable to express any HOT about the state in question. Barring exceptional factors, we can perform a speech act when, and only when, we have a thought that has the relevant content and mental attitude, a thought that the speech act would express.

So the best explanation of our inability to report mental states when they are not conscious is that in those cases no relevant HOT occurs. Conscious states must be accompanied by suitable HOTs, and nonconscious mental states are not so

---

[14] See, e.g., Marcel, "Conscious and Unconscious Perception: Experiments on Visual Masking and Word Recognition," *Cognitive Psychology*, 15 (1983): 197–237; Lawrence Weiskrantz, *Consciousness Lost and Found: A Neuropsychological Exploration*, Oxford: Oxford University Press, 1997; and Philip M. Merikle, Daniel Smilek, and John D. Eastwood, "Perception without Awareness: Perspectives from Cognitive Psychology," *Cognition*, 79, 1–2 (April 2001): 115–134, esp. p. 132.

[15] For more on the way that what fixes the extension of 'conscious state' may depart from what's essential to such states, see "Two Concepts of Consciousness," §IV and "A Theory of Consciousness," §II.

accompanied. We can conclude that a mental state's being conscious consists in its being accompanied by a suitable HOT.[16]

Not all mental states are conscious. And the HOTs the theory posits will themselves seldom be conscious. When these HOTs are conscious, introspective consciousness results; we are introspectively conscious of a mental state when we are aware of being conscious of that state. But it's rare that we are aware of our HOTs. And that is to be expected; for a second-order thought to be conscious, we must have a yet higher-order thought about that second-order thought, and it's reasonable to assume that this seldom happens.[17]

It is in any case no objection that we are typically unaware of having any such HOTs. Indeed, the theory predicts that this would be so. Since those thoughts are rarely conscious, we are seldom aware of their presence; we come to be aware of them only in those rare cases in which we introspect.

The foregoing argument reinforces the conclusion of section II that, if I say 'I think it's raining', my speech act expresses my HOT that I think it's raining, and not simply my thought that it's raining. This is important for the present theory. There can be no doubt that saying that I think it's raining reports the thought that it's raining. If, in addition, that speech act also expressed that thought, the very distinction between expressing and reporting would collapse. We then could not infer from an intentional state's being conscious to the occurrence of a HOT.

Collapsing the distinction between reporting and expressing would thus undermine the foregoing argument for an account of consciousness in terms of HOTs. Indeed, it would undermine the account itself, since it would encourage a reflexive conception of consciousness on which consciousness is an intrinsic feature of every

---

[16] A HOT's being suitable requires that it have the content that one is in the state in question and that it not depend on any conscious inference.

Suppose that one has a HOT that one is not conscious of as depending on any inference, and one then comes to be conscious of an inference that leads to that HOT. That would not result in the target state's no longer being conscious so long as one continued to have the HOT independently of that conscious inference, i.e., so long as one would still have the HOT without that conscious inference.

[17] Third-order thoughts do occur when we introspect; can fourth-order thoughts also occur? There is reason to think so. Sometimes we are actually conscious of our introspecting, and that means having a fourth-order thought about the third-order thought in which such introspecting consists. And we may occasionally even consciously think that we're introspecting, which would take it a step higher.

Still, it seems implausible that thoughts with explicitly fourth-order content ever occur; a thought whose explicit content is that one has a thought that one has a thought that one is in some particular state would at best be difficult to process. But the concept of introspection helpfully short circuits the explicit hierarchy. The thought in virtue of which my introspecting is conscious very likely has the explicit content simply that I'm introspecting, since it's unlikely that such a thought explicitly represents the relevant first- or second-order states. Similarly, if such a thought is itself conscious, the explicit content of the HOT in virtue of which it is conscious is very likely simply that I have a thought that I am introspecting. We needn't countenance contents with the iterative character of explicitly fourth- or fifth-order thoughts.

On difficulties with iterative content, see n. 28, below.

I am grateful to Josef Perner (personal communication) for pressing me on this issue.

conscious state, rather than a distinct state of being aware of one's conscious states. Saying that one thinks that p expresses one's consciousness of one's thought that p.[18] So, if saying that p amounted to the same thing as saying that one thinks that p, expressing a state would be the same as expressing one's consciousness of that state, which would encourage identifying mental states with one's consciousness of them.

There is another way we can put the connection between consciousness and collapsing the distinction between reporting and expressing. It's tempting to think that we can express any intentional state we are in, and a mental state is conscious just in case we can noninferentially report it. And we can assume that if expressing and reporting were the same, reporting would be noninferential, and expressing would be verbal. So, if expressing and reporting were the same, every mental state, by being verbally expressible, would be noninferentially reportable, and hence conscious. Nor, then, would there be any problem about why a verbally expressed intentional state is always conscious, since in verbally expressing a state one would thereby also express one's consciousness of that state.

The reflexive conception of consciousness, on which the property of a state's being conscious is intrinsic to that state, was championed by Descartes and Brentano, among others.[19] But it is also evident in Wittgenstein, who regards the idea of mental states that aren't conscious as involving a novel use of terms for such states.[20] Wittgenstein's reliance on performance conditions to the exclusion of such semantic considerations as truth conditions also leads him to hold that ostensible reports of mental states actually just express those states.[21] So it's tempting to think that his exclusive reliance on use and the consequent assimilation of reporting to expressing led to his rejection of mental states that aren't conscious.

But the exclusive reliance on performance conditions misleads. Considerations of mental attitude and illocutionary force, which undermined the claim that ostensibly higher-order remarks express first-order thoughts, also tell against the view that consciousness is intrinsic to mental states. Since the illocutionary force of 'I doubt it's

---

[18] At least when saying that one thinks that p does not rely on any conscious inference, which is the usual case.

[19] René Descartes, *Fourth Replies*, *The Philosophical Writings of Descartes*, tr. John Cottingham, Robert Stoothoff, and Dugald Murdoch (vol. III with Anthony Kenny), Cambridge: Cambridge University Press, 1984–91, II, 171; and *Second Replies*, II, 112.

Descartes also evidently collapses the distinction between expressing and reporting, as when he argues that nonlinguistic creatures have no thoughts because the lack of linguistic ability shows that they could not in any way even express thoughts; Letter to More, February 5, 1659, III, 366; the French is *exprimer*. See also *Discourse* (I, 140–1), and Letters to Marquess of Newcastle, III, 302–304, and to More, III, 364–367.)

And Franz Brentano, *Psychology from an Empirical Standpoint*, ed. Oskar Kraus, English edn., ed. Linda L. McAlister, tr. Antos C. Rancurello, D. B. Terrell, and Linda L. McAlister, London: Routledge & Kegan Paul, 1973 (original 1874), pp. 121–138.

[20] Ludwig Wittgenstein, *The Blue and Brown Books*, Oxford: Basil Blackwell, 1958, 2nd edn. 1969; pp. 22–3 in respect of sensations and pp. 57–8 in connection with thoughts.

[21] *Philosophical Investigations*, ed. G. E. M. Anscombe and R. Rhees, tr. G. E. M. Anscombe, Oxford: Basil Blackwell, 1953, §§244, 256, and 310 on sensations, and Part II, §x, p. 190 on thoughts.

going to rain' is assertoric, it cannot express the nonassertoric doubt that it's going to rain. Similarly, since no intentional state has two distinct mental attitudes, the assertoric HOT that I doubt that it's going to rain cannot be part of the nonassertoric doubt itself.[22]

IV. THE SOLUTION

The connections between consciousness and expressing just described provide the resources to answer the questions posed at the outset. Let me begin with the problem of why intentional states are conscious whenever we express them verbally.

As noted above, when I say that *p*, and thereby verbally express my thought that *p*, my speech act has the same performance conditions as those which would govern a speech act of saying that I think that *p*. Whenever it is appropriate to say that it's raining, it is also appropriate to say I think it is, and conversely.[23]

It is crucial for present purposes that this performance-conditional equivalence is not something we need to think through or figure out. Indeed, the ability we have to report our mental states noninferentially makes this equivalence wholly automatic for us. Whenever one says that it's raining, one could as easily have said that one thinks that it's raining, and conversely. In general, whenever we verbally express an intentional state, we might just as easily have reported that state, and whenever we noninferentially report an intentional state, we could just as easily have verbally expressed it. And, because reporting a state is no less automatic for us than verbally expressing it, any report of a state we make when we might equally have verbally expressed that state will be noninferential. We insensibly slip from saying one thing to saying the other, and indeed we often recall incorrectly which of the two we did say. The performance-conditional equivalence of reporting and verbally expressing is a matter of well-entrenched linguistic habit.

Whenever one says anything at all, one expresses an intentional state with the content of one's speech act. But, so far as performance conditions alone are concerned, saying that *p* amounts to the same thing as saying that one thinks that *p*, and this

---

[22] The foregoing section briefly summarizes the argument of "Thinking that One Thinks," ch. 2 in this volume.

For more on the idea that reporting intentional states is the same as expressing them, see §IV of that chapter. For reasons to think it's unlikely that an intrinsic theory allows an informative explanation of consciousness, see "A Theory of Consciousness," §III.

Chris D. Frith and Uta Frith cite brain-imaging studies in which subjects' being asked to report their mental states results in cortical activation in medial frontal cortex. The states reported are of many different sorts, and the cortical areas that subserve those states are all distinct from medial frontal cortex. Since reporting a mental state expresses a HOT in virtue of which one is conscious of that state, these findings suggest that such consciousness, and the higher-order content that figures in it, are extrinsic to the states themselves. See "Interacting Minds—A Biological Basis," *Science*, 286, i5445 (November 26, 1999): 1692–1695, p. 1693.

[23] If saying or thinking that one thinks it's raining does indicate a measure of hesitation not present in simply saying or thinking that it's raining, saying that *p* performance conditionally implies saying that one thinks that *p*, but not conversely. As noted earlier, this would not affect the present argument.

equivalence is second nature. So, even though the ability to express one's mental states verbally is distinct from the ability to report those states, for creatures like us the two abilities go hand in hand.

Indeed, the automatic, second-nature character of this performance-conditional equivalence is seen in our equally automatic rejection of statements such as 'It's raining but I don't think so'. Asserting such a sentence would involve expressing the thought that it's raining and going on in the very same speech act to deny that one has that thought. And that would conflict with the performance-conditional equivalence of reporting one's thoughts with verbally expressing them.

But being able to report a mental state noninferentially coincides with that state's being conscious. So being able to express an intentional state verbally will also coincide with that state's being conscious. It is because saying that p and saying that one thinks that p are performance conditionally equivalent and this equivalence is second nature for us that verbally expressing a thought normally suffices for that thought to be conscious.

It's tempting to see the connection between verbally expressing intentional states and their being conscious as somehow built into the very nature of consciousness and speech. But that connection is actually due only to the well-entrenched, habitual character of the performance-conditional equivalence between saying that p and saying that one thinks that p. It is that well-entrenched linguistic habit that underwrites the connection between verbally expressing a thought and its being conscious.[24]

The very same considerations allow us also to answer the second question, about why this connection doesn't hold when we express an intentional state nonverbally. Unlike speech acts, nonverbal expressions of intentional states do not in any straightforward way have performance conditions. It may be inappropriate when one sees that it's a clear day without a cloud in sight to say that it's going to rain or that one thinks it is. But simply taking one's umbrella in such circumstances is not inappropriate in that way. The illocutionary force of each speech act figures along with its intentional content in determining the conditions for the appropriate performance of that speech act. But because nonverbal actions have no illocutionary force, they seldom if ever have such performance conditions.

Since nonverbal actions lack performance conditions, they cannot be performance conditionally equivalent to speech acts of reporting the intentional states those nonverbal actions express. So there is no well-entrenched habit of treating the nonverbal expressions of intentional states as interchangeable with reports of those states. Nonverbal behavior that expresses intentional states accordingly does not coincide with those states' being conscious.

Perhaps a piece of nonverbal behavior could become so well-entrenched in our social interactions that it came to have specific performance conditions. Suppose

---

[24] "For use can almost change the stamp of nature" (*Hamlet*, III, iv, 168).

I'll argue in §V, however, that this well-entrenched linguistic habit is itself grounded in the way we conceive of thinking and speech. Roughly, because we think of thoughts as states that can be expressed in speech, it's second nature for us to assume that whenever one says that p, one has the thought that p. So it's also second nature whenever one says that p actually to think that one thinks that p.

that happens with the action of taking one's umbrella; that action comes to mean, in a quasilinguistic way,[25] that it's going to rain. Then my taking my umbrella would be performance conditionally equivalent to my reporting my thought that it's going to rain. Even so, it's unlikely that my nonverbally expressing my thought that it's going to rain by taking my umbrella would result in that thought's being conscious. For such nonverbal expressing to result in the thought's being conscious, the performance-conditional equivalence between taking my umbrella and reporting my thought would have to become second nature. And it's at best difficult to imagine that happening. The factors that result in one's saying that it's going to rain being automatically interchangeable with saying one thinks it going to rain would be unlikely to apply in this case.[26]

It is difficult to see how any account of consciousness other than that of the previous section could explain this difference between verbal and nonverbal expressing. A theory on which we're conscious of our conscious states by sensing them plainly won't do. Though we can report states of sensing things, no speech acts express sensations; so there would be no verbal expressions of our consciousness of intentional states with which the verbal expressions of those states could be performance conditionally equivalent.

Perceiving, unlike mere sensing, does have intentional content, and so it can be verbally expressed. But higher-order perceiving would simply mimic the explanatory efficacy of HOTs in respect of the difference for consciousness between the verbal and nonverbal expressing of intentional states.[27] And any explanation of that difference must presumably appeal to the automatic interchangeability of reporting with verbally expressing, and hence to higher-order states of some sort.

One might seek to explain the difference for consciousness between verbally and nonverbally expressing our intentional states by appeal to the idea that conscious mental functioning never occurs in creatures without language. But there are problems with the appeal to that Cartesian doctrine. For one thing, that view implausibly implies that nonlinguistic creatures have no conscious mentality, and we have no independent reason to think that that's so. It's also unclear how the explanation might go; even assuming that language is a prerequisite for conscious mental functioning, how does that assumption explain why verbally expressed thoughts are conscious but thoughts expressed nonverbally need not be? Appeal to a Cartesian link between language and consciousness, like the naive explanation of section II, simply calls attention to that tie, rather than actually explaining it.

Finally, because the blanket Cartesian claim allows of no exceptions to the connection between consciousness and speech, it will have trouble with the case

---

[25] Not simply in the sense of Paul Grice's "natural" meaning. See Grice, "Meaning," *The Philosophical Review*, LXVI, 3 (July 1957), 377–88.

[26] On those factors, see §V.

Wincing and other so-called pain behavior (e.g., Wittgenstein, §244) would not be performance conditionally equivalent to saying that something hurts, since those types of nonverbal behavior are not even voluntary performances. That makes it all the harder to imagine nonverbal expressions of pain coming to be automatically interchangeable with verbal reports of pain.

[27] On difficulties with higher-order perceiving, see "Varieties of Higher-Order Theory," §III.

of verbally expressed HOTs. As noted earlier, when I say that I think it's going to rain, thereby verbally expressing my thought that I think it's going to rain, the thought that's usually conscious is not my HOT that I think it's going to rain, but rather my thought that it's going to rain. The Cartesian doctrine about language and consciousness leaves that exception unexplained.

The Cartesian would doubtless urge that such cases are not really exceptions at all, and that even here verbally expressed thoughts are always conscious. The thought that's conscious when one says one thinks that *p* is generally not the thought that one thinks that *p*, but simply the thought that *p* itself. So the Cartesian would urge saving the generalization that verbally expressed thoughts are all conscious by adjusting what thought we take such speech acts to express. When one says that one thinks it's going to rain, the thought one's speech act expresses is not, on this line, a thought that has the same content; it is rather the thought that is conscious, namely, the thought that it's going to rain. Saying that one thinks that *p* expresses not the thought that one thinks that *p*, but just the thought that *p*.

Such gerrymandering of the thoughts our higher-order remarks express is congenial to Cartesian theorists, who see consciousness as intrinsic to all mental states. But this adjustment not only contravenes the correspondence of content between intentional states and the speech acts that express them, but the more decisive correspondence between mental attitude and illocutionary force. If saying that I think that *p* expressed not my thought that I think that *p*, but rather the first-order thought that *p*, then saying that I doubt or wonder something, which has assertoric illocutionary force, would express a mental attitude of doubting or wondering.

The Cartesian cannot explain why HOTs are an exception to the generalization that verbally expressed thoughts are conscious. But it's at least as important that the HOT theory be able to handle that exception. We are seldom aware of the HOTs that the theory posits; even when we report being in a conscious state, we are normally unaware of having any HOTs whatever. But we have compelling theoretical reasons to think that such HOTs occur, even when we are unaware of them. Conscious states are those we can noninferentially report, and reporting a mental state consists of verbally expressing a corresponding HOT. Still, we are in general aware of any intentional state that we verbally express. So, if we can't explain why we are seldom aware of the HOTs our reports of mental states seem to express, a doubt may remain about whether those HOTs occur at all.

But the HOT theory can readily explain the exception about the thoughts our higher-order remarks express, and do so without any gerrymandering of the data. One's verbally expressed thoughts are in general conscious because the speech acts that express them have the same performance conditions as reports about those thoughts, and that equivalence is second nature for us. How does this apply to the expressing of HOTs?

A second-order thought is conscious when one has a third-order thought that one has that second-order thought. And speech acts that express second-order thoughts are performance conditionally equivalent to those which express corresponding third-order thoughts. But here things are a lot less automatic. When one says that it's raining, one could just as easily have said that one thinks that it's raining. But when one says that one thinks that it's raining, it is by no means natural or second nature to say instead that one thinks that one thinks that it's raining.

This difference is easy to understand. We verbally express second-order thoughts often enough, indeed, whenever we report the states they are about. But we seldom have occasion to report those second-order thoughts. Because we have little use for speech acts that report those thoughts, there is little opportunity to form the habit of treating such reports as performance conditionally equivalent to verbal expressions of those thoughts. Indeed, higher-order remarks of the form ⌜I think that I think that p⌝ virtually never get said, except perhaps jokingly. And, despite their being fully grammatical, such third-order remarks strike us as being somewhat marginal as speech acts. So, though these remarks are performance conditionally equivalent to remarks of the form ⌜I think that p⌝, that equivalence is in no way second nature for us.

Indeed, the automatic performance-conditional equivalence of first-order remarks with second-order remarks very likely contributes to the difficulty of processing third-order remarks. Because saying that p is performance conditionally equivalent to saying that one thinks that p and that equivalence is automatic for us, the phrase 'I think that' strikes us as redundant, at least in respect of performance conditions. So the iteration of that phrase in third-order remarks distracts us, very likely interfering with the processing of those remarks as simply instances of the form ⌜I think that p⌝. The automatic performance-conditional equivalence between first- and second-order remarks makes the iterated phrase in ⌜I think that I think that p⌝ difficult to process.[28]

When we say things of the form ⌜I think that p⌝, there is no well-entrenched linguistic habit that makes it equally natural to say something of the form ⌜I think that I think that p⌝. Being disposed to express the HOT that one thinks it's raining does not automatically dispose one to report that one has that thought, which one would do by means of the awkward third-order remark that one thinks that one thinks that it's raining. Saying that one thinks that p does not dispose one to say that one thinks that one thinks that p; so verbally expressing a second-order thought does not dispose one to have a third-order thought about that second-order thought. One can accordingly express a second-order thought without its being conscious.

When we nonverbally express a thought, that thought may fail to be conscious because nonverbal behavior isn't performance conditionally equivalent to a report of the thought we express. When we verbally express a HOT, that verbal expression is performance conditionally equivalent to a report of that HOT, but the HOT still need not be conscious because that performance-conditional equivalence is not second nature for us.

---

[28] This may recall the difficulty we have in processing constructions with more than one level of center embedding, such as 'The rat the cat the dog chased bit died', since in both cases iteration makes a crucial difference. See Noam Chomsky and George A. Miller, "Introduction to the Formal Analysis of Natural Languages," *Handbook of Mathematical Psychology* vol II, ed. R. Duncan Luce, Robert R. Bush, and Eugene Galanter, 3 volumes, New York: John Wiley and Sons, 1963, pp. 269–321. But the processing difficulties in center embedding are doubtless due to different factors from those responsible for the difficulty with third-order remarks.

One could of course apply the argument of section III to figure out that, since one's thought that *p* is conscious, it must be that one also thinks that one thinks that *p*. But figuring that out would rely on conscious inference. So, if one then reported that one thinks that one thinks that *p*, the thought that speech act would express would rely on conscious inference. That inferential third-order thought would not make one conscious of one's second-order thought in a way that seems unmediated; so it would not result in that second-order thought's being conscious. Only when the performance-conditional equivalence is second nature for one will the relevant HOT be noninferential. The generalization that verbally expressed thoughts are conscious holds only for first-order intentional states, and not for HOTs as well.

Because HOTs are seldom conscious, it may be tempting to suppose that saying one thinks that *p* is simply a stylistic variant of saying that *p*. We take the content of our speech acts to match that of the thoughts they express. And when one says that one thinks that *p* but no HOT is conscious, the only thought one is aware of whose content might match the content of one's remark is one's thought that *p*. So it will then seem subjectively as though the content of one's ostensibly higher-order remark can only match that of one's first-order thought that *p*.

This subjective impression is reinforced by our assuming that, whenever we say anything at all, the thought we thereby express is conscious. We assume that even the thought expressed by saying that one thinks that *p* will be conscious. And the only relevant conscious thought is the first-order thought that *p*.

But we know that not all intentional states are conscious, and we have no reason to think that second-order thoughts might not be an exception to the generalization that verbally expressed thoughts are conscious. And, since we have compelling independent reason to hold that the thoughts our speech acts express have the same content as those speech acts, we should conclude that the thoughts our second-order remarks express frequently fail to be conscious.

It is likely that no other theory can explain why HOTs are an exception to the regularity that verbally expressed thoughts are conscious. Only an account that captures in a systematic and detailed way the connections between consciousness and verbal expression will be able to explain both the generalization and its exceptions.

It's worth briefly noting another exception to the generalization that all verbally expressed intentional states are conscious. Thoughts, desires, expectations, suspicions, and the like are not the only types of intentional state; emotions are intentional states as well. When somebody is joyous, angry, or sad, that person is joyous, angry, or sad about something, and joyous, angry, or sad that something is the case. But it may not be immediately obvious how we verbally express these affective intentional states. Saying that one is joyous, angry, or sad reports these states, but how do we verbally express them?

Typically we use evaluative words to express emotions verbally. One may express one's joy by describing something as wonderful, one's anger by saying that somebody acted badly, and one's sadness by characterizing something as unfortunate.[29] But

---

[29] Ethical emotivists have sought to capitalize on the use of evaluative remarks to express emotions when they claim that these remarks simply express feelings. But the term 'feeling' is used sometimes

whatever connections may hold between saying, for example, that one is angry and saying that somebody acted badly, no automatic, second-nature performance-conditional equivalence holds between speech acts of those two types.

The lack of an automatic performance-conditional equivalence between reports of emotions and the evaluative remarks that typically express them is useful in providing a mark for distinguishing the emotions from other intentional states, at least in the human case.[30] It may also explain the resistance many have to the idea that ascriptions of value simply express our emotions. Since evaluative remarks are not performance conditionally equivalent in a way that's second nature with reports of emotions, we resist thinking about value in terms of the emotions. Whatever the case about these things, because no automatic performance-conditional equivalence holds, emotions often fail to be conscious even when they are verbally expressed.[31]

V. CONSCIOUSNESS, THOUGHT, AND SPEECH

The performance-conditional equivalence of saying that p and saying that one thinks that p obtains because there are no circumstances in which it would be appropriate to say one but not the other. But that performance-conditional equivalence is by itself not enough for verbally expressed thoughts to be conscious; the equivalence must not just hold, but also be automatic and second nature. It must be a matter of well-entrenched linguistic habit.

This may seem to raise a difficulty. Well-entrenched linguistic habits often result simply from accidents of usage. But it's implausible that the consciousness of verbally expressed thoughts results from an accident of linguistic usage. It's overwhelmingly likely that it's due in some way to factors that have to do with the consciousness of intentional states and with what's involved in verbally expressing such states. Linguistic habits, however well-entrenched, seem to be the wrong kind of thing to invoke in explaining this generalization.[32]

But the well-entrenched linguistic habit that's operative here is no mere accident of usage. Our folk conception of intentional states characterizes them as states that

---

to refer to emotions and other times to refer to bodily sensations, such as pains. And emotivists have very often characterized the feelings they have in mind in solely qualitative terms. This has encouraged construing their view in terms of the expressing of bodily sensations, rather than the expressing of emotions, which have distinctive intentional content as well as qualitative character. For an especially pure example of this, see A. J. Ayer, *Language, Truth, and Logic*, New York: Dover Publications, 1952, ch. 6.

A more defensible version of ethical emotivism would rest on the recognition that evaluative remarks express emotions and that, in virtue of their intentional content, emotions have important ties to cognitive intentional states.

[30] An automatic performance-conditional equivalence might hold for being more self-conscious about their verbal expressions of emotion.

[31] For more on consciousness and the expressing of affective states, see "Consciousness and its Expression," ch. 11 in this volume, esp. §IV.

[32] I am grateful to David Chalmers for raising this challenge when he was discussant of an earlier, shorter version of this paper presented at the 2002 Barcelona meeting of the Association for the Scientific Study of Consciousness.

speech acts can express. It's likely that intentional states occur in many creatures with no linguistic ability. But the intentional states of those creatures are still such that, when states of that sort do occur in creatures that do have language, the speech acts of those creatures express those intentional states. Just as sincere speech acts always express intentional states, so intentional states are the kinds of thing that are express-ible by speech acts.[33]

Sincerely saying that p expresses an intentional state with the content that p. So, whenever somebody sincerely says that p, that individual thinks that p; if I sincerely say that p, you can correctly describe me as thinking that p. More important for present purposes, if I say that p, I can truly describe myself as thinking that p. Because all speech acts express intentional states, whenever one sincerely says that p, one could also truly say that one thinks that p.

This connection between saying that p and saying that one thinks that p holds because sincere speech acts always express intentional states. Moreover, our folk con-ception of speaking and thinking reflects that very connection; the connection is built into the way we think about thought and speech.

Simply having the capacity to have thoughts is not by itself sufficient for the con-nection between saying that p and saying that one thinks that p to be automatic. Creatures can have thoughts without having any concept of a thought; it takes far more mental sophistication to have a concept of an intentional state than simply to be in such states. Many creatures, moreover, might have a concept of an intentional state that's significantly less rich than ours; in particular, some creatures might well fail to conceive of intentional states as expressible by speech acts.

Suppose, however, that a creature with the capacity to have thoughts also has a concept of a thought, and does conceive of thoughts as states that speech acts can express. And suppose also that this creature has the ability to describe itself as being in intentional states. Then the connection between saying that p and saying that one thinks that p will be automatic and second nature. Because that creature conceives of thoughts as expressible by speech acts, it will be automatic and second nature for the creature that whenever it says that p it is disposed to describe itself as thinking that p. If speech acts always express thoughts, saying that p means expressing one's thought that p, and that applies to oneself no less than to others. So, even when that creature does not actually say that p but is simply inclined to do so, its concept of thoughts as states expressible by speech acts will very likely also dispose it to say that it thinks that p.

But this is exactly the well-entrenched connection to which the argument of section IV appealed between saying that p and saying that one thinks that p. So that well-entrenched linguistic habit is no mere accident of usage. Rather, it results from our very folk conception of the connection between speech acts and intentional states, together with our ability to describe ourselves as being in various intentional states.

---

[33] See "Intentionality," esp. §II.

If, as argued earlier, insincere utterances are degenerate speech acts, the qualification about sincerity is unnecessary. Still, I'll take that qualification for granted in what follows.

As noted at the close of section II, in ascribing content and mental attitude to intentional states we rely heavily on the content and illocutionary force of speech acts that would express those states. This is of a piece with our conceiving of intentional states as expressible by speech acts. Because speech acts express intentional states, we rely on the semantic and illocutionary properties of speech acts when we characterize states in intentional terms; we describe intentional states in terms of the speech acts that express them. Even when no speech act does express a particular intentional state, we describe that state by appeal to some speech act that would express the state.

Once again, Moore's paradox sheds light on the connection between thought and speech. It is second nature for us to think of thoughts as expressible in speech, so much so that we describe thoughts by reference to the speech acts that would express them. So it's also second nature to reject the possibility of genuine speech acts unaccompanied by corresponding thoughts. Our strong sense that one cannot assert 'It's raining but I don't think it is' is of a piece with that rejection, since in asserting such a sentence one would in one breath both say something and deny having the thought required for one to say that thing.

Speech acts that express HOTs and speech acts that express affective intentional states are exceptions to the regularity that verbally expressed thoughts are conscious, because in both cases the automatic performance-conditional equivalence fails to obtain. But, if the automatic character of that equivalence results from our folk conception of the connection between speech and thought, why does that folk conception fail in these two cases to generate an equivalence that's second nature for us?

Different factors explain the two exceptions. For speech acts that express HOTs, the exception is due not to anything about our folk conception, but rather to a processing limitation that figures in that case. Because the iteration of 'I think that' in ⌜I think that I think that p⌝ makes that remark difficult to process, we don't automatically process such remarks as special cases of the more general ⌜I think that p⌝.

Things are more complicated with the speech acts that express affective intentional states. The folk conception that characterizes cognitive intentional states as expressible by speech acts does not extend to affective intentional states. It's not part of our folk conception of emotions that speech acts with particular content express them. Though we conceive of cognitive intentional states in terms that largely match the speech acts that would express those states, we do not conceive of affective states that way.

Rather, we think about affective states mainly in terms of the nonverbal behavior that would express those states. The expressions we take to be distinctive of the various emotions are an individual's behavior toward others, and that individual's tone of voice, body language, and facial expressions. Though evaluative speech does also express emotions, our folk conception of the emotions makes relatively little of that connection. So our folk conception does not automatically dispose us to say that we're in particular affective states when we verbally express those states.

What about nonverbal expressions of affective states? People sometimes act in a joyous or angry way even though no relevant emotion is conscious. And our folk conception links the various emotions to distinctive nonverbal expressions of those states. So why doesn't that folk conception dispose us to think that we're joyous or angry when we nonverbally express those states in distinctive ways, thereby making us conscious of being in those states?

Our folk conception represents cognitive intentional states as expressible by speech acts whose differences in content and illocutionary force reflect the intentional differences among those states. And our folk conception similarly represents emotions as expressible by nonverbal behavior. But the differences among the types of nonverbal behavior that express the various emotions are far too coarse-grained to capture differences in content among the emotions. We can typically tell from nonverbal behavior whether a person is joyous, angry, or sad. But often we can tell, if at all, only from context or other background information what it is that the person is joyous, angry, or sad about. As with the nonverbal behavior that expresses cognitive intentional states, nonverbal expressions of the emotions reflect relatively few of the intentional properties of those states. So even though our folk conception ties the emotions to their nonverbal expressions, having that folk conception does not result in our being disposed to report specific emotions when we express them nonverbally. And because it doesn't, the nonverbal expressing of affective states does not automatically lead those states' becoming conscious.

The consciousness of verbally expressed intentional states is due to the automatic performance-conditional equivalence between saying that p and saying that one thinks that p. Those speech acts are performance conditionally equivalent in that automatic way because our folk conception represents cognitive intentional states as expressible by speech acts. That same folk conception also points toward an explanation of why we have HOTs about intentional states at all, and why those HOTs typically are reasonably accurate.

When we ascribe intentional states to ourselves, we almost always do so in a characteristically first-person way, relying on no conscious inference. But very occasionally we do ascribe intentional states to ourselves by consciously inferring from observation or theory. Imagine, then, a people who are particularly adept at ascribing intentional states to themselves solely by consciously inferring from theory and observation, and whose self-ascriptions of such states always consciously rely on such inferences.

Being highly skilled at such consciously inferential self-ascription, these people pass readily from being conscious of evidence that they think a particular thing to the self-ascriptive conclusion that they actually think that thing. Gradually their inferences from evidence to self-ascription come increasingly to be second nature for them. Saying that p, moreover, is itself evidence that one thinks that p. So, when these people say that p, the automatic character of their self-ascriptive conscious inferences disposes them also to say that they think that p. And their being so disposed reflects an underlying disposition to think that they think that p whenever they actually think that p.

As the disposition to say they think that p whenever they say that p becomes increasingly automatic, these people come correspondingly often to have HOTs about their first-order thoughts. As that disposition becomes more automatic, moreover, these people gradually cease being aware of the inference that leads to those HOTs. And their being thus unaware of that inference results in the relevant first-order thoughts' being conscious. The automatic character of the connection between these people's first- and second-order speech acts results in their first-order intentional states' coming to facilitate in them the occurrence of noninferential HOTs about those states.

We are never conscious of any inference on which the HOTs we have about intentional states seem to rely. Still, it's likely that, in learning to apply concepts for intentional states, we each passed through an earlier developmental stage in which we did apply those concepts to ourselves by consciously inferring from third-person considerations, including the things we find ourselves saying. We initially learned to apply concepts for intentional states to ourselves in just the way in which we apply them to others. The facilitation of noninferential HOTs about our own intentional states relies on an earlier stage in which our thoughts about our own intentional states generally did rely on conscious inference.[34]

Because of the awkward iteration in third-order remarks, that connection does not become automatic for second- and third-order remarks. So there is no similar facilitation of the third-order thoughts that occur when we introspect. This fits with what we know about introspection in the human case, namely, that it occurs relatively rarely and requires deliberate focus and some mental effort.

The facilitation by intentional states of HOTs about those states trades on a folk conception of intentional states as expressible by speech acts. So it won't occur in creatures without that folk conception, and hence not in creatures without language. We can accordingly expect that the intentional states of such creatures would seldom if ever be conscious, since no mental process would occur in them that facilitates HOTs about those states. This accords with pretheoretic intuition about such creatures. It's intuitively inviting to see nonlinguistic creatures as being in many conscious qualitative states, but intuition is arguably silent about whether their intentional states, if any, are also conscious.[35]

---

[34] The people just described, whose fluent self-ascriptions of intentional states always consciously rely on observation or theory, are in effect the people of Sellars' Myth of our Rylean Ancestors, just after they have become fluent in applying Jones's theory, which posits thoughts and other mental states ("Empiricism and the Philosophy of Mind," §§48–58).

Toward the end of "Empiricism and the Philosophy of Mind" Sellars writes: "[I]t turns out—need it have?—that [these people] can be trained to give reasonably reliable self-descriptions, using the language of the theory, without having to observe [their] own behaviour. ... *What began as a language with a purely theoretical use has gained a reporting role*" (§59, p. 189; emphasis in the original). We can explain how this last step in Sellars' story can occur by appeal to the facilitation of HOTs by intentional states, which results from the folk conception of intentional states as expressible by speech acts. Indeed, Jones's theory, as Sellars describes it, embodies that very folk conception. And the idea that individuals pass from giving only inferential reports to often making noninferential reports about their own intentional states accords with the present suggestion about our own individual cognitive development. For Sellars' own speculation about the cognitive development of individuals, see "The Structure of Knowledge, Lecture II: Minds," in *Action, Knowledge, and Reality: Critical Studies in Honor of Wilfrid Sellars*, ed. Hector-Neri Castañeda, Indianapolis: Bobbs-Merrill, 1975, pp. 316–331, §II.)

[35] More precisely, pretheoretic intuition holds that the mental states of such creatures are often conscious in respect of qualitative mental properties, but perhaps not in respect of intentional properties. Since perception involves both qualitative and intentional properties, the perceptions of nonlinguistic creatures might well be conscious only in respect of the qualitative properties of their perceptual states.

It is natural to assume that the qualitative states of many nonlinguistic creatures are conscious. And it turns out that a similar facilitation of HOTs operates in the case of qualitative states. But, since facilitation in that case relies on perception rather than linguistic ability, it can result in qualitative states' being conscious even in creatures that have no language. But that is beyond the scope of the present discussion.[36]

The automatic character of the performance-conditional equivalence of 'It's raining' with 'I think it's raining' explains more than just the quandaries we began with about verbal expressing and consciousness. It also helps us understand the hold on many that the traditional Cartesian picture of mind exerts. Basic to that picture is the idea that mental states are transparent to themselves, that the way mental states appear to consciousness is invariably the way they actually are.[37]

Because the performance-conditional equivalence of saying that *p* with saying that one thinks that *p* is second nature for us, there is a temptation to assimilate the reporting of intentional states to their verbal expression. And, as noted in section III, that assimilation encourages a conception of mental states on which their appearance and reality coincide, since reporting a thought tells us how it appears to one and verbally expressing the thought reveals its actual nature. The very idea that the mind is transparent to itself has appeal only because our folk conception of thoughts as expressible by speech acts makes it second nature for us that reports and verbal expressions of first-order thoughts have the same performance conditions.[38]

---

[36] See my "The Facilitation of Conscious States," forthcoming, and some brief remarks in "Sensory Qualities, Consciousness, and Perception," ch. 7 in this volume, §VI.

The HOT hypothesis puts forth a uniform treatment of what it is for a state to be conscious, whether that state is intentional or qualitative. Some theorists have held, to the contrary, that what it is for a state to be conscious is different in the two cases. It's likely that the temptation to hold that is a reflection of the different way in which HOTs are facilitated in the two kinds of case.

Because Sellars held that qualitative states are automatically conscious, he would not have seen the need in that case for factors that would facilitate consciousness.

[37] It is this claim which C. D. Broad aptly termed the "curious superstition" that introspection "must give exhaustive and infallible information" (*The Mind and its Place in Nature*, London: Routledge & Kegan Paul, 1925, p. 284).

Note the echo of this transparency claim in the idea that we have unmediated access to abstract propositions, which W. V. Quine rightly disparages as the myth of a museum of meanings ("Ontological Relativity," in *Ontological Relativity and Other Essays*, New York: Columbia University Press, 1969, p. 27).

[38] Substantially earlier versions of this chapter were presented at the Center for Interdisciplinary Research (ZiF) of the University of Bielefeld, Washington University in St Louis, and the Barcelona meeting of the Association for the Scientific Study of Consciousness. More recent versions were presented at North Carolina State University, the University of Alberta, and the Rutgers University Cognitive Science Colloquium. I am grateful to members of those audiences, and especially to Daniel Dennett, for helpful reactions.

11

Consciousness and Its Expression

Half a century ago it was often held that the emotions lack the intentional content that characterizes cognitive states. Logical empiricism had made popular the idea that certain sentences lack cognitive significance altogether and have only emotive meaning. Such sentences, it was held, simply express feelings, not cognitive states. And, since the content of speech acts reflects that of the mental states they express, if sentences that express emotions have no cognitive significance, those emotions themselves must lack the intentional content characteristic of propositional attitudes.

As the influence of these semantic doctrines has waned, however, it has become increasingly plain that a full description of the emotions does inevitably make reference to their intentional content. States such as joy, fear, anger, astonishment, sorrow, delight, and disappointment are all about things, and they all represent those things as having certain properties. The emotions, like cognitive states, do have intentional content.

But it is equally plain that the emotions are not just special cases of propositional attitudes, but are distinctive types of mental state. What is it, then, that distinguishes the emotions from cognitive states? Part of the answer doubtless lies with the phenomenal feel that emotions exhibit. There is normally a particular way one feels when one is angry, joyful, jealous, afraid, or sad, whereas the propositional attitudes have no such phenomenal aspect.

Although the occurrence of some phenomenal feel or other is characteristic of most emotions, phenomenal feel is a lot less central to the nature of those states than is often supposed. For one thing, emotions of different types frequently are not distinguishable in respect of their phenomenal feel. There is normally no discernible difference in phenomenal feel between fury and horror, devotion and compassion, fear and anger, disappointment and sorrow, though the emotions in each pair are strikingly different.

In any case, there are factors other than phenomenal feel that help distinguish the emotions from mental states of other sorts. One has to do with the centrality of the emotions for our understanding of the self. There is more to something's being a self than the collection of mental states it is in; those states must go together in a way that results in some characteristic unity and individuality. And it is arguable that the emotions are uniquely well suited to provide the needed unity and individuality.

For many emotions, very likely most, one cannot have the emotion without distinguishing oneself from other selves. This is not required for one to be in mental states of any other sort. Thoughts and desires can be about anything whatever, and sensations can represent any perceptible object, as well as states of one's body. And even when a thought, desire, or sensation does represent something that happens to be a self, the state need not represent that object as a self. By contrast, the very content of the emotions typically pertains to the interactions, real and notional, between oneself and other selves. Anger, envy, jealousy, indignation, affection, hatred, devotion, compassion, and contempt all normally concern other people. And although joy, fear, pride, disappointment, and disdain need not be about other people, interactions with others play a large role in the content of these states as well. Conceiving of oneself as a self in relation to other selves is necessary for most emotions.

Elsewhere, I have explored this characteristic connection between emotions and the self.[1] In what follows I focus on another feature that helps distinguish the emotions from cognitive states, a difference in the way the two sorts of state come to be conscious. Propositional attitudes have intentional content, and so can be expressed in speech. Similarly for the emotions; when we are delighted, angry, sad, or hopeful, we sometimes say things that express those emotions. But there is a difference between what happens when we express these two kinds of state in words. Whenever one verbally expresses a cognitive state, that state is conscious. We never, or almost never,[2] put thoughts in words without those thoughts' being conscious. By contrast, emotions can be verbally expressed without being conscious, and often they are. We say things that express our delight, anger, pleasure, or sadness even when these emotions are not conscious.

Why is it that cognitive and affective states differ in this way? Why should verbally expressing our cognitive states be sufficient for those states to be conscious, whereas verbally expressing our emotions is not? In what follows, I attempt to answer these questions. It turns out that the differences in the way cognitive and affective states behave with respect to consciousness and verbal expression is not due to any difference in what it is for the two kinds of state to be conscious. Rather, it is because of a difference in what happens when the two kinds of state are verbally expressed.

The link in the case of cognitive states between consciousness and being verbally expressed has doubtless encouraged the idea that an essential connection holds between language and mind. And, since consciousness has traditionally been regarded as central to the mind, that link may also have led to the insistence by some that cognitive states are the paradigmatic form of mental functioning. By the same token, the lack of any such link between consciousness and the verbal expression of emotions may be partly responsible for the comparative neglect of the emotions in most theoretical treatments of the mind.

According to psychoanalytic theory, the beneficial effect of treatment results largely from unconscious states' coming to be conscious. But why should talking about one's feelings be necessary to achieve this result? The foregoing considerations help provide a theoretically motivated answer. In the case of cognitive states, simply expressing the

---

[1] "Emotions and the Self," in *Emotion: Philosophical Studies*, ed. Gerald E. Myers and K. D. Irani, New York: Haven Publications, 1983, pp. 164–191.

[2] Because the minor exception to this generalization does not affect the contrast drawn here between cognitive states and the emotions, I shall usually not remark on it. See, however, n. 16, below.

states verbally is sufficient for them to be conscious. But this is not so for affective states, which matter more for therapeutic purposes. Simply expressing affective states in words cannot ensure that those states will be conscious. One must go farther and explicitly report or describe those states. For this reason, a satisfactory explanation of this difference between cognitive and affective states will very likely be relevant to psychoanalytic theory.

Accordingly, I occasionally consider in what follows certain aspects of Freud's own thinking about consciousness. After briefly reviewing some general issues that arise in explaining consciousness, I put forth and briefly defend a hypothesis about what it is for mental states to be conscious and about how conscious mental states differ from those which are not. Using that hypothesis, then, I develop an explanation of both why all verbally expressed cognitive states are conscious and why affective states may well fail to be conscious even when verbally expressed. I conclude with some brief remarks about how parapraxis relates to these conclusions.

I. FREUD AND CONSCIOUSNESS

Some things are so basic that they defy being explained in any useful way. And many have held that this is the case with consciousness—that consciousness is so fundamental that it resists being given any informative explanation. Our daily experience includes a constant stream of conscious thoughts, perceptions, and feelings. But simply having conscious thoughts, perceptions, and feelings does not help to explain what it is for these psychological states to be conscious. If all we can say about consciousness is how it subjectively appears to each of us, no truly explanatory account of consciousness is possible.

It is tempting to see the project of explaining consciousness as not just difficult or impossible, but also pointless. Everyday experience seems to encourage the traditional idea that all our thoughts, emotions, and perceptions are conscious. And if they are all conscious, it adds no information to say that such a state is conscious. If all psychological states are conscious, explaining consciousness is superfluous, once we have explained what thoughts, perceptions, and feelings are.

It hardly needs saying, however, that not all perceptions, thoughts, and emotions are conscious. There is much theoretical and experimental work in cognitive and developmental psychology, neuropsychology, psychoanalytic research and practice, theoretical linguistics, and the psychology of perception that establishes beyond question that mental functioning frequently occurs without being conscious. And this means that there is an explanatory task to do. Since some thoughts, feelings, and perceptions are conscious and others are not, we must explain what that difference consists in. My initial goal is to sketch briefly how this can be done.

Thoughts, perceptions, and emotions occur both consciously and nonconsciously. So one of those two ways of occurring must be the natural, default condition of these states. The natural condition of such states must be either the condition of being conscious or of not being conscious.

Settling which condition is the natural, default condition for thoughts, perceptions, and feelings is important because it determines what our explanatory task will be. If it is in the nature of psychological states to be conscious, we may well need no explanation of why some of them are conscious; that is simply their natural condition. But we would then need to explain why other such states are not conscious. If, on the other hand, psychological states are not in their nature conscious, we need not explain why the nonconscious ones are not conscious. But we would then have to discover what it is in virtue of which other such states are conscious.

It may, of course, be that some kinds of mental phenomena have as their natural, default condition that they are conscious, and others that they are not. Thus, some theorists have held that the default condition for cognitive states is not to be conscious, whereas affective states are in their nature conscious. I will come back to this possibility later. For now, I want merely to stress the more abstract point about what does and does not need explaining.

Perhaps nobody has been more intent to make theoretical room for mental states that are not conscious than Freud. So it is interesting to note a certain ambivalence in Freud's own thinking about consciousness. If psychological states are in their own nature conscious, we need not explain why some are conscious, but only why others are not. More important, if being conscious is the natural condition for mental states, their being conscious may well seem unexplainable. And this, somewhat surprisingly, seems to have been Freud's attitude. As he wrote in 1938, consciousness is a "unique, indescribable" quality of mental states,[3] and "the fact of consciousness" "defies all explanation or description."[4]

Still, with an exception I will note later on, Freud also explicitly held that the default condition for mental states is not the condition of being conscious. In his words, "mental processes are in themselves unconscious."[5] And again: "[t]he mental, whatever its nature may be, is in itself unconscious." Consciousness, he wrote, is "an inconstant quality" of mental occurrences, "one that is far oftener absent than present."[6] So it is puzzling that Freud should also have believed that consciousness "defies all explanation or description."[7]

It is tempting to speculate that Freud was led to this conclusion by the central place in his thinking of the mechanism of repression. Because of repression, certain mental states that would ordinarily be conscious are instead unconscious. Repression explains why those mental states are not conscious and what it is for them not to be conscious. By contrast, Freud had no similarly straightforward mechanism to explain what it is for conscious states to be conscious, and hence no explanation of consciousness. Still, if he was right about the general point that mental states are not in themselves conscious, we do need an explanation of why the conscious ones are conscious.

---

[3] "Some Elementary Lessons in Psycho-Analysis," in *The Complete Psychological Works of Sigmund Freud*, tr. and ed. James Strachey, London: The Hogarth Press, 1966–74 (henceforth "*Standard Edition*"), XXIII, pp. 279–86, at p. 283. In quoting Freud, I've throughout replaced 'psychical' in the Strachey translation by 'mental'.

[4] *An Outline of Psycho-Analysis, Standard Edition*, XXIII, pp. 141–208, at p. 157.

[5] "The Unconscious," *Standard Edition*, XIV, pp. 166–215, at p. 171.

[6] "Some Elementary Lessons," *Standard Edition*, XXIII, pp. 279–86, at p. 283.

[7] *An Outline of Psycho-Analysis, Standard Edition*, XXIII, pp. 141–208, at p. 157.

II. EXPLAINING CONSCIOUSNESS

I completely concur that the natural, default condition for mental states is not that of being conscious. Being conscious is an additional property that some psychological states have and others do not. How, then, can we explain the difference between those mental states which are conscious and those which are not?

At bottom, the difference between states that are conscious and those which are not is this: When a mental state is conscious, one is in some way conscious *of* that state. By contrast, when a mental state is not conscious, one is in no way conscious of it.

This preliminary characterization may, initially, sound circular, but it is not. We are conscious *of* lots of things. We are conscious of all the things we see and hear and taste and touch, and conscious in a different way of all the things we think about. Seeing and hearing Clinton and thinking about him are all ways of being conscious of Clinton.

Moreover, we are conscious not only of people and other objects, but of our own states of mind. I can be conscious that I want something to eat, or conscious that I am seeing Clinton, or conscious that I am thinking about Clinton. And that is just what happens when these states of mind are conscious—when, that is, my wanting something or seeing or thinking about somebody are conscious states. When these states are conscious, I am conscious, in a characteristic way, *of* those states. The reason this is not circular is that being conscious *of* things is a far more general property than a state's being conscious; so there is no problem in characterizing what it is for a state to be conscious in terms of our being conscious *of* that state.

Still, more must be said before we fully understand what it is for a psychological state to be conscious. Suppose I am angry at somebody, but unaware that I am. And suppose that my being angry becomes evident to somebody else, and that person informs me that I am angry. I believe that person, and so come myself to believe that I am angry. That is, I become conscious *of* my anger. Nonetheless, I may not come consciously to *feel* any anger; in that case, I am conscious *of* my anger, but my anger is not conscious. What's missing? What is it that is special about the way we are conscious of our mental states when those states are conscious?

What's special when my anger is conscious is that I am conscious of that anger in a way that seems and feels immediate. And that may well not happen when I simply take somebody else's word for it that I am angry. We can, moreover, explain what this apparent immediacy consists in. When it occurs, I am conscious of being angry in such a way that there *seems* to me to be nothing mediating between the anger and my being conscious of it. More generally, when any thought, feeling, or perception is conscious, one is conscious *of* that state in a way that seems to one to be unmediated in this way.

As I mentioned above, there are different ways we can be conscious of things. We are conscious of things when we see them or hear them or perceive them in some other way. And we are conscious of things when we have thoughts about them. So we must determine which of these ways of being conscious of things figures in our mental states' being conscious. When our feelings, thoughts, and perceptions are conscious, are we conscious of them because we sense them in some way, or because we have thoughts about them?

Many thinkers have found the first model inviting. Philosophers from Aristotle to John Locke and down to the present day have held that we perceive our conscious states by way of a kind of inner sense. Freud, too, seems to have adopted this model. Thus in his meta-psychological paper, "The Unconscious," he recommends that we "liken the perception of [mental processes] by means of consciousness to the perception of the external world by means of the sense-organs."[8]

I want to urge, however, that this is the wrong model. A number of considerations support this conclusion. For one thing, there is no dedicated sense organ for sensing our thoughts, perceptions, and affective states. Moreover, all sensing involves some distinctive sensory modality; indeed, there is a range of distinctive sensory qualities specific to each modality. Sensing by sight, for example, involves color qualities, and sensing by sound auditory qualities.

But the only qualities that figure when we are aware of our mental states are the qualities of the states we are aware of, not qualities that pertain to our awareness of those states. When we see something consciously, for example, the only relevant qualities are the color qualities of our visual sensations. Similarly for the other kinds of mental phenomena we are conscious of. There are no qualities that characterize our sensing of mental phenomena.[9]

For these and other reasons, we must reject the idea that, when our thoughts, feelings, and sensations are conscious, we are perceptually aware of those states. Still, we are conscious of them somehow. The only alternative is that we have thoughts about these states. Since these thoughts are about other mental states, I shall refer to them as higher-order thoughts (HOTs).

It goes without saying that we are seldom aware of having any such HOTs about our mental states. Almost all the conscious perceptions, thoughts, and feelings we have in ordinary waking life seem to us to be altogether unaccompanied by HOTs. Does this confute the HOT model? No. We will be aware of our HOTs only if those HOTs are *conscious* thoughts. And there is no reason to expect that in ordinary cases our HOTs will be conscious thoughts. Only when we focus introspectively on our mental states are those HOTs conscious.

One reason many thinkers have favored the perceptual model of how we are conscious of our conscious thoughts and feelings is that this model appears to explain why we are conscious of those states in a way that seems unmediated. When we see

---

[8] "The Unconscious," *Standard Edition*, XIV, pp. 166–215, at p. 171. See also my "Perceptual and Cognitive Models of Consciousness," *Journal of the American Psychoanalytic Association*, 45, 3 (Summer 1997): 740–746.

[9] One might urge that such qualities do occur, though we are not conscious of them. But when we introspect our mental states, we are conscious *of being conscious of* those states, and even then we are conscious of no quality belonging to our consciousness of those states. The only qualities we are conscious of are qualities of the states themselves.

Psychoanalytic clinicians might urge that there is sometimes an affective quality to the way we are conscious *of* our psychological states, but these cases are better explained as conscious affects associated with certain states' coming to be conscious.

and hear physical objects, nothing seems to mediate between the things we see and hear and our perceptual awareness of them. And that is how it seems when our mental states are conscious. This has led many to overlook the shortcomings of the perceptual model, with its commitment to a special sense and to mysterious sensory qualities.

But the HOT model can capture equally well the apparent immediacy of the way we are conscious of our conscious thoughts and feelings. When thoughts and feelings are conscious, the HOTs that make us conscious *of* those thoughts and feelings typically are not conscious. So we are aware of those thoughts and feelings without having any idea about *how* we are aware of them. Since our awareness of the states in these cases seems thus automatic, plainly nothing seems to us to mediate between those thoughts and feelings and our awareness of them.

When we focus introspectively on our conscious thoughts and feelings, however, we *are* conscious of having HOTs about those thoughts and feelings. Nonetheless, we remain completely unaware of any thought process that leads to our having those HOTs. So again it seems that nothing mediates between those thoughts and feelings and our consciousness of them. Insofar as our HOTs are conscious at all, those thoughts seem to us to be entirely spontaneous. This is unlike those cases in which the only way we are conscious of being angry, for example, is by believing what somebody tells us.

The HOT model explains exactly what's needed. It explains the difference between mental phenomena that are conscious and those which are not. On their own, thoughts, perceptions, and feelings are not conscious. Their sometimes being conscious consists in their being accompanied in those cases by suitable HOTs about them. By 'suitable', I mean that whenever the HOT is conscious, it seems spontaneous, and therefore unmediated. These HOTs make us conscious of our conscious thoughts, feelings, and perceptions, though typically the HOTs are not themselves conscious.[10]

Freud and others have sometimes held that, unlike thoughts and desires, emotions and bodily feelings cannot occur without being conscious. As Freud put it: "It is surely of the essence of an emotion, that we should be aware of it. ... Thus the possibility of the attribute of unconsciousness would be completely excluded so far as emotions, feelings and affects are concerned."[11] Freud noted that we "speak in a condensed and not entirely correct manner, of 'unconscious feelings' ";[12] but we do so, he held, only because the representational character of the feelings is repressed or misrepresented.[13]

[10] I have developed this hypothesis in a number of places. For general treatments, see "Two Concepts of Consciousness," ch. 1 in this volume; "Thinking that One Thinks," ch. 2 in this volume; "State Consciousness and Transitive Consciousness," *Consciousness and Cognition*, 2, 4 (December 1993): 355–363; "Consciousness and Metacognition," in *Metarepresentation: Proceedings of the Tenth Vancouver Cognitive Science Conference*, ed. Daniel Sperber, New York: Oxford University Press, 2000, pp. 265–295; and "A Theory of Consciousness," in *The Nature of Consciousness: Philosophical Debates*, ed. Ned Block, Owen Flanagan, and Güven Güzeldere, Cambridge, Massachusetts: MIT Press, 1997, pp. 729–753.
[11] "The Unconscious," *Standard Edition*, XIV, pp. 166–215, at p. 177.
[12] *The Ego and the Id, Standard Edition*, XIX, pp. 3–68, at p. 22.
[13] "The Unconscious," *Standard Edition*, XIV, pp. 166–215, at pp. 177–8.

Doubtless many cases of so-called unconscious feelings are of this sort, and therefore are not literally unconscious. Sometimes, for example, we are aware of being angry, but misdescribe or are unclear as to what that anger is about. Still, the unreportable anger described earlier gives us good reason to reject the general conclusion that affective states cannot literally fail to be conscious. Cases do occur in which a person is plainly angry but sincerely denies being angry. That sincere denial is compelling evidence that the anger simply fails to be conscious. Still, we can describe the person's anger in such cases in terminology that is characteristically mental; we can say whether the anger is intense or slight, and say what its object is, that is, what the person is angry about. And, as Freud noted for the case of cognitive states, the fact that we use the same terminology to describe the unconscious states as we use to describe conscious mental states is convincing evidence that the unconscious states are mental in nature.[14]

III. CONSCIOUSNESS AND REPORTABILITY

This, in broad strokes, is the HOT model of consciousness, and some of the reasons for thinking that it's true. For the rest of this discussion, I want to talk about some applications of the model, which provide useful confirmation of it. These applications should also help make the model somewhat more concrete.

When a person is angry, or thinking about somebody, or even perceiving something, the person's anger, thought, or perception may or may not be conscious. When it is conscious, the person can talk about it. The person can say, for example, such things as "I am angry," "I am thinking about that person," and "I see (or hear) that thing." These remarks will be based on no conscious inferences, either from what others have told the person or anything else. They will be spontaneous remarks about the person's own states of mind.

Even when one's anger, thought, or perception is not conscious, however, one may well behave in ways that reveal the anger, thought, or perception. But when those states are not conscious, one cannot tell others about them. At least, one cannot tell others about those states in the spontaneous way that's characteristic for the case of conscious states. One might still say things in a way that reveals these unconscious states; one might, for example, speak with an angry tone. But if one's anger is not conscious, one cannot spontaneously report to others that one is angry.

The HOT model provides the best explanation of this connection between consciousness and spontaneous reportability. To see this, consider the general connection that invariably holds between the statements we make and the thoughts those

[14] Freud called such cognitive states mental acts: "[A]ll the categories which we employ to describe conscious mental acts, such as ideas, purposes, resolutions, and so on, can be applied" equally well to unconscious mental states. Indeed, he continued, "the only way in which" many of "these latent [i.e., unconscious] states differ from conscious ones ... is precisely in the lack of consciousness." ("The Unconscious," *Standard Edition*, XIV, p. 168. The Strachey edition has 'some' such states; Cecil M. Baines's translation has 'many' [in *Freud: General Psychological Theory*, ed. Philip Rieff, New York: Collier Books, 1962, pp. 116–150, at p. 116].)

statements express. Suppose I say to you, "Clinton will win." My remark expresses my thought to the effect that Clinton will win. And in general, whenever one says anything at all, one's remark expresses some thought one has to the same effect as the remark itself.

Suppose, now, that I am consciously angry and I say that I am. My remark, "I am angry," expresses a thought I have. That thought is the thought that I am angry. It is a HOT about my anger. Saying that I am angry invariably expresses a HOT to the effect that I am angry.

When my thoughts and feelings are conscious, I can spontaneously tell others about those states; when my thoughts and feelings are not conscious, I cannot. The best explanation of this difference is that, when my thoughts and feelings are conscious, I have HOTs about those thoughts and feelings. Because I have these HOTs, I can express them in speech, by saying explicitly that I have those thoughts and feelings. And when my thoughts and feelings are not conscious, we can best explain my inability spontaneously to say these things by appeal to the absence in these cases of any such HOTs. I cannot express HOTs that I do not have.

These observations corroborate the hypothesis that a thought or feeling's being conscious is a matter of its being accompanied by a HOT about that thought or feeling. Moreover, this hypothesis applies equally to cognitive and to affective states. As noted earlier, it is true of both types of state that I can spontaneously report them if they are conscious, whereas I cannot if they are not conscious. And for both types of state, the reason we can spontaneously report them when they are conscious but not when they are not is that only the conscious ones are accompanied by suitable HOTs. It is these HOTs that we express when we spontaneously report our conscious states. The very same factor is responsible for the consciousness of both our cognitive and our affective states.[15]

IV. CONSCIOUSNESS AND EXPRESSION

What it is to be conscious is the same for cognitive and affective states. Nonetheless, it turns out that there are interesting and important differences in the way this model applies to the two types of state.

I mentioned earlier that, although I cannot spontaneously report my mental states when those states are not conscious, still, I may behave in a way that manifests those states. Suppose I am angry; even if my anger is not conscious, my facial expressions, manner, and bodily movements may well betray that anger. These things serve to *express* my anger, but they express it *nonverbally*. Things are the same way with thoughts and other cognitive states. My facial expressions and bodily movements may well reveal what I am thinking. For a trivial example, taking my umbrella may express nonverbally my belief that it's raining.

Often, of course, we reveal our thoughts and feelings verbally, by our use of words. When I tell you what I think or feel, I reveal those thoughts and feelings. But explicitly saying what one thinks and feels is not the only way we reveal in words what

---

[15] Contrary to Freud; see, e.g., *The Ego and the Id, Standard Edition*, XIX, pp. 3–68, at pp. 22–3.

thoughts and feelings we have. We also *express* those thoughts and feelings in words. As we shall see, it is crucial to distinguish *verbally expressing* our thoughts and feelings both from explicitly *reporting* those states and from expressing the states *nonverbally*.

Let's begin with thoughts and other cognitive states. Suppose I think it's raining. I can express that thought verbally by saying "It's raining." Or I could explicitly report my thought, by saying "I think it's raining." Or, again, I can express the very same thought nonverbally, by taking my umbrella. The question I want to focus on is how these differences relate to consciousness.

When I report my thought, by explicitly saying "I think it's raining," we have seen that that thought must be a conscious thought. Reporting the thought that it's raining expresses my HOT that I think it's raining, and that HOT makes me spontaneously conscious of my thought that it's raining. By contrast, if I nonverbally express my thought that it's raining, that thought need not be conscious. Though my taking my umbrella manifests my thought that it's raining, that thought may well not be conscious. I might take the umbrella absently, as we colloquially say, "without thinking"—that is, without *consciously* thinking.

What about the intermediate case, in which I neither report my thought explicitly nor express it nonverbally, but rather express it verbally? I verbally express my thought that it's raining by simply saying, "It's raining." And it turns out that, when I express my thought verbally in this way, the thought is always conscious. Similarly with all our thoughts and other cognitive states. Saying "Clinton will win" expresses verbally my thought that Clinton will win; and whenever I do verbally express that thought, the thought is conscious. Indeed, with a certain exception that I will disregard here,[16] we never, as noted above, say anything that expresses a thought or other cognitive state without that cognitive state's being conscious.

Let's now switch our attention to affective states. Suppose I am angry at you for doing a certain thing. If my anger is conscious, I might explicitly report the anger, by saying "I'm angry with you." Or I might express my anger nonverbally, say, by some facial expression or body language. And, as with cognitive states, when I *nonverbally* express my anger, the anger may or may not be conscious.

But how, then, might I *verbally* express my anger? Verbally expressing the different kinds of cognitive state relies on distinct forms of speech which reflect the kind of state being expressed. If I wonder something, I express my wondering of that thing by asking a question; if I believe something, I express that with an assertion; if I want you to do something, I can speak in the imperative mood; if I wish for something, I speak in the subjunctive or optative. But there exist no set forms of speech corresponding to the different kinds of affective state.[17]

This difficulty cannot be handled by explicitly mentioning the affective state in question. Recall that when I say "I am angry" I report my anger; I do not verbally express it. Saying something that explicitly mentions my anger constitutes a report of

---

[16] The exception concerns the verbal expression of HOTs themselves. On that exception, see "Why Are Verbally Expressed Thoughts Conscious?", ch. 10 in this volume.

[17] An exception might be gratitude, which I can express by saying "Thank you."

the anger. So the question remains as to how we verbally express our anger, as opposed to reporting it.

The answer is that I verbally express my anger at what you did by saying such things as "You shouldn't have done that" or "What you did was bad (or unacceptable, or uncalled for, and the like)." Saying these things expresses my anger, but without explicitly mentioning it—without, that is, reporting it. It may be that these things are sometimes also said without any hint of underlying indignation, that they are said as pure, objective judgments of the lack of merit in what you did. But that is probably rare. In any event, all that is needed for present purposes is a form of speech that in many cases, even if not in all, verbally expresses one's anger and does so with no explicit mention of that anger.

Whenever I say "It's raining," thereby verbally expressing my thought that it's raining, that thought is conscious. But things are importantly different when I verbally express my anger and other affective states. When I verbally express my anger at what you did, by saying, for example, "What you did was uncalled for," the underlying anger may or may not be conscious. Verbally expressed cognitive states are invariably conscious; verbally expressed affective states need not be.

As we have seen, the HOT model of consciousness explains why the mental states we explicitly report must be conscious. Can the model also explain the difference I have just drawn attention to between cognitive and affective states? Why is it that verbally expressed affective states need not be conscious but verbally expressed cognitive states must be?

In the case of affective states, such as anger, the HOT model plainly predicts the right thing. When I verbally express my anger by saying "What you did is inappropriate [or the like]," there is no reason to think that I must have any HOTs about my anger. Even if I am angry, it may be that the only relevant thought I have is that what you did is inappropriate. I may be wholly unaware of my anger. Saying "What you did is inappropriate" may express my anger without my in the least realizing that it does so. In this way, verbally expressing anger resembles expressing anger nonverbally, say, by one's body language or facial expression. There, too, one may be wholly unaware of one's anger, and so wholly unaware that one's body language or facial expression expresses it. Clearly, the HOT model explains why we can verbally express affective states even when those states are not conscious.

What we need, then, is an explanation of why things are different with cognitive states. When I say "It's raining," I verbally express my thought that it's raining. But my remark does not express any HOT about my thought that it's raining. It expresses only my thought that it's raining. Why, then, are all verbally expressed thoughts conscious? And can the HOT model explain why they are, given that saying "It's raining" verbally expresses only my thought that it's raining, and not any HOT?

When a person thinks it's raining, there are two distinct ways the person might convey this thought in words. The person might simply say, "It's raining," thereby verbally expressing the thought that it's raining. Or the person might say "I think it's raining," thereby reporting that thought. In saying "It's raining," one explicitly refers only to the weather, whereas the remark "I think it's raining" refers explicitly to one's *thought* about the weather.

But even though the two remarks literally mean different things, they have the same colloquial force. Saying "I think it's raining" is literally describing what one thinks, but the obvious conversational effect is to convey something about the weather. The two remarks are distinct semantically, but conversationally and pragmatically they are equivalent. Any differences between the two in respect of the degree of confidence expressed can be readily cancelled, or even reversed, by change of emphasis or context.

Even more crucial for our purposes, this equivalence is entirely second nature for anybody who understands how we talk about our thoughts. It is a bad joke to take the remark "I think it's raining" to be not about the weather, but just about the person's thoughts. It is a bad joke because the conversational equivalence between that remark and the remark "It's raining" is completely automatic to anybody with ordinary abilities to speak and understand. Because of this automatic conversational equivalence, it is largely a matter of indifference whether somebody says "It's raining" or "I think it's raining." Indeed, we typically may not recall, even a moment later, which of the two was said, either by us or by somebody else.

This has important implications about verbal expressions and consciousness. Suppose I think it's raining. If, then, I say "I think it's raining," I express a HOT *about my thought that it's raining.* My thought that it's raining would then have to be a conscious thought.

But the automatic conversational equivalence just described tells us that, even when I say "It's raining," I might equally well have said "I think it's raining." That is, I might equally well have verbally expressed a HOT about my thought that it's raining. Since I might equally well have expressed that HOT, I must have had the HOT, even though all I actually said was that it's raining. The automatic conversational equivalence of saying "It's raining" with saying "I think it's raining" means that the HOT will be present whichever of the two I say. Even when we verbally express our thoughts, those thoughts must be conscious.

When we express our thoughts nonverbally, however, no such automatic conversational equivalence applies. If I take my umbrella, thereby expressing my thought that it's raining, no automatic equivalence holds between my act of taking the umbrella and my saying "I think it's raining." So no reason exists in that case to think that I have any HOT about my thought that it's raining. The thoughts we express nonverbally need not be conscious thoughts.

The automatic conversational equivalence that does the work here is also absent when we express our affective states, even when we express those states verbally. Suppose I am angry at you and I verbally express that anger by saying "What you did was uncalled for." There is no automatic conversational equivalence between making that kind of remark and saying "I am angry with you." So, again, we have no reason in this case to think that one has a HOT about one's anger. Verbally expressing our cognitive states is enough to make one conscious of them; verbally expressing affective states is not. And, since the consciousness of affective states is assured only when we explicitly describe them, affective states are, Freud and others to the contrary (see the end of section II), one step further removed from consciousness than cognitive states.

Sometimes, when I say such things as "You shouldn't have done that" or "What you did was bad (or unacceptable, or uncalled for)," I express my anger at you. But it is also possible to say these things wholly dispassionately and without any feeling, whether conscious or not. In such a case, I simply express my thought that you should not have done that, or that what you did was bad (or unacceptable, or uncalled for). In yet other situations, my remark may do both things; it may at once express my anger and express my thought about the unfortunate character of your behavior.

Our occasional use of remarks of this kind to express dispassionate thoughts with no accompanying emotion makes it easy, when these remarks do express emotions, to remain unaware of those emotions. Saying "What you did was wrong" sometimes expresses only a dispassionate appraisal of somebody's action, with no angry feeling. So, even when the remark does express anger, one may regard oneself as expressing only a dispassionate thought; one may see oneself as simply commenting on the unmeritorious character of an action. In such a case one will have a HOT to the effect that one regards the action as unfortunate, but no HOT that one is angry. One's HOTs neglect the affective aspect of the mental states expressed by one's remark. One's speech act verbally expresses anger that is not conscious.

My remark that what you did was wrong may express my anger or my dispassionate thought or both. When it expresses my thought or both thought and anger, the thought is invariably conscious. But even when my remark expresses only my anger, I will have a HOT to the effect that I have the thought that what you did was wrong. That is so whether or not I am also conscious of my anger. The remark "What you did was wrong" is performance conditionally equivalent to saying "I think what you did was wrong," and that equivalence is second nature for us. So whenever I say that what you did was wrong, I have a HOT to the effect that I think that thing.

Many speech acts function in these two ways, sometimes as an expression of some emotion and other times as an expression of a dispassionate judgment about something's merits. This double role is part of what underlies the logical empiricists' insistence that apparent normative judgments are no more than verbal expressions of emotions. Speech acts have the same content as the mental states they express.[18] So, since anger, for example, can be verbally expressed by statements such as "You shouldn't have done that," the normative content of these remarks reflects the very content of the state of anger that such remarks sometimes express. Similarly for other emotions and their verbal expressions.

These considerations cannot, however, sustain the logical empiricists' contrast between cognitive and emotive meaning. As noted earlier, the emotions themselves do have intentional content; so their verbal expressions have cognitive significance, just like other, nonevaluative statements. Moreover, the speech acts that verbally express emotions also often double as verbal expressions of cognitive states.[19]

[18] See "Intentionality," ch. 3 in this volume. [The content of a speech act may be only roughly the same as that of the intentional state it expresses; see "Content, Interpretation, and Consciousness," ch. 12 in this volume, §§II–III. —Added in 2005.]

[19] It is in any case likely that the logical empiricists' contrast between cognitive emotive significance relied on a false assimilation of the emotions to bodily sensations such as pain, since the term 'feeling' applies to both.

Affective states may not be conscious even when they are verbally expressed. So getting these states to be conscious requires more than just their being expressed in words. As noted earlier, this is relevant to understanding the therapeutic benefit of psychoanalytic and related treatments. Simply giving verbal expression to our affective states need not produce therapeutic results. To make our affective states conscious, we must report—that is, we must explicitly describe and talk about—those states.

Indeed, simply expressing one's affective states in words may actually interfere with those states' coming to be conscious. Suppose I express my anger by saying that what you did was uncalled for. I may regard my remark as no more than a dispassionate comment about your behavior, and my seeing my remark that way may lead me to be reluctant to regard what I said as expressing my anger at you. This is especially likely since such remarks will invariably seem to express thoughts, whether or not we are also conscious of them as expressing an emotion. My interpretation of my state of mind, embodied in the HOT that I hold a certain dispassionate judgment about your behavior, may keep me from acknowledging, and hence from being conscious of, the way I feel about that behavior. For that reason, bracketing moral and other evaluative considerations can sometimes facilitate one's becoming aware of one's own affective states.

V. PARAPRAXIS AND CONSCIOUSNESS

Let me conclude by briefly applying these results to the phenomenon of parapraxis. I have said that verbally expressing our thoughts is enough for those thoughts to be conscious. But don't our verbal remarks in parapraxis express unconscious thoughts, thoughts of which we are not aware? I would argue not. For one thing, the states my verbal slips reveal are seldom cognitive states; normally they are affective states. The latent content of one's speech performance in these cases is one's anger or desire, not some latent belief about things.

Perhaps, however, such slips do sometimes reveal cognitive states. Perhaps an unintended word intrudes into my saying something, revealing some unconscious thought or belief.[20] But when this does happen, the intrusion of that word is best construed not as an integral part of what I am saying, but as a piece of nonverbal behavior. The intrusive word reveals my unconscious thought much as that thought might be revealed by my tone of voice or other aspects of how I make the relevant utterance. As noted earlier, the way we say things often reveals thoughts without thereby verbally expressing those thoughts. The unconscious latent thought in these cases is an internal causal factor that interferes with the seamless expression of my conscious thought, much as such a thought might unconsciously affect my nonverbal behavior.[21]

One might urge, however, that the speaker's latent thought is expressed not just by the intrusion of a single word, but by the entire speech performance. Consider

---

[20] Often in this kind of case the thought is conscious; but it need not always be.

[21] Thus we must take care to distinguish between what thought a speech act expresses and the various other thoughts that figure in its production. One factor to consider is the speaker's own point of view. When the latent thought is actually unconscious, the speaker will take the relevant speech performance to express the corresponding conscious thought, not the latent thought. Even

Freud's frequently cited case, in which the president of the Lower House of the Austrian Parliament said "I . . . declare the sitting *closed*," rather than open.[22] A plausible interpretation of this situation is that the president had an unconscious intention to close the meeting. And, since the content of that intention matches exactly the content of the actual speech performance, it may seem plausible to suppose that this speech performance expresses the corresponding unconscious intention.

But this interpretation is untenable. The president plainly also had a conscious intention to open the meeting.[23] And, if we see the entire utterance as expressing a latent intention to close the meeting, we cannot explain the connection between that speech performance and the corresponding conscious intention. We can do full justice to the situation only by construing the full speech performance as expressing that conscious intention. The latent intention to close the meeting—or, better, the latent wish not to have it open—exploits the expression in speech of the conscious intention, by injecting the word, 'closed'. It is only that single word that reveals, and therefore expresses, the unconscious intention. The slips of parapraxis do not undermine the generalization that all verbally expressed cognitive states are conscious.

Accordingly, the HOT model does well in explaining the things that need explaining. It explains why some cognitive and affective states are conscious, given that it is not in their nature to be conscious. And it also explains why conscious states, both affective and cognitive, are just the states we can spontaneously tell others about. Further, the model explains why verbally expressing cognitive states suffices for those states to be conscious, whereas this is not so for affective states. We can conclude that the model provides a promising framework for further research.[24]

---

when a suitable explanation of the slip is tendered, the speaker standardly feels as though the latent thought distorted the attempt to express verbally the manifest thought.

But there are more decisive considerations. Take a simple case: A speaker says "That was bad," where "That was nice" would have been socially appropriate. And the speaker avows having at that time thought only that it was nice; i.e., the speaker's thought that it was bad was, at the time, wholly unconscious. In what aspect of the speech performance does the parapraxis consist? If one says the parapraxis is the whole utterance, "That was bad," it may be tempting to conclude that the speech act expresses the unconscious thought that it was bad. But that construal does not do justice to the situation. The speaker *meant*, in *some* sense, to say "That was nice"; so the speech act as a whole must be connected with that conscious, if self-deceptive, thought. The parapraxis consists not in the speaker's overall speech performance, but in the unintended (i.e., *consciously* unintended) intrusion of the word 'bad' into that speech performance.

[22] *The Psychopathology of Everyday Life, Standard Edition*, VI, pp. 1–289, at pp. 59–60; also "Some Elementary Lessons," *Standard Edition*, XXIII, pp. 279–86, at p. 284, and elsewhere.

[23] Freud correctly notes that "there can be no doubt that what the President intended to say was 'opened' " ("Some Elementary Lessons," *Standard Edition*, XXIII, pp. 279–86, at p. 284).

[24] An earlier draft of this paper was read to the Division of Psychoanalysis (39) of the American Psychological Association, April 1996. I am grateful for useful discussion at that meeting.

12

Content, Interpretation, and Consciousness

I. FIRST-PERSON OPERATIONALISM AND HIGHER-ORDER THOUGHTS

We are all familiar with situations in which memory distorts some current experience. I may see a person I don't know at all, but my memory of an old friend causes me to misperceive that person as my friend; the conscious experience that results is of seeing the friend. Perhaps, for example, my friend wears glasses and the person now before me doesn't. Although I see a person without glasses, my memory of the friend intrudes and I seem, so far as consciousness is concerned, to see a person wearing glasses.

Folk psychology accommodates two distinct explanations of such cases. My memory of the earlier experience might contaminate the current visual information before it even reaches consciousness; if so, I in effect hallucinate the glasses. But perhaps, instead, I begin by consciously seeing the person as having no glasses, but the memory then immediately revises the experience by adding the glasses and also overwrites any current memory of the new visual experience without glasses.

These are the two scenarios that Dan Dennett and Marcel Kinsbourne labeled Stalinesque and Orwellian, respectively, famously arguing that the distinction between them is spurious. When it comes to consciousness, they urge, we cannot distinguish between appearance and reality. So, if the two scenarios are indistinguishable to consciousness, they are indistinguishable in reality, as well. Since consciousness cannot fix the time of contamination as being before or after the new visual information reaches consciousness, the two hypotheses differ only verbally. Folk psychology, by allowing for distinct scenarios, misleads us into thinking that this kind of case can occur in two different ways.[1]

As Dennett puts their view, "there is no reality of consciousness independent of the effects of various vehicles of content on subsequent action (and hence, of course, on memory)" (*CE* 132). So "there are no fixed facts about the stream of consciousness independent of particular probes" (*CE* 138; cf. 275). Dennett usefully calls this view *first-person operationalism* (*CE* 132), since it holds that the facts about consciousness are wholly fixed by the effects consciousness has on other things.

---

[1] Daniel C. Dennett and Marcel Kinsbourne, "Time and the Observer: The Where and When of Consciousness in the Brain," *The Behavioral and Brain Sciences*, 15, 2 (June 1992): 183–201; Open Peer Commentary, pp. 201–234, and Dennett and Kinsbourne's Author's Response, "Escape from the Cartesian Theater," pp. 234–247; and Dennett, *Consciousness Explained*, Boston: Little, Brown & Co., 1991 (henceforth *CE*), chs. 5 and 6.

Because theory outstrips observation, a satisfactory theory can often settle questions that won't yield to observation alone. So even if the Stalinesque and Orwellian scenarios are indistinguishable to consciousness itself, perhaps a reasonable theory of consciousness will, in principle at least, show us how to tell which scenario any particular case conforms to.

I have argued elsewhere[2] that we can do just this on a theory according to which a mental state is conscious just in case it is accompanied by a higher-order thought (HOT) to the effect that one is in that state. We do not regard as conscious any mental state of which we are wholly unaware. So we must in some way be conscious of every conscious state, and having a thought about a state is one way of being conscious of it. Intuitively, it seems that the way we are conscious of our conscious states is direct. We can explain this intuition by hypothesizing that we remain unaware of any inferences or other antecedent factors that might lead to HOTs or explain their occurrence; HOTs seem to arise spontaneously.[3] Indeed, HOTs need not themselves be conscious, and typically won't be.[4]

On this theory, a mental state becomes conscious at the onset of the relevant HOT. So whether my unrevised visual sensation reaches consciousness depends solely on whether the contamination occurs before or after the onset of some HOT. Since HOTs are determinate states, their exact moment of occurrence is determinate, whether or not we can discover it in practice.

At the same time, however, the HOT model explains why we should feel a certain reluctance to classify particular cases as being Stalinesque or Orwellian. Suppose a sensation occurs and very quickly becomes conscious. But then, almost immediately, the sensation changes, and a moment after that one becomes conscious of the change. Is this revision Stalinesque or Orwellian? That depends on whether we focus on the sensation in its original or changed form. The case is Stalinesque relative to the changed sensation, since that change occurred before the sensation became conscious in its new form. But relative to its original form the case is Orwellian, since the sensation was conscious in that original form before it changed. The case looks Stalinesque if we regard the revised sensation as a new, distinct state, and Orwellian if we see the revised sensation as just a later stage of the original state.

---

[2] "Multiple Drafts and Higher-Order Thoughts," *Philosophy and Phenomenological Research*, LIII, 4 (December 1993): 911–918; "Multiple Drafts and Facts of the Matter," in *Conscious Experience*, ed. Thomas Metzinger, Exeter, UK: Imprint Academic, 1995, pp. 275–290; and "First-Person Operationalism and Mental Taxonomy," ch. 8 in this volume.

[3] Though HOTs are noninferential from a first-person point of view, they might still result sometimes from inferences we are unaware of. We need not suppose that the way we are conscious of our conscious states actually is unmediated to explain our intuitive sense that it is.

[4] They will be conscious only when we are conscious of target states in the deliberate, attentive way we call introspection.

For development of this HOT model, see "A Theory of Consciousness," in *The Nature of Consciousness: Philosophical Debates*, ed. Ned Block, Owen Flanagan, and Güven Güzeldere, Cambridge, Massachusetts: MIT Press, 1997, pp. 729–753; "Thinking that One Thinks," ch. 2 in this volume; "State Consciousness and Transitive Consciousness," *Consciousness and Cognition*, 2, 4 (December 1993): 355–363; and "Two Concepts of Consciousness," ch. 1 in this volume.

But the choice between these two descriptions is in most cases unprincipled, since it will typically rely on artificially precise identity conditions for mental states. Whether such a case is Stalinesque or Orwellian hinges on arbitrary questions about taxonomizing our mental states themselves. Still, this does not show that it's not determinate when states with specific content properties become conscious, nor that the facts about when revision occurs and when states become conscious are exhausted by how things appear to consciousness.

II. THINKING, SPEECH, AND PROBES

"[T]here are," according to Dennett, "no fixed facts about the stream of consciousness independent of particular probes." One of the most intriguing applications of this challenging claim has to do with the connection between thinking and speech.

When we speak, we express the thoughts we have. Our speech acts, moreover, reflect the content of those intentional states. It is natural to hold that this correspondence of content is exact; whenever we say anything, the speaker's meaning of our speech act is the same as the content of the intentional state we express.

We all have experienced how putting our thoughts into words can appear to tighten up those very thoughts. It's usually assumed that this happens because the process of finding suitable words for one's thoughts clarifies the thoughts themselves. On that account, the clarifying speech act does not actually outstrip, in respect of content, the antecedent intentional state it expresses. It's just that fixing on the right words results in a new intentional state, whose content is more fine grained than one's original thought. So goes our ordinary, folk-psychological description of these cases, and so it seems to us from a first-person point of view. We have a robust first-person sense that our speech acts exactly match in content the antecedent intentional states they express. Whether or not the match is exact, it seems that way to us.

We will see below that folk psychology and our first-person sense of things overestimate the exactness of this match of content. But it is worth considering certain ostensible counterexamples to the idea that our first-person impression is always that an exact match obtains. We do sometimes discover as we say something that what we're saying does not really reflect our thoughts after all. We may have changed our mind, or even find that we never actually thought that thing at all, but said it only conversationally or from habit. But when this type of thing happens, our first-person sense is not of really saying the thing in question, but something like "as if" saying. We don't sense ourselves saying the thing with full illocutionary force, but simply producing the relevant utterance. In Wilfrid Sellars' apt metaphor,[5] the utterance is produced parrotingly, as with mere recitations, from causes that are tangential to what one thinks. We do sense in these cases a divergence between our speech and what we

---

[5] First used in a letter to Roderick Chisholm, published in Roderick M. Chisholm and Wilfrid Sellars, "Intentionality and the Mental," *Minnesota Studies in the Philosophy of Science*, II, ed. Herbert Feigl, Michael Scriven, and Grover Maxwell, Minneapolis: University of Minnesota Press, 1958, pp. 507–539, at p. 524.

think, but the speech productions do not seem to us, from a first-person point of view, to be full-fledged illocutionary acts.[6]

As we saw, an exact match in content between full-fledged illocutionary acts and the thoughts they express can accommodate cases in which our speaking seems to clarify our thoughts. But these cases seem to fit equally well with another interpretation, which itself lends support to Dennett's first-person operationalism. Perhaps putting our thoughts into words clarifies our thinking not because it results in our having clearer thoughts, but because speech acts themselves actually fix the content our thoughts have. Speech acts, on this view, are one sort of probe that determines the facts of consciousness. This is the "pandemonium model" of speech production that Dennett develops in chapter 8 of *Consciousness Explained*,[7] on which there are no determinate intentional states prior to the occurrence of verbal expressions. It is not simply that our choice of words often influences the content of our thoughts.[8] Rather, many forces occur in the intentional arena and compete for expression. The speech act that ultimately wins out in effect results from the vector product of those forces, rather than from some single, antecedently existing state with the relevant determinate content.

The folk-psychological view that speech acts always mirror the content of the intentional states they express reflects our subjective impression of these situations. It always seems, from a first-person point of view, that what we say exactly matches the content of some intentional state we are in. But Dennett's pandemonium model also does justice to this subjective impression. After all, if speech acts do fix the content of the intentional states they express, we will sense a perfect fit between them.

In addition to squaring with our subjective impressions, these two models both capture important aspects of the connection between thinking and speech. But the aspects they capture are different. One aspect has to do with what it is for a speech act to be meaningful. Two things are needed. One is that the sentence uttered have semantic meaning. But even so, no utterance is meaningful if it's a mere recitation without underlying thought, if, as Sellars put it, it is produced parrotingly. We can, of course, distinguish tolerably well between meaningful and parroting speech production, independent of any appeal to theory. But if we want to explain what that difference consists in, we must appeal to the idea that meaningful speech acts express intentional states, whereas parroting utterances do not.

The folk-psychological picture of the relation between speech and thought reflects this explanation. Nonparroting speech productions express antecedent intentional states, and expressing an intentional state means that the semantic meaning of

---

[6] Insincere speech and the speech productions of actors playing a part are also like this. See my "Intentionality," ch. 3 in this volume, §V. Thus J. L. Austin notes that if I insincerely say 'I promise', I don't strictly speaking promise, but only say I do ("Other Minds," in *Philosophical Papers*, 2nd and 3rd edns., Oxford: Oxford University Press, 1970 and 1979, pp. 76–116, at pp. 101–103 [1st edn., pp. 44–84, at pp. 69–71]). Similarly, Frege remarks that "stage assertion is only sham assertion" (Gottlob Frege, "Thoughts," in *Logical Investigations*, tr. P. T. Geach and R. H. Stoothoff, New Haven: Yale University Press, 1977, pp. 1–30, at p. 8).

[7] Page 240. See also pp. 245 and 247, and ch. 10, §5, esp. 315.

[8] Which Dennett suggests also happens (*CE* 247).

the speech act matches to some suitable degree the content of that intentional state. Such an explanation is unavailable on the pandemonium model. If speech acts fix the content of our intentional states, it cannot be that expressing an antecedent intentional state with roughly the same content is what makes a speech act nonparroting.

One might reply that the pandemonium model can, after all, explain the difference between parroting and nonparroting speech productions. Speech is nonparroting if it results from the forces competing in the intentional arena for expression; otherwise it is parroting.[9] Whether this reply works depends on just what those intentional forces are that the pandemonium model posits. If they are merely subpersonal events that resist folk-psychological taxonomy as full-fledged intentional states, the reply fails, since parroting utterances also result from the interaction of subpersonal events that resist folk-psychological taxonomy.

But perhaps the pandemonium model actually posits full-fledged intentional states operating in the intentional arena. Speech acts, then, simply settle which of these states wins out in the competition for expression, rather than converting subpersonal events of content fixation[10] into genuine intentional states. Then the model can explain speech as nonparroting if it results from such intentional states. But the pandemonium model so construed does not differ relevantly from the folk-psychological picture, which also posits antecedent intentional states, and regards nonparroting speech as that which results from such states. Any satisfactory explanation of how parroting and nonparroting utterances differ must invoke the intentional states posited by the folk-psychological model.

There is good reason, in any case, to construe Dennett's pandemonium model as positing only subpersonal events of content fixation, rather than full-fledged intentional states. Thus he writes:

We replace the division into discrete contentful *states*—beliefs, meta-beliefs, and so forth— with a *process* that serves, over time, to ensure a good fit between an entity's internal information-bearing events and the entity's capacity to express (some of) the information in those events in speech.[11]

The forces whose interaction results in speech acts are properly speaking proto-intentional, and precipitate into intentional states only when they issue in speech acts or in reactions to some relevant probe. Moreover, just which speech acts and intentional states these subpersonal forces issue in depends to some extent on factors irrelevant to the intentional content at hand. Events of content fixation determine speech performances more in the manner of instructions in aleatory music than fully developed scores.

---

[9] I owe this idea to Tim Kenyon, in conversation.

[10] Dennett speaks throughout *CE* of such nonconscious, subpersonal events that subserve mental states taxonomized folk psychologically. Because they occur nonconsciously, "their onsets do *not* mark the onset of consciousness of their content" (113; emphasis Dennett's). And he holds that, unlike mental states taxonomized folk psychologically, "content-fixations ... are [each] precisely locatable in both space and time" (113).

[11] *CE* 319, emphasis Dennett's. Cf. "The Message is: There is no *Medium*," *Philosophy and Phenomenological Research*, LIII, 4 (December 1993): 919–931, pp. 930–1.

Nonetheless, the folk-psychological model arguably exaggerates the match in content between speech act and intentional state, and the pandemonium model provides a useful corrective. If the content of an intentional state corresponds exactly to the semantic meaning of the speech act that expresses it, thinking must itself exhibit a language-like structure; perhaps thinking even takes place in a language of thought whose syntax and semantics echo those of overt natural language.[12] Such a picture, however, arguably underestimates the extent to which what we think and how we think it are affected by the way we express our thoughts in speech. The pandemonium model seeks to capture the effect our putting words to our thoughts has on the thoughts themselves.

Is there a view that preserves the virtues of both models, allowing us to explain the difference between parroting and nonparroting speech without tempting us to adopt an unqualified language of thought? Arguably yes. Perhaps meaningful, nonparroting speech acts always express intentional states with antecedently fixed content, but the speech acts are nonetheless often richer and more fine grained in content than the intentional states expressed. The content of the speech acts rules out more possibilities and invokes more distinctions than the less refined content of the intentional states those speech acts express.

How would this work? Which speech acts we perform is of course largely determined by the intentional states they express. But speech acts express those states in words that have, to some extent, an independent semantic life.[13] So, although the content of speech acts derives mainly from the intentional states expressed, the words used in expressing that content often go beyond it, making for speech acts whose semantic meaning is correspondingly enriched and refined.

Our thoughts, by contrast, seldom need to respect the fine-grained semantic distinctions inherent in natural language. Any intentional state can typically be expressed equally well by a range of speech acts whose semantic meanings are not exactly the same. So it's reasonable to regard the content of our intentional states as neutral among the distinct semantic meanings of those various possible speech acts. Any particular choice of words, then, produces a speech act with semantic meaning more fine grained than the content of the corresponding intentional state. Some match of content is required for a speech act to count as expressing an intentional state, but the match need not be exact.

What words we choose to express an intentional state may itself sometimes be due to some other intentional state. In these cases we might regard the resulting speech act as expressing both intentional states: that which led to some such speech act's being

---

[12] Most forcefully and impressively defended by Jerry A. Fodor in, e.g., *The Language of Thought*, New York: Thomas Y. Crowell, 1975; "Propositional Attitudes," *The Monist*, LXI, 4 (October 1978): 501–523; "Why There Still Has to Be a Language of Thought," Appendix in *Psychosemantics: The Problem of Meaning in the Philosophy of Mind* (Cambridge, Massachusetts: MIT Press/Bradford Books, 1987); "A Theory of Content," in *A Theory of Content and Other Essays*, Cambridge, Massachusetts: MIT Press/Bradford Books, 1990; and *The Elm and the Expert: Mentalese and its Semantics*, Cambridge, Massachusetts: MIT Press/Bradford Books, 1994.

[13] Partly for reasons developed in compelling detail by Tyler Burge, "Individualism and the Mental," *Midwest Studies in Philosophy*, IV (1979): 73–121, "Individualism and Psychology," *The Philosophical Review*, XCV, 1 (January 1986): 3–45, and elsewhere.

performed and also that which influenced the particular choice of words. The speech act would be more fine grained in content than either intentional state, but might not outstrip the two combined. But choices of words are doubtless often arbitrary, resulting from no mental factor at all. Mere habit or word pattern might determine what words we use; indeed, it is likely that this is what typically happens. In such cases, our speech act does outstrip in content any relevant antecedent intentional states. And, since the content of intentional states can be less fine grained than the meaning of the speech acts that express those states, there is less temptation on this view to suppose that thinking fully mirrors the syntactic and semantic properties of natural language.

Indeed, it may sometimes be difficult to capture our more coarse-grained thoughts in words, especially with the intentional states we ascribe to nonlinguistic animals. Dennett therefore concludes that the " 'thought' [of such an animal] might be inexpressible (in human language) for the simple reason that expression in a human language *cuts too fine.*" But Dennett concedes that "we may nevertheless exhaustively describe what we can't express."[14] But if we can exhaustively describe the content of a thought, we can use those very words to frame a sentence that would, however awkwardly, express that thought. If the content of some thought elides various distinctions inherent in human language, suitable disjunctions can provide neutrality in respect of those distinctions. Even when no straightforward sentence could express the content of thought, some complex compound should succeed.[15]

A speech act expresses an intentional state only if its content matches that of the intentional state, but the match need not be exact. How close must that match be? No precise answer is possible, but neither should we expect precision. For one thing, it is unclear just how finely we can differentiate intentional states and speech acts in respect of content. In addition, the distinction between parroting and nonparroting speech productions itself doubtless admits of an intermediate gray area. Nor, finally, should we expect to be able to specify with precision just which speech acts express which intentional states. Some reasonably close match of content is required even though the precise degree of correspondence eludes specification. It is an advantage of the present model that it does not aim for such precision.

III. CONSCIOUSNESS AND VERBALLY EXPRESSING OUR THOUGHTS

Let's call this third picture of the relation between thinking and speech the *refinement model.* Arguably, it avoids the disadvantages of both the folk-psychological and

---

[14] *Kinds of Minds: Toward an Understanding of Consciousness*, New York: Basic Books, 1996, p. 42. See also his "How to do Other Things with Words," in *Thought and Language*, ed. John Preston, Cambridge: Cambridge University Press, 1997, pp. 219–235.

[15] It is possible that many human thoughts have content that makes them better suited to being expressed by specific nonverbal actions than by speech; doubtless this is true of the thoughts of nonlinguistic animals. One might have a thought, e.g., that is expressed by one's getting in out of the rain. Deliberate cases of such actions are not merely automatic behavior, since they have among their causes intentional states with suitable content. It may not be clear in these cases just what that content is—whether it is, e.g., to get out of the rain, to seek shelter, to stop getting wet, or what. But it would be surprising if that content could not be captured, in some gerrymandered way, in human language.

pandemonium models, by allowing us to explain the difference between parroting and nonparroting speech performances while circumventing the temptation to hypothesize a full-fledged language of thought. The refinement model shares with the pandemonium model the recognition that speech often outstrips our thoughts in content. But unlike the pandemonium model, the refinement model preserves both our folk-psychological taxonomy and the traditional view that speech acts express antecedent intentional states.

Nonetheless, the refinement model appears to face a difficulty that both the pandemonium and folk-psychological models avoid. As noted earlier, whenever we express our thoughts in words, our subjective impression is that what we say exactly matches the content of the intentional state we express. It never seems, from a first-person point of view, that our speech act is richer or more fine grained in content than our antecedent intentional state. The folk-psychological and pandemonium models both reflect this, since both posit an exact correspondence of content between speech act and intentional state, differing only about whether the intentional state fixes the content of the speech act or the other way around. Either way we would seem to sense a perfect fit between them.

Folk psychology generally trades, of course, on such conformity to our subjective impressions. And in this case the pandemonium model follows suit. Can we defend the refinement model despite its departure from our subjective impressions about thinking and speech?

A slight detour here will be useful. As noted earlier, putting our thoughts into words sometimes seems to clarify those very thoughts. By itself, however, the clarifying effect of verbally expressing our thoughts does not tell against an exact match of content between thought and speech. It could simply be that the process of finding words to express our thoughts forces us to clarify those very thoughts. As we mentally hear ourselves say what it is that we think, we find it confused or unclear, and so revise on the fly what we think. But by adjusting our words as we go, we get the right thought out. The content of the resulting speech act could still match exactly that of the suitably revised thought.

There is, however, another way in which putting words to our thoughts might have a clarifying effect on those thoughts. Rather than leading us to clarify the thoughts themselves, it could result instead in our becoming clearer about just what those thoughts are. We would know better, having spoken, just what it was that we had been thinking all along. We discover what we think only as we say it.

Dennett takes this kind of case to support the pandemonium model, on which the content of our thoughts is fixed only when we speak (*CE* 245); hence his striking epigram from E. M. Forster: "How do I know what I think until I see what I say?" (*CE* 193) But our discovering what we think only as we say it does not, by itself, support the pandemonium model, since it does not show that our thoughts lacked fixed content until we spoke. It could instead simply be that our thoughts often are not conscious in the relevant way until we express them in words. Even if the speech act results from an antecedent intentional state whose content exactly matches that of the speech act, perhaps it's only as we speak that we become conscious of the intentional state *as having that content*.

These considerations help with the problem the refinement model faced. On that model, our speech acts often outstrip the intentional states they express in respect of content. But that is never how it seems from a first-person point of view. Our subjective impression is always that our speech acts exactly match in content the intentional states they express.

But these first-person impressions may not accurately reveal the content of our intentional states. It could be that our speech acts do often outstrip our intentional states in content, but that we are nonetheless conscious of those intentional states *as having the richer content.* We might subjectively sense an exact match in content not because such a match obtains, but because that is how we are conscious of our verbally expressed thoughts. Because we are conscious of such a thought as expressed by a particular speech act, we in effect read back the content of the speech act onto the intentional state it expresses. We interpret the intentional state as having the content exhibited by the speech act.

The idea that we interpret our thoughts in the light of our speech acts fits well with the spirit of Dennett's pandemonium model. To some extent at least, we rely on the same considerations others do in determining what we think. As Dennett notes, in cases when we discover what we think only as we say it, "we are . . . in the same boat as our external . . . interpreters, encountering a bit of text and putting the best reading on it that we can find" (*CE* 245). Hence Dennett's heterophenomenological method, on which our theorizing about mind seeks to do justice to the verbal reports people make about their mental states.[16]

The pandemonium model, however, takes these self-interpretations to be the last word about the content of our thoughts.[17] This squares with Dennett's first-person operationalism, which rejects the idea that there can be a difference between how things seem and how they seem to seem (*CE* 132). Intentional states are subjective states; they are a matter of how things seem to us. And how things seem to us in virtue

---

[16] *CE* 72–85; also ch. 4, *passim*, and Dennett's "Two Approaches to Mental Images," in his *Brainstorms*, Cambridge, Massachusetts: MIT Press/Bradford Books, 1978, pp. 174–189.

[17] The heterophenomenological method relies on the reports people make of their mental states; such reports in effect constitute self-interpretations. Dennett also regards cases in which we learn what we think by seeing what we say as involving a kind of self-interpretation (*CE* 245). But there self-interpretation occurs by way of speech acts that verbally express our intentional states, rather than explicitly reporting them.

Seeing verbal expressions of intentional states as self-interpretations as well as reports suggests that Dennett may be tacitly assimilating reports to verbal expressions. And that, in turn, may help explain why he regards self-interpretation as the last word about the content of our thoughts. Even if speech acts can differ in content somewhat from the intentional states they express, one might plausibly regard such expressions as better than any other evidence could be about the content of those states. So, assimilating reports of intentional states to their verbal expressions will make such self-interpreting reports themselves seem to be decisive about the content of the states those reports are about.

Assimilating the reporting of intentional states to their verbal expression also encourages the idea that mental states are all conscious, since the content of every mental state would itself then affirm, as reports do, that one is in that state. This idea may, moreover, be implicit in first-person operationalism, on which a state's mental properties are determined by how that state appears to consciousness.

of our being in some intentional state is a matter of the content that state has. So there is no difference, on first-person operationalism, between the content one's intentional states seem to one to have and the content they actually have. If it seems to one that an intentional state has a certain content, that's the content it has.

This approach saves an explanatory step. Why, if our speech acts outstrip in content the intentional states they express, do the intentional states subjectively seem to us to have the richer content of the speech acts? The pandemonium model avoids having to answer that question by positing that the intentional states really do have that richer content.

But even if the content of our speech acts does outstrip that of the thoughts they express, we can readily explain why those thoughts and speech acts seem, subjectively, to have the same content. As remarked earlier, a speech act counts as expressing a thought only if it has roughly the same content.[18] But we also sometimes convey our thoughts by actually reporting them—by saying literally that we have those thoughts. Suppose I think that it's raining. I verbally express that thought by saying, simply, that it's raining, whereas I report that very same thought by saying, instead, that I think that it's raining.

Indisputably, two such speech acts differ semantically, since they have distinct truth conditions. Still, they are easily conflated, since, with minor qualifications about degree of conviction that won't matter here, we can appropriately say one thing whenever we can appropriately say the other. This equivalence of performance conditions, moreover, is second nature for us; any time I actually do say it's raining, I might as easily have said that I think that it's raining, and conversely.

Suppose, then, I think that p and I express my thought with the somewhat richer, more refined statement that p'. The richer statement that p' is, then, performance conditionally equivalent to the statement that I think that p'. And because this equivalence is second nature, I might as easily have said that I think that p'. But if I had made the higher-order remark that I think that p', my statement would have expressed a thought that has roughly the same content; it would have expressed the HOT that I think that p'. And, since I might just as easily have made that statement, I must have had the HOT that the statement would have expressed.

The upshot is that, whenever I say that p', I have a HOT that I think that p'. And that HOT determines how I am conscious of the thought my speech act expresses. So, whatever the actual content of my thought, I am conscious of that thought *as having the content that p'*. We can explain why, even though my speech act may be somewhat richer and more refined in content than the thought it expresses, I am conscious of the thought *as having* the richer, more refined content.[19]

---

[18] It is arguable that, in addition, the intentional state must be causally implicated in producing the speech act. See my "Intentionality."

[19] These considerations explain, more generally, why it is that all verbally expressed cognitive intentional states are conscious. Whenever I express my thought that p by saying that p, I could as easily have said that I think that p. So I must have had the HOT I think that p, and on the HOT model my thought that p will accordingly be conscious. It is unlikely that any other model can explain why verbally expressed cognitive states are conscious. For more, see my "Why Are Verbally

But a difficulty looms for this explanation. If first-order conscious thoughts can be less fine grained than the speech acts that express them, why can't the same happen with HOTs as well?[20] And if our verbal report of a first-order thought might outstrip in content the HOT that report expresses, the HOT need not, after all, reflect the richer content of that report. And then we wouldn't be conscious of the first-order thought as having that richer content.

Perhaps this is all so. But recall that we are not trying to show that speech acts invariably have more fine-grained content than the thoughts they express, but only that this may sometimes happen, despite our subjective sense that it never does. And we have no reason to think it ever does actually happen with HOTs.

Indeed, it is highly unlikely that it ever happens there. We think that first-order thoughts have less fine-grained content than their verbal expressions because it seems clear that what we think could have been expressed equally well by distinct, semantically nonequivalent speech acts. But that's not the case with the HOTs that accompany our verbally expressed intentional states. Suppose I verbally express my first-order thought that *p* by the more fine-grained remark that *p'*. How I express my HOT about my less fine-grained, first-order thought that *p* is now dictated by the performance-conditional equivalence between saying the more fine-grained *p'* and saying that I think that *p'*. So I will now express that HOT only by saying that I think that *p'*. Verbally expressing my thoughts constrains the way I am conscious of them.[21]

IV. THE REFINEMENT MODEL AND FIRST-PERSON OPERATIONALISM

On the refinement model, speech acts often outstrip in content the intentional states they express. To explain how this squares with our subjective impressions, we must distinguish the content those states have from the content they seem to us to have. But the content of intentional states is a matter of how things seem to us. So this explanation conflicts with Dennett's first-person operationalism, which denies any

---

Expressed Thoughts Conscious?", ch. 10 in this volume. In "Consciousness and its Expression," ch. 11 in this volume, I show how these considerations also explain why affective states, unlike cognitive states, are often verbally expressed without being conscious.

[20] This echoes a challenge Dennett raises for the HOT model, that the pandemonium model should apply at higher levels as well; "the second-order state," he claims, "comes to be *created* by the very process of framing the report" (315, emphasis Dennett's). Also: "The emergence of the [verbal] expression [of a higher-order thought] is precisely what creates or fixes the content of higher-order thought expressed" (315).

[21] Dennett notes with approval Elizabeth Anscombe's argument that it is "wrong to claim that we *know* what our intentions are; rather we just *can say* what our intentions are" (*CE* 315 n. 10; see G. E. M. Anscombe, *Intention*, 2nd edn., Oxford: Basil Blackwell, 1963). The present explanation reflects this primacy of verbal expressions. On that explanation, the verbal expression of a thought constrains, by the performance-conditional equivalence, the content of our HOT about the target first-order thought, and hence how we are conscious of that target thought.

difference between things' seeming a certain way and their seeming to seem a certain way.[22]

But there is reason to reject that denial. Consider the game Dennett describes of "Hide the Thimble," which dramatizes how we can look straight at an object we're trying to find and yet fail consciously to register it (*CE* 334). This kind of case invites us to distinguish our seeing something consciously from our seeing it without being conscious of seeing it; things may seem a certain way even though they don't consciously seem that way.

The striking and subjectively surprising limits on parafoveal resolution that Dennett cites take us even farther. Parafoveal vision can produce only low-resolution sensations of most of the Warhol Marilyns,[23] but it seems subjectively that we are aware of them all in a clear and focused way. What it's like for one to have a particular conscious sensation is a function of how one is conscious of that sensation. So the best explanation of this case is that we have blurry parafoveal sensations of most Marilyns, but the way we are aware of those blurry sensations represents them as having high resolution.[24] What our sensations of the Marilyns is like for us is a function of how we're conscious of those sensations.[25] And, if the way we're conscious of our sensations sometimes goes beyond their mental properties by in effect refining them or

---

[22] The hierarchy of levels ends up, he claims, in our "having to postulate differences that are systematically undiscoverable by any means, from the inside or the outside," distinctions that are "systematically indiscernible in nature" (*CE* 319).

[23] *CE* 354. See *CE* 53–4 for Dennett's striking illustration of the limits on parafoveal vision in attempting to discern the color of playing cards seen parafoveally at arm's length.

[24] Similarly, in the thimble case; there is a conscious sensation in our visual field corresponding to the location of the thimble, since no subjective gap occurs there, but we are not conscious of that sensation *as* a sensation of a thimble.

We may also be conscious of sensations in ways that leave out aspects of their qualitative character, as when a throbbing pain is conscious only as painful and not as throbbing, or a sensation of red is conscious as red but not in respect of any particular shade. So, even though visual sensations appear to us to be "ultimately homogeneous," in Wilfrid Sellars' useful phrase, it may well be that their sensory qualities are actually composed of many pixels representing specific characteristics; their ultimately homogeneous appearance may be due only to the way our HOTs represent collections of such pixels. We are conscious of our sensations in a way that smooths them out, so to speak, and elides the details of their particulate, bit-map nature. (Wilfrid Sellars, "Philosophy and the Scientific Image of Man," in *Frontiers of Science and Philosophy*, ed. Robert G. Colodny, Pittsburgh: University of Pittsburgh Press, 1962, pp. 35–78; reprinted in *Science, Perception and Reality*, pp. 1–40, at p. 36.)

For more on sensations' diverging from the way we are conscious of them and the way HOTs function in that connection, see "The Independence of Consciousness and Sensory Quality," "Sensory Quality and the Relocation Story," and "Sensory Qualities, Consciousness, and Perception" (chs. 5, 6, and 7 in this volume), "Consciousness and Metacognition," in *Metarepresentation: A Multidisciplinary Perspective*, Proceedings of the Tenth Vancouver Cognitive Science Conference, ed. Daniel Sperber, New York: Oxford University Press, 2000, pp. 265–295, and "Explaining Consciousness," in *Philosophy of Mind: Classical and Contemporary Readings*, ed. David J. Chalmers, New York: Oxford University Press, 2002, pp. 406–421.

[25] Consider the striking results John Grimes reports, in which subjects fail consciously to notice dramatic changes of color and shape in a salient object if the change occurs during a saccade (John Grimes, "On the Failure to Detect Changes in Scenes across Saccades," *Perception*, ed. Kathleen Akins, New York: Oxford University Press, 1996, pp. 89–110). Our subjective sense that conscious

touching them up, it is highly likely that the same happens with our intentional states, as well.[26]

On the pandemonium model, our intentional states come to have determinate content only when expressed by a speech act, or fixed by some other sort of probe. This applies equally, Dennett argues, to the higher-order states in virtue of which we are conscious of our conscious states; those higher-order states themselves "[come] to be *created* by the very process of framing the report."[27] Such "heterophenomenological reports" are the verbal pronouncements people make about their own mental states, to which Dennett's heterophenomenological method seeks to do justice. Since framing those reports fixes the higher-order content, Dennett holds that sincere heterophenomenological reports are constitutive of what it's like for the subject at that time and, hence, constitutive of that subject's consciousness. It is those heterophenomenological reports, rather than any antecedently occurring intentional states, that fix the contents of consciousness.

This conclusion might seem tempting because we are seldom conscious of the higher-order states in virtue of which we are, in turn, conscious of our conscious mental states. So our first-person impression will be that heterophenomenological reports alone determine how we are conscious of those states. But this first-person appearance is unreliable. We are in many intentional states of which we are not conscious, and we should expect that we typically remain unaware of the HOTs in virtue of which we are conscious of our conscious states. Such HOTs would be conscious only if we had third-order thoughts about them, and we can safely assume that that seldom happens.

Moreover, we are occasionally conscious of our HOTs, wholly independently of whether we express them in heterophenomenological reports. Focusing introspectively on some particular state makes us aware not only of that state but also of the reflective, higher-order state of being aware of the lower-order target. The only reason to hold that heterophenomenological reports, rather than the HOTs they express, fix the contents of consciousness is Dennett's rejection of the folk-psychological model, on which speech acts generally express antecedent intentional states.

HOTs not only determine what it's like for us to be in various mental states; they also are, in effect, subjectively spontaneous interpretations of the mental states we are in.[28] Indeed, there is an important connection between consciousness and

---

experience is continuously responsive to changes in what we see outstrips the extent to which we actually track changes in our visual sensations. This lends support to the conclusion, argued for by Dennett (*CE* ch. 11), that our subjective sense of great detail throughout our visual field is also illusory. The way we are conscious of our sensations goes beyond those sensations themselves.

[26] Because what it's like to be in conscious states is sometimes informationally richer than the states themselves and that additional informational content is occurrent, we must posit occurrent states of higher-order awareness of the states, and not just dispositions to be aware of them.

[27] *CE* 315, emphasis Dennett's. Also: "The emergence of the [verbal] expression is precisely what creates or fixes the content of higher-order thought expressed" (ibid.).

[28] Subjectively spontaneous because we are unaware of any antecedent factor that might explain their occurrence. Because HOTs are not themselves typically conscious, we will seldom be explicitly aware of engaging in the self-interpretations these HOTs embody.

our seemingly spontaneous self-interpretations. When we spontaneously interpret ourselves as being in certain states, we are conscious of ourselves *as being in those states*. What it's like for us to be in particular states is a function of how we spontaneously interpret those states. In the absence of any such spontaneous self-interpretations, our mental states simply aren't conscious; there is nothing it's like for us to be in them.

First-person operationalism is also interpretationist, but it imposes a special constraint all its own. Mental states are conscious, on first-person operationalism, only when accompanied by intersubjectively accessible probes. Because we have no access to the mental states of others apart from these probes, such probes provide our sole basis for interpreting what states others are in. So tying the consciousness of mental states to the occurrence of probes means that mental states are conscious only when they are available for interpretation by others. First-person operationalism holds that the consciousness of mental states is a function of interpretation, but only third-person interpretations matter.[29]

But this third-person constraint is gratuitous. The self-interpretations that HOTs provide are by themselves sufficient for one's mental states to be conscious. Indeed, one might well wonder how third-person interpretations could have any bearing at all on the consciousness of mental states. The key is the denial by first-person operationalism of any difference between mental states and their being conscious—between how things seem and how they seem to seem. Given that denial, an interpretation of somebody as being in a particular state serves indifferently as reason to think that the person is in that state and that the state is conscious. First-person operationalism restricts itself to third-person interpretations because it denies the distinction between mental states and their being conscious.

Rejecting first-person operationalism allows us to distinguish being conscious of our mental states from the states we are conscious of. And that opens the way to explaining the consciousness of mental states along lines different from those invoked in explaining other mental properties. In particular, it may well be that mental states have determinate content even though the way we are conscious of those states is a function of the subjectively spontaneous self-interpretations embodied in HOTs. So, too, for the HOTs themselves; what it's like for us to be in various mental states is just a matter of the self-interpretations our HOTs embody, but those HOTs can themselves be determinate in content.[30] Interpretationism can be true about what it's like

---

[29] And such third-person interpretations cannot distinguish between a state's never coming to be conscious and its coming to be conscious too briefly to affect memory.

[30] As well as determinate as to time of occurrence, which makes it determinate when our mental states come to be conscious.

The HOT model may sometimes count a state as conscious even though there is nothing it's like for one to be in that state, e.g., in some cases where we find it hard to decide between Stalinesque and Orwellian explanations. The occurrence of a HOT would be decisive in any event, regardless of first-person impressions; it is standard for well-established theories to resolve problem cases when the empirical input, including first-person impressions, does not suffice.

for us to be in mental states without thereby holding for their content or other mental properties.[31]

[31] Work on this paper began in 1998 at the Center for Interdisciplinary Research (ZiF), University of Bielefeld, Germany. I am grateful to the Center for congenial and stimulating surroundings and to a PSC-CUNY Research Award for supporting my stay there. I am also grateful for helpful reactions to an earlier draft from the participants in the November 1998 Memorial University of Newfoundland Conference on Dennett and from members of the CUNY Cognitive Science Symposium.

PART IV

SELF-CONSCIOUSNESS

13

Unity of Consciousness and the Self

I. THE PROBLEM

One of the most central and important phenomena a theory of consciousness must explain is the sense of unity we have in respect of our conscious mental states. It seems that, for mental representations to be mine, they must, as Kant put it, "all belong to one self-consciousness" (*K.d.R.V.*, B132). Indeed, it was just such mental unity to which Descartes appealed in Meditation VI in arguing for the real distinction between mind and body. Whereas the geometrical essence of body guarantees its divisibility, the unity of consciousness ensures that mind is indivisible.

The unity of consciousness is the unity of an individual's conscious mental states. So understanding our sense of such unity requires knowing what it is for a mental state to be a conscious state. I've argued in a number of places that a state's being conscious consists in its being accompanied by what I've called a *higher-order thought* (HOT)—a thought to the effect that one is in the state in question. Let me briefly sketch the idea.

Suppose that one is in some mental state—one has, say, a thought or desire or emotion—but one is in no way whatever aware of being in that state. It will then subjectively seem to one as though one is not in any such state. But a state that one seems subjectively not to be in is plainly not a conscious state. So it's a necessary condition for a state to be conscious that one be aware, or conscious, of being in that state.[1]

In what way, then, are we aware of our conscious mental states? The traditional explanation appeals to inner sense; we are aware of our conscious states in something like the way we are aware of the things we see and hear.[2] It turns out that this idea is

---

[1] So there is no reason to suppose mental states, of whatever type, cannot occur without being conscious.

Ned Block's notion of phenomenal consciousness tacitly embodies the contrary assumption for qualitative states, since he holds that every qualitative state is phenomenally conscious. See "On a Confusion about a Function of Consciousness," *The Behavioral and Brain Sciences*, 18, 2 (June 1995): 227–247, and "Paradox and Cross Purposes in Recent Work on Consciousness," *Cognition*, 79, 1–2 (April 2001): 197–219.

[2] The phrase 'inner sense' is Kant's: *K.d.R.V.*, A22/B37. Locke uses the related 'internal Sense' (*An Essay Concerning Human Understanding*, edited from the fourth [1700] edition by Peter H. Nidditch, Oxford: Oxford University Press, 1975, II, i, 4, p. 105. For prominent modern exponents of the inner-sense model, see D. M. Armstrong, "What is Consciousness?", in Armstrong, *The Nature of Mind*, St Lucia, Queensland: University of Queensland Press, 1980, pp. 55–67; and William G. Lycan, *Consciousness and Experience*, Cambridge, Massachusetts: MIT Press/Bradford Books, 1996, ch. 2, pp. 13–43, and "The Superiority of HOP to HOT," in *Higher-Order Theories*

hard to sustain. Sensing occurs in various modalities, each with a characteristic range of mental qualities. But there is no distinctive range of mental qualities by way of which we are conscious of our conscious states.

The only other way we are conscious of things is by having thoughts about them as being present. So that must be how we are aware of our conscious states; a state is conscious if one has a HOT about that state. We seem to be conscious of our conscious states in a direct, unmediated way. We can capture that intuitive immediacy by stipulating that HOTs seem to one to rely on no inference of which one is conscious. We are seldom aware of any such HOTs. But we can explain that by supposing that it's rare that HOTs are accompanied by third-order thoughts, and hence rare that HOTs are, themselves, conscious.

The atomistic character of this model, however, may seem to prevent it from being able to explain our sense of the unity of consciousness. If each conscious state owes its consciousness to a distinct HOT, how could we come to have a sense of such unity? Why would all our conscious states seem to belong to a single, unifying self?[3] Why wouldn't a conscious mind seem instead to consist, in Hume's famous words, of "a mere heap or collection of different perceptions"?[4] It's this challenge that I want to address in what follows.

The challenge arguably poses a difficulty not just for an atomistic theory, such as one that appeals to HOTs, but for any account of the way we are actually conscious of our own conscious states. As Kant observed, "the empirical consciousness that accompanies different representations is by itself dispersed and without relation to the identity [that is, the unity] of the subject."[5] Because such empirical consciousness cannot explain unity, Kant posits a distinct, "*transcendental* unity of self-consciousness" (B132).[6] But it's unclear how any such transcendental posit could explain the appearance of conscious mental unity, since that appearance is itself an empirical occurrence.

In what follows, I consider whether the HOT model itself can explain the robust intuition we have that our conscious mental states constitute in some important way a unity, whether, that is, the model can explain why it seems, subjectively, that such unity obtains. One might counter that what matters is actual unity, not the mere subjective impression of unity. And Kant's observation about the dispersed character

of Consciousness, ed. Rocco W. Gennaro, Amsterdam and Philadelphia: John Benjamins Publishers, 2004, pp. 93–113. See also my "Varieties of Higher-Order Theory," in Gennaro, pp. 17–44, §§ II and III.

[3] I am grateful to Sydney Shoemaker for pressing this question, in "Consciousness and Co-consciousness," in *The Unity of Consciousness: Binding, Integration, and Dissociation*, ed. Axel Cleeremans, Oxford: Clarendon Press, 2003, pp. 59–71.

[4] David Hume, *A Treatise of Human Nature* [1739], ed. L. A. Selby-Bigge, Oxford: Clarendon Press, 1888, I, IV, ii, p. 207. Cf. Appendix, p. 634. For the famous "bundle" statement, see I, IV, vi, p. 252.

[5] If so, the way we are conscious of our conscious states cannot yield a sense of mental unity. Immanuel Kant, *Critique of Pure Reason*, tr. and ed. Paul Guyer and Allen W. Wood, Cambridge: Cambridge University Press, 1998, B133.

[6] And he warned against what he saw as the traditional rationalist error of relying on our subjective sense of unity to infer that the mind as it is in itself is a unity (First Paralogism, *K.d.R.V.*, B407–413).

of empirical consciousness suggests that no empirical account can help explain such actual unity.

But, whatever the reality, we must also explain the appearance of unity. And absent some implausible thesis about the mind's being transparent to itself, we cannot explain that appearance simply by appeal to the reality.[7] In any case, it is arguable that the appearance of conscious unity is, itself, all the reality that matters. The consciousness of our mental lives is a matter of how those mental lives appear to us. So the unity of consciousness simply is the unity of how our mental lives appear. We need not independently address the challenge to explain any supposed actual underlying unity of the self. Actual unity will seem important only on the unfounded Cartesian thesis that, for the mind, appearance and reality coincide.

II. CLUSTERS, FIELDS, AND INFERENCE

Our goal is to see whether the HOT model can explain the subjective impression we have of mental unity. One factor that helps some is that HOTs often operate not on single mental states, but on fairly large bunches. For evidence of this, consider the so-called cocktail-party effect, in which one suddenly becomes aware of hearing one's name in a conversation that one had until then consciously experienced only as part of a background din. For one's name to pop out from that seeming background noise, one must all along have been hearing the separate, articulated words of the conversation. But, since one was conscious of one's hearing of the words only as an undifferentiated auditory experience, the HOT in virtue of which one was conscious of one's hearing all those words must have represented the hearing of them *as* a single undifferentiated bunch, that is, as a background din. Doubtless this also happens with the other sensory modalities. That HOTs sometimes operate in this wholesale way helps explain our sense of mental unity; HOTs often unify into a single awareness a large bunch of experiences, on any of which we can focus more or less at will.

There is another, related kind of mental unity. When qualitative states are conscious, we typically are conscious of them not just individually, but also in respect of their apparent spatial relations to other states, of both the same sensory modality and others. We experience each conscious sensation in relation to every other, as being to the right or the left or above or below each of the others.[8] And, by calibrating such apparent locations across modalities, so that sights and sounds, for example, are coordinated in respect of place, we yoke the sensory fields of the various modalities together into what seems to us to be a single, modality-neutral field. Qualitative states are related in this way even when they are not conscious. But when we are conscious of the relevant mental qualities as being spatially related, this also contributes to our sense of having a unified consciousness.

---

[7] Indeed, the need to appeal to transparency makes any such explanation circular, since whatever plausibility such transparency may have rests in part on the apparent unity of consciousness.

[8] For problems about the way we are conscious of qualitative states as spatially unified within sensory fields, see my "Color, Mental Location, and the Visual Field," *Consciousness and Cognition*, 9, 4 (December 2000): 85–93, § IV. See also "Sensory Qualities, Consciousness, and Reception," ch. 7 in this volume, § VII.

A third factor that contributes to this sense of mental unity is conscious reasoning. When we reason consciously we are aware of our intentional states as going together to constitute larger rational units. We not only hold mental attitudes toward individual intentional contents; we also hold what we may call an *inferential attitude* towards various groups of contents. We hold, in effect, the attitude that we would never mentally deny some particular member of a group while mentally affirming the rest. This inferential attitude often fails to be conscious. But awareness of such rational unity not only results in an impression of causal connection among the relevant states; it also contributes to our sense of the unity of consciousness, since it makes one conscious in one mental breath of distinct contents and mental attitudes.

Indeed, it seems that most of our intentional states, perhaps all of them, fall into groups towards which we are disposed to hold such inferential attitudes. This encourages the idea that some special mental unity of the sort stressed by Descartes and Kant underlies all our intentional states. But the HOT model suffices to explain such unity; we can explain our consciousness of such inferential connections as resulting from HOTs' representing our intentional states as being thus connected.

III. THE SELF AS RAW BEARER

Wholesale operation of HOTs, of these sorts and others, doubtless helps to induce some conscious sense of unity among our mental states. But that will only go so far. Since no single HOT covers all our conscious states, the basic problem remains. How can we explain a sense of unity that encompasses states made conscious by distinct HOTs?

A HOT is a thought to the effect that one is in a particular mental state or cluster of states. So each HOT refers not only to such a state, but also to oneself as the individual that's in that state. This reference to oneself is unavoidable. Having a thought about something makes one conscious of it only when the thought represents that thing as being present. But being conscious of a state as present is being conscious of it as belonging to somebody. And being conscious of a state as belonging to somebody other than oneself would plainly not make it a conscious state.[9]

By itself, however, such reference to a bearer will not give rise to a sense of unity, since each HOT might, for all we know so far, refer to a distinct self. A sense of unity will result only if it seems, subjectively, that all our HOTs refer to one and the same self.

HOTs characterize their target states in terms of mental properties such as content, mental attitude, and sensory quality. But HOTs have far less to say about the self to

---

[9] Might there be types of creature for which the impersonal thought simply that a pain occurs would make that pain conscious, assuming no conscious inferential mediation? (I owe this suggestion to Jim Stone, personal communication.) Perhaps so, if there are creatures that literally don't distinguish themselves in thought from anything else. But all the nonlinguistic creatures we know of do seem to draw that distinction in a robust way, and few theorists now endorse the speculation that even human infants fail to do so.

One might question whether having a thought about something makes one conscious of that thing only if the thought represents it as being present. But independent of that, unless HOTs assign their target states to some specific individual, those HOTs will only be about mental-state types, as against individual tokens.

which they assign those states. A HOT has the content: I am in a certain state. So each HOT characterizes the self to which it assigns its target solely as the bearer of that target state and, by implication, as the individual that thinks that HOT itself. Just as we understand the word 'I' as referring to whatever individual performs a speech act in which the word occurs, so we understand the mental analogue of 'I' as referring to whatever individual thinks a thought in which that mental analogue occurs.

We must not construe HOTs as actually having the content that whoever thinks this very thought is also in the target state. The word 'I' does not literally mean *the individual performing this speech act*. Though each token of 'I' refers to the individual that uses it in performing a speech act, it does not do so by referring to the speech act itself.[10] We determine the reference of each token of 'I' by way of the containing speech act, but 'I' does not actually refer to that speech act. David Kaplan's well-known account suggests one way in which this may happen. The reference of 'I', he urges, is determined by a function from the context of utterance to the individual that produces that utterance; 'I' does not refer to the utterance itself.[11]

Similarly, every thought we could express by such a speech act refers to the individual that thinks that thought, but not because the thought literally refers to itself. What the mental analogue of 'I' refers to is determined by which individual thinks the thought, but not because that mental analogue actually refers to the containing thought. This is important because, if HOTs were about themselves, it would then be open to argue that each HOT makes one conscious of that very HOT, and hence that all HOTs are conscious. But as noted earlier, we are seldom aware of our HOTs.[12] Still, since we would identify what individual a token mental analogue of 'I' refers to as the individual that thinks the thought containing that token, we can regard the thought as in effect characterizing that referent as the individual who thinks that very thought. Each first-person thought thus disposes us to have another thought that identifies the self as the thinker of that first-person thought.

HOTs make us conscious not only of their target states, but also of the self to which they assign those targets. And, by seeming subjectively to be independent of

---

[10] *Pace* Hans Reichenbach, "Token-Reflexive Words," *Elements of Symbolic Logic*, New York: Macmillan, 1947, § 50.

[11] David Kaplan, "Demonstratives," in *Themes From Kaplan*, ed. Joseph Almog, John Perry, and Howard Wettstein, with the assistance of Ingrid Deiwiks and Edward N. Zalta, New York: Oxford University Press, 1989, pp. 481–563, pp. 505–507. Kaplan posits a character of 'I', which is a function whose value, for each context, is the speaker or agent of that context.

[12] In "Two Concepts of Consciousness," I wrongly suggested that we could so construe the content of HOTs (*Philosophical Studies*, 49, 3 [May 1986]: 329–359, § 11, pp. 344 and 346; reprinted as ch. 1 in this volume), and Thomas Natsoulas subsequently drew attention to the apparent consequence that all HOTs would be conscious ("What is Wrong with the Appendage Theory of Consciousness?", *Philosophical Psychology*, VI, 2 [June 1993]: 137–154, p. 23, and "An Examination of Four Objections to Self-Intimating States of Consciousness," *The Journal of Mind and Behavior*, X, 1 [Winter 1989]: 63–116, pp. 70–72). But a HOT need not explicitly be about itself to represent its target as belonging to the individual we can independently pick out as thinking that HOT.

It is also arguable that even if HOTs had the content that whoever has this thought is in the target state, HOTs still wouldn't refer to themselves in the way required to make one conscious of them. See my "Higher-Order Thoughts and the Appendage Theory of Consciousness," *Philosophical Psychology*, VI, 2 (June 1993): 155–167.

any conscious inference, HOTs make it seem that we are conscious of our conscious states in a direct, unmediated way. But that very independence HOTs have from conscious inference also makes it seem that we are directly conscious of the self to which each HOT assigns its target.

Every HOT characterizes the self it refers to solely as the bearer of target states and, in effect, as the thinker of the HOT itself. Nothing in that characterization implies that this bearer is the same from one HOT to the next. But there is also nothing to distinguish one such bearer from any other. And our seeming to be aware in a direct and unmediated way of the self each HOT refers to tilts things towards apparent unity. Since we seem to be directly aware of the self in each case, it seems subjectively as though there is a single self to which all one's HOTs refer, a single bearer for all our conscious states.

HOTs are not typically conscious thoughts; no HOT is ever conscious unless one has a third-order thought about it. So long as HOTs are not conscious, one will not be conscious of their seeming all to refer to a single self. But HOTs do sometimes come to be conscious; indeed, this is just what happens when we are introspectively conscious of our mental states. Introspective consciousness occurs when we are not only conscious of those states, but also conscious that we are.[13]

When HOTs do become conscious, we become aware both of the sparse characterization each HOT gives of the self and of the unmediated way we seem to be conscious of that self. So introspecting our mental states results in a conscious sense of unity among those states even when the states are conscious by way of distinct HOTs. This helps explain why our sense of unity seems to go hand in hand with our ability to engage in introspective consciousness. Indeed, being conscious of our HOTs when we do introspect leads even to our being conscious of the self those HOTs refer to as something that's conscious of various target states, and thus to the idea of the self as a conscious being, a being, that is, that's conscious of being aware of things.[14] Introspective consciousness results in a sense of one's conscious states as all unified in a single conscious subject.

It's worth noting in this connection that Hume's famous problem about the self results from his tacit adoption of a specifically perceptual model of introspecting; one cannot find a self when one seeks it perceptually.[15] The HOT model, by contrast,

---

[13] For more on introspective consciousness, see "Introspection and Self-interpretation," ch. 4 in this volume.

Occasionally we are even conscious of introspecting, which suggests the occurrence of fourth-order thoughts. But, though such thoughts would be about third-order thoughts, their explicit content would very likely be simply that one is introspecting. And if so, they would not have explicitly fourth-order content, which would arguably at best be difficult to process.

[14] This notion of a conscious being goes well beyond a creature's simply being conscious rather than, say, asleep or knocked out, what I have elsewhere called *creature consciousness*. A creature is conscious in this weaker way if it is awake and mentally responsive to sensory input. Creature consciousness thus implies that a creature will be conscious of some sensory input, but in principle that could happen without any of its mental states being conscious states.

[15] *Treatise*, I, IV, vi, p. 252. Similarly, various contemporary theorists seem to assume that introspective access to our mental states must be perceptual. See, e.g., Fred Dretske, "Introspection," *Proceedings of the Aristotelian Society*, CXV (1994/5): 263–278, and *Naturalizing the Mind*, ch. 2;

provides an informative explanation of the way we do seem to be introspectively conscious of the self.

Still, we have a sense of conscious unity even when we are not introspecting. We often become conscious of ourselves, in a way that seems direct, as being in particular mental states. And that leads us to expect that we could readily become conscious of all our mental states, more or less at will. We expect, moreover, that any such consciousness of our mental states will seem direct and unmediated. And that expectation amounts to a tacit sense that our conscious states form a unity even at moments when we are not actually conscious of any such unity. This tacit sense of mental unity arises in just the way our being disposed to see objects in particular places leads to a tacit, dispositional sense of where those objects are and how they fit together, even when we are not actually perceiving or thinking about them. We not only have an explicit sense of the unity of our conscious states, but a dispositional sense of unity as well.

The idea of being thus disposed to see our conscious states as unified may recall Peter Carruthers's view that a mental state's being conscious is a matter not of its being accompanied by an actual HOT, but rather of its being disposed to be so accompanied. This will not do, since being disposed to have a thought about something doesn't make one in any way conscious of that thing.[16] But we needn't adopt the dispositional HOT model to recognize that our sense of conscious unity can in part be dispositional; our sense of how things are is often a matter of how we are disposed to find them.

IV. THE BATTERY MODEL

The seemingly direct awareness each HOT gives us of the bearer of its target state leads to an initial sense that there is a single bearer to which all our conscious states belong. And the sparse way HOTs characterize that bearer bolsters that sense of unity. But this sparse characterization is not enough to identify ourselves; we do not, *pace* Descartes, identify ourselves simply as bearers of mental states. Still, it turns out that the way we do identify ourselves reinforces in an important respect our sense of the unity of consciousness.

John R. Searle, *The Rediscovery of the Mind*, Cambridge, Massachusetts: MIT Press/Bradford Books, 1992, pp. 96–7 and 144; Gilbert Harman, "Explaining Objective Color in terms of Subjective Reactions," *Philosophical Issues: Perception*, 7 (1996): 1–17, p. 8; reprinted in Alex Byrne and David Hilbert, eds., *Readings on Color, volume 1: The Philosophy of Color*, Cambridge, Massachusetts: MIT Press/Bradford Books, 1997, pp. 247–261; and Sydney Shoemaker, "Introspection and Phenomenal Character," *Philosophical Topics*, 28, 2 (Fall 2000): 247–273.

[16] See, e.g., my "Thinking that One Thinks," ch. 2 in this volume, and "Consciousness and Higher-Order Thought," *Macmillan Encyclopedia of Cognitive Science*, Macmillan Publishers, 2002, pp. 717–726. For Carruthers's view, see Peter Carruthers, *Phenomenal Consciousness: A Naturalistic Theory*, Cambridge: Cambridge University Press, 2000, and "HOP over FOR, HOT Theory," in *Higher-Order Theories of Consciousness*, ed. Gennaro, pp. 115–135. For difficulties in Carruthers's defense of that view, See my "Explaining Consciousness," in *Philosophy of Mind: Contemporary and Classical Readings*, ed. David J. Chalmers, New York: Oxford University Press, 2002, pp. 406–421, at pp. 410–11, and "Varieties of Higher-Order Theory," § IV.

We identify ourselves as individuals in a variety of ways that have little system-atic connection, relying on considerations that range from personal history, bodily features, and psychological characteristics to current location and situation. There is no magic bullet by which we identify ourselves, only a vast and loose collection of considerations, each of which is by itself relatively unimpressive, but whose combin-ation is enough for us to identify ourselves whenever the question arises.

Identifying oneself consists of saying who it is that one is talking or thinking about when one talks or thinks about oneself, that is, when one has first-person thoughts or makes the first-person remarks that express those thoughts. And one picks out the individual those first-person thoughts are about by reference to a diverse collec-tion of contingent properties, such as those just mentioned. For any new first-person thought, the reference that thought makes to oneself is secured by appeal to what many other, prior first-person thoughts have referred to, and this process gradually enlarges the stock of self-identifying thoughts available to secure such reference. Just as we take distinct tokens of a proper name all to refer to the same individual unless something indicates otherwise, so each of us operates as though all tokens of the men-tal analogue of 'I' in one's first-person thoughts also refer to the same individual. It is not easy, moreover, to override this default assumption.[17] The word 'I' and its mental analogue refer to whatever individual says or thinks something in first-person terms, but absent some compelling countervailing reason we also take them to refer to one and the same individual from one thought or speech act to the next.

The analogy with proper names may recall G. E. M. Anscombe's well-known view that 'I' does not function at all like a proper name. According to Anscombe, the first-person thought that I am standing, for example, does not predicate the concept *stand-ing* of any object, but exhibits instead a wholly unmediated conception of standing.[18] But this view cannot accommodate various fundamental logical relations, such as the incompatibility of my thought that I am standing with your thought that I am not. Even on the sparse characterization of the referent of 'I' described earlier, these logical relations demand that 'I' function as some type of referring expression.

Having a conscious sense of unity does not require having an explicit, conscious thought that all occurrences of the mental analogue of 'I' refer to a single thing. We typically have a sense that we are talking about one and the same individual when we use different tokens of a proper name even though we seldom have any actual thought to the effect that such coreference obtains. The same holds for talking or thinking about oneself using different tokens of 'I' or its mental analogue.

HOTs are first-person thoughts, and these considerations all apply to them. We appeal to a broad, heterogeneous collection of contingent properties to specify the individual each HOT represents its target as belonging to, and we take that battery of descriptions to pick out a single individual. Since this process extends to our HOTs, it enriches our description of the self to which our HOTs assign their target states, thereby reinforcing and consolidating the subjective sense each of us has that our

[17] Perhaps as in cases of so-called Multiple Personality or Dissociative Identity Disorder.
[18] "The First Person," in *Mind and Language: Wolfson College Lectures 1974*, ed. Samuel Guttenplan, Oxford: Clarendon Press, 1975, pp. 45–65.

conscious states all belong to a single individual. There is nothing special about the way we are conscious of our mental states or of the self they belong to that issues in this subjective sense. It results simply from an extension of our commonsense assumption that the heterogeneous collection of ways in which we identify ourselves combine to pick out one individual, that the 'I' in all our first-person thoughts and remarks refers to a single self.

It might be thought that the way we are conscious of ourselves must be special, since we identify ourselves, as such, by being conscious of ourselves, and identifying oneself, as such, is a precondition for identifying anything else.[19] But no informative identification of ourselves, as such, is needed to identify other things. Perceptually identifying objects other than oneself relies on some relationship that holds between oneself and those other objects, but the relevant relationship consists in the perceiving itself, and one needn't identify oneself to perceive something else. Perhaps in identifying an object relative to other things we often use as a fixed point the origin of one's coordinate system, and that may make it seem that identifying oneself is a precondition for perceptually identifying anything. But we do not ordinarily identify things perceptually relative to ourselves, but relative to a larger scheme of things that contains the target object. When appeal to that larger framework fails for whatever reason, nothing about the way we identify ourselves independently of that larger framework will come to our rescue.

Since this reinforced sense of unity results from our HOTs' functioning just as other first-person thoughts do to pick out a single individual, we are conscious of that reinforcement only when some of our HOTs are, themselves, conscious.[20] Introspective consciousness is once again pivotal for our conscious sense of mental unity.

Each HOT represents its target state as belonging to some individual. One secures reference to that individual by way of other first-person thoughts, each of which contributes to the heterogeneous collection of contingent properties by way of which we identify ourselves. We thereby identify the individual to which each HOT assigns its target as being the same from one HOT to the next. Since introspecting consists in being conscious of our HOTs, it results in our being conscious of those HOTs *as* seeming all to assign their targets to some single individual. One becomes conscious of oneself as a center of consciousness. Indeed, this provides an answer, which Hume despaired of giving, to his challenge "to explain the principles, that unite our

---

[19] On the idea that self-identification is a precondition for identifying anything else, see, e.g., Sydney Shoemaker, "Self-Reference and Self-Awareness," *The Journal of Philosophy*, LXV, 19 (October 3, 1968): 555–567, reprinted with slight revisions in Shoemaker, *Identity, Cause, and Mind: Philosophical Essays*, Cambridge: Cambridge University Press, 1984, expanded edition, Oxford: Clarendon Press, 2003, pp. 6–18 (references below are to the reprinted version); David Lewis, "Attitudes *De Dicto* and *De Se*," *The Philosophical Review*, LXXXVIII, 4 (October 1979): 513–543, reprinted in Lewis, *Philosophical Papers*, I, New York: Oxford University Press, 1983, pp. 133–159; and Roderick M. Chisholm, *Person and Object: A Metaphysical Study*, La Salle, Illinois: Open Court, 1976, ch. 1, §5, and *The First Person*, Minneapolis: University of Minnesota Press, 1981, ch. 3, esp. pp. 29–32.

[20] Simply operating as though 'I' has the same referent in all one's first-person thoughts is enough, however, to produce the tacit sense of unity mentioned at the end of § III.

successive perceptions in our thought or consciousness" (*Treatise*, Appendix, p. 636). HOTs lead to our interpreting the states they are about as all belonging to a single conscious self.

It is important to stress that the single subject which we're conscious of our conscious states as belonging to may not actually exist. It may be, for one thing, that there is no subject of which we actually have direct, unmediated consciousness. Perhaps the subject one's HOTs refer to isn't even the same from one HOT to the next. Even though the mental analogue of 'I' refers in each first-person thought to whatever individual thinks that thought, perhaps the relevant individual is different, even for a particular person's HOTs, from one HOT to another. For present purposes, however, these possibilities don't matter. As noted at the outset, the aim here is not to sustain the idea that a single, unified self actually exists, but to explain our compelling intuition that it does.

V. THE ESSENTIAL INDEXICAL

There is, however, a well-known reason to question whether we do actually identify ourselves by way of a heterogeneous battery of contingent properties. The reason has to do with the special way in which we sometimes refer to ourselves when we speak using the first-person pronoun and frame thoughts using the mental analogue of that pronoun.

Consider John Perry's vivid example, in which I see a trail of sugar apparently spilling from somebody's grocery cart. Even if I am the one spilling it, my thinking that the person spilling sugar is making a mess does not imply that I think that I, myself, am making a mess.[21] Reference to oneself, as such, uses what Perry dubs the essential indexical, also called by traditional grammarians the indirect reflexive, because it plays in indirect discourse the role played in direct quotation by the first-person pronoun.[22] And such reference to oneself seems to operate independently of any contingent properties in terms of which one might describe and identify oneself.[23]

Every HOT refers to the self in this essentially indexical way. A HOT cannot represent its target as belonging to oneself under some inessential description; it must represent that target as belonging to oneself, as such. But a thought's being about

---

[21] John Perry, "The Problem of the Essential Indexical," *Noûs* XIII, 1 (March 1979): 3–21. See also P. T. Geach, "On Beliefs about Oneself," *Analysis*, 18, 1 (October 1957): 23–4, reprinted in Geach, *Logic Matters*, Oxford: Basil Blackwell, 1972, pp. 128–9; A. N. Prior, "On Spurious Egocentricity," *Philosophy*, XLII, 162 (October 1967): 326–335; G. E. M. Anscombe, "The First Person," in *Mind and Language*, ed. Samuel Guttenplan, Oxford: Oxford University Press, 1975, pp. 45–65; Steven E. Boër and William G. Lycan, "Who, Me?", *The Philosophical Review*, LXXXIX, 3 (July 1980): 427–66; Hector-Neri Castañeda, "On the Logic of Attributions of Self-Knowledge to Others," *The Journal of Philosophy*, LXV, 15 (August 8, 1968): 439–56; Roderick M. Chisholm, *The First Person*, chs. 3 and 4; and David Lewis, "Attitudes De Dicto and De Se."

[22] And indirect discourse matters here in specifying intentional content.

[23] For an argument that this type of self-reference conflicts with the HOT model, see Dan Zahavi and Josef Parnas, "Phenomenal Consciousness and Self-Awareness: A Phenomenological Critique of Representational Theory," *Journal of Consciousness Studies*, 5, 5–6 (1998): 687–705, § III.

oneself, as such, seems not to rely on any battery of contingent properties. How, then, does the idea that we identify ourselves in terms of such collections of contingent properties square with the requirement that one's HOTs refer to oneself, as such?

Mental states are conscious, when they are, in virtue of being accompanied by HOTs, and each HOT in effect represents its target as belonging to the individual who thinks that HOT. This representing is tacit, since as we saw two sections ago, it is not mediated by any actual reference to the thought itself.

Essentially indexical self-reference occurs not just with HOTs, but with all our first-person thoughts. Suppose I think that I, myself, have the property of being *F*. My thought that I, myself, am *F* in effect represents as being *F* the very individual who thinks that thought. In this way I refer to myself, as such. I refer to myself, as such, when I refer to something, in effect, as the individual that does the referring. No additional connection between first-person thoughts and the self is needed.

In Perry's case, I begin by thinking that somebody is spilling sugar and I come to realize that I, myself, am that person. What I discover when I make that realization is that the individual who is spilling sugar is the very same as the individual who thinks that somebody is spilling sugar; the person being said or thought to spill is the very person who is saying or thinking that somebody spills. By identifying, in effect, the individual a thought purports to be about with the individual who thinks that thought, the essential indexical tacitly links what the thought purports to be about to the very act of thinking that thought.

HOTs are just a special case of first-person thoughts, and all the same things apply to them. Each HOT tacitly represents its target as belonging to the individual that thinks that very HOT. In this way, every HOT represents its target as belonging to oneself, as such.

Reference to oneself, as such, seems to be independent of any particular way of describing or characterizing oneself. But we can now see that there is one type of characterization that is relevant to such reference. When I think, without any essentially indexical self-reference, that the person spilling sugar is making a mess, my thought is, as it happens, about the very individual who thinks that thought, though not about that individual, as such. By contrast, when I think that I, myself, am spilling sugar, my thought then does ascribe the spilling of sugar to the very individual who thinks that thought, as such. As I've stressed, that essentially indexical thought does not explicitly refer to itself. Reference to the thinker, as such, is secured not by descriptive content, but because it's that individual who holds a mental attitude toward the relevant content. The essential indexical ties intentional content to mental attitude.[24]

This connection between the individual that's thought to be spilling sugar and the individual doing the thinking obtains solely in virtue of the tie between content and mental attitude. So it's independent of any other contingent properties one may think of oneself as having. That connection, moreover, is all one needs to refer to oneself, as such. The mental analogue of the word 'I' refers to whatever individual thinks a thought in which that mental analogue occurs.

---

[24] Any account, such as Kaplan's, that relies on context to determine the referent of 'I' and its mental analogue, will appeal to the performing of the relevant speech act or mental act.

In the first person, the essential indexical in effect identifies the self it refers to as the individual who thinks a thought or performs a speech act. This thin way of identifying oneself provides almost no information. But, by the same token, there is no conflict between our referring to ourselves in this way and the battery model of how we identify ourselves. The essential indexical picks something out as the individual that thinks a particular thought; the battery model provides an informative way of saying just which individual that is. This is why we seem unable ever to pin down in any informative way what the essential indexical refers to. The essential indexical refers to the thinker of a thought; an informative characterization of the self depends on one's applying some battery of descriptions to oneself in an essentially indexical way.

A thought about oneself, as such, refers to the individual that thinks that thought, but its content does not explicitly describe one as the thinker of the thought. Since essentially indexical thoughts refer independently of any particular description that occurs in their content, it's tempting to see them as referring in an unmediated way, which might then even provide the foundation for all other referring.[25] But such reference is not unmediated and cannot provide any such foundation. Reference to the thinker, as such, is mediated not by descriptive content, but by the tie the essential indexical tacitly forges between a thought's content and its mental attitude.

There is a sense we sometimes have of ourselves that makes it hard to see how, as conscious selves, we could find ourselves located among the physical furniture of the universe.[26] It's sometimes urged that essentially indexical self-reference is responsible for that appearance of mystery about being the subject of conscious experience, since the essential indexical occurs ineliminably only in describing such subjects. The present account suggests an explanation. It may be that the self seems difficult to fit into our ordinary objective framework because essentially indexical reference to the self is secured not by a thought's descriptive content, but by a tie between that thought's content and its mental attitude.

Reference to somebody, as such, occurs in cases other than the first person. I can describe others as having thoughts about themselves, as such, and the same account applies. Thus I can describe you as thinking that you, yourself, are *F*, and your thought is about you, as such, just in case your thought, cast in the first person, refers to an individual in a way that invites identifying that individual as the thinker of that thought.

Thoughts need not be conscious, and essentially indexical reference to oneself can occur even when they are not. I realize that I, myself, am the one spilling sugar if I would identify the person I think is spilling sugar with the person that thinks that thought. If that thought fails to be conscious, my realization will fail to be as well.

Still, when a thought is about oneself in that essentially indexical way, there is a tendency for it to be conscious over and above whatever tendency exists for thoughts

[25] See references in n. 19.

[26] Consider the puzzled cognitive disorientation Wittgenstein writes of "when I, for example, turn my attention in a particular way on my own consciousness, and, astonished, say to myself: THIS is supposed to be produced by a process in the brain!—as it were clutching my forehead" (*Philosophical Investigations*, ed. G. E. M. Anscombe and R. Rhees, tr. G. E. M. Anscombe, Oxford: Basil Blackwell, 1953, § 412).

that aren't about oneself in that way.[27] When one essentially indexically thinks that one is *F*, one is disposed to identify the person one thinks is *F* with the person who thinks that thought. So one is disposed to have a thought about that essentially indexical thought, and so to be conscious of that thought.

When an essentially indexical thought about myself is conscious, the HOT I have about that conscious thought describes it as being about the individual that thinks the thought. That HOT also in effect describes its target state as belonging to the very individual that thinks the HOT, itself. So, when a conscious thought is about oneself, as such, one is in effect conscious of that thought as being about the individual that not only thinks the thought but is also conscious of thinking it.

Does essentially indexical self-reference make a difference to the way beliefs and desires issue in action? Kaplan's catchy example of my essentially indexical thought that my pants are on fire[28] may make it seem so, since I might behave differently if I thought only that some person's pants are on fire without also thinking that I am that person. Similarly, my thinking that I, myself, should do a certain thing might result in my doing it, whereas my merely thinking that DR should do it might not result in my doing it if I didn't also think that I was DR.

Such cases require care. My doing something when I think I should arguably results from that belief's interacting with my desire to do what I should. Since I very likely would not desire to do what DR should do if I didn't think that I was DR, I would then have no desire that would suitably interact with my belief that DR should do that thing. And if, still not recognizing that I am DR, I nonetheless had for some reason a desire to do what DR should do, my belief that DR should do something would then very likely result in my doing it. The need here for a belief to make essentially indexical self-reference is due solely to the essentially indexical self-reference made by the relevant desire.

The situation is similar with thinking that one's pants are on fire. Even disregarding perceptual asymmetries, the desires that would pertain to my belief that my pants are on fire will doubtless differ in relevant ways from desires that would pertain to my belief that your pants are on fire, and so to my belief that DR's pants are on fire if I don't know that I am DR.

Many of one's beliefs and desires, however, do not refer to oneself at all, as such or in any other way. I might want a beer and think that there is beer in the refrigerator. The content of that desire might refer to me; it could be a desire that I have a beer. Things might well then be different if I had instead a desire only that DR have a beer. But the desire need not refer to me at all; its content could instead be simply that having a beer would be nice.[29] And that desire would likely lead to my acting, not because

[27] On the tendency of thoughts in general to be conscious when they occur in creatures with suitable ability to think about their own thoughts, see "Why Are Verbally Expressed Thoughts Conscious?", ch. 10 in this volume.

[28] "If I see, reflected in a window, the image of a man whose pants appear to be on fire, my behavior is sensitive to whether I think, 'His pants are on fire' or 'My pants are on fire', though the object of thought may be the same" ("Demonstratives," p. 533).

[29] Affective states, such as happiness, sadness, anger, and the like, also have intentional contents cast in such evaluative terms. See my "Consciousness and its Expression," ch. 11 in this volume, § IV.

the content of the desire refers to me, but because I am the individual that holds the desiderative attitude towards that content. Essentially indexical self-reference is not needed for beliefs and desires to issue in action.[30]

According to David Lewis, the objects toward which we hold attitudes are best understood as properties. Holding an attitude, he urges, consists in self-ascribing a property. And he argues that this account not only handles attitudes toward essentially indexical contents, which he calls attitudes *de se*, but also provides a uniform treatment for the attitudes, whatever their content.

Lewis's main concern is to say what kind of thing the objects of the attitudes are. And he seems to take as primitive the notion of self-ascribing invoked in this account. But it's still worth examining just what would be needed to ascribe a property to oneself, as such. In particular, does one need explicitly to think about or to represent oneself, as such?

Lewis holds that all ascribing of properties to individuals takes place under a description, which in the relevant kind of case is a relation of acquaintance. Self-ascribing, then, is the special case in which one ascribes a property to oneself "under the relation of identity," which he characterizes as "a relation of acquaintance par excellence" (543/156; see n. 19).

Lewis goes on, then, to construe all ascribing of properties to individuals as the ascribing of some suitable property to oneself. The ascribing of a property, P, to some individual under a relation of acquaintance, R, is the ascribing to oneself of the property of bearing R uniquely to an individual that has that property, P.[31] The property one self-ascribes specifies the content of the attitude one thereby holds. And, since the relation of acquaintance, R, figures in the property one self-ascribes, it is part of the content toward which one holds an attitude. One explicitly represents the individual one thinks has property P as the individual with which one is acquainted in the relevant way.

Because regress would occur if one applied this account to the special case of self-ascribing, it is not obvious how the relation of acquaintance is secured in that case. Still, self-ascribing is the special case of the ascribing of properties in which the

---

[30] When action results from a desire whose content is simply that having a beer would be nice, an interaction between mental attitude and content is again operative: It's my holding that desiderative attitude that results in action. So it may well be that some such interaction between attitude and content is needed for belief-desire pairs to lead to action, whether or not that interaction issues in essentially indexical self-reference.

Philip Robbins has suggested (personal communication) that HOTs might operate, as do desires, without first-person content, in which case HOTs also would not need to be cast in essentially indexical terms. But explaining the consciousness of mental states makes heavier representational demands than explaining action. To explain an action we need a belief-desire pair that would plausibly cause that action; my holding a desiderative attitude toward the content that having a beer would be nice would plausibly do so. To explain a state's being conscious, however, we must explain an individual's being conscious of being in that state, and that means actually representing oneself as being in that state, at least for creatures that distinguish in thought between themselves and everything else (see n. 9).

[31] "Postscripts to 'Attitudes *De Dicto* and *De Se*'," *Philosophical Papers*, I, New York: Oxford University Press, 1983, pp. 156–159, at p. 156.

relation of acquaintance is identity. If self-ascribing follows that model, the content toward which one holds an attitude in self-ascribing will explicitly represent the individual to which one ascribes a property as being identical with oneself. And it is unclear how this might occur unless the attitude explicitly represents that individual as being identical with the individual doing the ascribing. And this, we saw in section III, would cause trouble for the HOT model, since if HOTs explicitly refer to themselves, each HOT would make one conscious of that very HOT, thereby making all HOTs conscious.

But, since Lewis seems to take the notion of self-ascribing as primitive, it needn't follow the general model of the ascribing of properties. And if it doesn't, we can construe the identity between the individual to which a property is ascribed and the individual doing the ascribing as built into the act of self-ascribing, rather than its content. It would then be the performing of that act, rather than some explicit representing, that secures the identity. And the potential difficulty for the HOT model would thereby be averted.

VI. IMMUNITY TO ERROR THROUGH MISIDENTIFICATION[32]

The essential indexical apart, there is another concern about whether we actually identify ourselves by way of a heterogeneous collection of contingent properties. Some of our first-person thoughts appear to be immune to a particular type of error, and it may not be obvious how such immunity is possible if we identify ourselves by way of a battery of contingent properties.

One can, of course, be mistaken in what one thinks about oneself and even about who one is; one might, for example, think that one is Napoleon. And I've argued elsewhere that one can also be mistaken about what mental states one is in, even when those states are conscious. One can be conscious of oneself *as being* in mental states that one is not actually in. The HOT model readily explains this as being due to the having of a HOT that is mistaken in the mental state it ascribes to one.[33]

It's tempting to think that the phrase 'is conscious' is factive, so that one's being conscious of something implies that that thing exists. But even if this is so, one could still be conscious of states that one isn't actually in. Plainly one can be conscious of an actual object as being different from the way it actually is; one can be conscious, for example, of a red object as being green. And one's having a HOT that describes one

---

[32] This section is significantly recast over the original; see also "Being Conscious of Ourselves," *The Monist*, 87, 2 (April 2004): 159–181, §IV.

[33] See, e.g., "Sensory Qualities, Consciousness, and Perception," ch. 7 in this volume, §V; "Explaining Consciousness," §V; "Consciousness and Metacognition," in *Metarepresentation: A Multidisciplinary Perspective*, Proceedings of the Tenth Vancouver Cognitive Science Conference, ed. Daniel Sperber, New York: Oxford University Press, 2000, pp. 265–295, §V; "Consciousness, Content, and Metacognitive Judgments," *Consciousness and Cognition*, 9, 2, Part 1 (June 2000): 203–214, §V; and "Metacognition and Higher-Order Thoughts," *Consciousness and Cognition*, 9, 2, Part 1 (June 2000): 231–242, §IV.

as being in a state that one is not actually in simply makes one conscious of an existing object, namely, oneself, as being in a state that that object is not actually in.[34]

Even if we can be in error about who we are and what conscious states we are in, perhaps there are other ways in which some of our first-person thoughts cannot be mistaken. Suppose that I consciously feel pain or see a canary. It may be that I can be wrong about whether the state I am in is one of feeling pain or seeing a canary. But if I do think that I feel pain or see a canary, perhaps it cannot then be that I am right that somebody feels pain or sees a canary but wrong that it is I who does so. Sydney Shoemaker has forcefully urged that a range of first-person thoughts cannot be in error in this specific way. And he describes those thoughts in a now classic phrase as being "immune to error through misidentification," specifically with respect to reference to oneself.[35]

Not all first-person thoughts are immune to error in this way. In particular, no first-person thought is thus immune if one comes to have it in the way we come to have thoughts about the mental states of others. Shoemaker recognizes this, noting that one might wrongly take a reflection one sees in a mirror to be a reflection of one-self, and thereby misidentify oneself as the person one sees in the mirror (7). And, if one thought that the person in the mirror is in a particular mental state, one might conclude that one is, oneself, in that state; one could then be right that somebody is in that state, but wrong that it is oneself that is in the state. So Shoemaker does not claim immunity to error whenever one has a thought that one has a particular property, but only when one's thought arises from the special way we have access to our own conscious states.

Even confining ourselves to these cases, however, such immunity to error would threaten the battery model. On that model, we identify the individual each first-person thought refers to by appeal to a heterogeneous collection of contingent properties. But it could turn out that any or, indeed, all of the properties in such a battery do not actually belong to one. So, if we do identify ourselves in that way, then

---

[34] One might further object, as Elizabeth Vlahos has ("Can Higher-Order Thoughts Explain Consciousness? A Dilemma," MS), that in such a case there is no state that's conscious. This, too, is not a problem. We can simply construe the conscious states our HOTs thus refer to as the notional objects of those HOTs. Or we could equally well say instead that we are conscious in these cases of some relevant occurrent state but in an inaccurate way. Either move effectively meets the objection. See "Metacognition and Higher-Order Thoughts," §I.

[35] Sydney Shoemaker, "Self-Reference and Self-Awareness," p. 8. Shoemaker thinks such immunity applies even when I think I'm performing some action. See also Gareth Evans, "Demonstrative Identification," in Evans, *Varieties of Reference*, ed. John McDowell, Oxford: Clarendon Press, 1982, pp. 142–266.

James Pryor's useful distinction between *de re* misidentification and *wh*-misidentification hinges on the epistemic grounds for holding the relevant beliefs, which are not relevant to what follows ("Immunity to Error through Misidentification," *Philosophical Topics*, 26, 1 and 2 [Spring and Fall 1999]: 271–304.

I have profited from discussion of these issues with Roblin Meeks, and with Michael Martin when an earlier version of this paper was presented at the June 23, 2003, meeting of the Aristotelian Society. See also Meeks, "Identifying the First Person," unpublished Ph.D. dissertation, The City University of New York Graduate Center, 2003, chs. II–IV.

whatever state I think I am in and whatever my basis for thinking that, I could be right that somebody is in that state but wrong that I am the person who's in that state. If immunity to error through misidentification holds, the battery model is wrong.

But there is reason to doubt that such immunity does actually obtain, even for the first-person thoughts under consideration. One might in certain circumstances have such strong empathy with another person that one becomes confused about a mental state of that person, and takes oneself to be in the state. So one might in this way go from seeing another person in some form of emotional elation or anguish to being conscious of oneself as being in that state.

Such overwrought empathy might in some cases lead one actually to be in a felt state of elation or anguish. But that need not happen. It might instead be that no such affective state occurs in one, but one comes nonetheless to be conscious of oneself as being in such a state. This is what would happen if one were conscious of oneself as feeling elation or anguish and yet displayed none of the other characteristic signs of the state one was conscious of oneself as being in.

Suppose I think that I am in pain in what seems to be the characteristic first-person way in which we have access to our own pains. And suppose that there is some pain my thought is about. Why does it seem that I can't be wrong about whether I'm the one who's in pain, as opposed to you? The temptation to think that must stem from the assumption that being conscious of a pain or other state in the relevant subjective way in some way guarantees that I can't be wrong about whether I'm the individual I'm conscious of as being in that state. Subjective access may not guarantee that I'm right about the character of the state I'm conscious of myself as being in, but on this view it does ensure that I'm the one who's in that state if anybody is. One might indeed wonder what else it could mean for one's access to a state to be subjective. If some individual is in a state to which I have subjective access, how could it be somebody other than me who is in that state?

One might simply stipulate that this guarantee is part of what it is for access to be subjective; access is subjective only if it is in this way access to oneself. But it is a substantive question whether the thoughts under consideration are immune to error through misidentification, and it begs that question to assume that all access that seems subjective is actually subjective in this stipulated sense.

Part of what makes access to something seem subjective is that it appears spontaneous and unmediated. And it may be tempting to think that access that seems thus spontaneous and unmediated can occur only in connection with the transparency of the mind to its own states. But the appearance of spontaneity and of lack of mediation is not due to any actual transparency. Access to things often seems spontaneous and unmediated without actually being so; perceiving typically seems spontaneous and unmediated, though we know that it isn't. So, even when we seem to have spontaneous, immediate access to our own mental states, the appearance of spontaneous immediacy may be due solely to the noninferential character of the way we're aware of those states. Our access to these states appears spontaneous and unmediated only because we are unaware of any mediation between the states and our awareness of them.

I have subjective access to a pain when I have a HOT that I am in pain, a HOT that does not appear to me to rely on any inference. And such a HOT can arise, as with all our thoughts, in ways that result in its being erroneous. I can have a seemingly noninferential HOT that I am in pain or some other mental state even though I am not. And, as the empathy case illustrates, I can have such a HOT even though it is you that is actually in that state, rather than I. Immunity to error through misidentification does not obtain. The battery model faces no difficulty from that quarter.

Shoemaker appeals to a passage in which Wittgenstein urges that the first-person pronoun is used differently in statements such as 'I have a broken arm' from the way it's used in statements such as 'I am in pain'.[36] Wittgenstein claims that, though one plainly could be wrong about whether it is one's own arm that's actually broken, "[t]o ask 'are you sure that it's *you* who have pains?' would be nonsensical" (67, emphasis original). Doubtless such a question is typically out of place, but remarks that are typically out of place need not on that account be nonsensical. And, as the example of extreme empathy shows, such a question will in exceptional cases be appropriate, even if rather surprising.

It's tempting to hold that immunity to error obtains because the seemingly spontaneous, unmediated character of the access we sometimes have to mental states seems to guarantee that those states cannot belong to anybody other than oneself. But, since we have no reason to think that this access is actually spontaneous and immediate, as against merely apparent, no such guarantee holds.

The temptation to think that this guarantee does hold rests on the assumption that being conscious of a mental state in the relevant subjective way ensures that I'm not wrong about whether I'm the individual I'm conscious of as being in that state. And this assumption suggests a weaker form of immunity that does hold, despite cases of extreme empathy. I may think in that seemingly immediate way that I am in pain and be right that somebody is in pain, and yet be wrong that I'm the one who's in pain. But I cannot in such a case be wrong about whether it is I who I think is in pain. Similarly, if I think in that seemingly immediate way that I believe or desire something, I cannot be mistaken about whether it is I who I think has that belief or desire. Because this constraint is weaker than the immunity to error Shoemaker describes, I'll refer to it as *thin* immunity to error through misidentification.

Such thin immunity seems unimpeachable; how could one be mistaken in such a case about whether the individual one thinks is in some particular state is oneself? But it may seem that even such thin immunity may threaten the battery model about how we identify ourselves. Suppose, as that model holds, that we do identify the individual each first-person thought refers to by appeal to a heterogeneous collection of contingent properties. Any or even all of the properties in such a battery might turn out not to belong to one. So identifying oneself in that way seems to leave open the possibility that, when I take myself to be in pain or to have some belief, I could be mistaken even about who the individual is that I think is in pain or has that belief.

[36] Shoemaker, "Self-Reference and Self-Awareness," p. 7; Ludwig Wittgenstein, *The Blue and Brown Books*, Oxford: Basil Blackwell, 1958, 2nd edn. 1969, pp. 66–7.

What exactly does this thin immunity guarantee? When I have a conscious pain, I cannot be wrong about whether it's I who I think is in pain, though I can of course be wrong about just who it is that I am; I may, for example, think that I'm Napoleon. How can we capture this delicate distinction? What exactly does thin immunity ensure that I cannot be wrong about?

When I have a conscious pain, I am conscious of being in pain. The error I cannot make is to think that the individual I think is in pain is distinct from the individual that's conscious of somebody's being in pain. The misidentification I cannot make is to take myself be to somebody distinct from the individual doing the identifying. Nonetheless, such thin immunity does leave it open for me to be wrong in some substantive way about who I am, for example, by thinking that I am Napoleon.

The HOT model provides a natural explanation of thin immunity. The mental analogue of the pronoun 'I' refers to whatever individual thinks a thought in which that mental analogue occurs. So each HOT in effect[37] represents its target state as belonging to the individual that thinks that very HOT. When a pain is conscious, the individual the relevant HOT represents that pain as belonging to is the same as the individual that thinks that HOT. So one cannot be wrong about whether the individual that seems to be in pain is the very same as the individual for whom that pain is conscious.

When I think I am in pain, there is no way to go wrong about whether it's I who I think is in pain. So there is no way to misidentify the individual I think is in pain as somebody else. I am conscious of a single individual both as being in pain and, in effect, as the individual that's conscious of being in pain. And I use the mental analogue of 'I' to refer to that one individual.

This thin immunity is no more than an echo of the immunity Shoemaker describes, and the error against which it protects is not substantive. I cannot represent my conscious pain as belonging to somebody distinct from me because a pain's being conscious consists in one's being conscious of oneself as being in pain. And that in turn is simply a matter of one's being conscious of the pain as belonging to the individual that's conscious of it. The thin immunity to error that results consists only in the impossibility of one's being conscious of being in a state and yet conscious of that state as belonging to an individual other than the individual who is conscious of being in it.

Thin immunity doesn't protect against substantive errors about who I am; I might still think I'm Napoleon. So there is no conflict with the battery model. One is trivially immune to error only about whether the individual one is noninferentially conscious of as being in pain is the individual that's conscious of the pain. The battery of contingent properties, by contrast, enables us to distinguish that individual from others, described in terms of various distinguishing properties.[38] Thin immunity has no bearing on error in respect of the contingent properties in such a battery.

---

[37] In effect, once again, because, although thoughts that contain the mental analogue of 'I' do not actually refer to themselves, still every first-person thought disposes one to have another thought that identifies the referent of that mental analogue as the thinker of the first-person thought. Every first-person thought in that way tacitly, i.e., dispositionally characterizes the self it is about as the thinker of that very thought.

[38] Essentially indexical self-reference also enables one to distinguish oneself from every other individual, but again only in a thin way. It allows me to distinguish myself from others only relative

According to Shoemaker, when one introspectively knows that one is in pain or that one believes something, there is no "role for awareness of oneself as an object to play in explaining my introspective knowledge" of those states. This, he suggests, is of a piece with the immunity to error of our first-person thoughts about our own mental states.[39] And, if awareness of oneself as an object does not figure in introspective access, there is no way for such access to go wrong in respect of which object is in the introspected state.

But this doesn't accurately reflect the way we're conscious of our conscious states. Being conscious of a state on its own, and not of the state as belonging to some individual, is being conscious only of a state type, and not of any particular token. States are perforce states of objects; only types of states are independent of particular objects. It's for that reason that HOTs must make one conscious of mental states as belonging to a particular individual, namely, oneself. And those HOTs will accordingly make one conscious of oneself as the object that is in those states.

As noted at the outset, the perceptual model of the access we have to our own mental states makes a mystery of how we could be aware of a self. But we no more perceive our mental states than we perceive the self to which they belong. Construing introspective awareness in terms of conscious HOTs explains how awareness of oneself occurs. One is introspectively aware of a state in virtue of having a conscious thought that one is in a particular state, and one is thereby aware of oneself as being in that conscious state. Introspective awareness involves conscious thoughts that ascribe mental states to oneself.

Shoemaker writes that "[m]y use of the word 'I' as the subject of [such] statement[s as that I feel pain or see a canary] is not due to my having identified as myself something" to which I think the relevant predicate applies (9). But one is disposed to identify the individual one takes to do these things as the individual who takes somebody to do them. So one is disposed, in this thin way at least, to identify as oneself the individual one takes to feel pain or see a canary.

As noted above, Shoemaker is clear that the strong immunity to error he describes would not hold for all first-person thoughts. I might see somebody's reflection in a mirror and wrongly take myself to be that person. Error through misidentification is plainly possible in that case. Only thoughts that result from transparent access to our mental states would be immune to error in Shoemaker's strong way; such immunity hinges on our being conscious of states in that special way.

Thin immunity, by contrast, does not depend on subjective access or on any special properties such access supposedly has. Rather, thin immunity is a function solely

---

to my thinking of a particular essentially indexical thought; I am distinct from everybody else in that no other individual is in that token intentional state.

[39] "Self-Knowledge and 'Inner Sense'," The Royce Lectures, *Philosophy and Phenomenological Research*, LIV, 2 (June 1994): 249–314; reprinted in Shoemaker, *The First-Person Perspective and Other Essays*, Cambridge: Cambridge University Press, 1996, pp. 201–268, at p. 211.

Shoemaker's claim here echoes Wittgenstein's idea that, whereas 'I have a broken arm' involves "the use [of 'I'] as object," 'I have a toothache' involves instead "the use [of 'I'] as subject" (*The Blue and Brown Books*, p. 66). Cf. also Anscombe's view, mentioned in §IV, that there is no object of which first-person thoughts predicate concepts.

of how one's awareness of oneself as being in some state represents the individual that one is thereby conscious of. So far as thin immunity goes, the mirror case is on a par with one's being aware of oneself by having first-person access to some conscious state.

If I think that I'm the person I see in a mirror, I can be wrong about whether that image is actually of me. I could even be wrong in a certain way about who it is that I think I see; I might think I'm Napoleon and so think that I see Napoleon. But there is a thin way in which my identifying myself even there is immune to error. If I think I see myself in a mirror, I cannot be wrong about who it is I think the individual in the mirror is. I identify the individual in the mirror as the very individual whom I could also pick out as doing the identifying. In that thin way, I in effect identify the person I am visually conscious of as the individual who is visually conscious of that person, and I use the mental analogue of 'I' to refer to that one individual.

Such thin immunity is plainly trivial. But the thin immunity that holds when I think that I am in pain or that I believe something is no less so. I can be wrong about whether the individual I think is in pain is DR or Napoleon; what I can't be wrong about is whether the individual I think is in pain is the very individual that thinks that somebody is. I cannot be wrong about whether the individual I take to be in pain is the individual who is conscious of somebody as being in pain.

Similarly, suppose I think I am Napoleon because I see somebody in a mirror suitably dressed and wrongly take myself to be the person I see. Though I misidentify myself as that person, I do not misidentify who it is that I think is Napoleon; it is I, myself, that I think is Napoleon. No error is possible about whether the individual I think is Napoleon is the very individual I could also identify as having that thought.

The substantive immunity to error Shoemaker describes does not obtain. But things would be different if a mental state's being conscious were an intrinsic property of that state. It would then be intrinsic simply to one's being in a conscious state that one is disposed to regard as being in that state the individual that takes somebody to be in that state. Since it would be intrinsic to one's being in a conscious state that it is oneself that one takes to be in that state, one's identifying oneself as the individual that is in the state would not be the result of any process. It would result simply from one's being in the state, since the state is intrinsically conscious. Since there would be no identifying process that might go wrong, there would be no way for one to be right in thinking that somebody is in a conscious state but wrong that it is oneself that is in the state.

So, if consciousness were an intrinsic property of our conscious states, Shoemaker's strong immunity would hold. But we cannot assume without argument that a state's being conscious is an intrinsic property of that state. And that view faces serious difficulties. For one thing, it requires that we can only individuate conscious states so that being conscious of the state is an intrinsic part or aspect of the state itself. But one need not individuate conscious states in that way; one gets an entirely satisfactory method of individuation by taking the property of being conscious to be extrinsic to every conscious state. And if we can individuate conscious states both in ways that make consciousness intrinsic and in ways that do not, consciousness is intrinsic only nominally, relative to an optional method of individuation. And that is not enough to sustain strong immunity.[40]

Other considerations also tell against the idea that consciousness is intrinsic to conscious states. A single mental state may well have more than one content, but no single state can exhibit more than one mental attitude; no single intentional state could, for example, be both a case of doubting and an assertoric thought. Since an assertoric mental attitude figures in one's being conscious of one's mental states, the consciousness of any intentional state whose mental attitude is nonassertoric must be distinct from the state itself.[41] Since the Cartesian idea that consciousness is intrinsic to conscious states is untenable, it cannot sustain the strong immunity Shoemaker describes. Only thin immunity obtains.

Thoughts can make essentially indexical self-reference whether or not they are conscious thoughts. Does thin immunity to error occur only with conscious states? Or does such immunity affect nonconscious mental states as well?

Suppose I see in a mirror somebody limping. I am not in conscious pain. But I take that person to be me and, since I acknowledge the occurrence of pains that aren't conscious, I conclude that I am in a nonconscious state of pain. I can be wrong about whether the person I see is me. But here again I cannot be wrong about whether the individual I take to be in pain is the individual that's thought to be in pain. The mirror case shows that thin immunity extends to the self-ascription not only of non-mental properties, but in the same way to the self-ascription of mental states that are not conscious.

VII. UNITY AND FREEDOM

The present approach to unity also suggests natural ways to explain various failures of unity, such as the puzzling phenomenon of Multiple Personality, now more often known as Dissociative Identity Disorder.[42] It also helps explain one other important source of intuitions about the unity of consciousness.

---

[40] Shoemaker urges that the functional roles definitive of mental states sustain "a conceptual, constitutive connection between the existence of certain sort of mental entities [states] and their introspective accessibility" ("Self-Knowledge and 'Inner Sense'," Lecture II, "The Broad Perceptual Model," p. 225). Though he insists that this connection is weaker than the transparency of the mind to itself, it may be enough to support a taxonomy of conscious states on which their being conscious is an intrinsic property of those states. See Lecture II *passim*, and "On Knowing One's Own Mind," *Philosophical Perspectives: Epistemology*, 2 (1988): 183–209, reprinted in Shoemaker's *The First-Person Perspective and Other Essays*, pp. 25–49.

Still, since the connection with introspective accessibility is a matter of functional role, we need not regard that connection as a necessary part of taxonomizing mental states as such. Shoemaker's taxonomy may make consciousness an intrinsic property of conscious states, but that taxonomy is optional. These issues are also discussed in "Moore's Paradox and Consciousness," ch. 9 in this volume, §IV.

[41] See "Thinking that One Thinks," §IV. For more reasons to reject the idea that consciousness is intrinsic to mental states, see "Two Concepts of Consciousness," §II, and "Varieties of Higher-Order Theory," §V.

[42] The compelling appearance of distinct selves presumably results in part from there being disjoint sets of beliefs, desires, emotions, and other intentional states specific to the apparent selves, though

People have a compelling experience of many of their actions as being free, and that experience of seeming freedom encourages the idea of a unified, conscious self as the source of such actions. The HOT model provides a natural explanation of these Kantian ideas about freedom that doesn't posit any underlying unity of the self.

Even when we experience actions as free, we typically experience them as resulting from conscious desires and intentions. We do not experience the actions as being uncaused, but rather as being due to conscious desires and intentions that seem not, themselves, to be caused.[43] Actions appear to be free when they appear to result from spontaneous, uncaused desires and intentions.

Because our mental states are not all conscious, we are seldom if ever conscious of the mental antecedents of our conscious states. And conscious desires and intentions whose mental antecedents we are not conscious of seem to us to be spontaneous and uncaused. The sense we have of free agency results from our failure to be conscious

---

many general desires and background beliefs will be shared. But it's also very likely due to there being distinct sets of HOTs, each operating on a distinct group of intentional states. And, because each disjoint group of HOTs operates on a distinct set of first-person thoughts, that group of HOTs will assign its targets to an apparent self characterized by the battery that derives from that set of first-person thoughts. Such an individual will accordingly be conscious of itself in dramatically different terms, depending on which set is active.

It is worth noting that such failures of unity are failures of apparent unity of consciousness, and do not by themselves speak to the issue raised at the outset about some underlying actual unity of consciousness. We can speculate that such apparent unity may also be diminished or even absent altogether in creatures whose mental lives are less elaborate in relevant ways. I am grateful to Josef Perner (personal communication) for pressing the question about absence or failure of unity.

[43] As always, it is crucial to distinguish the mental state one is conscious of from our being conscious of it, in this case, the event of desiring or deciding from our consciousness of that event. Indeed, robust experimental findings support this distinction, by establishing that our subjective awareness of decisions to perform basic actions occurs measurably later than the events of deciding of which we are conscious. See Benjamin Libet, Curtis A. Gleason, Elwood W. Wright, and Dennis K. Pearl, "Time of Conscious Intention to Act in Relation to Onset of Cerebral Activity (Readiness Potential)," *Brain*, 106, Part III (September 1983): 623–642; and Benjamin Libet, "Unconscious Cerebral Initiative and the Role of Conscious Will in Voluntary Action," *The Behavioral and Brain Sciences*, 8, 4 (December 1985): 529–539. This work has been replicated and extended by Patrick Haggard, Chris Newman, and Edna Magno, "On the Perceived Time of Voluntary Actions," *British Journal of Psychology*, 90, Part 2 (May 1999): 291–303; Patrick Haggard, "Perceived Timing of Self-Initiated Actions," in *Cognitive Contributions to the Perception of Spatial and Temporal Events*, ed. Gisa Aschersleben, Talis Bachmann, and Jochen Müsseler, Amsterdam: Elsevier, 1999, pp. 215–231; and Patrick Haggard and Martin Eimer, "On the Relation between Brain Potentials and Awareness of Voluntary Movements," *Experimental Brain Research*, 126, 1 (1999): 128–133. For more on the connection between this research and intuitions about free will, see my "The Timing of Conscious States," *Consciousness and Cognition*, 11, 2 (June 2002): 215–220.

Related considerations have been advanced by Daniel Wegner, who presents experimental evidence that the experience of conscious will results from our interpreting our intentions as the causes of our actions. Wegner argues that such an interpretation arises when we are conscious of the intention as prior to and consistent with the action and we are conscious of no other cause of the action. See Daniel M. Wegner, *The Illusion of Conscious Will*, Cambridge, Massachusetts: MIT Press/Bradford Books, 2002, and Daniel Wegner and Thalia Wheatley, "Apparent Mental Causation: Sources of the Experience of Will," *American Psychologist*, 54, 7 (July 1999): 480–492.

of all our mental states. It does not point to any underlying metaphysical unity of the self.

This conclusion receives support from a certain type of weakness of will. Consider what happens when one is conscious of oneself as wanting to do something or withhold from doing it, but the desire one is conscious of oneself as having is not efficacious in producing or blocking that action. Doubtless in some cases one does not actually have the desire or intention one is conscious of oneself as having, or in any case not in the decisive way one is conscious of oneself as having it. In other cases the desire or intention may be present, but still not lead to action.[44] These cases all lead to a diminished subjective sense of freedom of the will, since one comes to see that causes one is unaware of sometimes play a decisive role in determining one's behavior. We become aware that the desires and intentions we are conscious of ourselves as having diverge somewhat from the actual mental determinants of our actions. Our diminished sense of freedom in these cases reinforces the hypothesis that our full sense of freedom on other occasions results simply from our being unaware of any causal determinants of the conscious desires and intentions that seem to lead to our actions.

These considerations also help explain the compelling sense we have that the consciousness of our thoughts, desires, and intentions makes a large and significant difference to the role those states are able to play in our lives. It's often held that our ability to reason, make rational choices, and exercise our critical capacities is enhanced by the relevant intentional states' being conscious. This inviting idea doubtless underlies Ned Block's explication of what he calls access consciousness in terms of a state's being "poised to be used as a premise in reasoning, . . . [and] for [the] *rational* control of action and . . . speech."[45]

But on the face of it, this idea should strike us as perplexing. The role that thoughts and desires can play in our lives is a function of their causal relations to one another and to behavior. And presumably those causal relations are due solely, or at least in great measure, to the intentional contents and mental attitudes that characterize the states. So it will not significantly matter to those causal interactions whether the states are conscious. Accompanying HOTs will of course add some causal relations of their own, but these will be minor in comparison to those of the target states.[46] Why, then,

---

[44] Is this the sort of thing Aristotle calls *akrasía* (*Nicomachean Ethics*, VII, 1–10)? *Akrasía*, as he describes it, occurs when one perceives some path as good and passion leads one to follow instead some other course. But perceiving the good, on his account, itself functions desideratively; the perception that a particular kind of thing is good together with the belief that something is of that kind leads to action. So, if passions can sometimes occur nonconsciously, the kind of case envisaged here will comfortably fall under Aristotle's notion of *akrasía*. I am grateful to Eric Brown for having raised this issue.

[45] "On a Confusion about a Function of Consciousness," p. 231; emphasis Block's.

It's arguable that Block's well-known distinction between phenomenal and access consciousness is best seen not as a distinction between two types of consciousness, but between two types of mental state, each of which can occur consciously. See my "How Many Kinds of Consciousness?", *Consciousness and Cognition*, 11, 4 (December 2002): 653–665.

[46] Nor, if content and mental attitude determine the interactions intentional states have with behavior and each other, should their being conscious matter much on any other explanation of what that consciousness consists in.

should consciousness seem, subjectively, to make such a difference to our ability to reason and make rational choices?

The answer lies in the connection consciousness has to the apparent freedom of our conscious thoughts, desires, and intentions. It's plausible that a state's arising freely would make a significant difference to the role it can play in our lives. And our conscious thoughts, desires, and intentions seem to us to arise freely because of the way we are conscious of them. So it seems, in turn, that our intentional states' being conscious must itself somehow make a significant difference to the role those states can play in our lives. It is because the way we are conscious of our intentional states often makes it seem that they are free and uncaused that their being conscious seems to matter to our ability to reason and make rational choices.[47]

[47] Earlier versions of this paper were presented as the Clark-Way Harrison Lecture at Washington University in St Louis, and at the Duke University meeting of the Association for the Scientific Study of Consciousness, the University of Salzburg, and Stanford University. Some work on this paper occurred during a semester's visit in the Program in Philosophy, Neuroscience, and Psychology at Washington University in St Louis; I am grateful for their support and hospitality.

Select Bibliography

Anscombe, G. E. M., "The First Person," in Samuel Guttenplan, ed., *Mind and Language*, Oxford: Clarendon Press, 1975, pp. 45–65.

Aristotle, *de Anima: Books II, III* (with passages from Book I), tr. D. W. Hamlyn, Oxford: Clarendon Press, 1968; with a report on recent work and a revised bibliography by Christopher Shields, Oxford: Clarendon Press, 1993.

Armstrong, D. M., *A Materialist Theory of the Mind*, New York: Humanities Press, 1968; 2nd revised edn., London: Routledge & Kegan Paul, 1993.

—— "What is Consciousness?", *Proceedings of the Russellian Society*, 3 (1978): 65–76; reprinted in expanded form in Armstrong, *The Nature of Mind*, St Lucia, Queensland: University of Queensland Press, 1980, pp. 55–67.

Austin, J. L., "Other Minds," in Austin, *Philosophical Papers*, 3rd edition, Oxford: Oxford University Press, 1979, pp. 76–116; 1st edition, 1961, pp. 44–84.

Berkeley, George, *The Works of George Berkeley*, ed. A. A. Luce and T. E. Jessop, London: Thomas Nelson & Sons Ltd., 1948–1957.

Block, Ned, "On a Confusion about a Function of Consciousness," *The Behavioral and Brain Sciences*, 18, 2 (June 1995): 227–247, with Author's Response, "How Many Concepts of Consciousness?", 272–287.

—— "Paradox and Cross Purposes in Recent Work on Consciousness," *Cognition*, 79, 1–2 (April 2001): 197–219.

—— Owen Flanagan, and Güven Güzeldere, eds., *The Nature of Consciousness: Philosophical Debates*, Cambridge, Massachusetts: MIT Press/Bradford Books, 1997.

Brentano, Franz, *Psychology from an Empirical Standpoint*, ed. Oskar Kraus, English edition ed. Linda L. McAlister, tr. Antos C. Rancurello, D. B. Terrell, and Linda L. McAlister, London: Routledge & Kegan Paul, 1973 (original 1874).

Carruthers, Peter, *Phenomenal Consciousness: A Naturalistic Theory*, Cambridge: Cambridge University Press, 2000.

—— "HOP over FOR, HOT Theory," in Gennaro, ed., *Higher-Order Theories of Consciousness*, pp. 115–135.

Chisholm, Roderick M., *The First Person*, Minneapolis: University of Minnesota Press, 1981.

Clark, Austen, *Sensory Qualities*, Oxford: Clarendon Press, 1993.

—— *A Theory of Sentience*, Oxford: Clarendon Press, 2000.

Dennett, Daniel C., *Content and Consciousness*, New York: Humanities Press, 1969.

—— *Brainstorms*, Cambridge, Massachusetts: MIT Press/Bradford Books, 1978.

—— *The Intentional Stance*, Cambridge, Massachusetts: MIT Press/Bradford Books, 1987.

—— *Consciousness Explained*, Boston: Little, Brown & Co., 1991.

Descartes, René, *The Philosophical Writings of Descartes*, tr. John Cottingham, Robert Stoothoff, and Dugald Murdoch (vol. III with Anthony Kenny), 3 volumes, Cambridge: Cambridge University Press, 1984–91.

Dienes, Zoltán, and Josef Perner, "Assumptions of a Subjective Measure of Consciousness: Three Mappings," in Gennaro, ed., *Higher-Order Theories of Consciousness*, pp. 173–199.

Dretske, Fred, "Conscious Experience," *Mind*, 102, 406 (April 1993): 263–283; reprinted in Dretske, *Perception, Knowledge, and Belief*, pp. 113–137.

Dretske, Fred, *Naturalizing the Mind,* Cambridge, Massachusetts: MIT Press/Bradford Books, 1995.

____ *Perception, Knowledge, and Belief,* Cambridge: Cambridge University Press, 2000.

Frankfurt, Harry G., "Freedom of the Will and the Concept of a Person," *The Journal of Philosophy,* LXVIII, 1 (January 14, 1971): 5–20.

Freud, Sigmund, *The Complete Psychological Works of Sigmund Freud,* tr. and ed. James Strachey, London: The Hogarth Press, 1966–1974.

Frith, Chris D., and Uta Frith, "Interacting Minds—A Biological Basis," *Science,* 286, i5445 (November 26, 1999): 1692–1695.

Geach, P. T., "On Beliefs about Oneself," *Analysis,* 18, 1 (October 1957): 23–4; reprinted in Geach, *Logic Matters,* Oxford: Basil Blackwell, 1972, pp. 128–9.

Gennaro, Rocco J., ed., *Higher-Order Theories of Consciousness,* Amsterdam and Philadelphia: John Benjamins Publishers, 2004.

Grice, Paul, "Utterer's Meaning and Intentions," *The Philosophical Review,* LXXVIII, 2 (April 1969): 147–177.

Grimes, John, "On the Failure to Detect Changes in Scenes across Saccades," in Kathleen Akins, ed., *Perception,* New York: Oxford University Press, 1996, pp. 89–110.

Harman, Gilbert, "The Intrinsic Quality of Experience," in James E. Tomberlin, ed., *Philosophical Perspectives, 4: Action Theory and Philosophy of Mind,* Atascadero, California: Ridgeview Publishing Co., 1990, pp. 31–52.

____ "Explaining Objective Color in terms of Subjective Reactions," in Enrique Villanueva, ed., *Philosophical Issues: Perception,* 7, Atascadero, California: Ridgeview Publishing Co., 1996, pp. 1–17; reprinted in Alex Byrne and David Hilbert, eds., *Readings on Color, volume 1: The Philosophy of Color,* Cambridge, Massachusetts: MIT Press/Bradford Books, 1997, pp. 247–261.

Kant, Immanuel, *Critique of Pure Reason,* tr. Werner S. Pluhar, Indianapolis: Hackett Publishing Co., 1996.

Kripke, Saul A., "Identity and Necessity," in Milton K. Munitz, ed., *Identity and Individuation,* New York: New York University Press, 1971, pp. 135–164.

____ *Naming and Necessity,* Cambridge, Massachusetts: Harvard University Press, 1980; originally as "Naming and Necessity," in Donald Davidson and Gilbert Harman, eds., *Semantics of Natural Language,* Dordrecht: D. Reidel Publishing Co., 1972, pp. 253–355 and 763–769.

Levine, Joseph, "Materialism and Qualia: The Explanatory Gap," *Pacific Philosophical Quarterly,* LXIV, 4 (October 1983): 354–361.

____ "On Leaving Out What It's Like," in Martin Davies and Glyn W. Humphreys, eds., *Consciousness: Psychological and Philosophical Essays,* Oxford: Basil Blackwell, 1993, pp. 121–136.

____ *Purple Haze: The Puzzle of Consciousness,* New York: Oxford University Press, 2000.

Lewis, David, "An Argument for the Identity Theory," *The Journal of Philosophy,* LXIII, 1 (January 6, 1969): 17–25; reprinted with additional material in Lewis, *Philosophical Papers,* vol. I, New York: Oxford University Press, 1983, pp. 99–107.

____ "Psychophysical and Theoretical Identifications," *Australasian Journal of Philosophy,* 50, 3 (December 1972): 249–58.

____ "Attitudes *De Dicto* and *De Se,*" *The Philosophical Review,* LXXXVIII, 4 (October 1979): 513–543; reprinted with postscripts in Lewis, *Philosophical Papers,* vol. I, New York: Oxford University Press, 1983, pp. 133–59.

—— "Reduction of Mind," in Samuel Guttenplan, ed., *A Companion to the Philosophy of Mind*, Oxford: Basil Blackwell, 1994, pp. 412–431; reprinted in Lewis, *Papers in Metaphysics and Epistemology*, Cambridge University Press, 1999, pp. 291–324.

Loar, Brian, "Phenomenal States," in Block, Flanagan, and Güzeldere, eds., *The Nature of Consciousness: Philosophical Debates*, pp. 597–616.

Locke, John, *An Essay Concerning Human Understanding*, edited from the 4th (1700) edn. by Peter H. Nidditch, Oxford: Clarendon Press, 1975.

Lycan, William G., *Consciousness and Experience*, Cambridge, Massachusetts: MIT Press/Bradford Books, 1996.

—— "The Superiority of HOP to HOT," in Gennaro, ed., *Higher-Order Theories of Consciousness*, pp. 93–113.

Malcolm, Norman, "Thoughtless Brutes," *Proceedings and Addresses of the American Philosophical Association*, 1972–3, XLVI (November 1973): 5–20; reprinted in Malcolm, *Thought and Knowledge*, Ithaca: Cornell University Press, 1977, pp. 40–57.

Marcel, Anthony J., "Conscious and Unconscious Perception: Experiments on Visual Masking and Word Recognition," *Cognitive Psychology*, 15 (1983): 197–237.

—— "Conscious and Unconscious Perception: An Approach to the Relations between Phenomenal Experience and Perceptual Processes," *Cognitive Psychology*, 15 (1983): 238–300.

—— "Slippage in the Unity of Consciousness," in Gregory R. Bock and Joan Marsh, eds., *Experimental and Theoretical Studies of Consciousness*, Ciba Foundation Symposium No. 174, Chichester: John Wiley & Sons, 1993, pp. 168–186.

Mellor, D. H., "Conscious Belief," *Proceedings of the Aristotelian Society*, LXXVIII (1977–8): 87–101.

—— "Consciousness and Degrees of Belief," in Mellor, ed., *Prospects for Pragmatism: Essays in Memory of F. P. Ramsey*, Cambridge: Cambridge University Press, 1980, pp. 139–73; reprinted in Mellor, *Matters of Metaphysics*, Cambridge: Cambridge University Press, 1991, pp. 30–60.

Merikle, Philip M., Daniel Smilek, and John D. Eastwood, "Perception without Awareness: Perspectives from Cognitive Psychology," *Cognition*, 79, 1–2 (April 2001): 115–134.

Metzinger, Thomas, ed., *Conscious Experience*, Exeter, UK: Imprint Academic, 1995.

Moore, G. E., "A Reply to My Critics," in Paul Arthur Schilpp, ed., *The Philosophy of G. E. Moore*, New York: Tudor, 1942, 2nd edn., 1952, pp. 533–677.

—— "Russell's 'Theory of Descriptions'," in Paul Arthur Schilpp, ed., *The Philosophy of Bertrand Russell*, New York: Tudor, 1944, pp. 175–226.

Nagel, Thomas, "What Is It Like to Be a Bat?", *The Philosophical Review*, LXXXIII, 4 (October 1974): 435–50; reprinted in Nagel, *Mortal Questions*, Cambridge and New York: Cambridge University Press, 1979, pp. 165–180.

Natsoulas, Thomas, "What Is Wrong with the Appendage Theory of Consciousness?", *Philosophical Psychology*, VI, 2 (June 1993): 137–154.

Nisbett, Richard E., and Timothy DeCamp Wilson, "Telling More than We Can Know: Verbal Reports on Mental Processes," *Psychological Review*, LXXXIV, 3 (May 1977): 231–259.

Palmer, Stephen E., "Color, Consciousness, and the Isomorphism Constraint," *The Behavioral and Brain Sciences*, 22, 6 (December 1999): 923–943, and Author's Response, "On Qualia, Relations, and Structure in Color Experience," 976–989.

Peacocke, Christopher, *Sense and Content*, Oxford: Clarendon Press, 1983.

—— "Colour Concepts and Colour Experiences," *Synthèse*, LVIII, 3 (March 1984): 365–381.

Perry, John, "The Problem of the Essential Indexical," *Noûs*, XIII, 1 (March 1979): 3–21.

Prior, A. N., "On Spurious Egocentricity," *Philosophy*, XLII, 162 (October 1967): 326–335.

Quine, W. V., *Word and Object*, Cambridge, Massachusetts: MIT Press, 1960.
_____ *Ontological Relativity and Other Essays*, New York: Columbia University Press, 1969.
Raffman, Diana, "On the Persistence of Phenomenology," in Thomas Metzinger, ed., *Conscious Experience*, pp. 293–308.
Rensink, Ronald A., "Change Detection," *Annual Review of Psychology*, 53, 1 (2002): 245–277.
Rorty, Richard, "Incorrigibility as the Mark of the Mental," *The Journal of Philosophy*, LXVII, 12 (June 25, 1970): 399–424.
_____ *Philosophy and the Mirror of Nature*, Princeton: Princeton University Press, 1979.
Rosenthal, David M., "Talking about Thinking," *Philosophical Studies*, 24, 5 (September 1973): 283–313.
_____ "Mentality and Neutrality," *The Journal of Philosophy*, LXXIII, 13 (July 15, 1976): 386–415.
_____ "Keeping Matter in Mind," *Midwest Studies in Philosophy*, V (1980): 295–322.
_____ "Reductionism and Knowledge," in Leigh S. Cauman, Isaac Levi, Charles Parsons, and Robert Schwartz, eds., *How Many Questions?: Essays in Honor of Sidney Morgenbesser*, Indianapolis: Hackett Publishing Co., 1983, pp. 276–300.
_____ "Emotions and the Self," in Gerald E. Myers and K. D. Irani, eds., *Emotion: Philosophical Studies*, New York: Haven Publications, 1983, pp. 164–191.
_____ "Armstrong's Causal Theory of Mind," in Radu J. Bogdan, ed., *Profiles: David Armstrong*, Dordrecht: D. Reidel Publishing Co., 1984, pp. 79–120.
_____ "Will and the Theory of Judgment," in Amélie O. Rorty, ed., *Essays on Descartes' Meditations*, Berkeley: University of California Press, 1986, pp. 405–434.
_____ "Judgment, Mind, and Will in Descartes," Report No. 29/1990, Center for Interdisciplinary Research (ZiF), University of Bielefeld.
_____ "Higher-Order Thoughts and the Appendage Theory of Consciousness," *Philosophical Psychology*, VI, 2 (June 1993): 155–167.
_____ "Multiple Drafts and Facts of the Matter," in Thomas Metzinger, ed., *Conscious Experience*, pp. 275–290.
_____ "A Theory of Consciousness," in Block, Flanagan, and Güzeldere, eds., *The Nature of Consciousness: Philosophical Debates*, pp. 729–753.
_____ "Apperception, Sensation, and Dissociability," *Mind and Language*, 12, 2 (June 1997): 206–222, part of a multiple review of Norton Nelkin, *Consciousness and the Origins of Thought*, Cambridge: Cambridge University Press, 1996.
_____ "Perceptual and Cognitive Models of Consciousness," *Journal of the American Psychoanalytic Association*, 45, 3 (Summer 1997): 740–746.
_____ "The Colors and Shapes of Visual Experiences," in Denis Fisette, ed., *Consciousness and Intentionality: Models and Modalities of Attribution*, Dordrecht: Kluwer Academic Publishers, 1999, pp. 95–118.
_____ "Consciousness and Metacognition," in Daniel Sperber, ed., *Metarepresentation: A Multidisciplinary Perspective*, New York: Oxford University Press, 2000, pp. 265–295.
_____ "Consciousness, Content, and Metacognitive Judgments," *Consciousness and Cognition*, 9, 2, Part 1 (June 2000): 203–214.
_____ "Metacognition and Higher-Order Thoughts," *Consciousness and Cognition*, 9, 2, Part 1 (June 2000): 231–242.
_____ "Color, Mental Location, and the Visual Field," *Consciousness and Cognition*, 9, 4 (April 2001): 85–93.

—— "Explaining Consciousness," in David J. Chalmers, ed., *Philosophy of Mind: Classical and Contemporary Readings*, New York: Oxford University Press, 2002, pp. 406–421 (previously circulated in MS also as "State Consciousness and What It's Like").

—— "Moore's Paradox and Crimmins's Case," *Analysis*, 62, 2 (April 2002): 167–171.

—— "The Timing of Conscious States," *Consciousness and Cognition*, 11, 2 (June 2002): 215–220.

—— "Consciousness and the Mind," *Iyyun, The Jerusalem Philosophical Quarterly*, 51, 3 (July 2002): 227–251.

—— "How Many Kinds of Consciousness?", *Consciousness and Cognition*, 11, 4 (December 2002): 653–665.

—— "Persons, Minds, and Consciousness," in Randall E. Auxier and Lewis E. Hahn, eds., *The Philosophy of Marjorie Grene*, La Salle, Illinois: Open Court, 2002, pp. 199–220.

—— "Varieties of Higher-Order Theory," in Gennaro, ed., *Higher-Order Theories of Consciousness*, pp. 17–44.

—— "Subjective Character and Reflexive Content," *Philosophy and Phenomenological Research*, 68, 1 (January 2004): 191–198.

—— "Being Conscious of Ourselves," *The Monist*, 87, 2 (April 2004): 159–181.

—— "Consciousness, Interpretation, and Higher-Order Thought," in Patrizia Giampieri-Deutsch, ed., *Psychoanalysis as an Empirical, Interdisciplinary Science: Collected Papers on Contemporary Psychoanalytic Research*, Vienna: Verlag der österreichischen Akademie der Wissenschaften (Austrian Academy of Sciences Press), 2005, pp. 119–142.

Schwartz, Robert, *Vision: Variations on Some Berkeleian Themes*, Oxford: Blackwell, 1994.

Searle, John R., *Intentionality: An Essay in the Philosophy of Mind*, Cambridge: Cambridge University Press, 1983.

—— "Consciousness, Explanatory Inversion, and Cognitive Science," *The Behavioral and Brain Sciences*, 13, 4 (December 1990): 585–696, and Author's Response, "Who is Computing with the Brain?", 632–642.

—— *The Rediscovery of the Mind*, Cambridge, Massachusetts: MIT Press/Bradford Books, 1992.

Sellars, Wilfrid, "Empiricism and the Philosophy of Mind," in Sellars, *Science, Perception and Reality*, pp. 127–196; republished as *Empiricism and the Philosophy of Mind*, with commentary by Robert Brandom and Richard Rorty, Cambridge, Massachusetts: Harvard University Press, 1997, and in Willem deVries and Timm Triplett, *Knowledge, Mind, and the Given*, Indianapolis and Cambridge, Massachusetts: Hackett Publishing Co., 2000, pp. 205–276.

—— *Science, Perception and Reality*, London: Routledge & Kegan Paul, 1963, and Atascadero, California: Ridgeview Publishing Co., 1991.

—— "Notes on Intentionality," *The Journal of Philosophy*, LXI, 21 (November 12, 1964): 655–665; reprinted with minor changes in Sellars, *Philosophical Perspectives: Metaphysics and Epistemology*, Atascadero, California: Ridgeview Publishing Co., 1977, pp. 128–140.

—— *Science and Metaphysics*, London: Routledge & Kegan Paul, 1968, and Atascadero, California: Ridgeview Publishing Co., 1992.

—— "Foundations for a Metaphysics of Pure Process," The Carus Lectures, *The Monist*, LXIV, 1 (January 1981): 3–90.

Shoemaker, Sydney, "Self-Reference and Self-Awareness," *The Journal of Philosophy*, LXV, 19 (October 3, 1968): 555–567; reprinted in Shoemaker, *Identity, Cause, and Mind: Philosophical Essays*, pp. 6–18.

Shoemaker, Sydney, "Functionalism and Qualia," *Philosophical Studies*, XXVII, 5 (May 1975): 292–315; reprinted with minor revisions in Shoemaker, *Identity, Cause, and Mind: Philosophical Essays*, pp. 184–205.

_____ "The Inverted Spectrum," *The Journal of Philosophy*, LXXIX, 7 (July 1982): 357–381; reprinted with postscript in Shoemaker, *Identity, Cause, and Mind: Philosophical Essays*, pp. 327–357.

_____ *Identity, Cause, and Mind: Philosophical Essays*, Cambridge: Cambridge University Press, 1984; expanded edn., Oxford: Clarendon Press, 2003.

_____ "Self-Knowledge and 'Inner Sense'," The Royce Lectures, *Philosophy and Phenomenological Research*, LIV, 2 (June 1994): 249–314; reprinted in Shoemaker, *The First-Person Perspective and Other Essays*, pp. 201–268.

_____ *The First-Person Perspective and Other Essays*, Cambridge: Cambridge University Press, 1996.

Simons, Daniel J., "Current Approaches to Change Blindness," *Visual Cognition*, 7, 1/2/3 (2000): 1–16; reprinted in Simons, ed., *Change Blindness and Visual Memory*, Philadelphia, Pennsylvania: Psychology Press, 2000, pp. 1–16.

_____ and Ronald A. Rensink, "Change Blindness: Past, Present, and Future," *Trends in Cognitive Sciences*, 9, 1 (January 2005): 16–20.

Treisman, Anne, "Features and Objects in Visual Processing," *Scientific American*, 255, 5 (November 1986): 114–125.

Van Gulick, Robert, "A Functionalist Plea for Self-Consciousness," *The Philosophical Review*, XCVII, (April 1988): 149–181.

Vendler, Zeno, *Res Cogitans*, Ithaca, New York: Cornell University Press, 1972.

Weiskrantz, Lawrence, *Blindsight: A Case Study and Implications*, Oxford: Clarendon Press, 1986.

Weiskrantz, Lawrence, *Consciousness Lost and Found: A Neuropsychological Exploration*, Oxford: Oxford University Press, 1997.

Wittgenstein, Ludwig, *Philosophical Investigations*, ed. G. E. M. Anscombe and R. Rhees, tr. G. E. M. Anscombe, Oxford: Basil Blackwell, 1953.

Index

absent qualities 9, 14, 149–52, 157–9, 170, 176–7, 209
access consciousness 113 n., 157, 158 n., 190, 192, 362
  see also Block
Albritton, Rogers 257 n., 258 n., 265 n., 274 n., 281 n.
Alston, William 49 n., 69 n.
anomalous monism 83–4
Anscombe, G. E. M. 34 n., 52 n., 331 n., 346, 348 n., 358 n.
appearance and reality of mental states 8, 43–5, 115, 138 n., 233, 240–6, 254, 305, 321–3, 329–32, 341
Aristotle 5, 26, 65, 78, 96, 122 n., 145 n., 167 n., 170 n., 171 n., 182 n., 196 n., 208 n., 311, 362 n.
Armstrong, D. M. 27 n., 47, 108 n., 113, 118 n., 141 n., 161 n., 165 n., 182, 222 n., 339 n.
Arnauld, Antoine 260 n.
Atherton, Margaret 45 n., 68 n.
Atlas, Jay David 272 n.
Austin, J. L. 51 n., 70 n., 90, 263–4, 272, 324 n.
Ayer, A. J. 300 n.

Baron-Cohen, Simon 212 n.
Berkeley, George 140 n., 196 n., 220 n.
Bieri, Peter 148 n.
binding problem 200, 248 n.
Black, Max 50 n., 257 n., 272 n.
blindsight 109, 179, 181, 185, 238
  see also Weiskrantz
Block, Ned 112–13, 149, 157, 158 n., 176, 184 n., 190–4, 339 n., 362
bodily sensations 38–9, 52–5, 66, 109, 136–7, 140–1, 162–3, 165, 198, 300 n., 318 n.
Boër, Steven E. 52 n., 348 n.
Boghossian, Paul A. 121
Bopp, James 206 n.
Bouwsma, O. K. 260 n.
Brentano, Franz 35 n., 65–7, 145 n., 179 n., 180 n., 184, 247 n., 293
Bridgeman, Bruce 288 n.
Broad, C. D. 305 n.
Brown, Eric 362 n.

Burge, Tyler 326 n.
Burnyeat, M. F. 50 n., 271 n.

Carruthers, Peter 110, 111 n., 128 n., 174 n., 185 n., 207 n., 345
Cartesian conception of mind 22–3, 28–35, 38, 40, 43, 45, 49, 360
  as against non-Cartesian conception 23, 26
  as engendering a regress for HOTs 9, 35, 38
  as regards consciousness, speech, and thought 71, 261, 265, 293 n., 296–7
  transparency of the mind to itself 2, 66 n., 130–1, 207 n., 239, 260–3, 305, 341, 355, 358, 360 n.
  see also mark of the mental
Cartesian Theater 230, 242–3
cerebral celebrity 251–2
Chalmers, David J. 194, 300 n.
change blindness 113–14, 156, 210, 332 n.
Chisholm, Roderick M. 24, 52 n., 77–8, 81–2, 85, 88, 143 n., 323 n., 347 n., 348 n.
Chomsky, Noam 298 n.
Church, Jennifer 163 n.
Churchland, Patricia Smith 229
Churchland, Paul M. 23 n.
Clark, Austen 153 n., 169 n., 199–200, 201 n., 225 n.
Clark, James J. 114 n.
cocktail-party effect 128, 136 n., 341
cogito 73 n., 258–9, 262, 264, 276 n.
color constancy 216
commonsense intuitions 22–3, 33, 143, 166–7, 229–30, 234, 237
concepts:
  comparative 11–12, 146, 188–9, 204–7, 214
  purely recognitional 207
confabulation, *see* misrepresentation by consciousness
conscious states:
  contrast with nonconscious states 3–4, 181, 186, 308–12
consciousness:
  as apparently essential to mental states 1, 10, 13, 21, 22, 25–32, 36, 39–47, 64, 98–9, 108, 111, 135–9, 144–8, 152, 155, 159, 164, 174, 175–7, 179, 217, 265, 308